H A N D B O O K S

UTAH

W. C. McRAE & JUDY JEWELL

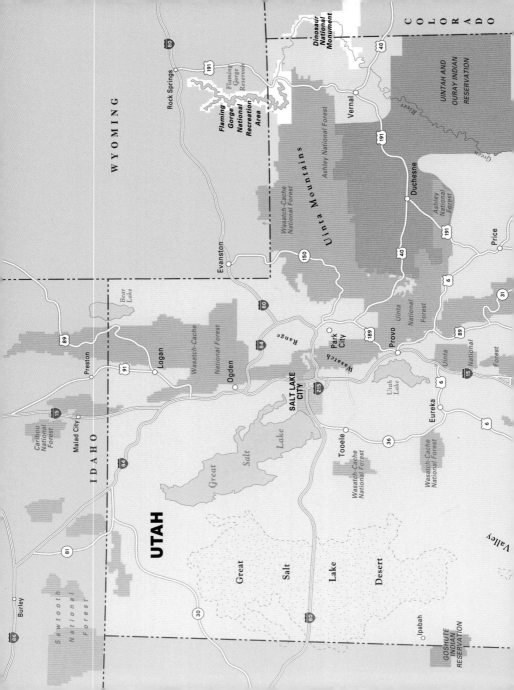

© AVALON TRAVEL

DISCOVER UTAH

The story goes that in 1847, when the trail-weary

Mormon leader Brigham Young surveyed the green Salt Lake Valley from Emigration Canyon high in the Wasatch Range, he declared, "This is the place." Since the founding of Salt Lake City and the settlement of Utah, many other people have taken a look at this dramatically scenic state and agreed: Yes, this *is* the place!

Few places on earth combine such spectacular terrain and unusual history as does Utah. The state hosts the majestic splendor of the Rocky Mountains, the colorful canyonlands of the Colorado Plateau, and the remote deserts and arid mountain ranges of the Great Basin. This region beckoned as the "Promised Land" to members of the struggling Church of Jesus Christ of Latter-day Saints in the 1840s – a place where those faithful to the Book of Mormon could survive and prosper in a land of their own. Today, this once insular state has put out the welcome mat – Utah's extravagant scenery and superlative recreational opportunities lure sightseers,

the temple at Brigham Young University

mountain bikers, hikers, and skiers from around the world, many of whom stay on to make this beguiling state their home.

Utah presents some curious statistics: It is the most urban state in the nation, a startling fact when you consider how utterly vacant — though dramatically beautiful — much of the landscape is. The unyielding deserts, craggy mountains, and imposing slickrock formations that cover much of the state aren't really fit for human habitation, and the vast majority of citizens live in just a few large cities — the sprawling metropolitan area called the Wasatch Front, which runs from Provo north to Ogden and includes Salt Lake City, counts a population of nearly 1.4 million.

Also, the majority of people living in Utah are practicing Mormons. To outsiders, the social homogeneity of smaller towns far from Salt Lake City, Park City, and Moab can seem off-putting, but the strong religious and cultural bonds that tie families and communities together in Utah are themselves noteworthy and increasingly rare

San Rafael horses

in the fast-paced modern world. The uniformity of the population stands in stark contrast to the diversity of the landscape and the abundance of opportunities for outdoor recreation.

Salt Lake City is the state capital, home to a major university and seat of a major religion – a rare combination of attributes that makes for a certain amount of civic gravitas and self-focus. But to visitors, Salt Lake City presents a near-unique natural and built environment where all-seasons, big-as-all-outdoors recreation coexists with the sophisticated comforts of urban living. And as one of the fastest-growing metropolitan areas in the nation, Salt Lake City's population is increasingly diverse and cosmopolitan.

In the Wasatch Mountain valleys behind Salt Lake City, superb snow conditions and friendly ski resorts combine to offer some of the best skiing in North America. In fact, several of these resorts helped host the 2002 Winter Olympics, which introduced an international focus and a bit of glitz to the local skiing scene. In Park City and Deer Valley, upscale amenities, fine dining, and plenty of après-ski

stained glass in the entrance to The Gateway in Salt Lake City

hangouts compete with stellar ski slopes for the attention of skiers and boarders from around the globe.

Southern Utah encompasses the Colorado Plateau, a vast sedimentary deposit that's been carved into canyons, arches, hoodoos, and chasms by millennia of erosion. This extremely dramatic landscape is preserved in five spectacular national parks and several national monuments. Zion National Park presents stunning contrasts, with barren, towering rock walls deeply incised by steep canyons containing a verdant oasis of cottonwood trees and wildflowers. Bryce Canyon National Park is famed for its abundance of red and pink hoodoos, delicate fingers of stone rising from a steep mountainside.

A large section of the Grand Staircase–Escalante National Monument preserves the dry washes and slot canyons trenched by the Escalante River and its tributaries as they drop toward the Colorado River. Long-distance hikers descend these sinuously beautiful, high-rock-walled cathedrals of stone to experience the

the Utah Field House of Natural History State Park Museum

near-mystical harmony of flowing water and stone. In Capitol Reef National Park, the Fremont River carves a magnificent canyon through Waterpocket Fold, offering hikers and explorers a leafy, well-watered sanctuary from the park's otherwise arid landscapes.

In vast Canyonlands National Park, the Colorado River begins to tunnel its mighty – and soon to be grand – canyon through an otherworldly landscape of deep red sandstone. The beauty is more serene and mystical at Arches National Park, where hundreds of delicate rock arches provide vast windows into the solid rock. High-spirited Moab is the recreational mecca of southeastern Utah. It's a boisterous community that's known for its mountain-bike lifestyle and comfortable – even sophisticated – dining and lodging.

And this is just the beginning of Utah's abundant wonders. From incredibly varied canyon country, remote and rugged mountain ranges, and glistening salt flats to ancient Native American rock art and cliff dwellings, fossilized dinosaur footprints, and old mining towns, this handbook will help you discover the many fascinating sights and experiences of Utah.

Arches National Park

Contents

The Lay of the Land 16
Planning Your Trip 20
Explore Utah 22
The Best of Utah 22
Camp It Up 24
Jurassic Utah 25
Touring the National Parks 26
Summer Music Festivals 28
Pictographs and Petroglyphs 29

Salt Lake City 31

Sights 36
Arts and Entertainment 51
Shopping 55
Sports and Recreation 56
Accommodations 61
Food 68
Information and Services 75

Park City and the Wasatch Range 79
Big Cottonwood Canyon 82
Little Cottonwood Canyon 88
Park City 97
North of Park City 116
Heber City and Vicinity 117

Northern Utah 121
The Great Salt Lake 125
Ogden 127
Vicinity of Ogden 137
Golden Spike National Historic Site 144
Logan and Vicinity 146

Great Basin Desert 157
Great Salt Lake Desert 160
Tooele 164
South of Tooele 166
Eureka and Tintic Mining District 172
Delta to Milford 175

Provo and Central Utah 183
Provo 186
Northwest of Provo 191
North of Provo 193
South of Provo Along I-15 196
South of Provo Along U.S. 89 203
Fish Lake and Vicinity 209

Dinosaur Country 211

Uinta Mountains 214
Vernal 220
North of Vernal 224
Flaming Gorge National Recreation Area 227
Dinosaur National Monument 233
South of Vernal 238
West of Vernal 239
Price 243
North of Price 246
East of Price... 248
The Castle Valley and North San Rafael Swell 250
Green River and Vicinity 256

Zion and Bryce.. 261

Bryce Canyon National Park 265
Vicinity of Bryce Canyon National Park 275
Along U.S. 89: Panguitch to Kanab 278
Kanab and Vicinity 282
Zion National Park 285
Vicinity of Zion National Park................................. 304
St. George.. 309
Vicinity of St. George 315
Pine Valley Mountains 318
Cedar City.. 321
The Markagunt Plateau 326

The Escalante Region...... 334
Grand Staircase-Escalante National Monument 338
Escalante 360
Boulder...... 364
Capitol Reef National Park 366
Torrey 379
East of Capitol Reef National Park...... 381
Glen Canyon National Recreation Area...... 384
Page, Arizona...... 389

Canyonlands...... 391
Moab 394
Moab Area Recreation 409
Arches National Park 419
Canyonlands National Park 426
Utah's Southeastern Corner 443

Background...... 460
The Land...... 460
Flora and Fauna...... 466
History 470
People and Culture 475
Arts and Entertainment...... 478

Essentials 480
Getting There and Around 480
Recreation 483
Accommodations 486
Food and Drink 486
Conduct and Customs 487
Tips for Travelers 488
Health and Safety 489
Information and Services 492

Resources 494
Suggested Reading 494
Internet Resources 496

Index 498

MAP CONTENTS

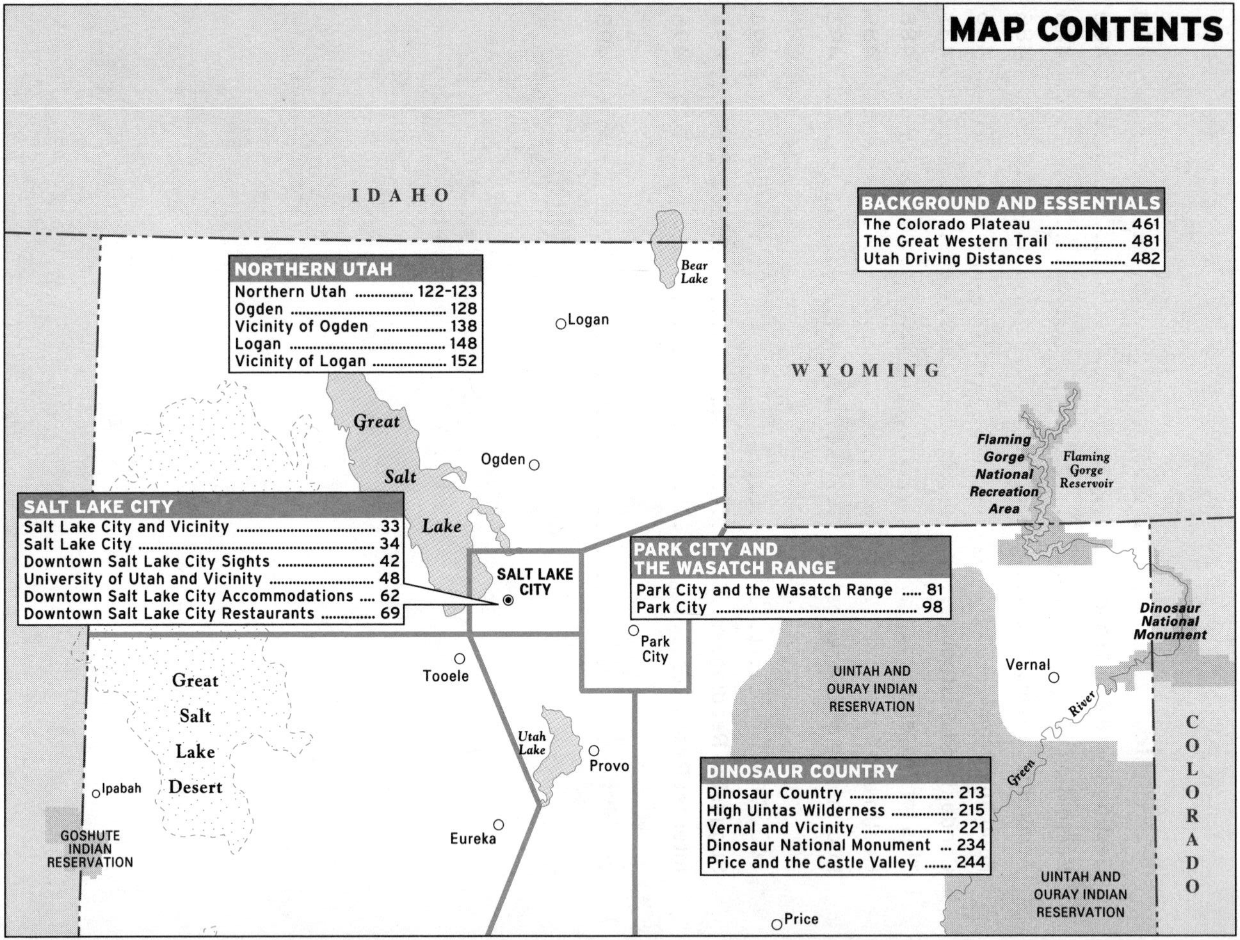

BACKGROUND AND ESSENTIALS

The Colorado Plateau 461
The Great Western Trail 481
Utah Driving Distances 482

IDAHO

WYOMING

COLORADO

Bear Lake

Logan

Great Salt Lake

Ogden

SALT LAKE CITY

Flaming Gorge National Recreation Area

Flaming Gorge Reservoir

Dinosaur National Monument

Green River

Vernal

UINTAH AND OURAY INDIAN RESERVATION

UINTAH AND OURAY INDIAN RESERVATION

Park City

Provo

Utah Lake

Tooele

Eureka

Price

Great Salt Lake Desert

Ibapah

GOSHUTE INDIAN RESERVATION

PARK CITY AND THE WASATCH RANGE

Park City and the Wasatch Range 81
Park City 98

DINOSAUR COUNTRY

Dinosaur Country 213
High Uintas Wilderness 215
Vernal and Vicinity 221
Dinosaur National Monument 234
Price and the Castle Valley 244

NORTHERN UTAH

Northern Utah 122-123
Ogden 128
Vicinity of Ogden 138
Logan 148
Vicinity of Logan 152

SALT LAKE CITY

Salt Lake City and Vicinity 33
Salt Lake City 34
Downtown Salt Lake City Sights 42
University of Utah and Vicinity 48
Downtown Salt Lake City Accommodations 62
Downtown Salt Lake City Restaurants 69

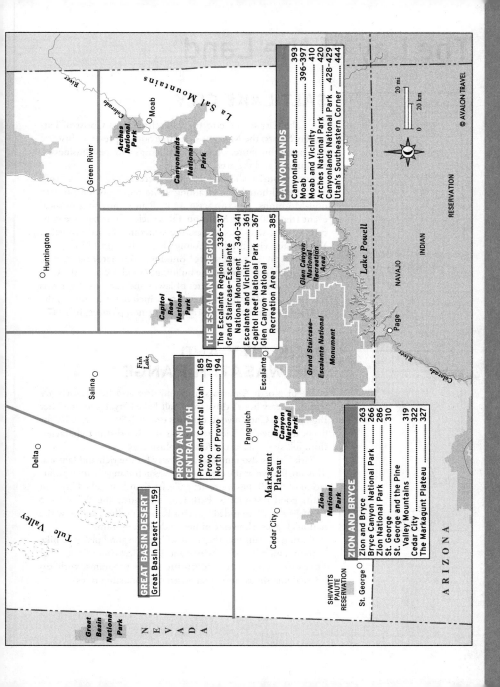

GREAT BASIN DESERT

Great Basin Desert 159

PROVO AND CENTRAL UTAH

Provo and Central Utah ...185
Provo 187
North of Provo 194

THE ESCALANTE REGION

The Escalante Region 336-337
Grand Staircase-Escalante
    National Monument ... 340-341
Escalante and Vicinity 361
Capitol Reef National Park ... 367
Glen Canyon National
    Recreation Area 385

CANYONLANDS

Canyonlands 393
Moab 396-397
Moab and Vicinity 410
Arches National Park 420
Canyonlands National Park ... 428-429
Utah's Southeastern Corner ... 444

ZION AND BRYCE

Zion and Bryce 263
Bryce Canyon National Park ... 266
Zion National Park 286
St. George 310
St. George and the Pine
    Valley Mountains 319
Cedar City 322
The Markagunt Plateau 327

© AVALON TRAVEL

The Lay of the Land

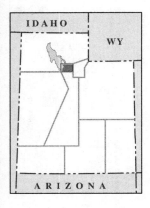

SALT LAKE CITY

Salt Lake City is home to the Church of Jesus Christ of Latter-day Saints, the Mormons. Temple Square preserves historic religious architecture, while the city booms with new businesses, restaurants, and the arts.

Every tourist should visit the sacred sights of **Temple Square.** Although the gleaming white temple is not open to non-Mormons, the **tabernacle** is. Plan to attend a musical event (the 320-voice Mormon Tabernacle Choir has free concerts twice a week) to witness the structure's famed acoustics. You can also visit Brigham Young's home, built in 1854.

The **Utah State Capitol** Building dominates the skyline just north of downtown. The building is modeled after the U.S. Capitol and sits amid 40 acres of lawns and gardens. Nearby is the **Pioneer Memorial Museum,** which tells the story of the 2,000-mile journey of the original Mormon pioneers in 1847.

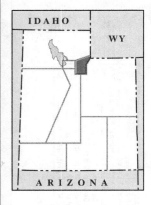

PARK CITY AND THE WASATCH RANGE

Some of North America's finest **skiing** and best resorts are within an easy hour's drive from Salt Lake City. Head up either Big or Little Cottonwood canyons or out I-80 to Park City for deep, dry powder. Each resort has its own distinct character, from folksy yet ski-crazy **Alta** to plush **Deer Valley.**

Park City is also famed as a getaway for the rich and famous. This small town at the crest of the Wasatch Range, with a population of 6,500, has more art galleries than Salt Lake City and many good restaurants. Park City also hosts the **Sundance Film Festival,** founded by actor Robert Redford and now the nation's biggest showcase of new independent films.

During the summer the ski areas become good places to hike or mountain bike—**Snowbird** and **Park City Mountain Resort** offer summertime adventure-sports programs, with zip lines, alpine slides, and other adrenaline-boosting rides.

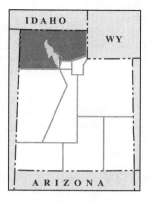

NORTHERN UTAH

Ogden, once a thriving rail hub, is now practically subsumed as a suburb of Salt Lake City. The city's old downtown area retains early-20th-century storefronts, which are now home to restaurants and shops. Ogden's huge and handsome rail station at the head of 25th Street no longer receives rail passengers, but it does house four museums, a restaurant, and an art gallery.

Logan is located in a green fertile valley and hedged by towering peaks. Its small downtown area has charming Victorian storefronts. **Summer festivals** make Logan a lively place: The nationally acclaimed Utah Festival Opera brings big voices to town; Festival of the American West brings in buckskin-clad mountain men and cowboy poets; and the Old Lyric Theater hosts a season of musicals and comedies.

Bear Lake, on the Idaho border, is a large, high-altitude lake with good fishing and cool summer temperatures.

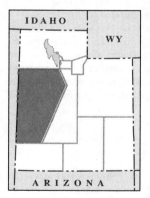

GREAT BASIN DESERT

This is the place to visit if you want to get away from it all. The Great Basin Desert alternates with arid mountain ranges, and only a few paved roads even cross this forlorn landscape. Many visitors travel through on I-80, getting a long look at the **Bonneville Salt Flats** in the state's northwestern corner.

Utah's west-central region is the best place in the state for **rockhounding,** and there's lots of history in the old mining **ghost towns** of Ophir, Gold Hill, and others. The **Pony Express** crossed this lonely stretch of desert, and remnants of old stations and inns can still be seen. If you're looking for solitude, backpacking trails lead into the little visited Deep Creek and House Mountain Ranges.

Just across the Utah border in Nevada is **Great Basin National Park,** with Lehman Caves (tours daily year-round), archaeological sites, and alpine hiking.

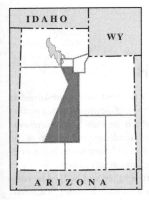

PROVO AND CENTRAL UTAH

Provo, home to **Brigham Young University,** is a good base for exploring the dramatic Wasatch peaks that rise directly behind the city. An especially nice back road is the **Alpine Scenic Loop,** which climbs up to 7,500 feet through dramatic mountain scenery. Along the way you'll pass **Sundance Resort,** noted for its skiing and good restaurants and **Timpanogos Cave National Monument,** open in summer for tours by serious hikers.

South of Provo are small sleepy towns. To the east, paralleling I-15, U.S. 89 follows the Sanpete River, which lies in a lovely agricultural valley flanked by mountains. The little towns along the route are showcases of historic **Mormon architecture.**

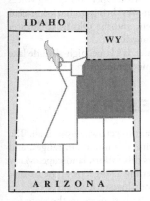

DINOSAUR COUNTRY

For dinosaur lovers, **Vernal** and **Price** each have dinosaur museums and easy access to dinosaur digs and paleontology labs, and the remote **Cleveland-Lloyd Dinosaur Quarry** has a visitors center and trails to dig sites; and **Dinosaur National Monument** offers many good hiking trails and scenic drives.

Beyond dinosaurs, the lofty but rounded **Uinta Mountains** are noted for their high-country, trout-rich streams and lakes. The **Green River** cuts a mighty canyon through these mountains, exposing cliffs of deep red and ochre. Called the **Flaming Gorge,** the canyon now contains a reservoir that's the center of a national recreation area. This region also has excellent ancient **Native American rock art,** particularly along the Nine Mile Canyon Backcountry Byway.

ZION AND BRYCE

Bryce Canyon National Park has famous vistas across an eroded amphitheater of pink sandstone hoodoos. Trails lead to a wonderland of fanciful formations and outcrops.

Cedar Breaks National Monument has formations similar to Bryce Canyon, only without the crowds. **Red Canyon** is adjacent to Bryce Canyon and shares its geology, but since it's not a national park you can mountain bike and ride horses amid the red-rock formations.

Hiking trails at **Zion** National Park lead up narrow canyons cut into massive stone cliffs, passing quiet pools of water and groves of willows. Zion is so awe inspiring that the early Mormons named it for their vision of heaven.

St. George, at the tip of the Sonoran Desert, makes the most of its year-round sun as a retirement and golf center. Just to the north, Cedar City is known for its summer Utah Shakespearean Festival, with eight plays a season.

THE ESCALANTE REGION

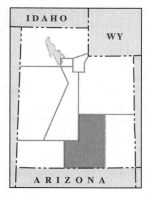

The Grand Staircase-Escalante National Monument preserves some of the Southwest's best canyon hiking. Numerous long-distance hiking trails follow the slot canyons of the Escalante River system. Back-road driving enthusiasts follow the Hole-in-the-Rock Road or the Burr Trail to visit some of the same landscape; just following scenic Highway 12 across Escalante country in a car is an eye-popping experience to most travelers.

Even though Highway 24 runs along the northern edge of Capitol Reef National Park and gives access to a historic Mormon orchard town, much of this park remains remote and unvisited. The long Waterpocket Fold formation that forms the southern two-thirds of the park is an excellent destination for long-distance hikers seeking solitude in the often busy Utah national parks.

CANYONLANDS

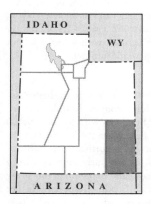

Moab is the center of the vast recreational area known as the canyonlands. Mountain biking is spectacular here; rafting down the Colorado and Green Rivers is nearly mandatory.

Just up the road from Moab is Arches National Park, with its famous rock bridges. Canyonlands National Park is remote and otherworldly. A visit that involves more than just a drive to a vista point requires a little planning and forethought. This area offers a wealth of rock art, Anasazi ruins, and vertical desert landscapes—a perfect place for a multiday backpacking trip.

The far southeastern corner of Utah is home to red-rock towers at Monument Valley, plus the charming town of Bluff. From here explore nearby rock-art sites, or take a rafting trip down the San Juan River. If all this desert has you hankering for water, visit Lake Powell, a reservoir on the Colorado River and a houseboating paradise.

Planning Your Trip

Most Utah-bound travelers will fly into the Salt Lake City airport: It's well served and convenient as a jumping-off point to most of the state, and if you're after the Utah experience, Salt Lake City is undeniably a big part of it. But travelers bound for the southern tier of the state might consider using the Las Vegas airport—it's an easy drive from Zion National Park.

Most visitors to Utah come with a specific destination or activity in mind, such as touring the national parks and monuments in the southern part of the state or skiing the Wasatch Range, and, indeed, it's impossible to see the entire state on a typical one-week vacation. But it is often possible to explore your chosen destination and then dip into another place or two that's not too far off your route. For instance, if you're visiting Bryce Canyon National Park, it would be a shame to miss the nearby Red Canyon and Kodachrome Basin State Park.

Some really cool destinations, such as the granaries and rock art in remote Nine Mile Canyon, require quite an effort to reach. And sometimes, a place that may seem merely unavoidable, such as Salt Lake City, can become a place you're eager to return to.

Southern Utah's parks and monuments are all within an easy day's drive of one another, and a week is long enough to begin to get acquainted with this area. Of course, after a week, you'll leave with a long list of hikes and river trips you'll want to take next time around. Two weeks will give you enough time to take some of those trips into the backcountry or to check out other areas, such as the dinosaur fossils and rock art in northeastern Utah.

Even if you only have a long winter weekend, it's easy to fly into Salt Lake in the afternoon and be skiing the next morning. Whether you base yourself in Salt Lake City (cheaper) or at a resort in Park City or Big or Little Cottonwood Canyon, there will be plenty of time to spend on the slopes. This is also about the only kind of trip to Utah where you can easily get away with not having a car. City buses and private shuttles run frequently to mountain resorts, but the rest of the state is barely served by bus or rail.

WHEN TO GO

For most purposes, spring (April–early June) and, especially, fall (September–October) are the most pleasant times to visit. Except in the mountains, summer heat can rapidly drain your energy.

Spring

The desert country shines with wildflowers in early spring, a choice time to visit. Each year's floral display depends on both the amount and timing of rains in the preceding winter. The same rain showers that bring spring flowers can also dampen trails and turn dirt roads to absolute muck. Especially in the higher elevations, clouds and rain can last for several days, so always have in mind a rainy-day alternative to hiking. Arm yourself with insect repellent from late spring to midsummer.

Summer

Summer travelers should look to the higher elevations to find relief from the heat that can envelop the state. Bryce Canyon, at 6,600–9,100 feet, is a good bet, as are the Uintas and the Flaming Gorge area in northeastern Utah.

Thunderstorms are fairly common from late July through early September and bring the threat of flash flooding, especially in slot canyons. In Canyonlands, Arches, and Moab, summer temperatures can easily get into the 100s. Carrying (and drinking) water becomes critical then; carry at least one gallon per person per day.

Autumn

Nearly the entire state enjoys warm and dry weather, though hot temperatures can linger into October at the lowest elevations, and the possibility of snow gradually increases on the plateaus and mountains. Aspens turn to gold in the high country in late September and early October, followed by colorful displays of oaks, cottonwoods, and other deciduous plants in canyons lower down. This can be the best time of year to travel in Utah.

Winter

Travel to Utah doesn't let up in the winter—the ski areas here are some of the nation's best, and very easy to get to from Salt Lake City. If you're traveling to other places in the state, inquire about travel conditions because snow and ice occasionally close roads and trails at higher elevations.

Brigham Young established his winter home in St. George, near present-day Zion National Park, for good reason. Winters are generally warmer here than in other parts of the state, and this southwest Utah town has become a retirement hotspot, with golf courses possibly outnumbering places of worship (and certainly far outnumbering bars and taverns).

Winter can be a great time to visit the high country around Bryce, where cross-county skiers take to the park roads. Around Escalante, the canyons can be quite nice in the winter during the day, but nights are freezing. In Canyonlands and Arches, winter days tend to be bright and sunny, but nighttime temperatures can dip into the teens or lower.

WHAT TO TAKE

No matter what time of year, remember to bring lots of sunscreen. Even in winter, the sun packs a wallop at high elevations. In summer, be prepared for blazing sun; unless you want to return from Utah looking like a leather handbag, buy and use a sunscreen with a high sun-protection level.

If you are planning on a lot of hiking, bring broken-in hiking shoes or boots. Lightweight sports or walking shoes won't provide much support in the rugged conditions of Utah's slickrock trails or rocky canyons.

If you're a birder, you won't forget to pack binoculars and a field guide, but other travelers should also consider bringing these along.

Even in summer, there can be wide variations in temperature. Nights in the desert can be very chilly even when summer highs soar above 100 degrees. Especially if you're planning on hiking or backpacking, plan to bring clothes than can be removed or put on in layers, as needed. Zip-off pants work especially well.

There's no need to pack dressy clothes. Nearly without exception, casual clothes are acceptable everywhere, even in what passes for classy restaurants. You'll find it difficult to underdress.

Alcohol presents another issue. If you think you'll want a drink, especially away from Salt Lake City or tourist destinations around the national parks, pack a flask or a bottle of wine, especially if you have discerning tastes. While many restaurants in the towns around these parks now offer a selection of alcoholic beverages, including good wine and Utah microbrews, Utah is not a drinking culture, to put it mildly. If you're accustomed to a cocktail or a nightcap, you might want to bring a bottle along on your trip.

And sure, you can bring your cell phone, but don't count on it working over large parts of Utah's backcountry.

Explore Utah

THE BEST OF UTAH

Utah's top sights form a ring within the state, making it easy and logical to take a 10-day-loop road trip that connects the state's most alluring attractions and sights. Think of this as a sampler of Utah's varied destinations. On your next trip—and chances are you'll want to come back to explore more deeply—you can focus on your favorites.

This trip assumes that you begin and end your trip in Salt Lake City. But because most of it is a loop, you can join it at any of several natural entry points: near Moab, if you're coming in on I-80 from Denver; or near Zion, if you're coming in on I-15 from Las Vegas.

Day 1

Arrive in **Salt Lake City.** Take in the Mormon historical sites at **Temple Square,** wander through the historic neighborhoods along South Temple Street, and, depending on the weather, attend a free evening concert at the Mormon Assembly Hall, the tabernacle, or at Gallivan Square. Spend the night at Hotel Monaco.

Day 2

Drive north on I-15 to **Ogden.** Walk along the historic storefronts—now antique shops and cafes—on 25th Street at the heart of 1890s Ogden. After lunch, continue north to the **Golden Spike** National Historic Site, a brief journey back in time into the Utah outback to the spot at Promontory Point where the transcontinental railroads were joined in 1869.

After checking out the visitors center and the steam trains, drive to **Logan** in the verdant Cache Valley, home to Utah State University and, in summer, the Utah Festival Opera. Find an excuse to eat some delicious Aggie ice cream, made by the university's dairy school. Spend the night at the Best Western Weston Inn.

Day 3

Return south toward Salt Lake City on I-15, this time stopping by **Antelope Island** State Park, the largest island in the Great Salt Lake and reached by a seven-mile causeway. It's one of the few areas where you can get close to the **Great Salt Lake,** and, if you wish, you can hike up to viewpoints, or rent a boat or take a swim at one of the state park beaches.

Hose the salt off your body and continue south, passing through Salt Lake City to **Park City,** Utah's top ski resort and film festival center. The old town area of Park City

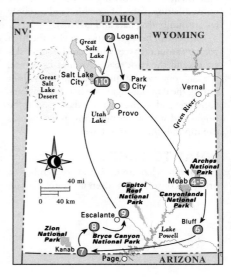

is a long and narrow street that remains from the town's beginnings as a mining camp. Shop the boutiques and pick out a fabulous restaurant for dinner. Main Street is lined with good choices; if budget's no matter, try The Riverhorse Cafe or Chimayo. Stay at the Hotel Park City.

Day 4

Today you'll put quite a few miles on the car. Drive from Park City to Provo on Hwy. 189, through the very scenic **Provo Canyon.** Continue south on Hwy. 6, first to Price and then to the town of Green River. After a brief drive along I-80, turn south on U.S. 191 to Moab.

You've earned a reward for driving five hours, so treat yourself to a night at **Sorrel River Ranch,** a luxury guest ranch east of Moab with a great dining room and decks that overlook the **Colorado River.**

Day 5

You're in the midst of national parks, so start exploring. **Arches** is an easy drive from Moab; you'll have time to hike to **Delicate Arch,** explore the **Devils Garden,** and stop at every scenic viewpoint along the way.

Spend the night at the Gonzo Inn in **Moab,** a major center for recreation in southeast Utah. In the evening, enjoy Moab's lively scene: good restaurants, brew pubs, and hoards of bicyclists.

Day 6

From Moab, drive south on U.S. 191. Unfortunately, time doesn't allow for exploration of all the far-flung districts of **Canyonlands,** but at least pull off U.S. 191 40 miles south of Moab at the road to Needles District and drive 10 miles to **Newspaper Rock Historical Monument,** one of the finest and most accessible petroglyph sites in Utah.

Return to U.S. 191 and continue south 78 miles to Blanding. From south of town, follow Hwy. 262 and back roads to **Hovenweep National Monument,** Utah's most impressive

Anasazi ruin, dating from 1200 A.D. Wander through the many stone structures, most in remarkably good repair, and ponder the mysterious disappearance of the farming Anasazi people.

Back on U.S. 191 continue south to the charming small town of **Bluff,** where you'll stay at the Desert Rose Inn.

Day 7

From Bluff, drive to aptly named Mexican Hat and drop into the **Navajo Reservation.** Soon the dramatic spires of **Monument Valley** fill the skyline. These lonely fingers of stone rising from the barren desert are practically metonyms of the Old West (at least in old Western films and modern SUV advertisements). After snapping hundreds of photos, continue southwest and drop into Arizona via Hwy. 163.

At Page, you'll cross the Colorado River on the **Glen Canyon Dam.** Stop and peer south over the 710-foot-high concrete dam at the beginning of the Grand Canyon. After leaving Page, you'll re-enter Utah. Your final destination? The Parry Lodge in Kanab.

Day 8

Two national parks in one day? No problem! From Kanab, get an early start and drive Hwy. 89 and then Hwy. 9 to **Zion,** where you'll drop off the car and ride the shuttle bus along the Virgin River parkway. Hop off and on, taking short hikes in the mighty Zion canyon.

Stop for lunch at the Zion Park Lodge, then backtrack to Hwy. 89 and continue north. Make the turn on Hwy. 12 for **Bryce Canyon.** Check into Bryce Canyon Lodge, then catch a free afternoon shuttle along the parkway. You'll want to catch the sunset on the park's mysterious pink and orange hoodoos.

Day 9

From Bryce Canyon, continue east along Hwy. 12 to **Escalante** for a day of hiking. It's your choice: the easy, mostly level hike to **Lower**

Calf Creek Falls, or more intense clambering and canyoneering through the Dry Fork of Coyote Gulch. After a day of outdoor recreation, enjoy great food and comfortable lodging at Boulder Mountain Lodge in Boulder.

Day 10

Today, return to Salt Lake City by following Hwy. 24 to Salina, then Hwy. 50 to I-15, which will get you to the Utah state capital in time for dinner.

CAMP IT UP

Utah is flush with campgrounds, including many in great state parks. For this tour, you'll have a long day's drive on Day 1, if you fly into Salt Lake City, or on the final day, if you're using the Las Vegas airport.

Night 1

Snow Canyon State Park is a beautiful spot just outside busy St. George. Even though it's at a higher elevation than the town, this area gets very hot in the summer, when the campground is fairly lightly used. But during spring, it's quite popular; reserve a site well in advance.

Nights 2-3

Head to Zion National Park, where you can find good spots in either of the two park-maintained campgrounds. If you're planning

in advance, some sites in Watchman can be reserved. Spend a couple of nights there to really see the park.

Night 4

The campgrounds at Bryce Canyon National Park are perfectly nice, but the high elevation of this park means cold nights in the spring and fall. (There are significant patches of snow on the ground in early May.) Find a warmer spot at Kodachrome Basin State Park, about 20 miles south of Bryce. Kodachrome is quite scenic in itself, with great campsites and several hiking trails.

Night 5

Two campgrounds near Escalante make a good base for exploring the northern edge of the Grand Staircase–Escalante National Monument. Of the two, the Calf Creek campground, east of town, is more scenic, but Escalante Petrified Forest State Park, just west of town, is larger and has showers.

Night 6

Don't skip a visit to Capitol Reef. The most noteworthy thing about the park's Fruita campground is its easy access to the local fruit trees (available for picking in the right season) and hiking trails. Because no reservations are accepted, it's best to arrive here early in the day to claim a spot.

Night 7

Head east to Hanksville and north along U.S. 191. Stop to visit Goblin Valley State Park, and either pitch your tent here or continue north to Green River State Park, in the town of Green River. If you're ready for a meal in town, have a burger and a beer at Ray's.

Night 8

Make your way northwest through Price and Provo to Jordanelle State Park, north of Heber City. Camp by the reservoir here or walk in to campsites at the Rock Cliff Reservoir unit. Another good local spot is Wasatch Mountain State Park, west of Heber City. From here, it's only about an hour's drive back to Salt Lake City.

JURASSIC UTAH

About 145–200 million years ago, when Utah's climate was wet and warm, dinosaurs laid down footprints (and their dead bodies) in sand and mud. These traces were covered and hardened under the pressure of overlying sediments. As mountains uplifted, the sedimentary layers were propped up and exposed to erosion, eventually revealing the fossilized bones and footprints.

Day 1

Vernal, on the eastern edge of the state, is a good place to begin exploring Utah's dinosaurs. In particular, start at the Utah Field House of Natural History State Park and Museum, with its interesting introductory video and great collection of dinosaur bones and fossilized plants and mammals from the later Eocene Epoch. After a visit to the museum, head north to the northern edge of Red Fleet State Park and take a three-mile round-trip hike to see dinosaur tracks.

Dinosaur National Monument, although a great place to explore, isn't really a dino-bone highlight these days—its Dinosaur Quarry (a wall of bones) is closed for at least several years due to structural problems.

Day 2

Perhaps you don't think you're ready for another dinosaur museum, but get used to it! There are a few along this route, and not a one of them boring. Visit the College of Eastern Utah Prehistoric Museum in Price to see locally dug fossils, including the Utahraptor. (Remember *Jurassic Park?*) After the museum, drive east from Huntington to the Cleveland-Lloyd Dinosaur Quarry to see an excavation site.

Day 3

Stop by the Museum of the San Rafael in Castle Dale for more bones and a replica of a fossilized egg, then head east to Moab for a look at tracks of a theropod and meat-eating sauropods. Check out the collection at the Dan O'Laurie Museum, which includes a very gnarly looking dinosaur replica and other historical exhibits—it really is worth a stop.

Days 4-5

OK, so there's The Dinosaur Museum in Blanding, south of Moab, and an excellent exhibit at the visitors center in remote Big Water, on Hwy. 89 at the southern edge of the Grand Staircase–Excalante National Monument, but for these two days we'll give you the option of simply exploring the national parks and monuments from Arches, near Moab, to Zion, just east of St. George.

Day 6

Just east of St. George, the St. George Dinosaur Discovery Site at Johnson Farm is a must-see. Recently discovered tracks show early Jurassic dinosaurs absolutely running amok across the former lakebeds here. It's considered one of the world's best dinosaur-tracks sites.

Day 7

As you drive north on I-15, pull off at Thanksgiving Point, where the Museum of Ancient Life has a huge collection of dinosaurs and other fossils and shows IMAX movies with computer-generated dinosaurs. Wind up your trip in Salt Lake City, where the Museum of Natural History is pretty darn good, even for the jaded fossil-watcher.

TOURING THE NATIONAL PARKS

Although the national parks of Utah are located in a geographically compact area, connecting the dots and visiting each of them isn't as straightforward as it might seem. The extremely rugged topography of the area has made road building difficult, so visiting all of the parks requires a lot of driving. Get into a road-trip frame of mind, cue up some good music, and head out. The following 10-day itinerary will only scratch the surface of what there is to see, but after this sampler, you'll know where to focus your next Utah adventure.

Days 1-2

Start in Moab, the recreation hub of southeast Utah. This small town is also the most convenient base for visiting both Arches and Canyonlands National Parks. You can tour Arches in half a day if you take only short hikes to viewpoints; if you want to visit all of the sites along the park road and hike to famed Delicate Arch, you'll spend most of a day in the park.

Devote Day 2 to exploring Canyonlands' Island in the Sky District, taking in the astonishing vista points (particularly Grand View Point) and saving time for a hike to the cliff edge. In the evenings, check out Moab's vibrant nightlife.

Day 3

From Moab, get an early start and drive south on U.S. 191. This day will require quite a bit of driving—roughly 200 miles. Pull off U.S. 191 40 miles south of Moab and drive toward the Needles District of Canyonlands. If you're short on time, you probably won't make the trip west to the park itself (it's 38 miles to the park gate), but at least follow the park access road for 10 miles to Newspaper Rock Historical Monument, one of the finest and most accessible petroglyph sites in Utah.

Return to U.S. 191 and continue south 78 miles, passing the ranching towns of Monticello and Blanding before turning west on

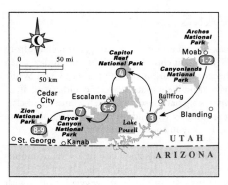

Hwy. 95 to reach Natural Bridges National Monument. Often overlooked, this small park is a gem, with three massive rock bridges and an Anasazi cliff dwelling.

Back on Hwy. 95, continue eight miles to the junction of Hwy. 276, then follow this route 40 miles to Halls Crossing Marina on Lake Powell, which offers car-ferry service across the lake. After a half-hour crossing, you'll reach Bullfrog Marina on the west side of the lake, with accommodations in the Defiance House Lodge.

Day 4

From Bullfrog, you can follow the well-maintained Notom-Bullfrog backcountry road to Hwy. 24 and the entrance to Capitol Reef National Park (80 miles), or you can follow paved Hwys. 276 and 95 to Hanksville and enter the park along Hwy. 24 (117 miles). Either way, you'll end up in Capitol Reef.

You'll want to explore the old pioneer town of Fruita, hike to see petroglyphs, and drive the scenic park road. Add a hike up the Chimney Rock Trail or along Capitol Wash.

Torrey, a small town just west of the park, has a profusion of hotels and is the best base for exploring the Capitol Reef area.

Day 5

From Torrey, follow Hwy. 12 south through the Grand Staircase-Escalante National Monument. The 61-mile trip between Torrey and Escalante is one of the most scenic routes in all of Utah—don't plan to drive this in an hour! Take in all the scenery and sights, including a visit to the prehistoric ruins at Anasazi State Park and a hike up dramatic Lower Calf Creek Falls Trail.

Spend the night at a motel in the town of Escalante or at the Escalante Petrified Forest State Park campground.

Day 6

Explore more of the Escalante River canyons. Drive 12.5 miles south from Hwy. 12 and turn onto Hole-in-the-Rock Road to traipse around Devil's Garden. You can also visit the canyons of Dry Fork of Coyote Gulch, 26 miles south of Hwy. 12. Return to Escalante for the night.

Day 7

From Escalante, continue west 42 miles on Hwy. 12 to Bryce Canyon. Leave the car and spend the day riding the park shuttle to vista points and exploring hoodoos from trailheads along the road.

Camp in the park or stay at the historic park lodge or one of the motels just outside the park entrance.

Days 8-9

Get up in time to see the rising sun light up the hoodoos, then drive west on Hwy. 12 to U.S. 89, and south from there to Hwy. 9. At Hwy. 9, turn west and enter Zion via the dramatic Zion-Mt. Carmel Highway (Bryce to Zion is 84 miles), then find a campsite or check into the lodge or a motel in Springdale. Ride the park shuttle for a quick overview of Zion Canyon.

Spend a second day exploring the canyon and its many enchanting hikes, including the Riverside Walk and the Emerald Pools trails.

SUMMER MUSIC FESTIVALS

Mormon Utah has a long tradition of music making and music appreciating, dating back from the raising of Salt Lake City's tabernacle and its attendant choir in the 1860s until today, when outdoor music concerts and festivals form a backdrop to summer in all parts of Utah. While the realities of scheduling and festival dates make it unlikely that a traveler could attend all of the following concerts in a typical summer's trip, taking part in some of the live music and classical music festivals available in Utah during the summer will add burnish to a trip otherwise dedicated to sunburned hiking or river-running in canyon country.

Salt Lake City

The amount of live music available in Salt Lake City in the summer is prodigious. In addition to ongoing music performances at the tabernacle, there are the LDS-sponsored Concert Series at Temple Square (801/240-3318, www.lds.com), concerts of classical and religious music, some of which take place outdoors.

The Roman Catholic Cathedral of the Madeleine presents the Madeleine Arts and Humanities Program (801/328-8941, www.saltlakecathedral.org), which offers classical music in a stunning 1909 place of worship.

For more modern music in an outdoor setting, head to Gallivan Center (www.gallivanevents.com) in the heart of downtown, where in addition to free summer weekday noontime and (mostly) Wednesday and Thursday night concerts, there's also an evening of opera arias on the first Saturday night after Labor Day.

Park City

During the summer, the Utah Symphony and other classical music performers grace the stage at Deer Valley's outdoor amphitheater (435/649-1000, www.deervalley.com).

The Park City International Music Festival (435/649-5309, www.pcmusicfestival.com) brings classical music to the Park City area year-round, with an emphasis on concerts in July at The Canyons resort.

Logan

In summer, Logan is Utah's music festival center. This lovely small city in a verdant mountain valley plays host to the Utah Festival Opera (800/830-6088, www.ufoc.org), with fully staged professional operas performed in an intimate performing arts center that was once a movie palace and vaudeville hall (the season runs mid-July–mid-August).

Another historic theater in Logan has been updated to serve as home base for the Old Lyric Repertory Theatre (888/878-2931, www1.usu.edu/lyric), which produces musicals and other theatrical productions in June, July, and August.

In addition, there are regular musical events in local parks and at the Logan Tabernacle (see www.tourcachevalley.com for a calendar of summer events).

Springdale

At the outdoor O. C. Tanner Amphitheater (www.dixie.edu/tanner), you'll find a summertime series of concerts ranging from bluegrass, jazz, and folk to classical music.

St. George

The Tuacahn Amphitheater (800/746-9882, www.tuacahn.org) was once devoted to uplifting Mormon-themed musicals, but more recently this dramatically located outdoor theater amid 1,500-foot cliffs near St. George features a July–December season of Broadway musicals and other musical events.

Moab

The Moab Music Festival (435/259-7003, www.moabmusicfest.org) offers concerts of classical chamber music, traditional music, vocal music, works of living composers, and jazz performed by acclaimed artists late August–mid-September. Performances take place in indoor and outdoor venues ranging from historic Star Hall in Moab to the banks of the Colorado River.

Outside the summer season, Moab offers the **Moab Folk Festival** in November (435/259-3198, www.moabfolkfestival.com).

PICTOGRAPHS AND PETROGLYPHS

Utah contains a rich tapestry of pictographs (drawings painted on rock using natural dyes) and petroglyphs (images carved into stone). Searching out rock-art panels can easily become an obsession, and it's a good one, since it will lead you far off the beaten path and deep into canyons that were once central for the area's ancient inhabitants.

The earliest known images are in the Barrier Canyon Style, which may date back 8,000 years. Interestingly, these very early images are frequently of ghostly apparitions and horned, robed creatures, and seem to have had ritual significance.

Rock art in the Fremont Style was created nearly 1,000 years ago, and is more abstract and stylized, often with geometric shapes and ciphers.

Ute Style images are comparatively recent—from the last 400 years—and often feature hunters on horseback, buffalo, and other game animals.

Day 1

Start your rock-art tour east of Cedar City at **Parowan Gap,** a narrow rock pass where ancient artists chiseled images more than 1,000 years ago. Who knows what kinds of meanings these pictographs—of geometric designs, lizards, bear claws, and human figures—had for travelers through this pass.

Day 2

Make your way east along Hwy. 12, which runs past Bryce Canyon. Stop between the towns of Escalante and Boulder at the **Boynton Overlook** and scan the cliff face across the river to see a pictograph of many handprints. It's possible to scramble up for a closer look from the parking area where Hwy. 12 crosses the Escalante River.

Continue east, then north up to **Capitol Reef.** Petroglyphs of horned mountain sheep and humans in feathered headdresses are easily viewed from a parking area along Hwy. 24 in **Fremont River Canyon.** These are some of the most easily reached rock-art panels in Utah.

Day 3

From the Capitol Reef area, cut south along Hwy. 95 to Blanding. From there, continue southeast to the **Hovenweep National**

Monument, one of Utah's best-preserved Anasazi villages. There, among the ruins, you'll find many petroglyphs.

The most interesting are in the **Holly Ruins,** where a series of spirals and concentric rings served as a calendar for ancient farmers. Shafts of light from the rising sun illuminate the petroglyphs. By aligning the designs, the Anasazi were able to mark the summer solstice and the fall and spring equinoxes.

Day 4

From the Blanding area, drive north on U.S. 191 to the entrance road of the Needles District of Canyonlands. Drive west a few miles toward the park to find **Newspaper Rock,** another easily reached showcase of rock art. The immense rock face is a collage of fantastic creatures, footprints, abstract designs, hunters on horseback, and wild animals—in all, 2,000 years of art on a boulder.

Continue north to Arches. On the hiking trail to **Delicate Arch** is an often overlooked panel of Ute Style rock-art images. Images like these, of mounted horsemen hunting mountain sheep, are clearly from the historical period, since horses reached America from Spanish colonies.

Day 5

The town of Green River is a good home base for today's touring. One of the most important rock-art sites in the United States is the **Great Gallery** in Canyonlands' **Horseshoe Canyon Unit.** In fact, the park service created the unit specially to protect this trove of incomparable art. Human-sized images of ghost spirits cover the walls—this was clearly a sacred place for thousands of years. That it's reached after a half day of backcountry driving and hiking only adds to the magic.

Depending on how long you spend in Horseshoe Canyon, make the trip to **Sego Canyon** on the same day or the following morning (it's half an hour east of Green River on I-80). Sego Canyon is a vast gallery of prehistoric art, where you'll find hundreds of etched images, starting with 8,000-year-old figures of ghostly, shamanic-looking creatures right out of sci-fi movies and extending up to the historic period, when Utes created images of humans using firearms, probably from the 18th century.

Day 6

Continue north on U.S. 191 to near Price, where you will take back roads to **Nine Mile Canyon.** Few people travel these dusty (but perfectly passable in dry weather) roads, but the rewards are great: There are a number of excellent rock-art panels and ancient grain caches tucked into the cliffs, and the scenery in the always deepening canyon is spectacular.

Day 7

After the previous day's back-road adventure, today's trip to **Dry Fork Petroglyphs** seems relatively simple. Yet these easily reached rock-art galleries, found northwest of Vernal, are also rarely visited. These spectacular images of life-sized human figures, many adorned with elaborate headdresses, are considered to be some of the best in the nation and resemble those in Horseshoe Canyon, which are reached only after a four-hour hike.

SALT LAKE CITY

In 1847 the Mormon prophet Brigham Young proclaimed this site the "right place" for a new settlement. Today, many residents and visitors would still agree. Modern Salt Lake City offers an appealing mix of cultural activities, historic sites, varied architecture, shopping, sophisticated hotels, and elegant restaurants. About 180,000 citizens live in the city, making it by far the largest and most important urban center in Utah, while more than one million people reside nearby in the city's sprawling suburbs.

Salt Lake City enjoys a physical setting of great visual drama. The city lies on the broad valley floor and terraces once occupied by prehistoric Lake Bonneville. The Great Salt Lake, the largest remnant of that ancient inland sea, lies just northwest of the city. The Wasatch Range rises immediately to the east; these rugged mountains, with many peaks exceeding 11,000 feet, are cut by steep canyons whose streams provide the area's drinking and irrigation water. Just minutes from downtown you can be skiing on some of the world's best powder in winter, or hiking among wildflowers in summer. On the other side of the valley, to the west, Lewiston Peak (elev. 10,626 feet) crowns the Oquirrh Mountains.

Salt Lake City's strong sense of self-focus and purposefulness comes from a near unique combination of attributes. It's a state capital, major university center, the largest city for hundreds of miles, and the seat of a wealthy and powerful worldwide religion.

By far the most popular tourist site in Salt

HIGHLIGHTS

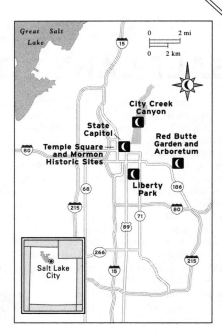

◖ **Temple Square and Mormon Historic Sites:** The epicenter of the Mormon faith, Temple Square offers museums, visitors centers, public gardens, concerts, and eye-popping architecture. Whether you're a believer or not, you'll enjoy the spectacle (page 36).

◖ **State Capitol:** Modeled on the U.S. Capitol building, Utah's seat of government is grandly scaled and brimming with granite and marble stones. From the steps leading to the building, views of the city and the Wasatch peaks are breathtaking (page 44).

◖ **Red Butte Garden and Arboretum:** An oasis of green in arid Salt Lake City, these gardens cover 30 acres. Plus, there's 200 acres of adjacent woodlands networked with trails for hiking and jogging (page 49).

◖ **Liberty Park:** This lovely park, with playgrounds, a lake, and lots and lots of manicured lawns, is located south of downtown. Liberty Park is also beloved for its Tracy Aviary, a bird zoo with falconry events (page 50).

◖ **City Creek Canyon:** The most accessible hiking and cycling path in Salt Lake City starts right downtown and winds up in City Creek Canyon along a rushing stream and past wooded glens. Bring a picnic and enjoy an island of nature in the midst of the city's urban sprawl (page 59).

LOOK FOR ◖ TO FIND RECOMMENDED SIGHTS, ACTIVITIES, DINING, AND LODGING.

Lake City is Temple Square, the spiritual center of the Mormon Church. Utah's political life centers on the imposing capitol, which overlooks the city from a hill just north of downtown. The University of Utah serves a major role in education and research from its 1,500-acre campus in the foothills east of the city. Another high point of any visit to Salt Lake City should be a tour of the city's historic architecture. The early Mormons' pride in their City of Zion is clearly seen in the old residential districts, with their beautiful Victorian mansions, and the downtown's ornate storefronts and civic structures. Few cities in the West retain such a wealth of period architecture.

Once a prosperous, though inward-looking, trade center for local farmers and ranchers—and a virtual theocracy—Salt Lake City in the last 50 years has emerged from its isolation to join the ranks of the leading cities of the American West. A measure of the city's new prestige is the fact that Salt Lake City hosted the 2002

Winter Olympics, the largest city ever to have hosted the winter games. Post-Olympics, the infrastructure now seems overbuilt, with vacant storefronts and closed restaurants attesting to the boom-and-bust economics of Olympic fever. However, Salt Lake and its surrounding ski and winter recreation centers are a relatively good value for Olympic-level snow sports, and its hotels and restaurants frequently offer exceptional deals on quality lodging and food.

PLANNING YOUR TIME

To see the sights in Salt Lake City requires at least three full days, and because the city is easily the most sophisticated place to stay and eat for hundreds of miles around (with the possible exception of Park City), it's also a comfortable and convenient hub for exploring the scenery and recreation of northern Utah.

You could easily spend a day visiting just the Latter-day Saints museums, religious and

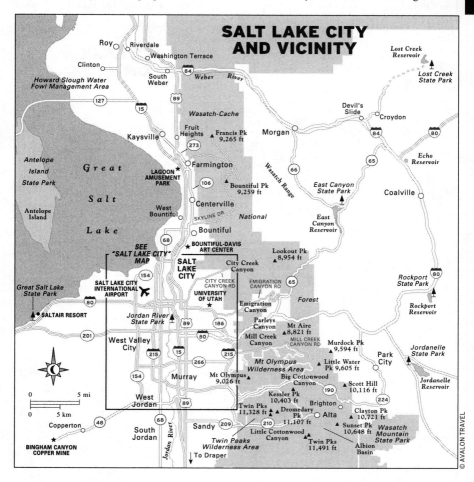

SALT LAKE CITY AND VICINITY

© AVALON TRAVEL

historical sites, and administrative buildings that front Temple Square. Many people budget in time to perform genealogical research while here—the church has extensive genealogical records and allows visitors to research family records free of charge.

A second day in Salt Lake City can be divided among visits to the state capital and the nearby Pioneer Memorial Museum, plus a stop by the Salt Lake Art Center. Add in a picnic at Liberty Park and a visit to the Tracy Aviary, a

bird zoo with live falconry displays, and you'll have a full and varied day.

Depending on the season, skiing or hiking in the Wasatch mountains directly behind the city should definitely be a part of every traveler's itinerary. A number of hiking trails begin right in the city: City Creek Canyon and Red Butte Garden and Arboretum, for example, are within reach of almost any downtown hotel. Day-trip options include Antelope Island State Park, an island in the Great Salt Lake linked

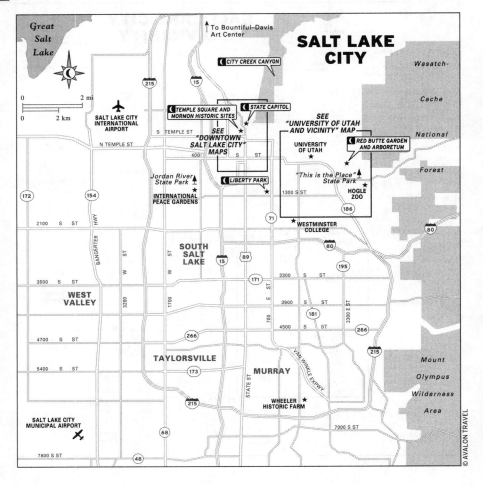

© AVALON TRAVEL

to the mainland by a seven-mile causeway, and Park City, a historic mining camp now turned glittering world-class ski resort.

HISTORY
The Vision

Salt Lake City began as a dream—a utopia in which the persecuted Latter-day Saints would have the freedom to create a Kingdom of God on earth. Their prophet, Brigham Young, led the first group of 143 men, three women, and two children to the valley of the Great Salt Lake in July 1847. The bleak valley, covered with sagebrush and inhabited mainly by lizards, could best be described as "the land nobody wanted." Many Mormon settlers wanted to continue under Young's leadership to the rich lands of California. But Young saw the value in staying: He declared that the Kingdom of God should be independent of gentiles, and this land's remoteness would protect them from enemies.

Settlement

The pioneers put their doubts aside and set to work digging irrigation canals, planting crops, constructing a small fort, and laying out a city as nearly 2,000 more immigrants arrived that first summer.

Through trial and error, farmers learned techniques of irrigating and farming the desert land. Then, in 1848, disaster struck. A plague of "crickets" (actually a flightless grasshopper, *Anabrus simplex*) descended from the hills to the east and began devouring the crops, nearly ending chances for the community's survival. But flocks of California seagulls appeared out of the west to feed on the insects. Considered a miracle by the Mormons, the seagull intervention saved part of the crops and gave the pioneers hope that life in the Great Salt Lake Valley would eventually be fruitful.

Meanwhile, the city continued to grow. Immigrants from Europe and the eastern United States poured in, many under the sponsorship of the Perpetual Emigrating Fund Company. Tanneries, flour mills, blacksmith shops, stores, and other enterprises developed under church direction. Beautiful residential neighborhoods sprang up, reflecting both the pride of craftsmanship and the sense of stability encouraged by the church. Workers commenced to raise the temple, the tabernacle, and the other religious structures that still dominate the area around Temple Square. Colonization of the surrounding country proceeded at a rapid pace.

As the Mormons' earthly City of Zion, Salt Lake City came close to its goal of being a community devoted to God. Nearly all aspects of political, economic, and family life came under the influence of the church during the first 20 years. Of all the utopian social experiments ever tried in the United States, the Mormon settlements at Salt Lake have had the greatest and most lasting success.

Coming of the Gentiles

The isolation that had shielded Salt Lake City from outside influence began to fade around 1870. Deracinated Civil War soldiers prospected for gold and found enough of it to encourage a mini–gold rush. Completion of the transcontinental railroad through Utah in 1869 encouraged non-Mormons to seek opportunity in the territory.

Even in this new social climate, Mormons and gentiles remained largely segregated. Each group developed its own social and political organizations and its own schools. Political life had been very dull during the first decades, when only a single set of church-appointed candidates appeared on the ballots. Voters had the option of voting "no," but they knew that their numbered ballots could be traced. The church discouraged political parties, believing they would lead to corruption and disharmony, and that civil government should be an arm of the church.

With the rising power of the gentile population in the 1870s, the church founded the People's Party to counter the anti-church Liberal Party. Salt Lake City's two major newspapers date from this time, with the *Deseret News* stating Mormon views and the *Salt Lake Tribune* representing the gentiles. Such fine shades of the political spectrum as the Republican or

Democratic Party rarely entered the picture. The Mormons steadily lost control of their city; from a 93 percent majority population in 1867, they slipped to just 50 percent by 1891. In 1889 the first non-Mormons were elected to city offices.

Modern Times

Wealth from successful mining operations fueled much of the development in Salt Lake City's business district, located in the blocks south of Temple Square. As a rule, the blocks nearest the temple had affiliations with the church, while those farther south belonged to non-Mormons. In the early 1900s, skyscrapers began sprouting high above East Temple Street—which was rechristened Main Street.

Exchange Place became the non-Mormon financial center.

The Depression was hard on Salt Lake City, as the dust bowl droughts sapped an already precarious water supply. The local economies picked up during World War II, as federal spending began to pour in and military installations took shape in the deserts west of Salt Lake City. Suburban growth began, providing the first exodus from the city's older neighborhoods. By the 1970s, the LDS Church began to spend money on revitalization of the city's downtown core. And the spending continues: the church has pledged $1.5 billion to redevelop parts of three blocks just south of Temple Square as City Creek Center, an enormous live/work/shop complex.

Sights

Although Salt Lake City is a sprawling urban area, fortunately the majority of tourist destinations are concentrated in a easy-to-negotiate area in and near the downtown core. Excellent public transport makes it simple to forego a rental car and just hop the light rail or bus.

◖ TEMPLE SQUARE AND MORMON HISTORIC SITES

Easily Salt Lake City's most famous attraction, this complex (open daily 9 A.M.–9 P.M.) has a special meaning for Mormons: It is the Mecca or the Vatican of the Church of Jesus Christ of Latter-day Saints. Brigham Young chose this site for Temple Square in July 1847, just four days after arriving in the valley. Nearby, Young built his private residences; the tabernacle, visitors centers, museums, and a host of other buildings that play a role in LDS church administration also line the streets around Temple Square. You're welcome to visit most of these buildings, which provide an excellent introduction to the LDS religion and Utah's early history.

Enthusiastic guides offer several tours of Temple Square, which covers an entire block in the heart of the city. A 15-foot wall surrounds

the square's 10 acres; you can enter through wrought-iron gates on the south, west, and north sides. All tours, exhibits, and concerts are free. Foreign-language tours are available, too—ask at the North Visitor Center. Smoking is prohibited on the grounds.

Musical Concerts

Temple Square is the site for an ongoing series of free musical concerts. Organists demonstrate the sounds and versatility of the tabernacle's famous instrument in half-hour recitals held Monday–Saturday at noon and 2 P.M. and on Sunday at 2 P.M. in the summer months. The rest of the year, the recitals are at noon Monday–Saturday and 2 P.M. on Sunday.

The renowned Tabernacle Choir sings on Sunday mornings at 9:30 A.M. (you must be in your seat by 9:15 A.M. and remain seated during the entire performance). You can also hear the choir during rehearsals 8–9:30 P.M. on Thursday evenings (you can come and go during the rehearsals). In June, July, August, and December, rehearsals and broadcasts are held across the street in the Conference Center, which can accommodate the larger summer

© W. C. MCRAE

The Salt Lake Temple rises above downtown.

.visittemplesquare.com, or call 801/240-2534 or 800/537-9703 for programs and times.

Temple Square Historical Tour

Guides greet you at the gates of the square and offer an introduction to Salt Lake City's pioneers, the temple, tabernacle, Assembly Hall, and historic monuments. The free 40-minute tours begin every 10 minutes during the summer season and every 15 minutes the rest of the year; hours are usually 9 A.M.–9 P.M. Custom group tours can be scheduled in advance. Points of interest, which you may also visit on your own, include the Seagull Monument (commemorating the seagulls that devoured the plague of "crickets" in 1848); a bell from the abandoned Nauvoo Temple; sculptures of Christ, church leaders, and handcart pioneers; an astronomy observation site; and a meridian marker (outside the walls at Main and South Temple Streets) from which surveyors mapped out Utah. Although tour leaders don't normally proselytize, the tours do give the guides a chance to witness their faith.

The Salt Lake Temple

Mormons believe that they must have temples within which to hold sacred rites and fulfill God's commandments. According to the LDS faith, baptisms, marriages, and family-sealing ceremonies that take place inside a temple will last beyond death and into eternity (prior to entering a temple, members prepare for a spiritual experience by dressing in white clothing, which represents purity). The temple is used only for these special functions; normal Sunday services take place in local stake or ward buildings—in fact, the temple is closed on Sunday.

Only LDS members who meet church requirements of good standing may enter the sacred temple itself; others can learn about temple activities and see photos of interior rooms at the South Visitor Center. Non-Mormons are not allowed to enter the temple or its grounds. However, you can get a good look at the temple's east facade from the Main Street gates.

The plan for Salt Lake City's temple came first as a vision to Brigham Young when he still

and Christmas season crowds. Broadcasts are also held in the Conference Center during LDS semiannual General Conferences, which take place on the first Sunday of October and April. Admission on these two Sundays is available only to Conference ticket holders. Occasionally, when the choir is on tour, a youth choir, youth symphony, or other group replaces it.

In addition, the Temple Square Concert Series presents complimentary hour-long concerts in the Assembly Hall featuring local and international artists every Friday and Saturday evening at 7:30 P.M. Tickets are not required, but admittance is for those eight years of age and older. From June through August, the Temple Square Concert Series presents Concerts in the Park, held in the Brigham Young Historic Park on the southeast corner of State Street and Second Avenue. These outdoor concerts begin at 8:00 P.M. during June and July and 7:30 P.M. in August.

For additional activities, check the bulletin boards as you enter Temple Square, ask any of the guides, check the Events section at www

lived in Illinois. Later, Young's concept became a reality with help from church architect Truman O. Angell; construction began in 1853. Workers chiseled granite blocks from Little Cottonwood Canyon, 20 miles southeast of the city, then hauled them by oxen and later by railroad for final shaping at the temple site. Dedication took place on April 6, 1893—40 years to the day after work began.

The foundation alone required 7,478 tons of stone. Walls measure nine feet thick at the base and taper to six feet on the second story. The tallest of the six slender spires stands 210 feet and is topped by a glittering statue of the angel Moroni with trumpet in hand. The 12.5-foot statue is made of hammered copper covered with gold leaf.

The Tabernacle

Pioneers labored from 1863 to 1867 to construct this unique, dome-shaped building. Brigham Young envisioned a meeting hall capable of holding thousands of people in an interior free of obstructing structural supports. His design, drawn by bridge-builder Henry Grow, took shape in massive latticed wooden beams resting on 44 supports of red sandstone. Because Utah lacked many common building supplies, the workers often had to make substitutions. Wooden pegs and rawhide strips hold the structure together. The large organ pipes resemble metal, balcony pillars appear to be marble, and the benches look like oak, yet all are pinewood painted to simulate these materials.

The tabernacle has become known for its phenomenal acoustics, due to its smooth arched ceiling, and its massive pipe organ is regarded as one of the finest ever built. From 700 pipes when constructed in 1867, the organ has grown to about 12,000 pipes, five manuals, and one pedal keyboard. Daily recitals (noon and 2 P.M. Mon.–Sat. and 2 P.M. Sunday in summer, noon Mon.–Sat. and 2 P.M. Sun. the rest of the year) demonstrate the instrument's capabilities. Temple Square tours include a stop in the tabernacle for a short presentation on the history of the building; an

acoustic demonstration shows that a dropped pin can be heard even in the back rows—170 feet away!

Important church conferences take place in the tabernacle every spring and autumn, but the seating capacity of about 6,500—considered huge when it was built—is now far too small, despite the addition of a balcony. The renowned Mormon Tabernacle Choir, 320 voices strong, is heard on the Sunday morning national radio show *Music and the Spoken Word*. Visitors may also attend choir rehearsals Thursday evenings at 8 P.M. or the broadcast performance on Sunday at 9:30 A.M. (be seated by 9:15 A.M.); both are free.

Assembly Hall

Thrifty craftspeople built this smaller, Gothic Revival structure in 1877–1882 using granite left over from the temple construction. The truncated spires, reaching as high as 130 feet, once functioned as chimneys. Inside the hall, there's seating for 1,500 people and a choir of 100. The baroque-style organ, installed in 1983, has 3,500 pipes and three manuals; of particular note are the organ's horizontal pipes, called trumpets. Initially the Salt Lake Stake Congregation met here; now the building serves as a concert hall and hosts church functions.

North Visitor Center

Wander around on your own or ask the ever-present tour guides for help. Exhibits focus on the life and ministry of Jesus Christ and the importance of ancient and modern prophets, including those from the Bible and Book of Mormon. An interesting exhibit is a scale model of Jerusalem as it may have looked at the time of Christ. A spiraling ramp leads to the upper level, where *Cristus,* an 11-foot replica of a sculpture by Bertel Thorvaldsen, stands in a circular room whose wall mural depicts the universe.

South Visitor Center

Two new exhibits cover the building of the Salt Lake Temple and "Strengthening the

SALT LAKE CITY FOR KIDS

© W. C. MCRAE

Discover Gateway is hands-on.

DISCOVER GATEWAY

None of the exhibits at this children's favorite (in the Gateway complex at 444 West 100 South, 801/456-KIDS, 10 A.M.-6 P.M. Mon.-Sat., until 9 P.M. Mon. and Fri., noon-6 P.M. Sun., $9.50, $8.50 for Utah residents, free for children under 1) display Do Not Touch signs; in fact, most of the displays are hands-on. Formerly the Children's Museum of Utah, Discovery Gateway provides engaging interactive activities that inspire learning in children and fun for the whole family. Kids get to take part in activities such as putting on a play, hosting the morning TV news, or making a short animated film. They can also take part in a mock Life Flight or rescue operation in an authentic life-sized helicopter.

LAGOON AMUSEMENT PARK AND PIONEER VILLAGE

History, recreation, and thrilling rides come together at this attractively landscaped park (801/451-8000 or 800/748-5246) 16 miles north of Salt Lake City. Lagoon traces its own history back to 1887, when bathers came to Lake Park on the shores of the Great Salt Lake, two miles west of its present location. The vast Lagoon Amusement Park area includes roller coaster rides, a giant Ferris wheel, and other midway favorites. There are also musical performances and miniature golf. Lagoon A Beach provides thrilling water slides and landscaped pools.

Pioneer Village brings the past to life with authentic 19th-century buildings, stagecoach and steam-train rides, a Ute museum, a carriage museum, a gun collection, and many other exhibits. Wild West shoot-outs take place several times daily. Food booths are scattered throughout the park, or you can dine at the Gaslight Restaurant near the Opera House.

Lagoon Amusement Park, Lagoon A Beach, and Pioneer Village are all open 11 A.M.-11 P.M. or midnight Sunday–Friday, open at 10 A.M. Saturday. The complex is open Saturday and Sunday early April–Memorial Day weekend, daily between Memorial Day and Labor Day weekends, then Saturday and Sunday through September. An all-day ride pass is $37 adults, $32 for children over age 4 and up to 50 inches in height, $21 for children 3 and under, and $25 for seniors. The all-day pass includes Lagoon A Beach privileges. An additional $7 is charged for parking. Take I-15 to the Lagoon exit and follow signs.

WHEELER HISTORIC FARM

Kids enjoy a visit to this working farm (6351 South 900 East, 801/264-2241, www.wheelerfarm.com, 9:30 A.M.-5:30 P.M. in spring and fall, daily 9:30 A.M.-8 P.M. in summer, 1-5 P.M. in winter, free) to experience the rural life of milking cows, gathering eggs, churning butter, and feeding animals. Hayrides (sleigh rides in winter) take visitors around the farm. Henry and Sariah Wheeler started the farm in 1887 and developed it into a prosperous dairy and ice-making operation. Tour guides take you through the Wheelers' restored Victorian house, built 1896-1898, the first in the county to have an indoor bathroom. Signs on other farm buildings recount their history and use. The Ice House now sells crafts and snacks.

The Salt Lake County Recreation Department operates the farm and offers special programs for both youngsters and adults. There's no admission charge to the farm, but you'll pay for individual activities. A tour costs $2 adults, $1.50 children 3-11 and seniors 65 and up; milking the cow costs just $0.50. Though it was once on the outskirts of town, suburbs now surround Wheeler Historic Farm.

Family." Exhibits on the main level include paintings of prophets and church history, a baptismal font supported by 12 life-size oxen (representing the 12 tribes of Israel) as used in temples, photos of the Salt Lake Temple interior, and a scale model of Solomon's Temple. Head downstairs to see replicas of the metal plates inscribed with the Book of Mormon, which Mormons believe were revealed to Joseph Smith in 1823. Ancient plates of Old World civilizations and stone boxes from the Americas are exhibited to support the claim that the plates are genuine. LDS literature can be obtained at a desk near the entrance.

Museum of Church History and Art

Brigham Young encouraged the preservation of church history, especially when he saw that Salt Lake City's pioneering era was drawing to a close. The collection of church artifacts, begun by the Deseret Museum in 1869 and now housed in this modern museum (45 N. West Temple, 801/240-4615, 9 A.M.–9 P.M. Mon.–Fri. and 10 A.M.–7 P.M. Sat–Sun. and holidays except New Year's Day, Easter, Thanksgiving, and Christmas; free), includes the plow that cut the first furrows in the Salt Lake Valley. Exhibits document each of the past church presidents and religious paintings and sculpture. Perhaps the most striking piece is the gilded 11.5-foot statue of Moroni, which crowned a Washington, D.C., chapel from 1933 to 1976. Temporary exhibits also display Mormon artistry and themes in photography, abstract art, textiles, furniture, and woodworking.

Step outside to see the 1847 log cabin, one of only two surviving from Salt Lake City's beginnings. The interior has been furnished as it might have been during the first winter here.

Family History Library

This library (35 N. West Temple, 801/240-2331, 8 A.M.–5 P.M. Mon., 8 A.M.–8 P.M. Tue.–Sat., closed federal holidays) houses the largest collection of genealogical information in the world. Library workers have made extensive travels to many countries to micro-

CITY CREEK CENTER REMAKES DOWNTOWN

Why are there massive holes in the center of Salt Lake City? Work is underway on an ambitious $1.5 billion civic renovation at the heart of downtown Salt Lake City. The City Creek Center will sprawl 20 acres along South Temple Street at Main and State Streets, including the better part of three blocks and encompassing the former locations of the ZCMI Center, Crossroads Plaza, and the Inn on Temple Square hotel. The entire project is funded by the LDS Church, which owns the land on which City Creek Center will be built. City Creek Center will offer premier retail space, with anchor stores such as Nordstrom, Macy's, and Dillards, plus restaurants, offices, and residential development. City Creek Center will also include approximately six acres of gardens and landscaped green space, water features, and open walkways. Fountains and artificial streams will represent the historic south fork of City Creek that ran through the downtown area when pioneer settlers first arrived in 1847. The City Creek Center project is slated for completion in 2011.

film documents and books. More than 125 employees are assisted by over 400 volunteers to keep track of the records. The LDS Church has gone to this effort to enable members to trace their ancestors, who can then be baptized by proxy. In this way, according to Mormon belief, the ancestors will be sealed in the family and the church for eternity. However, the spirits for whom these baptisms are performed have a choice of accepting or rejecting the baptism.

The library is open to the public. If you'd like to research your family tree, bring what information you have and get the library's *A Guide to Research* booklet. A brief slide presentation explains what types of records are kept and how to get started. Staff will answer questions. In most cases the files won't have information about living persons because of rights to privacy. The church leaves nothing to chance in preserving its genealogical records and history—master copies on microfilm rest in vaults deep within the mountains southeast of Salt Lake City.

If you are new to genealogical investigation, you may want to start your research at the FamilySearch Center (15 E. South Temple Street, 801/240-4085, same hours as Family History Center), on the main floor in the Joseph Smith Memorial Building (formerly Hotel Utah). The center has individual computer stations with access to family history resources and staff is available to help you free of charge.

Conference Center

Completed in 2000, this block-square, 10-acre building (60 W. North Temple, 801/240-0075) is used both as a performance space and a place of worship. The main auditorium, which seats 21,000, serves as a meeting hall for large LDS assemblies. The building is fronted by white granite. The many-tiered design incorporates four acres of landscaping, with trees, flowers, fountains, and waterfalls. From a distance the building looks like the Hanging Gardens of Babylon. Free tours are offered 9 A.M.–9 P.M.

Brigham Young Monument

This monument, standing in the middle of Main near North Temple Street, celebrates the first 50 years of settlement in Salt Lake City. Unveiled on July 24, 1897, it portrays Brigham Young, in bronze, atop a granite pedestal with figures below representing a Native American, a fur trapper, and a pioneer family. A plaque lists the names of the first group of 148 Mormon pioneers. The statue is also the originating point for the city's street-numbering system.

Joseph Smith Memorial Building

Built of white terra-cotta brick in modern Italian Renaissance style, this building (15 E. South Temple, open Mon.–Sat., closed Sun. except to those attending worship services) opened in 1911 as a first-class hotel for church and business leaders. However, in 1987 the LDS Church, which owned the hotel, converted it into an office building and a memorial to LDS founding father Joseph Smith. The opulent lobby, with its massive marble columns, chandeliers, and stained-glass ceiling, remains intact; you definitely should walk through the lobby and admire the grand architecture.

On the ground floor, the **FamilySearch Center** (801/240-4085) has computers available to trace family ancestry. **Nauvoo Cafe** (801/539-3346, 8 A.M.–8 P.M.) offers light meals and food to go. Also on the ground floor is the large-screen **Legacy Theater** (801/240-0080 for reservations), which screens LDS-themed films. Admission is free, but you'll need a ticket for entry (obtained at the information desk at the building's Main Street entrance). The 10th floor offers observation areas, the formal **Roof Restaurant** (801/539-1911), and the less formal **Garden Restaurant** (same phone).

© W. C. MCRAE

The former Hotel Utah is now the Joseph Smith Memorial Building, housing the FamilySearch Center.

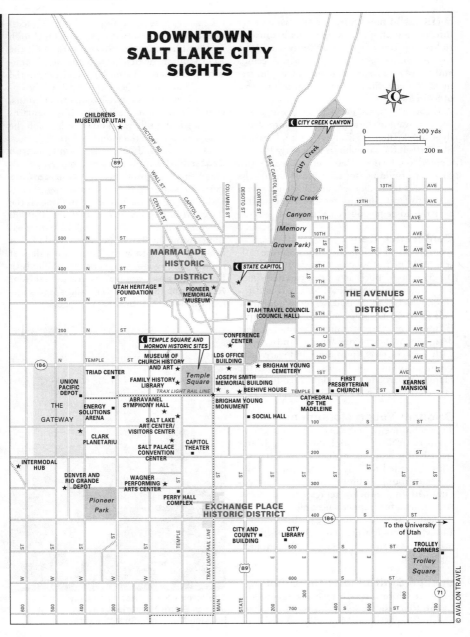

DOWNTOWN SALT LAKE CITY SIGHTS

LDS Office Building

Day-to-day running of the massive LDS Church organization is centered in the 28-story tower (50 E. North Temple, 801/240-2190, 9 A.M.– 5 P.M. Mon.–Fri., until 4:30 P.M. Oct.–Mar.) east of Temple Square. Such a volume of correspondence takes place that the building has its own zip code. Free tours begin in the main lobby and explain a bit about the work here, but the big attraction is a visit to the 26th-floor observation deck. You'll see Temple Square and the whole city spread out below like a map. Weather permitting, the valley, the Great Salt Lake, and the surrounding mountains stand out clearly. Tours last about 30 minutes, depending on how long you want to take in the panorama. The main lobby has some noteworthy artwork, including a giant 66- by 16-foot mural of Christ appearing to his apostles just prior to his ascension. Gardens and fountains grace a small park behind the building.

Beehive House

This former house of Brigham Young (67 E. South Temple, 801/240-2671, tours every 10 minutes 9 A.M.–9 P.M. Mon.–Sat., free) was built in 1854 and occupied by Young and his family until his death in 1877. The adobe and brick structure stood out as one of the most ornate houses in early Salt Lake City. Free tours lasting 30–40 minutes take visitors through the house and tell of family life within the walls. The interior has been meticulously restored with many original furnishings. A beehive symbol, representing industry, caps the house and appears in decorative motifs inside. Brigham Young had about 27 wives, but only one at a time stayed in this house; other wives and children lived next door in the Lion House. Downstairs in the main house, Young's children gathered in the sitting room for evenings of prayer, talks, and music. Upstairs, he entertained guests and dignitaries in a lavish reception room called the Long Hall. Other rooms to see include the kitchen, family store, bedrooms, playroom, and the "fairy castle," where small children could peer through a window at grown-ups in the hallway below.

The **Lion House** (63 E. South Temple), next door, was built in 1855–1856 of stuccoed adobe; a stone lion guards the entrance. Brigham Young used it as a supplementary dwelling for his many wives and children. Today, the pantry and basement of the building are open to the public as the **Lion House Restaurant.**

Brigham Young Cemetery

Church president, founder of Utah, colonizer, and territorial governor, Brigham Young rests here with five of his wives and his eldest son. Several monuments on the grounds honor the pioneers and Young's family. From State Street near Beehive House, travel a half block east on First Avenue.

Eagle Gate

This modern replacement of the original 1859 gate spans State Street just north of South Temple Street. It once marked the entrance to Brigham Young's property, which included City Creek Canyon. The bronze eagle has a 20-foot wingspan and weighs two tons. The present gate, designed by Brigham Young's grandson, architect George Cannon Young, was dedicated in 1963.

OTHER DOWNTOWN SIGHTS
Abravanel Concert Hall

One of the most striking modern buildings in Salt Lake City, Abravanel Concert Hall (123 W. South Temple, 801/355-2787) glitters with gold leaf, crystal chandeliers, and more than a mile of brass railing. Careful attention to acoustic design has paid off: The concert hall is one of the best in the world. The Utah Symphony Orchestra inaugurated its new home in 1979 after $12 million and three years of construction; the Utah Opera also performs here. An illuminated fountain flows outside on the plaza during concerts.

Salt Lake Art Center

This civic gallery (20 S. West Temple, 801/328-4201, 10 A.M.–5 P.M. Mon.–Sat., until 9 P.M. Fri., 1–5 P.M. Sun., by donation) hosts a changing lineup of traveling and thematic

© W. C. MCRAE

The Salt Palace hosts many conventions, including the huge Outdoor Retailers trade show.

exhibits, including displays of painting, photography, sculpture, ceramics, and conceptual art. Diverse art classes and workshops are scheduled along with films, lectures, poetry readings, musical concerts, and theater. A gift shop offers art books, posters, crafts, and artwork.

Salt Palace Convention Center

This enormous structure (between 200 South and South Temple along West Temple, 801/534-4777) just keeps getting larger. After a recent $58 million expansion that enlarged the facility by 40 percent, the Salt Palace encompasses 515,000 square feet of exhibit space and 164,000 square feet of meeting space, including a 45,000-square-foot ballroom and 66 meeting rooms. Even in the sprawling scale of downtown Salt Lake City, this is a big building. The center also houses the Salt Lake Convention and Visitors Bureau and the **Visitor Information Center** (90 S. West Temple, 801/521-2822, www.visitsaltlake.com).

Clark Planetarium

This planetarium and science center (110 South 400 West, 801/456-7827, www.clarkplanetarium.org, 10:30 A.M.–9 P.M. Mon.–Thurs., until 11 P.M. Fri.–Sat., until 8 P.M. Sun., most exhibits free, IMAX movies require payment), in the new Gateway shopping center, combines a 3D IMAX theater with a five-story screen, plus popular family-oriented science and space exhibits. A highlight is the Hansen Star Theatre, which employs state-of-the-art technology to project a star show on a 360-degree 55-foot dome. Also in the Star Theatre are *Cosmic Light Shows,* which combine computer animation, special effects, and a 12,000-watt digital surround-sound system.

UTAH STATE CAPITOL AND VICINITY
◖ State Capitol

Note that the Utah Capitol building will be closed for seismic renovation until late 2008; call to confirm opening dates.

© W. C. MCRAE

Utah's state capitol as seen by a buffalo

Utah's granite capitol (300 North and State Street, 801/538-3000, 8 A.M.–8 P.M. daily) occupies a prominent spot on a hill just north of downtown. The architectural style may look familiar; the building was patterned after the national capitol. The interior, with its Ionic columns, is made of polished marble from Georgia. Murals depict early explorers and pioneers; smaller paintings and statues show all of the territorial and state governors and prominent Utah figures of the past. The Gold Room, used for receiving dignitaries, provides a formal setting graced by chandeliers, wall tapestries, elegant furniture, and cherubs on the ceiling. Enter the chambers of the House of Representatives, Senate, and Supreme Court from the mezzanine. Photo exhibits of the state's scenic and historic spots, beehive memorabilia, mining, and agriculture line hallways on the ground floor.

Forty acres of manicured parks and monuments surround the capitol. From the steps leading to the building, you can look out over Salt Lake City and straight down State Street, which runs south about 28 miles without a curve. From near the Mormon Battalion Monument, east of the capitol, steps lead down into a small canyon and **Memory Grove,** another war memorial, and a series of streamside parks.

Free tours in summer depart every half hour 9 A.M.–4 P.M. Monday–Friday. Meet in front of the large map on the first floor; call 801/538-1563 for tour details. Visitors are welcome to dine at the circular cafeteria (7 A.M.–4 P.M. Mon.–Fri.) behind the capitol. Annual legislative sessions begin in January and last about 45 days.

Pioneer Memorial Museum

Descendants of Utah's Mormon pioneers have packed all four levels of this museum (300 N. Main St., 801/538-1050, open 9 A.M.–5 P.M. Mon.–Sat., 1–5 P.M. Sun. June–Aug., closed on major holidays, free but donations appreciated), with a huge collection of pioneer artifacts, portraits, and memorabilia that tell the story of the 2,000-mile exodus from Nauvoo, Illinois, to Salt Lake City. A video shown on request introduces the collection.

While some exhibits here are of interest mostly to Mormons (for example, the personal effects of Brigham Young), other displays in the museum's four floors provide insights into the daily life of frontier Utah. The two-story **Carriage House,** connected to the museum by a short tunnel, displays pioneer-era conveyances, including a mule-drawn streetcar, stagecoaches, and the wagon in which Brigham Young is believed to have arrived in the Salt Lake Valley. Free parking is available at a lot between the museum and the State Capitol.

Council Hall

The venerable Council Hall lies across the street from the capitol. Dedicated in 1866, the brick building served as the city hall and a meeting place for the territorial and early state legislatures. Council Hall used to stand downtown before being moved here in 1963.

SALT LAKE CITY'S HISTORIC ARCHITECTURE

Salt Lake City boasts some of the best-preserved historic architecture in the American West. From the magnificent public buildings to the craftsmanship of humble workers' cottages, the city's structures say a lot about early citizens' pride in their earthly City of Zion.

The **Utah Heritage Foundation** (355 Quince St., 801/533-0858, 9 A.M.–5 P.M. Mon.–Fri.) has information and self-guided tour brochures on Salt Lake City's historic districts. In addition to Temple Square and the State Capitol, any tour of the city's historic architecture should include the following:

South Temple Street was probably the most prestigious street address in all of early Utah. Many religious and business leaders owned stately mansions along South Temple, once known as Brigham Street. (A number of these homes are now B&Bs.) Twin towers and gargoyles embellish the imposing Catholic **Cathedral of the Madeleine** (331 E. South Temple, 801/328-8941, open daily year-round and for concerts Sunday evenings in spring and summer). Adjacent is the equally impressive **First Presbyterian Church** (347 E. South Temple). The palatial **Kearns Mansion** (603 E. South Temple, 801/538-1005) now serves as the official governor's residence. Thomas Kearns, noted for his silver-mining wealth, be-

came a U.S. senator and publisher of the *Salt Lake Tribune*. The Kearns Mansion is open for free tours Monday–Saturday in summer and on a limited schedule the rest of the year.

Just north of South Temple Street is the district known as **The Avenues,** where the majority of Salt Lake City's early Catholics lived. While most of these homes aren't grand mansions, they are excellent examples of Victorian workers' homes. Streets in the **Marmalade District** on the hillside west of the capitol bear the names of fruit trees – hence the term "marmalade." Many residences date from the 19th century. The **McCune Mansion** (200 N. Main) is one of the city's most eye-catching old houses. The turn-of-the-20th-century turreted structure features a tiled roof and exceptional interior woodwork.

Downtown's grandest building is undoubtedly the **City and County Building** (400 South and State Street). This confection of a building resembles a fanciful Scottish castle right out of *Brigadoon* and once served as the Utah State Capitol; it's now the seat of SLC's local government. Across the street at Main and 400 South is the **Exchange District,** a clutch of grandly handsome office towers that served as the banking center for turn-of-the-20th-century Salt Lake City.

It is now the home of the **Utah Travel Council.** Drop in to see the staff of the **Utah Tourism and Recreation Information Center** (801/538-1030 or 800/200-1160, open 8 A.M.–6 P.M. Mon.–Fri., 9 A.M.–5 P.M. Sat.) on the main floor for information on sights, services, and events in the state. The 1883 Gothic Revival building just to the east was also moved here. Formerly the 18th Ward Chapel of the LDS Church, it's now **White Memorial Chapel** and is used for community events.

UNIVERSITY OF UTAH AND VICINITY
Gilgal Gardens
On the way to the university from downtown

is one of the newest, and oddest, of Salt Lake City's public parks. The Gilgal Gardens (749 East 500 South, 8 A.M.–dusk daily, free) is a colossally weird sculpture garden created by an LDS bishop whose spiritual seekings led him to create stone-carved monuments and engrave stones with Biblical and other religious verses.

Thomas Child began Gilgal Gardens in 1945, and work on the gardens and its sculpture continued until his death in 1963. The carvings and statues illustrate a curious mix of Mormon, Old Testament, and Egyptian influences: A Sphinx has the head of LDS founder Joseph Smith, while other sculpture vignettes represent Nebuchadnezzar's dream and a mon-

© W. C. MCRAE

This sphinx, located in the Gilgal Gardens, has the face of LDS church founder Joseph Smith.

ument to the masonry trade. In all, there are 13 carved stone sculptures, plus innumerable flagstones with etched quotes within a garden setting. It's all very strange and oddly moving, and if you're attracted by people's curious spiritual journeys, you should make this one of your SLC stops—there's no other garden quite like this one.

University of Utah

Mormon pioneers established a university in their short-lived town of Nauvoo, Illinois, and they brought its books with them to Utah. The University of Deseret opened in 1850, just two and a half years after the first colonizers reached the Salt Lake Valley. It was renamed the University of Utah (201 Presidents Circle, 801/581-7200) in 1892 and moved to its present site on a terrace east of town in 1900. The state-assisted institution now sprawls across a 1,500-acre campus. A giant "U" on the hillside lights up during sporting events, and if the university team wins, the lights flash.

About 28,000 students study a wide range of fields including the liberal arts, business, medicine, science, engineering, and architecture—some 16 colleges and schools in all. The adjacent Research Park is a partnership of the university and private enterprise involving many students and faculty. A center of culture, the University of Utah is home to the Utah Museum of Natural History, the Utah Museum of Fine Arts, musical concerts, and theater groups. Visitors are welcome at cultural and sporting events, libraries, bookstore, movie theater, and Olpin Union food services. Most recreational facilities are reserved for students. For a campus map, a list of scheduled events, and other information, drop by the Park Building (801/581-6515) at the top of President's Circle or the Olpin Union (801/581-5888) just north of Central Campus Drive. On-campus parking is available at metered spaces around the grounds and in pay lots next to the Olpin Union and the Marriott Library; free parking can be found off campus on residential streets.

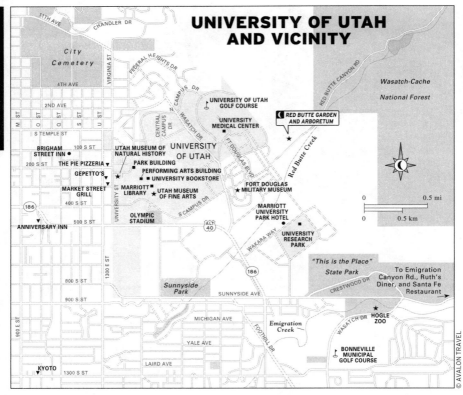

UNIVERSITY OF UTAH AND VICINITY

Utah Museum of Natural History

This large and varied collection of geology, biology, and anthropology exhibits (1390 E. President's Circle, 801/581-6927, www.umnh.utah .edu, 9:30 A.M.–5:30 P.M. Mon.–Sat., noon–5 P.M. Sun. and holidays, $6 adults, $3.50 children 3–12 and seniors 65 and up), off University Street (1350 East), tells the natural and early Native American history of Utah. Impressive natural history models include dinosaurs, early mammals, and the varied wildlife of the present day. Look for the exhibit of California gulls *(Larus californicus)* devouring the plague of grasshoppers. Exhibits display artifacts and trace the development of prehistoric cultures and their replacement by modern tribes such as the Ute and the Navajo. A reproduction of the huge Barrier Canyon Mural pictograph shows early Native American art. Other exhibits illustrate Utah's mining history and feature specimens of the state's more than 600 minerals. A gift shop sells animal souvenirs for the kids, fossil and mineral specimens, books on Utah and natural history, and posters. Free validated parking is available in front.

Utah Museum of Fine Arts

This ambitious museum (410 Campus Center Dr., 801/581-7332, www.umfa.utah .edu, 10 A.M.–5 P.M. Tues.–Fri., until 8 P.M. Wed., 11 A.M.–5 P.M. Sat–Sun., $5 adults, $3 youths 6–18 and seniors) displays a little of everything, from 5,000-year-old Egyptian art to works by contemporary artists. Permanent exhibitions include art of China, India, Southeast Asia, Europe, Africa, pre-Columbia, and the early American West. Three large galleries host visiting exhibitions; there's also a pleasant café. Free parking validation in university parking lots.

◀ Red Butte Garden and Arboretum

Utah's largest botanical garden (300 Wakara Way, 801/581-4747, www.redbuttegarden.org, open year-round with irregular hours and days, $6 adults, $4 seniors and children 3–17, free access to hiking trails in the natural area) offers 30 acres of floral displays, ponds, waterfalls, and four miles of mountain nature trails in a 200-acre natural area. The garden visitors center features botanical gifts and books, and the Courtyard Garden is an excellent place for a family picnic.

To reach the garden from I-15, take the Sixth South exit, which will take you east, then turn north two blocks to Fourth South and head east past where Fourth merges into Fifth South. After rising up a hill, take the left onto Wakara Way and continue east to the Red Butte Garden and Arboretum exit.

Fort Douglas Military Museum

At the Fort Douglas Military Museum (32 Potter St., 801/581-2151, noon–5 P.M. Tues.–Sat., noon–4 Sun., free), artifacts and historical photos take visitors back to the days of the Nauvoo Legion, the Mormon Battalion, and U.S. Army life in Utah during pioneer days. In late 1862, Colonel Patrick Connor marched to this site with his California-Nevada volunteers and built Camp Douglas. Officially the post defended the mail route and kept check on local tribes of Native Americans. Connor also felt it necessary to keep an eye (and cannon) on the Mormons, whom he and other federal officials distrusted. The colonel wasted no time in seeking Native Americans to fight. In January 1863, just months after his arrival, Connor's troops ambushed several hundred Shoshoni on the Bear River in northern Cache Valley. The event advanced Connor's career but ranks as one of the bloodiest slaughters in the history of U.S.–Native American conflicts. Later, in a more peaceable mood, the colonel and some of his soldiers pioneered the development of Utah's minerals near Park City and elsewhere in the territory.

The museum's exhibits show the unique histories of Fort Douglas and other military bases in Utah. A World War I room includes photos of German POWs once interned here. Other exhibits illustrate the big military buildup during World War II, when Utah even had a naval base.

The museum building, officers' row, and some of the other structures at Fort Douglas date from the 1870s and 1880s and are built in an architectural style termed Quartermaster Victorian. Pick up a walking-tour leaflet of the fort at the museum; a map shows the nearby post cemetery, where Colonel Connor, soldiers, and German POWs are buried. Fort Douglas, formerly used by the military as administration and recruitment offices, is now part of the University of Utah. Turn north on Wasatch Drive from 500 South and travel one-half mile to the museum.

"This Is the Place" State Park

It is believed that Brigham Young gazed onto the Salt Lake Valley for the first time from this spot (2601 Sunnyside Ave., 801/582-1847, visitors center open 9 A.M.–5 P.M. Mon.–Sat., park open dawn–dusk daily, free), southeast of the University of Utah near the mouth of Emigration Canyon. He spoke the famous words, "This is the right place. Drive on." Exactly 100 years later, on July 24, 1947, a crowd gathered to dedicate the massive *This Is the Place* monument. Twelve-foot bronze statues of Brigham Young flanked by Heber C. Kimball and Wilford Woodruff stand atop a central pylon. The park has a pleasant picnic area, and the monument honors not only the Mormon pioneers but also the Catholic missionaries from Spain, fur trappers and traders, government explorers, and California immigrants who contributed to the founding of an empire in "the top of the mountains." Sculptures, bas-reliefs, and plaques around the base of the monument illustrate Utah's beginnings. A visitors center displays a mural depicting major events on the migration of the "Saints" from Nauvoo, Illinois, to their promised land. An eight-minute narration recounts the journey; narration in a foreign language can be requested, too.

Old Deseret (10 A.M.–5 P.M. daily Memorial Day–Labor Day, $6 adults, $4 children and seniors, family pass available for $20), on the grounds near the monument, re-creates a Utah pioneer village. During the summer it comes alive with farming and crafts demonstrations and wagon rides. Most of the dozen buildings that were moved here are original, some of the first in the valley. Some notable structures include Brigham Young's forest farmhouse, the 1847 Levi Riter cabin, and the Charles Rich house, designed in the 1850s for polygamous family living.

Hogle Zoo

Utah's state zoo (2600 E. Sunnyside Ave. 801/582-1631, www.hoglezoo.org, 9 A.M.–5 P.M. daily, until 4 P.M. in winter, $8 adults, $6 children 3–12 and seniors 65 and over), an especially popular spot with the kids, is on the eastern edge of town and across from "This Is the Place" State Park. Children like to ride the miniature train (closed in winter, $1) and see exhibits in the Discovery Center. Many of the large-animal enclosures have natural settings; here you'll see the familiar elephants, rhinos, and hippos. The apes and monkeys carry on almost all the time, though mornings are best to hear the songs of the white-handed gibbons of Southeast Asia. Exhibits on tropical, temperate, and desert zones contain deadly cobras and vipers, aardvarks, Australian kookaburras, brightly colored birds in a walk-in aviary, and dozens of other exotic species. The cats include lions, leopards, tigers, and ocelots.

SOUTH OF DOWNTOWN
◖ Liberty Park

This large park (southeast of downtown and bordered by 900 and 1300 South and by 500 and 700 East) is the jewel of the city's public park system and contains abundant recreational facilities in addition to an excellent aviary, an arts center, and 80 acres of grass and shady boulevards. A fun addition to the park is a conceptual "map" of northern Utah that re-creates the rivers, lakes, and mountains as a series of fountains and wading pools.

The Children's Garden—playground, amusement park, snack bar, and large pond with rental boats—sits in the southeast corner of the park (all closed in winter). The tennis center on the western side of the park offers 16 lighted courts and instruction; an outdoor swimming pool adjacent to the tennis center is open in summer.

Birds have taken over the southwest corner of Liberty Park. **Tracy Aviary** (589 East 1300 South, 801/596-8500, www.tracy aviary.org, 9 A.M.–6 P.M. daily Mar.–Oct., 9 A.M.–4:30 P.M. the rest of the year, adults $5, students and seniors $4, children 4–12 $3) houses more than 400 individual birds of 135 species and offers bird shows with trained free-flying birds such as falcons. Birds on display include majestic golden and bald eagles, showy flamingos and peacocks, the hyacinthine macaw (the world's largest parrot), the golden pheasant of China, and hundreds of other feathered friends. Emus from Australia prance across fields while ducks, geese, swans, and other waterfowl keep to the ponds. You'll also get to meet Utah's only native vulture, the turkey vulture.

Bird shows can change from year to year, so call or check the website to verify what's happening. Shows are traditionally presented during the summer at 11 A.M. and 1 P.M. Tuesday–Saturday, 11 A.M., 1, and 3 P.M. Saturday, and at 1 and 3 P.M. Sunday and holidays.

The Chase Mill, just north of the aviary entrance, was built by Isaac Chase in 1852 and is one of the oldest buildings in the valley. Free flour from the mill saved many families during the famine of 1856–1857. The mill is open periodically for special events. Formal gardens lie north of the mill.

Chase's adobe brick house (built 1853–1854), farther to the north, has been restored. Go inside to see exhibits of the **Chase Home Museum of Utah Folk Art** (801/533-5760, noon–5 P.M. Mon.–Thurs., 2–7 P.M. Fri.–Sun. Memorial Day–Labor Day, noon–5 P.M. weekends only mid-Apr.–Memorial Day and Labor Day–mid-Oct., free) sponsored by the Utah Arts Council. On display is contemporary Utah folk art, including quilts, rugs, woodcarvings, ethnic arts, and Native American works.

International Peace Gardens

With wishes for world peace, the Salt Lake Council of Women created this unusual garden (900 West and 1000 South) in the northwest corner of Jordan Park. Members of Salt Lake City's various ethnic and national groups were invited to design and plant a garden that reflected their cultural heritage. Currently, nearly 25 groups have taken part; you'll find Dutch windmills, pagodas, and Buddhist temples scattered around the grounds. The Peace Gardens are a lovely place for a stroll in summer.

Arts and Entertainment

Salt Lake City offers a wide variety of high-quality arts and cultural institutions; classical and religious music venues are particularly noteworthy. Jazz, blues, and alternative music clubs and dance bars are also numerous. In short, there's a lot more going on here than you might think at first glance.

Local publications are the best places to check for information on what's happening. The *City Weekly* is the largest and most comprehensive free newspaper, with lots of arts and entertainment coverage. The daily papers, *Deseret News* and *Salt Lake Tribune,* both have listings in their Friday Weekend and Sunday Art and Entertainment sections. The visitors center website (www.visitsaltlake.com) also has a lengthy listing of events and entertainment options.

Most of Salt Lake City's top-flight music and arts performances take place in a handful of venues, themselves world-class facilities worthy of a visit. When you know the dates of your visit, contact the Salt Lake County Center for the Arts (801/355-2787 or 888/451-2787, www.artix.org), which handles ticketing for most of the city's arts offerings, to find out what's going on while you're here.

The city's main performance space is the **Capitol Theatre** (50 West 200 South,

801/534-6364), a glittering vaudeville house from the turn of the 20th century that's been refurbished into an elegant concert hall. The **Abravanel Concert Hall** (between the Salt Palace and Temple Square at 123 W. South Temple, 801/533-5626) has fantastic acoustics and is home to the Utah Symphony and other classical music performances. The new **Rose Wagner Performing Arts Center** (138 West 300 South, 801/323-6800) has three performance spaces and is home to several local dance and theater troupes.

In **Temple Square** (800/537-9703), the Mormon tabernacle and the Assembly Hall host various classical and religious musical concerts, including performances by the famed Mormon Tabernacle Choir.

NIGHTLIFE

Nearly all nightclubs and music bars that serve alcohol in Salt Lake are private clubs, and you'll end up paying a temporary membership charge (usually $5) in addition to the cover charge (even if you don't have a drink). Clubs open to the public (no membership needed) are so noted. The best way to check out the club scene is to pick up a copy of *City Weekly,* a free and widely available news and entertainment weekly.

If you're just looking for a beer and a chance to chat with the locals, try one of the brewpubs listed in the *Food* section. There's no membership charge at Salt Lake brewpubs.

Monk's House of Jazz (19 East 200 South, 801/350-0950) was formerly the city's premier jazz club; now it offers a mix of live dance bands, Djs, and karaoke. The **Tavernacle Social Club** (201 East 300 South, 801/519-8900) is a hipper-than-thou piano bar, with an updated lounge act that features dueling pianos, sing-alongs, and karaoke on Sundays and Tuesdays.

To explore the live-music club scene, start at **Mo's Neighborhood Grill** (358 S. West Temple, 801/359-0586). Mo's is a friendly club with a wide range of live music most nights, including jazz, folk, and rock, plus a couple evenings a week of comedy. Another spot for local bands is the **Urban Lounge** (241 South 500 East, 801/746-0557).

If you're looking for a singles-oriented, collegiate crowd and some danceable live music, check out the **Port O' Call** (78 West 400 South, 801/521-0589). Touring national acts stop at **The Depot** (in the Gateway Center at 400 S. West Temple, 801/355-5522), a nightclub in the cavernous Union Station; it's also a good spot for meeting friends when there's no live band.

In the category of high-spirited, only-in-Salt-Lake fun, try out **Bar Deluxe** (666 S. State Street, 801/521-5255), with live music, karaoke, or other hijinks nightly, and **Burt's Tiki Lounge** (726 S. State St., 801/521-0572), with live music and such mayhem as Sunday Night Karaoke Swilldown and the Thursday Voodoo organist.

If you just want to dance, SLC offers a number of options. **Area 51** (400 West 451 South, 801/534-0819) has theme nights (Gothic, Techno, DiverseCity, etc.). The vast, multi-floored **Elevate/Hotel** complex (155 W. 200 South, 801/478-4310) has enough dance floors and bar areas to fill an entire night's worth of fun.

Salt Lake City isn't known for its vibrant gay scene, but there is a growing number of gay clubs. A good place to start the evening is **The Trapp** (102 South 600 West, 801/531-8727), with a nice outdoor deck and a cruisy atmosphere, or **Try-Angles** (251 West 900 South, 801/364-3203), with a pleasant patio for drinks and sunning. **MoDiggity's** (3424 S. State St., 801/332-9000) is mostly a women's club, but everyone is welcome.

THEATER

Pioneer Theatre Company (801/581-6961, www.pioneertheatre.org), one of Salt Lake City's premier theater troupes, offers a seven-show season running September–May. The company performs a mix of contemporary plays, classics, and musicals. Although the company operates from the University of Utah's **Pioneer Memorial Theatre** (300 South and University Street), it is not part of the university itself. The Pioneer Memorial Theatre is also the site of University of Utah student productions and the Young People's Theatre, which produces plays for children.

The city's cutting-edge theater group is the **Salt Lake Acting Company** (168 West 500 North, 801/363-7522, www.saltlakeacting company.org). This well-established troupe doesn't shy away from controversy: Their excellent production of Tony Kushner's *Angels in America* raised eyebrows and stirred strong reactions. Besides presenting new works from around the world, the company is also committed to staging plays by local playwrights; there are performances year-round.

The **Grand Theatre** (1575 S. State St., 801/957-3459 or 801/957-3263, www.thegrand.org), on the Salt Lake City Community College campus, is home to a year-round program of theatrical performances (mostly musicals) by both student and semiprofessional troupes.

For something spoofier, the **Off Broadway Theatre** (272 S. Main, 801/355-4628, www .theobt.com) is the place for "improv" competitions, Broadway comedies, and topical farces. At the **Desert Star Playhouse** (4861 S. State,

801/266-7600, www.desertstar.biz), you'll find old-fashioned melodramas and cabaret-style comedy skits.

CLASSICAL MUSIC AND DANCE

From its modest beginnings in 1940, the **Utah Symphony** (www.utahsymphony.org) has grown to be one of the best-regarded orchestras in the country. Each season, the symphony performs in the glittering Abravanel Hall (123 W. South Temple, 801/533-NOTE for tickets) in Salt Lake City and travels to Snowbird, Deer Valley, Ogden, Provo, Logan, and other cities.

The **Utah Opera Company** (www.utahopera.org), founded in 1978, stages four operas during its October–May season. The Utah Opera and the Utah Symphony now share administrative offices and contact information (see above).

Another center for classical music and performance is the **University of Utah** (801/581-6772, www.utah.edu/home/artsculture). The university's Symphony Orchestra, Chamber Orchestra, jazz ensembles, opera, bands, and ballet, dance, and choral groups present regular concerts and performances on and off campus; the season runs September–May.

Ballet West (801/323-6900, www.balletwest.org) began in Salt Lake City in 1963 as the Utah Civic Ballet, but as the group gained fame and began traveling widely it chose its present name to reflect its regional status. This versatile group's repertoire includes classical, modern, and foreign works. Most Utah performances take place at downtown's Capitol Theatre, September–May.

The professional **Ririe-Woodbury Dance Company** (801/323-6801, www.ririewoodbury.com) has one of the most active dance programs outside New York City. The varied repertoire includes mixed media, eye-catching choreography, and humor. The group also shares its expertise by teaching production and dance skills to students and professionals. Ririe-Woodbury Dance Company is based at the Rose Wagner Performing Arts Center, as is the **Repertory Dance Theatre**

(801/534-1000, www.rdtutah.org), a professional company focusing on classical American and contemporary dance.

CONCERT SERIES AND MUSIC FESTIVALS

The **Concert Series at Temple Square** (801/240-3318 or 801/240-2534) presents hundreds of performances a year for the public; all are free. The LDS Church sponsors the varied musical fare to provide a common meeting ground of great music for people of all faiths. You might hear chamber music, a symphony, operatic selections, religious choral works, piano solos, organ works, a brass band, or a percussion ensemble. Programs last about an hour and usually take place at 7:30 P.M. Friday and Saturday evenings in either the Assembly Hall or the tabernacle. The same group presents summer outdoor concerts at Temple Square June–August. Organists present 25-minute **Organ Recitals** in the tabernacle at noon (and at 2 P.M. in summer) Monday–Saturday and at 2 P.M. Sunday. The **Mormon Tabernacle Choir** sings in the tabernacle on Sunday mornings at 9:30 A.M. (be seated 15 minutes before) for a 30-minute radio broadcast. You're also welcome to attend rehearsals by the Mormon Tabernacle Choir on Thursday evenings at 8 P.M. At the same hour on Wednesday evenings, the Mormon Youth Symphony rehearses in the tabernacle, and on Tuesday evenings the Youth Chorus rehearses. Schedules of all musical events are posted in Temple Square and available at www.visittemplesquare.com.

The **Madeleine Arts and Humanities Program** is held in the historic Cathedral of the Madeleine (331 E. South Temple, 801/328-8941, www.saltlakecathedral.org, all events are free.). This series of choral, organ, and chamber music concerts takes place on Sunday evenings throughout the spring and summer. Lectures, theatrical performances, and dance concerts are also held.

In June, the **Gina Bachauer International Piano Competition** (801/521-9200, www.bachauer.com) takes over Salt Lake City. More than 60 young pianists from around the world gather to perform a two-week-long series of performances both as solos (early in the competition) and with the Utah Symphony (only the finalists). The winners compete for recording contracts, a Steinway piano, and thousands of dollars in cash. It's a good chance to enjoy the musicianship of tomorrow's rising piano stars and to savor the thrill of musical competition.

Summer Concerts and Festivals

Salt Lake City is filled with free music concerts in summer, when local parks and public spaces become makeshift concert halls. Check local media or the visitors center for details on the following ongoing concert series.

Gallivan Center Concerts and Films features free noontime concerts on weekdays, plus free live music concerts on Thursday evenings. **Monday in the Park Concerts** are free concerts at the Chase Home Museum in Liberty Park. **Creekside Concerts** are held outdoors every Saturday evening in summer at Westminster College (1840 South 1300 East, 801/832-2437).

The Utah Symphony (801/533-5626, www .utahsymphony.org) also offers an extensive summer series of concerts at Wasatch Front ski areas, a short drive from downtown Salt Lake City.

MOVIES

First-run multiplexes are spread around downtown Salt Lake City; check the daily newspapers for listings. The city is lucky to have the Salt Lake Film Society, which sponsors a "year-round film festival" with art and foreign films at the **Broadway Centre** (111 East 300 South, 801/321-0310), and the **Tower Theatre** (876 East 900 South, 801/328-1645). The **Utah Film and Video Center** (20 S. West Temple, 801/534-1158), in the Salt Lake Art Center, also screens independent documentaries, animation, and experimental films.

Brewvies (677 South 200 West, 801/355-5500) is a brewpub/cinema combo where you can buy an ale and a burger and watch a first-run or cult favorite film.

For a selection of major release first-run movies, check out the following multiplexes in the downtown area: **Megaplex 12 at The Gateway** (165 S. Rio Grande, 801/325-7500) and **Trolley Corners Theatre** (515 South 700 East, 801/364-6183).

EVENTS

Concerts, festivals, shows, rodeos, and other special events happen here nearly every day, and the Salt Lake Convention and Visitors Bureau (90 S. West Temple, 801/521-2822, www .visitsaltlake.com) can tell you what's going on. Also check the Visitors Bureau's *Salt Lake Visitors Guide* for some of the best-known annual happenings.

The first weekends of April and October see the annual **General Conference of the Church of Jesus Christ of Latter-day Saints,** held at Temple Square (801/240-2531). The church president (believed to be a prophet of God) and other church leaders give guidance to members throughout the world. (Hotel rooms are in short supply at this time.)

Cinco de Mayo is celebrated in May with a party and concerts at Gallivan Center (801/538-3247) the week of May 5. A larger celebration of multiculturalism comes the third weekend of the month, when the grounds of the Salt Lake City and County Building at State Street and 400 South erupt with the **Living Traditions Festival** (801/596-5000). Enjoy dances, food, and entertainment of the many different cultures that make up the Utah mosaic.

The **Scottish Festival and Highland Games** (801/969-7030) starts June off on a lively step with manly contests, bagpipe music and dancing, and ethnic food; held at Murray Park. The **Utah Arts Festival** (801/322-2428, www.uaf .org) takes place the last weekend in June and includes lots of music, dance, literary readings, art demonstrations, craft sales, and food booths. The event is held at Library Square.

The summer's single largest festival is in July. The **Days of '47 Celebration** (801/247-8545) commemorates the arrival of Mormon pioneers here on July 24, 1847. The city celebrates with three parades, including the huge 24th of July Pioneer Parade (the day is a state holiday), a marathon, lots of fireworks, and the year's biggest rodeo, held at the Delta Center.

The **Greek Festival** (Hellenic Center at 300 South 300 West, 801/328-9681) in September celebrates Greek culture with food, music, folk dancing, and tours of the historic Holy Trinity Greek Orthodox Cathedral. The festival is held the weekend after Labor Day. The **Utah State Fair** (held at the state fairgrounds (North Temple and 1000 West, 801/538-8441) is a celebration of the state's agricultural heritage and features rodeos, livestock shows and judging, arts and crafts exhibits, musical entertainment, and a midway.

Shopping

If you're a shopper already familiar with Salt Lake City, you'll note a few changes during your next visit. The enormous ZCMI and Crossroads Plaza shopping centers, which anchored downtown shopping and fronted Temple Square, have been demolished (see the sidebar *City Creek Center Remakes Downtown*). In their place, the City Creek Center development is scheduled for completion in 2011.

As in most large U.S. cities, shoppers in Salt Lake take much of their business to suburban malls. Cottonwood Mall, at Highland and Murray Holiday Roads south of the city, and Valley Fair Mall, at I-215 Exit 18 southwest of the city, are two popular malls, each containing more than 100 stores. Salt Lake City also boasts several unique shopping areas and unusual stores, including some excellent boutique centers and one large downtown mall. *Remember that many shops are closed on Sunday.*

The Gateway

Just west of downtown, on the site of the former rail yards, The Gateway (between 400 and 600 West, between 200 South and North Temple, 801/456-0000) was built in the run-up to the 2002 Winter Olympics as a destination boutique shopping mall, entertainment center, and condo development. The shops, restaurants, and entertainment venues line a winding pedestrian street that is designed to resemble a developer's idea of Olde Worlde. Here you'll find chain stores such as Abercrombie and Fitch, J. Crew, Barnes and Noble, and Virgin Megastore, plus the Megaplex 12 cinema (801/325-7500), and an impressive selection of restaurants and bars.

Trolley Square

Salt Lake City's most unusual shopping center came about when developers cleverly converted the city's old trolley barn. Railroad magnate E. H. Harriman built the barn in 1908 as a center for the city's extensive trolley system. The vehicles stopped rolling in 1945, but their memory

The Gateway shopping area is an easy walk from the Temple Square area.

© W. C. MCRAE

lives on in Trolley Square (corner of 500 South and 700 East, 801/521-9877, open daily, including Sunday afternoons). Inside, you'll see several trolleys, a large stained-glass dome, salvaged sections of old mansions and churches, and many antiques. More than 100 shops and restaurants call this gigantic barn home. Watch movies at Cineplex-Odeon Theatres (four screens, 801/363-1183) and Flick 2 (two screens, 801/521-6113). **Trolley Corners** (515 South 700 East), across the street, is a smaller shopping area with shops, restaurants, and Trolley Corners Theatres (801/364-6183).

TP Gallery

Crafts and art by Native Americans are featured here (252 S. Main St., 801/364-2961, 10 A.M.–6 P.M. Mon.–Sat.). Look for beadwork and leather items (Utes), jewelry (Navajo, Hopi, and Zuni tribes), pottery (Hopi and New Mexico Pueblo tribes), kachina dolls (Hopi), baskets (Papago), sand paintings, books, and cassettes.

Recreational Equipment, Inc. (REI)

If you suddenly realize you need a new tent pole, some zip-off pants, or any other gear for hiking, camping, bicycling, skiing, river-running, rock climbing, and travel, swing by this large store (3285 East 3300 South, 801/486-2100, 10 A.M.–9 P.M. Mon.–Fri., 9 A.M.–7 P.M. Sat., 11 A.M.–6 P.M. Sun.). Gear can be rented,

too. The book section is a good place to look for regional outdoor guides. Topo maps cover the most popular hiking areas of Utah.

Gardner Village

This attractive shopping village (1100 West 7800 South, 801/566-8903) in West Jordan, 12 miles south of downtown Salt Lake City, offers a restaurant and crafts shops in the refurbished Gardner Mill, built in 1877. Old houses and cabins have been moved to the grounds and restored for additional shops. Step into the silo to dine at **Archibald's Restaurant** (801/566-6940, open daily for lunch and dinner, and Saturday and Sunday for breakfast) for American and continental food. The village also has a small museum of historic exhibits. Take I-15 Midvale Exit 301 (7200 South), turn west, and follow signs to the Gardner Mill.

Bookstores

Sam Weller's Zion Book Store (254 S. Main, 801/328-2586, 10 A.M.–8 P.M. Mon.–Sat., 10 A.M.–6 P.M. Sun.) claims to be one of the West's largest, with more than half a million new and used books covering many topics. If you're a book lover, you'll want to check out the impressive selection of quality used books. The **University of Utah's Bookstore** (270 South 1500 East, 801/581-6326, 8 A.M.–5:30 P.M. Mon.–Fri., 9 A.M.–4 P.M. Sat.) has a varied selection on many subjects.

Sports and Recreation

In Salt Lake City, a glimpse at the horizon and the craggy, snow-covered Wasatch Mountains tells you that outdoor recreation is very close at hand. Even on a short visit to the Salt Lake area, you'll want to get outdoors and enjoy a hike or a bike ride up a mountain canyon. You won't be alone: The city's newest immigrants, young professionals, are as attracted to the city's right-out-the-back-door access to the great outdoors as to the region's vibrant economy.

Skiing has always been Utah's biggest recreational draw, and as host of the 2002 Winter Olympics the Salt Lake City area drew the attention of international skiing and winter sports lovers. Summer visitors will find lots to like after the snow melts: Most ski areas remain open for warm-weather recreation, including mountain biking, hiking, trail rides, tennis, and plain old relaxing. The U.S. Forest Service manages Mill Creek and Big and Little

Cottonwood Canyons as part of the Wasatch National Forest. Located just east of the city, these canyons provide easy access to hiking and biking trail systems and to popular fishing streams.

DOWNHILL SKIING

Utah's "Greatest Snow on Earth" lies close at hand. Within an hour's drive from Salt Lake City you can be at one of seven downhill areas in the Wasatch Range, each with its own character and distinctive skiing terrains. (Coverage of the individual resorts follows in the *Park City and the Wasatch Range* chapter.) The snow season runs from about mid-November to April or May. Be sure to pick up the free *Utah Ski Vacation Planner* from Ski Utah, Inc. (150 West 500 South, Salt Lake City, UT 84101, 801/534-1779 or 800-SKI-UTAH, snow conditions at 801/521-8102, fax 801/521-3722) or from most tourist offices in Utah. Or check out the website at www.skiutah.com). The planner lists most Utah resorts and has diagrams of the lifts and runs, lift ticket rates, and detailed information on lodging.

Salt Lake City–area ski resorts are grouped quite close together. Although they are in different drainages, Solitude and Brighton ski areas in Big Cottonwood Canyon and Snowbird and Alta ski areas in Little Cottonwood Canyon, they all share the high country of the Wasatch Divide with Park City, Deer Valley, and The Canyons ski areas. There is no easy or quick route between the three different valleys, however, and traffic and parking can be a real hassle. Luckily, there are plenty of options for convenient public transport between Salt Lake City and the ski areas and between the resorts themselves.

Alternatively, you can ski between the various ski areas with **Ski Utah Interconnect** (801/534-1907, www.skiutah.com/interconnect), which provides a guide service for backcountry touring between Wasatch Front ski areas. Skiers should be experienced and in good physical condition because of the high elevations (around 10,000 feet) and the need for some walking and traversing. Touring is with

downhill equipment. On Monday, Wednesday, Friday, and Sunday, tours start at Deer Valley Resort and ski through Solitude, Brighton, Alta, and Snowbird via the backcountry terrain between them. On the other three days (Tuesday, Thursday, and Saturday), the trip starts at Snowbird and goes through Alta, Brighton, and Solitude. The cost of $195 a day includes the guide's services, lunch, and all lift tickets.

Transportation to Ski Areas

Salt Lake City's public bus system, the UTA (801/287-4636, www.utabus.com), has regularly scheduled service to the four resorts on the west side of the Wasatch Range: Solitude, Brighton, Snowbird, and Alta. You can get on the buses downtown (they connect with the TRAX light rail), at the University of Utah, or at the bottoms of the canyons. A couple of early-morning buses run up to the ski areas every day; return buses depart the ski areas around 5 P.M.

Lewis Brothers Stages (801/359-8677 or 800/826-5844, www.lewisstages.com) offers a Ski Express from the Salt Lake City Airport and downtown hotels to all Wasatch Front ski areas, including Park City, Deer Valley, The Canyons, Brighton, Solitude, Snowbird, and Alta. Book a $52 round-trip ticket through a hotel or call Lewis Brothers directly. Lewis Brothers also operates the Canyon Jumper, which connects Park City to Snowbird, Alta, Solitude, and Brighton. Optional ski packages include transportation and lifts at a discount. Similar services are offered by other transportation companies, including All Resort Express (435/649-3999 or 800/457-9457), and Park City Transportation (435/649-8567 or 800/637-3803).

CROSS-COUNTRY SKIING

During heavy snowfalls, Salt Lake City parks and streets become impromptu cross-country ski trails, and any snowed-under Forest Service road in the Wasatch Range is fair game for Nordic skiers. The Mill Creek Canyon road is a favorite. If you don't mind cutting a trail or skiing ungroomed snow, ask at ski rental shops for hints on where the backcountry snow is good.

Otherwise, there are numerous organized cross-country ski areas in the Salt Lake City area. The Mountain Dell Golf Course in Parley's Canyon (off I-80 toward Park City) is a favorite place to make tracks. There are cross-country facilities at Alta and Solitude (see the *Park City and the Wasatch Range* chapter) as well as at the White Pine Touring Center in Park City.

HIKING, JOGGING, AND BIKING

The four miles of trails outside **Red Butte Garden** east of the University of Utah are a quiet place for a walk or a jog (see the *University of Utah and Vicinity* section). The hiking trails wind through wildflower meadows and past old sandstone quarries. You don't need to pay the admission to the gardens proper to hike the trails.

Joggers also favor the shady oasis of **Liberty Park** and the rolling terrain of **Sugarhouse Park**. (See *Parks* in the *Other Activities* section for more information.)

Mill Creek Canyon

For hiking trails in the nearby Wasatch Range, simply drive up Mill Creek or Big or Little Cottonwood Canyon (entrance at Wasatch Boulevard and Mill Creek Road, 3800 South) and look for trailheads. Contact the Wasatch-Cache National Forest Recreation Information, in the REI store (3285 East 3300 South, 801/466-6411), for maps and advice. Also see the *Big Cottonwood Canyon* and *Little Cottonwood Canyon* sections in *Park City and the Wasatch Range* chapter.

Great mountain biking, plentiful picnic areas, and many hiking possibilities lie along Mill Creek just outside Salt Lake City. You may bring your dog along, too—this is one of the few canyons where pets are welcome. In fact, odd-numbered days are designated "leash-free" days in Mill Creek Canyon. However, these off-leash regulations are fiercely contested and may change. Obey the posted regulations when

you begin your hike. Bicycles are allowed in Mill Creek Canyon only on even days—days when dogs must be leashed.

Picnic sites are free and available on a first-come, first-served basis; most lack water. The first one, **Church Fork Picnic Area,** is three miles in at an elevation of 5,700 feet; **Big Water Picnic Area** is the last, 8.8 miles up at an elevation of 7,500 feet. A $2.25 per vehicle usage fee is charged in Mill Creek Canyon.

Salt Lake Overlook on Desolation Trail is a good hiking destination for families. The trail climbs 1,200 feet in two miles for views of the Salt Lake Valley. Begin from the lower end of Box Elder Picnic Area (elev. 5,760 feet) on the south side of the road. Energetic hikers can continue on Desolation Trail beyond the overlook to higher country near timberline and go all the way to Desolation Lake (19 miles). The trail runs near the ridgeline separating Mill and Big Cottonwood Canyons, connecting with many trails from both canyons. Much of this high country lies in the Mount Olympus Wilderness. See Mt. Aire and Park City West 7.5-minute topo maps.

Alexander Basin Trail winds to a beautiful wooded glacial bowl below Gobblers Knob; the trailhead (elev. 7,080 feet) is on the south side of the road eight miles up Mill Creek Canyon, 0.8 mile beyond Clover Springs Picnic Area. The moderately difficult trail begins by paralleling the road northwest for a few hundred feet, then turns southwest and switchbacks one mile to the beginning of Alexander Basin (elev. 8,400 feet). The trail to Bowman and Porter Forks turns right here, but continue straight one-half mile for the meadows of the upper basin (elev. 9,000 feet). The limestone rock here contains many fossils, mostly shellfish. From the basin it's possible to rock-scramble to the summit of Gobblers Knob (elev. 10,246 feet). (The name comes from an attempt by the mine owners to raise turkeys after their ore played out; the venture ended when bobcats ate all the birds.) See the Mt. Aire 7.5-minute topo map.

Bikers should continue to the end of the Mill Creek Canyon road, then set out on the Big

Water Trail. The Great Western Trail (a 3,000-mile ridgetop trail, stretching from Canada to Mexico) intersects Big Water at 1.5 miles. Bikers can turn off of Big Water and follow the Great Western Trail to the ridgetop divide overlooking The Canyons Ski Resort. Here, the route turns south and follows the Wasatch Crest Trail along the ridge and around the head of the upper Mill Creek basin. To avoid conflicts with hikers, Big Water, Little Water, and the Great Western Trail are closed to mountain bikes on odd-numbered calendar days.

City Creek Canyon
In the city itself, a pleasant and relaxing route for a stroll or a jog follows **City Creek Canyon,** a shady, stream-filled ravine just east of the State Capitol. The road that runs up the canyon is now closed to most traffic and extends more than five miles from its beginnings at **Memory Grove,** just northeast of the intersection of E. North Temple and State Street, to Rotary Park at the top of the canyon.

Since pioneer days, people have obtained precious water from City Creek and enjoyed the diverse vegetation, wildlife, and scenery. Because City Creek is still part of the city's water supply, regulations prohibit dogs, horses, and overnight camping.

Hikers and joggers may travel on the road every day. In summer (Memorial Day weekend–September 30), bicyclists may enter only on odd numbered days, motorized vehicles may drive up only on even calendar days and only with reservations (usually for a picnic); a gate at the bottom controls entry. No motorized vehicles are allowed the rest of the year, but bicycles can use the road daily then. A $3 charge applies if you drive through to the trailhead at the upper end (no reservation needed).

The big attraction for many visitors is a stop at one of the picnic areas along the road. Picnickers can reserve sites with the Water Department (801/483-6797). Sites are sometimes available on a first-come, first-served basis (midweek is best). Picnic permits cost $3 and up depending on the size of the group. The entrance to City Creek Canyon is reached via

Bonneville Boulevard, a one-way road. From downtown Salt Lake City, head east on North Temple, which becomes Second Avenue after crossing State Street, then turn left (north) 1.3 miles on B Street, which becomes Bonneville Boulevard after 11th Avenue, to City Creek Canyon Road. Returning from the canyon, you have to turn right on Bonneville Boulevard to the State Capitol. Bicyclists and joggers may approach City Creek Canyon from either direction.

A popular hiking destination from the trailhead at road's end (elev. 6,050 feet) is City Creek Meadows, four miles away and 2,000 feet higher. After 1.5 miles, you'll pass Cottonwood Gulch on the left; a side trail leads up the gulch to an old mining area. After another one-half mile on the main trail, a spring off to the right in a small meadow is the last reliable source of drinking water. During the next mile, the trail grows steeper and winds through aspen groves and then passes two shallow ponds. The trail becomes indistinct here, but you can continue one mile northeast to the meadows (elev. 8,000 feet); a topo map and compass help. For splendid views of the Wasatch Range, climb north one-half mile from the meadows up the ridge to where Davis, Salt Lake, and Morgan counties meet. Hikers also enjoy shorter strolls from the trailhead along the gentle lower section of trail.

OTHER ACTIVITIES
Parks
Salt Lake City has lovely parks, many of which have facilities for recreation. For information about the city's park system, contact the Parks and Recreation office at 801/972-7800; for county park information, call 801/468-2560.

There are abundant reasons to spend time at **Liberty Park** (southeast of downtown and bordered by 900 and 1300 South and by 500 and 700 East, 801/538-2062), including the Tracy Aviary, the children's play area, and the acres of shade and lawn. The park also affords plenty of opportunity for recreation. The tennis center on the western side offers 16 lighted courts. The outdoor swimming pool adjacent to the tennis center is open in summer. During the sweltering Salt Lake summer, the shady boulevards provide a cool environment for jogging. You'll find horseshoe pits to the north of the park's historic Chase House.

Mormon pioneers manufactured beet sugar at **Sugarhouse Park** (1300 East and 2100 South, 801/467-1721), on the southeast edge of Salt Lake City, beginning in 1851; the venture later proved unprofitable and was abandoned. Today, expanses of rolling grassland in the 113-acre park are ideal for picnics, strolling, and jogging. The park has a playground and fields for baseball, soccer, and football. In winter, the hills provide good sledding and tubing. A lake attracts seagulls and other birds for bird-watching. Sweet smells rise from the Memorial Rose Garden in the northeast corner.

Swimming Pools and Gymnasiums

Two of the best and most central outdoor public pools are at **Liberty Park** (1300 South and 700 East) and **Fairmont Park** (2361 South 900 East). Serious lap swimmers should check out the **Salt Lake City Sports Complex** (near the University of Utah at 645 S. Guardsman Way, 801/583-9713); it has a 25-meter indoor pool and a lovely 50-meter outdoor pool with great views of the mountains.

For an even bigger splash (at a far heftier price than the public pools listed above), try **Raging Waters** (1200 West 1700 South, 801/972-8300), a water-sport theme park that features water slides and a wave pool. The children's area has waterfalls, geysers, a "dinosaur beach," and a small wave pool.

Tennis

Seventeen city parks have courts; call the Salt Lake City Parks and Recreation Department (801/972-7800) for the one nearest you. **Liberty Park** (1300 South and 500 East) has 16 courts.

Golf

Salt Lake City claims to have the highest number of golf courses per capita in the na-

tion, with more than a dozen in the metro area. There's a course for every level of expertise, from city-owned nine-hole courses for beginners to championship-level courses like the 27-hole private **Stonebridge Golf Club** (4415 Links Drive, West Valley City, 801/957-9000, www.golfstonebridgeutah.com) and the 36-hole, par-71 or -72 public **Mountain Dell Golf Course** (I-80 Exit 134, 801/582-3812, www .slcgov.com/publicservices/Golf), each with challenging terrain and incredible mountain views. Other courses include **Bonneville** (954 Connor St., 801/583-9513), east of downtown, an 18-hole, par-72 course. **University** (on the University of Utah campus at 100 South 1900 East, 801/581-6511) is a nine-hole, par-33 executive course. **Forest Dale** (2375 South 900 East, 801/483-5420), near Sugarhouse Park, is a nine-hole, par-36 course. **Nibley Park** (2730 South 700 East, 801/483-5418) is a nine-hole, par-34 course. **Glendale** (1603 West 2100 South, 801/974-2403) is an 18-hole, par-72 course. **Rose Park** (northwest of downtown at 1386 N. Redwood Rd., 801/596-5030) is an 18-hole, par-72 course.

Skating

Cottonwood Heights Recreation Center (7500 South 2700 East, 801/943-3160) offers year-round ice-skating and lessons, indoor and outdoor pools, racquetball courts, and a weight room. Roller skate at the **Utah Fundome** (4998 South 360 West in Murray, 801/293-0800) and **Classic Roller Skating Centers** (9151 South 255 West in Sandy, 801/561-1791).

Canoeing

A canoe trip through **Jordan River State Park** (office at 1084 N. Redwood Rd., 801/533-4496, 8 A.M.–5 P.M. Mon.–Fri.) reveals birds and other wildlife in a peaceful setting that you wouldn't expect so close to downtown Salt Lake City. A green canopy of willow, Russian olive, and Siberian elm overhangs the river for much of its length. Canoeists can stop at the International Peace Gardens and other parks along the way. The state park office can advise on boating conditions and places to rent canoes, paddles, and life jackets. Park rangers enforce the rule that each boater must wear a Coast Guard–approved life jacket. Put-in is at 1200 West 1700 South (across from Raging Waters); take-out is at 1000 North 1525 West.

You'll need two cars or someone to pick you up at trip's end. Allow at least 2.5 hours (without stops) for the six-mile route. This is the only section of the river open to boats. It's a good idea to call the park before a trip to check on possible river obstructions. Off-season boating isn't recommended because of the greater likelihood of hazards blocking the way.

Rock Climbing

Rockreation (2074 East 3900 South, 801/278-7473) offers instruction, equipment rental, and a massive rock gym with 6,700 square feet of climbing terrain. Day passes are available; there's also a weight and fitness room at the complex.

Equipment Rental

Utah Ski and Golf (134 West 600 South, 801/355-9088) rents golf clubs in summer and ski equipment when the snow falls. Rent bicycles at **Canyon Bicycle** (3969 S. Wasatch Blvd., 801/278-1500). For hiking, camping, climbing, and ski rentals, try **REI** (3285 East 3300 South, 801/486-2100). Another all-sport rental outfit is **Wasatch Touring** (702 East 100 South, 801/359-9361).

SPECTATOR SPORTS
Professional Sports

Utah professional sports fans love their **Utah Jazz,** which are usually strong contenders in the NBA's Western Division. The team plays at the EnergySolutions Center (300 West at South Temple). Tickets are hard to come by at the last minute, but it's worth a call to the team's box office (801/355-SEAT) to inquire. Otherwise, you'll need to rely on scalpers or ads in the classifieds. The **Salt Lake Bees** (801/485-3800) is the AAA affiliate of baseball's Anaheim Angels. Games are played at the impressive Franklin Quest Field April–September; it's hard to imagine a more astonishing backdrop to a game of baseball than the craggy Wasatch Front. The **Utah Grizzlies** (E Center at 3200 S. Decker Street, 801/988-8000) are Salt Lake City's International League ice-hockey team.

University of Utah

University athletic teams (1825 E. South Campus Dr., 801/581-UTIX) compete in football, basketball, baseball, softball, tennis, track and field, gymnastics, swimming, golf, skiing, and other sports.

Bonneville Raceway Park

For roaring engines, smoking tires, and checkered flags, visit the raceway in West Valley City (6555 West 2100 South, 801/250-2600) during its April–October season.

Accommodations

Salt Lake City has the best selection of accommodations in Utah, with many new hotels built for the 2002 Winter Olympics. Unless you're on a really tight budget, you'll probably be more comfortable if you avoid the cheapest motels along West Temple or State Street. Many of these older motor-court units have become residential lodgings, and the owners don't put much effort into upkeep. However, you should have a pleasant stay at all of the following accommodations.

There are several major lodging centers. Downtown Salt Lake City has the advantage of being close to Temple Square, EnergySolutions Arena, the Salt Palace, and most other visitor attractions. South of downtown, near 600 South and West Temple, is a clutch of hotels and motels, including several business-oriented hotels. While these lodgings are only six blocks from the center of the city at Temple Square, remember that blocks are very long in SLC.

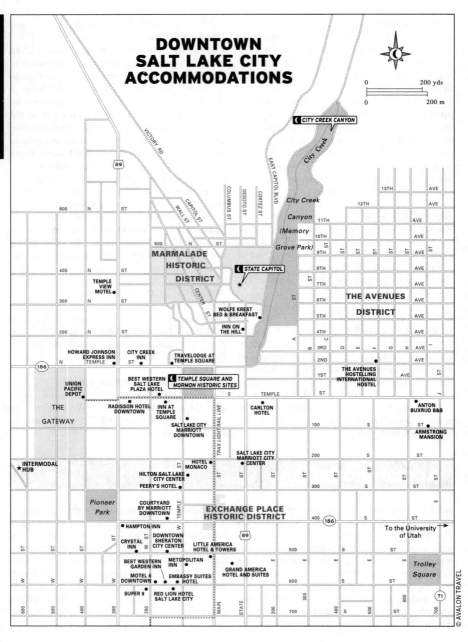

DOWNTOWN SALT LAKE CITY ACCOMMODATIONS

CITY CREEK CANYON

STATE CAPITOL

MARMALADE HISTORIC DISTRICT

City Creek Canyon (Memory Grove Park)

THE AVENUES DISTRICT

TEMPLE VIEW MOTEL

WOLFE KREST BED & BREAKFAST

INN ON THE HILL

HOWARD JOHNSON EXPRESS INN

CITY CREEK INN

TRAVELODGE AT TEMPLE SQUARE

THE AVENUES HOSTELLING INTERNATIONAL HOSTEL

UNION PACIFIC DEPOT

BEST WESTERN SALT LAKE PLAZA HOTEL

TEMPLE SQUARE AND MORMON HISTORIC SITES

THE GATEWAY

RADISSON HOTEL DOWNTOWN

INN AT TEMPLE SQUARE

CARLTON HOTEL

ANTON BUXRUD B&B

SALT LAKE CITY MARRIOTT DOWNTOWN

ARMSTRONG MANSION

INTERMODAL HUB

HOTEL MONACO

SALT LAKE CITY MARRIOTT CITY CENTER

HILTON SALT LAKE CITY CENTER

PEERY'S HOTEL

Pioneer Park

COURTYARD BY MARRIOTT DOWNTOWN

EXCHANGE PLACE HISTORIC DISTRICT

To the University of Utah

HAMPTON INN

DOWNTOWN SHERATON CITY CENTER

CRYSTAL INN

LITTLE AMERICA HOTEL & TOWERS

Trolley Square

BEST WESTERN GARDEN INN

METOPOLITAN INN

MOTEL 6 DOWNTOWN

EMBASSY SUITES HOTEL

GRAND AMERICA HOTEL AND SUITES

SUPER 8

RED LION HOTEL SALT LAKE CITY

© AVALON TRAVEL

Another cluster of hotels and motels is west along North Temple, the primary surface street leading to the airport. If your trip to Salt Lake City involves visiting students or conducting business at the university, there are a couple of good lodging options near the campus.

In general, room rates can be rather high, though quality is good. The prices listed below are standard rack rates. You can frequently beat these prices by visiting the hotel's website to check for specials. Also, due to hotel overbuilding for the Olympics—63 new hotels were built in the Salt Lake area after the city won the Olympic nod—you can frequently find real deals on SLC lodgings at Internet booking sites if there's not a convention in town. Prices can alter by as much as $100 a night within the same week, so take the following prices as guidelines only.

If you have trouble locating a room, consider using the city's free reservation service (800/847-5810, www.visitsaltlake.com).

DOWNTOWN NEAR TEMPLE SQUARE
Under $50
There aren't many good budget-class accommodations in this prime area, but if cheap is what you're looking for, try the **Temple View Motel** (325 North 300 West, 801/521-9525, $46 and up), slightly north of the city center; there are three kitchen units.

$50-100
You can find several good moderately priced motels near Temple Square. The **Howard Johnson Express Inn** (121 North 300 West, 801/521-3450 or 800/541-7639, $66 and up) is an older but well-maintained motor-court motel with a pool, complimentary continental breakfast, and free HBO. The **City Creek Inn** (230 W. North Temple, 801/533-9100 or 866/533-4898, www.citycreekinn.com, $58) is a well-kept little motor court motel just two blocks from the temple.

Just east of Temple Square is the pleasant, well-maintained **Carlton Hotel** (140 E. South Temple, 801/355-3418 or 800/633-3500, www .carltonhotel-slc.com, $75 and up). The Carlton is an older hotel in a great location, and offers a guest laundry, exercise room, sauna, hot tub, and in-room VCRs with free movies; there are also five suites.

$100-150
Both of the following have family-style restaurants on premises. Overlooking Temple Square is the **Best Western Salt Lake Plaza Hotel** (122 W. South Temple, 801/521-0130 or 800/366-3684, http://plaza-hotel.com, $119 and up), which offers a pool in addition to its great location.

The first of SLC's historic older hotels to be refurbished into a natty, upscale lodging was the **Peery Hotel** (110 West 300 South, 801/521-4300 or 800/331-0073, $110 and up). Its 1910 vintage style is preserved in the comfortable lobby, while the guest rooms are completely updated, nicely furnished, and quite spacious. There are two restaurants on the premises, as well as an exercise room.

Some of Salt Lake's most grand heritage homes sit on Capitol Hill, just below the State Capitol Building. Surely one of the most eye-catching is the red sandstone mansion now called the **Inn on the Hill** (225 N. State St., 801/328-1466, www.innonthehillslc.com, $119 and up). Built in 1906 by a local captain of industry, the inn has 14 guest rooms decorated with period detail, but all with modern amenities like private bathrooms. Practically every room has views over all of Salt Lake City. Full gourmet breakfasts are included.

$150-200
One block west of the temple is the **Radisson Salt Lake City Hotel Downtown** (215 W. South Temple, 801/531-7500 or 888/201-1718, $159 and up). At this modern, 15-story hotel, you'll find a pool and conference, business, and exercise facilities; children under 12 stay free. The **Salt Lake City Marriott City Center** (220 S. State St., 801/961-8700, $179 and up) was completed just before the Olympics; it sits above Gallivan Plaza, an urban park and festival space. A luxury-level business hotel, the

Marriott has an indoor pool, recreation area, and a fine dining restaurant.

Over $200

The **[C] Hotel Monaco** (15 West 200 South, 801/595-0000 or 877/294-9710, www.monaco-saltlakecity.com, $229 and up) occupies a grandly renovated historic office building in a very convenient spot in the middle of downtown; on the main floor is **Bambara,** one of the most sophisticated restaurants in Utah. Rooms are sumptuously furnished with real élan: This is no anonymous business hotel in beige and mauve. Expect wild colors and contrasting fabrics, lots of flowers, and excellent service. Facilities include on-site fitness center, meeting rooms, plus concierge and valet services. Each room comes with two-line phones, CD stereo, in-room fax, printer, and copier, plus an iron and board. Pets are welcome, and if you forgot your own pet, the hotel will deliver a companion goldfish to your room. If you want to splurge on a hotel in Salt Lake, make it this one.

One of SLC's best hotels, the **Hilton Salt Lake City Center** (255 S. West Temple, 801/328-2000 or 800/HILTONS, $214 and up) is a huge complex with an indoor pool, two fine-dining restaurants, a private club, fitness facilities, valet laundry, and convention facilities for small groups.

The **Salt Lake City Marriott Downtown** (75 S. West Temple, 801/531-0800 or 800/228-9290, $219 and up) is directly across from the Salt Palace Convention Center. At this high-quality hotel there's an indoor/outdoor pool, sauna, fitness center, a good restaurant, lounge, and private nightclub (available to hotel guests). Weekend rates are often deeply discounted.

SOUTH DOWNTOWN

Just south of the religious sites and convention areas downtown is a large complex of hotels and motels (mostly representatives of large chains) with rooms in almost every traveler's price range. These lodgings aren't entirely convenient for travelers on foot, but if you have a car or intend to ride buses (unfortunately, the free bus zone doesn't extend this far south, but the zone is just a short walk from these hotels), then these are some of the newest and nicest places to stay in the city.

Under $50

Directly south of downtown a couple of miles is the **International Ute Hostel** (21 E. Kelsey Ave., AKA 1160 South, just east off State Street, 801/595-1645, www.internationalute hostel.com, $20–45). Beds are available in dorm-style or private rooms, and there's full access to kitchen facilities and common areas.

$50-100

Motel 6 Downtown (176 West 600 South, 801/531-1252 or 800/466-8356, $53 and up) is a standard motel, but it does have a pool. Pets are allowed at the **Super 8 Motel** (616 South 200 West, 801/534-0808 or 800/800-8000, $75 and up). The **Metropolitan Inn** (524 S. West Temple, 801/531-7100 or 800/578-7878, $76 and up) offers nicely maintained rooms, all with coffeemakers and access to a heated pool and hot tub. Pets are accepted.

If you're looking for comfortable rooms without breaking the bank, the **Little America Hotel and Towers** (500 S. Main St., 801/363-6781 or 800/304-8970, $95 and up) is a great place to stay. This large lodging complex (with nearly 850 rooms) offers three room types. Courtside rooms and garden suites are scattered around the hotel's nicely manicured grounds, with most rooms overlooking a pool or fountain. Tower suites are executive-level suites in a 17-story block offering some of SLC's best views. All guests share the hotel's elegant public areas, two pools, health club, and workout facility. The restaurant here is better than average, and there is free airport transport.

The **Best Western Garden Inn** (154 West 600 South, 801/521-2930 or 800/521-9997, $89 and up) offers a pool, fitness room, restaurant, guest laundry, and free airport shuttle.

Holiday Inn Downtown (999 S. Main, 801/359-8600 or 800/933-9678, $89 and up) is three blocks farther south than the other lodgings in this listing but offers facilities that make it stand out, such as a putting green, tennis courts, basketball court, and a playground for children in addition to the usual pool and exercise facilities. Besides, there's a free downtown shuttle service to whisk guests to the center of things (free airport transportation is offered as well). Rooms are very nicely appointed.

$100-150

Red Lion Hotel Salt Lake Downtown (161 West 600 South, 801/521-7373 or 800/325-4000, $100 and up) has a pool, spa, exercise facilities, room service, guest laundry, and free airport transportation.

One of the nicer-for-the-money hotels in this part of Salt Lake City is the **Crystal Inn** (230 West 500 South, 801/328-4466 or 800/366-4466, $110 and up). Rooms here are very large and nicely furnished; all come with refrigerators and microwaves. There's a free hot breakfast buffet for all guests. For recreation, there's an indoor pool, exercise room, sauna, and hot tub.

$150-200

Sheraton City Center Hotel (150 West 500 South, 801/532-3344 or 800/421-7602, $149 and up) is one of the city's best addresses for high-quality comfort and service. The lobby areas are very pleasant, and facilities include a great pool, exercise room, and spa. The rooftop restaurant and lounge are also notable. The Hilton offers free airport and downtown shuttles.

One of the best situated of all the south downtown motels is **Courtyard by Marriott Downtown** (130 West 400 South, 801/531-6000, $159 and up). It's very central to all the restaurants and happenings in the city's fast-changing warehouse/loft district. There's a pool, hot tub, fitness facility, and airport shuttle.

If you're in Salt Lake for an extended time, or are traveling with a family, consider the **Embassy Suites Hotel** (110 West 600 South, 801/359-7800 or 800/362-2779, $169 and up). All suites have efficiency kitchens (with coffeemakers) and separate living and sleeping areas; there are two two-bedroom units. Facilities include a pool, sauna, exercise area, restaurant, and lounge.

Hampton Inn (425 South 300 West, 801/741-1110 or 800/HAMPTON, $159 and up) offers complimentary hot breakfast, indoor pool, hot tub, and high-speed wireless Internet access.

Over $200

A 2001 addition to the Salt Lake hotel scene—and to the skyline—is the **C Grand America Hotel and Suites** (555 S. Main St., 801/258-6000 or 800/621-4505, $304 and up). This behemoth of a hotel is a full Salt Lake City square block (remember, that's 10 acres), and its 24 stories contain 775 rooms, more than half of them suites. Rooms have luxury-level amenities; expect all the perks and niceties that modern hotels can offer delivered in an over-the-top package that borders on the indulgences of Las Vegas hotels.

EAST OF DOWNTOWN

There aren't many lodging choices in this part of the city, but this is a pleasant residential area without the distinct urban jolt of much of the rest of central Salt Lake City.

This is also where most of the city's bed-and-breakfasts are located. Salt Lake City contains a wealth of beautiful residential architecture, especially in the historic neighborhoods east of downtown and near the capitol. Early politicians, Mormon leaders, and wealthy merchants especially favored South Temple Street, east of downtown. Many of their mansions have been restored, and some are now high-quality B&Bs.

Most B&Bs have a range of room prices, so use the rate headings as just a guideline; most have suites at a higher price.

Under $50

The Avenues (one mile east of Temple Square, on the corner of 107 F St. and 2nd Ave., 801/363-3855, $17–34) offers dorm rooms with use of a kitchen, TV room, and laundry. Information-packed bulletin boards list city sights and goings-on, and you'll meet travelers from all over the world. Beds are available in the dorm (includes sheets), or in private rooms (only half have private baths). Reservations (with first night's deposit) are advised in the busy summer-travel and winter-ski seasons. From downtown, head east on South Temple Street to F Street, then turn north two streets.

$50-100

The **Anton Boxrud Bed and Breakfast** (57 South 600 East, 801/363-8035 or 800/524-5511, www.antonboxrud.com, $85 and up) offers seven guest rooms (with a mix of private and shared baths) in a grand 1901 Victorian brick home. The house has been restored to its original splendor and features hardwoods, wood-paneled walls, stained glass, and period furnishings. There's also a hot tub, and breakfasts are notably good.

The **Brigham Street Inn** (1135 E. South Temple, 801/364-4461 or 800/417-4461, $89 and up) is a fabulous Queen Anne mansion. When the architect-owners refurbished the home, they engaged 12 local designers and gave each a room to make over—the result is an eclectic showcase of sensitive historic renovation. There are nine guest rooms, each with private bath. One deluxe room has a private garden entrance, kitchen, and whirlpool tub.

$100-150

The **Armstrong Mansion** (667 East 100 South, 801/531-1333 or 800/708-1333, www.armstrongmansion.com, $119 and up) is another Queen Anne mansion converted to a comfortable B&B. Each of the 14 rooms has a private bath and is decorated with full Victorian flair.

The **Anniversary Inn** (460 South 1000 East, 801/363-4900 or 800/324-4152, www.anniversaryinn.com, $139 and up) caters to couples and newlyweds interested in a romantic getaway. All 32 rooms are imaginatively decorated according to theme: Beds may be in a covered wagon or a vintage rail car, and bathrooms may be in a "sea cave." Chances are good that your room will have its own private waterfall. You get to pick your suite from choices

that include "the lighthouse," "the opera house," "South Pacific," and "Venice." These rooms aren't just filled with kitsch—they are luxury-class rooms, with big-screen TVs, hot tubs, stereos, and private bathrooms. Rates vary widely according to the room. If you'd like to check out these clever theme rooms before signing up, call the inn for information on early afternoon tours, which are held daily except Sunday. There's a second Anniversary Inn at 678 East South Temple (same website for information).

$150-200

Right on the University of Utah's research park, the **Marriott University Park Hotel and Suites** (480 Wakara Way, 801/581-1000 or 800/637-4390, $199 and up) is one of the city's best-kept secrets for luxurious lodgings in a lovely setting. You can't miss with the views: All rooms either overlook the city or look onto the soaring peaks of the Wasatch Range directly behind the hotel. Rooms are very nicely appointed—the suites are some of the nicest in the city. All rooms have minibars, refrigerators, and coffeemakers; there's a pool and exercise room, and bicycles are available for rent.

A block from the recent commercial development at Trolley Square is the **Chase Suite Hotel by Woodfin** (765 East 400 South, 801/532-5511 or 800/237-8811, $159 and up). All rooms have separate sleeping and living spaces and come with full kitchens—just the thing if you're in town for a few days or traveling with a family. There's also a pool, hot tub, and sport court.

WEST DOWNTOWN TO THE AIRPORT

Nearly all of the following offer transportation to the Salt Lake City Airport. Hotels with the smallest addresses on W. North Temple are closest to downtown.

$50-100

Gateway Motel (819 W. North Temple, 801/533-0603 or 877/388-8311, $49 and up) was spiffed up for the 2002 Winter Olympics.

It's on the road to the airport but still quite close to downtown.

Although it's on the road to the airport, the **Econo Lodge** (715 W. North Temple, 801/363-0062 or 800/877/233-2666, $69 and up) is also convenient to downtown, as it's just west of the I-15 overpass. The motel offers a courtesy car to downtown or the airport and has a pool and guest laundry. Of the many older motor-court motels along North Temple, perhaps the best-maintained is the **Overniter Motor Inn** (1500 W. North Temple, 801/533-8300 or 800/914-8301, $75 and up), with an outdoor pool and clean rooms. Moderately priced rooms are also available at **Days Inn** (1900 W. North Temple, 801/539-8538 or 800/329-7466, $92 and up), and at the **Motel 6 Airport** (1990 W. North Temple, 801/364-1053, $53 and up), where there's a pool. In the same price range but closer to the airport, the **Airport Inn** (2333 W. North Temple, 801/539-0438, $79 and up) has a pool and guest laundry.

The **Quality Inn SLC Airport** (1659 W. North Temple, 801/533-9000, $89 and up) offers nicely furnished rooms, a restaurant and private club, and a pool and spa. Practically next door to the terminal is the **Ramada Salt Lake City** (5575 W. Amelia Earhart Dr., 801/537-7020 or 800/272-6232, $79 and up), with a pool and spa.

$100–150

The **Radisson Hotel Salt Lake City Airport** (2177 W. North Temple, 801/364-5800 or 800/333-3333, $139 and up) is a very attractive, lodge-like building with nicely furnished rooms. Guests receive a complimentary continental breakfast and newspaper, and in the evenings there's a "manager's reception" with free beverages. Facilities include a pool, spa, and fitness room. Suites come with a loft bedroom area. There's quite a range in room prices, though package rates and promotions can bring down the rates dramatically.

$150–200

At the **Airport Hilton** (5151 Wiley Post Way,

801/539-1515 or 800/999-3736, $1 rooms are very spacious and nicely and facilities include two pools, a putting green, sports court, and an exercise room and spa. The hotel even has its own lake.

CAMPGROUNDS

Camp VIP (1400 W. North Temple, 801/328-0224, $27 for tents or RVs without hookups, with hookups $36) offers tent and RV sites year-round with showers, swimming pool, game room, playground, store, and laundry. From I-15 northbound, take Exit 311 for I-80, go west 1.3 miles on I-80, exit north one-half mile on Redwood Road (Highway 68), then turn right another one-half mile on North Temple. From I-15 southbound, take Exit 313 and turn south 1.5 miles on 900 West, then turn right 0.8 mile on North Temple. From I-80 either take the North Temple exit or exit on Redwood Road (Highway 68) and go north one-half mile, then right one-half mile on North Temple.

Hidden Haven Campground (435/649-8935, year-round, tent and RV sites without hookups $16.50, with hookups $21.75), 18 miles east of Salt Lake City near Park City, has showers, a store, laundry, and a trout stream. Take I-80 Exit 143, then go east 1.6 miles on the north frontage road (or take Park City Exit 145 and go west one mile on the north frontage road).

Pioneer Village Campground (801/451-8100, mid-Apr.–mid-Oct., tent and RV sites without hookups $25, with hookups $29–35), 16 miles north of Salt Lake City in Farmington, at Lagoon Amusement Park, has showers, a store, laundry, and discounts on rides. Take I-15's Lagoon exit and follow the signs.

Cherry Hill Camping Resort (1325 S. Main in Kaysville, 801/451-5379, mid-Apr.–mid-Oct., some activities operate only Memorial Day–Labor Day weekends, tent or RV sites without hookups $28, with hookups $34), 18 miles north of Salt Lake City, features a water slide, innertube ride, swimming pool, Pirates Cove (for young children), restaurant, miniature golf, and a variety of games, as well as a large campground with showers, a store, and laundry. Take I-15 Lagoon/Farmington Exit 327 and go north two miles on U.S. 89.

Reservations for Forest Service campsites can be made by calling 877/444-6777 or by visiting www.reserveamerica.com. There are two campgrounds in Big Cottonwood Canyon about 15 miles southeast of downtown Salt Lake City. Both have drinking water and cost $16 a night. **Spruces Campground** (elev. 7,400 feet, 9.1 miles up the canyon) is open early June–mid-October. The season at

Redman Campground (elev. 8,300 feet) lasts mid-June–early October. It's between Solitude and Brighton, 13 miles up the canyon.

Little Cottonwood Canyon (about 19 miles southeast of downtown Salt Lake City) has two campgrounds with drinking water. **Tanners Flat Campground** (elev. 7,200 feet, 4.3 miles up the canyon) is open mid-May–mid-October ($16). **Albion Basin Campground** lies high in the mountains (elev. 9,500 feet) and is open early July–late September ($16). Go 11 miles up the canyon (the last 2.5 miles are gravel).

Food

Travelers will be pleased with the quality of food to be found in Salt Lake City. If you've been traveling around the more remote areas of the state, the abundance of ethnic restaurants especially will be a real treat.

Most of the following restaurants serve alcohol, though you may need to ask specifically to see the drinks menu. At the time of publication, none of the restaurants in the listings below were private clubs (which require a membership to get in), but these things change. Several of the more popular restaurants have private clubs adjacent to the dining areas.

The free *Salt Lake Visitors Guide* also lists dining establishments. Dinner reservations are advisable at the more expensive restaurants. Also note that most restaurants are closed Sunday; if you're going to be in Salt Lake over the weekend, ascertain that your hotel has a restaurant, or you may be wandering the streets looking for an eating establishment that's open on the Sabbath.

COFFEEHOUSES AND BREAKFAST

If you've fallen victim to the nation's obsession with gourmet coffees, you'll discover that lattes and cappuccinos are more scarce in Utah than elsewhere because of Mormon strictures on caffeine. However, several fine coffeehouses exist in Salt Lake City. The **Salt Lake Roasting Co.** (329 East 400 South, 801/363-7572, 6:45 A.M.–midnight daily) offers a wide selection of coffees, fresh baked European-style pastries, a vaguely "alternative" atmosphere, and a pleasant outdoor patio in good weather. At **Cup of Joe** (353 West 200 South, 801/363-8322, 7 A.M.–midnight Mon.–Fri., 8 A.M.–midnight Sat., 9 A.M.–8 P.M. Sun.), the atmosphere is sleek and industrial; however, you'll also find comfortable couches, stacks of reading material, and free Wi-Fi. Joe's also serves lunchtime panini sandwiches and is open till midnight with entertainment—poetry readings, acoustic music, conversation clubs—most evenings.

For one of Salt Lake's favorite breakfasts, drive (or ride your bike) a couple of miles east of the city to **Ruth's Diner** (2100 Emigration Canyon, 801/582-5807, open for three meals Mon.–Sat.). The restaurant's namesake was a cabaret singer in the 1920s who opened her own restaurant in 1931. Ruth's Diner has been in continuous operation ever since (the ads read "70 years in business…Boy am I tired!"). Ruth's is full of atmosphere and overlooks a rushing stream. It's a great place to go for an old-fashioned breakfast or a hearty lunch. Live music is featured at Sunday brunch. Another

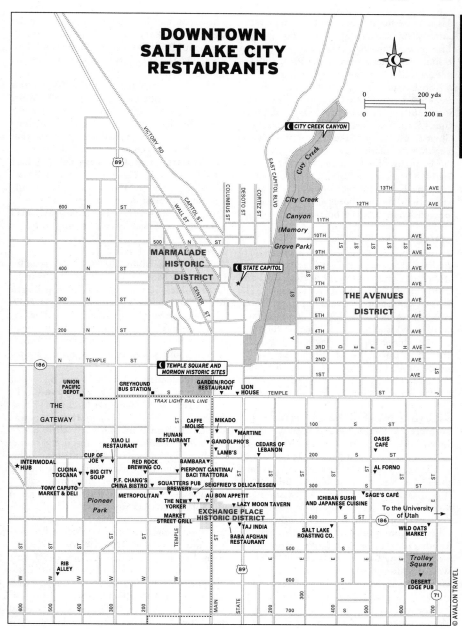

DOWNTOWN
SALT LAKE CITY
RESTAURANTS

| 0 | | 200 yds |
| 0 | | 200 m |

CITY CREEK CANYON

VICTORY RD

89

600 N

COLUMBUS ST
DESOTO ST
CORTEZ ST
EAST CAPITOL BLVD
CAPITOL ST
WALL ST

City Creek

City Creek
Canyon
(Memory
Grove Park)

500 N ST

**MARMALADE
HISTORIC
DISTRICT**

STATE CAPITOL

400 N ST

CENTER ST

300 N ST

200 N ST

13TH AVE
12TH AVE
11TH
10TH
9TH AVE
8TH AVE
7TH
6TH AVE
5TH AVE
4TH AVE
3RD AVE
2ND AVE
1ST AVE

**THE AVENUES
DISTRICT**

186

N TEMPLE ST

TEMPLE SQUARE AND
MORMON HISTORIC SITES

UNION
PACIFIC
DEPOT

GREYHOUND
BUS STATION

GARDEN/ROOF
RESTAURANT

LION
HOUSE

TEMPLE

**THE
GATEWAY**

TRAX LIGHT RAIL LINE

CAFFE
MOLISE

MIKADO

100 S ST

HUNAN
RESTAURANT

MARTINE

GANDOLPHO'S

CEDARS OF
LEBANON

OASIS
CAFÉ

XIAO LI
RESTAURANT

LAMB'S

200 S ST

CUP OF
JOE

INTERMODAL
HUB

RED ROCK
BREWING CO.

BAMBARA

CUCINA
TOSCANA

BIG CITY
SOUP

PIEPONT CANTINA/
BACI TRATTORIA

AL FORNO

P.F. CHANG'S
CHINA BISTRO

SQUATTERS PUB
BREWERY

SEIGFRIED'S DELICATESSEN

300 S ST

TONY CAPUTO
MARKET & DELI

METROPOLITAN

THE NEW
YORKER

AU BON APPETIT

ICHIBAN SUSHI
AND JAPANESE CUISINE

SAGE'S CAFÉ

LAZY MOON TAVERN

Pioneer
Park

MARKET
STREET GRILL

**EXCHANGE PLACE
HISTORIC DISTRICT**

400 S ST

186

To the University
of Utah

TAJ INDIA

BABA AFGHAN
RESTAURANT

SALT LAKE
ROASTING CO.

WILD OATS
MARKET

500 S

TEMPLE ST

89

RIB
ALLEY

MAIN
STATE

600 S

Trolley
Square

DESERT
EDGE PUB

71

600 W
500 W
400 W
300 W
200 W

300 S
700 S
200 S
400 S
500 S
600 S
700 S

classic place for an old-fashioned breakfast is **Lamb's** (169 S. Main, 801/364-7166, open for three meals Mon.–Sat.), which hasn't changed its look or its menu since the 1930s. Lamb's is an easy walk from most downtown hotels.

Another pleasant place for a traditional breakfast is the **Park Cafe** (604 East 1300 South, 801/487-1670, breakfast and lunch Tues.–Sat.). The Park is directly across from Liberty Park, which makes a great pre- or post-breakfast destination. Closer to downtown, in the Exchange District, the **Market Street Grill** (48 Market St., 801/322-4668, open for three meals daily) is best known for its excellent seafood dinners but is also a favored spot for stylish and delicious breakfasts.

Brunch

If you're looking for Sunday brunch, most of the hotel restaurants have buffets, but for the brunch of champions, head to the lodges and resorts up nearby Wasatch Front canyons. The **Silver Fork Lodge** (11 miles up Big Cottonwood Canyon, 435/649-9551, open for three meals daily) is a favorite destination for a scenic brunch, perhaps followed by a hike. The brunch at **La Caille at Quail Run** (at the mouth of Big Cottonwood Canyon, 801/942-1751, dinner nightly, brunch on Sun.) is where to head if you feel like putting on the ritz.

DELIS AND FOOD MARKETS

Siegfried's Delicatessen (69 West 300 South, 801/355-3891, 9 A.M.–6 P.M. Mon.–Fri., 9 A.M.–5 P.M. Sat.) has a great selection of sausages, cold cuts, breads, pastries, and cheeses. A New York–style deli, **Gandolfo's** (158 S. Main, 801/322-3354, 7 A.M.–8 P.M. Mon.–Fri., 10 A.M.–8 P.M. Sat.) offers favorites like meatball and pastrami sandwiches in a dining room hung with sports memorabilia. Another good place to stop to provision a picnic is (**Tony Caputo Market and Deli** (308 West Broadway, 801/531-8669, 9 A.M.–7 P.M. Mon.–Fri., 9 A.M.–5 P.M. Sat., 11 A.M.–3 P.M. Sun.), with great sandwiches, Italian-style sausage and cheese, loads of olives and other Mediterranean temptations, and a park nearby

where you can have an impromptu picnic. **Carlucci's Bakery** (next door at 314 West 300 South, 801/366-484, 7 A.M.–7 P.M. Mon.–Fri., 7 A.M.–5 P.M. Sat.) offers European-style breads and pastries.

On summer Saturdays, the **Salt Lake Farmers Market** (300 South and 300 West, 8 A.M.–1 P.M. Sat., June–Oct.) takes over Pioneer Park. The market offers a wide variety of ethnic and to-go eating options, along with a selection of fresh fruits, vegetables, and baked goods.

Wild Oats Natural Food Market (645 East 400 South, 801/257-9866, 7 A.M.–10 P.M. Mon.–Sat., 8 A.M.–10 P.M. Sun.) is an all-natural grocery store that also features a very good vegetarian café, plus an expansive salad bar with lots of healthy carry-out options.

AMERICAN FARE

Lamb's (169 S. Main, 801/364-7166, open for three meals Mon.–Sat., $13–15) claims to be Utah's oldest restaurant; it started in Logan in 1919 and moved to Salt Lake City in 1939. You can still enjoy the classic 1930s diner atmosphere as well as the tasty food. The menu offers seafood, steak, chops, chicken, and sandwiches; Lamb's is an especially good place for breakfast.

For moderately priced food and history of a different sort, try the **Lion House** (63 E. South Temple, 801/363-5466, 11 A.M.–8 P.M. Mon.–Sat., $8–18). Built in 1856, this was one of Brigham Young's homes, where his 26 wives and 56 children spent most of their time. High-quality cafeteria-style meals are available for lunch and dinner in the basement dining room, formerly the household pantry.

For a lunch of soup and sandwiches, go to **Big City Soup** (235 South 400 West, 801/333-SOUP, 11 A.M.–4 P.M. Mon.–Sat., $5–8). If fast food is more your style, then at least try the local purveyor: **Crown Burgers** (convenient locations to downtown are at 377 East 200 South and 118 North 300 West, 10 A.M.–10:30 P.M. Mon.–Sat., burgers $4 and up) with many outlets throughout the Salt Lake area, is the local favorite for char-grilled burgers and good fries.

The Lion House restaurant was once Brigham Young's home.

Two excellent options for barbecue and soul food are **Sugarhouse Barbecue Co.** (2207 South 700 East, 801/463-4800, lunch and dinner daily, $9–15), with dry-rubbed ribs and pulled pork, and **Rib Alley** (533 South 500 West, 801/359-9926, lunch and dinner Mon.–Fri., dinner Sat., $9–15), with Southern country cooking like barbecue ribs and catfish.

FINE DINING

Salt Lake City has a number of upscale restaurants where high rollers can flex their credit cards and eat world-class cuisine. **Metropolitan** (173 W. Broadway, 801/362-3472, lunch Mon.–Fri., dinner nightly, $25–30) is easily Salt Lake City's most ambitious restaurant, taking "fusion cuisine" to new lengths. In this high-design dining room (reserve tables near the fireplace-cum-water-sculpture), the foods of the world meet and mingle on your plate in preparations that are sometimes unexpected but always stylish. Seared venison medallions appear with tem-

pura vegetables, venison-laced spring rolls, morel mushrooms, and a reduced sake sauce. A crabmeat Napoleon is served with caviar and fresh lobster sauce.

Bambara (in the Hotel Monaco, 202 S. Main, 801/363-5454, open for three meals daily, $20–25) is another exciting fixture to the Salt Lake dining scene. The menu emphasizes the freshest and most flavorful of local meats and produce, with preparations in a wide-awake New American style that's equal parts tradition and innovation. This is easily the most beautiful dining room in the city. Highly recommended.

Martine (22 East 100 South, 801/363-9328, lunch weekdays, dinner Mon.–Sat.) offers equally delicious food in a less formal atmosphere. The antique high-ceilinged dining room is coolly elegant, and the cooking and presentation subtly continental. You have a choice of ordering tapas-style—$6.50–7.50 for lime and garlic calamari or tarragon halibut cakes with saffron aioli—or ordering fixed-price multi-course dinners, featuring delicacies such as duck breast with coriander and black current glaze, starting at $23 for two courses.

For classic French cuisine, **La Caille at Quail Run** (near Little Cottonwood Canyon at 9565 Wasatch Blvd., 801/942-1751, dinner nightly, brunch on Sun., $30–40 per person for dinner) offers superb pastry, crepes, seafood, and meat dishes in an 18th-century rural French atmosphere. Vineyards, gardens, ponds, and manicured lawns surround the re-created French chateau—hard to believe it's Utah. Antique furnishings grace the dining rooms and halls. Dress is semiformal; reservations are advised.

VEGETARIAN

Even a meat-loving place like SLC offers a selection of dining options for vegetarians. **Sage's Café** (473 East 300 South, 801/322-3790, lunch and dinner daily, breakfast Sat.–Sun., $12–15) serves satisfying organic vegetarian cuisine, while the wine list emphasizes organic wines. **Oasis Café** (151 South 500 East, 801/322-1162, three meals daily,

$13–21) serves an ambitious all-organic menu that borrows tastes and preparations from around the world; while most dishes are vegetarian, fresh fish and some organic meats are also served. **Evergreen House** (755 State St, 801/328-8889, 11:30 A.M.–6 P.M. Mon.–Sat., $6–13) prepares all-vegetarian Chinese dishes. The café at **Wild Oats Market** (645 East 400 South) serves a vegetarian menu.

BREWPUBS

Brewpubs are often the most convenient places in Utah to enjoy good food and drink, as there's no private-club rigmarole. Each of the following pubs is open for both lunch and dinner daily; main courses range $8–15.

The state's oldest brewpub is **(Squatters Pub Brewery** (147 W. Broadway, 801/363-2739). In addition to fine beers and ales, the pub (part of Salt Lake Brewing Company) serves sandwiches, burgers, and other light entrées in a handsome old warehouse. In summer, there's seating on the back deck.

Very popular and kind of a scene, the **Red Rock Brewing Company** (254 South 200 West, 801/521-7446) offers pasta, salads, and sandwiches, including an excellent variation on the hamburger (baked in a wood-fired oven inside a bread pocket). There's often a wait to get in the door, but the food and brews are worth it. The Red Rock is unusual for Salt Lake in that it serves food late—till midnight on weekends.

Desert Edge Brewery (700 East and 500 South, 801/521-8917), in Trolley Square, is also known simply as "The Pub." The menu is inexpensive, with sandwiches and salads available all day; some of the ales are cask-conditioned. In the evening, several zippy entrées, such as grilled salmon with spinach and chicken with citrus chipotle chili glaze appear on the menu. The atmosphere is retro industrial chic, and there's a second-floor outdoor veranda.

PIZZA

At these fine SLC pizzarias, a slice ranges from $2.75–4. **Gepetto's** (230 South 1300 East, 801/583-1013, lunch and dinner Mon.–Sat.),

near the University of Utah, serves pizza, lasagna, sandwiches, and salads. Live entertainment is offered Thursday–Saturday.

The Pie Pizzeria (1320 East 200 South, 801/582-0193, lunch and dinner daily), downstairs from the University Pharmacy, offers New York–style hand-thrown pizza. There's live music Monday and Tuesday evenings.

For pizza in a more atmospheric setting, try the gourmet pies at **Rusted Sun** (2010 S. State St., 801/483-2120, lunch and dinner Mon.–Sat., dinner only Sun.), with New York–style pizza and calzone, or **Settebello Pizza** (260 S 200 West, 801/322-3556, lunch and dinner Mon.–Sat.).

STEAK AND SEAFOOD

For the best fish and seafood in SLC, go to the **Market Street Grill** (48 Market St., 801/322-4668, open for three meals daily, $14–33), featuring fresh seafood plus steak, prime rib, chops, chicken, and pasta. Adjacent is an oyster bar. Three-course, early-bird specials are available for $18 before 6:30 P.M. A second location is near the university (260 South 1300 East, 801/583-8808).

The New Yorker (60 Market St., 801/363-0166, lunch Mon.–Fri, dinner Mon.–Sat., $22–38) is yet another fine dining house in a historic storefront. Here the emphasis is on seafood and excellently prepared certified Angus beef and fresh American lamb. If you're not up to a full meal, there's also a café menu; or just go to the oyster bar and fill up on bivalves. The atmosphere is lively; it's in Salt Lake's financial district, so expect an audience of stockbrokers and businessmen.

Other steakhouse choices include **Spencers** (in the downtown Hilton, 255 S. West Temple, 801/238-4748, lunch and dinner daily, $23–42), which has a big reputation as the city's best high-rolling steak house, and **Ruth's Chris Steakhouse** (134 W. Pierpont Ave., 801/366-4000, dinner nightly, $22–38).

DINING WITH A VIEW

Some of the best views in the city are from the top of the 10-story Joseph Smith Memorial

Building (15 E. South Temple), the former Hotel Utah, where you'll find two excellent restaurants. The **Garden Restaurant** (801/539-1911, lunch and dinner Mon.–Sat., $10–18) offers unparalleled views onto Temple Square and downtown Salt Lake City. What's more, the restaurant is reasonably priced, offering sandwiches and salads for lunch and steaks, seafood, and continental dishes at dinner. With even better views onto Temple Square, the **Roof Restaurant** (801/539-1911, dinner Mon.–Sat., $34 adults, $15 children 11 and younger) offers an upscale buffet with prime rib, salmon, ham, shrimp, salads, desserts, and all the trimmings. Reservations are recommended; no alcohol is served.

MEXICAN AND SOUTHWESTERN

◖ Red Iguana (736 W. North Temple, 801/322-1489, lunch and dinner daily, $6–11) is one of the city's favorite Mexican restaurants; it offers excellent south-of-the-border cooking with a specialty in Mayan and regional foods. Best of all, flavors are crisp, fresh, and earthy. The Red Iguana is very popular, so arrive early—especially at lunch—to avoid the lines.

Hector's Miramar (342 West 1300 South, 801/484-2877, lunch and dinner daily, $7–15) serves traditional Mexican tortilla-based dishes, but its real focus is the excellent cuisine of other Latin and South American regions. Seafood dishes are a specialty. The food is authentic (for example, they offer a selection of ceviche, deep-fried whole fish, and *menudo*—tripe soup), so expect exciting and unusual flavors.

Right downtown, **Blue Iguana** (165 S. West Temple, 801/533-8900, lunch and dinner Mon.–Sat., dinner only Sun., $6–15) offers high quality Mexican cooking in a lively basement dining room. In addition to standard tacos and burritos, you'll find seven different moles.

For Mexican fast food, the local chain **La Frontera** (1236 West 400 South, 801/532-3158; 1434 South 700 West, 801/974-0172, and other metro locations; open for three meals daily, $4–9) serves burritos, enchiladas, tacos, *huevos rancheros,* and other Mexican favorites.

CONTINENTAL

Salt Lake City has a couple top-notch Italian restaurants. Not far from downtown, **◖ Cucina Toscana** (307 W. Pierpoint Ave., next to Caputo's Market, 801/328-3463, dinner nightly, $12–25) offers high-quality grilled meats, salads, and pasta in a coolly elegant dining room. Reservations are a must as Cucina Toscana is frequently jammed—for the best service, try to avoid peak dining hours.

Many people feel that **Fresco Italian Cafe** (1513 South 1500 East, 801/486-1300, 5–10 P.M. Mon.–Sat., 5–9 P.M. Sun.) is SLC's finest Italian eatery, if not the city's best overall restaurant. The pleasant setting features an intimate dining room entered through a garden, and the property is on a quiet street a few miles south of the city center. The main courses are full-flavored yet subtle: Cheese tortellini is served with fresh peas, roasted red peppers, sage, and tomato butter ($16), and the house specialty is grilled lamb medallions served with roasted garlic-rosemary demi-glace ($19).

Other Italian restaurants of note include downtown's **Caffé Molise** (55 West 100 South, 801/364-8833, lunch and dinner Mon.–Fri., dinner Sat., $10–17) with a bistro atmosphere and tasty mid-priced Italian specialties, including pasta and grilled chicken and beef dishes. Another good value for classic Italian pasta dishes is **Al Forno** (239 South 500 East, 801/359-6040).

Stoneground (249 E. 400 South, 801/364-1368, lunch and dinner Mon.–Sat., dinner Sun.) has at least dual personalities—it's both a hipster hangout with pool tables and a reasonably priced Italian restaurant and pizzeria. The atmosphere is industrial but windows look out onto a gorgeous view of the Wasatch Front. Pizzas are excellent, and pasta dishes are flavorful and full of character.

For excellent French cuisine, drive a few miles south of downtown to the **◖ Paris Bistro** (1500 S. 1500 East, 801/486-5585, dinner nightly, $16–29), a lovely dining room in gold and burgundy that serves up classics such as duck confit, steak au poivre, mussels moulinere, plus pasta and wood-fired pizza.

MIDDLE EASTERN AND INDIAN

For something unusual, try **Baba Afghan Restaurant** (55 East 400 South, 801/596-0786, lunch Mon.–Fri., dinner nightly, $9–12). Afghani food is like a mix of Indian and Middle Eastern cuisines. There are a number of vegetarian dishes.

Cedars of Lebanon (152 East 200 South, 801/364-4096, lunch and dinner Mon.–Sat., $7–14) has exotic Mediterranean flavors from Lebanon, Morocco, Armenia, Greece, and Israel—many vegetarian items, too. Belly dancers enliven the scene on Friday and Saturday nights.

Tandoori and northern Indian cooking is the specialty at **Taj India** (3540 S State St., 801/268-2423, lunch Mon.–Fri, dinner Mon.–Sat., $7–14). The nan breads are wonderful, and there is a large selection of vegetarian dishes. Near the university is a good Indian restaurant, the **Bombay House** (1615 S. Foothill Dr., 801/581-0222, lunch and dinner Mon.–Sat.). The **Star of India** (177 East 200 South, 801/363-7555, lunch Mon.–Sat., dinner nightly) is another favorite for tandoori-roasted meats and full-flavored curries.

ASIAN

Salt Lake City has a couple upscale Chinese restaurants that update the classics. At **P. F. Chang's China Bistro** (174 West 300 South, 801/539-0500, lunch and dinner daily, $12–20), in a historic building just south of the convention center, the cuisine is a split between traditional Chinese and modern ingredients cooked in a Chinese method. This is a busy place, so reservations are a good idea. The **Butterfly** (13 N. 400 West, in The Depot at The Gateway, 801/456-8999, lunch and dinner daily, $12–32) is an ambitious restaurant,

taking traditional Chinese ingredients and re-imagining them through the lens of cutting edge French cuisine. Duck confit egg rolls and tea-smoked quail are two favorites.

Thai food is popular in SLC. **Bangkok Thai** (1400 S. Foothill Dr., 801/582-8424, lunch and dinner Mon.–Fri., dinner Sat. and Sun., $12–19) is a ways from downtown, but worth the drive for intensely flavored red curries and other traditional Thai specialties. In The Gateway Center, **Thaifoon** (7 N 400 W, 801/456-8424, lunch and dinner daily, $9–17) has a stylish dining room (think indoor waterfall and patio with fire pits) that highlights the upscale Thai and Thai-influenced cooking here. Expect delicious and temptingly named dishes such as Evil Jungle Prince Shrimp and Firecracker Chicken—this is also a good spot for drinks and appetizers, with excellent coconut shrimp.

There are several good Japanese restaurants. At the **Happy Sumo** (in The Gateway at 153 S. Rio Grande St., 801/456-7866, lunch and dinner daily, "special rolls" $9–17), traditional sushi mixes with eclectic pan-Asian dishes in a lively, upscale setting. The outdoor patio features live music most evenings. Under new ownership, **Mikado** (67 West 100 South, 801/328-0929, lunch Mon.–Fri., dinner Mon.–Sat., $12–23) features excellent sushi specialties such as shabu-shabu, and updated fusion dishes such as miso and sake marinated sea bass with wasabi mashed potatoes. Reservations recommended.

Ichiban Sushi and Japanese Cuisine (336 South 400 East, 801/532-7522, dinner nightly, $10–19) is a transplant from Park City, where it had a huge reputation as a superlative sushi house. Its reputation has only grown since its move to Salt Lake, where it's currently housed in a converted Lutheran church.

Cafe Trang (307 W 200 South, 801/539-1638, lunch and dinner daily, $9–18) is a top-rated Vietnamese restaurant with wonderful food, and lots of choices for vegetarians.

Information and Services

Salt Lake City's visitors centers are well stocked with information and enthusiastic volunteers. Coupled with excellent public transportation, you'll find the city and surrounding areas easy to negotiate despite its intimidating sprawl.

INFORMATION
Tourist Offices

Volunteers at the **Salt Lake Convention and Visitors Bureau** (downtown in the Salt Palace at 90 S. West Temple, Salt Lake City, UT 84101, 801/521-2822 or 800/541-4955, www .visitsaltlake.com, 8 A.M.–5 P.M. Mon.–Fri. and 9 A.M.–4 P.M. Sat.) will tell you about the sights, facilities, and goings-on in town. The office also has many helpful magazines and brochures. At the airport, the Visitors Bureau has branches near the baggage claim areas in both Terminal 1 and Terminal 2, which are staffed only during the day.

The **Utah Travel Council** (300 N. State St., 801/538-1900 or 800/200-1160, fax 801/538-1399, www.utah.com, 8 A.M.–5 P.M. Mon.–Fri. and 10 A.M.–5 P.M. weekends and holidays) publishes a well-illustrated *Utah Travel Guide,* travel maps (both state maps and a series of five detailed maps covering the state), and other helpful publications. There are specialized guides to biking and rafting holidays as well. (You can also find these publications at the Salt Lake Convention and Visitors Bureau and local chambers of commerce.) The staff at the Travel Council information desk provides advice and literature about Utah's national parks and monuments, national forests, Bureau of Land Management areas, and state parks as well as general travel in the state.

Wasatch-Cache National Forest

Although visiting the Forest Service headquarters or a ranger station is always an option, travelers may find it easier to go to REI (3285 East 3300 South, 801/486-2100), where the Forest Service has a recreation information

kiosk (801/466-6411, 10:30 A.M.–7 P.M. Tues.–Sat.). The staff here is often more customer-service oriented to outdoor recreationalists than those found in ranger stations. A full selection of maps and printed material is available.

The Wasatch-Cache National Forest **supervisor's office** (downtown on the eighth floor of the Federal Building, 125 S. State St., Salt Lake City, UT 84138, 801/524-3900, www.fs.fed.us/wcnf, 7:30 A.M.–4:30 P.M. Mon.–Fri., until 5 P.M. in summer) has general information and forest maps for all the

USEFUL NUMBERS

- Highway Emergency Assistance: 801/576-8606 or *71 (mobile phones)

- Lawyer Referral Service (Utah State Bar Association): 801/531-9075

- Physician Referral Service (Utah State Medical Association): 801/355-7477

- Police (Salt Lake City): 801/799-3000

- Road Conditions: 801/964-6000

- Salt Lake Convention and Visitors Bureau (local travel information): 801/521-2822 or 800/541-4955

- Sheriff (Salt Lake County): 801/535-5441

- Utah Division of Wildlife Resources: 801/538-4700

- Utah Recreation/Ski Report: 801/521-8102

- Utah State Parks: 801/538-7220

- Utah Transit Authority (UTA): 801/287-4636

- Utah Travel Council (statewide travel information): 801/538-1030

national forests in Utah; some forest and wilderness maps of Nevada, Idaho, and Wyoming; and regional books.

For detailed information on hiking and camping in the nearby Wasatch Range, visit the **Salt Lake Ranger District office** (6944 South 3000 East, Salt Lake City, UT 84121, 801/943-1794, 8 A.M.–5 P.M. Mon.–Fri.). The district includes the popular Mill Creek, Big Cottonwood, and Little Cottonwood Canyons in the Wasatch Range, the Wasatch Range east of Bountiful and Farmington, and the Stansbury Mountains west of Tooele. Large reference books cover nearly every recreational activity and trail. The foresters here will likely have personal knowledge of the area you're heading to.

Libraries

The large **city library** (210 East 400 South, 801/524-8200, 9 A.M.–9 P.M. Mon.–Thurs. and 9 A.M.–6 P.M. Fri.–Sat.) contains a wealth of reading material, a children's library, records, and audio- and videotapes. Special collections include Western Americana and Mormon history. Puppet shows and story hours entertain children. The architecture of the library building is striking and effective—full of natural light, it's a great place to read, then glance up at the mountains. See the telephone blue pages or call for locations of the five branch libraries.

The **Marriott Library** (at the University of Utah, 801/581-6085 or 801/581-8558, 7 A.M.–10 P.M. Mon.–Thurs., 7 A.M.–5 P.M. Fri., 9 A.M.–5 P.M. Sat., shorter hours during summer and school breaks) ranks as one of the leading research libraries of the region. The large map collection has topo maps of all 50 states as well as maps and atlases of distant lands. Hikers can photocopy maps of areas they plan to visit. The public is welcome to use the library; a Library Permit Card can be purchased to use materials outside of the library.

Media

The *Salt Lake Tribune* morning daily reflects the city's non-LDS viewpoints. The LDS-owned *Deseret News* comes out daily in the afternoon with a conservative viewpoint and greater coverage of LDS Church news. The free *City Weekly* describes the latest on art, entertainment, events, and social spots and covers local politics and issues.

Salt Lake City has good public radio stations. KUER 90 FM offers a good musical mix along with National Public Radio news. KCPW, at both 88.3 and 105.1 FM, offers more NPR news and programming as well as foreign news programs. KRCL, at 91 FM, is a community radio station with progressive news and locally produced programming.

SERVICES

The main **downtown post office** is at 230 West 200 South, 801/974-2200. The University of Utah has a post office in the bookstore.

Salt Lake City is a major regional banking center, and you'll have no trouble with most common financial transactions. As elsewhere in the world, ATMs are everywhere and make monetary exchange easy. If you are depending on foreign currency, consider changing enough for your trip around Utah while in Salt Lake City. Exchanging currency will be much more difficult in smaller, rural towns. Change foreign currency at **Wells Fargo** (79 S. Main, 801/246-1069).

Minor medical emergencies can be treated by **IHC** (55 N. Redwood Rd. and six other area locations, 801/321-2490), just west of downtown. Hospitals with 24-hour emergency care include **Salt Lake Regional Medical Center** (1050 E. South Temple, 801/350- 4111), **LDS Hospital** (Eighth Ave. and C St., 801/350-4111), **St. Mark's Hospital** (1200 East 3900 South, 801/268-7111), and **University Hospital** (50 N. Medical Dr. 1800 East, 801/581-2121). For a physician referral, contact one of the hospitals or the Utah State Medical Association (801/355-7477).

For a 24-hour pharmacy, try **Rite Aid** (5540 South 900 East, 801/262-2981). If you're looking for a drugstore, check the phone book for

Smith's Pharmacy; there are more than 25 in the Salt Lake metro area.

The **American Automobile Association** (AAA) offices are at 560 East 500 South, 801/541-9902.

TRANSPORTATION
Air
Salt Lake City International Airport is conveniently located seven miles west of downtown; take North Temple or I-80 to reach it. All major U.S. carriers fly into Salt Lake City. Salt Lake City is the western hub for Delta Air Lines, which is the region's air-transport leader.

SkyWest Airlines (800/453-9417), Delta's commuter line, flies to Vernal, Cedar City, and St. George in Utah and to smaller cities in adjacent states.

The airport has three terminals; in each you'll find a ground-transportation information desk, a cafeteria, motel/hotel courtesy phones, auto rentals (Hertz, Avis, National, Budget, and Dollar), and a ski-rental shop. Terminal 1 also houses Zion's First National Bank (currency exchange), an ice-cream parlor, and gift shops. Utah Information Centers are found in Terminals 1 and 2 (801/575-2800). Terminal 3 is dedicated to foreign arrivals and departures. Staff at the ground-transportation information desks will know the bus schedules into town and limousine services direct to Park City, Sundance, Provo, Ogden, Brigham City, Logan, and other communities. UTA Bus #50 is the cheapest way into town. It leaves the airport daily except holidays every hour from about 6:30 A.M. to about 11:30 P.M. (less frequently and only to about 5:30 P.M. on Sundays).

Train
Amtrak trains (information and reservations 340 South 600 West, 800/872-7245) stop at a new depot called the "Intermodal Hub," which also serves as a terminus for local buses and commuter trains. The only Amtrak train that currently passes through the city is the Cali-fornia Zephyr, which heads west to Reno and Oakland and east to Denver and Chicago four times a week. Call for fares, as Amtrak prices tickets as airlines do, with advance-booking, special seasonal, and other discounts available. Amtrak office hours (timed to meet the trains) are irregular, so call first.

Long-Distance Bus
Salt Lake City sits at a crossroads of several major freeways and has good **Greyhound** bus service (300 S 600 West, 801/355-9579 or 800/231-2222). Generally speaking, buses go north and south along I-15 and east and west along I-80. One bus daily leaves from Salt Lake City for Yellowstone National Park (summer only).

Local Bus and Light Rail
Utah Transit Authority (UTA) provides inexpensive bus and light rail train service in town and to the airport, the University of Utah, and surrounding communities. Buses go as far north as Ogden, as far south as Provo and Springville, and as far west as Tooele. TRAX light rail trains connect the Delta Center, the University of Utah, downtown Salt Lake City, and the southern suburbs. No charge is made for travel downtown within the "Free-Fare Square" area (bounded by North Temple, 400 South, West Temple, and 200 East). During the winter ski season, skiers can hop on the Ski Bus Service to Solitude, Brighton, Snowbird, and Alta ski areas from downtown, the University of Utah, and other locations. A bus route map and individual schedules are available at www.rideuta.com and from the ground transportation information desk at the airport, the Salt Lake Convention and Visitors Bureau downtown, Temple Square visitors centers, or by calling UTA (801/287-4636 or BUS-INFO, 6 A.M.– 7 P.M. Mon.–Sat. Free transfers are given on request when the fare is paid. On Sunday, only the airport, Ogden, Provo, and a few other destinations are served. UTA shuts down on holidays. Fares are $1.60 for two

TRAX light rail train

© W. C. MCRAE

hours of travel on both TRAX or the buses; a day pass is $4.25.

Auto Rentals

All the major companies and many local outfits are eager to rent you a set of wheels. In winter you can find "skierized" vehicles with snow tires and ski racks ready to head for the slopes. Many agencies have an office or delivery service at the airport: Avis Rent A Car, Salt Lake International Airport (801/575-2847 or 800/331-1212), Budget Rent A Car (641 North 3800 West, 801/575-2586 or 800/527-0700), Dollar Rent-A-Car (601 North 3800 West), Salt Lake International Airport (801/575-2580 or 800/421-9849), Enterprise Rent-A-Car (151 East 5600 South, 801/266-3777, 801/534-1888, or 800/RENT-A-CAR), Hertz, Salt Lake International Airport (775 North Terminal Dr., 801/575-2683 or 800/654-3131), National Car Rental, Salt Lake City International Airport (801/575-2277 or 800/227-7368), and Payless Car Rental (1974 W. North Temple, 801/596-2596 or 800/327-3631).

Taxis

The following have 24-hour service: City Cab (801/363-8400), Ute Cab (801/359-7788), and Yellow Cab (801/521-2100).

PARK CITY AND THE WASATCH RANGE

Immediately east of Salt Lake City, the Wasatch Range soars to over 11,000 feet. These mountains are characterized by their steep canyons and abundant snowfall, the combination of which makes for legendary skiing. Big Cottonwood Canyon, home to Solitude and Brighton ski and snowboard areas, is just south and east of the city; the next canyon south, Little Cottonwood, has Snowbird and Alta, two world-class ski resorts (snowboarding is permitted at Snowbird, but not at Alta). When the snow melts, the hiking is every bit as great as the skiing and boarding.

About 45 minutes east of Salt Lake via I-80, and a thriving city in its own right, Park City is home to three major ski areas: Park City Mountain Resort, The Canyons, and Deer Valley. Park City hosted many events during the 2002 Winter Olympics (the Cottonwood Canyon resorts stayed out of the Games) and is also well known as the site of the annual Sundance Film Festival.

Though the entire Northern Wasatch region is within commuting distance from Salt Lake, skiers who can afford the somewhat pricey accommodations should try to spend at least a couple of nights at one of the many lodges, which range from Alta's friendly, down-home places to Deer Valley's equally friendly but ultra-chic digs.

When the snow melts, many of the resorts have summer operations, with lift-assisted mountain biking being the most popular activity. There are also hiking trails, picnic areas, and campgrounds across the region.

Even in the summer, nights can be cold in

© JUDY JEWELL

PARK CITY

HIGHLIGHTS

◖ **Snowbird Ski and Summer Resort:** In addition to being a great place to ski (be sure to make it over to the Mineral Basin), Snowbird's summer activities mean that the adrenaline never stops flowing. If you want to relax, stay at the swank Cliff Lodge and indulge at the Cliff Spa, one of the nicest in the state (page 88).

◖ **Alta Ski Area:** Here's where old skiers come to...ski their rear ends off! Don't be surprised if a 70-year-old helps you up from a fall. Alta is a haven for skiers – no snowboarding allowed – and the accommodations are homey and extra-friendly (page 93).

◖ **Deer Valley Resort:** When you need to show off your new ski outfit, do it at Deer Valley. But don't feel intimidated by the occasional fur-trimmed jacket; although you may ride the lift with a big-time CEO, you're just as likely to cruise down a perfectly groomed run with the fun-loving members of a blue-collar town ski club (page 101).

◖ **Utah Olympic Park:** Bobsled, luge, and ski jump competitions were held here during the 2002 Winter Olympics. Now, winter or summer, come here to watch freestyle ski jumping or take a bobsled ride. Guided tours of the competition sites are also available (page 106).

◖ **Ski Interconnect:** Expert skiers can really learn the local geography by skiing a challenging daylong guided backcountry tour between Snowbird, Alta, Solitude, Brighton, and Park City Mountain Resort (page 107).

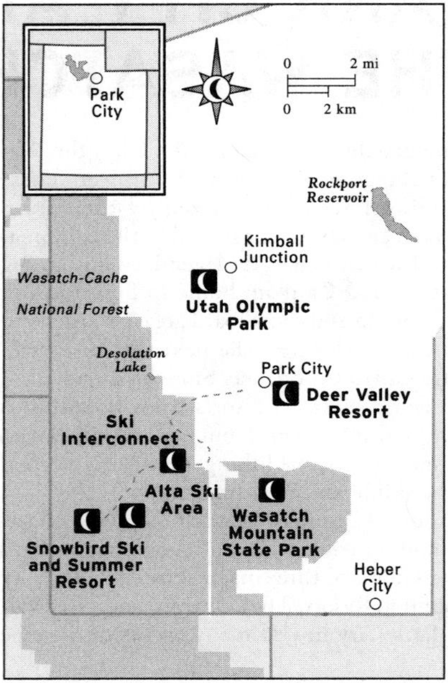

◖ **Wasatch Mountain State Park:** This is Utah's largest state park, and along with camping, hiking, and great scenic views, it has one of the best public golf courses you'll find anywhere (page 117).

LOOK FOR ◖ TO FIND RECOMMENDED SIGHTS, ACTIVITIES, DINING, AND LODGING.

---

the mountains, and even in the winter, sunny days can bring warm afternoons where it's possible to unzip your parka and bask in the thin-aired glow.

PLANNING YOUR TIME

In the winter, if you have only a few days, it's best to pick an area—Big Cottonwood Canyon, Little Cottonwood Canyon, or Park City—and base yourself there for skiing and boarding. It's not really necessary to have a car, especially in the Cottonwood Canyon areas; if you want to explore another ski area for a day, it's generally cheaper to use a shuttle service than to rent a car. If not everybody in your group is interested in skiing all day long, Park

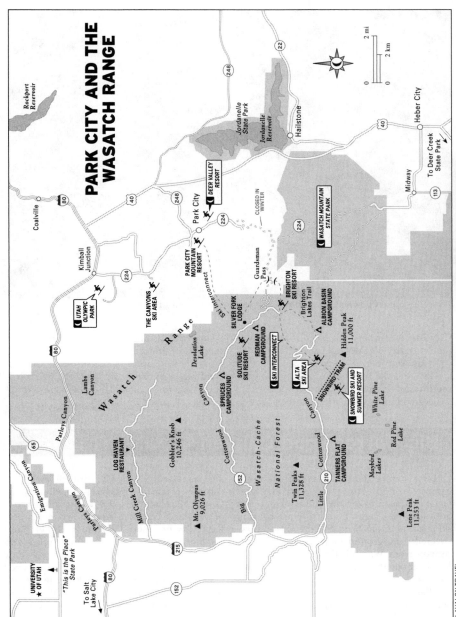

PARK CITY AND THE WASATCH RANGE

© PAUL LEVY

Park City quiets down in the summer, but there's still plenty to do.

City is the best bet—it's a real town with as much activity off the slopes as on them.

In the summer, it's nice to have a car (or a bike!) and the freedom to poke around the mountains. Increasingly, the ski areas have structured summer activities, but there are also plenty of trails and a real sense of relaxation that sets in. Indeed, the Cottonwood Canyon areas are very quiet in the summer, and are good places to camp and hike. Early July is a good time to catch wildflowers, but evenings can be cold any month of the year.

Big Cottonwood Canyon

Cliffs towering thousands of feet form the gateway to Big Cottonwood Canyon. Skiers come in season to try the downhill slopes at Solitude and Brighton and to cross-country ski at the Solitude Nordic Center or on snow-covered campground loop roads. Enter the canyon from Wasatch Boulevard and 7000 South, about 15 miles southeast of downtown Salt Lake City. The 14-mile drive to Brighton Basin reveals splendid vistas at each turn while climbing to an elevation of 8,700 feet.

The summertime-only Guardsman Pass Road turns off just before Brighton and winds up to Guardsman Pass (elev. 9,800 feet) at the crest of the Wasatches, then drops down into either Park City or Heber City on the other side; the mostly unpaved road is usually open late June–mid-October.

Eight picnic areas lie along Big Cottonwood Creek. You'll come first to **Oak Ridge Picnic Area,** one mile from the entrance, followed by **Dogwood Picnic Area** (elev. 5,200 feet), 1.1

miles from the entrance, and finally to **Silver Lake Picnic Area** (elev. 8,720 feet) near road's end, 14.5 miles up the canyon. Silver Lake offers full access to fishing and picnic sites.

SOLITUDE MOUNTAIN RESORT

The best thing about Solitude (801/534-1400 general info or 801/536-5777 snow report, www.skisolitude.com, $53 adult lift ticket) is reflected in its name—it's rarely crowded. Even on a snowy Saturday in February, it's often possible to ski right up to the base area lifts and hop on, with no line. The other thing that makes this ski area distinctive is the European-style village at the base area. The village square is closed to cars—day visitors park in a lot about a five-minute walk away and underground parking lots stow condo guests' vehicles—and the inn and several condos face the pedestrian area. From all the lodgings, it's only a short walk to the lifts.

Ski season at Solitude runs from about Thanksgiving until the third week in April, depending on snow.

History

This area was originally called Solitude by silver miners in the early 1900s. It became a ski area served by two chairlifts in 1957, and in 1989 the Emerald Express became Utah's first high-speed quad lift. Until the Creekside condominiums opened in 1995, Solitude was entirely a day-use area. Solitude is privately owned by one family; Intrawest was brought in to develop some of the lodgings but has no equity interest in the resort.

Terrain and Lifts

Skiers can choose from a wide variety of runs—there are plenty of nice wide blue cruisers, and, when conditions are favorable, gates open to expert terrain, including Honeycomb Canyon, containing more than 400 acres of ungroomed powder skiing on the back side of the resort. The Honeycomb lift, a fixed quad, makes this challenging, largely natural area relatively accessible.

One of the nice things about Honeycomb Canyon is that, along with all the 50-degree-slope double-black-diamond tree runs, there's one run that's accessible to strong intermediate skiers and snowboarders. Woodlawn, a blue-black run, starts at the top of the Summit lift and goes right down the center of the canyon. There's one short, steep section and a lot of moguls before it reaches the bottom of the Honeycomb lift, but on a clear day with good snow conditions, it's a great challenge for an advancing skier. (In less than perfect conditions, it's terrifying and best left to experts.) Another good, challenging intermediate run is Dynamite, also starting at the top of the Summit lift.

Of the seven lifts, only one—Eagle Express—is a high-speed quad, which may partly explain why Solitude is not swamped with people. (The Powderhorn lift is especially long and slow.)

Day skiers (as opposed to resort guests)

Solitude's lifts take skiers and snowboarders through some lovely aspen groves.

© JUDY JEWELL

generally head out from the Moonbeam base area, where a quad lift shuttles skiers and boarders up to a network of green and blue runs. A large day lodge at the Moonbeam base has lockers, a café and bar, and a comfortable area to sit and wait for your die-hard companions to come off the mountain.

In all, there are over 1,200 skiable acres, rated 20 percent beginner, 50 percent intermediate, and 30 percent advanced. The green and blue runs are mostly clumped together, which makes it difficult for an expert and a novice to ski in the same area and meet up for lift rides together. The Eagle Express, which is the one high-speed quad, accesses a nice network of blue runs.

Adult lift tickets cost $53 (multiday and half-day tickets offer slight discounts, as do various frequent-skier deals). Seniors above age 70 pay $25. Lift tickets for children (7–13) are $32; ages 6 and under ski free. The Solbright pass, which allows access to both Solitude and Brighton, is $63; this pass is available only when the trail connecting the two resorts is open. From the top of Solitude's Summit lift, you can catch the Sol/Bright run over the Evergreen lift at Brighton.

Solitude also has "per ride" lift ticket packages; a ten-ride pass costs $55 (purchase more and the price per ride goes down) and can be used throughout the season.

Lifts run 9 A.M.–4 P.M. daily. For more information, check www.skisolitude.com.

Solitude has a ski school, rentals, and a program called Back Tracks, where ski patrollers take you on a backcountry tour outside area boundaries.

Solitude Nordic Center

Plenty of snow and nicely groomed tracks make Solitude's Nordic Center (Silver Lake Day Lodge, 801/536-5774 or 800/748-4754, ext. 5774, www.skisolitude.com, 9 A.M.–4:30 P.M. daily mid-Nov.–mid-Apr., $15 adults, $10 after 12:30 P.M., free for children under 11 and seniors 70 and over) of the best places in Utah for both traditional cross-country skiers and skate skiers. The 20 miles of groomed trails are relatively easy to ski, with level loops for beginners and rolling terrain for more experienced skiers. An additional 6.2 miles of trails are groomed for snowshoers. Don't hesitate to try the gentle, mostly downhill ski from the Nordic Center lodge to the downhill skiing base area at Solitude.

The Nordic Center is in the Silver Lake Day Lodge, about two miles up the road from Solitude's downhill area, almost all the way to Brighton. The shop's staff offers rentals (touring, racing, telemark, and snowshoes), sales, instruction, day tours, and advice on backcountry touring and avalanche hazards. Tickets can be purchased here or at Solitude's downhill ski area. The ski area is 12 miles up Big Cottonwood Canyon and only a 28-mile drive southeast of downtown Salt Lake City.

If you're not so fussy about skiing on groomed trails, explore the loop trails at **Spruces** campground, 9.1 miles up Big Cottonwood Canyon. These trails are also popular with snowshoers.

Summer Activities

During the summer the Sunrise lift operates 1–6 P.M. Wednesday–Friday and 10 A.M.–4 P.M. on weekends. A single ride costs $6 for a person (without a bike).

MOUNTAIN BIKING

Twenty miles of single-track within the resort area, plus easy access to nearby Wasatch National Forest roads and trails, make Solitude a fun place to bike. Bicycles are permitted on the Sunrise lift, which runs on weekends during the summer ($25 for the day, $26 for a two-hour bike rental and two lift rides). Full-suspension mountain bikes are available for rent, as are "mountain scooters," burly, knobby-tired cousins of razor scooters ($10 per hour, two-hour minimum).

DISC GOLF

The 18-hole course is free, though you may want to ride the Sunrise lift ($6 per ride) to get to the first hole, which is at 9,000 feet (a pretty good hike up the mountain from the base area).

Accommodations

Most lodgings at Solitude are in the European-style ski village at the base of the slopes and are owned and managed by Solitude Mountain Resort (801/534-1400 or 800/748-4754, www .skisolitude.com). Rates at all of the Solitude-owned lodgings drop by at least half during the summer.

The **Inn at Solitude** ($269–359) is a few steps away from the base area lifts. As ski resort hotels go, it's rather intimate, with 46 rooms, a fancy restaurant and private club bar, a spa, and other amenities.

The **Village at Solitude Condominiums** offers condo units in three different developments: Creekside (about $400 for a one-bed unit) is right next to the base area lifts; Powderhorn ($260 and up) is only a few steps farther; and Eagle Springs ($260 and up), while a slightly longer walk to the lifts, has easy access to Club Solitude's indoor pool and exercise room. All have fireplaces, full kitchens, TVs and VCRs, private decks, and come with one, two, or three bedrooms. Just outside the main village area find **The Crossings,** with three-bedroom townhouses (about $700), and **Alpine Creek,** with spacious one-bedroom units for a few dollars less than the in-village places.

About a mile from Solitude, and not part of the resort village, is the **Silver Fork Lodge** (11332 E. Big Cottonwood Canyon, 801/649-9551 or 888/649-9551, $135–185), with eight rustic B&B rooms without TV or telephones. The Silver Fork is largely known for its restaurant.

Food

The Inn at Solitude's restaurant, **St. Bernard's** (801/536-5508, breakfast and dinner daily during ski season, dinner reservations recommended, dinner entreés $26–32, breakfast buffet $14 adults, $8 children), is the place to go for an elegant (and expensive) dinner. The menu leans toward country French. **Creekside Restaurant** (801/536-5787, dinner Thurs.– Sun. during ski season, $14–28) is a better bet for families or anyone who doesn't want a fancy dinner; it features very good Italian fare, including wood-fired pizzas. The **Thirsty Squirrel,** a private club facing the square, is a popular après-ski bar, with typical pub food.

For a quick slice of pizza, an espresso, or good ice cream, stop by the **Stone Haus Pizzeria and Creamery** (801/536-5767, breakfast, lunch, and dinner year-round, small pizza $10) right in the village square. During the summer, you'll be able to notice the distinctive grass roof—in the winter it's where cross-country skiers gather for a free shuttle back to the Nordic area.

Cross-country ski or snowshoe (approximately three-quarters of a mile) along easy trails to the trailside █ **Yurt** (801/536-5709) for a five-course dinner ($100). Only 20 people are seated each evening, and reservations are required (it's best to make them well in advance).

Outside the main resort complex, the **Silver Fork Lodge** (11332 E. Big Cottonwood Canyon, 801/649-9551 or 888/649-9551, breakfast, lunch, and dinner daily, $15–22) uses a 50-year-old sourdough starter to make pancakes. For dinner, you can get your Caesar salad topped with a 14-ounce steak or stick with a pasta dish or a more traditional meat-and-veggies meal.

Transportation

From Salt Lake City, take I-80 East to I-215 South. Take I-215 to Exit 6 (6200 South) and follow 6200 South, which becomes Wasatch Boulevard. Follow the signs to Big Cottonwood Canyon; Solitude is 14 miles up Big Cottonwood Canyon.

UTA buses (801/743-3882, www.rideuta .com, $1.60 one-way) run between Salt Lake City, with stops at many hotels and park-and-rides, and Solitude. Canyon Transportation (800/255-1841, www.canyontransport.com,

GETTING TO THE SLOPES

Don't assume that you'll need a rental car for your ski trip to Utah, even if you want to visit more than one resort. The cheapest way to arrange a ski trip is to stay in Salt Lake City and take the UTA bus (www .utabus.com) to the mountains. From downtown, take the TRAX light rail south to either the 7200 South or 10000 South station, then catch a bus to the slopes. Buses 92 and 93 travel up Big Cottonwood Canyon; 97 and 98 go up Little Cottonwood. Fares are about $2 each way; during the winter, buses run throughout the day.

Even easier is taking a bus – either public or private – to a ski resort where you'll stay in resort lodgings. From the airport, Canyon Transportations runs regular shuttles to the ski areas (about $64 round-trip).

Once you get to your destination, don't feel like you're tied to your chosen ski area. It's easy to take UTA buses between Snowbird and Alta, or between Solitude and Brighton. For longer trips, private shuttle buses travel between Big and Little Cottonwood canyons and the Park City resorts.

$33 one-way) runs shuttle buses up Big Cottonwood Canyon, with stops at both Solitude and Brighton.

BRIGHTON SKI RESORT

Brighton (801/532-4731 or 800/873-5512, www.skibrighton.com, 9 A.M.–4 P.M. daily mid-Nov.–mid-Apr., night skiing 4–9 P.M. Mon.–Sat. early Dec.–Mar., $47 adult daytime lift ticket) is a long-time favorite with local families for the excellent skiing and friendly, unpretentious atmosphere (no Euro-village resort atmosphere here—it's all about being on the mountain). It's also the most snowboard-friendly of the Cottonwood resorts and is the only place near Salt Lake with a real night-skiing program. The resort, which is in the Wasatch-Cache National Forest, does not have a commercial summer season; however, there are plenty of places to hike in the area.

History

Brighton is Utah's oldest ski resort, dating from 1936, when ski club members built a "skier tow" from half-inch wire rope and an old elevator drum. Two years later, a T-bar tow was erected, and in 1946 the area's first actual chairlift traveled up Mount Millicent. Brighton is now owned by CNL Income Properties Inc., a Florida-based real estate investment trust. Boyne, USA, which also owns Crystal Mountain Resort in Washington and Big Sky in Montana, operates the resort.

Terrain and Lifts

While 21 percent of the runs are beginner and 40 percent intermediate, Brighton does offer some difficult powder-bowl skiing and steep runs. Four high-speed quads (Milly, Great Western, Crest, and Snake Creek), one triple chairlift, and three double chairs climb as high as 10,500 feet for a 1,745-foot vertical descent to the base. In addition to the more than 60 runs and trails at Brighton, you can hop on the Sol-Bright run to visit Solitude ski area; a lift there will put you back on a trail to Brighton. Night skiing is offered Monday–Saturday.

Absolute beginners can step onto the Magic Carpet and be gently carried up to the Explorer area, which is also served by a slow-moving (and thus easy to mount and dismount) lift. Beginners with a few runs behind them and cautious intermediate skiers and boarders should venture onto the Majestic lift, which serves a good network of wide, tree-lined green and blue runs. More advanced folks will prefer the bowls in the Millicent and Evergreen areas. One of the things that makes Brighton so popular with snowboarders (besides the fact that they're welcome here) is its lack of long runouts. It also has an open-backcountry policy, though it's unwise to head off into the backcountry unless you're with a Salt Lake native who grew up skiing and boarding here.

Brighton's terrain parks are among some of the best in the West. Snowboarders looking for a challenge should head up the Crest Express quad and play around the My-O-My and Candyland terrain parks. Just down the slope from these areas are two more terrain parks and a half pipe.

Brighton has a ski and snowboard school, rentals, ski shops, and three cafeterias. Many Utah residents learned to ski at Brighton, and its snowboard classes are considered to be especially good.

Adults ski for $47 a day, $40 half-day, and $30 at night. Seniors over 70 and children ages 7–10 pay $10, and kids 6 and under ski free with a paying adult.

Accommodations

Adjacent to the slopes is resort-owned **Brighton Lodge** (800/873-5512, $125–175), which offers accommodations with a heated outdoor pool and spa; restaurant adjacent. It's much smaller than most ski-resort lodges, and very casual. A few hostel bunks (shared bath) are available for $99. If you want a more posh setting, it's best to stay just down the hill at Solitude. A short walk from Brighton's lifts, off the Brighton Loop Road, **Brighton Chalets** (801/942-8824 or 800/748-4824, www.brightonchalets.com, winter rates $100 and up) rents out a range of cottages and chalets. Each chalet comes with a furnished kitchen, fireplace, and cable TV and sleeps at least six people.

Food

Slope-side restaurants include the **Alpine Rose** (801/532 4731 ext. 252, 8 A.M.–4 P.M. daily year-round, open until 9 P.M. Mon.–Sat. mid-Dec.–mid-Mar., $8–10), a good lunch spot; the **Millicent Chalet** (801/532 4731 ext. 219, 8 A.M.–4 P.M. daily, $6–8) at the foot of Mount Millicent; and **Molly Green's** (801/532-4731 ext. 206, 11 A.M.–8 P.M. daily year-round, open until 11 P.M. Mon.–Sat. mid-Dec.–mid-Mar., club membership $5, dinner $12–14), a private club.

Information

Contact Brighton Ski Resort at 801/532-4731 or 800/873-5512, www.skibrighton.com.

Transportation

Brighton is at road's end, two miles past Solitude in Big Cottonwood Canyon. From Salt Lake City, take I-80 East to I-215 South. Take I-215 to Exit 6 (6200 South) and follow 6200 South, which becomes Wasatch Boulevard. Follow the signs to Big Cottonwood Canyon; Brighton is 16 miles up Big Cottonwood Canyon.

UTA buses (801/743-3882, www.rideuta.com, $1.60 one-way) run between Salt Lake City and Brighton, with stops at many hotels and park-and-rides. Canyon Transportation (800/255-1841, www.canyontransport.com, $33 one-way) also runs shuttle buses up Big Cottonwood Canyon, with stops at both Solitude and Brighton.

HIKING BIG COTTONWOOD

Mineral Fork Trail follows an old mining road past abandoned mines, cabins, and rusting equipment to a high glacial cirque. Waterfalls, alpine meadows, wildflowers, and abundant birdlife make the steep climb worthwhile. The signed trailhead is on the south side of the road six miles up the canyon (0.8 mile past Moss Ledge Picnic Area). You'll climb 2,000 feet in three miles to the Wasatch Mine, whose mineralized water makes up much of the flow of Mineral Fork Creek. Another two miles and 1,400 feet of climbing lead to Regulator Johnson Mine. A loop trip can be made by climbing the ridge west of Regulator Johnson (no trail) and descending Mill B South Fork Trail to Lake Blanche and the main road, coming out 1.5 miles west of the Mineral Fork Trailhead. See Mount Aire and Dromedary Peak 7.5-minute topo maps.

Brighton Lakes Trail winds through some of the prettiest lake country in the range. Families enjoy outings on this easy trail, which begins in Brighton behind the Brighton Lodge. Silver Lake has a boardwalk giving full access to fishing docks. The first section follows Big Cottonwood Creek through stands of aspen and evergreens. The trail continues south across meadows filled with wildflowers, then climbs more steeply to Brighton Overlook, one mile from the start. Dog Lake, surrounded by old mine dumps, lies 200 yards to the south. Continue on the main trail one-half mile to Lake Mary, a large, deep lake below Mount Millicent. Lake Martha is another one-half mile up the trail. Another mile of climbing takes you to Lake Catherine, bordered by a pretty alpine meadow on the north and by the steep talus slopes of Sunset and Pioneer Peaks on the south. Total elevation gain for the three-mile hike to Lake Catherine is 1,200 feet. Hikers can also go another one-half mile to Catherine Pass and descend 1.5 miles to Albion Basin in Little Cottonwood Canyon. Sunset Peak (elev. 10,648 feet) can be climbed by following a one-half-mile trail from the pass. See the Brighton 7.5-minute topo map.

Campgrounds

At an elevation of 7,500 feet, **Spruces Campground** (9.7 miles up the canyon, 877/444-6777, www.reserveamerica.com, late May–mid-Oct., has water) is the largest campground in the area. Except for a couple of group sites, all of the campsites at **Redman Campground** (13 miles up the canyon, mid-June–early Oct., has water), located between Solitude and Brighton at an elevation of 8,300 feet, are first come, first served. **Jordan Pines** has several large group camping sites (8.8 miles from the canyon entrance, 877/444-6777, www.reserveamerica.com, has water) available by reservation only. Please note that, in order to preserve the Salt Lake City watershed, dogs are not permitted at these campgrounds. This is strictly enforced!

Little Cottonwood Canyon

The road through this nearly straight glacial valley ascends 5,500 feet in 11 miles. Splendid peaks rise to more than 11,000 feet on both sides of the canyon. In winter and spring, challenging terrain attracts skiers to Snowbird and Alta ski areas. Enter Little Cottonwood Canyon from the junction of Highway 209 and Highway 210, four miles south of the entrance to Big Cottonwood Canyon.

Granite rock for the Salt Lake Temple came from quarries one mile up the canyon on the left. Here, too, are the Granite Mountain Record Vaults, containing genealogical and historical records of the LDS Church stored on millions of rolls of microfilm. Neither site is open to the public.

◖ SNOWBIRD SKI AND SUMMER RESORT

When you drive up Little Cottonwood Canyon, Snowbird (801/742-2222 or 800/232-9542, www.snowbird.com, $64 all-day tram and lift ticket, $84 Snowbird–Alta combination pass) is the first resort you get to. It's about a 40-minute drive from the heart of downtown Salt Lake City. Aside from sheer convenience,

Snowbird is known for its great snow—an average of 500 inches a year, and much of that classified as "champagne powder." It's a big, fun place to ski or board, with lots of varied terrain.

History

Snowbird's owner and developer, Dick Bass, is well known in mountaineering circles as the author of *Seven Summits,* his account of climbing the highest peak on every continent. He reportedly had the vision for the resort, including the deluxe Cliff Lodge, while he was holed up in a tent on Mount Everest. The soaring 11-story windowed atrium at the sturdy concrete Cliff imparts a sense of openness that was so sorely lacking in that Everest tent. Along with open space and light, Bass also had a vision of a spa.

It was important to Bass to build an environmentally friendly resort, and much effort was taken to preserve trees and improve the quality of the watershed, which had been degraded by mining. Mine tailings were removed and lodges built in their place to avoid harming existing trees and vegetation.

Terrain and Lifts

Snowbird is on the west side of the Wasatch Range, with ski runs mostly on the north face of the mountains. There are three distinct areas to ski at this large and varied resort: Peruvian Gulch, Gad, and—on the back side—Mineral Basin. And, if 2,500 skiable acres aren't enough to keep you busy, you can buy a special lift ticket that allows skiing between Snowbird and neighboring Alta.

Plenty of lifts serve Snowbird, including four high-speed quads and a tram that can ferry up to 125 skiers up to the top of Peruvian Gulch at one time. The runs here are long, too, meaning that you don't have to hop a lift every few minutes. Unless it's a powder day (when all the locals call in sick and head for the mountains), lines are rarely a problem, especially midweek. The one place that does get crowded is the tram; lines can be quite long here, especially first thing in the morning and just after lunchtime. But the tram really is the way to get up the mountain quickly, with access to the best territory.

PARK CITY

DEALING WITH HIGH ALTITUDE

Suppose skiers leave their sea-level hometown at 5 P.M. on Thursday, fly to Salt Lake City, and get the first tram up from the Snowbird base area at 9 A.M. on Friday. By 9:15, they're at 11,000 feet. No wonder they feel tired before they even start skiing.

It's hard to say who will be immobilized by the altitude. Men seem to have more problems than women, and athletes often feel worse than more sedentary people. But the altitude (and the dry air that goes along with it) can have a host of effects.

EFFECTS OF HIGH ALTITUDE

- Sleeplessness.

- Increased drug potency, especially with tranquilizers and sedatives.

- Increased UV radiation. People taking tetracycline are especially sensitive to the sun.

- Stuffy nose. The dry air can make your sinus tissues swell and feel stuffy. Antihistamines or decongestants just make the tissues swell more.

- Increased sensitivity to MSG.

- Increased flatulence.

- Slightly decreased fertility (decreased testosterone production in men; delayed ovulation in women).

- Slow-drying, thick nail polish.

TIPS

- Don't expect to go full steam all at once. Day two can be particularly rough . . . don't feel bad about knocking off early and taking a nap. Rest is good, even when sleep is difficult.

- Don't take it too easy. It's best to get some light exercise.

- Drink lots of water and avoid alcohol for the first two or three days.

- Decrease salt intake to prevent fluid retention.

- Breathe deeply.

- Wear sunglasses or goggles. It is easy to sunburn your eyes and damage the corneas.

- Use a vaporizer at night; most ski resorts have them in the rooms.

- Try not to arrive with a cold. (Ha!)

- If you're seriously prone to high altitude's ill effects, consult your doctor before your trip. Diamox, a prescription drug, stimulates the respiratory system and decreases fluid retention, easing the effects of high altitude.

Twenty-seven percent of the runs are classed as beginner, 38 percent intermediate, and 35 percent advanced. Plenty of ungroomed areas lie in the backcountry, too. Snowbird's ski and snowboard schools and separate "bunny hill" make it a good place to learn. The longest run is 3.5 miles and drops 3,200 feet.

Intermediate-level skiers should pick up a copy of the free *Intermediate Experience Guide*, a pocket-sized guide detailing a full-day tour of Snowbird, with good maps and clear instructions. Experts will find enough terrain to keep busy for days, including traverses that lead to incredibly steep chutes.

Snowbird has gone to some lengths to attract snowboarders—there's a super-pipe under the Mid-Gad lift and a large expert-level terrain park near the Baby Thunder lift. The terrain itself, with lots of natural chutes, lends itself to snowboarding.

Skiers and snowboarders alike should be sure to check out the Mineral Basin area. Reach it by taking the tram to the top of Hidden Peak (11,000 feet) then heading over to the back side of the mountain, or by riding the Peruvian Express lift, then riding a "magic carpet" through a 600-foot-long tunnel to Mineral Basin. Two high-speed quads serve a great network of runs on this side of the mountain.

Guided ski tours of about two hours (free with lift-ticket purchase) leave from the Snowbird Plaza deck daily at 10:30 A.M. and tour mostly blue runs. A particularly popular program is First Tracks, which allows people to pay an extra $50 and ride the tram before it officially opens in the morning. A mountain guide then escorts this small group of First Tracks patrons down the mountain. Reserve at least a day in advance by calling 801/933-2222, ext. 4135.

Wasatch Powderbird Guides (801/742-2800, www.powderbird.com) offers helicopter skiing in the peaks above the regular runs; rates start at $630.

Snowbird also offers a number of **adaptive ski programs.** Sit-skis, mono-skis, and outriggers make skiing possible for athletes with mo-

bility impairments. Instruction and programs are available for both children and adults.

In addition to its ski school, Snowbird offers rentals, a wide selection of shops, restaurants, snack bars, four lodges, swimming pools, health spa, and child-care services.

The exceptionally long season at Snowbird continues to mid-May, though many lifts close by May 1. Even confirmed Alta skiers head to Snowbird for their late spring skiing.

Standard lift tickets (including the tram) cost $64. Forgo the tram and your ticket price drops to $54; add access to Alta's lifts and you'll pay $71. Seniors pay $53 for tram and chairlift access, and two children 6 and under can ski free with each adult (lifts only; $15 for a pass that includes the tram). Half-day and multiday passes are also available.

Summer Activities

Snowbird offers a full array of family recreation and resort facilities to summer visitors. All lodging, spa, and recreational facilities remain open, as do all restaurants and retail outlets.

A summer favorite is the tram ride to Hidden Peak (elev. 11,000 feet) for a fantastic panorama of the Wasatches, the surrounding valleys, and the distant Uinta Mountains. Round-trip one-ride tickets are $10 adults, free for children under six.

The resort's summer commercial emphasis is on vaguely extreme sports (including the bizarre mechanical bull, $8 per ride), although there are also plenty of general fitness and outdoor activities. An all-day pass for activities, including the bull, bungee jump, a zip line, and more, goes for $32.

The Activity Center (near the tennis courts, 801/933-2147) is the hub for summer activities, and also rents mountain bikes and can arrange horseback rides in the Mineral Basin. A hiking map available at the center shows local trails and jogging loops. Guided hikes are available, and there's a nature trail adapted to guests with disabilities. If you're looking to relax, there's also the Cliff Spa and Salon, with beauty and massage treatments. Snowbird is also the site of frequent summertime musical and arts events.

Snowbird Expeditions

Winter and summer, outdoor adventurers can sign on with Snowbird Expeditions (www .snowbirdx.com), a program offering participants hands-on mountaineering instruction and guidance from some of the world's top experts and lodging at comfortable Cliff Lodge and a well-appointed backcountry camp. David Breashears, a world-famous climber, author, and cinematographer, designed these expeditions to combine the optimum blend of intense athletic activity, technical climbing instruction, mountaineering skills, world-renowned healthful cuisine, and restorative spa treatments.

Accommodations

All of Snowbird's accommodations are run by the resort; the best way to find out about the many options is simply to call the central reservation line (800/232-9542) or check the website (www.snowbird.com). Prices vary wildly according to season, day of week, and view but are generally quite expensive during the winter.

The poshest place to stay in Snowbird is the ski-in/ski-out **【 Cliff Lodge,** with more than 500 rooms, scores of incredible Oriental rugs, four restaurants, conference facilities, retail shops, a year-round outdoor pool, and a top-notch spa. One very nice practical detail is the ground-floor locker (complete with boot drier) assigned to each guest. The Cliff is swanky without being snobbish or stuffy—you don't have to look like the current season's Bogner catalog to fit in here (though many guests do). Standard winter room rates run $200–450, with package deals available.

The Cliff Spa (801/933-2225) offers all sorts of massage therapies, facials, manicures, yoga and Pilates classes, a weight room, cardio equipment, and its own outdoor pool. It's much nicer and more complete than most hotel spas. A day pass to the spa permits access to the classes and workout facilities; people who aren't staying at the Cliff are perfectly welcome. It's best to reserve massages and other treatments at least a day or two in advance.

The **Lodge at Snowbird,** the **Inn,** and the **Iron Blosam Lodge** are the resort's three condominium complexes. Though they aren't quite as grand as the Cliff, they're perfectly nice, and quite practical places to stay (the three are pretty similar) with guest laundries, pools, steam and sauna, restaurants, and many kitchen units. All of these places are a short walk from the tram loading area. Most are one-bedroom units, with prices ranging $275–350.

More condos are available through **Canyon Services** (888/546-5707, www.canyon services.com). These upscale accommodations are found between Snowbird and Alta, and are available in four different complexes and in units with 1–5 bedrooms (winter rates start at about $400).

If these prices seem prohibitive, remember that Salt Lake City is just down the hill, and city buses run up the canyon several times a day.

Food

Serious skiers will no doubt eat lunch either on the mountain at the **Mid-Gad Lodge** or at the **Forklift,** a sandwich-and-burger joint near the base of the tram. And while these places are perfectly acceptable refueling stations, be aware that there are a couple of very good restaurants at Snowbird.

The **【 Aerie** (801/933-2160 or ext. 5500, breakfast and dinner daily in winter, dinner nightly in summer, $20–52) is the Cliff's fancy 10th-floor restaurant, with excellent food with a slight Asian influence and fine sunset views of the mountains. Try the tea-marinated duck breast served with star anise and cinnamon polenta. If you'd like to partake of the Aerie's scenery but aren't up for such a splurge, check out the **sushi bar,** open during the winter in the Aerie's lounge. It's a friendly, casual atmosphere with really good fresh sushi and live jazz

PARK CITY

drifting over from the bar area. The Aerie also serves a big buffet breakfast.

The espresso bar in the Cliff's **Atrium** (801/933-2140, breakfast and lunch daily in winter, breakfast daily in summer, light breakfast less than $5) has granola, bagels, and fruit. It's quick and has a splendid view of the mountain. The Atrium is also a pleasant place to relax at the end of the day, with a good après-ski menu of sandwiches, vegetarian chili, and other light snacks.

For a not-too-extravagant dinner, the **El Chanate** (801/933-2025 or ext. 5100, dinner nightly, $9–17) has reasonably priced (but not wildly exciting) Mexican food and an astounding array of tequilas, especially for a state not known for high-end alcoholic beverages. It's tucked away in the bottom of Cliff Lodge.

In the Iron Blosam Lodge, **Wildflower Restaurant** (807/933-2230 or ext. 1042, dinner $12–28) has very good Italian-inspired dinners. It's not quite as expensive or elegant as the Aerie, but the food and views are nearly as good. Another relatively affordable dinner

restaurant is the **Lodge Bistro** (807/933-2145 or ext. 3042, $19–42), located in the Lodge at Snowbird. Dinners here have a French influence; however, the steamed mussels with a curry sauce are a hit.

Down at the bottom of the canyon, about 15 miles from Snowbird, find the **Market Street Grill** (2985 East Cottonwood Pkwy., 801/942-8860, lunch Mon.–Fri., dinner nightly, Sun. brunch, $20–25), an excellent seafood restaurant, and **La Caille** (9565 Wasatch Blvd., 801/942-1751, dinner nightly, $34–68), a romantic recreation of a French chateau, with correspondingly elegant French food. It's a little over the top (and the prices are way so), but if you're tired of Utah, it's cheaper than a plane ticket.

Information

For reservations and information on the skiing and year-round resort facilities, contact **Snowbird Ski and Summer Resort** (Snowbird, UT 84092, 801/742-2222, www.snowbird .com). For a snow report, call 801/933-2100.

Alta's deep powder is for skiers only – no snowboarders allowed.

© JUDY JEWELL

Transportation

The resort at Snowbird is six miles up Little Cottonwood Canyon and 25 miles southeast of downtown Salt Lake City. Snow tires are required November 1–May 1 (with tire chains in the car). During extremely heavy snowstorms the canyon may be temporarily restricted to vehicles with 4WD or chains.

It's easy to take **UTA transit** (801/743-3882, www.rideuta.com, $1.60 one-way) from Salt Lake to Snowbird. From downtown, take the TRAX light rail south to either the 7200 South or 10000 South station, then catch bus 97 or 98 to the slopes. The same buses continue up to Alta, providing an easy link between Snowbird and Alta.

Canyon Transportation (800/255-1841, www.canyontransport.com, $33 one-way) vans run regularly between the airport and Big and Little Cottonwood canyon resorts, and Park City.

Snowbird provides free shuttle service between the different areas of the resort during skiing hours.

◖ ALTA SKI AREA

Alta (office 801/742-3333, snow conditions 801/572-3939, www.alta.com, $59 adults, $30 children 12 and under, $84 Alta–Snowbird pass) has a special mystique among skiers. A combination of deep powder, wide-open terrain, charming accommodations, and the polite but firm exclusion of snowboards make it special, as does its clientele. Many Alta skiers have been coming here for years—it's not uncommon to share a lift with a friendly 70-year-old who, upon debarking the lift, heads straight for the steepest black run.

Do not come to Alta expecting to do anything but ski. There is no shopping, no nightlife, no see-and-be-seen scene.

Unlike Park City's resorts, there are no housing developments near Alta or Snowbird, which gives them a feeling of remoteness. The lack of development around Alta is largely due to Mayor Bill Levitt, owner of the Alta Lodge and mayor for 34 years (he stepped down in 2006 at the age of 88), who fought developers all the way to the U.S. Supreme Court.

THE GREATEST SNOW ON EARTH

What makes Utah's snow so great? In a word, geography. Storms come in from the Pacific, pushed by cold jet-stream air across the Great Basin. When these storm clouds encounter the Wasatch peaks, the jet stream forces them upwards into even colder air, where they release their moisture. The extremely cold temperatures ensure that this moisture falls as light, dry snow.

Storm fronts often become trapped in the Salt Lake Valley, laden with moisture and too heavy to rise out of the Great Basin. These heavy clouds make it partway out of the basin, dump snow on the nearby mountains, then drop back to the Great Salt Lake where they pick up more moisture. This cycle continues until the storm weakens and the clouds release enough moisture to float over the tops of the mountains and continue eastward.

Dogs are not permitted in the town of Alta, unless they receive a special permit. Appeal to the powers-that-be at the town offices, if necessary.

History

The little town of Alta owes its original reputation to rich silver veins and the mining camp's rip-roaring saloon life. Mining started in 1865 with the opening of the great Emma Mine and peaked in 1872, when Alta had a population of 5,000 served by 26 saloons and six breweries. Crashing silver prices the following year and a succession of deadly avalanches ended the boom. Little remains from the old days except abandoned mine shafts, a few shacks, and the cemetery.

By the 1930s, only one resident was left—George Watson—who elected himself mayor. Watson ran a small tourist business known as the Alta Scenic Railway, providing rides in the canyon on a jitney, a car mounted on the old railroad tracks. In 1938 he deeded 1,800 acres to the U.S. Forest Service. (There is some present-day speculation that Watson didn't ever really own the deeded land, but he did take advantage of the tax breaks he got by handing it over.)

Ski enthusiasts brought Alta back to life. The Forest Service hired famous skier Alf Engen to determine Alta's potential as a site for a future ski area. In 1939, Alta's Collins chairlift became the second lift in the United States; detractors complained that the $1.50 per day lift tickets reserved the sport just for the rich. (Some of the original Collins single chairs are still around; look for them in the Wildcat Base parking lot near the Goldminer's Daughter.)

For a closer look at Alta's colorful past, check out the Alta Historical Society's exhibit at the local community center/library, across the road from the Snowpine Lodge (801/742-3522).

Terrain and Lifts

The first thing to know about Alta is that it's for *skiers;* snowboards aren't allowed. And, even though it's right next door to Snowbird, it feels totally different. Whereas Snowbird feels big and brawny, Alta has an almost European quality. To keep the slopes from becoming too crowded, Alta limits the number of skiers allowed. (It's rare that anyone is turned away; this mostly happens during the holidays and on powder-filled weekends.)

Lifts include two high-speed quads, a high-speed triple, four slower chairlifts, and several tow ropes. Even though Alta has the reputation of being an experts' ski area, there is a fair amount of very nice beginner territory. Of the more than 40 named runs, 25 percent are rated beginner, 40 percent intermediate, and 35 percent advanced. The longest run is 3.5 miles and drops 2,020 feet. Skiers should keep their eyes open as they ride the lifts—porcupines are a common sight in the treetops here.

A good strategy for skiing Alta's 2,200 acres is to begin the day skiing from the Albion Base on the east side of the resort, perhaps even warming up on the mile-long green Crooked

Mile run near the Sunnyside lift before heading up the Supreme lift to fairly steep blue runs and some of Alta's famously "steep and deep" black runs. Later in the day, move over to the Wildcat side, after the sun has had a chance to soften the snow there.

Holders of the Alta–Snowbird pass can cut over to Snowbird's Mineral Basin area from the top of Alta's Sugarloaf lift. The cut-across is not difficult, and Mineral Basin is a fun place to ski.

Alta's season usually runs mid-November–April. Average total snowfall is about 500 inches per year, and snow levels usually peak in March, with depths of about 121 inches.

Alta's Alf Engen Ski School (801/359-1078) offers a wide variety of lessons; rentals and child-care services are also available. Guided snowcat skiing (and snowboarding) in the Grizzly Gulch backcountry is available for expert skiers and boarders with lots of off-trail experience. Five runs cost $200; call the ski school to reserve a spot.

Cross-Country Skiing

The **Alta Nordic Shop** (801/742-9722) is at the base of the Wildcat lift, near the western end of groomed cross-country trails. These trails, groomed for both classic and skate skiing, are not the world's most exciting—they essentially parallel the tow rope that runs between the Wildcat and Albion lifts—but they're a good place to learn cross-country techniques or get your legs in shape at the beginning of the season. A Nordic Pass ($10, available at the Nordic Shop) is required to ski these groomed trails. The Nordic Shop also sells and rents cross-country gear and snowshoes, and provides lessons.

More ambitious cross-country skiers can head up the unplowed summer road to Albion Basin. Snowcats often pack the snow. The road begins at the upper end of the Albion parking lot, then climbs gently to the top of Albion Lift, where skiers can continue to Albion Basin. Intermediate and advanced skiers can also ski to Catherine Pass and Twin Lakes Pass. Cross-country skiers may ski the beginner (green) Alta trails. Those heading for the backcountry should have proper equipment and experience; the Nordic Shop can advise on avalanche conditions.

Summer Activities

Other than a couple of hiking and yoga retreats, Alta doesn't offer any summer programs, though a number of area Forest Service trails attract hikers and bikers; lodges remain open.

Accommodations

Alta's accommodations are excellent though pricey: Even bunk beds in a dorm room are over $100! Note, however, that room rates at most lodgings include breakfast and dinner. Rates at all the lodges are comparable, from about $110–140 for a dorm bed to $450–500 for a large room with a view. In summer, room rates drop by nearly half. Please note that there's an additional room tax of over 12 percent, and most lodges tack on a 15 percent service charge, in lieu of tipping.

The easiest way to find a room is simply to call a reservation service: **Alta Vacations** (800/220-4067, www.altavacations.net) can make reservations at all lodgings and arrange transportation and ski packages.

In Alta, one of the most charming and most central places to stay is the **Alta Lodge** (801/742-3500 or 800/707-2582, www.alta lodge.com, $130–500), an old-fashioned ski lodge that oozes authenticity. Rates include breakfast and dinner. Alta Lodge, built in 1939, is not fancy. In fact, descending the four flights of wood-plank stairs from street level is a bit like entering a mine. Fortunately, at the bottom of this shaft guests are greeted by a friendly dog, engaging people, and a super-size bottle of SPF 45 sunscreen at the check-in window. The atmosphere is relaxed and the Sitzmark Club, the lodge's bar, is lively. There are no televisions in the rooms at Alta Lodge, but a game room off the lobby has a big-screen TV and nightly videos. The lodge also has a good ski-and-play program for kids.

The most luxurious place to stay in town is **Alta's Rustler Lodge** (801/742-2200 or 888/532-2581, www.rustlerlodge.com, bed in dorm room $123, standard room with bath $410), with heated outdoor pool, fine-dining restaurant, and spacious rooms. But even here, there's no pretense. Après-ski, it's common to see guests wandering around the lobby swathed in their thick hotel bathrobes. The Alta Day Spa, at the Rustler, offers massage, facials, and full-body skin care; call the lodge to book an appointment.

Alta's oldest place to stay is the **Snowpine Lodge** (801/742-2000, www.thesnowpine .com, bed in dorm room $120, standard room with bath $169–199 per person). It was built as a WPA project in 1938, and its original design was a smaller version of Timberline Lodge, on Oregon's Mount Hood, another WPA ski lodge. Since then, the Snowpine has been extensively remodeled, but it is still small, cozy, and a touch on the funky side. Like Alta Lodge, the Snowpine is an easy place to make friends—the lobby area, the outdoor hot tub, and the dining room are all very convivial.

The **Alta Peruvian Lodge** (801/742-3000 or 800/453-8488, www.altaperuvian.com, dorm bed $122, standard room $250 per person) is another good choice, with its large heated outdoor pool and grand lobby. Like most of the other local lodgings, the Peruvian has a colorful history. In 1947 its owner acquired two hospital barracks from Brigham City, over 100 miles to the north, hauled them to Alta, and hooked them together. Though the original structure still stands, the lodge has been considerably updated and modernized. Breakfast and a family-style dinner are included in the room rates.

The **Goldminer's Daughter Lodge** (800/453-4573, www.goldminersdaughter lodge.com, dorm room $137, small bedroom $187 single, $304 double) is right near the base of the Wildcat lift, near the large parking area, with easy ski-in, ski-out access. (All of Alta's lodgings have easy access from the slopes, but most are up-slope from the lifts, meaning that at the end of the day, you've got to be hauled back to your lodge on a tow rope.) While the Goldminer's Daughter doesn't have quite the history or ambience of many of Alta's lodgings, it's a shade less expensive and plenty comfortable.

In addition to the traditional ski lodges, there are condos available for rent. **Hellgate Condominiums** (801/742-2020, www.hell gate-alta.com) is between Snowbird and Alta; units sleeping 4–6 people go for about $400 a night. Be sure to pick up groceries in Salt Lake City; there are no food stores up here.

Food

Since virtually all of Alta's lodges include breakfast and dinner for their guests, Alta does not have a highly developed restaurant scene. All of the lodge dining rooms are open to the public; of these, the Rustler and Alta Lodge are particularly good places for dinner.

Stop for lunch on the mountain at **Watson's Shelter** (801/799-2296, lunch, $5–12), mid-mountain beneath the top of the Wildcat lift. Upstairs, **Collin's Grill** (801/742-3333, lunch, $8–20) is a sit-down restaurant; a coffee shop is downstairs.

Alta's one real restaurant of note is the **Shallow Shaft** (801/742-2177, dinner nightly in winter, Thurs.–Sun. in summer, $12–25), across the road from Alta Lodge. Although the place looks a little dubious from the outside, the interior has great views of the ski mountain. Along with good steaks and chops, there are several vegetarian options, and the wine list is as good as you'll find in Utah. The Shallow Shaft is one of Utah's best restaurants, and reservations are required.

Transportation

Alta is eight miles up Little Cottonwood Canyon. Snow tires are required in the canyon November 1–May 1 (with tire chains in the car). During extremely heavy snowstorms the canyon may be temporarily restricted to vehicles with 4WD or chains; occasionally it shuts down entirely.

Parking can be difficult in Alta. Pay attention to the No Parking signs, as parking regulations are enforced.

It's easy to take UTA transit from Salt Lake

to Alta. From downtown, take the TRAX light rail south to either the 7200 South or 10000 South station, then catch bus 97 or 98 to the slopes. The bus ride from the 7200 TRAX station to Alta takes a little over an hour.

Canyon Transportation (800/255-1841, www.canyontransport.com, $33 one-way) vans run regularly from the airport. Alta Shuttle (801/274-0225 or 866/274-0225, www.altashuttle.com, $29 any one-way trip) runs between the airport, Alta, and Park City resorts.

HIKING LITTLE COTTONWOOD

Before heading up for a hike in Little Cottonwood Canyon, make sure that your dog is not along for the trip. Because this heavily used canyon is part of the Salt Lake City watershed, environmental regulations prohibit domestic animals, even in the car.

White Pine, Red Pine, and **Maybird Gulch Trails** lead to pretty alpine lakes. Red Pine and Maybird Gulch lie in the Lone Peak Wilderness (www.fs.fed.us/r4/wcnf/). All three trails begin from the same trailhead, then diverge into separate valleys. On any one of them, you'll enjoy wildflowers and superb high-country scenery. Start from White Pine Trailhead (elev. 7,700 feet) 5.3 miles up the canyon and one mile beyond Tanners Flat Campground. The trail crosses a bridge over Little Cottonwood Creek and contours west, then southwest to White Pine Fork. The effects of several avalanches can be seen along this section. The trails divide after one mile, just before crossing White Pine Fork; turn sharply left for White Pine Lake or continue straight across the stream for Red Pine Lake and Maybird Gulch. Red Pine Trail contours around a ridge, then parallels Red Pine Fork to the lake (elev. 9,680 feet)—a beautiful deep pool ringed by conifers and alpine meadows. Energetic hikers can rock-scramble along the stream another one-half mile (no trail) to Upper Red Pine Lake. The upper lake sits in a glacial cirque devoid of trees. Trout lurk in the waters, though the lake may remain frozen until late June. Maybird Gulch Trail begins two miles up Red Pine

Trail from White Pine Fork and leads to tiny Maybird Lakes. From the trailhead, White Pine Lake is 3.5 miles (2,300-foot elevation gain), Red Pine Lake is the same (1,920-foot elevation gain), and Maybird Lakes are 4.5 miles (2,060-foot elevation gain). See the Dromedary Peak 7.5-minute topo map. This whole area is heavily used by hikers, so take great care with the environment. Please follow the Forest Service regulation that prohibits wood fires within one mile of the lakes.

Peruvian Gulch-Hidden Peak Trail gives you the advantage of hiking just one-way from either the top or bottom by using the Snowbird tram. From the top of Hidden Peak (elev. 11,000 feet), the trail crosses open rocky country on the upper slopes and spruce- and aspen-covered ridges lower down, then follows an old mining road down Peruvian Gulch. Elevation change along the 3.5-mile trail is 2,900 feet. The Dromedary Peak 7.5-minute topo map covers this area.

Cecret Lake Trail begins from the west side of Albion Basin Campground and climbs glacier-scarred granite slopes to a pretty alpine lake (elev. 9,880 feet) below Sugarloaf Mountain. Wildflowers put on colorful summer displays along the way. The trail is just one mile long and makes a good family hike; elevation gain is 360 feet. Continue another mile for fine views south to Mount Timpanogos from Germania Pass. It's no secret that early miners had trouble spelling Cecret Lake; you'll see two versions on maps!

Campgrounds

Tanners Flat Campground (mid-May–mid-Oct., $12, has water) is 4.3 miles up the Little Cottonwood Canyon at an elevation of 7,200 feet. **Albion Basin Campground** (late June–mid-Sept., $10, has water) lies 11 miles up the road near the head of the canyon at an elevation of 9,500 feet (the last 2.5 miles are gravel road). Both campgrounds accept reservations through www.reserveamerica.com or at 877/444-6777.

Park City

Park City is without a doubt the recreational capital of Utah. With three ski areas and the Utah Olympic Park located in the valley, the city (pop. about 8,000) is noted worldwide for its snow sports: The U.S. national ski team trains here, and many of the 2002 Winter Olympic competitions took place in the valley. In summer, guests flock to the resorts to golf and explore the scenic mountain landscapes on horseback, mountain bike, or foot.

However, there's a lot more to Park City than recreation: The well-heeled clientele that frequents the resorts has transformed this old mining town into the most sophisticated shopping, dining, and lodging center in Utah. However, such worldly comforts come at a cost. Condominium developments and trophy homes stretch for miles, encroaching on the beauty that brought people here in the first place.

Even if you're not a skier or hiker, plan to explore Park City's historic downtown. Late-19th-century buildings along Main Street and on the hillsides recall Park City's colorful and energetic past. Here you'll find a historical museum, art galleries, specialty shops, and fine restaurants. A busy year-round schedule of arts and cultural events (including the Sundance Film Festival), concerts, and sporting contests also help keep Park City hopping.

Orientation

Park City lies in a mountain valley at an elevation of 7,000 feet on the eastern side of the Wasatch Range, 31 miles east of Salt Lake City via I-80 and Highway 224. The principal exit for Park City is called Kimball Junction, and although Park City proper is seven miles south, the condominiums and shopping centers begin immediately. Just south of Kimball Junction is

PARK CITY

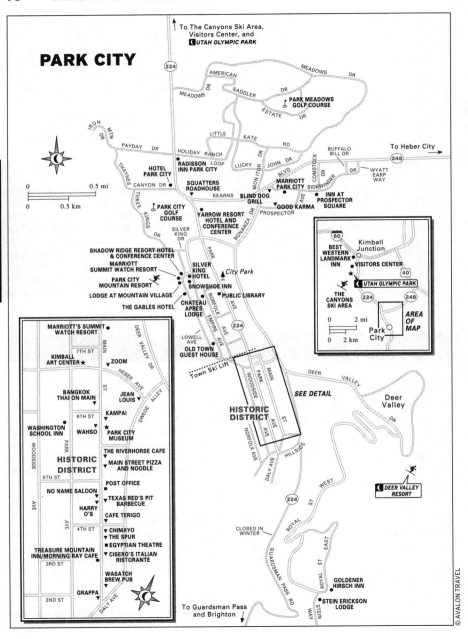

on a hillside two miles south of the present town site. Their sample assayed at 96 ounces of silver per ton, with lesser values of lead and gold. Two years later, the Flagstaff Mine began operation, and development of one of the West's richest mining districts took off. What had been a peaceful valley with grazing cattle now swarmed with hordes of fortune hunters and rang with the sound of pickaxes. In 1898, a hotel fire nearly brought an end to the young city. The fire raced along Main Street, reduced 200 businesses and houses to ashes, and left much of the population homeless. Determined citizens immediately set to work rebuilding and constructed a new downtown within three months. Many of the businesses you see along Main Street date from that time. The museum is in the old City Hall Building, built in 1885 and rebuilt after the 1898 fire. There are great photos of skiers from the 1930s, and a car from an old *underground* chair lift (remember, this was a mining town). Go downstairs to see the original jail, known as the "dungeon."

Historic buildings along Park City's Main Street house upscale shops and restaurants.

The Canyons Resort, with its mammoth new lodges, and the Utah Olympic Park, the ski-jump facility. In Park City proper, the Park City Mountain Resort is just west of downtown; most businesses stretch along historic Main Street. Two miles southeast of Park City is Deer Valley, both an upscale condo development and the state's most exclusive ski resort.

SIGHTS

No matter what else you do in Park City, spend an hour or two wandering along historic Main Street. Even with the inrush of galleries, gift shops, and trendy restaurants, there's still considerable Old West charm here.

Park City Museum

Drop in to this museum (528 Main St., 435/649-7457, www.parkcityhistory.org, 10 A.M.–7 P.M. Mon.–Sat., noon–6 P.M. Sun., free) to see historic exhibits on Park City's colorful past. In October 1868, with winter fast approaching, three off-duty soldiers from Fort Douglas discovered a promising outcrop of ore

Kimball Art Center

This large civic art center (638 Park Ave., 435/649-8882, www.kimball-art.org, 10 A.M.–5 P.M. Mon.–Fri., noon–5 P.M. Sat.–Sun., donations appreciated), at the corner of Heber and Park near the bottom of Main Street, exhibits works of noted artists and sponsors classes and workshops. Two galleries display monthly changing shows of paintings, prints, sculptures, ceramics, photography, and other media. The gift shop has many items for sale. Look for other art galleries along Main Street, too.

PARK CITY MOUNTAIN RESORT

The first great thing about Park City Mountain Resort (435/649-8111 office, 435/649-0493 or 800/222-7275 lodging reservations, 435/647-5449 snow phone, www.parkcitymountain.com, adult lift tickets $75–80) is its convenience to downtown Park City: The Town Lift loads right above Main Street! The other thing skiers and snowboarders love about this place is its expanse. There's a lot of terrain, good bowl skiing for experts, and some of Utah's best terrain parks and pipes for snowboarders. In spite of all this space, the resort can get very crowded, especially on weekends and holidays.

The price of lift tickets varies depending upon conditions and time of purchase (prepaying for a multiday pass offers the best deals). Purchase multiday tickets online or by calling guest services at 800/222-7275.

Ski season usually runs mid-November–mid-April. Lifts operates 9 A.M.–4 P.M. Night skiing runs 4–9 P.M. late December–March on the Payday and First Time lifts.

History

Though Park City locals began messing around on skis and building ski jumps in the 1930s, the resort didn't open until 1963. Skiers and snowboarders can check out signs erected by Park City Historical Society to mark old mining sites around the resort. Intermediate-level skiers and snowboarders can join a historian for a free two-hour Mountain History Tour; check the website or ask at the ticket counter about these tours.

Park City Mountain Resort hosted all the snowboarding events and the men's and women's giant alpine slalom in the 2002 Winter Olympics. The resort is owned by POWDR Resorts, which also runs Mount Bachelor in Bend, Oregon, and Killington in Vermont.

Terrain and Lifts

Though many people access the ski area via the Town Lift, the main base area is actually about half a mile north, at the Resort Center. This is where the main resort parking lot is, and from here, lifts can get you to various points on the mountain.

Four six-passenger high-speed lifts, two high-speed quads, six triple chairs, and four double chairs carry up to 28,400 skiers *per hour* high onto the eastern slope of the Wasatch Range. More than 100 trails range in length from 0.25 to 3.5 miles (16 percent easier, 45 percent more difficult, and 39 percent most difficult). Four terrain parks and a super-pipe are part of Park City's successful effort to at-

tract snowboarders. Experienced skiers and boarders can enjoy the powder in five open bowls near the top of the mountain—a total of 650 acres. The total drop is 3,100 feet in elevation from the top of Jupiter Bowl to the Resort Center.

Blue runs dominate the lower and mid-mountain. Intermediate skiers and boarders will appreciate the hillside full of blue cruisers off the King Con high-speed quad; even beginners can get a nice long run from the mid-mountain (it's easy to get to by riding first the Town Lift, then Bonanza) by following the Home Run trail back to the Town Lift base.

The Jupiter and McConkey's lifts ferry expert skiers and boarders to a series of steeper bowls. Actually, the lifts get you to only a couple of areas near the bowls; after debarking the lifts, many people hike along the ridges to find just the right run down.

For skiers and boarders who like a structured approach, the resort's website has a pretty slick planning feature (www.parkcitymountain .com/winter/pmt) that will help you select the best runs for your ability and energy level.

Mountain hosts are posted around this sprawling resort, helping visitors find their way back to the Town Lift base or over to the challenging Jupiter Bowl area. In addition to the Mountain History tours (see the *History* section), the resort offers special two-hour ski or snowboard tours for teenagers. Teens can join up with "Ride Guides" Fridays at 11 A.M. and 1:30 P.M., and Saturdays and Sundays at 10 A.M. and 1 P.M. at the top of the Bonanza lift.

Park City ski area and the adjacent resort village offer night skiing, a ski school, rentals, ski shops, ice-skating, and restaurants (three are on the slopes).

Skiing at Park City Mountain Resort is one of several outdoor activities that people with disabilities can learn with the help of the **National Ability Center** (435/649-3991 voice or TDD, www.discovernac.org), located on the edge of town. The center provides special equipment and instruction at affordable rates, offers programs to people of all ages, and is open for summer programs as well.

Mountain Coaster

Winter or summer, thrill-seekers can ride a toboggan on a elevated track (noon–9 P.M. Mon.–Thurs., 10 A.M.–10 P.M. Fri.–Sat., noon–6 P.M. Sun. mid-June–Labor Day, shorter hours mid-May–mid-June and Labor Day–mid-Oct., $17, small discount with lift ticket) through the aspen glades on an elevated track as it winds over a mile of curves, bends, and loops. Ride a lift to the top of the track, suck in your breath, and plummet downhill in this roller coaster–like ride.

Summer Activities

Although the Park City ski area shuts most of its lifts down for the summer, the resort remains open and maintains 30 miles of trails for mountain bikers, hikers, and horseback riders; for $11 you can ride up the Town or Payday Lift with your bike or picnic hamper. A free map of designated mountain-biking trails is available from the resort and local bike shops.

In addition to the Mountain Coaster, which runs on tracks, the ski area has an **Alpine Slide** (noon–9 P.M. Mon.–Thurs., 10 A.M.–10 P.M. Fri.–Sat., noon–6 P.M. Sun. mid-June–Labor Day, shorter hours mid-May–mid-June and Labor Day–mid-Oct., $11 adult per plunge, $3 passenger under 48 inches in height and older than 2 years), which is like a toboggan on a giant curving sliding board. A chairlift takes you to the start of a half-mile track that twists and winds down the hillside. No special skills are needed to ride the little wheeled sled.

Even more frightening is the **ZipRider** (hours as above, $19), a cable ride that makes a 60-second, 500-foot plunge along 2,300 feet. At its highest point, the rider is suspended 110 feet off the ground.

Other summer activities include a climbing wall, horseback rides, miniature golf, and hiking.

◖ DEER VALLEY RESORT

Deer Valley Resort (435/649-1000 or 800/424-3337, ski report 435/649-2000, www.deervalley.com, lifts open 9 A.M.–4:15 P.M. early Dec.–mid-Apr., $79 adult full day, $55 adult afternoon, $47 children 4–12 full day, $38 children afternoon; $56 seniors 65 and older full day, $39 seniors afternoon) is the crème de la crème of Utah ski areas. Here you'll find good uncrowded skiing on immaculately groomed trails with all the extras of posh accommodations, gourmet dining, attentive service, and polished brass everywhere. Lift operators steady the chairs as you plunk your bottom down, mountain guides lead free tours, and, at the top of nearly every lift, a friendly green-parka-clad host points you to a run that's right for you. And, in spite of its reputation as being a cushy, glitzy area for spoiled rich folks, the skiing here can be great, and the people riding the lifts are by and large friendly and interesting.

Deer Valley prohibits snowboards. The ski area is 1.5 miles south of downtown Park City (33 miles east of Salt Lake City), and free shuttle buses connect the resort and the town.

History

Although a small ski area, Snow Park, operated in this area 1947–1965, Deer Valley itself did not open until 1981. The owners, Edgar and Polly Stern, wanted to provide a resort that was both easy to get to and more luxurious than other ski areas. The Sterns were soon joined by Roger Penske; Edgar Stern and Roger Penske still own the resort.

Like Park City's other ski areas, Deer Valley was built on private land (as opposed to the Cottonwood areas, which are on U.S. Forest Service leases) and is fueled by development. It's rather like the typical golf course development, where expensive homes are built immediately adjacent to the area, meaning that you're frequently skiing past incredibly huge, expensive homes.

The 2002 Olympics slalom, mogul, and aerial events were held at Deer Valley.

Terrain and Lifts

Deer Valley spans four mountains: Bald Eagle Mountain, Bald Mountain, Empire Canyon, and Flagstaff Mountain. Though the main base area and parking is at Snow Park, the mid-mountain Silver Lake area is much more of a hub. In fact, at the end of the day, you can't just ski straight down to the parking area; instead you must make your way to Silver Lake, take a short ride on the Homestake lift out of the valley, then ski down Bald Eagle Mountain to the base.

The slopes are served by 22 lifts, including one four-passenger high-speed gondola and 11 high-speed quads, providing 99 runs, six bowls, and a vertical drop of 3,000 feet. The longest run is 2.8 miles. Twenty-seven percent of the skiing is rated easier, 410 percent more difficult, and 32 percent most difficult. Though Deer Valley has the reputation of coddling skiers (and it's true that they provide a green or blue way down from the top of every lift), there's plenty of challenging territory for advanced skiers, especially in Empire Canyon. The 2007–2008 season brought a new high-speed detachable quad chairlift, Lady Morgan Express, to the Empire Canyon area, opening up over 200 new skiable acres, 65 acres of gladed skiing, and nine new runs.

Deer Valley is famous for its meticulously groomed trails. To find out what's been groomed, check the boards at the top of every mountain. Mountain hosts can also steer you to freshly groomed trails (or onto ungroomed powder).

The majestic Snow Park Lodge (elev. 7,200 feet) contains the main ticket office, ski school, rentals, ski shop, child-care service, gift shop, and a restaurant. You can drive three miles and 1,000 feet higher to Silver Lake Lodge (parking here is more limited), a major hub of activity on the mountain, with more restaurants and luxury hotels.

Mountain guides lead tours of the mountain at 9:30 A.M. (for advanced skiers) and 10 A.M. (for intermediates) from the Snow Park Lodge and at 1:30 P.M. (intermediate and advanced skiers) from the Silver Lake Lodge.

Bald Eagle Mountain, near the Snow Park base, contains the main beginners' area and served as the site for 2002 Olympic events. Aspiring slalom skiers can take a run on the Know You Don't slalom course; the Champion mogul course is also open to the public. Not surprisingly, the White Owl run, site of the freestyle aerial jumps, is off-limits.

At 9,400 feet, Bald Mountain is steeper and more exposed; its intermediate and advanced runs have spectacular views but often get skied out in the afternoon. Find steep ungroomed trails in the Sultan and Mayflower areas.

On the right (west) side of Flagstaff Mountain (elev. 9,100 feet) the snow often holds up well, making its intermediate and beginner ski trails good bets for skiing later in the day. Blue runs off the Northside Express are good for intermediates. The Flagstaff area also has tree skiing and access to Ontario Bowl.

Empire Canyon (elev. 9,570 feet) has skiing for all abilities, including a family ski area off the Little Chief lift, challenging but skiable intermediate terrain, and some of the most advanced skiing at Deer Valley, including eight chutes and three bowls.

A mid-mountain course located on the Race Course ski run just above the Silver Lake Lodge offers a chance to race against the clock or another racer. Times are electronically displayed at the finish; $6 for one run, $10 for two.

The classic last run of the day is Last Chance, which goes past stunning ski houses and some fairly amazing yard art all the way to the parking area. (Tired skiers can also board the Silver Lake Express from the top and ride it back to the Snow Park base.)

To prevent overcrowded trails, Deer Valley restricts the number of skiers on the mountain and often needs to restrict ticket sales during Christmas, New Year's, and Presidents' Day weeks. If you're planning on skiing here during the holidays, reserve lift tickets at least a few days in advance.

Summer Activities

Mountain bikers, hikers, and sightseers can catch the Sterling and Silver Lake lifts (10 A.M.–5:30 P.M. daily mid-June–Labor Day, weekends only Labor Day–mid-Sept., $24 full-day pass, $16 single-ride bike pass, $13 hikers or sightseers, $10 child or senior scenic ride, $7 scenic ride on Silver Lake lift only) to explore more than 50 miles of trails running from the peak. Riders must wear helmets. Instruction, rentals, and tours are available; call the resort (800/424-3337) for more information. Summer is also the season for off-road cycling events, Utah Symphony concerts, and music festivals. For horseback rides, call Deer Valley Stables (435/645-7256).

Accommodations

There is an abundance of condominium lodgings in Deer Valley, many almost immediately adjacent to the slopes. The best way to book lodgings is to contact Deer Valley Central Reservations (435/645-6528 or 800/558-3337, www.deervalley.com) and let them guide you through the process. The website has a good interactive map that will give you an overview of the accommodations and prices. Another local booking service is Deer Valley Lodging (888/976-2732, www.deervalleylodging.com), with condominiums and private homes. Package deals are often available from both services, but rates at are still high—it's hard to find a condo for under $375. But remember, you're only a couple of miles from Park City and about an hour from Salt Lake. It's worth skiing Deer Valley even if you can't afford to sleep here.

Accommodations are in two main areas: Snow Park, the Deer Valley base area, which is about one mile from downtown Park City, and the Silver Lake area, located mid-mountain approximately 3.2 miles from the Snow Park base area. A short distance past Silver Lake is the Empire Pass area, with a few condos. Both Snow Park and Silver Lake lodges are themselves just day lodges.

If money is no object, book a room at the luxurious **Stein Ericksen Lodge** (7700 Stein Way, 435/649-3700 or 800/453-1302, www .steinlodge.com, $735 and up), mid-mountain in the Silver Lake area. The lodge is like a Norwegian fantasy castle built of log and stone. Rooms are exquisitely appointed, and there's a day spa with pool and fitness room. The restaurant here is one of the highest rated in the

area. You can book a room here either through the lodge itself or through Deer Valley Central Reservations.

Another extremely comfortable place is the **Goldener Hirsch Inn** (7570 Royal St. East, 435/649-7770 or 800/252-3373, www.goldener hirshinn.com, $450 and up) in exclusive Silver Lake Village; it's an Austrian style ski-in, ski-out inn with beautifully furnished rooms (the gorgeous hand-carved beds were imported from Austria), hot tubs, a sauna, lounge, meeting facilities, and underground parking. The restaurant here is also extremely good.

At the Snow Park Base, **The Lodges at Deer Valley** (book at Deer Valley Central Reservations, $280 and up hotel room, $585 and up condo apartment) includes hotel rooms with mini-fridge and toaster and full-kitchen condos; the complex has a year-round outdoor pool and hot tub. These are joined by many, many other condos. Central reservations can help you select a place.

Food

The mid-mountain lodges here are unique because you can actually drive to them. In the **Silver Lake Lodge,** several cafeteria-style restaurants make for a quick lunch. On a sunny day, stretch out in the lawn chairs on McHenry's Beach, the big sunny spot in front of the lodge, with a grilled portabello mushroom sandwich. There are also a couple of small coffee shops on the mountain—they serve Deer Valley's trademark turkey chili and good cookies. For a sit-down lunch, après-ski snacks, or dinner, the **Royal Street Cafe** (435/645-6724, lunch and dinner daily, lunch around $12–15), in the Silver Lake Lodge, is a good bet.

If you take an informal survey of lift riders here, the most popular meal in Deer Valley seems to be the **Seafood Buffet** at the Snow Park Lodge (435/645-6632, 6:30–9 P.M. Mon.–Sat. during the ski season, $58 adults, $29 children). Both quality and quantity are unstinting.

For fine dining, the award-winning **Mariposa** (435/645-6715, dinner Tues.–Sun. during ski season, most entreés over $30, reservations recommended) at Silver Lake Lodge is a good bet, preparing "classic and current" cuisine; fresh fish, rack of lamb, steaks, chicken, and other meats receive savvy sauces and preparations.

At the **Goldener Hirsch Inn** (435/649-7770, breakfast, lunch, and dinner daily, $18–36, reservations recommended) in Silver Lake Village, dishes reflect both an Austrian heritage and New World pizzazz: wienerschnitzel ($28) is the house specialty, and fondue is another popular option. At the Stein Ericksen Lodge, also at Silver Lake Village, the elegant **Glitretind Restaurant** (435/649-3700, breakfast, lunch, and dinner daily, plus Sunday brunch, $22–38, reservations recommended) serves contemporary cuisine with a few Asian touches.

THE CANYONS RESORT

Talk about infinitely expanding ski areas! The Canyons Resort (4000 The Canyons Dr., 435/649-5400, 435/615-3456 snow report, 888/226-9667 reservations, www.thecanyons .com), Utah's largest and fastest-growing resort, now sports an entire city's worth of buildings near the bottom of the lifts. More than $33 million has been spent on expanding and renovating the resort. Lifts—including more high-speed lifts than other Utah resorts—reach up to eight separate peaks along the Wasatch Mountains, serving more than 3,700 skiable acres, making The Canyons one of the largest ski areas in the United States. At the base of the slopes are three large lodge hotels. It's no surprise that, given all this development, ticket prices are pretty high.

The Canyons is 27 miles east of Salt Lake City via I-80 and Highway 224. A free shuttle bus runs between the resort area and Park City.

History

From a fairly small local resort called Park West, this area morphed into Wolf Mountain, and then, in 1997, became The Canyons. The Canyons is owned and operated by American Skiing Company, which also owns a number of ski areas in New England.

Though no Olympic events took place in The Canyons, the resort is extraordinarily proud of the fact that the *Today Show* was broadcast from the elegant Grand Summit Lodge.

Terrain and Lifts

The Canyons (lifts run 8:30 A.M.–4 P.M. Nov.–Apr., $76 adults, $44 seniors and children 12 and under, save a few dollars by purchasing online at least 14 days in advance) is the first Park City ski area you'll reach coming from Salt Lake City. Not counting the Cabiolet gondola from the day-use parking area and a couple of surface tows, the resort has 14 lifts, including an eight-passenger gondola, a detachable six-pack, and five high-speed quads. The 3,700 acres are spread out across eight mountains; the 152 ski trails are rated 14 percent beginner, 44 percent intermediate, 42 percent advanced and expert. The longest run is 2.5 miles and drops 3,190 feet. For snowboarders, there are seven natural half-pipes, one constructed pipe, and two terrain parks. Many locals who once skied at Park City have shifted allegiances to The Canyons, mostly because of the less-crowded slopes here. However, if the snow is iffy, it's usually better to head over to the Cottonwood canyons; when conditions aren't absolutely favorable, The Canyons seems to have the worst snow of any of the Wasatch resorts.

To begin a day at The Canyons, ride the cabriolet from the parking area to the resort base. From the base, you'll have to wait in line for the Flight of the Canyons gondola, which soars over mountains, valleys, and terrain parks to the Red Pine Lodge, the mid-mountain base. From here, ski down to the Tombstone Express, ride that lift, and from there continue working your way south (left on the trail map) to the top of the Dreamscape lift, which lets out onto a mountainside full of nice blue runs.

Expert skiers and boarders can go from Tombstone to Ninety Nine 90. Check out the runs off Ninety Nine 90, a high-speed quad serving expert runs. The views from the top are breathtaking, the trails there send you meandering through gladed steeps, open bowls, and narrow chutes. You could spend a whole

© JUDY JEWELL

The Canyons Resort is an expansive ski area, with plenty of room to ski or snowboard.

day there, especially after a big snowfall. Also, from there, you can access backcounty skiing on huge bowls way above the tree line. There is a short hike, but it's well worth it.

At the end of the day, ride up on the Super Condor Express, then cruise home on Upper Boa to Willow Drain, a long easy cruise marred only by an uphill walk at the end. (If you can't bear to walk, just ride the gondola back down to the base.)

The resort offers day care, supervised lunches, ski lessons, and rentals for the younger set. The Canyons includes a ski school, rental and sales shop, a half-dozen restaurants (three mid-slope), and a free shuttle service from lodges and hotels in Park City.

Summer Activities

The **Flight of the Canyons Gondola** (10 A.M.– 6 P.M. late June–Labor Day, $12 adults, $8 seniors, $6 children) lifts you up to the Red Pine Lodge, where you can eat lunch or embark on a day hike or mountain bike ride (bikes are permitted on the gondola, but dogs aren't). There's also a disc golf course (free) near the top of the gondola.

The resort can arrange backcountry horseback rides and hot air balloon rides.

Locals swing by the Cabiolet parking lot every Wednesday afternoon during the summer (2–7 P.M.) for a farmers market. Free concerts, usually featuring rock bands, held Saturday evenings late July–late August, can draw big crowds.

Accommodations

A major portion of the expansion at The Canyons (888/226-9667 central reservation line, www.thecanyons.com) has been the building of **Grand Summit Lodge, Sundial Lodge,** and **Silverado Lodge,** which sit at the base of the ski slopes. These enormous hotels are built to a scale unlike any other lodgings in Park City and vie with Canadian national park resorts in terms of grandness and scope. All of these lodges have a mix of hotel rooms and condos;

expect to pay upwards of $300 for the most basic (though luxurious by most travelers' standards) rooms during ski season. Be sure to book in advance for these "less expensive" hotel rooms. Condos can get quite elaborate and expensive, topping out at more than $1000 per night. Facilities at the Grand Summit, which fronts directly onto the gondola loading platform, include a full-service health club and spa including indoor/outdoor pool, three on-site restaurants, and bar and brewpub. The Sundial Lodge, about 100 yards from the gondola, has an outdoor heated pool, hot tub, and on-site exercise facility. The Silverado, which was completed during the 2007 season, is a few steps farther downhill and has the requisite outdoor heated pool, hot tub, and exercise room.

Although the resort lodgings are prohibitively expensive for many travelers, two of Park City's least expensive hotels, the Best Western Landmark and the Holiday Inn Express, are near Kimball Junction, about a mile from The Canyons.

Food

Mid-mountain, at the top of the gondola, the **Red Pine Lodge** (8:30 A.M.–3:30 P.M. daily, $5–10) is a good place to grab lunch without having to disrupt a day on the slopes. It serves the typical pizza, burgers, soup, and salad. Better food is served at the **Lookout Cabin** (435/615-2892, lunch daily, $10–20, reservations suggested) a sit-down restaurant at the top of the Lookout lift.

Dinner is served mid-mountain at the **Viking Yurt** (435/615-9878, www.parkcityyurts.com, dinner during winter, $100–150, reserve well in advance). To reach the yurt, dinner guests meet at 6 P.M. sharp to ride a sleigh up the ski runs, either directly to the yurt or to the Red Pine Lodge, where snowshoes or cross-county skis are doled out for the short trek to the yurt for a fixed-price five-course gourmet dinner.

In the Grand Summit Lodge, **The Cabin** (435/615-8060, breakfast, lunch, and dinner daily, lunch about $10, $18–38) is the elegant dinner restaurant; it's also a good place for lunch or an early après-ski dinner. If you're

not staying at the lodge, it's nice to have an excuse to go inside, take a break, and enjoy its atmosphere.

WINTER RECREATION
◖ Utah Olympic Park

Built for the 2002 Olympics, this was the site of the bobsled, luge, and ski jump competitions (near The Canyons at 3000 Bear Hollow Dr., 435/658-4200, www.olyparks.com/uop, 9 A.M.–6 P.M. daily year-round, free general admission). It is now open to the public for guided tours of the competition sites, including visits the top of the K120 ski jump and the bobsled run for panoramic views of the surrounding country.

The mission of the park is now to train aspiring athletes. Visitors can often watch athletes train. During the summer, freestyle skiers do acrobatic jumps and plunge into a huge swimming pool. On summer Saturday afternoons, there's a freestyle aerial show.

© PAUL LEVY

Freestyle ski jumpers spend the summer jumping into a huge swimming pool at the Utah Olympic Park.

It's also possible to actually *do* something here, such as take a vigorous (some would say harrowing) bobsled run (summertime rides age 14 and up only, $60; winter rides age 16 and up, $200, reservations highly recommended) with a professional driver, or ride a zip line ($20) or alpine slide ($15, $5 child with paying adult). In the winter, adults can choose from a spectrum of bobsled, skeleton, luge, and Nordic jumping classes and workshops ($75–1800). Three-day summer camps introduce ice hockey, speed skating, figure skating, luge, bobsled, ski jumping, biathlon, curling, freestyle, and skeleton to kids ages 9–14 ($395).

White Pine Touring

Park City's cross-country ski center (Park Ave. and Thaynes Canyon Dr., 435/649-6249, www.whitepinetouring.com, mid-Nov.–early Apr., $18 adults, $8 children 6–12, 6 and under free, equipment rentals available) offers rentals, instruction, and guided snowshoe tours. It has a touring center and about 12.4 miles of groomed trails right in town. White Pine also has a yurt in the Uinta Mountains that's available year-round ($79–99 winter, $59–69 summer). A year-round office and shop is at 1790 Bonanza Drive (435/649-8710).

🄲 Ski Interconnect

If you look at the map, you'll see that Snowbird, Alta, Solitude, Brighton, and Park City Mountain Resort are not that far from each other and can be linked by backcountry routes. Experienced skiers who are up for a challenging day can explore the backcountry between these ski areas in Big and Little Cottonwood Canyons and Park City with Ski Utah Interconnect (801/534-1907, www.skiutah.com, mid-Dec.–mid-Apr., $195, reservations required), which provides a guide service for extensive touring of Wasatch Front ski areas. Touring is with downhill equipment and requires legs of steel and the ability to ski ungroomed powder all day long and do a bit of hiking to reach those great bowls and chutes. Tours on Monday, Wednesday, Friday, and Sunday depart from Deer Valley and move on to Park City Mountain

Resort, Solitude, Brighton, Alta, and Snowbird. On Tuesday, Thursday, and Saturday, tours start at Snowbird and visit Alta, Brighton, and Solitude. Cost includes guide service, lunch, lift tickets, and transportation back to the point of origin.

Sleigh Rides

Riding a horse-drawn sleigh to a Western dinner or an evening of entertainment is quickly becoming a Park City tradition. One of the more elaborate activities is offered by **Snowed Inn Sleigh Company** (435/647-3310, www .snowedinnsleigh.com, $79 adults, $49 children, reservations required), which takes guests on a sleigh ride to a lodge where dinner is served; short rides without dinner are also available ($20 for ages 2 and up).

SUMMER RECREATION
Historic Union Pacific Rail Trail State Park

This state park (435/645-8036) consists of a multi-use, nonmotorized trail built to accommodate hikers, bicyclists, horseback riders, and cross-country skiers. The trail parallels I-80 and runs 27 miles from Park City through the town of Coalville to Echo Reservoir. In Park City, from Park Avenue, turn onto Kearns Boulevard, then right onto Bonanza Drive, and after about 200 yards, left on Prospector Avenue, where you can catch the trail behind the Park City Plaza (parking area on the right).

Mountain Biking

This is a favorite summer activity in the Park City area, with more than 350 miles of mountain bike trails. Some of the local landowners, including ski resorts and mining companies, have offered access to their land and have even built trail sections at their own expense. Helmets are always required when riding on private land. *Mountain Biking Park City and Beyond,* by Gregg Bromka, gives descriptions and maps of the trails open that summer. All three Park City resorts keep a lift open for bikers and hikers during the summer. Deer Valley's 55 miles

The slopes of Park City Mountain Resort rise up from town. In the summer, it's a nice place to hike.

of single- and double-track trails are stunning; Park City has 35 miles of trails. The Canyons also offers gondola rides to mountain bikers; from there they can access many trails.

Bikes are available to rent at nearly every resort and sports store (see the *Equipment Rental* section).

Golf

Park City has two 18-hole courses. The city-owned **Park City Golf Club** (435/615-5800, www.parkcitygolfclub.org, $43) is at Park Avenue and Thaynes Canyon Drive. An outstanding public course is at Wasatch Mountain State Park, a short distance away in Midway (see the *Heber City and Vicinity* section). Play **miniature golf** (435/649-8111, $6) at Park City Mountain Resort.

Hiking

The ski areas open their trails to hikers in summer; pick up a trail map and just head out. Deer Valley, Park City, and The Canyons resorts all offer lift-assisted hiking that takes walkers up

to the high country without an air-sucking foot ascent; see individual resorts for information. From downtown Park City, follow trail signs to the slopes; well-marked trails start just on the edge of town and head uphill. *Park City Trails,* by Raye Ringholz, describes many hiking and ski-touring possibilities in the area and offers a history and walking tour of Park City.

When hiking around Park City, stay clear of relics of the mining past that lie scattered about. You're likely to come across miners' cabins in all states of decay, hoist buildings, aerial tramway towers, rusting machinery, and great piles of mine tailings. Unlike other parts of the Wasatch Range, most of the land here belongs to mining companies and other private owners. Visitors need to keep a distance from mine shafts—which can be hundreds of feet deep—and respect No Trespassing signs.

Horseback Riding

Red Pine Adventures (2050 White Pine Canyon, 435/649-9445 or 800/417-7669, from $69) offers trail rides of varying lengths;

1.5-hour rides start several times a day. Horseback rides are also available at The Canyons (435/649-5400) and at Park City Mountain Resort (435/645-7256).

Ballooning

Though expensive, a flight aboard a hot air balloon is an exhilarating experience. Balloons take off in the early morning year-round, weather permitting, and trips typically include a continental breakfast and post-flight champagne toast. Cost is $125 for 30 minutes, $200 for one hour with either **Park City Balloon Adventures** (435/645-8787 or 800/396-8787, www.pcballoonadventures.com) or **Morning Star Balloons** (435/685-8555, www.morning starballoons.com).

Fishing

Fly-fishing is a favorite pastime in the mountain streams and lakes of the Wasatch Mountains. The Weber and Provo Rivers are well known for their wily native cutthroat, wild brown, and rainbow trout and Rocky Mountain whitefish. Get your fishing license, supplies, and a guide at **Park City Fly Shop** (805 Park View Dr., 435/645-8382 or 800/324-6778) or **Trout Bum 2** (4343 North Highway 224, Suite 101, 435/658-1166 or 877/878-2862). **Park City Outfitters** (435/647-0677 or 866/649-3337, www.parkcityoutfitters.com) and **Local Waters Fly Fishing** (435/655-5858 or 800/748-5329) also lead guided fly-fishing trips.

Other Activities

Two-hour **rafting** trips down the Provo River Canyon are offered by **High Country Rafting** (435/649-7678, www.highcountryrafting.com, May–Sept., $35 adults, $20 children 12 and under). Trips start at Frazier Park, 30 minutes from Park City. With similar prices, whitewater trips down the Weber River, north of Park City, are offered by **Park City Rafting** (435/655-3800, www.parkcityrafting.com). **Boating, water-skiing,** and **sailboarding** are popular activities at the Jordanelle, Rockport, and Echo Reservoirs.

The local yoga studio, **The Shop** (1167 Woodside Ave., 435/649-9339, www.park cityyoga.com), teaches Anusara yoga.

The **city park** next to the former miners' hospital has picnic tables, a playground, volleyball and basketball courts, and ball fields.

The upscale **Silver Mountain Sports Club** (2080 Gold Dust Lane, 435/649-6670) has two large swimming pools, spinning, weight room, saunas, hot tub, and classes. The city-owned recreation center at **Park City Racquet Club** (1200 Little Kate Rd., 435/615-5400) features two outdoor pools, indoor and outdoor tennis, racquetball, basketball, volleyball, aerobics, saunas, and massage.

Equipment Rental

Most sports stores in Park City (and there are lots of them) rent skis and related equipment in winter and bicycles and camping gear in summer. It's also easy to rent equipment, including mountain bikes in the summer, at the ski resorts.

White Pine Touring (1790 Bonanza Dr., 435/649-8710) rents cross-country skis, mountain-climbing equipment, camping gear, and mountain bikes.

Jans Mountain Outfitters (1600 Park Ave., 435/649-4949) and Wolf Mountain, Deer Valley, and Park City ski areas (435/649-4949 or 800/745-1020) has downhill, telemark, and cross-country rentals, snowboards, mountain bikes, in-line skates, and fly-fishing gear.

ARTS AND ENTERTAINMENT
Musical Concerts

Summer is music-festival time in Park City. The Utah Symphony and other classical performers take the stage at Deer Valley's outdoor amphitheater (435/649-1000) the third week of July through the third week of August for a summer concert series. The Canyons (801/536-1234, Sat. evenings late July–late Aug.) offers rock, country, and jazz concerts. The Park City International Music Festival (435/649-5309, July) offers chamber music at Kimball Art Center and Park City Community Church. And there are free concerts on Wednesday evenings 6–8 P.M. in summer at Deer Valley's Snow Park amphitheatre (435/901-7664).

Cinema

Of course the big event is the annual **Sundance Film Festival** (www.sundance.org, mid–late Jan.), which spotlights more than 200 films from around the world and involves at least as many parties as films. The **Park City Film Series** (435/615-8291, Sept.–June) offers art, foreign, and classic films at the Jim Santy Auditorium (1255 Park Ave).

Theater

The **Egyptian Theatre Company** puts on dramas, comedies, musicals, and children's theater year-round in the historic Egyptian Theatre (328 Main St., 435/649-9371).

Nightlife

As you'd expect in a ski resort, nightlife centers on bars and dance clubs. The principal hangouts are on Main Street, though all the lodges and resorts and most of the larger hotels have bars and clubs of their own. All are private clubs, requiring a small membership fee (usually around $5) to enter. The trendy **Harry O's** (427 Main St., 435/655-7579) is the largest music venue in town, with a large, crowded dance floor. The more down-home **No**

Name Saloon (447 Main St., 435/649-6667) has darts, pool, and live music nightly; duck down into **The Spur** (352 Main St., 435/615-1618) for rock, acoustic folk, or bluegrass and a friendly, convivial atmosphere. **The Sidecar** (333 Main St., 435/645-7468) is another low-key place with good live music most nights.

Cisero's (306 Main St., 435/649-6800) has live music Wednesday–Saturday and a big-screen TV for sports. Jazz and pop singers entertain nightly at the **Riverhorse Cafe** (540 Main St., 435/649-3536). You can drink a microbrew and chat with friends at **Wasatch Brew Pub** (250 Main St., 435/649-0900) or, north of the Main Street neighborhood, at **Squatter's Roadhouse** (1900 Park Ave., 435/649-9868).

Events

Contact the Park City Visitor Information Center (1826 Olympic Parkway, 435/658-9616, www.parkcityinfo.com) for the latest news on happenings around town. The year's biggest event is in January, when the stars come to town for the **Sundance Film Festival.**

The **Park City International Music Festival** (435/649-5309, www.pcmusicfestival

Park City's Egyptian Theatre Company stages plays year-round in this historic building.

© PAUL LEVY

SUNDANCE INSTITUTE FILM FESTIVAL

Robert Redford began this noted film festival in 1981 as a venue for independent films that otherwise had a difficult time reaching the screen or a mass audience. In subsequent years, the Sundance Festival has become the nation's foremost venue for new and innovative cinema. The festival is held the second half of January, at the height of the ski season, so Park City is absolutely packed and then some. (As the festival has grown, some films are now shown at the Tower Theatre in Salt Lake City.) Definitely make plans well in advance if you want to attend any of the screenings or festival activities.

Tickets to the screenings can be hard to come by, especially for films with advance reputations or big stars; if you can't get tickets, put your name on waiting lists or join the lines at the theaters for canceled tickets. However, tickets to less well-known films are usually available at the last minute. If you are coming to Park City expressly to see the films, inquire about package tours that include tickets.

Park City is exciting during the festival, as the glitterati of New York and Hollywood descend on the town. You'll see movie stars, some wild clothing, and lots of deal-making. For information on the Sundance Festival, call its information number (435/328-FILM) or check the website (www.sundance.org).

.com) presents concerts year-round with an emphasis on the festival's acclaimed summer concert series (throughout July at The Canyons).

Cowboys and cowgirls compete in the **Oakley Rodeo** Thursday–Saturday on the 4th of July weekend 15 miles east of Park City. In August, more than 200 artists exhibit their work on Main Street for the **Art Festival. Summit County Fair** in nearby Coalville has a parade, rodeo, horse show, roping, demolition derby, entertainment, and exhibits.

Ski areas open in November. In celebration, there's a big street dance, ski racing, and fireworks, usually near Thanksgiving.

Christmas in the Park presents carols, the lighting of a community tree, and a visit by Santa in December. Skiers descend the slopes with torches at Park City ski area for the **Christmas Eve Torchlight Parade.**

SHOPPING

Park City's primary shopping venue is historic Main Street, which is lined with upscale boutiques, gift shops, galleries, crafts shops, and sporting-goods stores. Don't miss **Mountain Body** (near the Town Lift at 825 Main St., 435/655-9342, 10 A.M.–10 P.M. daily) with locally made lotions and salves for dry, high-altitude skin and a wide variety of spa treatments.

Dolly's Bookstore (510 Main St., 435/649-8062, 10 A.M.–10 P.M. Mon.–Sat., 11 A.M.–8 P.M. Sun.) has a good selection of books for all ages and interests.

ACCOMMODATIONS

Park City is awash in condos, hotels, and B&Bs; guest capacity far exceeds the town's permanent population. Rates peak at dizzying heights during the ski season, when accommodations may also be hard to find. Most lodgings have four different winter rates, which peak at the Christmas holidays and in February and March; there are different rates for weekends and weekdays as well. Many lodgings have rooms in a wide range of prices (from hostel rooms to basic hotel rooms to multiroom suites), so remember that *the following price categories are for a standard double room in the winter high season.* Summer rates are usually about half of the rates below. During ski season, many lodgings ask for minimum stays—sometimes a weekend, sometimes a full week. Park City's hotel tax is 10.35 percent; add this to any rate you're quoted.

The following accommodations are in addition to the lodges and hotels operated by and located at Deer Valley and The Canyons. For rooms at these resorts, contact the central reservation phone numbers mentioned in those sections.

The Park City Area Chamber of Commerce has an online lodging locator (www.parkcity info.com).

Reservation Services

Undoubtedly the easiest way to find a room or condo in Park City is to call one of the many reservation services; most also offer ski, golf, or other recreational packages. For reservations in Deer Valley condos and private homes, contact **Deer Valley Central Reservations** (435/645-6528 or 800/558-3337, www.deervalley.com); it also represents some properties in Park City. Other Deer Valley properties are available through **Deer Valley Lodging** (888/976-2732, www.deervalleylodging.com).

Another good place to start your lodging search is **David Holland's Resort Lodging and Conference Services** (435/655-3315, www.davidhollands.com). This service owns an assortment of inns, condos, and lodges in Park City and represents other units and private homes, which makes it able to offer a variety of prices and facilities.

If you're here to ski, and ski widely, ask about the Silver Passport when you book your room. The Silver Passport, a single lift ticket to all three resorts in the Park City area, must be purchased prior to arrival in conjunction with lodging from participation lodging providers or Park City Mountain Reservations (800/222-7275).

Under $50

You'll have to give up your privacy to get an inexpensive room in Park City, but it is possible to sleep cheaply at **Chateau Après Lodge** (1299 Norfolk Ave., 435/649-9372, www.chateauapres .com, $35 dorm bed, $100 private double), which is a short walk from the Park City Mountain Resort Base and has a dedicated following among serious skiers. The rooms are far from elegant, but this is really Park City's best deal. The breakfast buffet is a great place to meet other skiers.

$50-100

Although it's not in town, the **Best Western**

Holiday Hills (200 S. 500 West, Coalville, 435/336-4444 or 866/922-7278, www.bw stay.com, $80) in Coalville, about 20 minutes from Park City, is a reasonable bet for travelers who want a comfortable room (and continental breakfast) that's only a few bucks more expensive than a lift ticket. It's located just off I-80 exit 162.

It's also possible to find high-quality lodgings in this price range in Heber City, also about 20 minutes from Park City.

$100-150

A homey option for skiers and other outdoors people is the **(Old Town Guest House** (1011 Empire Ave., 435/649-2642 or 800/290-6423, www.oldtownguesthouse.com, $99–229 including breakfast), owned by a woman who leads backcountry ski tours with Ski Interconnect. The old house is a comfortable, though not frou-frou, B&B; the upstairs McKonkey's suite is most spacious, and has the most privacy.

Park City's Old Town neighborhood was once full of tumbled-down miners' cottages. Many, including the one housing the Old Town Guest House, have been spruced up.

$150-200

Out at the Kimball Junction freeway exit is the **Best Western Landmark Inn** (6560 N. Landmark Dr., 435/649-7300 or 800/548-8824, www.bwlandmarkinn.com, $189), with a pool, spa, breakfast buffet, and a free shuttle to ski areas and downtown Park City. If you want a high-quality, reasonably priced (for Park City) hotel room, and don't mind being a bit removed from the action, this is a good bet. During the summer, rooms are about $100 cheaper. Also by the freeway and with similar facilities is the **Holiday Inn Express** (1501 West Ute, 435/658-1600, $216). Both of these hotels are close to The Canyons.

Among the lodging options clustered around the Park City Mountain Resort lifts is the **Lodge at the Mountain Village** (1415 Lowell Ave., 435/655-3315 or 888/727-5248, www.thelodgepc.com, $190 hotel room, $385 one-bedroom condo), which is run by David Holland's Resort Services; this is about as cheap as you'll find ski-in-ski-out lodgings in town.

Over $200

Right downtown is the **Treasure Mountain Inn** (255 Main St., 435/649-7334 or 800/344-2460, www.treasuremountaininn.com, $240 and up). Treasure Mountain is a large complex of three buildings with several room types, all with kitchens. The Treasure Mountain has seen a lot of use (when it was built in 1963 it was Park City's first condominium hotel), but refurbishment projects have been happening regularly and it's one of the more genuinely "green" hotels in town.

◀ **Marriott's Summit Watch Resort** (780 Main St., 435/647-4100 or 800/845-5279, www.marriott.com, $300 and up for hotel room with kitchenette) is a cluster of condominium hotels at the base of Main Street near the Town Lift. They are easily the nicest lodging options in the downtown district, with rooms ranging from studios to two-room villas. All rooms have kitchen facilities and luxury level amenities; there's a central pool, and all the dining that downtown Park City offers is within a five-minute stroll. Right at

the main base of the Park City Mountain Resort and just a few dollars more expensive is **Marriott's MountainSide** (1305 Lowell Ave., 800/845-5279, www.marriott.com, $314 for a kitchenette hotel room); if you are looking for top-notch ski-in-ski-out lodging, this is a good choice. Although you can walk to town from here, it's a bit of a schlep in the winter.

Park City has yet another plush Marriott, the **Marriott Park Hotel and Convention Center** (1895 Sidewinder Dr., 435/649-2900 or 800/234-9003, www.parkcitymarriott.com, $240), located in a business and condo development northeast of downtown. Designed with the small conference trade in mind, it offers swimming pool and spa facilities, two restaurants, and a lounge; in addition to hotel rooms, there are one- and two-bedroom units with kitchens.

The **Yarrow Resort Hotel and Conference Center** (1800 Park Ave., 435/649-7000 or 800/927-7694, www.yarrowresort.com, $260) is just below historic Main Street and close to the ski lifts. It's a little older, but the rooms are large and well kept; some rooms have kitchens, and there's also a restaurant, outdoor heated pool, hot tub, and exercise room.

A landmark Park City B&B is the **Washington School Inn** (543 Park Ave., 435/649-3800 or 800/824-1672, www.washingtonschoolinn.com, $285 and up). The quarried limestone inn was built in 1889 as the town's elementary school; after a complete remodel in the 1980s, the old Washington School emerged as one of the most luxurious lodgings in Park City. There are 12 large standard rooms and three suites, all with private baths and each uniquely decorated. There's an indoor hot tub, sauna, and ski lockers. Children 12 and over are welcome.

Adjacent to the Park City Ski Area is the **Shadow Ridge Resort Hotel and Conference Center** (50 Shadow Ridge St., 435/649-4300 or 800/451-3031, www.shadowridgeresort.com, $209 and up). Shadow Ridge offers a mix of hotel-style rooms and kitchen-equipped condos with 1–3 bedrooms. Facilities include a heated outdoor pool, sauna, and fitness center.

If you need post-ski massage treatments, Align Spa is in the resort's lobby.

The **Inn at Prospector Square** (2200 Sidewinder Dr., 435/649-7100 or 800/453-3812, www.allseasonsresortlodging.com, $200 hotel room, $380 two-bedroom condo) is one of several hotel/condominium complexes managed by All Season Resorts. Several different room types are scattered through eight different buildings about a mile from Main Street and the main Park City lifts; guests can use the adjacent Silver Mountain Sports Club.

Despite its pedestrian name, the **Hotel Park City** (2001 Park Ave., 435/940-5000, www .hotelparkcity.com, $700 suite) is quite sumptuous, even by Park City standards. This all-suite hotel has deluxe in-room CD and DVD players, comfy leather sofas, sumptuous bathrooms, a heated outdoor pool, a spa and fitness center, and a good restaurant.

At the foot of Main Street, the **Silver Queen Hotel** (632 Main St., 435/649-5986 or 800/447-6423, www.silverqueenhotel.com, $500 one-bedroom condo) has luxurious accommodations in a small older building that's convenient to restaurants and only a short walk from the Town Lift.

Campgrounds

Park City RV Resort (2200 W. Rasmussen Rd., 435/649-8935, www.parkcityrvresort .com, $20 tent, $30–35 hook-ups) offers seasonal tent and year-round RV sites with showers and laundry. From I-80, take Park City Exit 145 and travel west one mile on the north frontage road. The campground is about six miles from Park City.

There are good public campgrounds in the Heber City area. Jordanelle and Wasatch Mountain State Parks are both good places to pitch a tent in the summer. See the *Heber City and Vicinity* section for details on these state parks.

FOOD

Park City has the greatest concentration of good restaurants in Utah. The five blocks of historic Main Street alone offer many fine places to eat, and each of the resorts, hotels,

and lodges offers more options. Note that many of the restaurants close in May and November—the so-called "mud season." During ski-season weekends, dinner reservations are strongly recommended for all but the most casual restaurants.

Main Street

A favorite place for a traditional breakfast is the **Morning Ray Cafe** (255 Main, 435/649-5686, breakfast and lunch daily, $5–10) in the Treasure Mountain Inn complex, with fresh pastries, omelets, and hotcakes served till noon. For lunch, there are salads and sandwiches.

At the top of Main Street, **Wasatch Brew Pub** (250 Main St., 435/649-0900, lunch and dinner daily, $9–20) is a good place for a casual, inexpensive pub-style meal and excellent beers and ale; in good weather, there's a patio for outdoor dining.

One of Park City's most noted restaurants is **Chimayo** (368 Main St., 435/649-6222, dinner nightly, $28–40), the area's leading purveyor of contemporary Southwest cuisine. Halibut is pan seared with chipotle and served with a mango salsa, spaghetti squash, and roasted broccolini. Chimayo's sister restaurant, **Grappa** (151 Main St., 435/645-0636, dinner nightly, $27–38) is at the top of Main Street; here you'll find distinctive approaches to Italian standards, such as polenta with herb-encrusted rainbow trout ($27) or horseradish-encrusted salmon ($34). In the summer, there's a lovely deck.

One of the most romantic restaurants in Park City is 【 **Wahso** (577 Main, 435/615-0300, dinner nightly, $28–40). Its name is both Chinese and French (*oiseau,* meaning "bird"), as is the cuisine at this stylish, slightly formal restaurant. French sauces meet Chinese cooking techniques, and vice versa.

The inspiration for the food at pleasant **Cafe Terigo** (424 Main St., 435/645-9555, lunch Mon.–Sat., dinner nightly, $20–30) is Italian, but dishes such as porcini-dusted scallops on sweet corn risotto with roasted red pepper and arugula puree show that ingredients and techniques have been substantially updated. The atmosphere in the restaurant and on the side patio is simultaneously calming and fun.

Another signature Park City restaurant, the **The Riverhorse Cafe** (540 Main St., 435/649-3536, dinner nightly, $25–40) in the old Masonic building, serves carefully prepared American standards with a few restrained flourishes; after a day of skiing, splurge on the mixed grill here. The Riverhorse also features live musical entertainment.

New American cooking is the order of the day at **Zoom** (660 Main St., 435/649-7614, lunch and dinner daily, lunch $10–15, dinner entreés $18–36). The grilled meats are excellent, as is the trout. Zoom has perhaps the nicest patio dining in Park City. Zoom is housed in an old railroad depot at the foot of Main Street, and is owned by Robert Redford.

Tucked into an odd space around the corner at the foot of Main Street, **Jean Louis** (136 Heber Ave. #107, 435/200-0260, dinner nightly, $19–45) serves a broad range of "entreés du monde" as well as the Normandy-born chef's take on traditional American fare, such as roast duck or a soft-shelled crab po' boy.

Prospector Square and Beyond

A good, reasonably priced, and healthy bet for any meal of the day is **Good Karma** (1782 Prospector, 435/658-0958, breakfast and lunch Mon.–Fri., dinner nightly, $9–14), a sweet but tiny spot with a variety of Asian dishes (standard American fare is served at breakfast); go for the Indian food. In the summer, sit out back in the courtyard.

One of Park City's best restaurants is the **Blind Dog** (1781 Sidewinder Dr., 435/655-0800, dinner Mon.–Sat., $15–55). Don't let its bland setting fool you; the food here is seriously good, and though crab cakes ($29) are favorites here, the Dog also makes a mean meatloaf ($22). Right next door, the Blind Dog runs a sushi restaurant (same phone and hours, $6 and up), capitalizing on their good sources of fish.

For a Western steak-house atmosphere, go to **Grub Steak Restaurant** (2200 Sidewinder Ave., 435/649-8060, lunch Mon.–Sat., dinner nightly, $17–40) in the Inn at Prospector Square. The steaks, prime rib, grilled chicken, and seafood are excellent, and dinners come with a trip to the salad bar.

On Park Avenue at Kearns Boulevard is **Squatter's Roadhouse Grill** (1900 Park Ave., 435/649-9868, breakfast, lunch, and dinner daily, $8–22), a brewpub with above-average pub grub. Vegetarians should check out the char-broiled tofu tacos.

Off the beaten path but worth searching out, the sweetly romantic **Chez Betty** (1637 Short Line Dr., 435/649-8181, dinner nightly Dec.–March, Thurs.–Mon. Apr.–Nov., $11–34) in the Copperbottom Inn, serves lovely French-inspired dinners, including an excellent four-course chef's tasting menu ($52, $72 with wine). Several of the entrées are available in "petite" portions.

Even when ski season comes to a halt, it's worth checking out the **Baja Cantina** (435/649-2252, $12–16) at the main base of the Park City Mountain Resort lifts for zippy, full-flavored Mexican lunches and dinners in a colorful and bustling dining room. It's one of Park City's best budget choices.

INFORMATION AND SERVICES

A number of Main Street storefronts advertise "visitors information"; these places are almost invariably real estate offices, though they do have racks of brochures. For the best selection of info, and a genuinely helpful staff, visit the **Park City Visitor Information Center** (1826 Olympic Parkway, 435/658-9616, www.park cityinfo.com, 9 A.M.–6 P.M. daily) near Kimball Junction at the turnoff to the Utah Olympic Park. There's a branch office in the Park City Museum (528 Main Street).

The **post office** is downtown (450 Main St., 435/649-9191). **Park City Family Health and Urgent Care** (1665 Bonanza Dr., 435/649-7640) provides care 24 hours a day.

TRANSPORTATION

Park City Transit operates a trolley bus up and down Main Street (about every 10 minutes daily) and has several bus routes to other parts of town including Park City, The Canyons, and Deer Valley ski areas (about every 10–20 minutes daily). All buses are free; pick up a transit guide from the chamber/bureau, on any of the buses, or by calling Park City Transit (435/645-5130 recording). Parking can be extremely difficult in downtown Park City, so it's a good idea to hop a bus.

All Resort (800/457-9457, $32 one-way, 24-hour advance reservations recommended) makes regular runs between Park City and Salt Lake City Airport or downtown. They also offer car rentals in Park City. If you're not embarrassed to ride in a Hummer, **Park City Transportation** (435/649-8567 or 877/474-9109, from $89 one person, $99 two people) provides year-round service to downtown Salt Lake City and the SLC airport; ski shuttles depart from Park City and Salt Lake City in winter to Brighton, Solitude, Snowbird, Alta, Sundance, Snowbasin, and Powder Mountain ski areas; call 24 hours in advance for reservations and to check if a passenger minimum applies.

Call **Ace Transportation** (435/649-8294) for cabs.

North of Park City

Old ranching and mining communities dominate the mountain valleys that now serve as the I-80 and I-84 corridor east of Salt Lake City. The reservoirs here are popular with RV campers, boaters, and anglers.

Coalville and Vicinity

Coalville (pop. 1,380) lies 19 miles northeast of Park City on I-80 near the confluence of Chalk Creek and the Weber (pronounced WEE-ber) River. The **Best Western Holiday Hills** (200 S. 500 West, Coalville, 435/336-4444 or 866/922-7278, www.bwstay.com, $80) is a good alternative to lodgings in pricey Park City.

Rockport State Park

Rockport Reservoir (9040 N. Highway 302, Peoa, 435/336-2241 or 877/444-6777 reservations, year-round, $7 day use, $9–18 camping) is tucked in the Weber River Valley 13 miles south of Coalville. Visitors enjoy fishing, water-skiing, sailing, windsurfing, and swimming. The Weber River above and below the lake also has good fishing for trout and whitefish. The state park facilities are along the eastern shore and include a paved boat ramp, docks, three picnic areas with covered tables, eight primitive campgrounds, and the modern **Juniper Campground** (with showers). Reservations are recommended for Juniper Camp-

ground on summer weekends, though there's usually plenty of space in the reservoir's five primitive campgrounds. Rockport State Park is 45 miles east of Salt Lake City; take I-80 Wanship Exit 156 and go south five miles on U.S. 189.

Echo Reservoir

A small private resort operates a boat ramp and campground (435/336-9894, early May–Sept.) between Coalville and Echo in a grove of large cottonwood trees on the reservoir's eastern shore. Water-skiing and sailing are the most popular lake activities. Take I-80 Coalville Exit 164 and go north 3.5 miles (or take I-80 Echo Exit 169 and go south two miles).

East Canyon State Park

East Canyon Reservoir (801/829-6866, 877/444-6777 reservations, year-round, $7 day use, $9–21 camping) is one of the closest mountain lakes to Salt Lake City (38 miles). It's also close to Ogden (33 miles) and Morgan (12 miles). The 600-acre lake is about six miles long and one-half-mile wide; elevation is 5,700 feet. Power boating, water-skiing, and angling are the most popular activities. Fishing is good for rainbow trout in the lake and in East Canyon Creek. You'll find a marina and most of the state park facilities at the lake's north end. The marina has a store, snack bar, boat storage, slips, and boat rentals. A beach east of the marina is popular with swimmers and picnickers. Facilities at the north end of the lake include a paved boat ramp, picnic area, and campground (water and showers, but not much shade). Camping reservations are recommended for summer weekends.

Heber City and Vicinity

Its setting in a lush agricultural valley surrounded by high mountains has earned Heber City the title "Switzerland of America." Many of its people work at farming, raising livestock, and dairying—as their families have done since pioneer days, though it's also become the site of some fantastically expensive vacation homes. Heber City (pop. 9,775) makes a handy stop for travelers exploring the nearby Wasatch and Uinta Ranges or visiting the large Deer Creek and Strawberry Reservoirs. It also offers reasonably priced accommodations a short drive from Park City. Heber City merges almost seamlessly into the town of Midway, home to several upscale resorts.

SIGHTS
Heber Valley Historic Railroad
Ride a turn-of-the-20th-century train (450 South 600 West, 435/654-5601, www.heber valleyrr.org, year-round, $30 adults, $20 children 3–12, $23 seniors for Provo Canyon trip) pulled by steam locomotive #618 past Deer Creek Lake into scenic alpine Provo Canyon. A 90-minute dog-friendly trip goes to Soldier Hollow ($24 adults, $16 children, $18 seniors, $10 dogs).

Soldier Hollow
Soldier Hollow (435/654-2002, www.soldier hollow.com, $17 full-day trail pass adults, $9 children 7–17, $14 seniors), site of the 2002 Olympic and Paralympic cross-country skiing and biathalon events, offers roughly 20 miles of trails (including some easy ones added to the Olympic-level course) for cross-country skiing, snowshoeing, biathlon, and mountain biking. There's also a tubing hill ($17 for 2 hours ages 7 and up, $10 ages 3–6). Rentals are available at the lodge. From Heber City, head west on

100 South to Midway. Take a left on Center Street (Hwy. 113) in Midway and head south for 3.5 miles to Soldier Hollow.

Homestead Crater
Just northwest of the town of Midway, on the grounds of the Homestead Resort, is a large volcanic-like cone called the Crater. This geological curiosity is actually composed of travertine deposited by the local hot springs; water once flowed out of the top, but it's now piped to a 65-foot-deep, 95°F pool deep in the Crater's belly. The Crater (800/327-7220, 10 A.M.–7 P.M. daily, $11 swimming, $16 weekend, $8 guests of Homestead Resort, scuba from $22) is accessible for swimming, scuba diving, and snorkeling. Scuba classes and guided dives are also offered.

EVENTS
Horse shows and rodeos take place throughout the summer in the Heber City area. A **powwow** in late June brings tribes for dances and craft sales. The **Utah High School Rodeo Finals** are also held in June. **Wasatch Fair Days** features a parade, rodeo, exhibits, livestock show, entertainment, and demolition derby in early August. Labor Day weekend brings **Swiss Days** to Midway and a huge gathering of border collies to Soldier Hollow for the **International Sheepdog Championship.**

RECREATION
◖ Wasatch Mountain State Park
Utah's largest state park (435/654-1791, http://stateparks.utah.gov, 800/322-3770 or www.reserveamerica.com camping reservations, 435/654-0532 tee times, $5 day use, $12–21 camping, $27 18 holes golf) encompasses 22,000 acres of valleys and mountains on the

east side of the Wasatch Range. The excellent Lake and Mountain golf courses are in the main part of the park; the newer Gold and Silver courses are at Soldier Hollow, which occupies a corner of the park. To reach the main park entrance, from Heber City, drive west three miles to Midway, then follow signs north two miles.

Unpaved scenic drives lead north through Pine Creek Canyon to Guardsman Pass Road (turn right for Park City or left over the pass for Brighton), northwest through Snake Creek Canyon to Pole Line Pass and American Fork Canyon, and southwest over Decker Pass to Cascade Springs. Winter brings snow depths of 3–6 feet mid-December–mid-March. Separate cross-country ski and snowmobile trails begin near the golf course. **Homestead Cross-Country Ski Center** (at the Homestead Resort, 700 N. Homestead Dr., Midway, 435/654-1102) provides equipment for both sports.

The large **Pine Creek Campground,** just north of the golf course at an elevation of 5,600 feet, has showers and hookups from late April or early May to late October. A 1.5-mile **nature trail** begins near site #21 on the Oak Hollow Loop in Pine Creek Campground. **Little Deer Creek Campground** is a smaller, more secluded area in an aspen forest, open with water June–mid-September. It's also open earlier and later without water—check with the park office first; groups often reserve all the sites. You can get there by driving the seven-mile unpaved road to Cascade Springs, then turning north four miles on another unpaved road.

Jordanelle State Park

This large reservoir upstream of Heber City on the Provo River provides recreation for boaters and anglers. It's east of U.S. 40 six miles north of Heber. There are two recreation areas. **Rock Cliff Recreation Site** (435/782-3030, $7 day use, $15 walk-in campsite) is at the upper end of the east arm of the reservoir and has splendid walk-in camping sites with restrooms and hot showers, a nature center, boardwalks with interpretive displays, and pavilions for day use. **Hailstone Recreation Site** (435/649-9540 or 800/322-3770, www.reserveamerica.com, $9

A nature trail at Jordanelle State Park's Rock Cliff Recreation Site traverses a wetland.

day use, $15–18 camping) is a large campground with restrooms and showers, day-use shaded pavilions, a marina with 80 boat slips, a general store, a laundry, and a small restaurant. Facilities include wheelchair access with raised tent platforms.

Heber Valley RV Park Resort (435/654-4049, year-round, $15 and up), about six miles north of Heber City, offers camping sites, hot showers, a country store, and a launderette just below the Jordanelle Reservoir dam.

Deer Creek State Park

The seven-mile-long Deer Creek Reservoir (Deer Creek State Park, P.O. Box 257, Midway, UT 84049, 435/654-0171 or 800/322-3770, www.reserveamerica.com, $9 day use, $15–21 camping) lies in a very pretty setting below Mount Timpanogos and other peaks of the Wasatch Range. A developed area near the lower end of the lake has a campground with showers, picnic area, paved boat ramp, dock, and fish-cleaning station; elevation is

5,400 feet. **Island Beach Area,** 4.5 miles to the northeast, has a gravel swimming beach and a marina (open in summer with a store, snack bar, boat ramp, and rentals of fishing boats, ski boats, and personal watercraft); ice fishers can park here in winter. Rainbow trout, perch, largemouth bass, and walleye swim in the lake. Good winds for sailing blow most afternoons. You'll often see a lineup of catamarans at the sailboat beach near the campground and crowds of sailboarders at the Island Beach Area. The campground is just off U.S. 189 11 miles southwest of Heber City and 17 miles northeast of Provo.

Deer Creek Island Resort (Island Beach Area, 435/654-2155) has boat rentals, a store, and a restaurant.

Strawberry Reservoir

This 17,000-acre reservoir (435/654-0470) lies on a high rolling plateau 23 miles southeast of Heber City. Creation of the original Strawberry Reservoir began in 1906 as a federal reclamation project to divert water from the Colorado Basin west to the Utah Valley. Soldier Creek Dam (constructed in 1973) greatly increased the reservoir's size. A section of lake called "The Narrows" separates Strawberry Arm on the west from the smaller Soldier Creek Arm on the east. The water at this 7,600-foot elevation is cold for water-skiing, but hardy souls in wetsuits often brave it. Fishing is good all year (through the ice in winter) for rainbow and cutthroat trout and some brook trout and kokanee salmon. Several winter parking areas along U.S. 40 provide access for cross-country skiing, snowmobiling, and ice fishing.

The **Strawberry Visitor Center/Fish Hatchery** (435/548-2321, 7 A.M.–5:30 P.M. daily) sells maps and books and functions as a small museum. A 200-yard boardwalk with interpretive stations leads to the hatchery and an information kiosk.

The Forest Service maintains four campgrounds (435/548-2321, www.fs.fed.us/r4/uinta, www.recreation.gov reservations, late May–late Oct., $14–28) and three marinas around the lake.

Other Recreation Areas

Whiskey Springs Picnic Area is located near the mouth of Daniels Canyon, eight miles southeast of Heber City on U.S. 40; water is available in summer. Elevation is 6,400 feet; signs along the short **Whiskey Springs Nature Trail** identify plants.

Currant Creek Recreation Complex, on the southwest shore of **Currant Creek Reservoir** (elev. 8,000 feet), has a campground (435/548-2321, www.fs.fed.us/r4/uinta, www.recreation.gov reservations, late May–late Oct., $14 camping), paved boat ramp, and fishing access for people with disabilities. Anglers catch rainbow, cutthroat, and brook trout; ice fishing is good in winter. **Currant Creek Nature Trail** begins from Loop D of the campground and climbs 400 feet in a 1.25-mile loop; signs tell about the ecology. The best way to get here from Heber City is to drive southeast 42 miles on U.S. 40 past Strawberry Reservoir, just before **Currant Creek Lodge** (motel and café, 801/548-2226), turn northwest 19.5 miles along Currant Creek on Forest Route 083. High-clearance vehicles can take a slow, scenic route over Lake Creek Summit (elev. 9,900 feet); from Heber City, head east 31 miles on Center Street, which becomes Lake Creek/Currant Creek Road (Forest Route 083).

The primitive **Wolf Creek Campground** (435/548-2321, www.fs.fed.us/r4/uinta, early July–mid-Oct., $9) is located in an Engelmann spruce forest at 9,500 feet near Wolf Creek Pass 38 miles from Heber City. From Heber City, drive north and east to Francis, then head southeast about 22 miles on Highway 35 (part gravel); this scenic road continues on to Hanna and Duchesne in northeastern Utah.

ACCOMMODATIONS

Heber City motels are generally well-maintained and reasonably priced. A few miles west, in Midway, are several more expensive and luxurious resorts.

$50-100

All of the following have pools, and most also

have spas with saunas and whirlpools. Rooms at the **National Nine High Country Inn** (1000 S. Main, 435/654-0201 or 800/345-9198, $43–65) are a good deal; all come with refrigerators and microwaves. The **Swiss Alps Inn** (167 S. Main, 435/654-0722, $55–90) is a charming budget motel with an outdoor pool, a playground and two suites with full kitchens.

The **Holiday Inn Express** (1268 S. Main, 435/654-9990 or 800/315-2621, $76) is actually a pretty good choice for those who don't appreciate the quirks of small-town budget motels.

Over $100

Undoubtedly the truly unique place to stay in the Heber City area is the **Homestead Resort** (700 N. Homestead Dr., Midway, 435/654-1102 or 800/327-7220, www.homestead resort.com, $119 and up). This hot-spring resort is three miles west of town near Midway and features mineral baths, swimming, and accommodations. The natural hot-spring water is believed to be good for the skin, and if the water alone doesn't do the trick, the resort's spa services can probably help. The spacious grounds and stately buildings of the Homestead may remind you of an age long past, but the facilities are modern.

Golfers can play at the resort's 18-hole course ($55–65 18 holes) but should also note that excellent golf courses are right down the road at Wasatch Mountain State Park. Stables offer horseback riding, hayrides (and sleigh rides in winter), and bicycle rentals. Rooms should be reserved well in advance, especially for summer weekends. **Fanny's Grill** (888/327-7220, breakfast, lunch, and dinner daily, $8–17) has casual dining.

Another Midway resort, the **Blue Boar Inn** (1235 Warm Springs Rd., 435/654-1400 or 888/650-1400, $175 and up), is right near an entrance to Wasatch Mountain State Park

and the park's popular golf course. Each of the inn's 14 meticulously decorated rooms is devoted to a different poet or author; there's also a very good restaurant and a cozy pub on site.

FOOD

American-style cafés line Main Street, along with plenty of fast food to serve the skiing crowds. One particularly colorful place to stop for food and local color is the extra-convivial **Sidetrack Cafe** (98 S. Main, 435/654-0563, breakfast, lunch, and dinner daily, $4–9). Sandwiches are good here, and H&H bagels are flown in from New York.

Another fun, casual place with good food is **Spin Cafe** (220 N. Main St., 435/654-0251, lunch and dinner Mon.–Sat., Sun. brunch, $8–20); the barbeque is a specialty.

In a little strip mall in Midway is **Tarahumara** (380 E. Main, 435/654-3465, lunch and dinner Mon.–Sat., $8–18) where the Mexican food is surprisingly good. The dining room at the **Blue Boar Inn** (1235 Warm Springs Rd., 435/654-1400 or 888/650-1400, breakfast, lunch, and dinner daily, Sun. brunch, $26–36), which puts out elegant takes on standard dishes, is also highly regarded.

Information and Services

The **Heber Valley Chamber of Commerce** (475 N. Main, 435/654-3666, www.heber valleycc.org, 9 A.M.–5 P.M. Mon.–Fri., Sat.–Sun. June–Sept.) dispenses information on businesses in Heber City and Midway. **Heber Ranger District Office** (2460 S. U.S. 40, 435/654-0470, www.fs.fed.us/r4/uinta, 8 A.M.–5 P.M. Mon.–Fri.) manages the Uinta National Forest lands east and southeast of Heber City.

The **post office** is at 125 East 100 North (435/654-0881). **Wasatch County Hospital** is at 55 South 500 East (435/654-2500).

NORTHERN UTAH

Northern Utah is dominated by the sprawling suburbs of the Wasatch Front. However, there are plenty of things to do and see beyond the sights of the Utah state capital and seat of the LDS Church. One of the state's signature features is the Great Salt Lake, a remnant of a network of Ice Age lakes that once covered the West. It's not exactly easy to visit the lake itself—and at certain times of the year, not exactly pleasant—but this is a one-of-a-kind destination that merits a detour.

The region has a rich railroad history. Ogden was born of the railroads, and the city's historic downtown is dominated by Union Station, now home to multiple museums. The first transcontinental railway joined the Atlantic and Pacific coasts near here in 1869, at Promontory Summit. This windswept pass is preserved as the Golden Spike National Historic Site, with a visitors center and exhibits to beguile the student of history and the rails.

Logan is one of Utah's most pleasant towns, home to Utah State University and a profusion of summer festivals, including the Utah Opera Festival. The town's alpine setting and the surrounding dairy farms make the deserts and saline lakes of Utah seem far away.

PLANNING YOUR TIME

Northern Utah is close to Salt Lake City, and in fact many of the sights in this chapter could be visited on a day trip from the state capital.

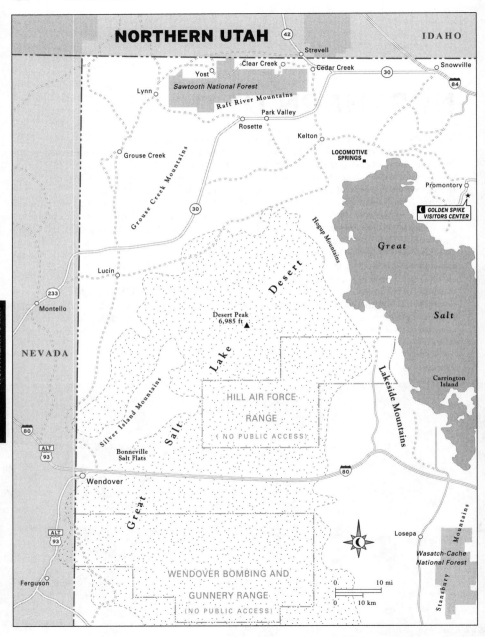

NORTHERN UTAH

IDAHO

Strevell

Clear Creek   Cedar Creek   Snowville

Yost

Sawtooth National Forest

Lynn   Raft River Mountains

Park Valley

Rosette

Grouse Creek   Kelton

LOCOMOTIVE SPRINGS

Promontory

GOLDEN SPIKE VISITORS CENTER

Grouse Creek Mountains

Great

Hogup Mountains

Lucin

Desert

233

Montello

Salt

Desert Peak
6,985 ft

NEVADA

Lake

Carrington Island

HILL AIR FORCE
RANGE
(NO PUBLIC ACCESS)

Silver Island Mountains

Salt

Lakeside Mountains

80

ALT
93

Bonneville
Salt Flats

Wendover

80

Great

Losepa

Mountains

Salt

Wasatch-Cache
National Forest

ALT
93

WENDOVER BOMBING AND

GUNNERY RANGE

(NO PUBLIC ACCESS)

Stansbury

Ferguson

0.   10 mi

0   10 km

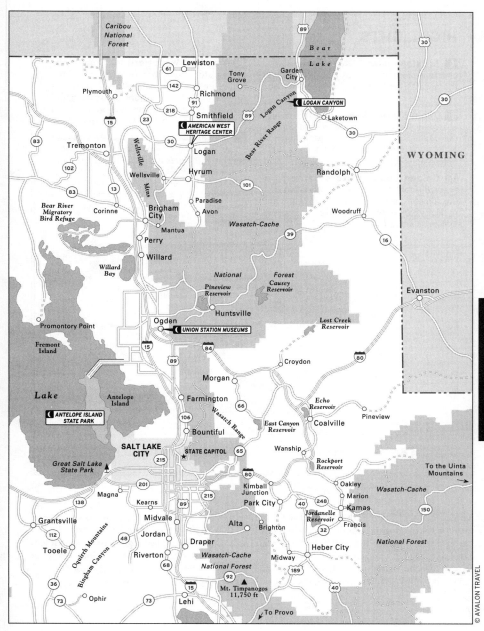

NORTHERN UTAH

HIGHLIGHTS

《 Antelope Island State Park: Hike or bike to explore the curious natural history of the largest island in the Great Salt Lake (page 126).

《 Union Station Museums: The cavernous Union Station is a glorious relic of Odgen's railroading past, and now serves as home to a clutch of interesting museums and collections (page 129).

《 Golden Spike Visitors Center: The first transcontinental rail lines were joined at this remote site in 1869; the visitors center and replica steam trains help recreate the epoch-making event (page 144).

《 American West Heritage Center: The living history museum enacts aspects of the Logan area's rich human history, from Native American culture to homestead farming. Seasonal celebrations and ritual events make for a year-round series of festivals (page 147).

《 Logan Canyon: Immediately behind Logan, Highway 89 winds up a steep, forested canyon in the Wasatch Mountains. The landscape is beautiful – picture perfect for picnicking or hiking – and the valley's end, at 7,800-foot Bear Lake Summit, offers incredible vistas of Utah, Wyoming, and Idaho (page 153).

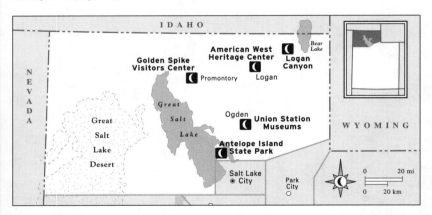

LOOK FOR 《 TO FIND RECOMMENDED SIGHTS, ACTIVITIES, DINING, AND LODGING.

Antelope Island State Park is a good destination for hiking and mountain biking—spend half a day exploring this island in the Great Salt Lake. Ogden's museums and old city center can also be visited as a side trip from Salt Lake City, but it's worth spending the night if you're heading as far as Logan to attend one of that city's many music and theatrical festivals. Logan also makes a good base camp if you are heading to more remote destinations, such as the Golden Spike National Historic Site or Bear Lake.

The Great Salt Lake

Since its discovery by fur trappers in the 1820s, this lake has both mystified and entranced visitors. Early explorers guessed that it must be connected to the ocean, not realizing that they had come across a body of water far saltier. Only the Dead Sea has a higher salt content. When Mormon pioneers first tried evaporating the lake water, they found the residue bitter tasting—the resulting salt is only 84 percent sodium chloride (table salt); the remaining 16 percent is a mix of sulfates and chlorides of magnesium, calcium, and potassium. The lake's northern arm, isolated by a railroad causeway, contains the highest mineral concentrations—about twice those of the southern arm. Bacteria and algae grow in such numbers that they sometimes tint the water orange-red or blue-green. A tiny brine shrimp *(Artemia salina)* and two species of brine fly *(Ephydra sp)* are about all that can live in the lake.

The lake is always changing—rising with spring snowmelt, then falling due to evaporation that peaks in late summer and autumn. These annual variations result in differences in lake levels of six to as much as 18 inches. Long-term changes have affected the lake, too: Climate variations and diversion of river water for irrigation have caused a 21-foot difference between record low and high levels, and the lake size has varied dramatically, between 900 square miles at the lowest water level to 2,500 square miles at the highest.

Great Salt Lake State Park

Bathers have enjoyed hopping into the lake ever since the 1847 arrival of Mormon pioneers. Extreme buoyancy in the dense water makes it impossible for a bather to sink—no swimming ability is needed! But put your head underwater and you'll quickly realize that the salty water

NORTHERN UTAH

© W. C. MCRAE

Antelope Island rises from the Great Salt Lake.

causes great irritation to the eyes, throat, and nose. During summer algae blooms, the odor of the water irritates the nose.

Beginning in the 1880s, several resorts popped up along the lake's east and south shores. Besides bathing, guests could enjoy lake cruises, dances, concerts, bowling, arcade games, and roller-coaster rides. **Saltair Resort** stood as the grandest of the old resorts. Completed in 1893, the Moorish structure rose five stories and contained a huge dance floor where as many as 1,000 couples could enjoy the orchestra's rhythms. A rail line from Salt Lake City ran out on a 4,000-foot pier to the resort, which stood on pilings over the water. After 1930, low water levels, the Great Depression, fires, and fewer visitors gradually brought an end to Saltair. Its buildings burned for the second time in 1970.

A developer has recently built a smaller replica (801/250-4400)of the Saltair Resort on the Great Salt Lake's southern shore near I-80 Exit 104. Despite floods of rising lake waters and wind damage, this Saltair is still open, though it is nowhere near as glamorous as the resort's earlier incarnations. The main structure has a smattering of gift shops (Christmas tree ornaments made of salt), food concessions, and a small museum; videos detail the history of the lake and promote the racecourse at Bonneville Salt Flats. A short causeway leads out into the lake, where you can get a good whiff of the brackish water. Saltair is also a popular site for concerts.

The adjacent **beaches** (801/250-1898, free) are popular in summer. Stop in at the nearby **Great Salt Lake visitors center** (801/533-4083, open 9 A.M.–4 P.M. daily year-round, free) to see a video and exhibits about the lake. A good selection of local travel information is available, too. From Salt Lake City, drive west nine miles on I-80, take Exit 111 (7200 West), and follow the north frontage road west to the beaches; or take I-80 Exit 104 (Magna) and turn east on the north frontage road.

Salt Island Adventures (801/252-9336, www.gslcruises.com) offers cruise-boat excursions on the Great Salt Lake. Cruises leave from the Great Salt Lake State Marina (I-80 Exit 104); the least expensive option is a one-hour sightseeing tour ($15 adults, $13 seniors, $10 children 2–12); a variety of dinner cruises and theme events are also offered. No sailings on Sunday or Monday; call for information on off-season events.

Antelope Island State Park

Though just a short distance offshore from Salt Lake City, Antelope Island (office at 4528 West 1700 South, Syracuse, UT 84075, 801/773-2941, $9 per vehicle) seems a world away. Its rocky slopes, rolling grasslands, marshes, sand dunes, and lake views instill a sense of remoteness and rugged beauty. An extension of the Oquirrh Mountains, Antelope Island is the largest of the lake's ten islands. It measures 15 miles long and 5 miles wide; Frary Peak (elev. 6,596 feet) rises in the center.

The entire island is a state park, accessible via a seven-mile paved causeway. Antelope Island is a great place for mountain biking; park trails are open to hiking, bicycling, and horseback riding, allowing access to much of the island; there's also a marina for sailboats and kayaks. Campsites run $12, including the toll and day-use fee (campsite reservations 800/322-3770). Showers and restrooms are available in the swimming area in the northwest corner of the island. Take I-15 Exit 335 (two-thirds of the way north to Ogden), then drive nine miles west to the start of the causeway and the entrance booth.

Archaeologists have found prehistoric sites showing that Native Americans came here long ago, perhaps on a land bridge during times of low lake level. In 1843, explorers John Frémont and Kit Carson rode their horses across a sandbar to the island and named it after the antelope (pronghorn) herds that the party hunted for food. In 1849, Brigham Young established a ranch here for the church's herds of cattle, sheep, and horses.

Antelope Island is now home to more than 600 bison, as well as deer, bighorn sheep, pronghorn, and other wildlife. The yearly bison roundup (early November) is a big event for both cowboys and visitors: The bison are driven to corrals on the north end of the island and given veterinary checkups. To keep the herd small enough to avoid overgrazing, some animals are culled out for sale or for hunt. Thanks largely to its population of brine flies and shrimp, the Great Salt Lake attracts a wide variety of birds and is an important migratory stop. Antelope Island is a good place to look for eared grebes, avocet, black-necked stilts, willets, sanderlings, long-billed curlews, burrowing owls, chukars, and all sorts of raptors.

Ogden

Located at the northern edge of the Wasatch Front urban area, Ogden (35 miles north of Salt Lake City off I-15) remains very much its own city even as it is engulfed by suburbs. Ogden was one of the West's most important rail hubs at the beginning of the 20th century, and in the downtown area vestiges of the city's affluence remain in the grand architecture and the impressive Union Pacific Depot.

Ogden is named for Peter Skene Ogden of the British Hudson's Bay Company. He explored and trapped in the upper reaches of the Ogden and Weber Valleys in 1828–1829, but he never descended to the site of the city that bears his name. In 1846, Miles Goodyear established an out-of-the-way trading post and stockade here, one of the first permanent settlements in Utah, and named it Fort Buenaventura.

When Mormons arrived at the site of Salt Lake City in 1847, Goodyear, a former mountain man, felt too crowded, so he sold out to the Mormons and left for California. In 1849, Brigham Young visited the site, then known as Brownsville, and thought it favorable for settlement. The following year he sent 100 families to found the town of Ogden.

Arrival of the transcontinental railroad in

downtown Ogden's historic architecture

© W. C. MCRAE

NORTHERN UTAH

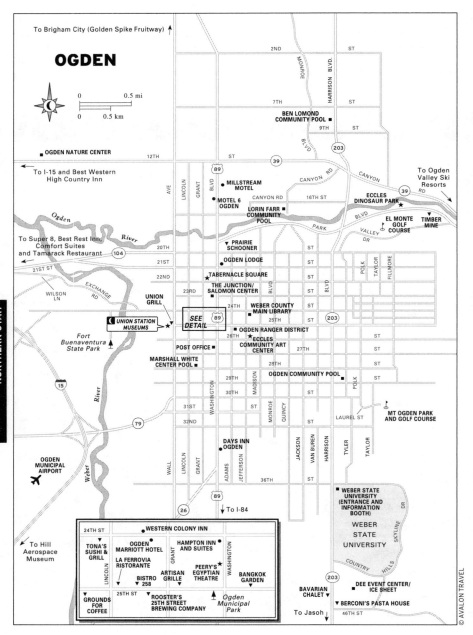

NORTHERN UTAH

OGDEN

To Brigham City (Golden Spike Fruitway)

0   0.5 mi
0   0.5 km

OGDEN NATURE CENTER

To I-15 and Best Western High Country Inn

To Super 8, Best Rest Inn, Comfort Suites and Tamarack Restaurant

To Hill Aerospace Museum

OGDEN MUNICIPAL AIRPORT

Fort Buenaventura State Park

UNION STATION MUSEUMS

UNION GRILL

MILLSTREAM MOTEL
MOTEL 6 OGDEN
LORIN FARR COMMUNITY POOL
PRAIRIE SCHOONER
OGDEN LODGE
TABERNACLE SQUARE
THE JUNCTION/ SALOMON CENTER
WEBER COUNTY MAIN LIBRARY
OGDEN RANGER DISTRICT
ECCLES COMMUNITY ART CENTER
POST OFFICE
MARSHALL WHITE CENTER POOL
OGDEN COMMUNITY POOL

BEN LOMOND COMMUNITY POOL

ECCLES DINOSAUR PARK
EL MONTE GOLF COURSE
TIMBER MINE

To Ogden Valley Ski Resorts

MT OGDEN PARK AND GOLF COURSE

DAYS INN OGDEN

WEBER STATE UNIVERSITY (ENTRANCE AND INFORMATION BOOTH)

WEBER STATE UNIVERSITY

DEE EVENT CENTER/ ICE SHEET
BAVARIAN CHALET
BERCONI'S PASTA HOUSE

To Jasoh

SEE DETAIL

SEE DETAIL

24TH ST
WESTERN COLONY INN
TONA'S SUSHI & GRILL
OGDEN MARRIOTT HOTEL
HAMPTON INN AND SUITES
LA FERROVIA RISTORANTE
PEERY'S EGYPTIAN THEATRE
BISTRO 258
ARTISAN GRILLE
BANGKOK GARDEN
25TH ST
GROUNDS FOR COFFEE
ROOSTER'S 25TH STREET BREWING COMPANY
Ogden Municipal Park

© AVALON TRAVEL

1869 changed Ogden forever. Although the railroad's Golden Spike had been driven at Promontory Summit, 55 miles to the northwest, Ogden earned the title "Junction City" as lines branched from it through Utah and into surrounding states. New industries and an expanding non-Mormon population transformed the sleepy farm town into a bustling city. Today Ogden, with a population of 80,000, serves as a major administrative, manufacturing, and livestock center for the intermountain West.

Ogden is worth exploring for its museums, historic sites, and access to scenic spots in the Wasatch Range, which looms precipitously just behind the city. Ogden Canyon, beginning on the east edge of town and leading into the Wasatch, leads up to lakes, campgrounds, hiking trails, and three downhill ski areas. Several 2002 Winter Olympic events took place in the Ogden area, including the downhill and super-G ski races and the men's and women's curling competition.

ORIENTATION

Mormon pioneers laid out the city in their typically neat fashion but adopted an unusual street system. Streets running east–west are numbered, from 1st Street in the north of town to 47th Street in the south; streets running north–south commemorate U.S. presidents and other historical figures. The streets were laid out before the city had found its center—today, the intersection of 25th Street and Washington Boulevard is usually considered the center of downtown.

SIGHTS

Visitors to downtown Ogden will notice a lot of building cranes in the next few years. The former Ogden City Mall, which formed the core of downtown, has been torn down and a new entertainment, retail, and residential complex called The Junction is being built on the site. First to open at The Junction is the Salomon Center, a sports, recreation and fitness center complete with Gold's Gym, wave pool large enough for surfing, Utah's largest climbing wall, and a vertical wind tunnel that

recreates the experience of free-fall skydiving. Also open at The Junction is a Megaplex 13 movie theater, to be followed by retail and condominium development over the coming years. The development is scheduled for completion in 2010.

◖ Union Station Museums

Travelers thronged into the cavernous Union Station Building (25th St. and Wall Ave., 801/629-8444, www.theunionstation.org) during the grand old days of railroading. Completed in 1924, it saw more than 120 trains daily during the peak World War II years. Today, the depot is mostly known for its fine museums and the **Ogden-Weber Convention and Visitors Bureau Information Center** (801/627-8288 or 800/ALL-UTAH, www.ogdencvb.org, 8 A.M.–8 P.M. Mon.–Sat. and 10 A.M.–7 P.M. Sun. Memorial Day weekend–Labor Day weekend, 8 A.M.–5 P.M. Mon.–Fri. the rest of the year), supplier of local travel information. In the same office, the **Forest Service Information Center** (801/625-5306, open 8 A.M.–4:30 P.M. Mon.–Fri., open Sat. in summer) provides recreation information for public lands in the Wasatch Range.

Union Station's museums and art gallery are well worth a visit. A single ticket gives admission to all exhibitions (10 A.M.–5 P.M. Mon.–Sat., until 6 P.M. Sun. in summer, $5 adults, $3 children 3–12, $4 seniors 65 and over).

The **Browning-Kimball Car Museum** displays a glittering collection of about a dozen antique autos ranging from a one-cylinder 1901 Oldsmobile to a 16-cylinder 1930 Cadillac sports sedan. Chicago gangsters once owned the 1931 Pierce Arrow, probably the museum's most famous car; note the built-in gun holster. Car exhibits rotate about three times a year. The Utah License-Plate Exhibit shows every tag from 1915, when they were first issued, to the present.

Wattis-Dumke Railroad Museum uses highly detailed dioramas to illustrate railroad scenes and construction feats. Eight model trains (HO scale) roll through the Ogden rail yard, wind through a model of the Sierra and

Humboldt Palisades, cross the Great Salt Lake on the Lucin Cutoff, and descend Weber Canyon. Exhibits and photos show railroading history and great trains, such as the "Big Boys," which weighed more than one million pounds and pulled heavy freights up the mountain ranges. A documentary film about the first transcontinental railroad is shown on request. Outside, just south of the station, at the **Eccles Railroad Center,** you can visit giant diesel locomotives and some cabooses.

The **Natural History Museum** displays beautiful rocks, minerals, and gemstones. Fossils reveal imprints of dinosaurs and other prehistoric life forms, and you can look at Native American artifacts and crafts. On display is a smoky quartz specimen weighing 19 pounds— over 44,000 carats—said to be the world's largest faceted stone.

Browning Firearms Museum (upstairs) contains the gun shop of and many examples of firearms invented by the Browning family. John M. Browning (1855–1926), a genius in his field, held 75 major gun patents. He developed the world's first successful automatic firearms, which used gases from the bullet to expel the old shell, load a new one, and cock the mechanism. The skillfully done exhibitions display both military and civilian handguns, automatic weapons, rifles, and shotguns.

The Gallery at the Station (also upstairs) displays paintings, sculpture, and photography in a former pigeon roost. Exhibitions rotate monthly.

The station also houses the Union Grill Restaurant, a model train store, and a gift shop.

Historic 25th Street

When Ogden was the railroad's main transport hub, 25th was the city's main street. Running like a wide boulevard between Washington Avenue and the palatial Union Pacific Depot, the street boasted the city's first grocery and hardware stores, blacksmith shops, livery stables, hotels, and restaurants, many of them run by immigrants attracted by the railroads. Most

© W. C. MCRAE

Historic 25th Street has long been Ogden's center for dining and drinking.

of the buildings were built for posterity in red brick and handsome vernacular styles.

After the city's residents came to rely less on the railway and more on the motor car, the city's orientation changed, and this historic precinct fell into disrepair and ill-repute. In the last twenty years, artists and small cafés have colonized the street because of its cheap rents, and a younger generation finds aesthetic value in the lovely historic commercial architecture. Twenty-fifth Street now serves as a combination gallery and restaurant row, while still functioning as the city's bowery. It's a pleasant place for a stroll, and many of the shops and cafés are worth a detour. Pick up a brochure detailing histories of many of these buildings from the tourist office in Union Station.

On summer Saturdays, the **25th Street Farmers and Art Market** (25th and Grant) takes over Ogden Municipal Park. Also in the park is the **Ogden Amphitheater**, with free events all summer, including free movies and classical music concerts on Monday nights.

© W. C. MCRAE

Be sure to step inside Peery's Egyptian Theater; the interior is as striking as the building's exterior.

NORTHERN UTAH

Peery's Egyptian Theater

You can't miss the unusual facade of this venerable building (near the corner of 25th St. and Washington Ave., 801/395-3200 or 800/337-2690). Looking suspiciously like an Egyptian sun temple, this old-time movie palace and vaudeville theater was built in 1924 in the "atmospheric" style during the fit of Egyptomania that followed the discovery of King Tut's tomb. After falling into disrepair for many years, the old theater has been completely refurbished and serves as Ogden's performing arts center. The interior of the hall is equally astonishing, with a sun that moves across the ceiling, floating clouds, and glittering stars. With columns, hieroglyphs, and mummies everywhere, the theater looks like the set for *Aida*. The Egyptian keeps very busy with a series of top-notch musical performances and regional theater productions.

Adjacent to the Egyptian Theater is the **David Eccles Conference Center** (801/395-3200), a handsome new building designed to harmonize architecturally with the theater. To-

gether the conference center and the theater form the core of Ogden's convention facility.

Weber County Daughters of Utah Pioneer Museum and the Miles Goodyear Cabin

Drop in to examine the furnishings, clothes, and crafts of Mormon pioneers at the Pioneer Museum (2148 Grant Ave., 801/393-4460, 10 A.M.–5 P.M. Mon.–Sat. Memorial Day–Labor Day, free). Walk behind the museum to see the Goodyear cabin, probably the oldest non–Native American structure in Utah. It was built in about 1845 of cottonwood logs and later moved here from its original site near the Weber River. The cabin can be seen even when the museum is closed. Pioneer Museum is in the former Weber Stake Relief Society Building (1902).

Ogden Temple and Tabernacle

The modern temple of white cast stone and reflective glass has a central gold spire much like that of the Provo Temple. In fact, both temples were designed by the same architect. Dedicated in January 1972, the Ogden Temple contains 283 rooms on four levels and efficiently accommodates many people while retaining a reverent atmosphere; only Mormons engaged in sacred ordinance work may enter. The white-steepled Ogden Tabernacle (2133 Washington Blvd., on Tabernacle Square, open 9 A.M.–5 P.M. Mon.–Sat. in the summer), completed in 1956, sits just to the north. Visitors are welcome inside the tabernacle when it's open.

Fort Buenaventura State Park

Miles Goodyear built the original Fort Buenaventura (office at 2450 South A Ave., 801/621-4808, 8 A.M.–dusk daily except in winter, $4 per vehicle or $1 per person to walk in) in 1846 to serve as a trading post and way station for travelers crossing the remote Great Basin region. Now a replica of the tiny fort provides a link with Utah's mountain-man past. The location, dimensions, and materials used for the stockade and three cabins inside closely follow the originals. Special programs are scheduled throughout the year, including a mountain-man rendezvous on Easter and Labor Day weekends and a pioneer skill show held on July 24. The 32-acre park has a picnic area and a pond popular for canoeing in summer (rentals are available). From downtown Ogden, take 24th Street west across the rail yard and Weber River, turn left on A Avenue, and follow signs to 2450 A Avenue.

Eccles Community Art Center

A series of monthly changing exhibitions in this historic mansion (2580 Jefferson Ave., 801/392-6935, 9 A.M.–5 P.M. Mon.–Fri. and 9 A.M.–3 P.M. Sat., free) display the best of regional paintings, sculpture, photography, and mixed media. The ornate mansion, once owned by the philanthropic Eccles family (whose name attaches to many arts centers in northern Utah), is an attraction in itself. Turrets, cut glass, and carved woodwork decorate the brick and sandstone structure, built in 1893 in a Richardsonian-Romanesque style. The car-

riage house in back contains a sales gallery, and the grounds are used as a sculpture garden.

Ogden Nature Center

The 127 acres of wildlife sanctuary (information at 966 W. 12th St., 801/621-7595, www.ogdennaturecenter.org, 9 A.M.–5 P.M. Mon.–Fri., 10 A.M.–1 P.M. Sat., $3 ages 12–64, seniors and children 3–11 $1.25), on the outskirts of Ogden, provide a place for children and adults to enjoy nature while learning. Hiking trails lead through woods, wetlands, and open fields. Deer, porcupines, muskrats, rabbits, snakes, and about 130 species of birds have been spotted here. Injured or orphaned animals are cared for at the center's rehabilitation center and then released into the wild. The new visitors center offers classes, workshops, displays, and activities year-round; the pillars used in construction are recycled from the railroad trestle that once spanned the Great Salt Lake. Visitors are welcome to use the picnic area. To get there, follow West 12th Street northwest from downtown.

Eccles Dinosaur Park and Museum

Paths at this leafy park (1544 E. Park Blvd., 801/393-3466 or 801/393-DINO, 10 A.M.–8 P.M. Mon.–Sat., noon–6 P.M. Sun. Labor Day–Memorial Day, closes earlier the rest of the year, $6 adults, $5 seniors and students, $4 ages 2–12) lead to 115 life-size, realistic replicas of dinosaurs, making this a favorite with children. Exhibitions are based on the most up-to-date studies of paleontologists, and the replicas are created by the same folks who build "dino-stars" for Hollywood films. A 16,000-square-foot museum expands the services and facilities of the park.

Hill Aerospace Museum

Construction of Hill Field began in 1940, just in time to serve the aircraft maintenance and storage needs of the military during the hectic World War II years. The decades since have seen a parade of nearly every type of bomber, fighter, helicopter, trainer, and missile belonging to the U.S. Air Force. At Hill Aerospace

Museum (five miles south of Ogden on I-15, 801/777-6818, 9 A.M.–4:30 P.M. daily year-round, by donation), about 50 of these can be seen close-up in outdoor and indoor exhibits, from the Stearman bi-wing trainer—which helped many servicemen and -women learn to fly during the late 1930s and early 1940s—to the super-fast (Mach 3.5) SR-71 *Blackbird* strategic reconnaissance plane. The Engine Room displays cutaway models of a 28-cylinder Pratt and Whitney R-4360 and several jet engines. Other exhibits inside include flight simulators, missiles, a Norden bombsight, uniforms, aircraft art, and model aircraft. Chances are you'll see jets from the adjacent Air Force base streaking overhead on training missions. To get there, take Roy Exit 341 and follow signs east.

WEBER STATE UNIVERSITY

Weber (WEE-ber) State University (801/626-6000) lies southeast of downtown on a bench of prehistoric Lake Bonneville; the Wasatch Range rises steeply behind. The university emphasizes undergraduate education, though the four-year school also offers a few graduate programs in education and business. The school began in 1889 as Weber State Academy under the LDS Church, became a state-supported community college in 1933, Weber State College in 1963, and Weber State University in 1991. It now operates on a four-quarter system with a student population of about 15,000 and faculty and staff of 1,200. The institution serves largely as a commuter university for Weber and Davis counties. Visitors are welcome on campus for the **Museum of Natural History** (801/626-6653, 8 A.M.–5 P.M. Mon.–Fri., free), Shaw Art Gallery (801/626-6455, 11 A.M.–5 P.M. Mon.–Fri.), library, student union with bookstore, and cultural and sporting events. **Swenson Gymnasium** (801/626-6466), on the south end of campus, provides swimming, racquetball, tennis, basketball, indoor track, and weight-room facilities to the public. **Wilderness Recreation Center** (801/626-6373, open 9 A.M.–5 P.M. Mon.–Fri., 8 A.M.–5 P.M. Sat., 2–5 P.M. Sun. year-round), next to Swenson Gymnasium, rents bicycles,

white-water kayaks, rafts, cross-country skis, camping gear, and other sports equipment. The Olympic curling competitions took place at the campus's new **Ice Sheet** (801/399-8750), an ice rink and stadium; call for a public skating schedule.

Obtain a free parking permit and map at the **information booth** (along the main entrance road off 3750 Harrison Boulevard, campus tours can be arranged by calling 801/626-6844). A clock tower at the center of campus makes a handy landmark, so it's hard to get lost.

ENTERTAINMENT AND EVENTS

Ogden has a busy calendar of theater, dance, festivals, shows, and sporting events. To find out what's going on, contact the Ogden-Weber Convention and Visitors Bureau Information Center (in Union Station, 801/627-8288 or 800/255-8824, www.ogdencvb.org).

In January, the **Winterfest/Hof Sister City Festival** celebrates winter and Ogden's German sister city, Hof, with ski and dogsled races and German food, music, and dancing.

June brings the **Taste of Ogden,** which takes place midmonth at Municipal Park and is a celebration of Ogden's restaurants.

Two of summer's biggest civic events are in July. **Pioneer Days** on July 24 has a parade, rodeo, and crowning of Miss Rodeo Utah, while **Ogden Street Festival** takes over 25th Street with a 10K run, dog-trick contests, chili cook-off, and a huge garage sale in the lot in front of Union Station.

August brings the **Weber County Fair,** with horse shows and racing, livestock sale, and exhibits. Every Saturday morning, there's a lively **Farmer's Market** on historic 25th Street.

The **Golden Spike Bicycle Classic** is a road race of about 85 miles from Promontory Summit to Ogden the weekend after Labor Day in September. Late in the month is the **Greek Festival,** which celebrates Ogden's Greek heritage with food, dancing, and entertainment at the Greek Orthodox Church of the Transfiguration (674 42nd St.).

RECREATION

Ogden has a new multi-purpose recreational center at the center of downtown's The Junction development. Called the Salomon Center (Kiesel Ave. between 23rd and 22nd St., 801/399-4653), the complex houses a Gold's Gym (801/399-5861), IFLY (801/528-5348), an indoor skydiving simulator, Flowrider (801/399-4653), an indoor surf wave pool, Irock Climbing Gym (801/399-4653), a bowling alley, and more.

Swimming

Year-round swimming is offered at Ben Lomond Community Pool (1049 7th St., 801/625-1100), Ogden Community Pool (2875 Tyler Ave., 801/625-1101), and Marshall White Center Pool (222 28th St., 801/629-8346). The outdoor Lorin Farr Community Pool (1691 Gramercy Ave., 801/629-8691) is open in summer.

Hiking

Hikers with time and a vehicle should head up into the Wasatch Range for **wilderness hikes** among the aspen forests and cliff-hung canyons; check with the Forest Service Information Center in Odgen's Union Station (801/625-5306) for trail maps. However, the city of Ogden provides its own excellent trail system, the **Ogden River Parkway**. This 3.1-mile trail system links a number of the city's major parks and attractions along the Ogden River, including Eccles Dinosaur Park and the Utah State University Botanical Gardens. Join the trail at any number of points along Park Avenue, Big D Sports Park, the Botanical Gardens, or off Valley Drive.

Golf

Enjoy golfing at any of these courses: 18-hole Ben Lomond (1800 N. U.S. 89, 801/782-7754); nine-hole El Monte (1300 Valley Dr. at the mouth of Ogden Canyon, 801/629-8333); nine-hole Golf City Family Fun Center (1400 East 5600 South, 801/479-3410), which also has a lighted 18-hole miniature golf course; 18-hole Mount Ogden Park and Golf Course (1787 Constitution Way, 801/629-8700); nine-hole Nordic Valley (15 miles east at 3550 Nordic Valley Way in Eden, 801/745-0306); 18-hole Schneiter's Riverside (5460 S. Weber Dr., 801/399-4636); 18-hole Valley View (2501 E. Gentile in Layton, 801/546-1630); 18-hole The Barn Golf Course (305 W. Pleasant View Dr. in North Ogden, 801/782-7320); and 18-hole Wolf Creek (15 miles east at 3900 N. Wolf Creek Dr. in Eden, 801/745-3365).

Skiing

You'll find good **downhill skiing** in the Wasatch Range 15–19 miles east of Ogden at Nordic Valley, Snowbasin, and Powder Mountain (see the *Vicinity of Ogden* section). **Cross-country skiers** can use the easy set tracks in Mount Ogden Park and Golf Course (30th and Taylor) or head into the mountains for more challenging terrain.

ACCOMMODATIONS

Rooms are relatively inexpensive in Ogden, which makes it a good base for exploring the area (remember, Salt Lake City is only 35 miles south).

Under $50

You'll find the city's cheapest rooms along Washington Boulevard, which was the main highway before the freeway went in. Quite a number of older motor-court motels still operate here, but caveat emptor: Some are in fairly grim shape, and for the same money you could find better values. If you're looking for an inexpensive room, try the **Millstream Motel** (1450 Washington Blvd., 801/394-9425, $30 and up); almost half the rooms have kitchenettes and there's a restaurant on the premises. Right across the street is the new **Motel 6 Ogden** (1455 Washington Blvd., 801/627-4560 or 800/466-8356, $42 and up), with a pool. Closer to the center of the city is **Ogden Lodge** (2110 Washington Blvd., 801/394-4563, $40 and up), a nicely maintained older motel with a pool, business center and complimentary breakfast. For an affordable stay in the city center, try the **Western Colony Inn** (234 24th

St., 801/627-1332, $40 and up), with kitchen-ettes and nicely maintained motel rooms.

$50-100

Most Ogden midrange lodgings are located near freeway exits. At I-15 Exit 346 is **Best Rest Inn** (1206 W. 21st St., 801/393-8644 or 800/343-8644, $57 and up), with a pool, 24-hour restaurant, and a convenience store. All rooms come equipped with microwaves and fridges. West of the freeway is the **Super 8 Motel of Ogden** (1508 West 2100 South, 801/731-7100 or 800/800-8000, $68 and up).

A few blocks south of downtown is **Days Inn Ogden** (3306 Washington Blvd., 801/399-5671 or 800/999-6841, $54 and up). This comfort-able hotel offers nicely decorated rooms (some poolside rooms are quite large), a restaurant, and a private club. Facilities include an indoor pool, spa, and fitness room.

At I-15 Exit 347 is the **Best Western High Country Inn** (1335 W. 12th St., 801/394-9474 or 800/594-8979, $96 and up), with a pool, spa, and fitness room. Pets are accom-modated, and there's a good restaurant in the motel. At the same exit, the **Comfort Suites of Ogden** (2250 South 1200 West, 801/621-2545 or 800/462-9925, $90 and up) has an indoor pool and fitness center; all rooms have efficiency kitchens and coffeemakers, and rates include continental breakfast.

$100-150

The only historic boutique hotel in Ogden is the **(Hampton Inn and Suites Ogden** (2401 Washington Blvd, 866/394-9400, $139 and up), a grand art deco souvenir of the early 20th century. In addition to comfortable rooms and gracious formal lobby, guests are offered exercise facilities, a business center, and a fine-dining restaurant. The Hampton Inn was completely renovated and refurbished for the Olympics—this is a charming place to stay, with frequent rate specials on hotel websites.

$150-200

Near the city center is **Ogden Marriott Hotel**

(247 24th St., 801/627-1190 or 800/421-7599, $159 and up), with an indoor pool, hot tub, guest laundry, and a business center; there's a lounge and restaurant on the premises.

For a unique lodging experience, consider the **(Alaskan Inn** (six miles east of Ogden at 435 Ogden Canyon, 801/621-8600 or 888/707-8600, www.alaskaninn.com, $159 and up). A log lodge and cabin complex, the Alaska Inn sits along the banks of a mountain stream. Lodging is either in suites in the cen-tral lodge building or in individual log cabins. The decor—hand-hewn pine furniture, brass lamps, Western art—is rustic and elegant. Breakfast is included in the rates.

Campgrounds

Century Mobile Home and RV Park (1399 W. 21st St. South, I-15 Exit 346, then one block west on Wilson Ln., 801/731-3800, year-round, $19 tents or RVs without hookups, $27 with hookups) has showers, swimming pool, game room, store, and laundry. There are a number of more rural campgrounds up Ogden Canyon (see the *Vicinity of Ogden* section).

FOOD

Quite a number of good restaurants line 25th Street, the slowly gentrifying Main Street of turn-of-the-20th-century Ogden. In addition to the dining options noted below, there are bakery cafés, a Greek restaurant, sushi joints, taverns with burgers, and home-style Mexican food. If you've got time, just saunter along 25th street and you'll be sure to find someplace to your fancy.

Breakfast and Light Meals

The **Tamarack Restaurant** (1254 W. 21st St., near I-15 21st St. exit, 801/393-8691), is good to know about; it's open 24 hours daily. If your idea of breakfast is strong coffee, fresh pastries, and the option of an omelet, plan on frequenting **Grounds for Coffee** (111 25th St., 801/629-0909), the city's best coffee shop; there's often entertainment in the evening. The coffee shop is in a beautifully preserved 19th-century storefront along historic 25th Street.

American Standards

One of the most youthful and lively places along 25th is **⟨ Rooster's 25th Street Brewing Company** (253 25th St., 801/627-6171, $8–15, lunch and dinner daily), a brew-pub with good food (burgers, pizza, ribs, fresh fish, and sandwiches) and good microbrews. In summer there's a pleasant shady deck.

If you're looking for modern American-style food—grilled fish, gourmet sandwiches, and salads—head to the Union Pacific Station and try the **Union Grill** (2501 Wall Ave., 801/621-2830, lunch Mon.–Fri., dinner Mon.–Sat., $11–18).

Fine Dining

⟨ Bistro 258 (258 25th St., 801/430-4287, lunch Mon.–Fri., dinner Mon.–Sat., $12–23) is one of Ogden's best fine-dining restaurants. The dishes are continental-influenced, though there's also a good selection of Utah beef. A house specialty is roasted balsamic herb chicken; filet mignon stuffed with spinach and Montrachet cheese is a standout.

The **Artisan Grille** (172 25th Street, 801/395-0166, lunch Mon.–Sat., dinner Tues.–Sat., $17–25) offers hand-crafted cuisine in a lovingly restored dining room. Choices range from pasta and wood-fired pizzas to up-scale dishes like sesame-crusted chicken and filet mignon with red shallot butter.

⟨ Jasoh (4590 Harrison Blvd. 801/399-0088, open for dinner Mon.–Sat., $12–40) is a stylish new restaurant focusing on "new American cooking," apparently meaning that the menu borrows equally from both Mediterranean and Asian food traditions. The local-boy-made-good chef/owner has cooked in top restaurants in New York, San Francisco, and Hawaii; the menu reflects his wide-ranging experience and eclectic tastes. Roast duck is served with guava sauce, and jerked chicken is stuffed with goat cheese and served with grilled shrimp. And talk about unusual—this is probably the only restaurant in Utah where you can order a Yak steak!

Western-Theme Restaurants

For good beef, seafood, and American-style dining, Ogden has a number of interesting choices. The **Graycliff Lodge** (508 Ogden Canyon, five miles up Ogden Canyon on the left, 801/392-6775, Sun. brunch and Tues.–Sun. dinner, $15–37) serves old-fashioned steak, lamb, prime rib, and seafood in a romantic creekside setting. **Prairie Schooner** (445 Park Blvd., 801/392-2712, lunch Mon.–Fri., dinner nightly, $12–32) serves steak, prime rib, and seafood in an informal Western atmosphere (dine in a covered wagon). For another take on the Western theme, try the **Timber Mine** (1701 Park Blvd., 801/393-2155, open for dinner nightly, $19–$38), which serves steak and seafood to diners in a mine shaft.

Ethnic Restaurants

As befits a town at the base of towering mountains, Ogden has a good and very popular German restaurant, the **Bavarian Chalet** (4387 Harrison Blvd., across from the Dee Event Center, 801/479-7561, dinner Tues.–Sat., $12–22). All your German favorites are here, including schnitzels, sauerbraten, and strudels. This is one of the city's most beloved restaurants; reservations are suggested.

La Ferrovia Ristorante (234 25th St., 801/394-8628, lunch and dinner Tues.–Sat., $12–18) offers an inexpensive selection of pasta, pizza, and calzone.

Bangkok Garden (465 E. 25th St. 801/621-4049, lunch and dinner Mon.–Sat., $8–15) has a good selection of spicy Thai cuisine, and it also serves up high-quality Chinese cooking. Just down the street, **Tona's Sushi and Grill** (210 25th St., 801/622-8662, lunch and dinner Tues.–Sat., $9–17) is an outpost of good Japanese cooking, with sushi, teriyaki and other delights.

INFORMATION AND SERVICES

The **Ogden-Weber Convention and Visitors Bureau Information Center** (Wall Ave. and 25th St., Ogden, UT 84401, 801/627-8288 or 800/ALL-UTAH, www.ogdencvb.org, 8 A.M.–8 P.M. Mon.–Sat., 10 A.M.–7 P.M. Sun. Memorial Day–Labor Day weekends, 8 A.M.–5 P.M. Mon.–Fri. the rest of the year), in Union Station, can tell you about the sights, facilities, and goings-on for Ogden and surrounding communities, including Davis, Morgan, and Box Elder Counties.

Visit the **Forest Service Information Center** at Union Station or the **Ogden Ranger District office** of the U.S. Forest Service (507 25th St. and Adams Ave., 801/625-5112, 8 A.M.–4:30 P.M. Mon.–Fri. and Sat. in summer at Union Station) to find out about local road conditions, camping, hiking, horseback riding, ski touring, snowshoeing, and snowmobiling.

Hospital care and physician referrals are provided by **McKay-Dee Hospital Center** (3939 Harrison Blvd., 801/627-2800) and **Columbia Ogden Regional Medical Center** (5475 South 500 East, 801/479-2111). Minor medical problems can be handled at **NowCare** (698 12th,

801/394-7753). The downtown **post office** is at (2641 Washington Blvd., 801/627-4184).

TRANSPORTATION

Utah Transit Authority (UTA) buses serve many areas of Ogden and head east to Huntsville and south to Salt Lake City and Provo; buses operate Monday–Saturday and offer some late-night runs. UTA has an **information booth** at its main downtown bus stop in Ogden Municipal Park (corner of 25th and Washington Blvd., 801/621-4636, open noon–5 P.M. weekdays). **Greyhound** provides long-distance service from the terminal (2393 Wall Ave, 801/394-5573).

Air travelers use the **Salt Lake City International Airport,** just 35 miles away.

Yellow Cab (801/394-9411) provides 24-hour taxi service.

Vicinity of Ogden

Ogden is at the northern edge of Salt Lake City, and from here it's quick to get out into the hinterlands of northern Utah. Ogden Canyon is particularly scenic, and leads to some of the best downhill-skiing slopes in Utah.

EAST OF OGDEN
Ogden Canyon
Cliffs rise thousands of feet above narrow Ogden Canyon, just barely allowing Highway 39 and Ogden River to squeeze through. In autumn, the fiery reds of maples and the golden hues of oaks add color to this scenic drive deep within the Wasatch Range. Ogden Canyon begins on the eastern edge of Ogden and emerges about six miles farther, at Pineview Reservoir in the broad Ogden Valley.

This fertile agricultural basin is a crossroads for recreationalists. In winter, skiers turn south from the reservoir to Snowbasin Ski Area and north to Nordic Valley and Powder Mountain ski areas. Summer visitors have a choice of staying at swimming beaches and campgrounds on the shore of Pineview Reservoir or heading

to canyons and mountain peaks in the Wasatch Range. Reach the canyon from Ogden by heading east on 12th Street (take I-15 Exit 347).

Pineview Reservoir
This many-armed lake on the Ogden River provides excellent boating, fishing, water-skiing, and swimming at an elevation of 4,900 feet. Campgrounds, picnic areas, and marinas ring the shore of this four-mile-long reservoir. For day-tripping, **The Bluffs** offers sandy beaches and shaded picnic areas at Cemetery Point on the lake's east side ($5 per vehicle, $1 per pedestrian, day use only); a marina with boat ramp, docks, and snack bar is nearby ($5 boat launch); follow Highway 39 to the Huntsville turnoff (10.5 miles east of Ogden), then turn west two miles. **Middle Inlet** is another beach area 1.5 miles north of Huntsville, on the lake's western shore, with a boat ramp, small store, dock, slips, fuel, and storage. **North Arm Wildlife Viewing Trail** makes a 0.4-mile loop at the north end of the reservoir, where the

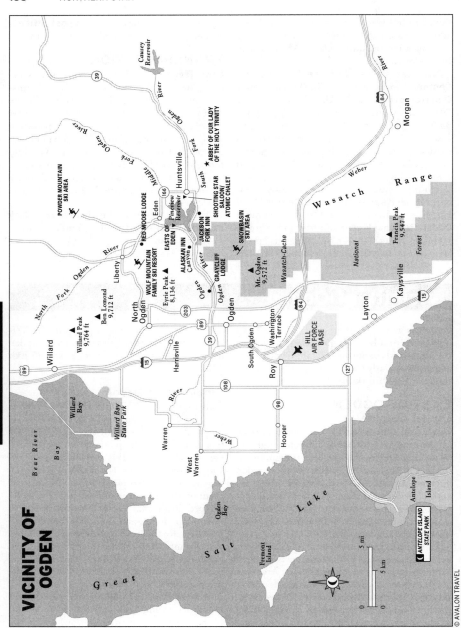

VICINITY OF OGDEN

Causey Reservoir

Morgan

POWDER MOUNTAIN SKI AREA

RED MOOSE LODGE

Huntsville

ABBEY OF OUR LADY OF THE HOLY TRINITY

Eden

Pineview Reservoir

SHOOTING STAR SALOON/ ATOMIC CHALET

Wasatch Range

Francis Peak 9,547 ft

Wasatch-Cache

National Forest

EASTS OF EDEN

JACKSON FORK INN

SNOWBASIN SKI AREA

Eyrie Peak 8,136 ft

WOLF MOUNTAIN FAMILY SKI RESORT

ALASKAN INN

GRAYCLIFF LODGE

Mt. Ogden 9,572 ft

Liberty

Ben Lomond 9,712 ft

North Ogden

Ogden Canyon

Kaysville

Willard Peak 9,764 ft

Ogden

Layton

Willard

Harrisville

South Ogden

Washington Terrace

HILL AIR FORCE BASE

Willard Bay State Park

Willard Bay

Roy

Bear River Bay

Warren

West Warren

Hooper

Ogden Bay

Salt Lake

Antelope Island

ANTELOPE ISLAND STATE PARK

Great

Fremont Island

5 mi

5 km

© AVALON TRAVEL

North Fork of the Ogden River joins the reservoir; the trail, built especially for wildlife viewing, lies off Highway 162.

Abbey of Our Lady of the Holy Trinity

This community of 30 Trappist monks welcomes visitors to its chapel and reception room (1250 South 9500 East, 801/745-3784, reception room open 8 A.M.–noon and 1–5 P.M. Mon.–Sat.). The monks explain the monastery's work and sell locally produced bread, honey, and farm products. Although no tours are given, a slide show illustrates the religious life and work of the community. You may attend the Mass and chants held daily in the chapel. Quonset buildings, originally just temporary, have proved both practical and unique for nearly all the monastery's needs. The founders chose this location for its seclusion and beautiful setting. The abbey is four miles southeast of Huntsville; follow signs for Monastery from Highway 39.

Accommodations

$50-100

The **Jackson Fork Inn** (Hwy. 39 at milepost 18 or 7345 East 900 South, Huntsville, 801/745-0051, $75 and up), offers rooms with private baths and unique decor—not bad for a dining room and lodge that started out as a barn. On the northern arm of Pineview Reservoir is a charming log B&B, the **Snowberry Inn** (1315 N. Hwy. 158 in Eden, 801/745-2634, www.snowberryinn.com, $89 and up). The inn overlooks the reservoir and provides access for water sports and swimming, while Ogden-area ski resorts are only 15 minutes away. All five guest rooms come with private baths; guests share a hot tub, billiard table, and TV room.

Another fun place to stay is the **⟨ Atomic Chalet** (5917 E. 100 South, Hunstville, 801/745-0538, www.atomicchalet.com, $85 and up), a B&B right on Pineview Reservoir. It's a lodge-like building with casual and relaxed vibe, and a favorite of skiers in winter.

© W. C. MCRAE

Monks at the Abbey of Our Lady of the Holy Trinity may soon move out of the Quonset huts they've used since 1947.

NORTHERN UTAH

All three guest rooms have private bathrooms, fridges, and TV/DVD players.

OVER $100

On the other side of the lake, near Eden, the **Red Moose Lodge** (2547 N. Valley Junction Dr., 801/745-0333 or 877/745-0333, www.theredmooselodge.com, $119 and up) is a handsome wood-structured lodge in the style of the 1930s (though it's newly constructed, with lots of modern luxuries like a spa, hot tubs, and free wireless Internet access). Rates include breakfast.

A number of condo developments have sprung up in the Ogden valley to serve the needs of skiers at the local ski areas. For a selection of condo options, check out the listings at www.destinationeden.com and www.wolflodgecondos.com.

Also see the **Alaskan Inn,** in the *Ogden* section, which is near the top of Ogden Canyon near Pineview Reservoir.

CAMPGROUNDS

The free **Maples Campground** (elev. 6,200 feet) is nestled among maples and aspens in the mountains near Snowbasin Ski Area. The season lasts late May–early September; there's no drinking water. Drive to the ski area's lower parking lot (marked Lower Shop), then turn west 1.5 miles on a gravel road.

Travel Highway 39 east from Huntsville to find eight Forest Service campgrounds within 10 miles. Most of these campgrounds have water; charges range $11–17. **Perception Park,** 7.5 miles east of Huntsville, was specially built to accommodate people with disabilities. Some sites can be reserved (877/444-6777).

The free (first come, first served) **Weber County Memorial Park** (801/399-8491) is one mile down the paved road to Causey Reservoir, a narrow crescent-shaped lake in the upper South Fork of the Ogden River. A paved road in the park crosses the river to individual sites; three group sites can be reserved through Weber County Parks and Recreation. Water is available late May–late September. Turnoff for Causey Reservoir is one mile east of Willows Campground on Highway 39. **Monte Cristo Campground** sits high in mountain forests of spruce, fir, and aspen at an elevation of 8,400 feet (between mileposts 48 and 49, 40 miles east of Ogden, 21 miles west of Woodruff on Highway 39); sites are open early July–late September and have drinking water.

Food

Some of the Ogden area's favorite places to eat are nestled in the bucolic Ogden Valley, just minutes from downtown Ogden. The **Jackson Fork Inn** (Hwy. 39 at milepost 18, 7345 East 900 South, 801/745-0051, Sun. brunch, dinner nightly, $12–21), used to be a dairy barn, though it's now a popular supper club with steaks, chicken, and pasta.

Also in the valley, the little town of Huntsville offers a couple of places to eat and Utah's oldest bar—in business since 1879—the **◖ Shooting Star Saloon** (7345 East 200 South, 801/745-2002, lunch and dinner daily, sandwiches $6–10). This is a favorite place to

Utah's oldest bar is still a good place to come for burgers.

come for burgers; TV's *Good Morning America* once named it one of the top five places for burgers in the United States. Interesting graffiti in the restrooms, and the bar boasts the stuffed head of an enormous dog that is rumored to be the original for Jack London's *Call of the Wild.*

A fun place to eat near Eden is **Eats of Eden** (2529 N. Hwy. 162, 801/745-8618, lunch and dinner Tues.–Sat., $8–18), serving good pizza, pasta, and sandwiches.

SNOWBASIN SKI AREA

Snowbasin (3925 E. Snowbasin Rd., Huntsville, UT 84317, 801/620-1000 or 888/437-5488, 801/620-1100 for snow report, www.snowbasin.com) was gussied up substantially for the 2002 Winter Olympics when it hosted the men's and women's downhill, super-G, and combined competitions. Snowbasin is now one of Utah's largest ski areas, with an excellent lift system, great panoramic views, and no crowds. Though it gets a bit less snow than the Cottonwood resorts, Snowbasin is well equipped with snow-making machines.

Terrain and Lifts

With more than 3,200 acres of terrain and relatively few other skiers and snowboarders, there's almost always room to roam here. The area is well covered with speedy lifts, meaning that you can spend more time skiing and less time standing in line or sitting on pokey chairlifts.

Four triple chairlifts and one double plus one quad and two gondolas and a short little tram serve 63 runs, of which 11 percent are rated beginner, 49 percent intermediate, and 40 percent expert; snowboarding is allowed. The longest run is three miles and drops 2,400 feet in elevation.

With 40 percent of trails marked with black diamonds, Snowbasin is clearly an expert skier's dream. The north side of the mountain (the John Paul area) has incredible expert terrain—long and *steep.* However, John Paul is sometimes closed for races. There are also extra-black chutes off the top of the Strawberry Express gondola.

But intermediate skiers can also have a good, non-terrifying time here. The Strawberry area in particular is full of nicely groomed long blue cruisers. Beginners will find only limited territory.

Ski season at Snowbasin normally runs Thanksgiving–mid-April. Adult lift tickets are $62 for a full day, $51 half day; children's rates are $39 full day, $31 half day; seniors pay $50/$35).

Snowbasin offers a ski school, ski shop, rentals, and three day lodges. Of particular note is the **outdoor ice rink** at Needles Lodge, at the top of the Needles gondola.

Cross-Country Skiing and Snowshoeing

Snowbasin maintains the Maples Nordic Loop, 11 miles of cross-country ski trails, groomed for both classic and skate skiers. This loop is west of the Grizzly Center and is free. Cross-country ski and snowshoe rentals are available at the Grizzly Center.

Accommodations and Food

There is no lodging at Snowbasin. Though most people drive up from Salt Lake City, the Ogden Valley lodgings are quite handy, with a number of B&Bs and condos catering to skiers.

Dining options are pretty limited: You can eat at the base lodge or you can eat at the mountain-top Needles Lodge (801/620-1021, lunch and dinner, 9 A.M.–4 P.M. Sun.–Fri., until 8 P.M. on Sat. in ski season, $6–20) or John Paul Lodge (801/620-1021, 9 A.M.–3 P.M. daily in ski season, $6–20).

Summer Activities

The lifts at Snowbasin remain open in summer for hikers and bikers, making it easy to reach the high country. In addition, Snowbasin sponsors a series of Sunday afternoon concerts at Earl's Lodge, located at the base of the ski runs.

NORTHERN UTAH

OTHER SKI AREAS

Wolf Mountain Family Ski Resort

The Wolf Mountain Family Ski Resort (P.O. Box 478, Eden, UT 84310, 801/745-3511, www.wolfmountaineden.com) is the closest to Ogden and is especially popular with families (Monday is family night). It's an unintimidating place to learn to ski. Two double chairlifts serve 19 runs, of which 30 percent are beginner, 50 percent intermediate, and 20 percent expert. Elevation drop is 1,000 feet. You can ski at night, too—all runs are under lights Monday–Saturday. Nordic Valley's season runs daily early December–late March. Adult lift tickets cost $26 full day, $22 half day, and $10 night. Nordic Valley has a ski school, ski shop, and a day lodge. It's 15 miles northeast of Ogden; go through Ogden Canyon, turn left at Pineview Dam, and follow signs. The lifts remain open in summer for mountain bikers, and a terrain park opened in 2007.

Powder Mountain Winter Resort

Two double chairlifts and one triple, plus one quad, reach two different peaks and serve more than 80 runs (10 percent beginner, 50 percent intermediate, and 40 percent expert) at Powder Mountain Winter Resort (P.O. Box 450, Eden, UT 84310, 801/745-3771 or 801/745-3772, www.powdermountain.com). Three surface tows supplement the chairlifts. High elevations of 6,895–8,900 feet catch plentiful powder snow. You can ski at night from the Sundown lift until 10 P.M. Powder Mountain's season lasts mid-November–late April. Adult lift tickets cost $53 full day, $45 half day, and $19 for night skiing. Facilities include a ski school, ski shops, rentals, and three day lodges. Powder Mountain is 19 miles northeast of Ogden; drive through Ogden Canyon, turn left at Pineview Dam, and follow signs. In summer, mountain bikers are free to use the trails, but there is no lift-assisted hiking or biking.

ACCOMMODATIONS

Powder Mountain's **Columbine Inn** (801/745-3773, www.powdermountain.com) has simple hotel-style rooms ($75–110) as well as condo suites with full kitchens and fireplaces ($150–300).

NORTH OF OGDEN

Most travelers driving north from Ogden will simply take the I-15 freeway. However, if you like life in the slow lane, you can follow the **Golden Spike Fruitway,** or old U.S. 89, as it winds north to Brigham City through orchards and farm land. Fruit stands, open during the July to mid-September season, offer a bountiful supply of cherries, apples, peaches, pears, apricots, plums, berries, and vegetables.

Willard Bay State Park

Two separate recreation areas along the eastern shore of freshwater Willard Bay (900 West 650 North, P.O. Box A, Willard, UT 84340, 435/734-9494 or 800/322-3770 for campground reservations, $9 day use, $15 camping) provide opportunities for water sports, camping, and nature study. Only two miles of Willard Bay's 15-mile circumference are natural shoreline; dikes enclose nearly all of the bay to keep out saltwater from the Great Salt Lake just to the west. Canals carry water into the bay during winter and spring, then out for irrigation during the growing season.

More than 200 species of birds have been observed near the park; common ones include the white pelican, California gull, snowy egret, Western grebe, killdeer, black-necked stilt, and American avocet; eagles visit in winter. Conditions are great for water-skiing and power boating, and anglers catch channel catfish, smallmouth bass, bluegill, crappie, and walleye. Winter visitors find good ice fishing in the bay mid-December–late February.

North Marina (just west of I-15 Willard Exit 360) features a sandy swimming beach, campground with showers, boat ramp, and dock. The developed campground's season is normally April 1 (or Easter, if it falls in March) through October, but an overflow area on the shore stays open year-round. Reservations are recommended on summer weekends and holidays.

South Marina has a boat ramp, docks, and campground with showers. The area is set up mostly for day use, as the open grassy areas used for camping lack designated sites. The dikes on this part of the bay prevent beaches and lake views, but you won't be so crowded here on summer weekends, and the campground nearly always has room. South Marina is open April 1 (Easter if it falls in March) through October; no reservations are taken here. Access is from I-15 Exit 354; follow signs west 2.5 miles.

Brigham City

Peaks of the Wasatch Range exceeding 9,000 feet form the backdrop to this agricultural center with a population of 17,000. There's not much here to delay the traveler, though students of history will enjoy the displays in the **Brigham City Museum-Gallery** (24 North 300 West, 435/723-6769, 11 A.M.–6 P.M. Tues.–Fri., 1–5 P.M. Sat., free) that show how residents lived in the 19th century. The art gallery features changing shows by local artists and artists from all over Utah. The **Brigham City Depot** (833 W. Forest, 435/723-2989), a late-19th-century railroad station, has been lovingly restored to its original condition, with separate waiting rooms for each gender and many antiques from railroading in the past. Many people think the Mormon **Box Elder Tabernacle** (251 S. Main St., 435/723-5376, tours 9 A.M.–9P.M. daily May–Oct.) is Utah's most beautiful building. Non-Mormons are welcome.

Amid the taco stands and fast-food restaurants along Main Street is a unique place to eat. The **Idle Isle Restaurant** (24 S. Main St., 435/734-2468, lunch and dinner Mon.–Sat.) is an ice-cream parlor, candy store, and diner little changed from the 1920s when it first opened. At lunch, there's soup, homemade rolls, and various sandwiches on the menu; in the evening, all meals—good American-style dishes like roast pork and chicken-fried steak—come with a piece of pie. The atmosphere is splendid.

Bear River Migratory Bird Refuge

Millions of birds drop in to feed or nest in the freshwater marshes created by the intersection of the Bear River and the Great Salt Lake; about 60 species nest in the Bear River Migratory Bird Refuge (office at 866 S. Main, in Breitenbeker's Plaza, Brigham City, UT 84302, 435/723-5887, 8 A.M.–4:30 P.M. Mon.–Fri.). In pioneer days, reports told of flocks of waterfowl blackening the sky. Flooding in the late 1980s closed the area and displaced many birds until receding waters allowed it to reopen in 1990. A four-mile loop gravel road is open to visitors. Head west 15 miles on Forest Street from Brigham City on a partly paved road.

Belmont Springs

Natural hot springs ponds have been developed into a swimming pool and hot tubs, a nine-hole golf course, and a campground. Volleyball and horseshoe equipment is available, too. In recent years, the hot springs ponds have also become popular with scuba divers. Belmont Springs (435/458-3200, 9 A.M.–9 P.M., golf hours 8:30 A.M.–dark, early May–early Oct., pool and hot tubs $5 adults, $3 children, camping $8 without hookups, $16 with hookups) lies 10 miles north of Tremonton and one mile south of Plymouth.

NORTHERN UTAH

Golden Spike National Historic Site

At 12:47 P.M. on May 10, 1869, rails from the U.S. East and West Coasts met for the first time. People across the country closely followed telegraph reports as dignitaries and railway officials made their speeches and drove the last spikes, then everyone broke out in wild celebration. The joining of rails at this windswept pass in Utah's Promontory Mountains marked a new chapter in the growth of the United States. A transcontinental railroad at last linked both sides of the nation. The far western frontier would be a frontier no more. Swift-moving Army troops would soon put an end to Native American troubles. Vast resources of timber, mineral wealth, and farmland lay open to development.

History

The Central Pacific and Union Pacific Railroads, eager for land grants and bonuses, had been laying track at a furious pace and grading the lines far ahead. So great was the momentum that the grader crews didn't even stop when they met but laid parallel grades for 250 miles across Utah. Finally Congress decided to join the rails at Promontory Summit and stop the wasteful duplication of effort. A ragged town of tents, boxcars, and hastily built wooden shacks sprang up along a single muddy street. Outlaws and crooked gambling houses earned Promontory Summit an awful reputation as a real "hell-on-wheels" town. The party ended six months later when the railroads moved the terminal operations to Ogden. Soon only a depot, roundhouse, helper engines, and other rail facilities remained. The Lucin Cutoff across the Great Salt Lake in 1904 bypassed the long twisting grades of Promontory Summit and dramatically reduced traffic along the old route. The final blow came in 1942, when the rails were torn up for scrap to feed wartime industries.

◖ Golden Spike Visitors Center

The Golden Spike National Historic Site, authorized by Congress in 1965, re-creates this momentous episode of railroad history. The visitors center (mailing address: P.O. Box 897, Brigham City, UT 84302, 801/471-2209, www.nps.gov/gosp, 9 A.M.–5:30 P.M. daily, closed Mon.–Tues. Oct. 21–April 30 and Thanksgiving, Christmas, and New Year's Day, $7 per vehicle or $4 per adult, whichever is less) offers exhibits and programs that illustrate the difficulties of building the railroad and portray the officials and workers who made it possible. A short slide show introduces Promontory Summit's history. A 20-minute program, *The Golden Spike,* presents a more detailed account of building the transcontinental railroad. Rangers give talks several times a day in summer. An exhibit room has changing displays on railroading, and historic markers behind the visitors center indicate the spot where the last spike was driven.

The two locomotives that met here in 1869, Central Pacific's Jupiter and Union Pacific's 119, succumbed to scrap yards around the turn of the 20th century. However, they have been born again in authentic replicas. Every day in summer the trains steam along a short section of track from the Engine House to the historic spot. You can't ride on the engines; they're here mostly for photo ops.

The annual Last Spike Ceremony reenacts the original celebration every May 10 with great fanfare. The Railroaders' Festival in August has special exhibits, a spike-driving contest, reenactments, handcar races, and entertainment. A sales counter offers a good selection of books on railroading, Utah history, and natural history, as well as postcards and souvenirs. Motels and restaurants are nearby in Brigham City and Tremonton. From the I-15 Brigham City Exit 368, head west on Highway 13 and Highway 83 and follow signs 29 miles.

Promontory Trail Auto Tour

Imagine you're riding the rails across Utah a century ago. This seven-mile scenic drive follows the old grades past many construction feats of hardy railway workers. You'll see the

GOLDEN SPIKE CEREMONY

In grade school, many of us learned that when the Union Pacific and Central Pacific Railroads met, a solid-gold ceremonial stake was driven to mark the spot. One yearns to go to Promontory and pry out that golden spike. But the real story tells us the event was marked with no fewer than two golden spikes, both from California; a silver spike contributed by the state of Nevada; and an iron spike with its body plated in silver and its cap plated in gold, courtesy of the state of Arizona.

A polished myrtlewood tie was placed at the site to receive the spikes, protecting the precious metals from the damage of driving them into the earth. At the ceremony, Central Pacific President Leland Stanford (founder of Stanford University) took the first swing at the final spike and missed it entirely – but did hit the tie. Union Pacific Vice President and General Manager Thomas C. Durant next tried his hand and missed not only the spike but the rail and the tie as well. A bystander was finally summoned from the crowd to tap the stake home.

Shortly after the formal ceremony concluded, the valuable spikes and tie were removed and standard fittings were substituted to link the nation by rail.

parallel grades laid by the competing Union Pacific and Central Pacific, clearings for sidings, original rock culverts, and many cuts and fills. Wildflowers, grass-covered hills, and views over the blue Great Salt Lake appear much the same as they did to early train travelers. A booklet available at the visitors center describes the features and history at numbered stops on the drive. There are two segments to the auto tour, a five-mile section to the west of the visitor center and a two-mile section to the east.

Big Fill Walk

An easy 1.5-mile hike leads farther down a railroad grade to the famous Big Fill and Big Trestle sites. Rugged terrain on this side of the Promontory Mountains posed some of the greatest construction challenges to both lines. The Central Pacific tackled an especially deep ravine here with a massive fill, 170 feet deep and 500 feet long, requiring about two months of work by 500 men and 250 teams of animals. The Union Pacific, pressed for time, threw together a temporary trestle over the gorge, paralleling the Big Fill.

VICINITY OF GOLDEN SPIKE NATIONAL HISTORIC SITE
Promontory Point

This peninsula that juts into the Great Salt Lake has no connection with the first transcontinental railroad but does make a pleasant scenic drive. A paved road follows the eastern shore of the peninsula below the Promontory Mountains for 22.5 miles, then becomes gravel for the last 17.5 miles around to the west side. There are good views of the Great Salt Lake, the Wasatch Range, and the Lucin Cutoff railroad causeway. Lake Crystal Salt Co. at road's end was a salt extraction plant (it's no longer in operation). There's no hiking or camping on Promontory Point—the land has been fenced and signed No Trespassing. The Promontory Point turnoff is six miles east of the Golden Spike visitors center.

Thiokol

Many buildings of this giant aerospace corporation lie scattered across the countryside about six miles northeast of the historic site. You're not likely to be allowed to tour the facility, but you can see a group of missiles, rocket engines, and a space-shuttle booster casing in front of administrative offices. Turn north two miles on Highway 83 at the junction with the Golden Spike National Historic Site road (eight miles east of the visitors center).

RAFT RIVER MOUNTAINS

Few Utah residents know about these mountains in the northwest corner of the state, despite

NORTHERN UTAH

their pretty alpine scenery. Panoramic views from the top of the Raft River Range take in the Great Salt Lake, barren desert, farmlands, and mountains in Utah, Nevada, and Idaho. The range runs east–west—something of a rarity in the region. The summit ridge isn't what you'd expect, either—it's a long ridge of gently rolling grasslands. Bull Mountain (elev. 9,931 feet) crowns the range, though it's hard to pick out from all the other grassy knolls.

Hikers haven't yet discovered the range—you'll find pristine forests and canyons but no real trails. Aspen, Douglas and subalpine fir, and limber pine thrive in the canyons and on the northern slopes below the summit ridge. Ranchers run cattle on the top and in other meadow areas. A road that requires a four-wheel drive vehicle climbs into the mountains from Yost.

Clear Creek Campground (elev. 6,400 feet) offers sites in a beautiful setting below the north slope of the Raft River Range. The roads leading to the campground also offer access to the range's best hiking. For information, contact the **Burley Ranger District office** of the Sawtooth National Forest (2621 S. Overland Ave., Burley, ID 83318, 208/678-0430).

Travelers can easily cross the lonely country of Utah's northwest corner on paved Highways 42 and 30. Park Valley, south of the Raft River Mountains, has a small store and gas station, and a café (all closed Sunday).

Logan and Vicinity

Without question one of the most appealing towns in Utah, Logan, with a city population of 49,000 and an area population of almost 110,000, lies surrounded by the lush dairy and farmlands of the Cache Valley and by the lofty peaks of the Bear River Range. Of all the mountain communities in the American West that advertise their Swiss or Bavarian aspirations, Logan comes closest to actually looking alpine.

The town itself is built on stair-like terraces, which mark ancient shorelines of Lake Bonneville. Utah State University lends a youthful energy to the town, and residents are notably trim and fit (the fact that some are performers from New York City doesn't hurt). Logan is also one of the state's festival centers: Theater, music, and performance series enliven the town in summer. As everywhere in Utah, the outdoors is never far away: The mountains provide abundant year-round recreation including scenic drives, boating on nearby Bear Lake, camping, fishing, hiking, and skiing.

SIGHTS

Logan has a lovely little downtown filled with handsome architecture, lined with trees, and flanked by parks. A walk along Main Street is a pleasant diversion, with numerous shops to visit, including bookstores, recreation stores, old-fashioned clothiers, and the mandatory Bluebird Restaurant, a traditional soda fountain.

Mormon Temple, Tabernacle, and History Museum

The distinctive castellated temple (175 North 300 East) rises from a prominent hill just east of downtown. After Brigham Young chose this location in 1877, church members labored for seven years to complete the temple. Architect Truman O. Angell, designer of the Salt Lake Temple, oversaw construction. Timber and blocks of limestone came from nearby Logan Canyon. Only Mormons engaged in sacred work may enter the temple, but visitors are welcome on the grounds to view the exterior.

The tabernacle also stands as a fine example of early Mormon architecture. Construction of the stone structure began in 1865, but other priorities—building the temple and ward meetinghouses—delayed dedication until 1891. The public may enter the tabernacle, which is downtown at Main and Center Streets.

At the **Cache Valley Historical Museum** (160 N. Main, 435/753-5139, 10 A.M.–4 P.M.

© W. C. MCRAE

Logan Tabernacle

Tues.–Fri. in summer, by appointment the rest of the year, free), exhibits show how Logan's early settlers lived. You'll see their tools, household furnishings, clothing, art, and photographs. It is also the Cache Valley tourist office. More of Logan's history can be seen on a walking tour; ask for the self-guided, 45-minute *Logan's Historic Main Street* brochure at the tourist office.

Willow Park and Zoo

This small free zoo (419 West 700 South, 8 A.M.–dark daily year-round, closed some holidays) displays exotic birds such as an Andean condor, a golden pheasant, a mitered conure, and more familiar golden and bald eagles, peacocks, swans, and ducks. In fact, Willow Park has one of the greatest waterfowl collections in the region, showcasing more than 100 species. The setting offers walkways along shady willow trees and children can feed the ducks, geese, and trout. See lemurs, red fox, coyotes, elk, deer, bobcats, and more. Willow Park also has picnic areas and a playground in amongst its large shady trees.

◖ American West Heritage Center

This institution (4025 S. Hwy. 89/91, 435/245-6050, www.americanwestcenter.org, 10 A.M.–5 P.M. Tues.–Sat., until 4 P.M. in winter, $5 adults, $4 seniors and students, $3 children 3–11), six miles southwest of Logan, combines the function of a visitors center with the history and culture of the Old West. The center is quite ambitious, and includes a permanent living history installation that highlights the lives and lifestyles of the native peoples of the Cache Valley, the fur-trapping mountain men who arrived here in the 1820s, and the pioneer Mormon farmers who settled here starting in the 1860s. The center used to have a big celebration in August called the Festival of the American West; now the festival events are scattered throughout the year. Check the calendar for events such as mountain man rallies, cowboy poetry recitations, art shows, harvest fairs, pioneer cooking contests, and so on. Also on premises is the Northern Utah Welcome Center, which provides tourist information, an introduction to local history, and a gift shop.

Adjacent to the center and incorporated into it is the **Ronald V. Jensen Living Historical Farm,** an outdoor museum that re-creates life on a Cache Valley family farm in 1917. Workers dress in period clothing to plow soil, thresh grain, milk cows, shear sheep, and butcher hogs. The men mostly worked in the fields while women stayed closer to home to cook, can, quilt, gather eggs from the henhouse, and pick vegetables from the garden. You'll see breeds of animals representative of early farms, a lineup of steam tractors, a giant early gasoline tractor, and many other pieces of farm machinery. Buildings here include an 1875 farmhouse, summer kitchen, root cellar, smokehouse, blacksmith shop, horse barn, sheep shed, and a privy or two. Special demonstrations take place all through the year, usually on Saturday; these range from planting the garden to shearing the sheep and harvesting the grain. In fall, the cornfield is converted into a maze.

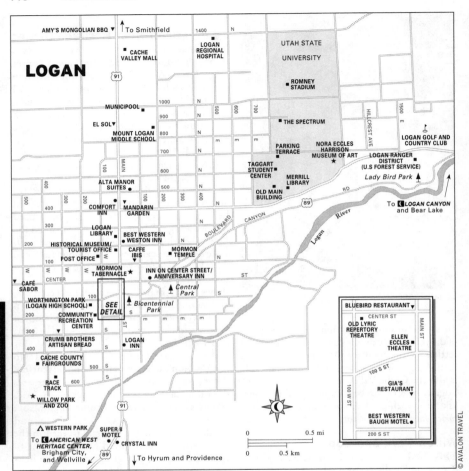

© AVALON TRAVEL

Utah State University

In 1888, a federal land-grant program opened the way for the territorial legislature to establish the Agricultural College of Utah. The school grew to become Utah State University (USU) in 1957 and now has eight colleges, 45 departments, and a graduate school. USU's "Aggies" number more than 20,000, led by 2,300 faculty and staff. The university has continued its original purpose of agricultural research while diversifying into atmospheric and space sciences, ecology, creative arts, social sciences, and other fields.

Attractions on campus include the **Nora Eccles Harrison Museum of Art** (650 North 1100 East, 435/797-0163, 8:30 A.M.–4:30 P.M. Mon.–Fri., free), one of the largest permanent collections of art in Utah; the student center; and several libraries. **Old Main Building,** with its landmark bell tower, was begun one year after the college was founded and has housed nearly every office and department in the school at one time or another. The oak-shaded campus sits northeast of downtown on a bench left by a northern arm of prehistoric Lake Bonneville.

Try USU's famous Traditional Aggie ice cream, available in the student center and at the USU Dairy Sales outlet (8710 University Blvd., 435/797-2109).

ENTERTAINMENT AND EVENTS

One of the best reasons to visit Logan is to catch the community's high-quality arts and music festivals. People from all over Utah and the intermountain West come to Logan to take in an opera, a chamber music concert, or an evening of theater in this scenic alpine valley. The Cache Valley Tourism Council (160 N. Main St., 435/752-2161, www.tourcachevalley.com) can fill you in on what's happening in the area.

Utah Festival Opera Company

This professional opera troupe (P.O. Box 3489, Logan, UT 84323-3489, 435/750-0300 or 800/830-6088, www.ufoc.org) takes over the beautifully restored Ellen Eccles Theatre (43 S. Main) in mid-July to August. The fact that a small Utah agricultural college town has its own prominent opera company is slightly unusual. Two factors account for the opera and its hearty success. Michael Ballam, a Logan-area native and professional opera singer, decided in 1993 to start an opera company in Utah; at the same time, Logan's old movie palace and vaudeville hall, the Capitol Theatre, was remodeled and transformed into a world-class performing arts center. Renamed the Ellen Eccles Theatre, the theater has excellent acoustics and an intimate yet formal atmosphere that perfectly suited Ballam's operatic vision. Utah Festival Opera currently stages four performances during its month-long season.

Old Lyric Repertory Theatre

The Old Lyric (28 W. Center, 435/797-1500 or 888/878-2931) provides a summer season of musicals, comedies, and dramas in a historic theater in downtown Logan. Visiting equity actors lead the shows produced by the Utah State University's drama department. Other Logan-area summer stock theaters also present light comedies and musicals.

Musical Events

Utah State University and Logan jointly sponsor a **Music in the Parks** series throughout the summer. The university also sponsors a **summer performing arts series,** which brings the Utah Symphony, dance troupes, and chamber musicians to the campus. For information on both series, call 435/797-0305. The **Capitol Arts Alliance** (435/752-0026) brings in musicals, events, and performances to the Ellen Eccles Theatre throughout the year.

Other Events

The **Mendon May Day Festival** takes place 11 miles west of Logan and features a maypole dance and other festivities.

June brings the **Summerfest Art and Jazz Festival** to downtown Logan, which features works by local artists, concerts, food, and a home tour.

The **Cache County Fair and Rodeo** has agricultural and craft exhibits along with PRCA rodeo action at the fairgrounds in Logan during August. At the Clarkstor Ampitheatre, 21 miles northwest of Logan, the **Martin Harris Pageant** re-creates pioneer and Mormon history.

In Wellsville, seven miles southwest of Logan, **Wellsville Founders Day Celebration,** on Labor Day in early September, commemorates the first pioneers to settle in Cache Valley.

RECREATION
Parks, Swimming, and Tennis

Willow Park (450 West 700 South) is a good place for a picnic and has the added attractions of a small zoo, playground, volleyball courts, and a softball field. **Bicentennial Park** (100 S. Main) offers picnic spots downtown. Swim year-round at the indoor **Municipool** (114 East 1000 North, 435/750-9890). The **Community Recreation Center** (195 South 100 West, 435/750-9877) features tennis and handball/racquetball courts, basketball, volley-ball, weight room, indoor track, table tennis, sauna, and whirlpool. **Tennis courts** are also available at Mount Logan Middle School (875 North 200 East), Central Park (85 South 300 East), and Worthington Park at Logan High School (162 West 100 South).

Golf

The cool and verdant Cache Valley is especially suited to golf, and there are some dandy courses in the Logan area. Play at the 18-hole **Logan Golf and Country Club** (710 North 1500 East, 435/753-6020), the **Logan River Golf Course** (550 West 1000 South, 435/750-0123), the 18-hole **Birch Creek Golf Course** (600 E. Center in Smithfield, seven miles north, 435/563-6825), or the nine-hole **Sherwood Hills** (Sardine Canyon, 13 miles southwest on U.S. 89/91, 435/245-6055). Sherwood Hills also offers a hotel (435/245-6424), one indoor and two outdoor pools, horseback riding, cross-country ski trails, racquetball, and tennis.

Winter Sports

Ice-skating is popular in winter at Central Park (85 South 300 East). The Logan Ranger District office (435/755-3620) has lists of cross-country ski tours in the area.

The **Beaver Creek Lodge** (435/753-1707 or 435/753-1076), 28 miles east of Logan on Hwy. 39, offers snowmobile rentals plus cross-country ski trails in winter. Just next door is the **Beaver Mountain Ski Area** (see the *Logan Canyon* section).

Equipment

Trailhead Sports (117 N. Main, 435/753-1541) has hiking and camping gear, cross-country ski rentals and sales, canoe and kayak rentals and sales, and topo maps. Outdoor sporting goods are also sold at **The Sportsman** (129 N. Main, 435/752-0211) and **Gart's Sporting Goods** (585 N. Main, 435/752-4287).

ACCOMMODATIONS
$50-100

Logan's motels are generally well maintained and moderately priced. For a basic, inexpensive room, try the **Super 8 Motel** (865 S. U.S. 89/91, 435/753-8883 or 800/800-8000, $59 and up). The **Logan Inn** (364 S. Main, 435/753-5623, $50 and up) provides a pool, some kitchen rooms, and a guest laundry. **Comfort Inn** (447 N. Main, 435/752-9141 or 800/228-5150, $70 and up) has a guest laundry, complimentary continental breakfast, pool, hot tub, and exercise room.

South of Logan, near Wellsville and the American West Heritage Center, is the **Ramada Limited** (2002 S. U.S. Hwy. 89, 435/787-2060 or 800/272-6232, $89 and up). Right downtown, the **Best Western Baugh Motel** (153 S. Main, 435/752-5220 or 800/462-4154, $85 price) offers large rooms, outdoor swimming pool, and exercise room. There's a restaurant adjacent. Also downtown, the attractive **⟨ Best Western Weston Inn** (250 N. Main, 435/752-5700 or 800/532-5055, $89 and up) has a pool, two hot tubs, a weight room, and complimentary breakfast.

History and luxury meet at **⟨ Providence Inn B&B** (three miles south of Logan at 10 S. Main in Providence, 435/752-3432, www.providenceinn.com, $99 and up). The inn is listed on the National Register of Historic Places; parts of the building were built as a stone church in 1869. Each of the grandly refurbished 17 guest rooms offers a private bath, TV and VCR, and phone.

Over $100

The **Crystal Inn** (853 S. Main, 435/752-0707 or 800/280-0707, $108 and up) offers a pool, hot tub, and nicely furnished rooms with efficiency kitchens.

One of the more unusual places to stay in Logan is **Inn on Center Street/Anniversary Inn** (169 E. Center, 435/752-3443, www.anniversaryinn.com, $139 and up), a complex of heritage homes with 22 themed rooms. Because this lodging was designed as a special occasion destination (hence the name), all rooms have private baths with jetted tubs and big-screen TVs, and breakfast is delivered to your room. No children; reservations required.

Campgrounds

To reach **Riverside RV Park** (435/245-4469, year-round), turn east on 1700 South from U.S. 89/91; it's just south of town and has showers and laundry. **Country Cuzzins RV Park** (1936 N. Main, 435/752-1025, year-round) has campsites, a laundry, convenience store, and hot showers; no tenting. **Hyrum State Park** offers camping, swimming, fishing, and boating seven miles south near the town of Hyrum (see the *Hyrum State Park* section), and the U.S. Forest Service operates many campgrounds beginning six miles east of town on U.S. 89 in Logan Canyon (see the *Logan Canyon* section).

FOOD

If you're looking for a cup of coffee, a pastry, or perhaps a salad for lunch, then head to **Caffe Ibis** (52 Federal Ave., 435/753-4777, 8 A.M.–9 P.M.). The atmosphere is pleasantly alternative, and the adjacent bakery and health food store are a nice plus. Another great spot for morning coffee and fresh-baked pastries is **Crumb Brothers Artisan Bread** (291 South 300 West, 435/792-6063, 8 A.M.–5 P.M.).

Like any college town, Logan has a full array of pizza and fast-food places; most of them are along N. Main. **Mandarin Garden** (432 N. Main, 435/753-5789, lunch Mon.–Fri., dinner nightly, $7–16) is the best of the many Chinese restaurants in town. At **Amy's Mongolian BBQ** (1537 N. Main, 435/753-3338, lunch and dinner Mon.–Sat., $9–17), you can enjoy Mongolian barbecue or a Chinese buffet, or order from the menu. For Mexican food, try **El Sol** (871 N. Main, 435/752-5743, lunch and dinner daily, $6–10).

For something uniquely Loganesque, try the **Bluebird Restaurant** (19 N. Main, 435/752-3155, breakfast, lunch, and dinner Mon.–Sat., $8–20), a beautifully maintained soda fountain, chocolatier, and restaurant that appears unchanged from the 1930s.

Also a Logan tradition, **Gia's Restaurant** (119 S. Main, 435/752-8384, lunch and dinner Mon.–Sat. $8–17) has an atmospheric dining room and is Logan's best bet for a traditional Italian meal.

For more up-to-date dining, **¡Cafe Sabor!** (600 W. Center, 435/752-8880, lunch and dinner Mon.–Sat., $7–18), at the west end of Center Street at, offers tasty Mexican and Southwest fare in Logan's old train depot. The tortillas and salsas are all made fresh on premises; there's outdoor dining on the shaded passenger platforms. Traditional Mexican dishes as well as grilled chicken, fish, and beef are served.

A new dining room for high quality northern Italian cooking is **Le Nonne Ristorante Italiano** (132 N. Main, 435/752-9577, lunch and dinner Mon.–Fri., dinner only Sat., $11–22). The chef/owner hails from Tuscany, and the cuisine reflects cooking learned from his *nonne* (grandmothers).

INFORMATION AND SERVICES

The **Cache Valley Visitors Bureau** (downtown at 199 North Main S., Logan, UT 84321, 435/755-1890 or 800/882-4433, www.tourcachevalley.com, 8 A.M.–5 P.M. Mon.–Fri., sometimes Sat. in summer) has maps and travel information for Cache and Rich Counties, including Logan and Bear Lake. To learn more of local history and architecture, ask for *Logan's Historic Main Street*, a brochure outlining a self-guided, 45-minute walking tour. For recreation information and maps of the surrounding mountain country, visit the **Logan Ranger District office** (1500 E. U.S. 89, 435/755-3620, 8 A.M.–4:30 P.M. Mon.–Fri., until 5 P.M. in summer). The district covers Logan Canyon, the Bear River Range, and the Wellsville Mountains.

Logan Regional Hospital (1400 North 500 East, 435/752-2050) provides 24-hour emergency care. The **post office** is at 151 North 100 West (435/752-7246).

VICINITY OF LOGAN
Hyrum State Park

The Little Bear River feeds this popular 450-acre reservoir beside the town of Hyrum. Boaters come to water-ski, sail, or paddle across the

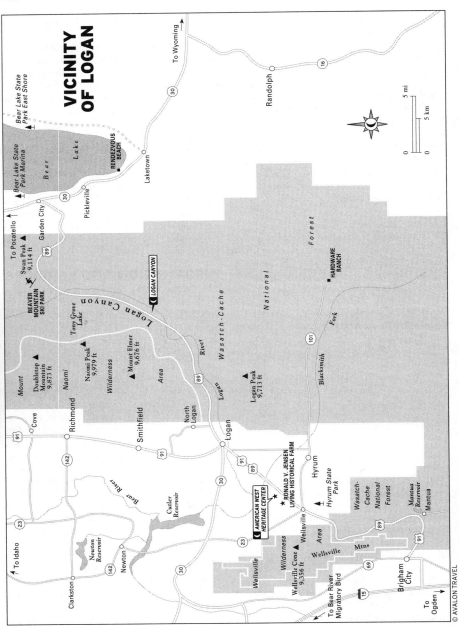

VICINITY
OF LOGAN

To Wyoming

Randolph

16

Bear Lake State
Park East Shore

Bear Lake State
Park Marina

Bear Lake

RENDEZVOUS
BEACH

Laketown

30

Pickleville

Garden City

To Pocatello

Swan Peak
9,114 ft

89

BEAVER
MOUNTAIN
SKI PARK

Logan Canyon

LOGAN CANYON

Tony Grove
Lake

Naomi Peak
9,979 ft

Mount Elmer
9,676 ft

Mount Naomi Wilderness Area

Doubletop
Mountain
9,873 ft

Logan River

Wasatch-Cache

National

Forest

HARDWARE
RANCH

101

Blacksmith Fork

Logan Peak
9,713 ft

91

Cove

Richmond

142

Smithfield

North
Logan

91

89

Logan

Hyrum

RONALD V. JENSEN
LIVING HISTORICAL FARM

AMERICAN WEST
HERITAGE CENTER

Hyrum State
Park

Wasatch
Cache
National
Forest

Mantua
Reservoir

Mantua

89

Bear River

Cutler
Reservoir

30

23

Wellsville

Wellsville
Wilderness
Area

Wellsville Cone
9,356 ft

Wellsville Mtns

69

91

Newton
Reservoir

Newton

142

23

91

To Idaho

Clarkston

To Bear River
Migratory Bird

Brigham
City

15

To
Ogden

5 mi

5 km

© AVALON TRAVEL

waters. Sandy beaches dot the shore, though no lifeguards watch over the area. Fishing in the lake isn't great, but anglers sometimes have good luck in the river just below the spillway during spring runoff.

The park has two developed areas on the north shore. The launch and campground area has picnic grounds, a beach, a boat ramp, docks, and the ranger office (405 West 300 South, Hyrum, UT 84319, 435/245-6866 or 800/322-3770 for campground reservations, day use $6, camping $15), but most park visitors head for the day-use area farther east along the shore for picnicking, lying on the beach, and swimming. It's reached by a half-mile drive (follow signs) or a half-mile foot trail from the campground. Campground reservations are advised on summer weekends. The park makes a good base for exploring the Cache Valley area; rangers can suggest places to go and provide snowmobiling information. From Logan, drive south seven miles on the Hyrum Road (Highway 165), which branches off U.S. 89/91 on the south edge of town, or go southwest six miles on U.S. 89/91, then turn east three miles on Highway 101 and follow signs.

Hardware Ranch and Blacksmith Fork Canyon

The Utah Division of Wildlife Resources (435/753-6206, http://wildlife.utah.gov/hardwareranch) operates this ranch in the midst of the northern Wasatch Range to provide winter feed for herds of elk. In winter, concessionaires offer sleigh rides ($5 adults, $3 children 4–8) for a closer look at the elk and wagon rides if there's not enough snow. A visitors center (435/753-6768, noon–5 P.M. Thurs.–Mon., from 10 A.M. Sat.) with displays is also open in winter. During the spring calving season, you might see newborn baby elk. You're not likely to see elk here in the summer months, but the drive in is still pretty.

The 16-mile paved road from Hyrum east to Hardware Ranch follows the scenic Blacksmith Fork Canyon past fishing spots (trout and whitefish), **Shenoah Picnic Area,** and **Pioneer Campground** (sites open late May–

late September, $10, has water). Two small campgrounds, **Friendship** and **Spring** (mid-May–late Oct., $5, no water) are to the north along the Left Hand Fork of Blacksmith Canyon. An extensive snowmobile trail system extends from Hardware Ranch as far as Logan Canyon to the north and the Monte Cristo area to the south, with many side trails.

◖ LOGAN CANYON

From its mouth on the east edge of Logan, Logan Canyon, with its steep limestone cliffs, winds more than 20 miles into the Bear River Range, a northern extension of the Wasatch Mountains. Paved U.S. 89 follows the canyon and is a designated Scenic Byway. If you're looking for a day-trip out of Logan, just head up the canyon; you'll pass lots of picnic areas, campgrounds, fishing spots, and trailheads where you can easily spend a few blissful hours.

Steep slopes on the west rise to rolling plateau country across the top of the range, and moderate slopes descend to Bear Lake on the east. The route climbs to an elevation of 7,800 feet at Bear Lake Summit, from which there's a good view of the lofty Uintas of northeastern Utah. In autumn, maples of the lower canyon turn a brilliant crimson while aspens in the higher country are transformed to gold. Roadside geologic signs explain features in Logan Canyon. Picnicking is free at picnic areas, but you have to pay to picnic at some campgrounds.

A mile-by-mile guide to the canyon is available from the Cache Valley travel office in Logan.

Skiing

Beaver Mountain Ski Area (435/753-4822 snow and road conditions, 435/753-0921 office, ski school, and lift tickets, www.skithebeav.com, 9 A.M.–4 P.M. daily early Dec.–late Mar.), operates three double chairlifts serving 22 runs, the longest of which is 2.25 miles and drops 1,600 vertical feet. A cafeteria, ski shop, rentals, and lessons are available at the day lodge. Adult lift tickets cost $38 full day, $30 half day; children under 12 ski for $30 full day, $25 half day. Go northeast 28 miles on U.S. 89, then north 1.5 miles on Highway 243.

Hiking

A number of easy to moderate hikes makes Logan Canyon a lovely and convenient destination for a little exercise and an eyeful of nature. Four miles up the canyon, **Riverside Nature Trail** winds along the Logan River between Spring Hollow and Guinavah Campgrounds, a 1.5-mile (one-way) stroll with good bird-watching opportunities. From Guinavah, you can loop back to Spring Hollow via the **Crimson Trail;** this more strenuous trail takes you up the limestone cliffs and down in another two miles. It takes its name from the autumn colors visible along the way. Five miles up is the **Wind Cave Trailhead.** Wind Cave, with eroded caverns and arches, is one mile and an 1,100-foot climb from the trailhead.

Jardine Juniper Trail begins at Wood Camp Campground, 10 miles up the canyon. The trail climbs 1,900 feet in 4.4 miles to Old Jardine, a venerable Rocky Mountain juniper tree. Still alive after 1,500 years, it measures about 27 feet in circumference and 45 feet high. The name honors a USU alumnus. A mile farther up the canyon is **Logan Cave,** a 2,000-foot-long cavern that hardy spelunkers can explore; bring at least two light sources.

At **Bear Lake Summit,** 30 miles from Logan, the **Limber Pine Nature Trail** originates at the parking area on the right and terminates at a massive limber pine 25 feet in circumference and 44 feet high. At one time this tree was thought to be the world's oldest and largest limber pine, but a forestry professor at USU discovered that it is really five trees grown together and "only" about 560 years old. The easy self-guided walk takes about an hour; Bear Lake can be seen to the east.

Accommodations

A handsome timber and stone lodge, **Beaver Creek Lodge** (435/753-1707 or 435/753-1076, $89 and up), not only offers rooms daily but also has horseback trail rides, snowmobile rentals, and cross-country ski trails in winter. The lodge is about 28 miles northeast on U.S. 89, just past the turnoff for Beaver Mountain Ski Area.

CAMPGROUNDS

There are 10 Forest Service campgrounds along U.S. 89 in Logan Canyon, so finding a place to pitch a tent shouldn't be difficult. The closest to Logan are **Bridger** and **Spring Hollow** campgrounds (877/444-6777, $10–14), three and four miles respectively from town.

BEAR LAKE

More than 28,000 years ago, faulting in massive blocks of the earth's crust created a basin 50 miles long and 12 miles wide. Bear Lake filled the entire valley during the last ice age but has now receded to cover an area 20 miles long and 8 miles wide at an elevation of 5,900 feet. About half the lake lies in Utah and half in Idaho. The lake's famed turquoise color is thought to be caused by limestone particles suspended in the water.

The ecology of Bear Lake has been upset somewhat by an enterprising irrigation system. In recent centuries, Bear Lake has dwindled in size so greatly that Bear River, which once fed the lake, now totally bypasses it. The lake is kept from becoming saline by farmers who canal water from the river back to the lake during spring runoff and then pump it back into the river during the summer irrigation season.

In recent years, thousands of summer homes and condo developments have sprouted along the shore and hillsides to take advantage of the scenery and water sports. Bear Lake State Park offers a marina and campground on the west shore, a large camping area on the south shore at Rendezvous Beach, and undeveloped campgrounds on the east shore. For information on Bear Lake, contact the Bear Lake Convention and Visitors Bureau (800/448-BEAR, www.bearlake.org).

Garden City and Vicinity

This small town (year-round pop. 400) on the

© W. C. MCRAE

ready for some four-wheeling at Bear Lake

east shore at the junction of U.S. 89 and Highway 30 comes to life in summer. There are a number of shops, restaurants, and hotels, as well as the **Pickleville Playhouse** (2.8 miles south of Garden City, 435/946-2918), which features family entertainment on summer evenings. A Western-style cookout precedes the show.

The town celebrates the harvest of its most famous crop with the **Raspberry Days Festival,** the first weekend in August, featuring a parade, the crowning of Miss Raspberry, a Little Buckaroo Rodeo, crafts, and entertainment. The **Mountain Man Rendezvous** reenacts the big gatherings of fur trappers and Native Americans that took place at Bear Lake in the summers of 1826 and 1827; the modern event is held the second weekend of September at Rendezvous Beach in Bear Lake State Park (435/946-3343).

Bear Lake State Park

The 71,000 acres of Bear Lake give plenty of room to water-ski, sail, or fish. Bear Lake State Park (435/946-3343 or 800/322-3700 for campground reservations) offers three recreation areas. The **marina** (year-round, $7 day use, $15 camping), one mile north of Garden City on U.S. 89, offers boat slips protected by a breakwater, a boat ramp, a swimming area, picnic tables, a campground with showers, and ranger offices.

Wide and sandy, **Rendezvous Beach** (early May–late Sept., $7 day use, $15 camping, $21 with hookups), eight miles south of Garden City near Laketown, attracts visitors to the lake's southern shore. The park has a day-use area with a boat-rental concession and several campgrounds with showers. Ask at the entrance station for recommended places to camp; some sites have lake views, some offer hookups, and some are set up mainly for RVs.

East Beach (year-round, $7 day-use, $9 camping) is on the lake's much less developed eastern shore. In addition to the state park boat ramps, six primitive campgrounds and day-use areas are about all that's here; outhouses are provided, but only South Eden has drinking water.

Bear Lake National Wildlife Refuge

This wetlands refuge occupies 17,600 acres of marshlands north of the lake and is a favored stopping place for sandhill cranes, herons, white pelicans, egrets, and many species of ducks. Four species of fish not found any other place in the world evolved in Bear Lake. One of these, the Bonneville cisco, attracts anglers by the thousands. During spawning in January, nets are used to dip the small (6–8 inches long), tasty fish from the icy water. Ice fishing is very popular; fish sought year-round by anglers include the native Bear Lake cutthroat and Bonneville whitefish and the introduced rainbow and Mackinaw trout and yellow perch. Keep an eye out for the Bear Lake monster—a dark dragonlike creature 90 feet long that spouts water!

Accommodations

UNDER $100

Bear Lake Motor Lodge (just south of the

BEAR LAKE MONSTER

When white settlers first arrived in the Bear Lake area, the local Native Americans warned them that a monster lived in the lake. The beast was described as being of the "legged serpent" variety and was said to have carried humans away. Few Native Americans of the area would bathe in the lake or camp nearby, but settlers scoffed – even after a few sightings by whites.

In 1868, no fewer than 20 people reported seeing the monster, all within a period of a few weeks. These included a few citizens of local repute and a wagonload of eight travelers. The monster gained fame and many believers, both in the area and beyond. Soon monsters were "spotted" in other lakes, including a 45-foot-long alligator that came out of the Great Salt Lake and smashed a campsite as the residents fled. This proliferation of tall tales began to cast doubts on the existence of Bear Lake's monster, and fewer sightings were reported.

There were even a few legends explaining the monster's demise. One farmer told of a huge creature from the lake that hungrily devoured part of his flock of sheep. As the surviving animals fled, the monster's eye caught a coil of barbed wire about the size and shape of huddled prey and swallowed it whole. By the farmer's account, the resulting pain drove the beast back into the lake and it was never seen again. Rangers at Minnetonka Cave offer another story. They maintain the monster was intimidated by the surrounding human population and sought refuge in the cave where it survived on cave popcorn and coral. In this version, the monster was felled by a collapsing cave wall, with all but a clenched claw buried under rubble. The existing trail was built over that rockfall and rangers today still point out a piece of flowstone just under the trail that strangely does resemble a large dragon claw.

highway junction at 50 S. Bear Lake Blvd., 435/946-3271, $65 and up) has basic rooms, some with kitchenettes, plus a restaurant and beach access. **Ideal Beach Resort** (2144 S. Bear Lake Blvd., 435/946-3364 or 800/634-1018, $70 and up), 3.3 miles south of Garden City, offers motel and condo accommodations (half-week or longer) year-round, plus camping and a restaurant. The Ideal also offers boat rentals, a beach, swimming pools, tennis, and miniature golf. The adjacent nine-hole **Bear Lake Golf Course** (435/946-8742),is open to the public.

OVER $100

Harbor Village Inn (900 N. Bear Lake Blvd., 435/946-3448 or 800/324-6840, year-round, $115 and up) offers suites with full kitchens and fireplaces, plus use of tennis courts, lap pool, and hot tub.

CAMPGROUNDS

In addition to the state park campgrounds, there's the **Bear Lake KOA** (435/946-3454, May–Oct.), 0.8 mile north of Garden City on U.S. 89 near the state park marina. It offers a swimming pool, miniature golf, tennis, store, showers, cabins and laundry.

Food

Each of the above three lodgings (Bear Lake Motor Lodge, Ideal Beach Resort, Harbor Village Inn) has its own restaurant. Additionally, **Bear Lake West** (208/945-2222) is 4.5 miles north of Garden City, just across the Idaho border three miles south of Fish Haven, and has a nine-hole golf course and a steak and seafood restaurant (Sun. brunch, dinner Thurs.–Sat. in summer).

GREAT BASIN DESERT

Utah's Wild West remains nearly as wild as ever. Rugged mountain ranges and barren desert valleys have always discouraged all but the most determined individuals. Explorers, pioneers in wagon trains, Pony Express riders, and telegraph linemen crossed this inhospitable land with only the desire to reach the other side. It took the promise of gold and silver to lure large numbers of people into the jagged hills. Fading ghost towns still show the industry of the early miners. Hardy ranchers also braved the isolation to grow hay and run their cattle and sheep. Shortage of water has always been the limiting factor to development, though the U.S. military has found these remote deserts to be alluring for weapons testing: Several bombing ranges and munitions depots dot the countryside.

Though west-central Utah is now one of the driest parts of the Great Basin, a far different scene existed some 10,000 years ago. Freshwater Lake Bonneville then covered 20,000 square miles—one-fourth of Utah—and forests blanketed the mountains that poked above the lake waters.

Today, clouds moving in from the Pacific Ocean lose much of their moisture to the Sierra Nevada and other towering mountain ranges in California and Nevada. By the time the depleted clouds reach west-central Utah, only the Deep Creek, Stansbury, and southern Wah Wah Mountains reach high enough (over 12,000 feet) to gather sufficient rain and snow to support permanent streams.

Availability of water determines the quantity and variety of wildlife. Of the larger mammals,

© JUDY JEWELL

HIGHLIGHTS

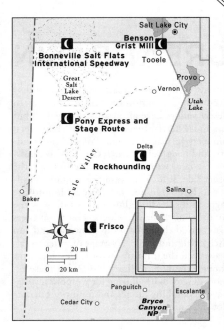

◖ Bonneville Salt Flats International Speedway: Even if you're not here during August's Speed Week races, you'll want to pull off the freeway to check out the perfectly flat salt flats, where land speed records are regularly set (page 162).

◖ Benson Grist Mill: This perfectly preserved grain mill from the 1850s offers a fascinating glimpse into the agrarian life of frontier Utah (page 165).

◖ Pony Express and Stage Route: Explore Utah's outback by following the route of the old Pony Express, which carried mail between Salt Lake City and California in the 1860s (page 167).

◖ Rockhounding: The deserts around Delta are filled with curious minerals and fossils, and local businesses rent shovels, hammers, and other tools to make your rockhounding experience rewarding (page 175).

◖ Frisco: One of the best-preserved ghost towns in Utah, Frisco is a photographer's delight. Walk the wind-blown streets to experience the reality of Old West mining camps (page 180).

LOOK FOR ◖ TO FIND RECOMMENDED SIGHTS, ACTIVITIES, DINING, AND LODGING.

mule deer and pronghorn are most widespread. Elk can be found in mountainous areas east of Delta. Rocky Mountain bighorn sheep have been reintroduced in the Deep Creek Range. Herds of wild horses roam the Confusion and House Ranges. Vast numbers of birds visit Fish Springs National Wildlife Refuge and other desert oases during early spring and late autumn migrations.

Nomadic Paleo-Indians entered this region about 15,000 years ago, as ice-age lakes such as Lake Bonneville began to shrink. These nomadic hunters and gatherers proved well

suited to the drying environment, relying on small game and wild plant foods. It's likely the modern Goshute—or Gosiutes—and Utes descended from these ancient peoples.

The Goshute once occupied northwest Utah and adjacent Nevada; they now live in the Goshute and Skull Valley Indian reservations. The Utes had the greatest range of all of Utah's tribes, extending from west-central Utah into Colorado and New Mexico; they now have reservations in northeast Utah and southwest Colorado.

In the early 1860s, prospectors found placer

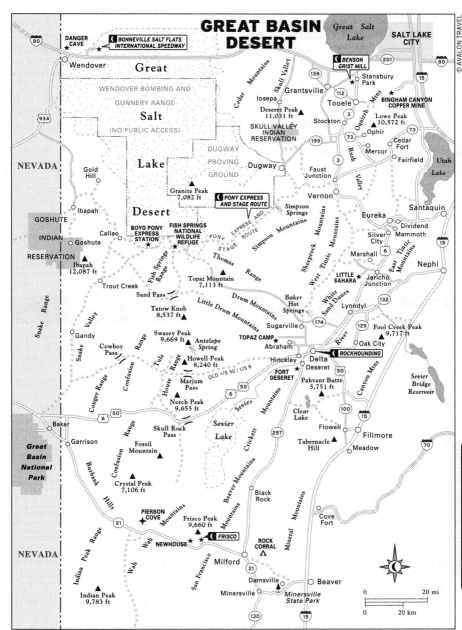

GREAT BASIN DESERT

gold deposits in the desert mountain ranges, though significant production had to wait for the arrival of the transcontinental railroad in 1869. Deposits of gold, silver, copper, lead, and zinc were found in quick succession. Active gold mining continues in the Mercur, Tintic, and Detroit districts.

PLANNING YOUR TIME

Admittedly, the barren deserts and arid mountain ranges of west central Utah won't lure many travelers away from the ski resorts of the Wasatch Range or the red rock canyons of Utah's national parks. However, if you enjoy solitude, expansive landscapes, and the thrill of exploring a land little changed since white explorers first arrived, this corner of Utah is for you. Most travelers will find it sufficient merely to cross the desert on one of the paved roads, either on I-80 between Salt Lake City and Wendover, Nevada, or one of the two highways that link to Great Basin National Park in eastern Nevada. As an add-on to a Utah road trip itinerary, this region should claim no more than a day of driving and exploration.

Roads do provide surprisingly good access for such a remote region. Paved I-80, U.S. 50, U.S. 6, and Hwy. 21 cross the Great Basin Desert, while dirt roads branch off in all directions. Following the Pony Express and Stage Route from Fairfield to Ibapah might be the most unique driving tour; you experience some of the same unfenced wilderness as did the tough young Pony Express riders. You can negotiate this and many other back roads by car in dry weather. For the adventurous, the wildly beautiful mountain ranges offer countless hiking possibilities—though you'll have to rough it. Hardly any developed trails exist.

Great Salt Lake Desert

Lake Bonneville once covered 20,000 square miles in Utah, Idaho, and Nevada; when the lake broke through the Sawtooth Mountains, its level declined precipitously, leaving the 2,500-square-mile Great Salt Lake and huge expanses of salt flats to its south and west. These salt-flat remnants of Lake Bonneville are almost completely white and level and go on for more than a hundred miles in some directions. It is commonly said that one can see the earth's curvature at the horizon, though this apparently takes a very discerning eye.

Other than the section traversed by I-80, most of the Great Salt Lake Desert is off-limits to ordinary travelers, as it is used by the military to test weapons of all sorts. Jet aircraft and helicopters occasionally break the silence in flights above the Wendover Bombing and Gunnery Range. Scientists and engineers at Dugway Proving Grounds work on chemical and biological weapons. The base received some notoriety in 1968 after 6,500 sheep died on neighboring ranches. The military never admitted that it had released toxic warfare chemicals, but it did compensate the ranchers. Just south of Tooele you'll see the neat rows of buildings across the vast Tooele Army Depot, which functions as a storage, maintenance, repair, and training center. In 1996, the Army began incineration of part of the U.S. chemical weapons cache at the depot.

WENDOVER AND VICINITY

Wendover began in 1907 as a watering station during construction of the Western Pacific Railroad. The highway went through in 1925, marking the community's beginnings as a travelers' stop. Wendover Air Force Base got its start in 1940 and soon grew to become one of the world's largest military complexes. During World War II, crews of bombers and other aircraft learned their navigation,

WHAT'S OUT THERE?

Two military installations – the Utah Training and Test Range and the Dugway Proving Ground – and the Tooele Army Depot, a chemical and biological weapons storage area, occupy much of the land in the Great Salt Lake Desert. They are all extremely high-security areas.

UTAH TRAINING AND TEST RANGE

The UTTR provides the huge amount of land necessary to train military air crews and test weapons. It is, put simply, a bombing range, with many mock targets erected for fighter pilots and their crews to practice on. The UTTR was created in 1979 for cruise missile testing. The large amount of land and airspace required for that purpose has made the UTTR a natural place to test smart munitions, long-range standoff weapons, remote controlled/unmanned air vehicles, boost-glide precision-guided munitions, air-to-air missiles, and autonomous loitering anti-radiation missiles.

The UTTR also has the largest overland contiguous block of supersonic authorized restricted air space in the continental United States. The airspace is situated over 2,624 square miles of Department of Defense land, of which 1,490 square miles are owned by the U.S. Air Force. The remainder is owned and managed by the U.S. Army at Dugway Proving Ground.

Though the UTTR quite obviously does not allow visitors, the Hill Aerospace Museum, located at the Hill Air Force Base just south of Ogden in the town of Roy, is open to the public and has many displays of military aircraft (see the *Northern Utah* chapter).

DUGWAY PROVING GROUND

The primary mission of Dugway Proving Ground is to evaluate, test, and develop chemical defense; biological defense; incendiary, smoke, and obscurant systems; and to conduct environmental technology testing. Dugway sells its services to all authorized customers, including United States and foreign governments, as well as nongovernmental organizations. In addition, Dugway is a major range and test facility for chemical and biological defense testing.

Dugway Proving Ground encompasses about 800,000 acres. In addition to chemical and biological defensive testing and environment characterization and remediation technology testing, Dugway is the Defense Department's leader in testing battlefield smokes and obscurants. The installation currently consists of more than 600 buildings with a total value of over $240 million.

As if all this weren't enough, Dugway has developed a following among UFOlogists, who suspect that the base's secret status, underground facilities, and low profile make it the perfect place for sequestering of "alien artifacts" and other items of extraterrestrial origin.

TOOELE ARMY DEPOT

In the summer of 1996, the army began burning part of the nation's store of chemical weapons at the Tooele Army Depot, located 10 miles south of the town of Tooele and 55 miles from Salt Lake City. The depot held the nation's single largest cache of chemical weapons, with 44 percent of the arsenal stored in underground bunkers called igloos. Part of the reason for burning the weapons, besides treaty requirements with the former U.S.S.R, was that there was a far greater risk of leakage and environmental damage in leaving the chemical agents in bunkers than there in incinerating them. The gases destroyed include sarin, mustard gas, nerve gas, and lewisite, a skin-blistering agent. The last of Tooele Army Depot's chemical weapons was destroyed in 2007.

GREAT BASIN DESERT

formation flying, gunnery, and bombing skills above the 3.5 million acres of desert belonging to the base. Only after the war ended did the government reveal that one of the bomber groups had been training in preparation for dropping atomic bombs on Japan. Little remains of the base—once a city of nearly 20,000 people. Hill Air Force Base, near Ogden, continues to use the vast military reserve for training air crews. Wendover now has the tacky grandiosity of a Nevada border town.

C Bonneville Salt Flats International Speedway

A brilliant white layer of salt left behind by prehistoric Lake Bonneville covers more than 44,000 acres of the Great Salt Lake Desert. For much of the year, a shallow layer of water sits atop the salt flats. Wave action planes the surface almost perfectly level—some say you can see the curvature of the earth here. The hot sun usually dries out the flats enough for speed runs in summer and autumn. Cars began running across the salt in 1914 and continue to set faster and faster times. Rocket-powered vehicles have exceeded 600 miles per hour. Expansive courses can be laid out; the main speedway is 10 miles long and 80 feet wide. A small tent city goes up near the course during the annual **Speed Week** in August; vehicles in an amazing variety of styles and ages take off individually to set new records in their classes. The salt flats, just east of Wendover, are easy to access: Take I-80 Exit 4 and follow the paved road five miles north, then east. Signs and markers indicate if and where you can drive on the salt. Soft spots underlain by mud can trap vehicles venturing off the safe areas. Take care not to be on the track when racing events are being held!

Silver Island Mountains

These rugged mountains rise above the salt flats northeast of Wendover. You can visit them and their rocky canyons on a 54-mile loop drive. Take I-80 Exit 4, go north 1.2 miles, turn left 0.8 mile on a gravel road, then turn right at the sign for the Silver Island Mountains. The road

loops counterclockwise around the mountains, crosses Lebby Pass, and returns to the junction near I-80. Another road goes north from Lebby Pass to Lucin in the extreme northwest corner of Utah. High-clearance vehicles do best on these roads, though cars can often negotiate them in dry weather. The *Benchmark Road and Recreation Atlas* to Utah shows approximate road alignments and terrain.

Practicalities

Wendover has a split personality—half the town lies in Utah and half in Nevada. On both sides you'll find accommodations and restaurants where you can take a break from long drives on I-80. Five casino hotels, eight motels, and two campgrounds offer places to stay. Six casinos on the Nevada side provide a chance to lose your money in the usual gambling games. Most of the town's visitor facilities line Wendover Boulevard, also known as State Highway, which parallels the interstate. Lodgings are cheaper on the Utah side. The **Day's Inn** (685 E. Wendover Blvd., 435/665-2215 or 800/329-7466, $60 and up) is the nicest place on the Utah side. The other lodgings are all well under $50; to really pinch pennies, the **Motel 6** (561 E. Wendover Blvd., 435/665-2267, about $35) is one of the chain's better efforts.

GRANTSVILLE

Here on the edges of the Great Salt Lake Desert, old buildings and tall Lombardy poplars reflect the pioneer heritage of this rural community, first settled in 1851 and named Willow Creek Fort. The museum in town offers a look at local history. Grantsville stretches along Hwy. 138 nine miles northwest of Tooele. For hiking and camping in the Stansbury Mountains, crowned by 11,031-foot Deseret Peak, head south 10 miles to South Willow Canyon Recreation Area.

Donner-Reed Pioneer Museum

Early residents built this one-room adobe schoolhouse within the Grantsville fort walls in 1861. Today it's a museum honoring the

IOSEPA

Now a ghost town in Skull Valley with little more than a cemetery, foundations, and a few houses, Iosepa once had a population of 226 Polynesian settlers. Devout Hawaiian Mormons who desired to live in the promised land of Utah began the settlement in 1889. All the good farmland around Salt Lake City had been taken, so the group wound up in this desolate valley west of the Stansbury Mountains. Undaunted by the harsh climate and scarcity of water, the Hawaiians laid out a townsite and named it Iosepa ("Joseph") after the sixth president of the LDS Church, Joseph F. Smith. Livestock was raised, crops and trees were planted, and roses bloomed in the new desert home. The islanders celebrated Pioneer Day on August 28, the date they arrived in Skull Valley, with feasts of poi and roast pig. Not all harvests produced a profit, however, and life here was hard. Leprosy appeared in 1896, and its several victims were forced to live in a separate building – Utah's only known leper colony. News in 1916 of plans to build a Mormon temple in Hawaii brought a wave of homesickness, and within a year the struggling settlement disbanded.

Today Iosepa is a large ranch along the road 15 miles south of I-80 Timpie Springs Exit 77. There's no sign at the ranch, but it's the largest in the area, with four houses along the road and several farm buildings. The two small frame houses belonged to the original Hawaiian settlement; two other surviving buildings are farther back. Residents don't mind people visiting the old townsite, but ask first. To see the cemetery, turn east past a group of mailboxes and the northernmost house, go through a gate, then keep left at a fork. The cemetery, marked by six flagpoles, is three-quarters of a mile in; the road may be too rough for cars. Time and the elements have reduced the graves to mounds of gravel with just a few marble headstones. Their Hawaiian names seem out of place in this lonely desert valley.

Donner-Reed wagon train of 1846. These pioneers crossed the Great Salt Lake Desert to the west with great difficulty, then became trapped by snow while attempting to shortcut through the Sierra Nevada to California. Of the 87 people who started the trip, only 47 desperate people survived the harsh winter—by eating boiled boots and harnesses and the frozen flesh of dead companions. Museum displays include a large collection of guns and pioneer artifacts found abandoned on the salt flats, pottery, arrowheads, and other Native American artifacts. Outside you can try out Grantsville's original iron jail and see an early log cabin, blacksmith shop, and old wagons. Another adobe building across the street served as a church and dates from 1866. The museum is open on request during the summer; free. To view the exhibits, visit or call Grantsville City Hall (corner of Park and Main, 435/884-3411, 8:30 A.M.–5 P.M. Mon.–Fri.). From the city hall, go two blocks west on Main to Cooley Street, then one block north to the museum.

Bonneville Seabase

Scuba divers can enjoy ocean-type diving in the middle of the mudflats. A natural pool here was found to have salinity so close to that of the ocean that marine creatures could thrive in it. Several dozen species have been introduced, including groupers, triggerfish, damsel fish, clown fish, and lobsters. The springs are geothermally heated, so winter cold is no problem. The original pool has been expanded and new pools were created by dredging. User fees run $15 per person; you can rent full equipment for scuba diving ($21) or snorkeling ($11). Bonneville Seabase (9390 W. Hwy. 138, 435/884-3874) is five miles northwest of Grantsville.

STANSBURY MOUNTAINS

Not all of western Utah is desert, as a visit to this section of the Wasatch National Forest southwest of Grantsville will show. Trails lead to Deseret Peak and other good day-hiking and backcountry destinations. Grantsville Reservoir, South Willow Canyon Recreation Area, and trailheads into the Deseret Peak Wilderness

GREAT BASIN DESERT

are accessed via the South Willow Canyon on the southeast slope of the Stansbury Mountains. Signs for Willow Creek Recreation Area on the west end of Grantsville will guide you south onto South Willow Road. Turn right onto a paved road after four miles and continue west up South Willow Canyon. For more information about the area, contact the Salt Lake Ranger District office (6944 South 3000 East, Salt Lake City, UT 84121, 435/524-5042).

Follow the paved road only a few miles from the South Willow Road junction to reach **Grantsville Reservoir,** popular for water sports, trout fishing, picnicking, and camping; campsites begin to appear after three miles.

More sites are available at the BLM's **Clover Creek Campground,** at the southern end of the Stansbury Mountains on a spring-fed creek. There's no developed water or fee. From Grantsville head out South Willow Canyon Road and continue past the recreation area turnoff to Hwy. 199 at Rush Valley.

Turn right onto Hwy. 199 and travel west; the campground is eight miles from the junction with Hwy. 36.

Deseret Peak Wilderness Area

Hikers enjoy expansive views amidst alpine forests and glacial cirques in the Deseret Peak Wilderness Area in the central portion of the Stansbury Mountains. The moderately difficult 3,600-foot climb to the summit is 7.5 miles round-trip. Most of the way is easy to follow, though it's recommended that you carry the USGS topo maps Deseret Peak West and Deseret Peak East (7.5-minute) or Deseret Peak (15-minute). The trail begins at Loop Campground at the end of the road up South Willow Canyon. On a clear day atop the summit you can see much of the Wasatch Range on the eastern horizon, the Great Salt Lake to the north, Pilot Peak in Nevada to the northwest, the Great Salt Lake Desert to the west, and countless desert ranges to the southwest.

Tooele

To sound like a native, pronounce the town's name "too-WILL-uh." Origin of the word is uncertain, but it may honor the Goshute chief Tuilla. The attractive town (pop. 22,500) lies 34 miles southwest of Salt Lake City in the western foothills of the Oquirrh (pronounced OH-ker) Mountains and has become a bedroom community for Salt Lake City workers. At its 4,900-foot elevation, Tooele offers fine views of the Great Salt Lake to the north and Tooele Valley and Stansbury Mountains to the west. Mormon pioneers settled here in 1849 to farm and raise livestock, but today the major industries are the nearby Tooele Army Depot—site of recently completed chemical-weapons incineration—the Dugway Proving Ground, and mining. Visitors wanting to know more about the region's history will enjoy the town's several museums. Other attractions in the area include a scenic drive and overlook in the Oquirrhs, the ghost town of

Ophir, and hiking and camping in the nearby Stansbury Mountains.

SIGHTS
Tooele Railroad Museum

A steam locomotive and a collection of old railroad cars surround Tooele's original (1909) train station, now the Tooele Railroad Museum (35 N. Broadway, 435/882-2836, 1–4 P.M. Tues.–Sat. Memorial Day–Labor Day weekends, by donation). Step inside to see the restored station office and old photos showing railway workers, steam engines, and trestle construction. You might also meet and hear stories from retired railway men who volunteer as museum guides. Mining photos and artifacts illustrate life and work in the early days at Ophir, Mercur, Bauer, and other booming communities now faded to ghosts. Much of the old laboratory equipment and tools on display came from the Tooele Smelter, built by

International Smelter and Refining Company in 1907–1909. The smelter processed copper, lead, and zinc until 1972. Ore came over the Oquirrh Mountains by aerial tramway from the Bingham Mine. More than 3,000 people worked here during the hectic World War II years. A highly detailed model shows the modern Carr Fork Mill, built near Tooele but used only 90 days before being dismantled and shipped to a more profitable site in Papua, New Guinea. Two railroad cars, once part of an air force mobile ballistic missile train, contain medical equipment and antique furniture. Outside, kids can ride the scale railway (Saturday only), check out a caboose, or explore a replica of a mine.

Daughters of Utah Pioneers Museum

Meet Tooele's pioneers through 128 framed pictures and see their clothing and other possessions at this downtown museum (39 E. Vine St.). The small stone building dates from 1867 and once served as a courthouse for Tooele County. The little log cabin next door, built in 1856, was one of the town's first residences. The Daughters of Utah Pioneers Museum (DUP) is open some Saturdays in summer and for groups on request; call the numbers on the front (the small DUP museums are run by volunteers and those who are on call to open the museums change from season to season and year to year).

C Benson Grist Mill

Pioneers constructed this mill (one block west of Mills Junction, eight miles north of Tooele, 435/882-7678, 10 A.M.–4 P.M. May–Nov.), one of the oldest buildings in western Utah, in 1854. Wooden pegs and rawhide strips hold the timbers together. E. T. Benson, grandfather of past LDS president Ezra Taft Benson, supervised its construction for the LDS Church. The mill produced flour until 1938, then ground only animal feed until closing in the 1940s. Local people began to restore the exterior in 1986. Much of the original machinery inside is still intact, and offers a fascinating glimpse of 19th century agricultural technology. Antique farm machinery, a granary, log cabin, blacksmith shop, and other buildings stand on the grounds to the east. Ruins of the Utah Wool Pullery, which once removed millions of tons of wool annually from pelts, stand to the west.

RECREATION
Sailboarding

Ten miles south of Tooele is the small town of Stockton on the shore of Rush Lake, where sailboarding has gained great popularity in recent years. Rush Lake's location between two mountain ranges and its proximity to Salt Lake guarantee sailboarders steady currents of south winds, with plenty of strong 8–15 mph blasts on hot days.

Mountain Biking

Soldier Canyon, six miles south of Tooele, draws mountain bikers. It's a four-mile climb to the mining ghost town of Jacob City, 9,000 feet above sea level.

Other Activities

The **city park** (corner of Vine and 2nd West, 435/882-3247) offers picnicking, playground, and an indoor swimming pool (year-round). During the summer months it may be more fun to swim in the outdoor pool at the **Stansbury Park Golf Course** (435/882-2426). Other golfing choices are the nine-hole **Oquirrh Hills Golf Course** (Seventh and Edgemont, 435/882-4220) on the east side of town, or the 18-hole course in **Stansbury Park** (435/882-4162) eight miles north on Hwy. 36.

ACCOMMODATIONS

All motels lie conveniently along Main Street (Hwy. 36). On the north end, the **Villa Motel** (475 N. Main, 435/882-4551 or 800/882-4551, $55 and up) has basic rooms, some with kitchenettes. The **Best Western Inn Tooele** (365 N. Main, 435/882-5010 or 800/448-5010, $81 and up) has an indoor pool, a spa, and a couple of rooms with kitchens. **American Inn and Suites** (491 S. Main, 435/882-6100 or 800/228-5150, $75 and up) offers free full breakfasts, kitchenettes and efficiency kitchens, laundry facilities, and a pool and spa. Rates are discounted on weekends. The new **Hampton Inn** (461 S. Main, 435/882-6102 or 800/HAMPTON, $125 and up) has a pool, hot tub, and free breakfast bar, and each room has an efficiency kitchen.

FOOD
Somewhat oddly in this prototypically Old West town, many of the good eating options are ethnic; main courses rarely top $10 at any of the following. Eat Chinese-Polynesian-American at the **Sun Lok Yuen** (615 N. Main, 435/882-3003, lunch and dinner Mon.–Sat.). **Athena's** (21 E. Vine, 435/882-8035, lunch and dinner Mon.–Sat.) serves Greek food. For Mexican try **Melina's Mexican Restaurant** (1205 N. Main, 435/843-1496, lunch and dinner daily).

Tracks (1641 N. Main, 435/882-4040, lunch and dinner daily), a private club with easy membership, has some of the best food and the liveliest atmosphere in town (nothing fancy, but it's good bar food) and microbrews on tap.

INFORMATION
The **Tooele Chamber of Commerce** (201 N. Main, 435/882-0690 or 800/378-0690, www.2wheelah.com, 9 A.M.–4 P.M. Mon.–Fri.) can tell you about the sights and services here. Its office is upstairs in the Key Bank.

TRANSPORTATION
Utah Transit Authority (UTA) (435/882-9031) buses connect Tooele with Salt Lake City and other towns of the Wasatch Front Monday–Saturday. The main bus stop is at Main and 4th South.

South of Tooele

GHOST TOWNS
Ophir
Picturesque old buildings and log cabins line the bottom of Ophir Canyon in the Oquirrh Mountains, which once boomed with saloons, dance halls, houses of ill repute, hotels, restaurants, and shops. In the 1860s, soldiers under General Patrick Connor heard stories of Native Americans mining silver and lead for ornaments and bullets. The soldier-prospectors tracked the mines to this canyon and staked claims. By 1870 a town was born—named after the biblical land of Ophir, where King Solomon's mines were located. Much of the ore went to General Connor's large smelter at nearby Stockton. Later the St. John and Ophir Railroad entered the canyon to haul away the rich ores of silver, lead, and zinc and small amounts of gold and copper. Ophir's population peaked at 6,000, but, unlike most other mining towns of the region, Ophir never quite died. People still live here and occasionally

prospect in the hills. The city hall and some houses have been restored, and the new **Ophir Gophir** (801/882-9903) sells groceries and refreshments, but canyon vegetation has claimed the rest of the old structures.

Paved roads go all the way into town. From Tooele, head south 12 miles on Hwy. 36 through Stockton, turn left five miles on Hwy. 73, then left 3.5 miles to Ophir.

Mercur Gold Mine
General Connor's soldiers also discovered silver in the canyon southeast of Ophir during the late 1860s. After a slow start, prospectors made rich strikes and the rush was on. The mining camp of Lewiston boomed in the mid-1870s, then busted by 1880 as the deposits worked out. Arie Pinedo, a prospector from Bavaria, began to poke around the dying camp and located the Mercur Lode of gold and mercury ore. He and other would-be miners were frustrated when all attempts to extract gold from

the ore failed. Then in 1890, a new cyanide process proved effective, and a new boomtown arose around the Golden Gate Mill five years later. Though fire wiped out the business district in 1902, Mercur was rebuilt and had an estimated population of more than 8,000 by 1910. Only three years later, the town closed up when ore bodies seemed depleted. Mining revived in the 1930s and again in the 1980s. Thanks to strip mining, virtually nothing remains of this ghost town.

◖ PONY EXPRESS AND STAGE ROUTE

Relive some of the Old West by driving the Pony Express route across western Utah. The scenic route goes from spring to spring as it winds through several small mountain ranges and across open plains, skirting the worst of the Great Salt Lake Desert. Interpretive signs and monuments along the way describe how Pony Express riders rode swiftly on horseback to bring the country closer together. The 140 miles between Fairfield in the east and Ibapah near the Nevada border provide a sense of history and appreciation for the land lost to motorists speeding along I-80.

Allow at least a full day for the drive and bring food, water, and a full tank of gas. The Bureau of Land Management has campgrounds at Simpson Springs and south of Callao. No motels or restaurants line the road, but Ibapah has two gas station/grocery stores. You can travel the well-graded gravel road by car; just watch for the usual backcountry hazards of wildlife, rocks, and washouts. Adventurous travelers may want to make side trips for rockhounding, hiking, or visiting old mining sites. Always keep vehicles on existing roads—sand and mud flats can be treacherously deceptive.

You can begin your trip down the historic route from the Stagecoach Inn at Fairfield (from Salt Lake City or Provo, take I-15 to Lehi, then go 21 miles west on Hwy. 73). You can also begin at Faust Junction, 30 miles south of Tooele on Hwy. 36, or Ibapah, 51 miles south of Wendover off U.S. 93A. The

A BRIEF HISTORY OF THE PONY EXPRESS

In 1860, Pony Express officials put together a chain of stations between St. Joseph, Missouri, and Sacramento, California. Relays of frontier-toughened men covered the 1,838-mile distance in 10 days. Riders stopped at stations spaced about 12 miles apart to change horses. Only after changing horses about six times did the rider complete his day's work. Despite the hazards of frontier travel, only one mail pouch was ever lost, and Native American conflicts held up service for only a single month. Historians credit the daring enterprise with providing communications vital to keeping California aligned with the Union during the Civil War and proving that the West could be crossed in all kinds of weather – thus convincing skeptical politicians that a transcontinental railroad could be built. The Pony Express operated for only 18 months; completion of the transcontinental telegraph in October 1861 put the riders out of work. The company, which received no government assistance, failed to make a profit for its owners.

BLM has an information kiosk and small picnic area 1.8 miles west of Faust Junction. For the latest road conditions and travel information, contact the BLM Salt Lake District office (2370 South 2300 West, Salt Lake City, UT 84119, 801/977-4300). The following are points of interest along the route.

Stagecoach Inn State Park and Camp Floyd

This two-story adobe and frame hotel was built by John Carson in 1858. The Stagecoach Inn was the first stop south of Salt Lake City on the Overland Stage Route and also a stop on the Historic Pony Express Route. Inside the restored inn you can see where weary riders slept and sat around tables swapping stories.

GREAT BASIN DESERT

Now part of Stagecoach Inn State Park (18035 West 1540 North in Fairfield, 801/768-8932, 9 A.M.–5 P.M. daily Apr.–Oct. 15, closed Sundays in winter, $2), the inn sits across from the remains of Camp Floyd, a Civil War–era military fort. Stagecoach Inn is 36 miles northwest of Provo.

Simpson Springs

Native Americans had long used these excellent springs before the first white men came through. The name honors Captain J. H. Simpson, who stopped here in 1859 while leading an army survey across western Utah and Nevada. About the same time, George Chorpenning built a mail station here later used by the Pony Express and Overland Express companies. A reconstructed stone cabin on the old site shows what the station looked like. Ruins of a nearby cabin built in 1893 contain stones from the first station. Foundations of a Civilian Conservation Corps camp lie across the road. In 1939, the young men of the CCC built historic markers, improved roads, and worked on conservation projects. The BLM campground higher up on the hillside has water (except in winter) and good views across the desert. A $3 per-vehicle fee is charged; do not drink the water. Sparse juniper trees grow at the 5,100-foot elevation. Simpson Springs is 25 miles west of Faust Junction and 67 miles east of Callao.

Fish Springs National Wildlife Refuge

The Pony Express station once located here no longer exists, but you can visit the 10,000 acres of marsh and lake that attract abundant bird- and wildlife. Waterfowl and marsh birds stop over in greatest numbers during their early-spring and late-autumn migrations. Many smaller birds nest here in late spring and early summer, though they're difficult to see in the

---

CROSSING THE GREAT BASIN DESERT

Imposing terrain and a scarcity of water discouraged early explorers from crossing the Great Basin region. In 1776, the Spanish became the first non-Indians to visit west-central Utah when members of the Dominguez-Escalante Expedition left the Utah Lake area and headed southwest, passing near the present-day towns of Delta and Milford.

Most American mountain men of the 1820s also kept to the Great Basin's edge — but not Jedediah Smith. With a party of 17 men, Smith set out in 1826 from northern Utah for Spanish California, searching for new fur-trapping areas. When Smith returned to Utah with two companions, the little group nearly perished in deep snows in the Sierra Nevada and from thirst in the desert.

Government explorer John C. Frémont named and made the first scientific studies of the Great Basin in 1845, putting to rest myths about the Great Salt Lake's monsters, whirlpools, and subterranean outlets to the Pacific.

In the following year, travelers began crossing the Great Basin as a shortcut to California. Horses and mules made the crossing safely, but the Donner-Reed wagon train met with disaster. Mud in the Great Salt Lake Desert slowed the group so much that they ran out of water and lost some of their wagons and oxen. The exhausted and demoralized group reached the Sierra Nevada late in the season, when snowstorms trapped and killed 40 of the 87 emigrants.

In 1859, Captain J. S. Simpson surveyed a military road to the south of the treacherous desert to connect Camp Floyd in central Utah with Carson Valley in western Nevada. Swift riders of the Pony Express used the road, known as the South-Central Overland Route, in 1860-1861, before the telegraph ended this brief chapter of American history. The Lincoln Highway, America's first designated transcontinental motoring route, included part of this road from 1910 to 1927.

thick vegetation. Opportunistic hawks and other raptors circle overhead. A self-guided auto tour makes an 11.5-mile loop through the heart of the refuge. Most of the route follows dikes between the human-made lakes and offers good vantage points from which to see ducks, geese, egrets, herons, avocets, and other water birds. The tour route and a picnic area near the entrance are open from sunrise to sunset; no camping is allowed in the refuge. Stop at the information booth near the entrance to pick up a brochure, see photos of birds found at the refuge, and read notes on the area's history. Fish Springs National Wildlife Refuge (435/831-5353) is 42 miles west of Simpson Springs and 25 miles east of Callao.

Boyd Pony Express Station

Portions remain of the station's original rock wall, and signs give the history of the station and the Pony Express. Find the station 13 miles west of Fish Springs and 12 miles east of Callao.

Callao

This cluster of ranches dates from 1859, when several families decided to take advantage of the desert grasslands and good springs here. The original name of Willow Springs had to be changed when residents applied for a post office—too many other Utah towns had the same name. Then someone suggested Callao (locally pronounced CAL-ee-o), because the Peruvian town of that name enjoys a similar valley-backed-by-high-mountain setting. Residents raise cattle, sheep, and hay. Children go to Callao Elementary School, one of the last one-room schoolhouses in Utah. Local people believe that the Willow Springs Pony Express Station site was located off the main road at Bagley Ranch, but a BLM archaeologist contends that the foundation is on the east side of town. Callao is 67 miles west of Simpson Springs and 28 miles east of Ibapah (via the Pony Express and Stage Route). A BLM campground at the site of a former CCC camp is four miles south beside Toms Creek; no water

or fee. The tall Deep Creek Range rises to the west.

Canyon Station

To get here, follow signs for Sixmile Ranch, Overland Canyon, and Clifton Flat between Callao and Ibapah. The original station used by Pony Express riders was in Overland Canyon northwest of Canyon Station. Native Americans attacked in July 1863, burned the first station, and killed the Overland agent and four soldiers. The new station was built on a more defensible site. You can see its foundation and the remnants of a fortification. A signed fork at Clifton Flat points the way to Gold Hill, a photogenic ghost town six miles distant (see the *Vicinity of Ibapah* section). Canyon Station is north of the Deep Creek Range, 13 miles northwest of Callao and 15 miles northeast of Ibapah.

Ibapah

Pronounce Ibapah "EYE-buh-paw" to avoid sounding like a tourist! Ibapah is about the same size as Callao—little more than a group of some 20 ranches. **Ibapah Trading Post** (435/234-1166) offers gas and groceries.

VICINITY OF IBAPAH

Continuing south a short way, the main road forks left to the Goshute Indian reservation, while the right fork crosses into Nevada to U.S. 93 (58 miles) on the old Pony Express and Stage Route. From Ibapah you can also go north to Gold Hill ghost town (14 miles) and Wendover (58 miles) or south to U.S. 50/U.S. 6 near Great Basin National Park via Callao, Trout Creek, and Gandy (90 miles).

Goshute Indian Reservation

The Goshute mastered living in the harsh desert by knowing of every edible seed, root, insect, reptile, bird, and rodent, as well as larger game. Their meager diet and possessions appalled early white settlers, who referred disparagingly to the Goshute as "diggers." Loss of land to ranchers and dependence on manufactured

GREAT BASIN DESERT

food put an end to the old nomadic lifestyle. In recent times the Goshute have gradually begun to regain independence by learning to farm and ranch. Several hundred members of the tribe live on the Goshute Indian reservation, which straddles the Utah-Nevada border. Most of the reservation is off-limits to nonmembers without special permission.

The isolated Goshute reservation has been in the national news in the last few years. Tribal elders have tentatively agreed to build a repository on their reservations for the nuclear waste from several out-of-state atomic energy generation facilities, in return for tens of millions of dollars in payments and infrastructure development. The federal government and Private Fuel Storage, a consortium of eight nuclear power companies, have worked out an agreement with the Goshute tribal leadership to lease reservation land for the nuclear storage facility, which could house up to 40,000 metric tons of highly radioactive fuel rods. Although licensed by the Nuclear Regulatory Council in 2005, the Interior Department effectively killed plans for the waste depository in 2006, when the BLM refused to allow the nuclear waste to be transported across public lands.

Gold Hill

Miners had been working the area for three years when they founded Gold Hill in 1892. A whole treasure trove of minerals came out of the ground here—gold, silver, lead, copper, tungsten, arsenic, and bismuth. A smelter along a ridge just west of town processed the ore. But three years later Gold Hill's boom ended. Most people lived only in tents anyway, and soon everything but the smelter foundations and tailings was packed up. A rebirth occurred during World War I, when the country desperately needed copper, tungsten, and arsenic. Gold Hill grew to a sizable town with 3,000 residents, a railroad line from Wendover, and many substantial buildings. Cheaper foreign sources of arsenic knocked the bottom out of local mining in 1924, and Gold Hill

began to die again. Another frenzied burst of activity occurred in 1944–1945, when the nation called once more for tungsten and arsenic. The town again sprang to life, only to fade just as quickly after the war ended. Determined prospectors still roam the surrounding countryside awaiting another clamor for the underground riches. Decaying structures in town make a picturesque sight. (Several year-round residents live here; no scavenging allowed.) Visible nearby are the cemetery, mines, railroad bed, and smelter site. The smaller ghost town of **Clifton** lies over the hill to the south but little remains; No Trespassing signs make visitors unwelcome. Good roads (partly dirt) approach Gold Hill from Ibapah, Wendover, and Callao.

DEEP CREEK RANGE

The range soars spectacularly above the Great Salt Lake Desert. Few people know about the Deep Creeks despite their great heights, diverse wildlife, and pristine forests. Ibapah Peak (elev. 12,087 feet) and Haystack Peak to the north (elev. 12,020 feet) crown the range. Glacial cirques and other rugged features have been carved into the nearly white granite that makes up most of the summit ridge. Prospectors have found gold, silver, lead, zinc, copper, mercury, beryllium, molybdenum, tungsten, and uranium. You'll occasionally run across mines and old cabins in the range, especially in Goshute Canyon. Of the six perennial streams on the east side, Birch and Trout Creeks still contain rare Lake Bonneville cutthroat trout that originated in the prehistoric lake; both creeks are closed to fishing. Other wildlife includes Rocky Mountain bighorn sheep (reintroduced), deer, pronghorn, mountain lion, coyote, bobcat, and many birds.

The Deep Creek Range gets plenty of snow in winter, so the climbing season runs late June–late October. Aspen and some mountain shrubs put on colorful displays in September and early October. Streams in the range have good water (purify first), but the lower canyons are often polluted by the organisms that accompany cattle excrement. Carry water while hiking on the dry ridges.

Main Climbing Routes

Most of the canyons have roads into their lower reaches. Four-wheel drive vehicles will be able to get farther up the steep grades than cars. Most hikers start up Granite or Indian Farm Creek and head for Ibapah or Haystack Peak. A trail along **Granite Creek** offers the easiest approach to Ibapah Peak, about 12.5 miles round-trip and a 5,300-foot elevation gain from the beginning of the jeep trail. The road to Granite Creek turns west off Snake Valley Road 10 miles south of Callao (7.8 miles north of Trout Creek Ranch). Keep left at a junction about one mile in, then follow the most-used track. The road enters Granite Canyon after three miles. The first ford of Granite Creek, a half mile into the canyon, requires a high-clearance vehicle; the second, 0.8 mile farther, may require four-wheel drive. The road deteriorates into a jeep track in another 0.6 mile at the border of Deep Creek Wilderness Study Area. Four-wheel drive vehicles can climb the steep grade another two miles. Continue two miles on a pack trail to the beginning of a large meadow at the pass, then head cross-country 1.5 miles to the small peak (11,385 feet) just before Ibapah. A small trail on the east side of this peak continues three-quarters of a mile to the summit of Ibapah.

Impressive panoramas take in the rugged canyons and ridges of the Deep Creek Range below and much of western Utah and eastern Nevada beyond. Remains of a heliograph station sit atop Ibapah. Early mapmakers measured the highest point in the range at 12,101 feet and named it "Haystack." A later survey determined the correct height to be 12,087 feet and renamed the peak "Ibapah"; the second-highest peak was given the old Haystack name by default.

Other Climbing Routes

Red Mountain (11,588 feet) can also be climbed from the pass above Granite Creek. The jeep trail to **Toms Creek** leads to a route to the head of the creek, from which Haystack Peak is about three miles south along the crest of the range; turnoff for Toms Canyon is 1.6 miles south of Callao and 8.4 miles north of the Granite Creek turnoff. A more direct route to Haystack Peak goes up through **Indian Farm Canyon.** Turnoff for this canyon is 4.3 miles south of Callao and 5.7 miles north of the Granite Creek turnoff. **Red Cedar Creek** in the heart of the Deep Creeks remains pristine—no trails, roads, or other developments. It's also very rugged; allow a day or two just to hike through one-way. **Trout Creek** is another good hiking area. A trail goes most of the way up the valley.

Approaches to the peaks from the Goshute Indian Reservation have been used less because of travel restrictions for non-Goshutes and because this western slope is much drier.

Information and Services

Hikers venturing into this remote range must be self-sufficient and experienced in wilderness travel. You'll need the 7.5-minute Ibapah Peak and Indian Farm Creek topo maps for the central part of the range, the 7.5-minute Goshute and Goshute Canyon maps for the northern part, and the 15-minute Trout Creek map for the southern part. The metric 1:100,000 Fish Springs quad covers the whole area, but with less detail. For firsthand information, contact the **BLM House Range Resource Area** (35 East 500 North, Fillmore, UT 84631, 435/743-6811).

All approaches to the Deep Creeks involve dirt-road travel and generally sizable distances. Ibapah has the nearest gas and groceries (38 miles from the Granite Creek turnoff).

GREAT BASIN DESERT

Eureka and Tintic Mining District

The lucky prospectors who cried "Eureka! I've found it!" had stumbled onto a fabulously rich deposit of silver and other valuable metals. Eureka sprang up to be one of Utah's most important cities and the center of more than a dozen mining communities. Much can still be seen of the district's long history—mine headframes and buildings, shafts and glory holes, old examples of residential and commercial architecture, great piles of ore tailings, and forlorn cemeteries. Exhibits at the Tintic Mining Museum in Eureka show what life was like. Paved highways provide easy access: from I-15 Santaquin Exit 248 (south of Provo) go west 21 miles on U.S. 6; from Delta go northeast 48 miles on U.S. 6; and from Tooele go south 54 miles on Hwy. 36.

History

Mormon stock herders began moving cattle here during the early 1850s to take advantage of the good grazing lands. Utes under Chief Tintic, for whom the district was later named, opposed the newcomers but couldn't stop them. Mineral deposits found in the hills remained a secret of the Mormons, as church policy prohibited members from prospecting for precious metals. In 1869, though, George Rust, a gentile cowboy, noted the promising ores. Soon the rush was on—ores assaying up to 10,000 ounces of silver per ton began pouring out of the mines. Silver City, founded in 1870, became the first of many mining camps. New discoveries kept the Tintic District booming. Gold, copper, lead, and zinc added to the riches. By 1910 the district had a population of 8,000 and the end was nowhere in sight. The hills shook from underground blasting and the noise of mills, smelters, and railroads. Valuable Tintic properties kept the Salt Lake Stock Exchange busy, while Salt Lake City office buildings and mansions rose with Tintic money. Mining began a slow decline in the 1930s but has continued, sporadically, to the

present. Most of the old mining camps have dried up and blown away. Eureka and Mammoth drift on as sleepy towns—monuments to an earlier era.

The ghosts of former camps can be worth a visit, too, though most require considerable imagination to see them as they were. Do not go near decaying structures or mine shafts. You'll also find sites of towns that exist mostly as memories. Diligent searching through the sagebrush may uncover foundations, tailing piles, broken glass, and neglected cemeteries. Yet behind many of the sites linger dramatic stories of attempts to win riches from the earth.

EUREKA

Mines and tailing dumps surround weather-beaten buildings. Eureka lacks the orderliness of Mormon towns; the main street snakes through the valley with side streets branching off in every direction. Few recent buildings have been added, so the town retains an authentic atmosphere from an earlier time. Eureka now has a population of about 600, down from the 3,400 of its peak years.

Tintic Mining Museum

The varied exhibits in this small museum (435/433-6842 or 435/433-6869, free) will give you an appreciation of the district and its mining pioneers. A mineral collection from the Tintic area has many fine specimens. You'll see early mining tools, assay equipment, a mine office, courtroom, blacksmith shop, a 1920s kitchen, many historic photos, and displays that show social life in the early days. One display is dedicated to the influence of Jessie Knight, a Mormon financier and philanthropist. Knightsville, now a ghost town site near Eureka, gained fame as one of the few mining towns in Utah without a saloon or gambling hall. Knight also promoted mine safety and closed his mines for a day of rest on

Sunday—both radical concepts at the time. You'll find the museum galleries upstairs in City Hall (built in 1899) and next door in the former railroad depot (1925). The *Tintic Tour Guide* sold here describes a 35-mile loop to some of the nearby ghost towns and mines. The Tintic Mining Museum is open sporadically—usually on summer weekends and some weekdays and on request at other times.

Bullion-Beck Mine

A large timber headframe on the west edge of town beside the highway marks one of the most productive mines in the district. John Beck arrived in 1871 and began sinking a shaft. At first people called him the "Crazy Dutchman," but the jeers ended when he hit a huge deposit of rich ore 200 feet down. The present 65-foot-high headframe dates from about 1890; originally a large wooden building enclosed it.

GHOST TOWNS
Dividend

Emil Raddatz bought this property on the east slope of the Tintic Mountains in 1907, believing that the ore deposits mined on the west side of the Tintics extended to here. Raddatz nearly went broke digging deeper and deeper, but the prized silver and lead ore 1,200 feet below proved him right. After his 1916 discovery, a modern company town grew up complete with hotel, movie theater, golf course, and ice plant. The miners, whose wages had been paid partly in stock certificates, chose the name Dividend because they had been so well rewarded. Mining continued until 1949, producing $19 million in dividends, but today only foundations, mine shafts, and large piles of tailing remain. A loop road east of Eureka will take you to this site and other mining areas. Walking or driving off the road is forbidden because of mine shafts and other hazards. Though the road is paved, some sections are badly potholed and need to be driven slowly. From downtown Eureka, go east 1.5 miles on U.S. 6 and turn right on the Divi-

dend road (0.1 mile east of milepost 141); the road climbs into hills and passes the Eureka Lily headframe and mine on the left after 2.5 miles. Continue 0.3 mile to Tintic Standard #1 shaft on right, then 0.3 mile more to the site of Dividend and the #2 shaft (signed); the road ends at a junction 0.9 mile farther; turn left 0.7 mile to U.S. 6 (four miles east of Eureka). The Sunshine Mining Company currently operates the Burgin Mine about one mile east of Dividend.

Mammoth

Prospectors made a "mammoth" strike over the hill south of Eureka in 1870. The town of Mammoth, more mines, mills, and smelters followed. The eccentric mining engineer George Robinson built a second town, immodestly named after himself, one mile down the valley. Both towns prospered, growing together and eventually becoming just Mammoth. Nearly 3,000 people lived here when activity peaked in 1900–1910. Then came the inevitable decline as the high-grade ores worked out. By the 1930s, Mammoth was well on its way to becoming a ghost town. People still live here and have preserved some of the old buildings. The Mammoth glory hole and mine buildings overlook the town at the head of the valley. Ruins of smelters and mines cling to hillsides. From Eureka, go southwest 2.5 miles on U.S. 6, then turn left (east) one mile on a paved road. Upper and lower towns can now be distinguished.

Silver City

Optimistic prospectors named their little camp for the promising silver ore, but a city it was not to be. The cost of pumping water out of the mines cut too deeply into profit margins, and a 1902 fire nearly put an end to the town. At that point LDS financier Jessie Knight stepped in to improve the mines and rebuild the town. He also built a smelter and later a mill. Silver City reached its peak about 1908 before declining to ghost town status in the 1930s. You can't miss the giant piles of tailing (light colored) and slag (dark colored) from the smelter and mill at the old townsite. Extensive concrete foundations show the complexity and size of the operations. Sagebrush has reclaimed the rest of the town, of which only debris and foundations survive. Some diehards still mine and prospect in the area, though; a new mining operation is currently reprocessing the old smelter waste products. Silver City ghost town site lies 3.3 miles southwest of Eureka (0.8 mile past the Mammoth turnoff) just off U.S. 6.

SHEEPROCK MOUNTAINS

Black Crook Peak (elev. 9,275 feet) tops this little-known range northwest of Eureka. Sheeprock Mountain Trail (Forest Trails 051 and 052) follows the crest of the mountains for most of their length. Several other trails connect from each side. See the Uinta National Forest map and the 7.5-minute Erickson Knoll, Dutch Peak, Lookout Pass, and Vernon topo maps. Mining, which peaked in the early 1900s, still continues on a small scale for silver, lead, and zinc. Bald eagles winter here approximately December–March; their numbers appear to fluctuate with the rabbit population. Anglers can try for brook and brown trout in Vernon Reservoir and Vernon and Bennion Creeks.

The small **Little Valley Campground** is open May–November; no water or charge. Although the Sheeprock Mountains are in the Wasatch National Forest, the Spanish Fork Ranger District office of the Uinta National Forest (44 West 400 North, Spanish Fork, UT 84660, 435/798-3571) manages this area, known as the Vernon Division.

To get to the Sheeprock Mountains, follow Hwy. 36 northwest 17 miles from Eureka (or south 42 miles from Tooele) to a junction signed Benmore, just east of Vernon; turn south five miles to Benmore Guard Station, then left 2.5 miles for Vernon Reservoir. Little Valley Campground is off to the right in a side valley 2.3 miles past the reservoir. A road in via Lofgreen is a bit rough for cars. None of these roads are recommended in wet weather.

LITTLE SAHARA RECREATION AREA

Sand dunes have made a giant sandbox between Eureka and Delta. Managed by the BLM, the recreation area covers 60,000 acres of free-moving sand dunes, sagebrush flats, and juniper-covered ridges. Elevations range from about 5,000 to 5,700 feet. Varied terrain provides challenges for dune buggies, motorcycles, and four-wheel drive vehicles. While off-road vehicles can range over most of the dunes, areas near White Sands and Jericho Campgrounds have been set aside for children. The Rockwell Natural Area in the western part of the dunes protects 9,150 acres for nature study.

The dunes originated 150 miles away as sandbars along the southern shore of Lake Bonneville roughly 10,000 years ago. After the lake receded, prevailing winds pushed the exposed sands on a slow trek northeastward at a rate of about 18 inches per year. Sand Mountain, however, deflected the winds upward, and the sand grains piled up into large dunes downwind. Lizards and kangaroo rats scamper across the sands in search of food and, in turn, are eaten by hawks, bobcats, and coyotes. Pronghorn and mule deer live here all year. Juniper, sagebrush, greasewood, saltbush, and grasses are the most common plants. An unusual species of fourwing saltbush (*Atriplex canescens*) grows as high as 12 feet and is restricted to the dunes area.

A visitors center near the entrance is open irregular hours. Three developed **campgrounds** with water (White Sands, Oasis, and Jericho) and a primitive camping area (Sand Mountain) are open all year. In winter, water is available only at the visitors center on the way in. Visitors to Little Sahara pay $8 per person, which includes use of campgrounds. For more information, contact the BLM office (15 East 500 North, Fillmore, UT 84631, 435/743-6811, www.ut.blm.gov/recsite/little.html).

The entrance road is 4.5 miles west of Jericho Junction, which lies 17 miles south of Eureka, 31 miles west of Nephi (I-15 Exits 222 and 228), or 32 miles northeast of Delta.

Delta to Milford

The barren Pahvant Valley along the lower Sevier River had long been considered a wasteland. Then, in 1905, some Fillmore businessmen purchased water rights from Sevier River Reservoir and 10,000 acres of land. The farm and town lots they sold became the center of one of Utah's most productive agricultural areas. Other hopeful homesteaders who settled farther from Delta weren't as fortunate. Thousands of families bought cheap land in the North Tract but found the going very difficult. Troubles with the irrigation system, poor crop yields, and low market prices forced most to leave by the late 1930s. A few decaying houses and farm buildings mark the sites of once-bustling communities. Farmers near Delta raise alfalfa seed and hay, wheat, corn, barley, mushrooms, and livestock. The giant coal-burning Intermountain Power Project (IPP) and the Brush Wellman beryllium mill have helped boost Delta's population to about 4,000. Miners have been digging into the Drum Mountains northwest of Delta since the 1870s for gold, silver, copper, manganese, and other minerals; some work still goes on there. The beryllium processed near Delta comes from large deposits of bertrandite mined in open pits in the Topaz and Spors Mountains farther to the northwest.

DELTA

For travelers, Delta (pop. 3,210) makes a handy base for visiting the surrounding historic sites, rockhounding, and exploring nearby mountain ranges. In downtown Delta, the **Great Basin Museum** (328 West 100 North, 435/864-5013, 10 A.M.–4 P.M. Mon.–Sat., free) presents a varied collection of pioneer photos and artifacts, arrowheads, a Topaz Camp exhibit, fossils, and minerals; antique farm machinery stands outside.

A **pioneer log cabin** (built 1907–1908), now on Main Street in front of Delta's municipal building, was the second house and the first

post office in Melville, which was later known as Burtner and finally as Delta in 1910. Historical markers near the cabin commemorate the Spanish Dominguez-Escalante Expedition, which passed to the south in 1776, and the Topaz Camp for Japanese Americans interned during World War II.

◖ Rockhounding

Beautiful rock, mineral, and fossil specimens await discovery in the deserts surrounding Delta. Sought-after rocks and minerals include topaz, bixbyite, sunstones, geodes, obsidian, muscovite, garnet, pyrite, and agate. Some fossils to look for are trilobites, brachiopods, horn coral, and crinoids. The chamber of commerce in Delta is a good source of local information.

You can see gemstones from the area at **West Desert Collectors** (278 W. Main, 435/864-2175) and **Tina's Jewelry and Minerals** (320 E. Main, 435/864-2444). A hat and plenty of water will add to your comfort and safety when enjoying the outdoors. Always be watchful when hiking to avoid rattlesnakes and mine shafts. Both are occasionally found in caves, where the dim light makes them harder to see.

Dig for trilobites and other marine fossils at **U-Dig Fossils** (350 East 300 South, 435/864-3638, 9 A.M.–6 P.M. Mon.–Sat. Apr. 1–Oct. 15), a private quarry. It's best to come prepared with work gloves, sturdy shoes, and protective eyewear; U-Dig provides hammers, buckets, and advice. One hour of digging goes for $6 adults 17 and older, $4 ages 8–16, free to children 7 and under. It's best to arrive by 4 P.M., because if business is slow, the quarry closes early.

Accommodations

All of Delta's motels are on or close to Main Street. **Diamond D Motor Lodge** (234 W. Main, 435/864-2041); **Deltan Inn** (347 E. Main, 435/864-5318); and the **Budget Motel**

GREAT BASIN DESERT

(75 South 350 East, 435/864-4533) each offer inexpensive, no-fuss rooms with $50 and up.

For a step up in style and amenities, the **Best Western Motor Inn Motel** (527 E. Topaz Blvd., 435/864-3882 or 800/354-9378, $86 and up) has a heated outdoor pool and allows pets.

CAMPGROUNDS
Antelope Valley RV Park (760 W. Main, 435/864-1813, Apr.–Nov., $12 tents, $17 RVs without hookups, $20 RVs with hookups) is on the west edge of downtown. **Oak Creek Campground** lies in a pretty wooded canyon in the Fishlake National Forest; sites have drinking water late May–early October; $7. Head east 14 miles on U.S. 50 and Hwy. 125 to Oak City, then turn right four miles on a paved road.

Food
Tops City Cafe (313 W. Main, 435/864-2148, breakfast, lunch, and dinner daily, $6–14) serves standard American fare. The **Rancher Motel** (171 W. Main, 435/864-2741, breakfast, lunch, and dinner daily, $5–18) has a café with American and Mexican food and a dining room upstairs serving steak and seafood.

Information and Services
Delta Chamber of Commerce (80 North 200 West, Delta, UT 84624, 435/864-4316, www.millardcountytravel.com, 10 A.M.–5 P.M. Mon.–Fri.) will tell you about services in town and sights in the surrounding area.

CANYON MOUNTAINS
East of Delta, the **Oak Creek Campground** (late May–early Oct., $7, has water) is a Forest Service campground (elev. 5,900 feet) that lies along the creek amid Gambel oak, cottonwood, maple, and juniper on the west side of the mountains. Canyon walls cut by Oak Creek reveal layers of twisted and upturned rock. Groups can reserve a large area with amphitheater, sports area, and shelter. Oak Creek usually has good fishing for rainbow trout. Much of its flow comes from a spring at the

upper end of the campground. From Delta go east 14 miles on U.S. 50 and Hwy. 125 to the small farming town of Oak City, then turn right four miles on a paved road.

WEST OF DELTA
Topaz Camp
Topaz is easily Utah's most dispirited ghost town site. Other ghost towns had the promise of precious metals or good land to lure their populations, but those coming to Topaz had no choice—they had the bad fortune to be of the wrong ancestry during the height of World War II hysteria. About 9,000 Japanese—most of whom were American citizens—were brought from the West Coast to this desolate desert plain in 1942. Topaz sprang up in just a few months and included barracks, communal dining halls, post office, hospital, schools, churches, and recreational facilities. Most internees cooperated with authorities; the few who caused trouble were shipped off to a more secure camp. Barbed wire and watchtowers with armed guards surrounded the small city—which was actually Utah's fifth-largest community for a time. All internees were released at war's end in 1945 and the camp came down almost as quickly as it had gone up. Salvagers bought and removed equipment, buildings, barbed wire, telephone poles, and even street paving and sewer pipes. An uneasy silence pervades the site today. Little more than the streets, foundations, and piles of rubble remains. You can still walk or drive along the streets of the vast camp, which had 42 neatly laid-out blocks. A concrete memorial stands at the northwest corner of the site.

One way to get here is to go west six miles from Delta on U.S. 50/U.S. 6 to the small town of Hinckley, turn right (north) 4.5 miles on a paved road (some parts are gravel) to its end, turn left (west) 2.5 miles on a paved road to its end in Abraham, turn right (north) 1.5 miles on a gravel road to a stop sign, then turn left three miles on a gravel road; Topaz is on the left.

House Range
This range about 45 miles west of Delta offers

great vistas, scenic drives, wilderness hiking, and world-famous trilobite fossil beds. Swasey Peak (elev. 9,669 feet) is the highest point. From a distance, however, Notch Peak's spectacular 2,700-foot face stands out as the most prominent landmark in the region. What the 50-mile-long range lacks in great heights, it makes up for in massive sheer limestone cliffs and rugged canyons. Precipitous drops on the western side contrast with a gentler slope on the east. Hardy vegetation such as juniper, piñon pine, mountain mahogany, and sagebrush dominates the dry slopes. Bristlecone pines grow on the high ridges of Swasey and Notch Peaks; the long-lived trees are identified by inward-curving bristles on the cones and by needles less than 1.5 inches long in clusters of five. Some of the high country also harbors limber pine, ponderosa pine, white fir, Douglas fir, and aspen.

Wildlife includes mule deer, pronghorn, chukar partridge, bald and golden eagles, and peregrine falcon. Wild horses roam Sawmill Basin to the northeast of Swasey Peak. Permanent water supplies are found only at a few scattered springs in the range. Limestone caves attract spelunkers, especially Antelope Spring Cave near Dome Canyon Pass (ask directions at the BLM office in Fillmore or from the Speleological Society of Utah). Council Cave on Antelope Peak (between Notch and Swasey Peaks) has an enormous opening, visible for more than 50 miles.

Mining in the range has a long history. Stories tell of finding old Spanish gold mines with iron tools in them that crumbled at a touch. More recent mining for tungsten and gold has occurred on the east side of Notch Peak. Outlaws found the range a convenient area in which to hide out; Tatow Knob (north of Swasey Peak), for example, was a favorite spot for horse thieves. Death Canyon got its name after a group of pioneers became trapped and froze to death; most maps now show it as Dome Canyon.

DRIVING IN THE HOUSE RANGE

The dirt roads here can be surprisingly good.

Often you can zip along as if on pavement, but watch for loose gravel, large rocks, flash floods, and deep ruts that sometimes appear on these backcountry stretches. Roads easily passable by car connect to make a 43-mile loop through Marjum and Dome Canyon Passes. You'll have good views of the peaks and go through scenic canyons on the west side of both passes. Drivers with high-clearance vehicles can branch off on old mining roads or drive past Antelope Spring to Sinbad Overlook for views and hiking near Swasey Peak.

Shale beds near Antelope Spring have given up an amazing quantity and variety of **trilobite fossils** dating from about 500 million years ago. Professional collectors have leased a trilobite quarry, so you'll have to collect outside. Trilobites can also be found near Swasey Spring and near Marjum Pass. Flat-edged rock hammers work best to split open the shale layers.

During World War I, a hermit took a liking to the House Range and built a one-room cabin in a small cave, where he lived until his death. He entertained visitors with a special home brew. Walk a quarter mile up a small side canyon from the road to see the cabin, which is on the right side of the road that comes down to the west from Marjum Pass.

Several roads connect U.S. 50/U.S. 6 with the loop through Marjum and Dome Canyon Passes. Going west from Delta on U.S. 50/U.S. 6, you have the choice of the following turnoffs: after 10 miles, turn right 25 miles at the fork for the unpaved old U.S. 50/U.S. 6; or after 32 miles, turn right 10 miles on a road signed Antelope Spring; or after 42 miles, turn right 16 miles on a road also signed Antelope Spring; or after 63 miles (30 miles east of the Utah-Nevada border), turn right 14 miles on a road signed Painter Spring.

HIKING IN THE HOUSE RANGE

Most hiking routes go cross-country through the wilderness. Springs are very far apart and sometimes polluted, so carry water for the whole trip. Bring topo maps and a compass; help can be a long way off if you make a wrong turn. Because of the light precipitation, the hiking season at the high elevations can last late April–late November. You can visit most destinations, including Swasey and Notch Peaks, on a day hike. These peaks offer fantastic views over nearly all of west-central Utah and into Nevada. For more information on the House Range, contact the BLM office (35 East 500 North in Fillmore, P.O. Box 778, Fillmore, UT 84631, 435/743-6811).

The trip to **Swasey Peak** makes a good half-day hike and is usually done as a loop. Total distance for the moderately difficult trip is about 4.5 miles with a 1,700-foot elevation gain to the summit (elev. 9,669 feet). Drive to the Antelope Spring turnoff, 2.5 miles east of Dome Canyon Pass, and follow the well-used Sinbad Overlook road 3.3 miles, passing the spring and trilobite area, up a steep grade to a large meadow below Swasey Peak. Cautiously driven cars might be able to get up this road, though it's safer to park low-clearance vehicles and walk the last 1.5 miles. (Nonhikers with suitable vehicles will enjoy driving to Sinbad Overlook for views at the end of the road.) From the large meadow at the top of the grade, head northeast on foot up the ridge, avoiding cliffs to the left. After 1.25 miles you'll reach a low summit; continue one-half mile along the ridgeline, curving west toward Swasey Peak. To complete the loop, descend one-half mile to the northwest along a ridge to bypass some cliffs, then head southwest three-quarters of a mile to the end of Sinbad Overlook road.

From here it's an easy 1.5 miles by road back to the start; Sinbad Spring and a grove of ponderosa pines are about halfway. No signs or trails mark the route, but hikers experienced with maps shouldn't have any trouble. Topo maps for this hike are the 7.5-minute Marjum Pass and Swasey Peak. Route-finding is easier when hiking the loop in the direction described. You'll get a close look at the mountain mahogany on Swasey Peak—some thickets of this stout shrub have to be crossed; wear long pants to protect your legs.

The 2,700-foot sheer rock wall on the western face of prominent **Notch Peak** is only 300 feet shorter than El Capitán in Yosemite. Most hikers prefer the far easier summit route on the other side via Sawtooth Canyon. This moderately difficult canyon route is about nine miles round-trip and has a 1,700-foot elevation gain. Bring water, as no springs are in the area. Like the Drum Mountains, Notch Peak has a reputation for strange underground noises. The 15-minute Notch Peak topo map is needed as much for navigating the roads to the trailhead as for the hiking. First take Antelope Spring Road to the signed turnoff for Miller Canyon, 4.5 miles north of milepost 46 on U.S. 50/U.S. 6 (42 miles west of Delta) and 11.5 miles south of old U.S. 50/U.S. 6 (35 miles west of Delta). Turn west 5.3 miles on Miller Canyon Road, then bear left to Sawtooth Canyon at a road fork.

A stone cabin 2.5 miles farther on the right marks the trailhead. The cabin is owned and used by people who mine in the area. Follow a rough road on foot into Sawtooth Canyon. After three-quarters of a mile the canyon widens where two tributaries meet; take the left fork in the direction of Notch Peak. A few spots in the dry creekbed require some rock-scrambling. Be on the lookout for flash floods if thunderstorms threaten.

After about three miles the wash becomes less distinct; continue climbing to a saddle visible ahead. From there, a short but steep quarter-mile scramble takes you to the top of 9,655-foot Notch Peak and its awesome drop-offs. Other ways up Notch Peak offer challenges for the adventurous. The other fork of Sawtooth Canyon can be used, for example, and a jeep road through Amasa Valley provides a northern approach.

Confusion Range

The Confusions lie in a long, jumbled mass west of the House Range. The sparse vegetation consists largely of piñon pine, juniper, sagebrush, shadscale, and cheatgrass. Some Douglas fir grow on the King Top Plateau, the highest area in the Confusion Range, where elevations reach 8,300 feet. Shortages of water and feed allow only small numbers of wild horses, pronghorn, deer, and smaller animals to eke out an existence.

Fossil Mountain, in the southeast part of the Confusions, has an exceptional diversity of marine fossils, many very rare. Thirteen fossil groups of ancient sea creatures have been found in rocks of early Ordovician age (350–400 million years ago). Fossil Mountain stands 6,685 feet high on the west edge of Blind Valley. A signed road to Blind Valley turns south off U.S. 50/U.S. 6 between mileposts 38 and 39 (54 miles west of Delta). Fossil Mountain is about 14 miles south of the highway.

SOUTH OF DELTA
Fort Deseret
What remains of this fort represents a fading piece of pioneer history. Mormon settlers hastily built the adobe-walled fort in only 18 days in 1865 for protection against Native Americans during the Black Hawk War. The square fort had walls 550 feet long and 10 feet high with gates in the middle of each side. Bastions were located at the northeast and southwest corners. Native Americans never attacked the fort, but it came in handy for penning up cattle at night. Parts of the wall and stone foundation still stand. From Delta go west five miles on U.S. 50/U.S. 6, then turn left (south) 4.5 miles on Hwy. 257. The site is on the west side of the road near milepost 65, about 1.5 miles south of the town of Deseret.

Great Stone Face
A natural rock formation seven miles southwest of Deseret bears a striking resemblance to the Mormon prophet Joseph Smith. To see the profile you have to view the rock from the west. From the town of Deseret, go south three miles on Hwy. 257, then turn right (west) four miles (should be signed) on a dirt road. A short hike at road's end leads up a lava flow to the stone face.

Clear Lake State Waterfowl Management Area
Lakes and marsh country offer ducks, Canada geese, and other birds a refreshing break from the desert. Roads cross Clear Lake on a causeway and lead to smaller lakes and picnic areas

to the north. The Utah Division of Wildlife Resources manages the area. From the junction of U.S. 50/U.S. 6 and Hwy. 257 west of Delta, go south 15.5 miles on Hwy. 257, then turn left (east) seven miles on a good gravel road.

Pahvant Butte
Locally known as Sugar Loaf Mountain, this extinct volcano rises 1,000 feet above the desert floor. Waters of prehistoric Lake Bonneville leveled off the large terrace about halfway up. Remnants of a crater, now open to the southwest, are on this level. Another terrace line is at the bottom of the butte. Hikers can enjoy the volcanic geology, expansive panoramas, and a visit to the curious ruins of a windmill. Construction of the wind-powered electric power station began in 1923 but was never completed. A large underground room and two concentric rings of concrete pylons give an eerie Stonehenge-like atmosphere to the butte.

The easiest way up is an old road on the south side that goes to the windmill site. From Clear Lake, continue east 3.3 miles to the second signed turn on the left for Pahvant Butte (Pahvant Butte Road: 3 miles, Sugarloaf Well #1: 8 miles). Turn left 3.5 miles at the sign, then turn left one-half mile on Pahvant Butte Road. Park before the road begins a steep climb. Daredevils in four-wheel drive vehicles have tried going straight up the slope from here, but the real road turns right and follows switchbacks 0.7 mile to the windmill site. This last 0.7 mile is closed to vehicles because of the soft volcanic rock, but it's fine for walking; elevation gain is about 400 feet. Pahvant Butte's highest point is about a half mile to the north and 265 feet higher; you'll have to find your own way across if headed there. Dirt roads encircle Pahvant Butte and go northeast to U.S. 50 and southeast to Tabernacle Hill and Fillmore. The Tabernacle Hill area provides good examples of volcanic features.

MILFORD
Miners on their way to Frisco and Newhouse crossed the Beaver River at a ford below a stamp mill, so Milford seemed the logical name for

GREAT BASIN DESERT

the town that grew up here. Most of Milford's businesses in the early days supplied the mining camps. Today the town serves as a center for the railroad, nearby farms, and a geothermal plant. Steam from wells at the Blundell Geothermal Plant, 13 miles northeast of town, produces electricity for Utah Power and Light. Travelers heading west will find Milford their last stop for supplies before the Nevada border. Milford (pop. 1,310) is at the junction of Hwy. 21 and Hwy. 257, 77 miles south of Delta and 32 miles east of Beaver. Baker, Nevada, is 96 miles northwest.

Accommodations and Food
In Milford, the **Station Motel** (100 West and 500 South, 435/387-2481, $50 and up) has basic rooms and a restaurant, the **Station Restaurant** (435/387-2804, breakfast, lunch, and dinner daily, $6–15). On the west edge of town, the new, pet-friendly **Oak Tree Inn** (777 W. Hwy. 21, 800/523-8460, $75 and up) has comfortable rooms with microwaves and refrigerators and a fitness center. Guests get a free breakfast next door at **Penny's Diner** (435/387-5266, $6–20), a pretty good 24-hour restaurant. **Pavilion Park** (300 West, year-round, has water) has a free camping area just beyond the high school grounds.

MINERSVILLE RESERVOIR PARK
The 1,130-acre reservoir (P.O. Box 1531, Beaver, UT 84713, 435/438-5472, $4 day use, $13 camping, has water electric hookups) here has good year-round fishing for rainbow trout and smallmouth bass (ice fishing in winter). Be sure to check with the rangers for information about fishing regulations for the park. Bait fishing is not allowed and there are special catch limits. Most people come here to fish, though some visitors go sailing or water-skiing. Park facilities include picnic tables, campsites (all with electric and water hookups), restrooms with showers, paved boat ramp, fish-cleaning station, and dump station. Fees are. Reservations are a good idea on summer holidays. In winter the restrooms may be closed but water is available. Minersville Reservoir lies just off Hwy. 21 in a sage- and juniper-covered valley eight miles east of Minersville, 18 miles southeast of Milford, and 14 miles west of Beaver.

GHOST TOWNS IN THE SAN FRANCISCO MOUNTAINS
Frisco Peak (elev. 9,660 feet) crowns this small range northwest of Milford. The Wah Wah Valley and Mountains lie to the west. Silver strikes in the San Francisco Mountains in the 1870s led to the opening of many mines and the founding of the towns of Newhouse and Frisco. By 1920 the best ores had given out and both communities turned to ghosts. A jeep road goes to the summit of Frisco Peak.

◖ Frisco
The Horn Silver Mine, developed in 1876 at the south end of the San Francisco Mountains, was the first of several prolific silver producers. Smelters, and charcoal ovens to fuel them, sprouted up to process the ore. A wild boomtown developed as miners flocked to the new diggings. The railroad reached Frisco in 1880 and later extended to nearby Newhouse. Frisco's population of 6,000 included quite a few gamblers and other shady characters. Twenty-three saloons labored to serve the thirsty customers. Gunfights became almost a daily ritual for a while, keeping the cemetery growing. But it all came to an end early in 1885, when rumblings echoed from deep within the Horn Silver Mine between shifts. The foreman luckily delayed sending the next crew down, and a few minutes later the whole mine collapsed with a deafening roar that broke windows in Milford, 15 miles away. Out of work, most of the miners and business people moved on. More than $60 million in silver and other valuable ores had come out of the ground in the mine's 10 frenzied years. Some mining has been done on and off since, but Frisco has died.

Today Frisco is one of Utah's best-preserved mining ghosts, with about a dozen stone or wood buildings surviving. A headframe and mine buildings, still intact, overlook the town from the hillside. Five beehive-shaped charcoal

© JUDY JEWELL

San Francisco Mountains

kilns stand on the east edge of Frisco. You can see the kilns and the townsite if you look north from Hwy. 21 (between mileposts 62 and 63) 15 miles west of Milford. Dirt roads wind their way in. A historical marker for Frisco is at the turnoff for the town; turnoff for the beehive kilns is 0.3 mile east. Hiking off the roads can be very dangerous near the old mines and time-worn buildings.

Newhouse

Prospectors discovered silver deposits in 1870 on the southwest side of the San Francisco Mountains but lacked the funds to develop them. Mining didn't take off until 1900, when Samuel Newhouse financed operations. A sizable town grew here as ore worth $3.5 million came out of the Cactus Mine. Citizens maintained a degree of law and order not found in most mining towns: Even the saloon and the working girls had to operate outside the community. Deposits of rich ore ran out only 10 years later and the town's inhabitants departed. The railroad depot was moved to a nearby ranch and other buildings went to Milford. Today, Newhouse is a ghostly site with about half a dozen concrete or stone buildings standing in ruins. Foundations of a smelter, mill, other structures, railroad grades, and lots of broken glass remain. A good dirt road turns north two miles to the site from Hwy. 21 (between mileposts 57 and 58), 20 miles west of Milford.

WAH WAH MOUNTAINS

Beyond the San Francisco Mountains, the Wah Wah Mountains extend south about 55 miles in a continuation of the Confusion Range. Elevation ranges from 6,000 to more than 9,000 feet. The name comes from a Paiute term for salty or alkaline seeps. Sparse sagebrush, juniper, and piñon pine cover most of the land. Aspen, white fir, ponderosa pine, and bristlecone pine grow in the high country. Mule deer, pronghorn, and smaller animals roam the mountains. Carry water, maps, and a compass into this wild country. Few people visit the Wah Wahs despite their pristine

GREAT BASIN DESERT

© JUDY JEWELL

Wah Wah Mountains

ecosystem. Here's your chance to get there before the crowds.

The snow-white pinnacle of Crystal Peak in the north end of the Wah Wah Mountains stands out as a major landmark. The soft white rock of the peak is tuff from an ancient volcano thought to predate the block-faulted Wah Wahs. The best way to climb the peak (elev. 7,106 feet) is to ascend the ridge just south of it from the east, then follow the ridge northeast up the peak.

The heart of the Wah Wahs has some fine scenery and opportunities for nature study.

Rugged cliffs mark the west edge of the range. A good hiking route begins at about 6,600 feet in elevation at the end of a dirt road going up Pierson Cove. Follow the dry wash upstream a short way to a split in the drainage, then take the left fork north through a canyon. After about two miles you'll come out of the canyon onto a high plateau. For the best views, turn northwest and continue climbing three-quarters of a mile to the summit of an 8,918-foot peak. See the 7-minute Wah Wah Summit topo map for back roads and hiking routes.

PROVO AND CENTRAL UTAH

In many ways, the geography and history of central Utah are extensions of the northern part of the state. The rugged Wasatch Range continues to act as an eastern boundary to the spread of the state's largest municipalities, which cluster at the base of the range. Here, smaller mountains and hills form a transition to the basin and range terrain to the west. The mountains of the Wasatch Range are steeper and higher than those to the north, perhaps even more majestic, and likely to be coated with snow.

Just two years after the founding of Salt Lake City, Mormon pioneers began settling both this area and the Wasatch Plateau south of the range. Today, Provo, the state's third-largest city (West Valley City, a Salt Lake City bedroom community, is number two) and home to bustling Brigham Young University, anchors the region's northern end, and quiet Mormon villages occupy much of the lower country.

PLANNING YOUR TIME

Unless you are planning extended backcountry explorations of the Tushar Mountains or taking a leisurely exploration of the Alpine Scenic Drive and Mount Timpanogos, it's unlikely that you'll be spending much time in central Utah. But it is worth stopping into the small towns along I-15 and U.S. 89 as you travel between Salt Lake City and southern Utah, and Provo is a good place to spend a night.

© PAUL LEVY

HIGHLIGHTS

⟪ Brigham Young University: There's a certain look to most universities, and BYU does not have that look. But in addition to what some might see as a cultural disconnect, there are several good museums scattered around the beautiful and sprawling campus (page 186).

⟪ Springville Museum of Art: Both the museum building and its collection make this small-town museum, located a short drive from Provo, worth visiting. The best time to come is in late April, when the Spring Salon shows the work of contemporary Utah artists (page 189).

⟪ Timpanogos Cave National Monument: Be prepared for a bit of a hike to these three limestone caves connected by tunnels. You'll be rewarded by branching helictites, icicle-like stalactites, rising stalagmites, and graceful flowstone formations in shades of green, yellow, red, or pure white (page 193).

⟪ Sundance Resort: Even if you lack the funds to spend the night here, it's worth visiting Sundance just to take a look around. The restaurants, shops, ski area, artist studios, and most other facilities are open to the public. Everything is very tasteful, and, to the extent possible in such a place, in accordance with nature (page 195).

⟪ Fremont Indian State Park: More than 500 excellent rock-art panels provide clues to

the lives of the Fremont people who lived here about 3,000 years ago. The village site was discovered and excavated in 1983, when I-70 was being built (page 207).

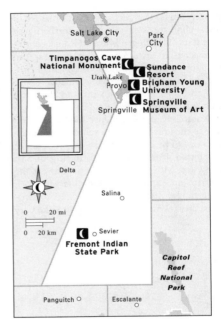

LOOK FOR ⟪ TO FIND RECOMMENDED SIGHTS, ACTIVITIES, DINING, AND LODGING.

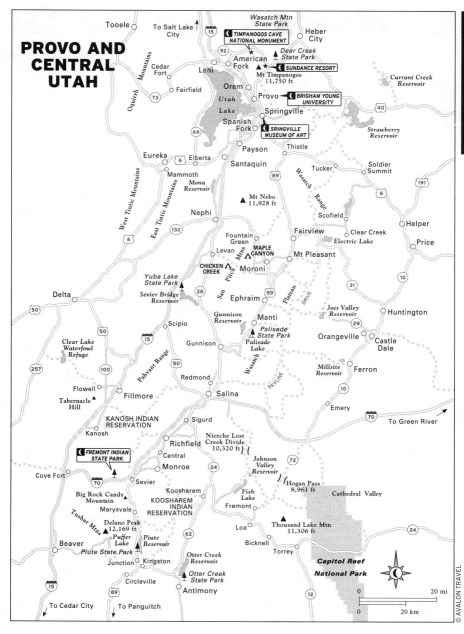

PROVO AND CENTRAL UTAH

Tooele
To Salt Lake City
15

Wasatch Mtn State Park
TIMPANOGOS CAVE NATIONAL MONUMENT

Heber City

92
American Fork
Deer Creek State Park
SUNDANCE RESORT

Cedar Fort
Lehi
Mt Timpanogos 11,750 ft

Currant Creek Reservoir

Oquirrh Mountains

Fairfield
73
Orem
Utah Lake
Provo
BRIGHAM YOUNG UNIVERSITY
40

Springville
SRINGVILLE MUSEUM OF ART

Spanish Fork
68
Strawberry Reservoir

Payson
Thistle

Eureka
6
Elberta
Santaquin
89
Tucker
Soldier Summit

Mammoth
Mona Reservoir
Wasatch Range
191
6

West Tintic Mountains
East Tintic Mountains

Mt Nebo 11,928 ft

Nephi
Scofield

132
Fountain Green
Fairview
Clear Creek
Electric Lake
Helper

6
Levan
Maple Canyon
San Pitch Mtns
Mt Pleasant
Price

CHICKEN CREEK
Moroni

Yuba Lake State Park
28
Ephraim
89
Plateau DRIVE
31
10

Delta
Sevier Bridge Reservoir
Gunnison Reservoir
Manti
Joes Valley Reservoir
Huntington

50
Scipio
Palisade State Park
Palisade Lake
29
Orangeville
Castle Dale

Clear Lake Waterfowl Refuge
50
15
Gunnison
Wasatch
SKYLINE
Millsite Reservoir
Ferron

257
100
Pahvant Range
50
Redmond
10

Flowell
Fillmore
Salina
Emery

Tabernacle Hill
KANOSH INDIAN RESERVATION
Sigurd
70
To Green River

Kanosh
Niotche Lost Creek Divide 10,320 ft

FREMONT INDIAN STATE PARK
Richfield
Central
Johnson Valley Reservoir
72

Cove Fort
70
Monroe
24

Sevier
Koosharem
KOOSHAREM INDIAN RESERVATION
Hogan Pass 8,961 ft
Cathedral Valley

Big Rock Candy Mountain
Marysvale
Fish Lake
Fremont

Tushar Mtns
Delano Peak 12,169 ft
62
Loa
Thousand Lake Mtn 11,306 ft
24

Beaver
Puffer Lake
Piute Reservoir
Bicknell

Piute State Park
Otter Creek Reservoir
Torrey

15
Junction
Kingston
Capitol Reef National Park

Circleville
Otter Creek State Park

89
Antimony
12
0   20 mi

To Cedar City
To Panguitch
0   20 km

© AVALON TRAVEL

Provo

Provo (pop. 114,000) has a striking setting on the shore of Utah Lake beneath the west face of the Wasatch Range. The city is best known as the home of Brigham Young University (BYU), a large, dynamic school sponsored by the Church of Jesus Christ of Latter-day Saints.

Provo also contains a rich architectural heritage. At the turn of the 20th century, this hard-working young city constructed its civic buildings with style and substance, and its residential areas are filled with Victorian mansions and vernacular workers' homes. The visitors center can provide self-guided tour brochures to the city's historic architecture.

Provo boasts one of the most majestic views of any of the Wasatch Front cities and easy access to the mountains, perhaps contributing to the city's consistently high marks in many publications' "livability" ratings.

◖ BRIGHAM YOUNG UNIVERSITY

The university (www.byu.edu) had a modest beginning in 1875 as the Brigham Young Academy, established under the direction of LDS Church president Brigham Young. Like the rest of Provo, BYU's population and size have grown dramatically in recent decades. BYU is one of the largest church-affiliated schools in the world. Students aren't required to be Mormons, but about 98 percent of the student body of 29,000 do belong to the LDS Church. High academic standards upheld by students and faculty have made the university a leader in many fields. Everyone attending the school must follow a strict dress and grooming code—something you'll notice immediately on a stroll across the pretty campus.

Exhibits and concerts are held in the **Harris Fine Arts Center** (just north of the Wilkinson Center, 801/378-7444 music ticket office or 801/378-4322 theater performances) and other locations on campus. BYU also goes all out to support its Cougars football and other athletic teams. Major sporting events take place in the 65,000-seat LaVell Edwards Stadium and the indoor 23,000-seat Marriott Center (801/378-2981 ticket office).

You're welcome to visit the more than 600 acres of BYU's vast campus. The big new **visitors center** (435/422-4678, 9 A.M.–4 P.M. Mon.–Fri.) provides literature and advice about things to see, events, and facilities open to the public.

Wilkinson Center serves as the social center for BYU, with cafeterias and snack bars, the campus bookstore, a movie theater, an art gallery, lounge areas, and an information desk. The **Skyroom Restaurant** on the sixth floor offers great views and fine dining (801/378-2049, lunch Mon.–Fri., $8–13). The lower level has **Outdoors Unlimited** (801/378-2708), with rentals of bicycles and equipment for camping, boating, snowshoeing, cross-country and downhill skiing, and other sports, and a **post office.**

The **Harold B. Lee Library** (801/378-2926, 7 A.M.–midnight Mon.–Sat.) has an impressive collection of books and maps on five levels; the genealogical library ranks second in size only to the one in Salt Lake City, which is the largest in the world.

Small collections on campus include a series of salt- and freshwater aquariums in the basement of the Widtsoe Building, and Earth Science exhibits and a Foucault pendulum in the lobby and hallways of the Eyring Science Center.

Museum of Art

BYU is home to one of the largest art museums (801/422-8287, http://moa.byu.edu, 10 A.M.–9 P.M. Mon.–Fri., noon–5 P.M. Sat., free except for occasional special exhibits) in the West, displaying famous works of art including Rembrandt's *Raising of Lazarus,* Gifford's *Lake Scene,* and Andy Warhol's *Marilyn.* The building itself is a work of art, with a polished granite exterior, hardwood floors, and high-ceilinged galleries bathed in natural light.

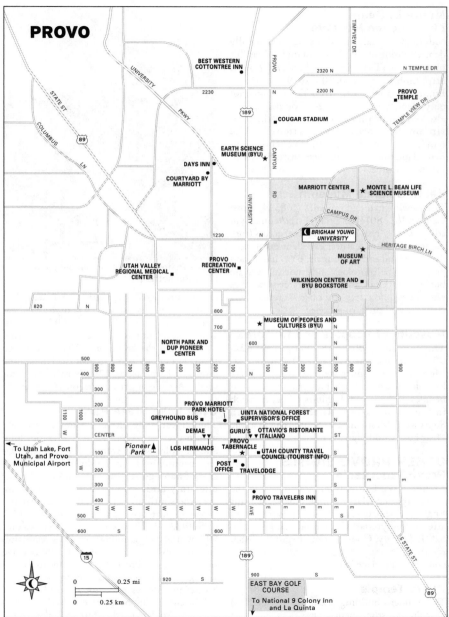

PROVO

BEST WESTERN COTTONTREE INN

PROVO

2320 N

N TEMPLE DR

UNIVERSITY PKWY

STATE ST

COLUMBUS LN

89

2230

2200 N

PROVO TEMPLE

TEMPLE VIEW DR

TIMPVIEW DR

189

N

COUGAR STADIUM

EARTH SCIENCE MUSEUM (BYU)

CANYON

DAYS INN

COURTYARD BY MARRIOTT

MARRIOTT CENTER

MONTE L. BEAN LIFE SCIENCE MUSEUM

RD

CAMPUS DR

UNIVERSITY

1230

N

BRIGHAM YOUNG UNIVERSITY

HERITAGE BIRCH LN

UTAH VALLEY REGIONAL MEDICAL CENTER

PROVO RECREATION CENTER

MUSEUM OF ART

WILKINSON CENTER AND BYU BOOKSTORE

820

N

800

N

700

N

MUSEUM OF PEOPLES AND CULTURES (BYU)

NORTH PARK AND DUP PIONEER CENTER

600

N

500

400

900 W
800 W
700 W
600 W
500 W
400 W
300 W
200 W
100 W

N

100 N
200 N
300 N
400 N
500 N
600 N
700 N
900 N

N

300

1100 W
1000 W

200

N

100

PROVO MARRIOTT PARK HOTEL

GREYHOUND BUS

UINTA NATIONAL FOREST SUPERVISOR'S OFFICE

N

CENTER

DEMAE

GURU'S

OTTAVIO'S RISTORANTE ITALIANO

ST

To Utah Lake, Fort Utah, and Provo Municipal Airport

100

Pioneer Park

LOS HERMANOS

PROVO TABERNACLE

UTAH COUNTY TRAVEL COUNCIL (TOURIST INFO)

S

200

POST OFFICE

TRAVELODGE

S

300

S

400

PROVO TRAVELERS INN

m

m

m

500

AVE

m
m
m
m
m
m

S

600

S

600

S

15

189

S STATE ST

0   0.25 mi

0   0.25 km

920

S

900

S

EAST BAY GOLF COURSE

To National 9 Colony Inn and La Quinta

89

Monte L. Bean Life Science Museum

Mounted animals and dioramas realistically depict wildlife of Utah and distant lands at this museum (645 East 1430 North, 801/422-5051, http://mlbean.byu.edu, 10 A.M.–9 P.M. Mon.–Fri., noon–5 P.M. Sat., free). The exhibits not only identify the many species on display but also show how they interact within their environments. Special presentations include movies, talks, workshops, and live-reptile, animal-adaptation, and other demonstrations; call for the schedule.

Earth Science Museum

This newly expanded museum (1683 N. Provo Canyon Rd., 801/422-3680, http://cpms.byu.edu, 9 A.M.–5 P.M. Mon.–Fri., free) across from Cougar Stadium features excellent exhibits of dinosaurs and early mammals; BYU has a good program in paleontology and students excavate bones from Utah and other western states. A viewing window lets you observe researchers cleaning and preparing bones.

Museum of Peoples and Cultures

This museum's (700 North 100 East, 801/422-0020, http://mpc.byu.edu, 9 A.M.–5 P.M. Mon.–Fri., free) purpose is to communicate knowledge about both modern and ancient peoples of the world. Exhibits reflect research in the Great Basin in Utah, the American Southwest, Mesoamerica, South America, the Near East, and Polynesia.

OTHER PROVO SIGHTS

Provo Tabernacle

Architect William Folsom, who designed the St. George and Manti Temples, patterned this English-style structure (100 S. University Ave.) after a Presbyterian Church he had visited in Salt Lake City. Construction, begun in 1883, required 15 years. Organ recitals and other concerts take place here.

Provo Temple

This modern building (2200 N. Temple Dr.) of white cast stone incorporates floral elements

© PAUL LEVY

Provo Temple is a striking building in a beautiful setting.

and a central golden spire. It's particularly impressive lit up against the sky at night. Dedication took place in 1972 with 75,000 people in attendance. Church members carry out sacred work within the 283 rooms. Visitors can't go inside but are welcome to visit the landscaped grounds. Turn east on 2230 North from University Avenue or drive north on 900 East.

Utah Lake State Park

The largest body of fresh water completely within the state, Utah Lake is 24 miles long and 11 miles wide. Average depth is only 9.4 feet. Mountains form the skyline in all directions. Swans, geese, pelicans, ducks, and other migratory birds stop by. Best bird-watching is at the south end of the lake and near the Provo Airport. The state park (801/375-0731 or 800/322-3770, www.reserveamerica.com, $9 day use, $18 camping) provides recreation facilities on the east shore, just a short drive from downtown Provo. Boaters come for water-skiing, sailboarding, and fishing; four paved boat ramps, docks, and slips are available.

The swimming beach offers another way to cool off. Anglers catch white and black bass, channel catfish, walleyed pike, carp, and other warm-water fish during most of the year. The lake usually freezes over by late December and has good ice fishing; trout descend from the mountain rivers during this season. A visitors center has ice-skating in winter. The campground is open mid-March–October with water and showers. Head west four miles on Center from downtown Provo or take the I-15 exit for West Center and go west three miles.

◖ Springville Museum of Art

The museum (126 East 400 South, Springville, 801/489-2727, http://sma.nebo.edu/museum. html, 10 A.M.–5 P.M. Tues.–Sat., 10 A.M.– 9 P.M. Wed., 3–6 P.M. Sun., free) started in the early 1900s as the collection of Springville High School, but when it began to receive gifts of major works from artists Cyrus Dallin and John Hafen, townspeople decided that a special building was needed. They built this fine Spanish-style structure during the Depression with federal and LDS Church assistance. The town is now also known as "Art City" for its patronage. The permanent collection contains 1,500 works including some of the best by early Utah pioneers and Native Americans as well

as the state's modern artists. Eleven galleries display visiting exhibits downstairs; a permanent collection is housed upstairs. The annual Spring Salon (late April) is a major show of Utah contemporary artists. From Provo, drive seven miles south on U.S. 89 (S. State St.) or take I-15 Exit 263 and go east.

ENTERTAINMENT AND EVENTS

Major annual events in the area include **Spring Salon,** which takes place in Springville in late April.

In July, Provo celebrates the Fourth with **Freedom Days** and an arts festival, music, a parade, a run, and other activities. Nationally recognized storytellers present traditional and new pieces on Labor Day weekend in the **Timpanogos Storytelling Festival.**

RECREATION
Parks, Gyms, and Water Parks

North Park (500 West 500 North, 801/379-6614) contains an outdoor pool and waterslide, picnic areas, playground, and a pioneer museum (801/852-6609, 1–4 P.M. Wed., Fri., Sat. in summer, free). **Provo Recreation Center** (1155 N.

© W. C. MCRAE

downtown Provo

University Avenue, 801/379-6610), next to Provo High School, has an indoor pool, racquetball and volleyball courts, and weight rooms.

The big **Seven Peaks Resort Water Park** (1330 East 300 North, 801/377-4386 or801/377-4FUN, www.sevenpeaks.com, 11 A.M.–8 P.M. Mon.–Sat. Memorial Day–Labor Day, $20 Mon.–Thurs., $22 Fri.–Sat. ages 12–64, $15.75/$16.50 ages 4–11, free ages 3 and under and 65 and over) contains 16 water slides, a huge wave pool, twisting tubes, and a variety of pools to cool off in. Guests can also engage in a wide variety of dry-land activities, including paintball, mechanical bull-riding, shooting cross-bows, and other equally frightening games. Turn east on Center Street to its end and follow signs.

Other Recreation

Play golf at the 27-hole **East Bay Golf Course** (1860 S. 380 East, 801/373-6262, turn east on East Bay Blvd. from South University Ave. near the I-15 interchange) or the nine-hole **Cascade Fairways Public Golf Course** (1313 East 800 North, Orem, 801/225-6677).

Year-round ice skating is possible at the **Peaks Ice Arena** (100 N. Seven Peaks Blvd., 801/377-8777, 8 A.M.–9 P.M. Mon.–Sat.), a 2002 Winter Olympics venue.

ACCOMMODATIONS

Most of Provo's newer accommodations are chain motels along South University Avenue, the long commercial strip that runs from I-15 Exit 266 to downtown. The downtown area offers older but well-maintained properties.

About $50

If you're concerned more with price than comfort, look for a string of budget motels at the south end of town. The **National 9 Colony Inn** (1380 S. University Ave., 801/374-6800 or 800/524-9999, about $50) has large rooms, with many kitchenette rooms, a sauna, pool, and hot tub, but a distinct budget-motel ambiance. Within an easy walk of the downtown restaurant row, the **Provo Travelers Inn** (70 East 300 South, 801/373-8973 or 800/321-0055, $50) has a pool.

$50-100

The **Travelodge** (124 S. University Ave., 801/373-1974 or 800/255-3050, $63) is a decently priced motel right in the center of town and has a pool.

Near the university, the **Days Inn** (1675 North 200 West, 801/375-8600 or 800/325-2525, $60) has a pool. The **Best Western Cottontree Inn** (2230 N. University Pkwy., 801/373-7044 or 800/662-6886, $86) is near the Provo River, with access to biking and walking paths; it has an indoor and outdoor pool, plus large rooms with lots of extras.

South of downtown, the **La Quinta** (1460 S. University, 801/374-9750, $80) has spacious rooms, an outdoor pool, and a good breakfast buffet.

Over $100

The **Provo Marriott Park Hotel** (101 West 100 North, 801/377-4700 or 888/825-3162, $150), in the heart of downtown, is an upscale business and conference hotel. Rooms are nicely appointed, and come with refrigerators and coffeemakers; facilities include a pool, spa, and weight room. Another good choice, and close to the university (Freedom Blvd. is the same as 200 West), is the **Courtyard by Marriott** (1600 N. Freedom Blvd., 801/373-2222, $150).

Campgrounds

Lakeside RV Campground (4000 W. Center, 801/373-5267, $18 tents, $25–27 RVs), just before Utah Lake State Park, has showers, pool, laundry, store, and canoe rentals; open year-round. **Provo KOA** (320 North 2050 West, 801/375-2994, $21 tent, $24–40 RV, mid-Apr.–mid.-Oct.) is a quarter mile west of I-15 on Center, then one block north.

FOOD

Downtown Provo has a pretty good restaurant row along Center, on both sides of University. It's easy just to wander down the street and select a place. Note that it's hard to find a place that's open for breakfast Sunday morning.

One of Provo's few fine dining restaurants is **C Ottavio's Ristorante Italiano** (69 E.

Center St., 801/377-9555, lunch and dinner daily, $10–20), a fun, old-fashioned Italian restaurant with a wide selection of excellent pasta and roast meat dishes and a strolling accordion player.

On the same block, find the almost-hip (in a yoga sort of way) **Guru's** (45 E. Center, 801/377-6980, lunch and dinner daily, $5–9), which serves good pasta, rice bowls, wraps, and salads, and where inspirational quotes and photos on the walls let you know that the meals are considered to be "food for the soul."

On the west side of center, **Demae** (82 W. Center, 801/374-0306, $4–20) has sushi (starting at $3) and big bowls of udon for $4. **Los Hermanos** (16 W. Center, 801/223-0108, lunch and dinner Mon.–Sat., $7–16) is a popular Mexican restaurant.

If you're looking for Mexican food, consider driving south of Provo to Springville. There, the somewhat ramshackle but *auténtico* **La Casita Mexican Restaurant** (333 N. Main St., 801/489-9543, $7–15) is the area's best bet for good traditional south of the border cooking; the restaurant has a liquor license. Also in Springville, **Ginger's Garden Cafe** (188 S. Main, 801/489-4500, $5–11) puts the emphasis on fresh, healthy food.

INFORMATION AND SERVICES

Utah Valley Convention and Visitors Bureau (111 S. University Ave., 801/851-2107 or 800/222-UTAH, www.utahvalley.org) offers advice on sights and services in Provo and the Utah Valley. Although mostly an administrative office, the **Uinta National Forest Supervisor** (88 West 100 North, 801/377-5780, www.fs.fed.us/r4/uinta) has general information about all districts in the forest.

The **post office** is at 95 West 100 South (801/275-8777). **Utah Valley Regional Medical Center** is at 1034 North 500 West (801/373-7850).

TRANSPORTATION

Utah Transit Authority (UTA, 801/375-4636, www.rideuta.com) provides local bus service in Provo and connects with Springville, Salt Lake City, Ogden, and other towns; buses don't run on Sunday and holidays except for a few lines on Sunday in Salt Lake City and Ogden. **Greyhound Bus** (124 North 300 West, 801/373-4211) has two northbound and two southbound departures daily. **Amtrak** trains (300 West 600 South, 800/872-7245) also serve Provo.

Northwest of Provo

Along the I-15 corridor between Provo and Salt Lake City are a few sights, ranging from the individual and quirky Hutchings Museum to the huge Thanksgiving Point enterprise.

John Hutchings Museum of Natural History

This amazingly diverse collection (55 N. Center St., Lehi, 801/768-7180, www.hutchings museum.org, 11 A.M.–5 P.M. Tues.–Sat., $3.50 adults, $2.50 children under 12) in the town of Lehi (LEE-high, 16 miles northwest of Provo on I-15) began as a family museum. Highlights include pioneer rifles, Native American crafts, glittering minerals, ancient fossils, mounted birds of Utah, and colorful tropical shells.

Thanksgiving Point

Also near Lehi, this vast park and education/entertainment center (801/768-2300 or 888/672-6040, www.thanksgivingpoint.com, 10 A.M.–8 P.M. Mon.–Sat., fees vary widely) between Utah Lake and I-15 contains everything from incredible gardens, a business park, golf course, formal garden, and paleontology museum to a petting zoo, plus loads of dining and shopping. Highlights of the park, which is the brainchild of the founders of WordPerfect, include **The Barn,** which serves as a performance and special events space; **Farm Country,** a farm and petting zoo, complete with wagon rides and lots of tame animals doing what comes naturally; **Thanksgiving Gardens,** containing 55 acres of formal gardens, plus a "waterfall amphitheater"; and a 200-acre, 7,728-yard **18-hole golf course.** The **Village at Thanksgiving Point** offers six restaurants and dining halls, and nearly 11 shops and stores. More than a million people visit each year, including tens of thousands of kids on school field trips.

Thanksgiving Point will either really appeal to you as a one-stop vacation wonderland or send you screaming in the other direction, in search of noncommercialized, unpackaged pastimes. However, one very good reason to make the stop is to visit the **Museum of Ancient Life,** which claims to be the largest dinosaur museum in the world. With over 122,000 square feet of exhibition space, this museum contains 60 complete dinosaur skeletons, with dozens of hands-on displays, research facilities, and a six-story IMAX theater. Most of the featured dinosaurs represent species that once strode across the alluvial sands of ancient Utah, including the first-ever displayed skeleton of a supersaurus, super-sized at 110 feet long.

The Thanksgiving Point compound is just west of I-15 Exit 287. Admission rates are a complex system of individual and combo tickets; check out the options on the website. An adult admission to the Museum of Ancient Life is $9.50, children 3–12 are $7.50. An Adventure Passport ticket to most facilities (including the museum, theater, gardens, and farm) is $25 adult, $19 children.

Camp Floyd Stagecoach Inn State Park

A restored inn, an old U.S. Army building, and a military cemetery (18035 West 1540

North, Fairfield, 801/768-8932, 9 A.M.– 5 P.M. daily summer, closed Sun. mid-Oct.– Mar., $2 per person, $6 family) preserve a bit of pioneer history at Fairfield, a sleepy village on the other side of Utah Lake from Provo. John Carson, who had been one of the first settlers of the site in 1855, built a family residence and hotel three years later. About the same time, troops of the U.S. Army under Colonel Albert Johnston marched in and established Camp Floyd nearby. The soldiers had been sent by President Buchanan to put down a rumored Mormon rebellion. Upon finding that no "Mormon War" existed, the colonel led his men to this site so as not to intimidate the major Mormon settlements. Fairfield jumped in size almost overnight to become Utah's third-largest city, with a population of about 7,000—including the 3,000 soldiers. Even for the times, it was rowdy—17 saloons served the army men. The camp (later named Fort Crittenden) served no real purpose, however, and was abandoned in 1861 so that troops could return east to fight in the Civil War.

Carson's hotel, later known as the Stagecoach Inn, continued to serve travelers on the dusty main road across Utah. Pony Express riders, stagecoach passengers, miners, sheepherders, and every other kind of traveler stopped here for the night until the doors closed in 1947.

Now the inn is a state park, furnished as in the old days and full of exhibits on frontier life. A shaded picnic area is beside it. The only surviving building of Camp Floyd has been moved across the street and contains a diorama of the fort and some excavated artifacts. Camp Floyd's well-kept cemetery is a three-quarter-mile drive west and south of Fairfield. From Provo or Salt Lake City, take I-15 to Lehi and turn west 21 miles on Hwy. 73.

North of Provo

The natural areas north of Provo could easily fill a week's worth of exploration, but they're also pretty easy to reach from town.

◖ TIMPANOGOS CAVE NATIONAL MONUMENT

Beautiful cave formations reward visitors who hike the trail to the cave entrance (801/756-5238, www.nps.gov/tica, 7 A.M.–5:30 P.M. May–Labor Day, 8 A.M.–5 P.M. Labor Day–mid-Oct., $3 per vehicle admission to monument, cave tours $7 adult, $5 ages 6–15, $3 ages 3–5) on the north side of Mount Timpanogos. Tunnels connect three separate limestone caves, each of which has a different character. The first was discovered by Martin Hansen in 1887 while he was tracking a mountain lion. Middle and Timpanogos Caves weren't reported until 1921–1922. Timpanogos Cave so impressed early explorers that a trail, lighting, and national monument protection came soon afterward.

Exhibits and a short slide show in the visitors center introduce the formation, history, and ecology of the caves. Be sure to obtain tickets here for the cave tour before starting up the trail.

Allow about three hours for the complete trip, including 45–60 minutes for the cave tour. The three-mile round-trip hike from the visitors center to the caves is moderately difficult; you'll climb 1,065 feet to an elevation of 6,730 feet. Points along the way have fine views up and down American Fork Canyon and out onto the Utah Valley. People with breathing, heart, or walking difficulties shouldn't attempt the trail; wheeled vehicles (including strollers) and pets aren't allowed.

Ranger-led tours wind about one-third mile through the caves. Underground temperature is about 45°F all year, so bring a sweater or jacket. The caves close during winter because snow and ice make the trail too hazardous; the season lasts May–mid-October. On Saturday (all day), Sunday afternoons, holidays, and midsummer weekdays, you may have a long wait. Call ahead to check hours and find out how busy the caves are. Tickets can also be purchased up to 30 day in advance by telephone. Tours often sell out mid-June–mid-August, when advance reservations are strongly recommended.

A snack bar at the visitors center is open in summer. Picnickers can use tables across the road from the visitors center and at a site a quarter-mile west.

The U.S. Forest Service has several campgrounds nearby. The visitors center is two miles up American Fork Canyon on the Alpine Scenic Loop (Hwy. 92). You can take I-15 American Fork Exit 279 if you're coming north from Provo or the I-15 Alpine Exit 287 if coming south from Salt Lake City.

ALPINE SCENIC LOOP

The narrow paved highway twists and winds through some of the most beautiful alpine terrain in Utah. Mount Timpanogos rises to 11,750 feet in the center of the loop and presents sheer cliff faces and jagged ridges in every direction. More than a dozen campgrounds and several picnic areas line the way. Anglers can try for trout in swift clear streams. Autumn brings brilliant gold to the aspen and scarlet to the maples. Winter snows close the loop at its higher elevations and attract skiers to Sundance Resort. The most scenic sections of the loop lie along American Fork Canyon and its South Fork, Provo Canyon, and its North Fork, and on the high pass between these drainages. A drive on U.S. 89 or I-15 completes the approximately 40-mile loop. With a few stops, a full day can easily be spent on the drive. If you'd like to see Timpanogos Cave on the way, begin the loop there to avoid waiting in ticket lines, especially on weekend afternoons.

Most of the picnic areas and campgrounds lie along American Fork Canyon at elevations of 5,400 to 6,200 feet. Higher recreation areas (801/785-3563 or 877/444-6777, www.recreation.gov, late May–Oct., $13) are **Granite Flat Campground** (elev. 6,800

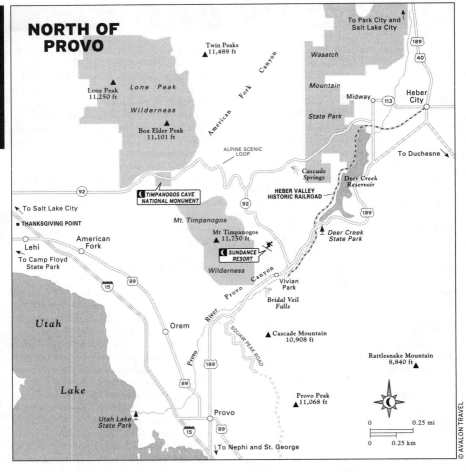

NORTH OF PROVO

To Park City and Salt Lake City

Twin Peaks ▲ 11,489 ft

Wasatch

American Fork Canyon

189

40

Lone Peak ▲ 11,250 ft

Lone Peak

Mountain

Midway

Heber City

113

Wilderness

State Park

Box Elder Peak ▲ 11,101 ft

ALPINE SCENIC LOOP

To Duchesne

Cascade Springs

Deer Creek Reservoir

92

TIMPANOGOS CAVE NATIONAL MONUMENT

HEBER VALLEY HISTORIC RAILROAD

92

189

To Salt Lake City

THANKSGIVING POINT

Mt. Timpanogos

Deer Creek State Park

American Fork

Mt Timpanogos ▲ 11,750 ft

Lehi

89

SUNDANCE RESORT

To Camp Floyd State Park

15

Wilderness

Provo Canyon

Vivian Park

Utah

Orem

River

Provo

Bridal Veil Falls

Cascade Mountain 10,908 ft

SQUAW PEAK ROAD

Rattlesnake Mountain 8,840 ft ▲

189

89

Lake

Provo

Provo Peak ▲ 11,068 ft

Utah Lake State Park

15

89

0   0.25 mi

0   0.25 km

© AVALON TRAVEL

To Nephi and St. George

---

feet), **Timpooneke Campground** (elev. 7,400 feet), **Mount Timpanogos Campground** (elev. 6,800 feet), and **Theatre in the Pines Picnic Area** (elev. 6,800 feet). **Pleasant Grove Ranger District office** (390 North 100 East, Pleasant Grove, 801/785-3563) of the Uinta National Forest has information and maps for recreation areas along the Alpine Scenic Loop and for the Lone Peak and Mount Timpanogos Wildernesses. (You'll pass the office if taking U.S. 89 and Hwy.

146 between Provo/Orem and the mouth of American Fork Canyon.)

Lone Peak Wilderness

The summit of Lone Peak rises to 11,250 feet on the divide between Little Cottonwood and American Fork Canyons. Despite its closeness to Provo and Salt Lake City, the wilderness (30,088 acres) offers good opportunities for solitude. Hikers sometimes spot mountain goats. A climb to the summit is a very strenuous day hike; many people prefer taking two days. Some routes have dangerous drop-offs and require mountaineering skills. Lower elevations have fine scenery as well as easier hiking. Lake Hardy (southeast of the summit) is a popular destination. Four main trailheads provide access to the wilderness: Bells Canyon from lower Little Cottonwood Canyon to the north, Draper Ridge to the west, Alpine to the south, and Granite Flat Campground (off American Fork Canyon) to the southeast.

Contact the Salt Lake City Ranger District for hiking information on the north slope, the Pleasant Grove Ranger District (390 North 100 East, Pleasant Grove, 801/785-3563) for the south side.

Mount Timpanogos Wilderness

The sheer cliffs of Mount Timpanogos tower 7,000 feet above the Utah Valley and present one of the most dramatic sights of the Wasatch Range. Trails to the heights lead past waterfalls, flower-filled alpine meadows, lakes, and permanent snowfields. One trail continues to the 11,750-foot summit for superb vistas of central Utah. The climb is strenuous, especially the last three miles, but requires no special skills. You'll see whole families—from grandchildren to grandparents—on this popular mountain. Even short hikes can be very rewarding. Take care to bring storm gear in case the weather suddenly turns bad. A shelter at Emerald Lake provides a refuge from storms. Hike either the **Timpooneke Trail** from Timpooneke Campground or the **Aspen Grove Trail** from the Theatre in the Pines Picnic Area; both trailheads lie just off the Alpine Scenic Loop. One-way distances to the summit are 9.1 miles on the Timpooneke Trail (4,350-foot elevation gain) and 8.3 miles on the Aspen Grove Trail (4,900-foot elevation gain). A hike on both trails (highly recommended) can be done with a car shuttle. If a trip to the summit sounds too ambitious, stick to the 12 miles between the trailheads via Emerald Lake (elev. 10,300 feet).

The **Summit Trail** branches off west of Emerald Lake, climbs a steep slope to the jagged summit ridge, then follows the ridge south-

east to the top. A large snowfield and the deep blue waters of Emerald Lake lie directly below. Chunks of ice break off the snowfield and float in the lake during even the hottest summer days. Local people often refer to the snowfield as a glacier, but technically it's just a snowfield. Some climbers continue southeast along the summit ridge and drop down onto the snowfield and slide or walk to Emerald Lake, but this can be a bit hazardous. Hiking season is mid-July–mid-October. In winter and spring, hikers must be equipped and experienced for snow travel. The Pleasant Grove Ranger District office (390 North 100 East, Pleasant Grove, 801/785-3563) can advise on hiking conditions.

Cascade Springs

Crystal-clear water emerges amidst lush vegetation and flows down a long series of travertine terraces at this beautiful spot. The springs produce more than seven million gallons of water daily. Boardwalks (some accessible for people with disabilities) and short trails with interpretive signs allow a close look at the stream and pools. Trout can be seen darting through the water (though fishing is prohibited). Plantlife includes maple, oak, aspen, willow, water birch, box elder, cattails, watercress, and wildflowers. The drive to Cascade Springs is also very pretty, either from the Alpine Scenic Loop or from Heber Valley. A paved road (Forest Route 114) branches off the Alpine Scenic Loop near its summit (between mileposts 18 and 19) and winds northeast seven miles to the springs. An unpaved road, passable by car if the road is dry, begins on the west edge of Heber Valley and climbs high above the valley with good views, then drops down to the springs; turn west seven miles on Hwy. 220 from Hwy. 113 (between Midway and Charleston) and follow signs.

◖ Sundance Resort

Since actor/director Robert Redford purchased this land in 1969, he has worked toward obtaining an ideal blend of recreation, the arts, and natural beauty. Sundance (801/225-4100 recorded information, 801/225-4107 or

800/892-1600 office, www.sundanceresort.com) sponsors a wide selection of summer arts and music events; workshops, exhibits, and artist residencies provide an intense artistic focus to this remote mountain Eden. Redford also founded the **Sundance Institute** in 1980 as a laboratory for independent filmmakers; the actual Sundance Film Festival is held in Park City.

DOWNHILL SKIING

Downhill skiing (801/223-4170, mid-Dec.–Apr.) is pretty relaxed at Sundance. The resort's three main lifts take skiers high on the southeast slopes of Mount Timpanogos. The 41 runs on 450 acres provide challenges for people of all abilities; total elevation drop is 2,150 feet. Ski instruction, rentals, accommodations, restaurants, and packages are available at the resort. On weekends, adult lift tickets cost $45 full day, $36 half day; children 12 and under ski for $20 full day, $18 half day; weekday prices are discounted around $10. **Sundance Nordic Center** ($14 adults, $9 ages 11–17) offers 26 miles of Nordic track, lessons, and rentals.

ACCOMMODATIONS AND FOOD

Rooms here are beautifully decorated (if you've ever received the Sundance catalogue, or shopped at their Salt Lake City outlet store, you'll know the sort of high Western romantic furnishings to expect). Standard rooms start at $227–300; suites run about $400–600, and large mountain houses are $700 and up. The resort's on-site spa books appointments in the evenings.

Sundance has three dining facilities in the main compound, including the **Foundry Grill** (801/223-4250, breakfast, lunch, and dinner Mon.–Sat., brunch and dinner Sun., brunch $27 adults, $15 kids, dinner entrees $13–35), the elegant **Tree Room** (801/223-4220, dinner nightly, reservations recommended, $24–46), and a deli. The food is very good.

GETTING THERE

The resort can easily be reached by taking U.S. 189 from Provo, Orem, or Heber City, then turning northwest 2.5 miles on Hwy. 92 (Alpine Scenic Loop).

Squaw Peak Road

This scenic drive follows the Wasatch Range east of Provo and offers many fine views over Utah Valley. The road turns south from U.S. 189 in Lower Provo Canyon, then climbs high into the mountains. Pavement ends after five miles at the turnoff for **Hope Campground** (801/785-3563 or 877/444-6777, www.recreation.gov, late May–Oct., $13, elev. 6,600 feet). The road continues south to the Left Fork of Hobble Creek east of Springville for a total of 26 miles one-way. Squaw Peak Road has some rough spots in the middle section, but cars with good clearance can usually be driven through in dry weather. The Pleasant Grove Ranger District office (390 North 100 East, Pleasant Grove, 801/785-3563) can advise on camping, hiking, and road conditions.

South of Provo Along I-15

Although the I-15 corridor is not particularly exciting, there are some good side trips off into the mountains to the east. The small towns just off the freeway offer glimpses into LDS history.

HOBBLE CREEK–DIAMOND FORK LOOP

Pleasant canyon and mountain views line this 34-mile scenic drive east of Springville. The road is open about mid-May–late October and is normally fine for cars—all but about the middle eight miles are paved. Along the way you'll pass picnic spots, campgrounds, hiking trailheads, and fishing holes. Back roads branch off to Squaw Peak Road, Strawberry Reservoir, and other destinations. Hikers can choose from a trail network totaling about 100 miles. Contact the **Spanish Fork Ranger**

District office (44 West 400 North, Spanish Fork, 801/798-3571) for maps and recreation information. Find Cherry and Balsam campgrounds (877/444-6777, www.recreation.gov, late May–Oct., $14) along this route. To drive the loop from Main Street in Springville (take I-15 Exit 263), head east three miles on 400 South to the mouth of Hobble Creek Canyon and follow Forest Routes 058 and 029.

NEBO SCENIC LOOP

This mountain drive loops off I-15 and winds into the heights of the southern Wasatch Range. You'll enjoy alpine forests, fine panoramas of the valleys below, and a close look at Mount Nebo—highest peak in the range. The entire 43-mile length from Payson to Nephi is paved; it's open mid-June–late October. In winter and spring, cross-country skiers and snowmobilers come up to glide across the snow. You can begin the drive from Payson in the north (I-15 Exit 254) or Nephi in the south (take I-15 Exit 222 or 228 and go east six miles on Hwy. 132). A partly paved road from Santaquin (I-15 Exit 248) goes southeast 11 miles via Santaquin Canyon to connect with the main drive.

More than 100 miles of trails lead into the backcountry. **Devil's Kitchen Geologic Area** lies at the end of a quarter-mile trail, 28 miles south of Payson; eroded layers of red-tinted river gravel and silt form spires and sharp ridges. **Mount Nebo Wilderness** is west of the drive and can be reached by several trails. Strong hikers can climb the south summit (elev. 11,877 feet) by trail on a day or overnight trip. The higher north summit (elev. 11,928 feet) is two peaks farther north along a knife-edged ridge (no trail).

The U.S. Forest Service maintains recreation facilities, trailheads, and overlooks along the Nebo Scenic Loop. Contact the **Spanish Fork Ranger District office** (44 West 400 North, Spanish Fork, 801/798-3571) for maps and information. If you're coming from the south, you can stop at the Forest Service's **Nephi Ranger District office** (635 N. Main, 435/623-2735) for info on the scenic loop. You can reserve

sites at Payson Lakes, Blackhawk, and Ponderosa campgrounds (877/444-6777, www.recreation.gov, late May–mid-Sept., $14).

NEPHI

This small town (pop. 5,200) serves as the commercial center for the region and the seat of Juab County. The first settlers arrived in 1851 and named the place for a patriarch in the Book of Mormon. Pleasant scents fill the air at the **Nephi Rose Garden,** one block east of Main on 100 North. North of Nephi, in Mona, **Young Living Family Farm** (435/623-8006) grows and distills herbs for essential oils (that's the distillery mentioned on the roadside sign).

Recreation and Events

Nephi's annual events are the **Ute Stampede and Rodeo** in July and the **Juab County Fair** in August. The **city park** at Main and 500 North has picnic tables, a playground, and an outdoor pool. The nine-hole **Canyon Hills Park Golf Course** (1200 East 100 North, 435/623-9930) lies up a canyon.

Accommodations

Right in town, the **Safari Motel** (413 S. Main, 435/623-1071, $45) has clean, inexpensive rooms plus a pool. It's a good alternative to the chain motels (Super 8, Motel 6) at the freeway exits.

Another local place is **Roberta's Cove Motor Inn** (2250 S. Main, 435/623-2629 or 800/456-6460, $50). Closer to downtown is the **Best Western Paradise Inn** (1025 S. Main, 435/623-0624 or 800/524-9999, $75), the nicest place you'll find to stay in town.

Food

The favorite place to eat in Nephi is **J. C. Mickelson's Restaurant** (2100 S. Main, 435/623-0152, breakfast, lunch, and dinner daily, $7 dinner specials) at I-15 Exit 222, with good American-style home cooking. The area's best Mexican restaurant is **Mi Rancherito Restaurant** (390 S. Main, 435/623-4391, lunch and dinner Mon.–Sat., $7–16). Head off

I-15 at exit 225 to find the **Salt Creek Steak House** (22 N. Sheep Ln., 435/623-0959, dinner Mon.–Sat., $12–28), a classic steak house.

Information and Services

The **Juab Travel Council** (4 S. Main, 435/623-5203 or 800/748-4361, www.juabtravel.com) is the best source for information on the area. The **Nephi Ranger District office** (635 N. Main, 435/623-2735) of the Uinta National Forest has information on the Nebo Scenic Loop. **Central Valley Medical Center** is at 48 West 1500 North (435/623-3000).

YUBA STATE PARK

Here at Yuba State Park (435/758-2611 ranger, 800/322-3770 or www.reserveamerica.com reservations, $7 day use, $9–15 camping) the Sevier Bridge Reservoir, 26 miles south of Nephi, is 22 miles long and 11,000 acres when full; its elevation is 5,014 feet. Minerals give the lake a turquoise tint that varies with the light. There's plenty of space for both water-skiers and anglers. Sailboarders often find good wind conditions here and warmer water in springtime than at most other Utah lakes. Anglers catch yellow perch, walleye, channel catfish, and northern pike; ice fishing, mostly for yellow perch, is done January–early March. North Sandy Beach (on the main road to the campground) and East Beach (reached from Hwy. 28) have the best swimming, but there's also a beach at the campground.

The name "Yuba" refers to the dam, begun in 1902 and originally named "U.B." Farmers who helped to build the dam received water rights from the Deseret Irrigation Company in payment for their labor; if they stopped working they lost their stock—if they kept working they had to do additional work to pay for an assessment. An old song lamented that "U.B. damned if you do and U.B. damned if you don't."

The campground (with showers), picnic area, and a paved boat ramp lie on the west shore; take I-15 Exit 202 and follow signs 4.3 miles. North Beach is off to the left 2.2 miles in; a small store here is open on summer weekends. If driving to the campground from the south, you can save eight miles by taking the I-15 frontage road (west side) from Scipio. East Beach and Painted Rocks Pictograph Site, both on the east shore, can be reached by boat or from Hwy. 28 (an unpaved road from North Beach provides a shortcut to Hwy. 28). Boaters can also use a boat ramp near Painted Rocks Pictograph Site. The park and campground stay open all year, though the campground showers close November–March.

FILLMORE

In 1851, Brigham Young and the Utah Territorial Legislature designated Fillmore as the territorial capital, even before the town was established. They chose this site in the Pahvant Valley because it lay in the approximate geographic center of the territory. Their plans didn't work out, but Fillmore (pop. 2,200) has become the center of a large agricultural region and the Millard County seat. A state historical museum in the Territorial Statehouse contains a wealth of pioneer history.

Territorial Statehouse State Park

Completed in 1855, the statehouse (50 W. Capitol Ave., 435/743-5316, 9 A.M.–4 P.M. Mon.–Sat., $3 adults, $1 ages 3–15, or $5 per vehicle) is Utah's oldest government building. Architect Truman O. Angell designed the three-story sandstone structure, originally planned to have four wings capped by a large Moorish dome. Only the south wing was completed, though, because antagonism between the U.S. government and the Mormons blocked the appropriation of expected federal funds. Several legislatures met here, but only the fifth session, in 1855, stayed for its full term; the sixth and eighth sessions opened here, then quickly adjourned to Salt Lake City's better-suited facilities.

Rooms are furnished to represent a typical pioneer bedroom, parlor, and kitchen. Other exhibits display clothing, tools, and Native American artifacts. Lawbreakers spent time in the jail—one of the building's many uses. Historic photos and paintings show pioneer families and leaders of the church and government in early Utah. You can visit a pair of 1880s log cabins on the grounds; one has pioneer furnishings, the other a wagon. Peek in the windows of the restored 1867 Little Rock School House nearby. The cabins and schoolhouse can be opened on request. Rose gardens flank the statehouse, which is downtown behind the Millard County Courthouse. Also part of this parklike complex are the municipal swimming pool and some lovely shaded picnic spots.

Accommodations and Food

A good bet in Fillmore is the **Inn at Apple Creek** (940 S. Hwy. 99, 435/743-4334, $65), a surprisingly nice (though not overly fancy) place for this small town. It has a small indoor pool and free breakfast. The **Best Western Paradise Inn** is at I-15 Exit 167 (905 N. Main St., 435/743-6895, $75) and has a heated pool and a good restaurant, the **Garden of Eat'n** (breakfast, lunch, and dinner daily, $6–23). Another good place for a bite to eat and some local atmosphere is **Cluff's Carhop Cafe** (260 N. Main, 435/743-5510, lunch and dinner Mon.–Sat., $5 burger), a cute retro-style burger joint with tables under shade trees.

CAMPGROUNDS

Open year-round, **Wagons West RV Campground** (545 N. Main, 435/743-6188, $23 and up RV) has showers, laundry, and a store; both tents and RVs welcome. **Fillmore KOA** (900 South 410 West, 435/743-4420, Mar.–early Dec., $18 tent, $22 and up RV, $32 cabin), one-half mile off the south end of the business loop near I-15 Exit 163, has showers, laundry, and a store.

Information and Services

Millard County Tourism (www.millardcounty.com) provides information on the county. **Fillmore Community Medical Center** is at 674 S. Hwy. 99 (435/743-5591).

TABERNACLE HILL

Volcanic eruptions in the desert 15 miles southwest of Fillmore have covered the land with cinder cones, a tuff ring, a collapsed caldera, spatter cones, pit craters, pressure ridges, and squeeze-ups. The first eruptions occurred 12,000-24,000 years ago, when Lake Bonneville covered the region. Explosive cinder and ash eruptions built a circular ring of tuff 3,000 feet across and 200 feet or more high, which rose above the lake waters. In a second period of eruptions 11,000-12,000 years ago, molten lava filled the tuff ring and spilled out to the north, forming a seven-square-mile island of black lava in the receding lake. About two-thirds of the tuff ring survives today. When viewed from the north, it resembles the Mormon Tabernacle in Salt Lake City – hence the name Tabernacle Hill. The collapsed caldera inside is 1,000 feet across and 60 feet deep. Two spatter cones near the hill represent the last gasps of the final eruption. A lava-tube cave, most of which lies west of the caldera, can be traced (on the surface) for about a mile. Bats live in some of the cave sections. You can enter the cave where its roof has collapsed, though rockfalls commonly block the passages. Watch for Great Basin rattlesnakes when exploring the caves and other features here.

You can visit Tabernacle Hill any time of year, but in summer try to visit early in the day. From Fillmore, go west six miles on 400 North (Highway 100) to Flowell, turn left (south) one mile, turn right two miles (pavement ends), turn left (south) 3.5 miles at the junction (the other road continues to cinder pits). Continue on the main track toward Tabernacle Hill in the distance; at a major gravel road, turn west, then immediately turn south again on a narrow dirt road – Tabernacle Hill is 2.5 miles farther. You may have to walk the last two miles, depending on road conditions. Tabernacle Hill can also be reached from Meadow, eight miles to the southeast. The BLM office in Fillmore (35 East 500 North, 435/743-3100) has maps and information helpful in exploring this and other areas of Utah's Great Basin.

VICINITY OF FILLMORE
Pahvant Range

These mountains east of Fillmore have seven summits over 10,000 feet; Mine Camp Peak (elev. 10,222 feet) is the highest. A network of trails and forest roads leads into the high country; contact the Fillmore Ranger District office (390 S. Main, 435/743-5721, www.fs.fed.us/r4/fishlake) for recreation information. Turn east six miles on 200 South from downtown Fillmore to reach four picnic areas along wooded Chalk Creek. They have water in summer; free. Elevations are 5,700–6,100 feet. Anglers catch rainbow and German brown trout in the creek. **Adelaide Campground** (late May–early Oct., $10, has water) lies along Corn Creek farther south near Kanosh. Cottonwood, piñon pine, juniper, spruce, and maple grow at the 5,500-foot elevation. From the southernmost east–west street in Kanosh, turn east five miles on a gravel road (Forest Route 106). The road continues through pretty country and descends Mud Spring Hollow to I-70. Corn Creek has fishing for rainbow and German brown trout.

Two recreation areas are in the northern part of the range: **Maple Hollow Picnic Area,** on the west side, has water late May–early October (elev. 6,900 feet); take the I-15 South Holden Exit 174 and go east six miles. Box elder, maple, oak, and fir trees grow in the hollow. **Maple Grove Campground** is open with water late May–early October (elev. 6,400 feet); $10. Turn west four miles on the signed paved road from U.S. 50 (near milepost 47 between Scipio and Salina). Maple, water birch, oak, piñon pine, juniper, and aspen grow in the valley; Ivie Creek has fishing for rainbow trout.

Cove Fort

In 1867, during the Black Hawk War, LDS Church president Brigham Young ordered construction of this fort (junction of I-15 and I-70, www.covefort.com, 10 A.M.–dusk early Apr.–mid-Oct., free) to protect travelers on the overnight journey between Fillmore and Beaver. Walls of volcanic basalt 13 feet high contained 12 rooms and a cistern and enclosed an area 100 feet square. Gunports at the two

© PAUL LEVY

Cove Fort was built as a defense during the Black Hawk War.

entrances and along the upper walls discouraged Native Americans from ever attacking the fort. Volunteers of the LDS Church lead informal tours and relate the fort's history. Cove Fort stands near the junction of I-15 and I-70; take I-15 Exit 135 and go southeast two miles or take I-70 Exit 1 and go northwest one mile.

BEAVER

Beaver (pop. 2,600) is a handy travelers' stop just east of I-15. Main Street (the I-15 Business Loop) has a good selection of motels and restaurants. Center Street (Hwy. 21) goes west to Minersville State Park (fishing and boating) and the desert country of west-central Utah. An entirely different world lies just to the east on Hwy. 153 (200 North St.)—wooded canyons, alpine lakes, and a ski area in Utah's third-highest mountain range, the Tushars.

Historic Buildings

More than 200 historic houses of architectural interest lie scattered around town. You'll see many of them by driving along the side streets. A large stone building remaining from Fort Cameron, constructed during a mining boom in 1872, still stands on the east edge of town across the highway from the golf course. The old **Beaver County Courthouse** (190 E. Center St., 11 A.M.–5 P.M. Tues.–Sat., free) with an ornate clock tower, represents the architectural splendor of its period. Building started in 1877, and the courthouse served Beaver County from 1882 until 1975. It now houses a historical museum; drop by to see pioneer portraits, historic documents, an 1892 wedding cake, other artifacts, and mineral specimens. Visit the courtroom on the top floor, then head down to the dungeon-like jail cells in the basement (check out the graffiti). The adjacent Historical Park, on Center one block east of Main, has a statue of Philo T. Farnsworth (1906–1971), the "Father of Television," who was born in a log cabin near Beaver.

Recreation and Events

City parks offer picnic tables and playgrounds

at Main and Center and at 400 East and 300 North. The second park also contains the indoor **Municipal Swimming Pool** (435/438-5066). **Tennis courts** are at the rodeo grounds on the east edge of town. Play golf at the nine-hole **Canyon Breeze Golf Course** (435/438-2601) on the east edge of town. There's good **rockhounding** in the Mineral Mountains northwest of town and in other areas to the west; a brochure that describes collecting sites is available from many local businesses.

Beaver City Birthday celebrates with historic programs on February 6. Early July brings the **Butch Cassidy Festival,** celebrating native son Robert Leroy Parker (a.k.a. Butch Cassidy) with a mountain man camp, pie-eating contest, hog-calling contest, and local bands. **Horse races** run through the summer. Beaver celebrates **Pioneer Day** on July 24 with a parade, fireworks, rodeo, horse racing, and games. The **Beaver County Fair** is held in August at the fairgrounds near Minersville to the west.

Accommodations

Several motels lie along the business route through town between I-15 Exits 109 and 112. Two places stand out as being especially comfortable. The **Best Western Butch Cassidy Inn** (161 S. Main, 435/438-2438, www.bw butchcassidyinn.com, $75) and the **Comfort Inn** (1540 S. Main, 435/438-6283, $75) are both very pleasant and have pools.

CAMPGROUNDS

At the north edge of town, **Beaver KOA** (Manderfield Rd., 435/438-2924 or 800/562-2912, Mar.–Oct., $20 tent, $29 RV) has showers, a store, laundry, and a pool (take I-15 Exit 112, go south 0.6 mile on the business loop, then turn left on Manderfield Rd.). **Beaver Canyon Campground** (1419 E. Canyon Road/200 North, 435/438-5654, May–Oct., $15 tent, $17 RV) has showers, laundry, and a Mexican restaurant (dinner nightly during camping season). **Minersville Reservoir** (435/438-5472, $4 day use, $13 camping) has a campground 14 miles west on Hwy. 21. The

Tushar Mountains have good camping, too (see *The Tushar Mountains* section).

Food

You'll find good old-fashioned American food at **Arshel's Cafe** (711 N. Main, 435/438-2977, breakfast, lunch, and dinner daily, $7–20). A fixture in Beaver since the 1930s, this is the kind of diner where you ought to save room for homemade pie after your meal.

Information, Services, and Transportation

The **Beaver Ranger District office** (575 S. Main, 435/438-2436, www.fs.fed.us/r4/fishlake) of the Fishlake National Forest provides information on camping, fishing, hiking, and road conditions in the forest lands of the Tushar Mountains to the east. **Beaver County Travel** (40 S. Main, 435/468-5438) can tell you more about sights and services in the area.

The **post office** is at 20 S. Main (435/438-2321). **Beaver Valley Hospital** provides medical care at 1109 North 100 West (435/438-7100).

THE TUSHAR MOUNTAINS

Although higher than the Wasatch Range, the Tushars remain relatively unknown and uncrowded. Travelers on surrounding highways get glimpses of their rocky summits, but people who hurry by rarely appreciate their size and height. Delano Peak (elev. 12,169 feet) crowns the Tushars and is the highest point in central Utah. From Beaver, Hwy. 153 (200 North Street) winds into the alpine country of the Fishlake National Forest; the first 19 miles are paved, followed by 21 miles of dirt. The road takes you through meadows and forests before making a steep descent to the town of Junction on U.S. 89. Forest Route 137 branches off Hwy. 153 10 miles from Beaver to Kents Lake, Anderson Meadow, and other pretty areas, then returns to the highway to complete a scenic loop (54 miles round-trip from Beaver). Drivers with high-clearance vehicles can journey amidst the summits on the Kimberly/Big John Road Backway between Hwy. 153 and the Kimberly Scenic Drive; much of this trip

goes above timberline with spectacular views of peaks above and canyons below. For recreation information and road conditions, contact the Beaver Ranger District (575 S. Main, 435/438-2436, www.fs.fed.us/r4/fishlake).

Camping and Picnicking

Most of the following campgrounds (435/438-2436, www.fs.fed.us/r4/fishlake) do not accept reservations; all have water in season. From Beaver, the first campground and picnic area reached is **Little Cottonwood** (May–Oct., $12) six miles east on Hwy. 153; elevation is 6,500 feet. **Ponderosa Picnic Area** (elev. 7,000 feet, $3 day use) is 2.5 miles farther up Beaver Canyon on Hwy. 153 in a grove of ponderosa pine. Little Cottonwood and Ponderosa lie along the rushing Beaver River, which has trout fishing. **Mahogany Cove Campground** (May–Oct., $8) overlooks Beaver Canyon 12 miles east of town on Hwy. 153. Its name comes from the abundant curl-leaf mountain mahogany; other trees at the 7,500-foot elevation include ponderosa pine, Gambel oak, juniper, and cottonwood. **Puffer Lake,** 21 miles from town on Hwy. 153, is set among forested hills of spruce, fir, and aspen at 9,700 feet. The lake, privately owned by **Puffer Lake Resort** (435/864-2751) on the other side of the highway has trout fishing, primitive camping, and a primitive boat ramp. The resort offers boat rentals, a small store, and cabins during warmer months.

To reach additional campgrounds or to drive the scenic loop, turn southeast on Forest Route 137 at a junction 10 miles east of town (near milepost 10 on Hwy. 153). The first eight miles are on a good gravel road (to Anderson Meadow), then there are seven miles of dirt road to Hwy. 153; the last half is passable when dry by cars with good clearance, but it can be too rough for RVs. **Little Reservoir Campground** (May–Oct., $10) is less than a mile in on Forest Route 137; sites are in a ponderosa pine forest at 7,350 feet. The reservoir here covers only three acres but often has good trout fishing. **Kents Lake Campground** (June–Oct., $10) overlooks Kents Lake five miles in on Forest Route 137. Sites are in a forest of spruce, fir, and aspen at 8,800 feet. The 100-acre lake offers trout fishing. **Anderson Meadow Campground** (June–Sept., $10) lies in high forests and meadows overlooking Anderson Meadow Reservoir at 9,500 feet, eight miles in on Forest Route 137. The reservoir has trout fishing. **La Baron Reservoir** is another popular fishing spot four miles farther (12 miles in on Forest Route 137), but it has only primitive camping; its elevation is 9,900 feet. Three miles farther you'll return to Hwy. 153; turn right for City Creek Campground and the town of Junction, left for Puffer Lake, Elk Meadows Resort, and Beaver.

The gravel and dirt section of Hwy. 153 from the town of Junction on U.S. 89 makes a relentless five-mile climb from the valley to the mountains—you'll need to use low gears going up and have good brakes coming down. This drive isn't recommended for trailers or RVs. The east side of Hwy. 153 is open late June until sometime in October. **City Creek Campground** (May–Oct., no fee) is near the bottom of the grade; from the turnoff five miles northwest of Junction, follow a side road in for one mile. Sites lie along City Creek in a diverse forest of cottonwood, aspen, ponderosa pine, piñon pine, Gambel oak, and juniper at an elevation of 7,600 feet.

Hiking

The **Skyline National Recreation Trail** is the main trail developed in the Tushars. Access to the trail is from the Big John Flat trailhead, 16 miles east of Beaver on Hwy. 153, or the Big Flat trailhead, 22 miles east of Beaver on Hwy. 153. Contact the Beaver Ranger District (575 S. Main, 435/438-2436, www.fs.fed.us/r4/fishlake) for maps (see the online map) and info; expect snow into early July.

Three peaks of the Tushars rise above 12,000 feet and make good climbing destinations—Delano Peak (elev. 12,169 feet), Mount Belknap (12,139 feet), and Mount Baldy (12,082 feet). Each involves an ascent of about 2,000 feet and can be reached on a day hike. Delano can be climbed by a route up its southwest slope, Belknap by a trail up its southeast side, and Baldy by a route from Blue Lake up its southeast side. (All three trails are reached from the Big John Flat Road, which turns north from Hwy. 153 between mileposts 16 and 17.) When dry, the dirt road is often okay for cars. Other climbing routes are possible, too.

Backcountry Ski Touring

A winter trip with **Tushar Mountain Tours** (435/438-6191, www.skitushar.com) is a great way to explore the Tushar backcountry. The guided tours ($99–149 per person for a full day with meals, or $40–85 to be skied in to a yurt) go where the snow (and the skier's ability) dictates, with nights spent in yurts ($100–140) or a condo ($60–225) at the erstwhile downhill ski area at Elk Meadows.

South of Provo Along U.S. 89

U.S. 89 parallels I-15, and is a pretty alternative to the interstate, with good views of the mountains and possibilities for diversions in the small towns along the route.

SKYLINE DRIVE

This scenic back road, nearly all of which is unpaved, follows the crest of the Wasatch Plateau for about 100 miles between U.S. 6 in the north and I-70 in the south. Few people travel the entire length; most do shorter sections reached from the many access roads. Much of the drive lies above 10,000 feet in vast meadows and alpine forests; above Ferron Reservoir, you'll reach the drive's summit at High Top (elev. 10,897 feet).

Probably the four most popular recreation areas on the plateau are **Scofield State Park, Huntington Canyon** (Hwy. 31), **Joes Valley Reservoir,** and **Ferron Reservoir.** Cars can normally reach Skyline Drive from these places when the roads are dry. The easiest access to the drive is paved Hwy. 31 between Fairview on the west and Huntington on the east; the road is kept clear in winter so that cross-country skiers, snowmobilers, and ice fishers can reach the plateau. Other roads may be too rough for low-clearance vehicles and even occasionally closed to all traffic; it's best to check with the Forest Service offices when planning a trip. A snowbank on Skyline Drive near Jet Fox Reservoir (east of Manti) often blocks traffic until middle or late July. The rest of the drive can usually be traveled mid-June to middle or late October. The drive may not be signed at either end; the north end is off U.S. 6 at a highway rest area near Tucker (between mileposts 203 and 204); the south end is reached from I-70 Ranch Exit 71.

Skyline Drive is in the Manti–La Sal National Forest. Get recreation information, forest maps, and road conditions from the **Price Ranger District office** (599 W. Price River Dr., Price, 435/637-2817) for the northeastern part of the Wasatch Plateau; the **Ferron Ranger District office** (115 W. Canyon Rd, Ferron, 435/384-2372) for the southeastern part of the plateau; and **Sanpete Ranger District office** (540 N. Main, Ephraim, 435/283-4151) for the western half of the plateau.

FAIRVIEW

Mormon farmers settled on the grasslands of the upper San Pitch (or Sanpete) River Valley in 1859, giving their community its original name of North Bend. Many pioneer buildings can still be seen in town. The unusual Fairview Museum of History and Art is worth a visit. Fairview (pop. 1,160) lies 42 miles south of Provo on U.S. 89; turn east on Hwy. 31 to reach the alpine lands of the Wasatch Plateau.

Fairview Museum of History and Art

Many of the varied exhibits at this local museum (85 North 100 East, 435/427-9216, 10 A.M.–6 P.M. Mon.–Sat., 2–6 P.M. Sun. mid-Apr.–mid-Oct., closes at 5 P.M. in winter, free) show a sense of humor. You'll see stern-faced

pioneer portraits, furniture, clothing, tools, telegraph and telephone equipment, mounted wildlife, Native American crafts, geology displays, and artwork. Noted Utah sculptor Dr. Avard Fairbanks donated much of the art including *Love and Devotion,* which depicts Peter and Celestia Peterson, Fairview residents who were married for 82 years.

San Pitch Mountains

This small range rises northwest of Ephraim. **Maple Canyon Campground** (877/444-6777, www.recreation.gov, late May–Oct., $8), on the east side at 6,800 feet, has pretty scenery but no water. You can hike from the campground up **Maple Canyon Trail** along the middle fork or up **Left Fork Maple Canyon Trail.** The trails can be done as a loop using a section of forest road. Maple Canyon is 3.75 miles west of Freedom.

EPHRAIM

The first settlers arrived in 1854 and named this place after a tribe mentioned in the Book of Mormon. A fort guarded against Native American attacks during the first six years. Pioneer structures that date back more than a century can be seen on Ephraim's side streets. Turkey-raising is big business here and in nearby towns; Ephraim is home to Snow College, a well-regarded junior college.

Ephraim (pop. 5,000) celebrates the **Scandinavian Festival** in May (Memorial Day weekend) with historic town tours, pioneer demonstrations, crafts sales, and a fun run. If you want to stay in town, the **Willow Creek Inn** (450 S. Main, 435/283-4566 or 877/283-4566, www.hotelwillowcreekinn.com, $72–104) is a medium-sized newer hotel.

Turn east 8.5 miles on 4th South for **Lake Hill Campground** (elev. 8,400 feet, 877/444-6777, www.recreation.gov, May–mid-Sept., $8). Beyond Lake Hill Campground lie other areas of the Wasatch Plateau—the road continues to Skyline Drive. The **Sanpete Ranger District office** (540 N. Main, Ephraim, 435/283-4151) has recreation and road information for the western half of the Wasatch Plateau and for the San Pitch Mountains.

MANTI

This town (pop. 3,180) dates from November 1849 and is one of the oldest in Utah. Brigham Young named it for a place mentioned in the Book of Mormon. An estimated 100 buildings built before 1880 can be seen on the side streets; Manti possesses some of the state's most splendid pioneer-era architecture. A rogue offshoot of the LDS Church, the polygamist The True and Living Church of Jesus Christ of Saints of the Last Days, has its headquarters in Manti.

The **Mormon Miracle Pageant** in July portrays the history of the Book of Mormon and of the pioneers and early church leaders. The extremely popular production takes place at night on Temple Hill; a large cast provides lots of action. **Sanpete County Fair** is held in August.

Manti Temple

This temple, on a small hill, has a commanding position over the town. Brigham Young dedicated the site in April 1877, just three months before his death. Workers labored 11 years to complete construction, using locally quarried blocks of oolitic limestone. The temple architecture combines several 19th-century styles in a rectangular plan similar to the first Mormon temples in the Midwest.

Accommodations

The town's best motel is **Manti Country Village** (145 N. Main, 435/835-9300 or 800/452-0787, www.manticountryvillage.com, $60–90), which has its own restaurant, a commodity in curiously short supply in the Sanpete Valley.

Given the town's wealth of period architecture, it's no wonder that the best places to stay are historic B&Bs. **Manti House Inn** (401 N. Main, 435/835-0161 or 800/835-7512, www.mantihouseinn.com, $69–129) provides bed-and-breakfast accommodations in an 1880 pioneer house; workers who built the temple stayed here in the 1880s. The **Yardley Inn** (190 West 200 South, 435/835-1861 or 800/858-6634, www.yardleyinnandspa, $65–130) is a turn-of-the-20th-century English-style home. All five rooms and one suite have private baths; two rooms have fireplaces, and the inn also has spa services (basically massage).

CAMPGROUNDS

In the Manti-La Sal National Forest, **Manti Community Campground** (877/444-6777, www.recreation.gov, late May–Oct., $8), seven miles east on 500 South/Manti Canyon Road, has a trout fishing pond (elev. 7,400 feet). From the campground, the road continues nine miles to Skyline Drive.

VICINITY OF MANTI

Palisade State Park

A pleasure resort here once featured a dance hall and a steam excursion boat. Now a state park (435/835-7275 ranger, 800/322-3770 or www.reserveamerica.com reservations, $6 day use, $15–21 camping, reservations recommended for summer weekends), the lake lies six miles south of Manti, then two miles east. Only non-motorized craft may be used. Canoeing (rentals available) and sailboarding are popular here. Anglers catch rainbow and cutthroat trout. The swimming beach and fishing conditions are best early in the season, before the water

© PAUL LEVY

Manti Temple

level drops. Cottonwoods shade the picnic area and campground.

The nine-hole **Palisade Golf Course** (435/835-4653), just beyond the state park entrance, has a clubhouse, pro shop, and driving range.

Gunnison Reservoir, three miles west of the state park, has good water-skiing and fishing for bass and perch; there are no developed facilities here, though people use the shore to launch boats (the west shore is best)—ask directions in Manti. **Nine Mile Reservoir** has a fine reputation for rainbow and other trout; the small lake is west of U.S. 89 and two miles south of Sterling.

Gunnison

The name honors Captain John Gunnison, an Army surveyor killed by Native Americans in 1853 near Sevier Lake. Gunnison (pop. 2,100) is an agricultural center with a couple of places to stay the night, including **Cedar Crest Inn** (435/835-6352, www.heavenlyplace.com, $55–85), a seven-room B&B in a rural mountain setting near Palisade State Park.

SALINA

Salina (pronounced suh-LINE-uh by locals) is a Spanish word for "salt mine," one of which is found nearby. The first pioneers arrived in 1863, but Native American conflicts forced them to evacuate the site from 1866 to 1872. Today, Salina is a handy travelers' stop, strategically located at the junction of U.S. 89 and I-70. You'll find several motels and places to eat downtown and near the I-70 interchange.

Accommodations

Downtown, the **Ranch Motel** (80 N. State St., 435/529-7789 or 800/695-8284, $32–48) is an acceptable budget place. Out by the freeway exit is **Shaheen's Best Western Motel** (1225 S. State St., 435/529-7455 or 800/528-1234, $69), with a small pool, guest laundry, and coffee shop. The **Scenic Hills Super 8** (75 East 1500 South, 435/529-7483 or 800/283-4678, $55–75) is also out by the freeway with a 24-hour Denny's restaurant adjacent (and a refrigerator and microwave for those leftovers).

Butch Cassidy Campground (1100 S.

State, 435/529-7400, $20 RV), between I-70 Exit 54 and downtown, offers sites for tents and RVs with showers, a store, and laundry.

Food

There are a number of chain restaurants at the freeway exit, but for a more unique experience, drive downtown to the popular **Moms Café** (10 E. Main St., 435/529-3921, breakfast, lunch and dinner daily, $5–19), with good home cooking, including Utah scones and a salad bar, in a vintage storefront and Mom presiding at a desk in the dining area.

RICHFIELD

The seat of Sevier County and the center of a large agricultural region, Richfield (pop. 7,100) has a few motels and restaurants; most are along the I-70 business route. This is the best-equipped town for travelers for miles around. It's also a major hub for ATV rides; the 260-mile-long **Paiute ATV Trail** is nearby.

Accommodations

Appletree Inn (145 S. Main St., 435/896-5481 or 800/528-1234, $65) is basically a budget motel, but one of the nicer ones in town. **Quality Inn** (540 S. Main St., 435/896-5465, $73) is a step up, with some kitchen units, an exercise room, and a free breakfast voucher for an adjoining restaurant. A good dog-friendly choice is the **Days Inn** (333 N. Main, 435/896-6476, $70). If you're willing to spend over $100, the **Hampton Inn** (1100 West 1350 South, 435/896-6666, $120) is the most upscale place in town.

CAMPGROUNDS

Richfield KOA (600 West 600 South, 435/896-6674 or 888/562-4703, $19 tent, $28 RV) is open all year with a pool, store, showers, and laundry.

Food

The **Little Wonder Café** (101 North Main St., 435/896-8960, breakfast, lunch, and dinner daily, $5–15) is a classic small-town place to go for old-fashioned breakfasts and homestyle meals. **Pepperbelly's Restaurant** (680 S. Cove View Rd., 435/896-2097, lunch and dinner daily, $7–12) is a lively Mexican-style restaurant with a '50s-theme dining room.

Information and Services

For travel info, contact the **Sevier County Travel Council** (250 N. Main, 435/893-0458, www.visitsevier.com). The **Richfield Ranger District office** of the Fishlake National Forest (115 East 900 North, 435/896-9233) has recreation and road information for the mountain country south and east of town.

The **Sevier Valley Hospital** is at 1100 N. Main (435/896-8271).

VICINITY OF RICHFIELD

Paiute All-Terrain Vehicle Trail

ATVers enjoy this 260-mile scenic loop trail and its many side trips in the scenic Pahvant Range, the Tushar Mountains, and the Monroe Mountains surrounding Richfield. Trail users travel among cool mountains, rugged canyons, and desert country. Access points include Beaver, Richfield, Fillmore, Fremont Indian State Park, Kanosh, Piute State Park, Marysvale, and Circleville. Information and a brochure are available from the Fishlake National Forest office (115 East 900 North, 435/896-9233). Information kiosks are also at some access points; see also www.marysvale.org/paiute_trail/contents.html for a good overview.

Monrovian Park

A paved road leads southeast from Monroe into this park in a pretty canyon. Cottonwoods and Gambel oaks shade picnic areas along gurgling Monroe Creek. Drinking water is available in summer. Four trails from the park area wind up onto the high Sevier Plateau above. Most spectacular is the trail that goes up Monroe Creek from the picnic areas, then follows Third Left Hand Fork to Scrub Flat Trail (six miles one-way); you'll have to do some wading. A narrow unpaved road with steep grades also climbs into the mountains. The Richfield Ranger District office in Richfield has detailed information about exploring this area. To reach the park, head south on Main Street in Monroe and follow signs four miles.

◖ FREMONT INDIAN STATE PARK

The prehistoric Fremont people had lived over much of Utah, but archaeologists weren't aware of this group's identity until 1931. Artifacts discovered along the Fremont River in central Utah indicated that the Fremont was a distinct culture. During construction of I-70 in 1983, a large site was discovered and excavated in Clear Creek Canyon. The Five Finger Ridge Village site probably had more than 150 occupants at its peak, around A.D. 1100; more people lived nearby in the canyon. The Fremont farmed in the canyon bottom and sought game and wild plant foods. They lived in pit houses and stored surplus food in carefully constructed granaries. More than 500 rock-art panels in the canyon depict the religious and hunting aspects of Fremont life in a cryptic form. Nothing remains at the village site, located across the canyon; workers constructing I-70 cut most of the ridge away to use as fill after the scientific excavations had been completed. Only an experienced eye can spot pit-house villages after nearly 1,000 years of weathering, so there was little to see at this village site anyway.

Although an even more remarkable Fremont site was discovered in eastern Utah in 2004, it is not open to the public.

Visitors Center

The park's visitors center (435/527-4631, 9 A.M.–6 P.M. daily in summer, 9 A.M.–5 P.M. the rest of the year, closed on winter holidays, $5 per vehicle) has excellent displays of artifacts found during excavations. Many aspects of Fremont life remain a mystery, but exhibits present ideas of how they could have lived here. Children can use a Fremont mano and metate to grind corn. A short video introduces the Fremont, their foods, events that may have caused their departure, and the excavation of Five Finger Ridge Village. The exhibit area also has short video programs on the Fremont. Models illustrate pit-house construction and how Five Finger Ridge Village may have looked. A full-size replica of a pit house includes audio explanations of the functions of the dwelling.

Three short trails begin outside the visitors center. **Show Me Rock Art Trail** (200 yards) leads past fine petroglyphs; the trail is level and graded and can be used by people with strollers or wheelchairs. **Discovery Trail** (200 yards) goes to more rock art and climbs a short way above the visitors center. **Canyon Overlook Trail** (1,000 feet) ascends about 500 feet above the visitors center for fine views of the canyon and surrounding mountains; this starts as a nature trail but continues another mile. Park staff can tell you of the many other trails and rock-art sites in the area.

The park is near I-70 Exit 17 in Clear Creek Canyon, five miles west of U.S. 89 and 16 miles east of I-15. You can camp at Castle Rock Campground. A short scenic drive follows the old highway nine miles through Clear Creek Canyon between the visitors center and I-70 Ranch Exit 8.

VICINITY OF FREMONT INDIAN STATE PARK
Castle Rock Campground

Clear Creek cut its canyon through tuff—a soft rock formed of hot volcanic ash from eruptions in the Tushar Mountains area. Erosion has carved towering buttresses and narrow canyons at Castle Rock, just off the main canyon. Campsites (435/527-4631, Mar.–Nov., $11) lie in a cottonwood and oak forest beside Joe Lott Creek. Register at the state park visitors center. Take I-70 Fremont Indian State Park Exit 17, turn onto the south frontage road, and follow it 1.3 miles.

Kimberly Scenic Drive

This unpaved 16-mile road climbs to about 10,000 feet on the north slopes of the Tushar Mountains with good views and cool forests of aspen and fir. Old Kimberly, a ghost-town site and once the center of the Gold Mountain Mining District, is reached about halfway. Little remains of the town, but you'll see mine shafts, tailing, mill ruins, and foundations. Prospectors haven't given up hope—more recent mining equipment can be seen along the road, too. Cars with good clearance can usu-

ally negotiate the road if it's dry; ask locally or check at the Beaver Ranger District office (corner of 190 North and 100 East, Beaver, 435/438-2436) of the Fishlake National Forest. Take I-70 Exit 17, turn west on the north frontage road and follow it under I-70; the drive ends at Marysvale on U.S. 89. Kimberly Scenic Drive connects with the Kimberly/Big John Road Backway (Forest Route 123) above Marysvale and winds through the alpine forests, rocky slopes, and meadows of the Tushar Mountains to Hwy. 153 (high-clearance vehicles recommended).

Big Rock Candy Mountain

This multicolored mountain, made famous in an old hobo song sung by Burl Ives, rises above the Sevier River. Cold mineral springs high on the mountainside are claimed to be very healthful and a cure for many ailments. The water, usually diluted before drinking, has a slight lemonade tang but no scent.

JUNCTION AND VICINITY

This tiny village (pop. 138) near the confluence of the south and east forks of the Sevier River is the Piute County seat. The entire county contains only 1,329 inhabitants. It's one of the smallest and most mountainous in the state, but local people say that if all the mountains were ironed out, the county would be one of Utah's largest. The outlaw Butch Cassidy grew up in this county and learned his first lawless ways here by altering cattle brands. The rustic cabin the Cassidys once called home still stands 2.5 miles south of Circleville (between mileposts 156 and 157 on U.S. 89). The bright red county courthouse dates from 1902–1903; drop in on weekdays for tourist information.

Vehicles with stout engines can follow Hwy. 153 up a long grade into the Tushar Mountains to Puffer Lake (18 miles) and other scenic spots, then descend to Beaver (40 miles); pavement ends just outside Junction, then there's 25 miles of dirt road before pavement begins again. This road isn't recommended for trailers or RVs. (See the *Tushar Mountains* section.) This whole area is very popular with ATV riders.

Piute State Park

The 3,300-acre Piute Reservoir (435/624-3268, $5 day use, $9 primitive camping) is one of the largest in central Utah. It's relatively undeveloped, however, with just an outhouse or two, a place to launch boats, and some docks. The park has no drinking water or established campground. Contact Otter Creek State Park for more information. From the town of Junction, drive north six miles on U.S. 89 and turn right 1.4 miles at the sign (near milepost 172).

Otter Creek State Park

Otter Creek Reservoir (435/624-3268 or 435/322-3770, www.reserveamerica.com, $5 day use, $15 camping) has some of the best trout fishing in Utah; it's 6.5 miles long and one-half to three-quarters of a mile wide (2,500 acres). Bird-watching is often good—especially in winter for raptors and swans and in spring for waterfowl and songbirds. Shore fishing can be productive in spring and autumn, but in summer you really need a boat because of moss near the shore and because the fish move to deeper waters. The park stays open all year and offers ice fishing and ice-skating in winter.

There are two campgrounds. The main campground (elev. 6,400 feet) has showers, windbreaks, boat ramp, dock, and a fish-cleaning station. The other is called Beach campground, and is more primitive.

From the town of Junction, go two miles south on U.S. 89, then turn east 13 miles on Hwy. 62. **Otter Creek RV Park Marina** (435/624-3292 or 800/441-3292) across the highway offers RV sites, a café (7 A.M.–7 P.M., $5–12), a store, showers, boat rentals, and fishing supplies; it's open March–October.

Fish Lake and Vicinity

You'll see expansive vistas, pristine meadows, sparkling streams, and dense forests on drives to and around Fish Lake. Hikers can reach remote spots, such as the 11,633-foot summit of the Fish Lake Hightop Plateau. Part of what's intriguing about Fish Lake is the mix of ecosystems: Sagebrush plateaus meet up with aspen forests at the water's edge.

Fish Lake formed when a block of the earth's crust dropped along faults. The water that filled the basin created one of Utah's largest natural lakes—six miles long and one mile wide. Anglers fish for lake (Mackinaw) and rainbow trout and splake (a hybrid of mackinaw and eastern brook trout). Swimming isn't recommended due to the cold water (50°F). Summers are cool at this 8,800-foot elevation, and the winter snows come early and last well into spring.

The lake and surrounding country lie in the Fremont Ranger District (138 S. Main, Loa, 435/836-2800) of the Fishlake National Forest. The **Forest Information Center** in Fish Lake Lodge (435/638-1033) is open daily in summer. Paved Hwy. 25 branches off Hwy. 24 (31 miles southeast of Richfield, 14 miles northwest of Loa) and climbs seven miles over a pass to the lake; the road is usually kept open year-round.

FISH LAKE CAMPGROUNDS AND RESORTS

Most of the Forest Service campgrounds (877/444-6777, www.recreation.gov, late May–mid-Sept., $9–13) lie just off Hwy. 25 along the lake's west shore. Dispersed camping isn't permitted near Fish Lake; head farther into the backcountry if you'd like an undeveloped spot. Campgrounds and other sites, with distances from the junction of Hwy. 25 and Hwy. 24, include the following:

• **Doctor Creek** (seven miles; in an aspen grove on the southwest shore; dump station)

• **Twin Creek Picnic Area** (8.8 miles; day use only; a ranger station is opposite the turnoff)

• **Mackinaw Campground** (nine miles; in an aspen grove overlooking the lake)

- **Bowery Creek Campground and Picnic Area** (10 miles; in an aspen grove overlooking the lake)

- **Joe Bush Fishermen Parking** (10.7 miles)

- **Pelican Promontory** (12 miles; turn left one mile for a panoramic view; not suitable for low-clearance vehicles)

- **Frying Pan Campground** (14.5 miles; on the edge of an aspen grove near Johnson Valley Reservoir)

- **Piute Parking Area** (14.8 miles; access to the reservoir)

At the junction just past the reservoir, you can turn north along Sevenmile Creek on Forest Route 640 to I-70 and Salina (36 miles) or south on Forest Route 036 to a boat ramp on Johnson Valley Reservoir (one mile), Fremont River (three miles), and Loa (20 miles). Both drives have exceptional scenery and go past many good spots for fishing and primitive camping; the roads are usually okay for cars.

Accommodations

Fish Lake Resorts (435/638-1000, www.fish lake.com) operates both the **Fish Lake Lodge** and **Lakeside Resort,** and each offers accommodations, a store, and a marina on the lake's southwest shore. The marinas rent fishing and pontoon boats and provide boat ramps, slips, bait, tackle, and boat gas. However, the accommodations are quite different at each of the resorts. **Lakeside Resort** (435/638-1000, cabins $85–140 year-round, RV sites with hookups $20 May 15–Oct. 15) is 7.3 miles in on Hwy. 25, where the highway first meets the lake. **Fish Lake Lodge** (1 North Hwy. 25, 435/638-1000, cabins year-round, $85–450), 1.2 miles beyond Lakeside Resort, is a huge, rambling log structure built in 1932; full of character, it has a dining area, dance hall, and a small store open Memorial Day weekend–Labor Day. The rustic dining room in the lodge has lake views and is open daily for breakfast and dinner. Showers are available to the public for a small fee. **Bowery Haven Resort** (435/638-1040

in-season or 435/943-7885 off-season, www .boweryhaven.com, May–Sept.) lies near Fish Lake about 10 miles in on Hwy. 25. Amenities include a marina (fishing boat rentals, ramp, slips, and supplies), cabins ($75 for a cabin with plumbing, $50 for a "rustic" cabin), motel rooms (starting at $75), RV park ($22 with hookups—no tents; has showers and laundry), café (open daily for breakfast, lunch, and dinner), and a small store.

THOUSAND LAKE MOUNTAIN

This high plateau rises above the Fremont River to an elevation of 11,306 feet at Flat Top. Panoramas from the rim take in the wooded valleys surrounding Fish Lake to the west and the colorful rock formations and canyons of Cathedral Valley in Capitol Reef National Park to the east. Roads and trails provide access to viewpoints and fishing lakes on the plateau. Forest roads lead to the heights from Hwy. 72 on the west and from the middle desert and Cathedral Valley on the east. For more information, contact the Fremont Ranger District office (138 S. Main, Loa, 435/836-2811).

Elkhorn Campground

This small campground (June–Oct., no fee) makes a good base for hikes to lakes and the Flat Top summit. Meadows and a forest of aspen, fir, and spruce surround the sites; elevation is 9,300 feet. From the north edge of Loa, turn east and north 12 miles on Hwy. 72 to Forest Route 206 and follow it eight miles to the campground. The winding mountain road is unpaved but passable by cars in dry weather. Desert View Overlook, three miles before the campground, has a fantastic view of Cathedral Valley and beyond. The road to Elkhorn Campground can also be approached from I-70 via Hwy. 72; this paved road climbs over Hogan Pass (elev. 8,961 feet), past meadows, groves of aspen, and fine views of Cathedral Valley and the surrounding country. Only vehicles with high clearance can drive up directly from Cathedral Valley via Forest Routes 020 and 022.

DINOSAUR COUNTRY

Northeastern Utah has an extremely diverse landscape comprising barren desert, deep canyons, high plateaus, and the lofty Uinta Mountains. Thousands of well-preserved bones unearthed in the region tell of a time about 140 million years ago when dinosaurs roamed the land in a relatively moist subtropical climate amid tree ferns, evergreens, and ginkgo trees. You can inspect the skeletons of these creatures in excellent museums in Vernal, Price, and Castle Dale, and visit bone excavations at the Cleveland-Lloyd Dinosaur Quarry.

The high country of the Uinta Mountains offers alpine scenery and good hiking. Kings Peak tops the range at 13,528 feet—the highest point in the state. Other popular recreation areas include Flaming Gorge National Recreation Area, Dinosaur National Monument, the Wasatch Plateau, and the San Rafael Swell. Anglers and boaters have a choice of many large reservoirs, and river-runners enjoy lively rides down the Green River through Red, Lodore, Whirlpool, Split Mountain, Desolation, and Gray Canyons.

You'll see two spellings in this region—Uinta and Uintah—both of which are pronounced "yoo-IN-tuh." Geographical terms (Uinta Mountains, Uinta Basin) don't have an "h"; political divisions (Uintah County and Uintah and Ouray Indian Reservation) usually do.

PLANNING YOUR TIME

Vernal makes a good base for exploring the Flaming Gorge and Dinosaur National Monument, though campers will find plenty of good sites in both of these areas. It's worth spending

© PAUL LEVY

DINOSAUR COUNTRY

HIGHLIGHTS

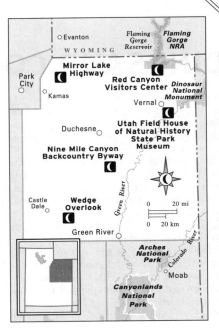

◖ Mirror Lake Highway: Get up into the western edge of the Uinta Mountains and to great campgrounds and hiking trails from this road, which stretches from Kamas into Wyoming. Its higher reaches are open spring, summer, and fall. In winter, this scenic road leads to snowmobile and ski trails (page 217).

◖ Utah Field House of Natural History State Park Museum: Don't pass through Vernal without a stop at this excellent museum, which has a great collection of dinosaur bones and exhibits to make even adults understand what's going on with them (page 220).

◖ Red Canyon Visitors Center: Here's a good place to admire the Flaming Gorge. A look out of the visitors center's huge picture window will make you want to walk the nearby trails at the gorge's rim (page 229).

◖ Nine Mile Canyon Backcountry Byway: This 40-some-mile dirt-road tour visits some outstanding Fremont Indian sites, including granaries, pictographs, and petroglyphs (page 248).

◖ Wedge Overlook: Follow good dirt roads east from the town of Castle Dale into the San Rafael Swell, where you'll have a good look at Utah's "Little Grand Canyon," with the San Rafael River far below (page 255).

LOOK FOR ◖ TO FIND RECOMMENDED SIGHTS, ACTIVITIES, DINING, AND LODGING.

at least two days here: one at the national monument and another at Flaming Gorge. If you have an extra day, plan to take a rafting trip on the Green River.

Another good hub is the town of Price, with a number of lodgings and good access to the San Rafael Swell and Cleveland-Lloyd Dinosaur Quarry. There are many dirt back roads in this area, so if your vehicle is up to it (consider touring via mountain bike), it's easy to spend another two or three days exploring here.

Finally, if hiking or backpacking is your

objective, the Uintas are the best place to spend your time…anywhere from a day trip out to the Mirror Lake Highway to a week-long backpacking trip.

In summer, come prepared for hot days and chilly nights; the valleys have average highs of about 90°F, which drop to the low 50s at night. The Wasatch Plateau and Uinta Mountains experience cool weather year-round. Above 10,000 feet, summer highs rarely exceed 70°F in the day and drop to the 30s and 40s at night; freezing weather may occur at any time of year.

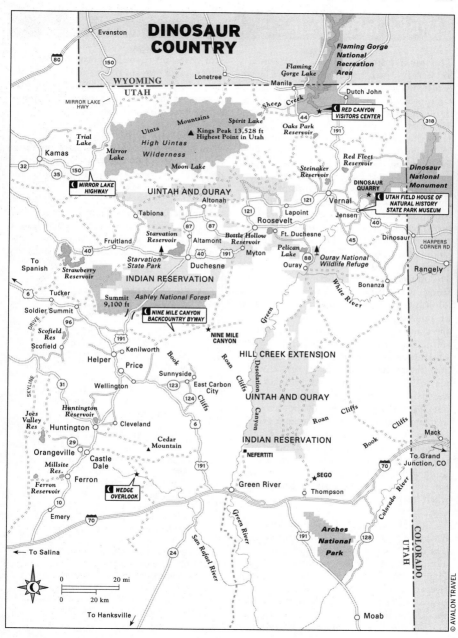

DINOSAUR COUNTRY

© AVALON TRAVEL

Uinta Mountains

This outstanding wilderness area contains lofty peaks, lush grassy meadows, fragrant coniferous forests, crystal-clear streams, and a multitude of tiny alpine lakes. The Uintas, unlike most other major ranges of the United States, run east–west. Underground forces pushed rock layers up into a massive dome 150 miles long and 35 miles wide. Ancient Precambrian rocks exposed in the center of the range consist largely of quartzite (metamorphosed sandstone). Outcrops of progressively younger rocks are found away from the center. Glaciers have carved steep ridges and broad basins and left great moraines. Barren rock lies exposed across much of the land, including the peaks and high ridges.

Trees, from 10,000 feet to timberline (about 11,000 feet), include limber pine, Engelmann spruce, and subalpine fir. Lower slopes (7,000–10,000 feet) support dense unbroken forests of lodgepole pine (the most common tree in the Uintas), aspen, Douglas fir, white fir, blue spruce, and scattered stands of ponderosa pine. Elk, moose, mule deer, and Rocky Mountain goat (reintroduced) come here to graze in summer. Also foraging for food are black bear, mountain lion, coyote, bobcat, raccoon, porcupine, badger, pine marten, snowshoe hare, marmot, and pika. Anglers seek out arctic grayling and native cutthroat, Eastern brook, rainbow, German brown, and golden trout. Aerial stocking keeps even the most remote lakes swimming with fish. Your luck at a lake or stream can range from lousy to fantastic, depending on when it was last stocked and how many other anglers have discovered the spot.

The remote setting of the Uinta Mountains has protected much of the forests from logging. The central part received protection in 1931 as a primitive area and designation in 1984 as the High Uintas Wilderness. Four of Utah's major rivers have their source in these mountains: the Bear and Weber Rivers on the north slope and the Provo and Duchesne on the south slope. Despite their great heights, the Uintas have a gentler terrain than the precipitous Wasatch Range. High plateaus and broad valleys among the peaks hold the abundant rain and snowfall in marshes and ponds, supporting large populations of wildlife and fish.

Visiting the Uintas

Winding over the western end of the range from the town of Kamas to the Wyoming border, Hwy. 150 offers splendid panoramas and access to fishing lakes and hiking trails. On the east, U.S. 191 and Hwy. 44 provide access to the Uintas and Flaming Gorge Reservoir from Vernal. Unpaved roads also lead to trailheads on all sides of the range. Developed and primitive campgrounds can be found along

"THE FIRST TIME I EVER SWORE"

In the 1870s and early 1880s, the LDS Church sent out calls for members to colonize lands east of the Wasatch Plateau. Though at first the land looked harsh and barren, crops and orchards eventually prospered with irrigation. Nevertheless, it was some time before the first families took a liking to this country. Mrs. Orange Seely of the Castle Dale area is credited with saying, "The first time I ever swore was when we arrived in Emery County and I said, 'Damn a man who would bring a woman to such a God-forsaken country!'" Individual families also came out on their own and started isolated farms and ranches in the Uinta Basin and along the eastern edge of the Wasatch Plateau to the south. Much of the land proved too dry or rugged for any use and remains in its natural state even today. Discoveries of coal in 1877 and oil in 1900 attracted waves of new people to the sleepy Mormon settlements east of the Wasatch Plateau. Immigrant miners fresh from Europe brought a new cultural diversity to the region.

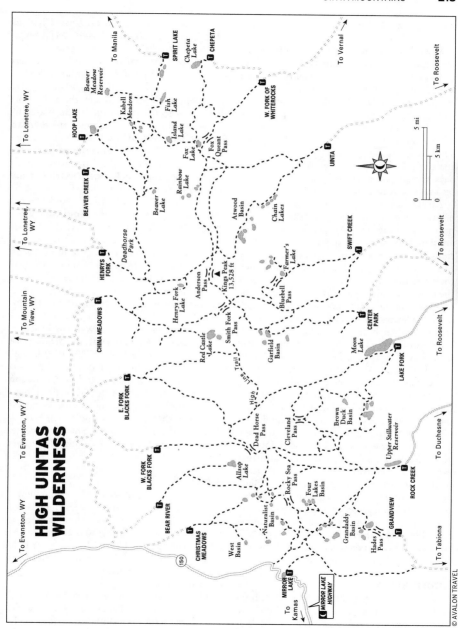

© AVALON TRAVEL

HIGH UINTAS WILDERNESS

To Evanston, WY

To Evanston, WY

To Lonetree, WY

To Lonetree, WY

To Mountain View, WY

To Kamas

To Manila

To Vernal

To Roosevelt

To Roosevelt

To Roosevelt

To Duchesne

To Tabiona

SPIRIT LAKE

Chepeta Lake

CHEPETA

W. FORK OF WHITEROCKS

UINTA

Beaver Meadow Reservoir

Fish Lake

Kabell Meadows

Island Lake

Fox Lake

Fox Lake

Queant Pass

Rainbow Lake

HOOP LAKE

BEAVER CREEK

Beaver Lake

Atwood Basin

Chain Lakes

SWIFT CREEK

Deadhorse Park

HENRYS FORK

Farmer's Lake

Henrys Fork Lake

Anderson Pass

Kings Peak 13,528 ft

Bluebell Pass

CENTER PARK

CHINA MEADOWS

Smith Fork Pass

Red Castle Lake

Garfield Basin

Moon Lake

LAKE FORK

E. FORK BLACKS FORK

High Line Trail

Dead Horse Pass

Cleveland Pass

Brown Duck Basin

Upper Stillwater Reservoir

ROCK CREEK

W. FORK BLACKS FORK

Allsop Lake

Rocky Sea Pass

Four Lakes Basin

GRANDVIEW

BEAR RIVER

CHRISTMAS MEADOWS

West Basin

Naturalist Basin

Grandaddy Basin

Hades Pass

MIRROR LAKE

MIRROR LAKE HIGHWAY

150

5 mi

5 km

these highways and at other locations including many of the trailheads.

Most people prefer to visit the Uintas mid-June–mid-September. Campers should be prepared for cold nights and freezing rain even in the warmest months. Afternoon showers are common in summer. Arm yourself with insect repellent to ward off the mosquitoes, especially in July. Snow stays on the ground until well into June, and the meltwater can make trails muddy until early July. The lakes and campgrounds along Hwy. 150 become crowded on summer weekends and holidays, though you can usually get off by yourself on a short hike into the backcountry.

An extensive trail system with about 20 trailheads goes deep into the wilderness and connects with many lakes. A great number of trips are possible, from easy day hikes to rigorous treks lasting weeks. Climbers headed for the summits can take trails to a nearby pass, then rock-scramble to the top. Kings Peak attracts the most attention because at 13,528 feet it's the highest point in Utah. The shortest approach is from Henrys Fork Trailhead on the north, which requires three days of hiking for the 32-mile round-trip; elevation gain is about 4,100 feet. Southern approaches from Swift Creek or Uinta Trailheads usually take an extra day. More than a dozen other peaks in the Uintas exceed 13,000 feet. No permits are needed for travel in the wilderness area, though it's recommended that you sign registers at the trailheads. Groups must not exceed 14 people. The High Uintas Wilderness, an area of about 450,000 acres, is closed to mechanized vehicles (including bicycles). Horses can use nearly all trails in the wilderness area. An exception is Bluebell Pass, which is impassable for them; other passes may be rough going depending on recent storms and trail maintenance. Winter snows close Hwy. 150 and the back roads, at which time snowmobilers and cross-country skiers come out to enjoy the snowy landscapes.

Information

The U.S. Forest Service manages the Uintas and surrounding forest lands. Northern and western parts are administered by the Wasatch-Cache National Forest (inside REI at 3285 East 3300 South, 435/446-6411, www .fs.fed.us/r4/wcnf). Most of the southern and eastern areas are part of the Ashley National Forest (355 N. Vernal Ave., Vernal, 435/789-1181, www.fs.fed.us/r4/ashley). For specific information, it's best to contact the district office closest to the trailhead. In the Wasatch-Cache National Forest, contact the **Kamas Ranger District office** (50 E. Center St., Kamas, 435/783-4338); for the western end of the range, including the Provo River drainage, contact **Evanston Ranger District office** (Evanston, WY, 307/789-3194); for the northern side including Smiths Forks and Henrys Fork drainages, contact the **Mountain View Ranger District office** (321 Hwy. 414, Mountain View, WY, 307/782-6555). In the Ashley National Forest, contact the **Flaming Gorge Ranger District office** (25 W. Hwy. 43, Manila, 435/784-3445) about the northeastern side including Spirit Lake and Sheep Creek; the **Vernal Ranger District office** (355 N. Vernal Ave., Vernal, 435/789-1181) for the southeastern end including Whiterocks River; the **Roosevelt Ranger District office** (244 W. U.S. 40, Roosevelt, 435/722-5018) for the southern end including Lake Fork, Yellowstone, and Uinta drainages; and the **Duchesne Ranger District office** (85 W. Main, Duchesne, 435/738-2482) for the southwestern end including Rock Creek and the North Fork of Duchesne drainages. All these offices have the forest maps and the High Uintas Wilderness topo map (1:75,000 scale).

KAMAS

Kamas is the start of what is probably Utah's most spectacular alpine drive. The Mirror Lake Highway (Hwy. 150) begins here at an elevation of 6,500 feet and climbs to the crest of the western Uinta Mountains at Bald Mountain Pass (elev. 10,678 feet) before descending on the other side and continuing to Evanston, Wyoming.

The nearest motels are in Heber City (17 miles southwest) and Park City (19 miles west). The **Kamas Ranger District office** (50 E.

Center, 435/783-4338) can advise on road conditions, campgrounds, hiking, cross-country skiing, and snowmobiling.

◖ MIRROR LAKE HIGHWAY

You can drive this scenic highway mid-June–mid-October. A $5 daily recreation pass, available at the start of the highway and at several points along the way, is required if you're going to park and hike. Campgrounds tend to fill on summer weekends, but some campsites can be reserved (877/444-6777, www.recreation.gov).

The first 25 miles of the highway are pretty, but relatively tame. Shortly after passing the Provo River Falls, the road climbs sharply and the views open up to include rugged mountain peaks.

Snowplows keep the highway cleared in winter to Soapstone, 15.5 miles from Kamas, to provide access for cross-country skiing and snowmobiling. Five trails used by both skiers and snowmobilers begin along the highway and at Soapstone. Skiers using snowmobile trails will find the most solitude on weekdays.

The scenic Mirror Lake Highway has many campgrounds and hiking trails into the Uinta Mountains.

© JUDY JEWELL

Beaver Creek Cross-Country Trail begins from Slate Creek (six miles east of Kamas) and parallels the highway to Pine Valley Campground, a distance of 5.5 miles one-way with an elevation gain of 440 feet. This trail is easy; branching off from it are other ski trails rated intermediate and advanced. You can obtain information and brochures for these and other skiing areas from the Kamas Ranger District office.

Mileages given below correspond to mileposts along the highway.

- **Mile 0.0:** Heading east on Hwy. 150 from the junction with U.S. 189 in Kamas.

- **Mile 0.1: Kamas Ranger District office.**

- **Mile 3.3: Kamas Fish Hatchery;** visitors welcome 8 a.m.–4 p.m. daily.

- **Mile 6.1:** Entering **Wasatch-Cache National Forest;** Slate Creek.

- **Mile 6.7: Yellow Pine Campground** (late May–late Oct., $6, no water), with sites in a forest of ponderosa and lodgepole pine and juniper at an elevation of 7,200 feet. **Yellow Pine Creek Trail** begins just north of the campground and goes up the creek to Lower Yellow Pine Lake (elev. 9,600 feet; four miles one-way) and beyond; this is a good hike early in the season.

- **Mile 8.2: Beaver Creek Picnic Area;** sites line both sides of Beaver Creek amid lodgepole pine and willow at 7,300 feet.

- **Mile 8.9: Taylor Fork ATV Campground** (water early June–mid-Sept., $10); **Taylor Fork-Cedar Hollow ATV Trail** begins here. Sites are along Beaver Creek in lodgepole pine and aspen at 7,400 feet.

- **Mile 9.3: Shingle Creek Campground and Picnic Area** (water early June–mid-Sept., $10); sites are in a mixed forest of aspen, pine, spruce, and fir at 7,400 feet.

- **Mile 9.9: Shingle Creek Trail** follows the creek upstream to East Shingle Lake (elev. 9,680 feet, 5.5 miles one-way) and Upper Setting Trail; this is a good early-season

DINOSAUR COUNTRY

hike. Past the trailhead, the highway climbs over a small pass to the Provo River and follows it upstream.

- **Mile 10.5: Lower Provo River Campground** (water early June–mid-Sept., $10) is one mile south on Pine Valley Road. Sites are along the Provo River in a pine and spruce forest at 7,600 feet. The nearby **Pine Valley Group Camping Area** is a group reservation area.

- **Mile 15.5: Soapstone Campground** (water early June–mid-Sept., $14), with sites along the Provo River amid lodgepole pine at 8,200 feet.

- **Mile 17.0: Shady Dell Campground** (water early June–mid-Sept., $12); sites lie along the Provo River at 8,200 feet.

- **Mile 17.7: West Portal of Duchesne Tunnel;** a sign describes this six-mile conduit that brings water from the Duchesne River to the Provo River. **Duchesne Tunnel Camping Area** is a group reservation site.

- **Mile 18.8: Cobblerest Campground** (water mid-June–mid-Sept., $12); sites are near the Provo River in a pine and spruce forest at 8,500 feet.

- **Mile 22.3: Slate Gorge Overlook.**

- **Mile 23.9: Provo River Falls Overlook.**

- **Mile 25.4: Trial Lake Campground** (water late June–early Sept., $14) is a quarter mile to the left on Spring Canyon Road. Sites are on the southeast shore of the lake in a pine and spruce forest at 9,500 feet. There's a parking area near the dam for anglers. Spring Canyon Road continues past the dam to Washington and Crystal Lakes and Crystal Lake Trailhead. **Notch Mountain Trail** begins at Crystal Lake Trailhead, goes north past Wall and Twin Lakes, through the Notch to Ibantik and Meadow Lakes, to the Weber River (elev. 9,000 feet, 6.5 miles one-way), and to Bald Mountain Pass (elev. 10,678 feet, 10 miles one-way). The **Lakes Country Trail** starts at the Crystal Lake Trailhead and goes west past Island, Long, and other lakes before joining the Smith-Morehouse Trail after three miles.

- **Mile 26.4: Lilly Lake Campground** (water early July–early Sept., $10); sites are in a spruce and fir forest at 9,800 feet. Lilly, Teapot, and Lost Lakes lie within short walking distances.

- **Mile 26.7: Lost Creek Campground** (water early July–early Sept., $14); sites are beside the creek in a spruce and pine forest at 9,800 feet. Lost Lake is a short walk to the southwest.

- **Mile 29.1: Bald Mountain Pass** (elev. 10,678 feet) and **Bald Mountain Picnic Area and Trailhead; Bald Mountain National Recreation Trail** climbs to the summit of Bald Mountain (elev. 11,947 feet) with great views all the way; the two-mile (one-way) trail climbs 1,269 feet, putting you in the midst of the Uinta Range's alpine grandeur. Expect a strenuous trip because of the high elevation and steep grades; carry rain gear to fend off the cold wind (even in summer) and possible storms. From the top, weather permitting, you'll enjoy panoramas of the High Uintas Wilderness, the Lakes Roadless Area, and the Wasatch Range. **Notch Lake Trail** also begins near the picnic area and connects with Trial Lake.

- **Mile 30.5: Moosehorn Campground** (water early July–early Sept., $14); sites are on the east and north shores of Moosehorn Lake in a spruce and fir forest at 10,400 feet. **Fehr Lake Trail** begins a quarter mile south and across the highway; it goes to Fehr Lake (one-half mile), Shepard Lake (1.5 miles), and Hoover Lake (1.5 miles).

- **Mile 31.2: Mirror Lake Campground and Picnic Area** (water early July–early Sept., $14) are a half mile to the right. This is the largest campground (91 sites) on the Mirror Lake Highway. Sites are near the lake in a forest of spruce, fir, and lodgepole pine at 10,200 feet. Anglers can park at the south end of the lake and at the Mirror Lake Trailhead. Boats can be hand-launched; no motors at all are permitted on the lake. **Highline and North Fork of the Duchesne Trails** lead from the trailhead to the High Uintas Wilderness.

- **Mile 32.1: Pass Lake Trailhead,** on the left, across the highway from Pass Lake. **Lofty**

Lake and Weber Canyon Trails begin here and connect with other trails. Weber Canyon Trail goes to Holiday Park Trailhead (elev. 8,000 feet, seven miles one-way), reached by road from Oakley.

- **Mile 33.9: Butterfly Lake Campground** (water early July–early Sept., $12); sites are on the south shore of the lake in a spruce, fir, and lodgepole pine forest at 10,300 feet.

- **Mile 34.2: Hayden Pass** (elev. 10,200 feet); **Highline Trailhead;** this is the closest point on the highway to the **High Uintas Wilderness.** The Highline Trail tends to be muddy, rocky, and heavily used. It winds east from here across the Uintas nearly 100 miles to East Park Reservoir north of Vernal. The highway makes a gradual descent from the pass along Hayden Fork of the Bear River. Contact the Evanston Ranger District offices for camping, hiking, and back-road travel in this area.

- **Mile 35.0: Ruth Lake Trailhead;** the lake is an easy three-quarter-mile hike west. There are only a few parking spots available.

- **Mile 38.9: Sulphur Campground** (water early June–mid-Sept., $12); sites lie near the Hayden Fork of Bear River in a forest of lodgepole pine, fir, and spruce at 9,000 feet.

- **Mile 41.8: Beaver View Campground** (water early June–mid-Sept., $12); sites overlook Hayden Fork of Bear River from a lodgepole pine and aspen forest at 8,900 feet; a beaver pond and lodge can be seen near the entrance station.

- **Mile 42.4: Hayden Fork Campground** (water early June–mid-Sept., $10); sites lie along Hayden Fork of Bear River in a lodgepole pine and aspen forest at 8,900 feet.

- **Mile 45.6: Stillwater Campground** (water early June–mid-Sept., $12); sites are in a lodgepole pine and aspen forest at 8,500 feet, near where Hayden Fork and Stillwater Fork meet the Bear River.

- **Mile 45.8: Christmas Meadow Road** goes right four miles to **Christmas Meadow**

Campground (water early June–mid-Sept., $12) and **Stillwater Trailhead.** Sites overlook a large meadow from a forest of lodgepole pine at 9,200 feet. Stillwater Trailhead, near the campground, is the starting point for hikes to lakes in Amethyst, Middle, and West Basins to the south.

- **Mile 46.5: Bear River Ranger Station** (435/642-6662, June–Oct.); stop here for recreation information about the northwestern part of the Uinta Range.

- **Mile 47.5:** A road turns right two miles to **Lily Lake.** Most of the route is unmaintained dirt road.

- **Mile 48.2: Bear River Campground** (water early June–mid-Sept., $10), with three sites along the Bear River just upstream from the East Fork confluence in a lodgepole pine and aspen forest at 8,400 feet.

- **Mile 48.3: East Fork Bear River Campground** (water early June–mid-Sept., $10); four sites along the Bear River just below the East Fork confluence in a lodgepole pine and aspen forest at 8,400 feet.

- **Mile 48.6:** Forest Route 058 goes right about 17 miles to **Little Lyman Lake Campground** (water early June–mid-Sept., $8). Sites are near the east shore of the lake in a lodgepole pine forest at 9,200 feet. Lyman Lake is just a short walk away. **Meeks Cabin Reservoir and Campground** (water early June–mid-Sept., $10) are two miles farther on Forest Route 058, then left about five miles on Forest Route 073. Sites here are along the southwest shore of the reservoir in a lodgepole pine forest at 8,800 feet.

- **Mile 48.7:** Leaving Wasatch-Cache National Forest. This is approximately the end of the scenic drive. The valley opens up and supports sagebrush and scattered aspen groves.

- **Mile 54.6: Wyoming border;** highway becomes Hwy. 150. Evanston is 23 miles ahead with several motels and two grocery stores.

Vernal

One of the oldest and largest communities in northeastern Utah, Vernal makes a handy base for travels to the many sights of the region. The perennial waters of Ashley Creek—named for mountain man William H. Ashley, who passed by in 1825—attracted the first settlers to the valley during the early 1870s.

Rugged terrain and poor roads isolated the area from the rest of Utah for years. In 1916, when a local businessman wanted to order a shipment of bricks from Salt Lake City for the facade of a new bank, he solved the problem of expensive shipping costs by having the bricks sent by parcel post! Freight cost $2.50 per hundred pounds while the postal service charged only $1.05. Other Vernal residents caught on to the post office's bargain rates and even started parcel-posting crops to market until the postal service changed its regulations.

Growth of the oil industry in recent decades has been a mixed blessing because of its boom-and-bust cycles. Vernal is the Uintah County seat and has a population of about 8,000.

SIGHTS
◖ Utah Field House of Natural History State Park Museum

This recently overhauled museum (496 E. Main, 435/789-3799, http://stateparks.utah. gov, 8 A.M.–7 P.M. daily Memorial Day weekend–Labor Day, 9 A.M.–5 P.M. daily in winter, $6 adults, $3 children, children 6 and under free) is a good place for both adults and children to learn about the dinosaurs that once roamed the Uinta Basin. Full-size models stalk or fly in the Dinosaur Gardens outside. Inside, the Geology and Fossil Hall has displays of 45-million-year-old skulls of ancient mammals, crocodiles, and alligators that once roamed across Utah. Other exhibits offer fossil specimens ranging in size from tiny insects to massive dinosaur bones. A colorful geologic mural shows the structure of rock layers in northeastern Utah. Other exhibits trace Utah's Native Americans from the Desert Culture through Anasazi and Fremont groups to the modern Ute. Don't skip the short video

© PAUL LEVY

The big guys outside the Utah Field House of Natural History State Park Museum are fake; the real goods are inside.

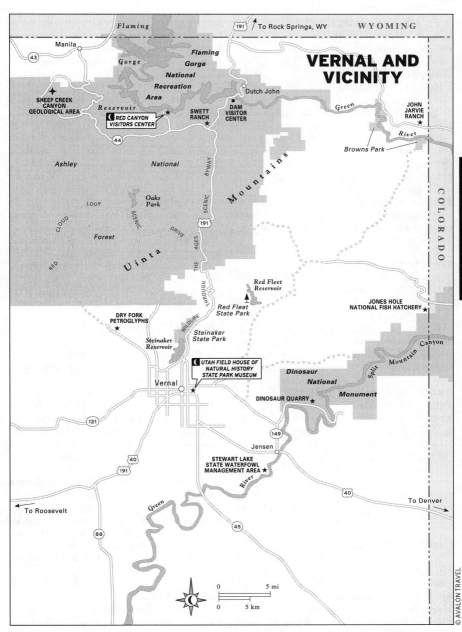

VERNAL AND VICINITY

Flaming To Rock Springs, WY **191** **WYOMING**

Manila

43

Flaming Gorge National Recreation Area

Gorge

Dutch John

SHEEP CREEK CANYON GEOLOGICAL AREA

Reservoir

RED CANYON VISITORS CENTER

SWETT RANCH

DAM VISITOR CENTER

Green

JOHN JARVIE RANCH

River

Browns Park

44

Ashley

National

SCENIC BYWAY

Mountains

COLORADO

DINOSAUR COUNTRY

Oaks Park

LOOP

SCENIC

DRIVE

191

CLOUD

Forest

THE AGES

RED

Uinta

THROUGH

Red Fleet Reservoir

JONES HOLE NATIONAL FISH HATCHERY

WILDLIFE

Red Fleet State Park

DRY FORK PETROGLYPHS

Steinaker Reservoir

Steinaker State Park

Split Mountain Canyon

UTAH FIELD HOUSE OF NATURAL HISTORY STATE PARK MUSEUM

Dinosaur

National

Vernal

DINOSAUR QUARRY

Monument

121

149

Jensen

STEWART LAKE STATE WATERFOWL MANAGEMENT AREA

40

191

River

40

To Denver

To Roosevelt

Green

88

45

0   5 mi

0   5 km

© AVALON TRAVEL

at the museum's entrance; it's interesting and kind of fun and will help you appreciate the museum's contents.

Daughters of Utah Pioneers Museum

Get to know Vernal's pioneers at the Daughters of Utah Pioneers Museum (across from the temple at the corner of 200 South and 500 West, open 10 A.M.–4 P.M. Wed.–Sat. June–Aug., free). The large collection includes a pioneer kitchen, spinning wheels, farm machinery, a buggy, old organs, clothing, guns, and a model of a Western town. You'll see Dr. Harvey Coe Hullinger's well-stocked medicine chest, last used in 1926 when he was 101 years old. One room of the museum is the stone tithing office, built in 1877.

Western Heritage Museum

The Western Heritage Museum (328 E. 200 South, 435/789-7399, 9 A.M.–5 P.M. Mon.–Fri., 10 A.M.–2 P.M. Sat., slightly longer hours in summer, free) is at the Western Park Complex, Vernal's convention center, amphitheater, equestrian center, and racetrack. This pioneer museum and art gallery places special emphasis on Utah's outlaw heritage (real or imaginary).

Ladies of the White House Doll Collection

Head for the Uintah County Library (155 E. Main St., 10 A.M.–9 P.M. Mon.–Thurs., 10 A.M.–6 P.M. Fri.–Sat.) to view a display of dolls fashioned after first ladies from Martha Washington through Nancy Reagan. Each wears a hand-sewn reproduction of the dress she wore at the Inaugural Ball. A brochure has to-the-point but often poignant biographies of each woman.

Dry Fork Petroglyphs

Several panels of famous petroglyphs are located along a sharp sandstone bluff about 10 miles northeast of Vernal. Considered to be some of the best rock art in the United States, what makes these carvings so notable is the fact that they contain dozens of nearly life-sized human figures, many with elaborate headdresses and ornamentation. The significance of these murals is unknown, though they were probably carved by the Fremont and are reckoned to be between 1,200 and 1,600 years old.

To reach the Dry Fork Petroglyphs (also called the McConkie Petroglyphs), drive west from Vernal on Main and turn north on 500 West. Follow the main road when it turns to the left onto Hwy. 121 and continue until the junction with 3500 West. Turn right (north) and follow this road for 6.8 miles. Watch for signs, and follow a private ranch access road to the marked parking area.

The petroglyphs are on private property, and donations are gladly accepted; there are no toilet facilities. Be sure to stay on the trails, and don't get immediately discouraged—the best of the carvings are about 15 minutes into the cliff-side hike. This area is very rich in petroglyphs, and you could easily spend hours wandering along the cliffs.

ENTERTAINMENT AND EVENTS

The **Outlaw Trail Theater** (Outlaw Trail Amphitheatre at Western Park, 302 E. 200 South, 888/240-2080, 8 P.M. nightly mid-June–early July) brings in some wild characters for original musical productions highlighting the area's Wild West past; Broadway musicals are also performed. The Outlaw Trail Festival also encompasses a juried art show in June and a juried photography show in September each year.

The **PRCA Dinosaur Roundup Rodeo** (800/421-9635, www.vernalrodeo.com) in mid-July pits man against beast. It's Vernal's biggest event of the year and includes a parade and country music showdown. A parade celebrates **Pioneer Day** on the 24th.

The **Uintah County Fair** comes to town in August.

RECREATION
River Tour Outfitters

River trips down the Green River's Split Mountain Gorge through Dinosaur National Monument provide the excitement of big rapids and the beauty of remote canyons. Experienced rafters will enjoy the challenge of the Class III–IV run down the Cross Mountain Gorge in the Yampa River. One-day and longer trips are offered by **Hatch River Expeditions** (435/789-4316 or 800/342-8243, www.hatchriver.com), **Adrift Adventures** (9500 E. 6000 South, Jensen, 800/723-8987, www.adrift.com) and **Dinosaur River Expeditions** (435/781-0717 or 800/345-7238, www.dinoadv.com). Expect to pay about $75 for day trips and about $175 per day for longer excursions; children usually get discounts.

The well-regarded **National Outdoor Leadership School** (3101 East 2500 South, 435/781-0305, www.nols.edu, $4220) runs a 21-day river guiding course for aspiring raft guides from its Vernal outpost. Shorter expeditions are also offered.

Other Recreation

Forget Moab—Vernal has great **mountain biking,** and far less hype. Check in at **Altitude Cycle** (580 E. Main, 435/781-2595, www.altitudecycle.com) for info on trails. The website has a frequently updated trail page.

An outdoor **swimming pool** sits next to Independence Park (170 South 600 West, 435/789-5775). Play **tennis** or **baseball** at the city park (corner of 400 North and 900 West). Golf at the 18-hole **Dinaland Municipal Golf Course** (675 South 2000 East, 435/781-1428).

ACCOMMODATIONS
$50-100

Right in the center of town, **Sage Motel** (54–56 W. Main St., 435/789-1442 or 800/760-1442, www.vernalmotels.com, $65–100) has comfortable rooms with refrigerators and microwaves, is pet-friendly, and is one of Vernal's least expensive lodgings.

Also downtown, **Weston Lamplighter Inn** (120 E. Main St., 435/789-0312, $69–140) has a pool and in-room microwaves and refrigerators. It's within easy walking distance of the dinosaur displays at the Utah Field House.

Well south of town along U.S. 191 is the **Weston Plaza Hotel** (1684 W. U.S. 40, 435/789-9550, $89–169), with an indoor pool and hot tub.

Vernal has one B&B, the **Landmark Inn** (288 East 100 South, 435/781-1800 or 888/738-1800, www.landmark-inn.com, $79–179 May–Sept., $59–179 Oct.–Apr.). This attractive brick house is just far enough off Main Street to be simultaneously quiet and convenient; rooms have TVs and private baths.

Over $100

Vernal's two Best Westerns are just a little fancier than other motels in town. The **Best Western Antlers Motel** (423 W. Main, 435/789-1202 or 800/528-1234, about $125) has a pool, hot tub, and fitness room; and **Best Western Dinosaur Inn** (251 E. Main St., 435/789-2660 or 800/528-1234, $111) has a pool, hot tub, and exercise room.

Campgrounds

Two state park campgrounds north of Vernal are located on reservoirs, making them popular swimming and boating spots: **Steinaker State Park** and **Red Fleet State Park** are described in the *North of Vernal* section. There's more camping 20 miles north in the Ashley National Forest and east at Dinosaur National Monument (23 miles).

Closer to town, **Dinosaurland KOA** (930 N. Vernal Ave, 435/789-2148, www.dinokoa.com, Apr.–Oct., $23 tent, $28 hookups) is on the north side of town. It has showers, a pool, laundry, and miniature golf (open May–Oct.). **Fossil Valley RV Park** (999 W. U.S. 40, 435/789-6450, www.fossilvalleyrvpark.com, Apr.–Nov., $20 tent, $26.50 hookups) has showers and laundry.

FOOD

Most of Vernal's restaurants are good, but pretty standard, small-town establishments. The local coffee joint is **Spoof's** (38 E. Main, 435/789-1154, 5:30 A.M.–10 P.M. Mon.–Fri., 6 A.M.–10 P.M. Sat., 8 A.M.–4 P.M. Sun.), which is right around the corner from the **Cobble**

DINOSAUR COUNTRY

DINOSAUR COUNTRY

Rock Restaurant and Brewpub (25 S. Vernal Ave., 435/789-8578, lunch and dinner daily, $7–12 sandwiches, $10–20 dinners), a casual family-run restaurant with good food (check out the pulled pork) and a couple of beers on tap (but hardly a brewpub). A favorite spot for a sandwich, burger, and Utah microbrew is the ❰ **Dinosaur Brew Haus** (550 E. Main, 435/781-0717, lunch and dinner daily, $6–13). On the road to Dinosaur National Park, **Naples Country Café** (1010 S. Hwy 40, 435/789-8870, breakfast, lunch, and dinner until 8 P.M. daily, $5–15) is a good place for breakfast or a sandwich.

Curry Manor (189 S. Vernal Ave., 435/789-2289, lunch Tues.–Fri., dinner Tues.–Sat., $12–25) is Vernal's gourmet restaurant, housed in a fine old Victorian brick home surrounded by flower gardens.

INFORMATION AND SERVICES

The **Utah Welcome Center** (435/789-6932, daylight hours daily) off U.S. 40 in Jensen, a few miles east of Vernal, has lots of information on northeastern Utah and the rest of the state. The Vernal Chamber of Commerce (134 E. Main, 435/789-1352, www.vernalchamber.com, 8 A.M.–5 P.M. Mon.–Fri.) can fill you in on local events. You can also contact the **Dinosaurland**

Travel Board (800/477-5558, www.dinoland .com) for tourist info and events.

Contact the **Vernal Ranger District office** (355 N. Vernal Ave., 435/789-1181, A.M.–5 P.M. Mon.–Fri.) of the Ashley National Forest for information about scenic drives, camping, hiking, cross-country skiing, and snowmobiling in the eastern Uinta Mountains. The **Bureau of Land Management Vernal District office** (170 South 500 East, 435/781-4400, www .ut.blm.gov/vernal, 7:45 A.M.–4:30 P.M. Mon.– Fri.) offers information on the John Jarvie Historic Ranch in the northeast corner of the state and areas south of Vernal, such as Pelican Lake and the White River; land-use maps and brochures on recreation areas are available.

Bitter Creek Books (684 W. Main, 435/789-4742) offers a selection of regional and general titles.

The **post office** is near the corner of Main and 800 West. **Ashley Valley Medical Center** provides hospital care at 151 West 200 North (435/789-3342).

TRANSPORTATION

Rent cars from **All Save Car Rentals** (2145 South 1500 East, 800/440-5776). **River Runners Transport** (417 E. Main, 435/781-4919 or 800/930-7238) offers shuttles.

North of Vernal

From Vernal, U.S. 191 heads north, up and over Uinta Mountain to Flaming Gorge, where a dam backs up the Green River. The drive is picturesque but not entirely pristine—views include vast phosphate mining operations and scars from off-road vehicles. For the best photos, head up here in the evening, when the light is beautiful.

WILDLIFE THROUGH THE AGES SCENIC BYWAY

This scenic interpreted route follows U.S. 191 and Hwy. 44 north from Vernal to Flaming Gorge Reservoir. As the road climbs, you cross

19 geologic formations—an exceptionally thick geologic layer cake—revealing rock layers from the period of the creation of the Uinta Mountains and on through the periods of erosion that followed. The 30-mile drive begins four miles north of town on U.S. 191; a tour map at a pullout shows the formations to be seen ahead. The helpful *Wildlife through the Ages* brochures are available at the Jensen Welcome Center and Forest Service and BLM offices. Signs on the drive identify and briefly describe each formation from the Mancos (80 million years old) to the Uinta Mountain Group (one billion years old).

STEINAKER STATE PARK

Water sports, camping, and picnicking at the park's 750-acre Steinaker Reservoir (435/789-4432 or 800/322-3770, www.reserveamerica.com, year-round, $5 day use, $12 camping) make this a popular place in summer. Anglers catch largemouth bass, rainbow trout, and a few brown trout. Water-skiers have plenty of room on the lake's two-mile length. Warm weather brings bathers to a swimming beach near the picnic area. Scuba divers find the best conditions from midsummer to late autumn, when visibility is up to 30 feet. In winter, visitors come to ice fish or cross-country ski. The campground (elev. 5,500 feet) is open with drinking water year-round; no showers or hookups. Other facilities include two covered pavilion areas and a paved boat ramp. From Vernal, go north six miles on U.S. 191, then turn left two miles.

RED FLEET STATE PARK

Colorful cliffs and rock formations, including three large outcrops of red sandstone, inspired the name of Red Fleet Reservoir (435/789-4432 or 800/322-3770, www.reserveamerica.com, year-round, $5 day use, $12 camping). Anglers catch largemouth bass, rainbow trout, and some brown trout and bluegill. Like the larger Steinaker Reservoir, Red Fleet stores water for irrigation and municipal use. A developed area offers covered picnic tables, water, restrooms, a fish-cleaning station, and a paved boat ramp. From Vernal, go north 10 miles on U.S. 191 to milepost 211, then turn right two miles on a paved road to its end.

A moderately rigorous 2.5-mile round-trip hike from the northern section of the park leads through desert landscape to a **dinosaur trackway** on the north shore of Red Fleet Reservoir. Three-toed, upright dinos laid down these tracks in a soft mud playa (now Navajo sandstone) about 200 million years ago. It's easiest to see these sometimes elusive tracks on a cloudy day or when the sun is low in the sky. Find the turnoff from U.S. 191 across from the big Simplot sign; follow this road 2.3 miles east to the trailhead.

JONES HOLE NATIONAL FISH HATCHERY

Make the long drive to Jones Hole (435/789-4481, www.fws.gov/joneshole) either to see the mass production of trout or to marvel at the scenery. Canyon walls tower 2,000 feet above Jones Hole, and springs supply water for the young trout raised here that will later go to Flaming Gorge Reservoir and other areas. The hatchery produces about three million rainbow, brown, brook, and cutthroat trout annually. Jones Hole is 38 miles northeast of Vernal via paved roads; head east on 500 North and follow the signs over Diamond Mountain Plateau.

Diamond Mountain is believed to be the site of a hoax played in the 1870s—two men salted the area with genuine diamonds, then sold out for a fortune; one culprit was caught, the other escaped. Unpaved roads connect Jones Hole Road with U.S. 191 and Browns Park. Hatchery staff discourage visits mid-November–mid-March because ice and drifting snow can make driving hazardous; it's best not to come then unless you call ahead, have four-wheel drive, and are prepared for winter camping.

A hiking trail begins below the raceways and follows Jones Hole Creek four miles to the Green River in Dinosaur National Monument. Hikers enjoy the spectacular canyon scenery, lush vegetation, a chance to see wildlife, and some Fremont pictographs. The creek has good fishing; special regulations (posted) include use of artificial lures and flies only. You may camp midway on the trail near the confluence with Ely Creek by first obtaining a backcountry permit from Dinosaur National Monument (970/374-3000). Ely Creek has good places to camp and explore. The trail begins at an elevation of 5,550 feet and descends 500 feet to the Green River in Whirlpool Canyon.

JOHN JARVIE RANCH

Browns Park, along the Green River in Utah's northeast corner and adjacent to Colorado, has always been remote. The Wild Bunch and other outlaws often used the area as a hangout. John Jarvie settled here in 1880 and stayed until his death in 1909. He ran a store, post office, and ferry and still had time to take care of the ranch and do some prospecting. A guided tour of the restored John Jarvie Ranch (435/885-3307 or 435/781-4400, 10 A.M.–4 P.M. daily May–Oct., free) takes in the original 1880s corral, blacksmith shop and tools, farm implements, crude dugout, stone house, and other structures. Jarvie's store has been reconstructed and filled with shelves of canned goods, dried food, pots and pans, tools, harnesses, barbed wire, and other necessities of late-19th-century ranch life. Exhibits also show artifacts dug up from the original store site.

Boaters on the Green River can easily stop off to see the ranch; a sign marks where to pull in. You can camp at **Bridge Hollow Recreation Site,** one-quarter mile downstream from the ranch (water available), and **Indian Crossing Recreation Site,** one-quarter mile upstream from the ranch (no water); the ranch also has drinking water.

Trucks or cars with good clearance can drive to the ranch on an unpaved road through scenic Crouse Canyon; this route branches off Jones Hole Road 26 miles from Vernal, goes north past Crouse Reservoir and into the canyon, winds west through hills and parallels the Green River (though the river is hard to see from the road), crosses a bridge over the swift-flowing Green, and turns left 0.3 mile; the distance from Jones Hole Road is 28 miles. Another way in is to go north from Vernal on U.S. 191 to 0.7 mile past the Wyoming border and turn right 22 miles on a gravel road; a steep 14 percent grade into Browns Park makes climbing back out difficult for RVs and other underpowered vehicles. A third approach is from Maybell, Colorado, on CO 318 (paved until the Utah border); this is the best road, especially in winter. Colorado 318 also provides access to Browns Park National Wildlife Refuge, a stopover point for migratory waterfowl in spring and autumn and a nesting habitat for ducks and Great Basin Canada geese. A gravel tour road goes through the refuge.

ASHLEY NATIONAL FOREST (VERNAL DISTRICT)

The southeastern part of the Uinta Mountains has very pleasant mountain country with scenic drives, fishing, hiking, camping, picnicking, and winter sports. Contact the U.S. Forest Service office in Vernal for road conditions and recreation information. Roads at the higher elevations open about the beginning of June and are often passable through October. Most roads to the campgrounds and reservoirs are okay for cars. Some areas may be closed to vehicle use because of wet conditions, wildlife habitat, sheep ranges, or erosion problems. One handy campground is **Lodgepole** (877/444-6777, www.recreation.gov, mid-May–late Sept., $14) offering sites with water at an elevation of 8,100 feet; it's 30 miles north of Vernal on U.S. 191 on the way to Flaming Gorge NRA. Nearby, **Red Springs** ($11) is another roadside campground.

Anglers will find rainbow trout in most of the lakes and streams. Brown trout and native cutthroat trout live in some areas. Most hiking trails are rocky with some steep sections; carry topo maps. Trails lead into the High Uintas Wilderness from Chepeta Lake and West Fork of Whiterocks trailheads; road distances to the trailheads are relatively long, then there's a hike of about 6–7 miles to the wilderness boundary. In winter, three cross-country ski trails lead west from U.S. 191 into the Grizzly Ridge and Little Brush Creek areas; signed trailheads are about 25 miles north of Vernal. Most of these trails are rated intermediate to advanced, though some sections are good for beginners, too. Snowmobilers have an extensive network of trails that mostly follow forest roads.

RED CLOUD LOOP SCENIC DRIVE

This 74-mile loop winds through scenic canyons and mountains northwest of Vernal. Allow about half a day for just the drive. Side roads go to East Park and Oaks Park Reservoirs, campgrounds, fishing streams, and hiking areas. Aspen trees put on a brilliant display in autumn. About half the drive follows un-paved forest roads, so it's a good idea to check road conditions first with the U.S. Forest Service office in Vernal. Cars with good clearance can usually make the trip if the roads are dry. Drive 20 miles north from Vernal on U.S. 191 (or 15 miles south from the junction of U.S. 191 and Hwy. 44 in Flaming Gorge NRA) and turn west on the paved East Park Reservoir Road at the sign that says Red Cloud Loop. Signs then show the rest of the way. The Jensen Welcome Center's brochure *Red Cloud Loop* describes points of interest.

It's easy to find a campsite along Red Cloud Loop. **East Park Campground,** at East Park Reservoir (elev. 9,000 feet), has water; go 20 miles north of Vernal on U.S. 191, then 10 miles northwest on forest roads (all but the last mile is paved). Other campgrounds include **Oaks Park, Paradise Park, Kaler Hollow,** and **Whiterocks.** Of these, only Whiterocks has drinking water.

Flaming Gorge National Recreation Area

The Flaming Gorge Dam impounds the Green River just south of the Wyoming border, backing up a reservoir through 91 miles of gentle valleys and fiery red canyons. The rugged land displays spectacular scenery where the Green River cuts into the Uinta Mountains—cliffs rising as high as 1,500 feet, twisted rock formations, and sweeping panoramas. Although much of the lake lies in Wyoming, most of the campgrounds and other visitor facilities, as well as the best scenery, are in Utah. Some of northeastern Utah's best mountain biking can be found around the Flaming Gorge area. Boating on the clear blue waters of the lake or the river below is one of the best ways to enjoy the sights. Water-skiers have plenty of room on

© PAUL LEVY

Lady Bird Johnson dedicated the Flaming Gorge Dam in 1964, telling the audience that natural beauty was their greatest resource and must be protected.

DINOSAUR COUNTRY

the lake's 66 square miles. Swimming is popular, too, as is scuba diving: **Atlantis Divers** (206 West Main St., Vernal, 435/789-3616) is the best resource for diving in the reservoir. Anglers regularly pull trophy trout and smallmouth bass from the lake and trout from the river. Rafting the lively Green River below the dam offers a thrilling ride that anyone with care and proper safety equipment can take—no special skills are needed. Be sure you're properly equipped before setting out. The U.S. Forest Service and private concessions offer boating facilities and about two dozen campgrounds in the recreation area.

Peace, quiet, and snow prevail in winter. Dedicated anglers still cast their lines into the Green River or fish through the lake ice. Cross-country skiers and snowmobilers make their trails through the woods. Campgrounds are closed, though snow campers and hardy RVers can stop for the night in parking areas.

Staff and volunteers at the **Flaming Gorge Ranger District Manila Headquarters office** (435/784-3445, www.fs.fed.us/r4/ashley/ recreation/flaming_gorge, 8 A.M.–4:30 P.M. daily in summer, 8 A.M.–4:30 P.M. Mon.–Fri. the rest of the year, $2 per vehicle day use) can answer your questions year-round at the junction of Hwy. 44 and Hwy. 43 in the center of Manila.

Information centers at Flaming Gorge Dam and Red Canyon Overlook have exhibits, video programs, maps, and literature. Flaming Gorge NRA can easily be reached by heading north 35 miles on U.S. 191 from Vernal. In Wyoming, head south on Hwy. 530 from the town of Green River or U.S. 191 from near Rock Springs.

Look for groups of graceful pronghorn in the open country east of the lake at Antelope Flat (north of Dutch John) and in the Lucerne area on the west side. Other wildlife in the area includes deer, elk, moose, mountain lion,

©PAUL LEVY

The Green River cuts into the Uinta Mountains at Flaming Gorge where the dam backs up a huge reservoir.

black bear, bighorn sheep, fox, bobcat, mink, and eagle.

FLAMING GORGE DAM AND VISITORS CENTER

Nearly a million cubic yards of concrete went into this dam, which was completed in 1962. The structure rises 502 feet above bedrock and is 1,285 feet long at the crest. The dam is open for self-guided tours daily from about the first weekend in April to the last weekend in September and for guided tours daily about early May–late September. Tours last 20–30 minutes and are free; check hours at the visitors center on the west end of the dam. You'll descend inside for a look at the three giant generators in the power-plant room, then go one floor below to where a shaft connects the turbine and generator of one of the units.

The visitors center (435/885-3135, 9 A.M.– 5 P.M. daily) has a large 3-D map of the area, exhibits, and video programs; books and maps are on sale and staff will answer your questions. The dam and visitors center are 6.5 miles northeast on U.S. 191 from the junction with Hwy. 44, or 2.8 miles southwest of Dutch John.

◖ RED CANYON VISITORS CENTER

Sheer cliffs drop 1,360 feet to the lake below. The visitors center (435/889-3713, 8 A.M.– 6 P.M. daily Memorial Day–Labor Day) has what may be Utah's best picture window; nearby viewpoints offer splendid panoramas up and down the canyon and to the lofty Uinta Mountains in the distance. A four-mile trail along the canyon rim connects the overlooks. Exhibits inside describe local wildlife and flora, geology, Native American groups that once lived here, and early history and settlement of the area. The visitors center is 3.5 miles west on Hwy. 44 from the junction with U.S. 191, then three miles in on a paved road. Three very nice campgrounds (435/784-3445 or 877/444-6777, www.recreation.gov, mid-May–mid-Sept., $15) are near the visitors center: **Red Canyon, Canyon Rim,** and **Greens**

DINOSAUR COUNTRY

The visitors center and trails around Red Canyon have great views.

Lake. At 7,400 feet, expect cool evenings and mornings.

SHEEP CREEK CANYON GEOLOGICAL AREA

Canyon walls on this scenic loop drive reveal rock layers deformed and turned on end by immense geological forces. The earth's crust broke along the Uinta North Fault and the south side rose 15,000 feet relative to the north. Fossils of trilobites, corals, sea urchins, gastropods, and other marine animals show that the ocean once covered this spot before the uplifting and faulting. Rock layers of yet another time preserve fossilized wood and tracks of crocodile-like reptiles.

The road through Sheep Creek Canyon is paved but has some narrow and rough places; it's closed in winter. The 13-mile loop branches off Hwy. 44 south of Manila between mileposts 14 and 15 and rejoins Hwy. 44 at milepost 22; the loop can be done in either direction. The *Wheels of Time* geology brochure, available at visitors centers and the Manila headquarters, describes geologic formations at marked stops. Three picnic areas—two in the lower part of the canyon and one in Palisades Memorial Park upstream where the road climbs out of the canyon—offer places to stop. Camping in the canyon has been restricted ever since a flash flood in 1965 killed a family of seven; Palisades Memorial Park marks the site. Only dispersed camping is allowed along the drive and only October 1–May 15. Two primitive campgrounds (outhouses but no water or established sites) lie just off Hwy. 44 along lower Sheep Creek a short way from the entrance to the scenic loop.

SWETT RANCH

Oscar Swett homesteaded near Flaming Gorge in 1909, when he was just 16 years old, then built up a large cattle ranch in this isolated region. With the nearest store days away, Oscar ran his own blacksmith shop and sawmill and did much of the ranch work; his wife Emma tended the garden, made the family's clothing, raised nine children, and helped with the ranch chores. You can experience some of the early homestead life on a visit to the ranch by joining Forest Service tours (435/784-3445, 10 A.M.– 5 P.M. daily Memorial Day–Labor Day). The house, cabins, spring house, root cellar, blacksmith shop, horse barn, cow shed, many other outbuildings, and farm machinery have been preserved. Drive north 0.3 mile on U.S. 191 from the Hwy. 44 junction (or south 1.6 miles from Flaming Gorge Lodge), then turn west and follow signs 1.3 miles on a gravel road.

BOATING ON FLAMING GORGE RESERVOIR

Three marinas along the lake's length offer rentals, fuel docks, guides, and supplies. Free paved boat ramps at these and several other locations are maintained by the Forest Service. Find **Cedar Springs Marina** (Dutch John, 435/889-3795, May–Sept.) two miles south of the dam at the lower end of the lake.

Lucerne Valley Marina (Manila, 435/784-3483, March–mid-Nov.) provides services on the broad central section of the lake near Manila; the marina has boat rentals (including houseboats). The marina is eight miles east of Manila on paved roads.

Buckboard Marina (307/875-6927, Apr.– Nov.) is on the west shore in Wyoming, 22.5 miles northeast of Manila on Hwy. 43/530, or 23.5 miles south of Green River on Hwy. 530.

Watch for strong winds on the reservoir; they can whip up large waves without warning—even on a clear day. Rock reefs may appear and disappear as the lake level changes.

THE GREEN RIVER BELOW FLAMING GORGE DAM

The Green bounces back to life in the Little Hole Canyon below the dam and provides enjoyment for boaters, anglers, and hikers.

Float Trips

Anyone in good shape with a raft, life jacket (must be worn), a paddle (and a spare), bailing bucket, and common sense can put in at the launch area just below the dam and float downriver to Little Hole (2.5 hours for seven river miles) or to Indian Crossing just above the John Jarvie Historic Ranch (5–8 hours for 14.5 river miles). It's also possible to continue 11 miles beyond Indian Crossing to Swallow Canyon take-out or 35 miles to Gates of Lodore on the Colorado side of the state line; these runs are mostly flat and have troublesome sandbars at low water. Gates of Lodore marks the beginning of some big rapids in Dinosaur National Monument; you'll need permits and whitewater experience here—or you can make prior arrangements to join a commercial river trip.

Visitors with canoes, kayaks, and dories can float all sections of the Green between the dam and Gates of Lodore, though river experience is needed for these craft. Have proper equipment before you get in and go. Raft rentals and shuttle services are provided by Flaming Gorge Resort (435/889-3773) and Flaming Gorge Recreation Services at the Dutch John Store (435/885-3191). Rentals typically cost $60–90 per day, depending on the size of the raft; vehicle shuttles cost about $39 to Little Hole.

Fridays, Saturdays, and holidays in summer often see large crowds on the river; you'll need reservations then for raft rentals and shuttles. For solitude, try to come Sunday to Wednesday. Guide services for boating and fishing trips can be contacted through the rental outfits. Life jackets (included with rentals) *must* be worn by all boaters—the water is too cold (57°F in summer, 40°F in winter) to swim in for long. The 10 Class II rapids between the dam and Little Hole lend some excitement to the trip but aren't usually dangerous. Red Creek Rapid below Little Hole is a Class III rapid and can be difficult; scouting before running is recommended (many groups portage this one). Camping is permitted downstream from Little Hole at established primitive sites or dispersed sites. Bring drinking water or obtain some at Little Hole. No motors are allowed between the dam and Indian Crossing. Water flow varies according to power needs; allow more time if the flow is small. Call the Bureau of Reclamation (435/885-3121) for present conditions.

The put-in is at the end of a 1.4-mile paved road (may not be signed) that turns off U.S. 191 one-third mile east of the dam. The parking area at the river is small and for unloading boats and passengers only. The main parking areas are 0.7 mile back up the road. Drivers can take either of two foot trails that descend from the parking lots to the river. The shuttle to Little Hole is only eight miles (paved) via Dutch John. The drive to Indian Crossing is much longer, 38 miles (25 of them unpaved); go north on U.S. 191 0.7 mile beyond the Wyoming state line, then turn east on a gravel road to Browns Park and follow signs; one section of this road has a 14 percent grade.

Fishing

Anglers can follow the **Little Hole National Recreation Trail** along the north bank of the Green River through Red Canyon for seven miles between the main parking area below the dam and Little Hole. Many good fishing spots dot the way. No camping, horses, ground fires, or motorized vehicles are allowed. The

Green River downstream from the dam has a reputation for some of western America's best river fishing. Modifications to the dam allow the ideal temperature mix of warmer water near the lake's surface and cold water from the depths. Special regulations apply here to maintain the high-quality fishing (check for current regulations). Anglers using waders should wear life jackets in case the river level rises unexpectedly; neoprene closed-cell foam waders are recommended for extra flotation and protection against hypothermia.

HIKING AND BIKING TRAILS

The **Canyon Rim Trail** is a popular 4.2-mile (one-way) hike or mountain-bike ride with trailheads at Red Canyon visitors center and the Greendale Overlook, a short distance from the junction of U.S. 191 and Hwy. 44. **Browne Lake** is a popular starting point for hikes outside the recreation area: Trail 005 goes to the **Ute Mountain Fire Lookout Tower,** a national historic site (two miles one-way); Trail 016 goes to **Hacking Lake** (seven miles one-way); Trail 012 goes to **Tepee Lakes** (five miles one-way) and **Leidy Peak** (elev. 12,028 feet, eight miles one-way); and Trail 017 goes to **Spirit Lake** (15 miles one-way). Browne Lake is 4.5 miles west on unpaved Forest Route 221 from the Sheep Creek loop drive, then 1.5 miles southeast on the Browne Lake road; see the Ashley National Forest map. Stop by Altitude Cycle in Vernal (580 E. Main, 435/781-2595) for a guide to mountain-bike trails in northeastern Utah. Rentals are available at the Flaming Gorge Resort and Red Canyon Lodge; they also host the Dinotrax mountain-bike festival every August. Visitors centers and Forest Service offices have maps of hiking and mountain-bike trails and can suggest dirt roads suitable for either activity. The USGS topo maps are recommended, too.

DUTCH JOHN

Dutch John has always been a government town. It sprang up in 1957–1958 to house workers during the construction of Flaming Gorge Dam and had a peak population of

DINOSAUR COUNTRY

about 3,000. About 150 current residents work in various state and federal agencies.

Flaming Gorge Recreation Service (435/885-3191), at the turnoff for Dutch John on U.S. 191, is basically a gas station (open year-round) with a snack bar (March–Oct.), store (March–Oct.), raft rental and shuttle services, and hot showers.

MANILA

The tiny town of Manila, just west of the recreation area, is the seat of Daggett County, the smallest and least-populated county in Utah. The name commemorates Admiral Dewey's capture of Manila in the Philippines, which occurred in 1898, while surveyors were laying out the Utah townsite. Manila is a handy, though rather bare bones, base for travel in the Flaming Gorge area. The town is 63 miles northwest of Vernal and 46 miles south of Green River, Wyoming.

ACCOMMODATIONS
Dutch John

Flaming Gorge Resort (1100 East Flaming Gorge Resort, 435/889-3773, www.fglodge .com, $90–140), seven miles southwest of Dutch John, offers motel rooms and condos year-round (with reduced winter rates) and a popular restaurant serving breakfast, lunch, and dinner daily year-round. The lodge also has a store, raft rentals, shuttles, and guided river fishing trips.

Red Canyon

The nicest place to stay in the Flaming Gorge area is **Red Canyon Lodge** (790 Red Canyon Rd., 435/889-3759, www.redcanyonlodge .com, early Apr.–late Oct. and winter weekends, $99–139), which sits beside Green's Lake a short distance from the Red Canyon visitors center. The lodge has an assortment of cabins (sleep up to six), some with kitchenettes, some with microwave and fridge. A restaurant opens daily for breakfast, lunch, and dinner; a store offers fishing supplies, a few groceries, bike rentals, horseback riding, and boat rentals on Green's Lake.

Manila

Aside from the houseboats and floating cabins at the **Lucerne Marina** (435/784-3483, www .flaminggorge.com, houseboats from $838 for three nights, cabins $175 per night), there are a couple of simple places to stay in Manila: **Twisted Timber Retreat** (Hwy. 44 and South Valley Rd., 435/784-3600, www.twisted timberretreat.com, $79), with rustic pine logs forming both cabin walls and furniture (all cabins have kitchenettes) and **Vacation Inn** (W. Hwy. 43, 435/784-3259 or 800/662-4327, Apr.–Oct., $75), where all rooms have kitchenettes.

Campgrounds

The camping season begins with the opening of **Lucerne Valley Campground** (877/444-6777, www.recreation.gov, May–Sept., $15), eight miles east of Manila. By Memorial Day, everything should be open. Campgrounds begin closing after Labor Day, though at least one is left open through October for hunters. If you're here early or late in the season, stop by or call the Manila Forest Service office or the Flaming Gorge Dam visitors center to find out what's available. Most campgrounds have water, and group sites and single-family units in some areas can be reserved. Two primitive campgrounds (outhouses but no water or established sites) lie just off Hwy. 44 along lower Sheep Creek. Some primitive campgrounds on the lake can be reached only by boat or trail; these include Kingfisher ($10), Hideout ($18), and Jarvies Canyon ($16). In Manila, the **Flaming Gorge KOA** (W. Hwy. 43, 435/784-3184, May–Oct., $22 tents, $26–30 hookups, $57 cabins) has showers, laundry, pool, playground, and cabins (bring sleeping bags).

VICINITY OF FLAMING GORGE

Spirit Lake has a beautiful setting in the high country of the Uintas. The lake (elev. 10,000 feet) offers fishing, boating, a campground, and a lodge. Hikers can take trails to nearby lakes (17 lie within three miles) and to the High Uintas Wilderness. **Spirit Lake**

Campground (mid-May–mid-Sept., no water, $9) is in a fir, spruce, and lodgepole pine forest. Also on the lake is **Spirit Lake Lodge** (435/783-2339, www.spiritlakeutah.com, $60–120), with simple, pet-friendly cabins (no electricity, cooking not allowed in cabins) housing up to eight.

Browne Lake (mid-May–mid-Sept., no water, $9) has a small campground (elev. 8,200 feet) and fishing for native cutthroat trout. Several trails start nearby (see the *Hiking and Biking Trails* section). Browne Lake is 4.5 miles west on unpaved Forest Route 221 from the Sheep Creek loop drive, then 1.5 miles southeast on the Browne Lake road; see the Ashley National Forest map.

Ute Mountain Fire Lookout Tower (elev. 8,834 feet, Fri.–Mon. Memorial Day–Labor Day), which has been restored as a historic site, has a good panorama of surrounding alpine lakes, Flaming Gorge Lake, and the Uintas. Turn west one mile on Forest Route 221 from the Sheep Creek loop drive, then 1.5 miles south on Forest Route 005.

Dinosaur National Monument

The monument (4545 E. U.S. 40, Dinosaur, CO, 970/374-3000, www.nps.gov/dino, $10, $5 for hikers, bicyclists, and motorcyclists, charged Apr.–Sept. on Utah side of monument) owes its name and fame to one of the world's most productive sites for dinosaur bones. More than 1,600 bones of 11 different dinosaur species cover a rock face at the quarry. The spectacular canyons of the Green and Yampa Rivers form another aspect of the monument. Harpers Corner Scenic Drive winds onto high ridges and canyon viewpoints in the heart of Dinosaur Monument. River-running allows a close look at the geology and wildlife within the depths and provides the bonus of thrilling rapids. Dinosaur National Monument straddles the Utah–Colorado border, but only the area around the quarry, in the western end of the monument, has dinosaur bones.

Unfortunately, in 2007 the Dinosaur Quarry, a huge attraction at the monument, was closed because of severe cracks in the building housing the wall of dinosaur bones. The quarry building was constructed in 1957 on unstable soil; since then, the structure has been falling apart because of the shifting ground.

Elevations range from 4,750 feet at the Green River near the quarry to 9,006 feet atop Zenobia Peak of Douglas Mountain. The high country is part of the east flank of the Uinta Mountains, whose geology is graphically revealed in the deep canyons of the Green and Yampa Rivers.

DINOSAUR QUARRY AREA

Although the quarry itself is closed indefinitely (at the very least until 2010), it is possible to hike about a half mile from the visitors center and see some dinosaur bones. If you are interested in the area's dinosaurs, be sure to visit the Utah Field House Museum in Vernal and the Cleveland-Lloyd Dinosaur Quarry east of Huntington.

QUARRY TO JOSIE MORRIS CABIN DRIVE

Stop at the visitors center or a roadside pullout for the booklet *Tour of the Tilted Rocks,* which describes points of interest for an auto tour to the Cub Creek area. The drive goes 10 miles past the quarry turnoff to a historic ranch, passing sites of Fremont rock art and the Split Mountain and Green River Campgrounds on the way. A small overhang known as the **"Swelter Shelter"** contains some petroglyphs; the pullout is one mile beyond the quarry turnoff; a trail leads 200 feet to the cave. **Sound of Silence Nature Trail** begins on the left 1.9 miles past the quarry turnoff; this unusual nature trail makes a three-mile loop up Red Wash, enters an anfractuosity (a

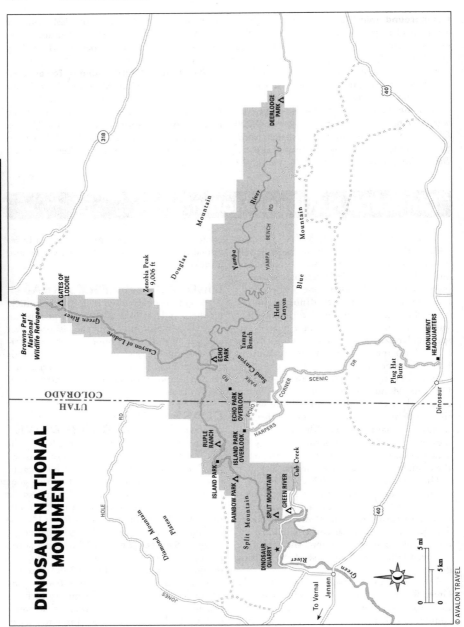

© AVALON TRAVEL

winding channel), crosses a bench and a ridge with fine panoramas, then descends through some slickrock back to Red Wash and the trailhead; you'll need the trail guide (best purchased at the quarry or headquarters) for this hike. Red Wash is also good for short strolls—just avoid it if thunderstorms threaten!

Continue on the drive to the Split Mountain Campground turnoff; the side road winds

DINOSAURS EXPOSED

A fortunate combination of sand and water preserved the bones of dinosaurs, turtles, crocodiles, and clam shells from about 145 million years ago at this spot in present-day Dinosaur National Monument. River floods washed the carcasses onto a sandbar, where they were buried and preserved. Pressure from thousands of feet of additional sediments above gradually turned the sand to rock, and the bones within it were partially mineralized. Later, uplift of the Rockies and Uintas tilted the sandstone layer nearly on edge and exposed the overlying rocks to erosion.

In 1909, Earl Douglass, of the Carnegie Museum in Pittsburgh, suspected that dinosaur bones might be found here because similar rock layers had yielded fine specimens in Colorado and Wyoming. He was right. A discovery the following year of eight Apatosaurus (a.k.a. brontosaurus) tail bones in their original positions became the first of many rewarding finds at the site. Douglass and other workers continued excavations until 1924, removing 350 tons of bones and attached rock that included 22 complete skeletons and parts of hundreds of other specimens. (Some of the best mounted skeletons can be seen at the Carnegie Museum.) After 1924, quarry work shifted emphasis from removing bones to exposing them in relief in their natural positions, which is what is preserved in the quarry building (currently closed because of structural infirmities).

down one mile to the campground at the Green River. The Green River emerges from Split Mountain Canyon here after some of the roughest rapids on the whole river. **Desert Voices Nature Trail** begins at the campground entrance and makes a two-mile loop; a trail brochure available at the quarry, headquarters, or near the start describes plants and geology seen along the way—allow 1.5–2 hours.

Back on the main road, a Green River overlook is on the left 1.2 miles past the Split Mountain Campground turnoff. The road to Green River Campground is a short way farther on the left. **Placer Point Picnic Area** is 1.1 miles beyond the junction, just before a bridge across the Green River. The main road continues past a private ranch, then pavement ends. A road fork on the right 2.7 miles past the bridge goes to Blue Mountain (high-clearance vehicles and good maps needed); keep left for the Josie Morris Cabin. A **petroglyph panel** is on the left beside the road 0.7 mile beyond the road fork. Continue past this panel 0.2 mile and park in a pullout on the right (may not be signed) for a look at no fewer than seven lizard petroglyphs on the cliffs above and to the left; a steep climb up the slope (no trail) allows a closer view of these and other figures. Large shade trees surround the **Josie Morris Cabin** at the end of the road, 0.9 mile farther. Josie grew up in Browns Park during the 1870s and 1880s and settled here about 1914. She spent much of the next 50 years alone at the ranch, tending the fields, garden, cows, pigs, and chickens. She was in her 90s when she died as a result of a hip broken in a riding accident. You can visit her cabin, outbuildings, orchards, and a nearby box canyon.

MONUMENT HEADQUARTERS

At the headquarters (4545 U.S. 40, Dinosaur, CO 81610, 970/374-2216, 8:30 A.M.–4:30 P.M. daily Memorial Day–Labor Day, 8:30 A.M.–4:30 P.M. Wed.–Sun. Sept.–Oct. and Mar.–May, closed Nov.–Feb.), located outside the monument in Colorado, a few exhibits and a 10-minute slide show introduce the monument's history, dinosaurs, and canyons. The

DINOSAUR COUNTRY

River Office here handles permits for groups running the Green or Yampa River within the monument. A self-guided scenic drive to Harpers Corner begins at the headquarters. You won't see any dinosaur exhibits in this part of the monument—the bones are only at the quarry area. From Vernal, go 35 miles east on U.S. 40 to the Colorado town of Dinosaur, then continue another two miles east to the monument headquarters. Dinosaur has a couple of small motels and places to eat.

HARPERS CORNER ROAD

This scenic drive begins at monument headquarters in Colorado and winds north past many scenic overlooks. The road opens in about early May and closes after the first big snowstorm in November, although it's kept clear to Plug Hat Butte overlook, 4.3 miles in. A booklet available at the monument headquarters has good background material on the area and describes the sights at numbered stops along the way. The paved road is 31 miles long (one-way); allow about two hours for the round-trip or half a day if you also plan to hike the two nature trails. You'll pass three picnic areas along the way, but no water or campgrounds are available. The road climbs a series of ridges with fine views of much of the monument, including Island Park, Echo Park, and the canyons of the Green and Yampa Rivers. You'll see spectacular faulted and folded rock layers and a complete range of vegetation, from the cottonwoods along the rivers far below to aspen and firs of the highlands.

Plug Hat Nature Trail is an easy half-mile loop in a piñon-juniper forest at a stop 4.3 miles from the beginning of the drive. At Island Park Overlook, about 26 miles along the drive, **Ruple Point Trail** heads west four miles (one-way) on an old jeep road to an overlook of the Green River in Split Mountain Canyon; carry water. The drive ends at Harpers Corner, a long and narrow peninsula. You can continue one mile on foot to the very tip by taking the **Harpers Corner Trail;** a brochure available at the start describes features visible from num-

bered stops. Cliffs on each side drop to a bend of the Green River at the beginning of Whirlpool Canyon, about 2,500 feet below. Echo Park, Steamboat Rock, and the sinuous curves of the Yampa River Canyon are visible, too. Allow 1.5–2 hours for the easy to moderately difficult walk. Binoculars come in handy for a better look at the geology and other features.

ECHO PARK

A rough dirt road branches off Harpers Corner Road 25 miles from monument headquarters and winds down more than 2,000 feet in 13 miles to Echo Park. The setting of Echo Park, near the confluence of the Green and Yampa Rivers, is one of the prettiest in the monument. The massive sandstone fin of Steamboat Rock looms into the sky across the Green River. Echo Park offers a campground, river access for boaters (permit needed), and a ranger station (open summer only). Cars with good clearance can often make this side trip, though it's better to have a truck. As with all dirt roads in Dinosaur National Monument, it shouldn't be attempted in any vehicle when it's wet. The clay surface becomes extremely slick after rains but usually dries out in 2–3 hours.

Hikers can follow an unmarked route from Echo Park along the banks of the Yampa River to the mouth of Sand Canyon; go up Sand Canyon until it opens out, cut across benchland to Echo Park Road in lower Pool Creek Canyon, and follow the road back to Echo Park. High water levels on the Yampa can block the route from about late May to late June; you'll need to do some rock-scrambling in Sand Canyon. The loop is 6–8 miles long, depending on the route taken.

Drivers with high-clearance trucks can also explore the backcountry on **Yampa Bench Road,** which turns off eight miles down the Echo Park Road. Yampa Bench Road has views of the Yampa River Canyon and Douglas Mountain to the north and Blue Mountain to the south; allow 4–5 hours to drive the 38 miles between Echo Park Road and U.S. 40. It's always a good idea to get directions and the latest road conditions from a ranger before driving into the backcountry. Rains occasionally cut off travel, so carry extra water, food, and camping gear.

OTHER AREAS

Gates of Lodore, on the Green River, has a campground, boat launching area for river-runners, and ranger station—all open year-round. **Gates of Lodore Trail** follows the river downstream to the dramatic canyon entrance, an easy 1.5-mile round-trip; get a trail leaflet at the ranger station or the trailhead. Gates of Lodore is 108 miles from monument headquarters via U.S. 40, Hwy. 318, and 10 miles of gravel road.

Rainbow Park and **Ruple Ranch** are on the west shore of the Green River at opposite ends of Island Park. Both offer places to launch or take out river boats. Easiest access is from the quarry area; distances are 26 miles to Rainbow Park and about another five miles to Ruple Ranch via the rough and unpaved Island Park Road. Cars with good clearance may be able to drive in, but the road is impassable during wet weather.

RIVER-RUNNING

Trips down the Green or Yampa River feature outstanding scenery and exciting rapids. All boaters in the monument must have permits or be with a licensed river-running company, even for day trips. A one-day trip on the Green gives a feeling for the river at a modest cost (see *Recreation* in the *Vernal* section). The most popular one-day run begins at Rainbow Park or Ruple Park; you bounce through the rapids of Split Mountain Canyon to take-outs at Split Mountain Campground.

Longer trips usually begin on the Green at Gates of Lodore in the north end of the monument. Names of rapids like Upper and Lower Disaster Falls, Harp Rapids, Triplet Falls, and Hells Half Mile in Canyon of Lodore suggest that this isn't a place for inexperienced boaters.

Canyon depths reach 3,350 feet, the deepest in the monument. Echo Park marks the end of Canyon of Lodore 19 river miles later. The Yampa River joins the Green here and noticeably increases its size and power. Whirlpool Canyon begins downstream with modest rapids for the next 17 miles, followed by an interlude of slow water at Island Park. The river picks up speed again on entering the warped walls of Split Mountain Canyon and roars through Moonshine, S.O.B., Schoolboy, and Inglesby Rapids on the eight miles to Split Mountain Campground. From here, the Green flows placidly for the next 100 miles through open country.

In 1869, John Wesley Powell lost one of his four boats and many supplies at Disaster Falls on his first expedition. As a result, the rest of the trip was too hurried to make all the scientific studies he had planned. Powell's second trip, in 1871, also had trouble when another boat was upset here.

The Yampa remains the last major undammed tributary of the Colorado River system. Snowmelt in the mountains of Colorado and Wyoming swells the Yampa to its highest and best levels May–mid-July. Most boaters put in at Deerlodge Park at the east end of the monument. The next take-out point is 46 miles downriver at Echo Park. A series of rapids culminates in Warm Springs Rapids, the Yampa's wildest. Where the water is shallow, boaters may have difficulties with sandbars and rocks.

Guided river trips are often best for first-time visitors. The raft companies listed in the *Vernal* section are among those authorized to guide trips in the monument. See a complete list at www.nps.gov/dino/planyourvisit/commercialguidedrivertrips.htm.

Private groups planning a trip on the Green or the Yampa should contact the River Unit (970/374-2468, www.nps.gov/dino/planyourvisit/privateriverrafting.htm) at monument headquarters far in advance; the office will let you know about equipment regulations and how to obtain the required permits. One-day permits are the easiest to obtain. The *Dinosaur River Guide,* by Laura Evans and Buzz Belknap, has maps and descriptions of both rivers in the monument.

CAMPGROUNDS

Dinosaur National Monument has two pleasant riverside campgrounds: Green River and Split Mountain. They're within about a mile of each other. **Green River Campground,** which is open only in summer and has water and a $12 fee, is five miles east of the Dinosaur Quarry. **Split Mountain Campground** is open only November–March while nearby Green River Campground is closed; no water or fee. It's four miles east of Dinosaur Quarry, then one mile north on the Split Mountain Road.

There are several other campsites in the monument—one of the nicest is the **Echo Park Campground,** 38 miles north of Monument Headquarters, with water and several walk-in tent sites ($8). The last 13 miles of the road to Echo Park are unpaved and impassable when wet. RVs and trailers are not recommended. A small campground at **Gates of the Lodore** has a boat launch and drinking water ($8, summer only). **Deerlodge Park Campground** ($8), at the east end of the monument, sits just upstream from the Yampa River Canyon. River trips on the Yampa usually begin here. The site is 53 miles from monument headquarters by paved roads. A primitive campground at **Rainbow Park** (free) is 26 miles from Dinosaur Quarry on an unpaved road.

All campsites in the monument are available on a first-come, first-served basis.

STEWART LAKE STATE WATERFOWL MANAGEMENT AREA

Birders might want to make a short side trip south of Jensen to visit their feathered friends. Abundant vegetation in the water and on the shore of this shallow lake provides food and shelter for birdlife. Take the small paved road south 1.4 miles from Jensen, then, when the paved road curves right, keep going straight on the gravel road for 1.2 miles. The road is okay for cars but is too narrow for large rigs or trailers.

South of Vernal

Few paved roads cross the vast area south of Vernal between U.S. 40 and I-70. The Green River flows south from here through the spectacular Desolation and Gray Canyons; most river-runners put in for this stretch at Sand Wash, accessible by dirt roads from Price or the crossroads hamlet of Myton (on U.S. 40 between Roosevelt and Duchesne) or by airplane from the town of Green River (there's an airstrip at Sand Wash).

The BLM office in Vernal can suggest other places to go in this remote desert. Fantasy Canyon contains eroded sandstone formations, but a high-clearance vehicle is needed to get in; contact the BLM for a map. The old Uinta Railway grade from Mack, Colorado, to the Utah ghost towns of Dragon, Watson, and Rainbow can be driven partway on a rough road. Gilsonite, a natural asphalt mined at these towns, provided the railway with most of its business. The narrow-gauge line operated 1904–1939 and had some of the steepest slick track and sharpest curves in the world.

OURAY NATIONAL WILDLIFE REFUGE

This desert oasis along the Green River provides a lush habitat for migratory and nesting waterfowl. Other birds and animals also find food and shelter in the brush, grass, marsh, and trees. More than 4,000 ducks nest in summer. Migratory populations peak in April and again in October.

A 12-mile self-guided auto tour follows gravel roads through a variety of habitats on the 11,480-acre refuge (435/545-2522, www .fws.gov/ouray). An observation tower gives a bird's-eye view of the marshlands. Hiking is permitted (take insect repellent). Some roads may close during spring flooding and autumn hunting, and those in the east part of the refuge may require four-wheel drive in wet weather. From Vernal, head southwest 14 miles on U.S. 40, turn south 14 miles on Hwy. 88, then turn into the refuge on a gravel road.

PELICAN LAKE

Birds also stop in large numbers at this shallow lake west of Ouray National Wildlife Refuge. The BLM has a campground (no water or fee) and a boat ramp on the south shore. From a junction northwest of the lake, go south on a narrow road (partly paved) that swings around the lake's west side to the campground and boat ramp. The lake has fishing for largemouth bass and bluegill. There's no swimming because of schistosomes (parasitic flatworms) in the water.

WHITE RIVER

The White has some of the best canoeing in Utah and is good for kayaking and rafting, too. The river originates in Colorado's White Mountains and meanders west to meet the Green River near the town of Ouray, Utah. The scenic ride through White River Canyon has only a few rapids, and they're easy. Trips can be a day to a week long, depending on where you put in and take out. Boat-ing provides good opportunities for viewing wildlife. Groves of cottonwoods make pleasant places to camp. The best time to go is during spring runoff, mid-May–June. No permits are needed—the BLM (district office at 170 South 500 East, Vernal, UT 84078, 435/781-4400) gives boaters the responsibility for proper boating, safety, and clean camping. Launch point is at the Bonanza Highway Bridge (40 miles south of Vernal), and take-out is at the Mountain Fuel Bridge, 40 river miles downstream. The shuttle between the two bridges is only 20 miles on graded dirt roads. The trip can be extended by putting in at Cowboy Canyon, nine miles upriver from Bonanza Highway Bridge on a very rough road, or by taking out at the confluence of the White and Green Rivers, 22 miles downriver from the Mountain Fuel Bridge. Both the confluence and Mountain Fuel Bridge take-outs are on Ute land; the tribe requires a permit to park or boat on its land (below Mountain Fuel Bridge). Contact the Utes (435/722-5511, www.utetribe.com, $10) for permits. Bring life jackets, a spare paddle, insect repellent, and drinking water. Obtain information on this trip from the BLM Vernal District Office (435/781-4400, www.blm .gov/utah/vernal/rec/white.html).

DINOSAUR COUNTRY

West of Vernal

Most travelers don't linger along the U.S. 40 corridor west of Vernal; however, there are good jumping off spots to the Uinta Mountains, north of the highway, along this route. If you just need a place to stop on U.S. 40, Starvation Reservoir is a good bet.

UINTAH AND OURAY INDIAN RESERVATION

The nomadic Utes moved into this part of Utah at about the same time that the older Fremont culture faded away, about 800 years ago, and practiced a hunting and gathering culture across much of the high-mountain basin country of Wyoming, Colorado, and Utah.

The first white contact was with the Spanish missionary-explorer Dominguez-Escalante and his expedition in 1776, and the Utes were the first Native American group encountered by the Mormons in Utah.

Mountain men and trappers traded with the tribe during the 1820s and 1830s, though most whites figured that this land, seemingly short of water and most other resources, was worthless. Pressures of settlements elsewhere in Utah and Colorado gradually forced more and more Utes from their traditional lands into the Uinta Basin. In 1861, President Lincoln issued an executive order making nearly the entire Uinta Basin into the Uintah Indian Reservation. By 1864, the U.S.

Army had moved almost all of the state's Utes onto the reservation. The Ouray Indian Reservation was established in 1881, then merged with the Uintah five years later.

Whites started having second thoughts, though, when they discovered coal and oil and realized the agricultural potential that irrigation held for the area. Much land was taken back. Beginning in 1905, heavily promoted homesteading programs brought in floods of settlers. The Utes recovered some cash awards for their lost lands during the 1950s and obtained the Hill Creek Extension south of the Uinta Basin. The reservation now covers approximately one million acres in the Uinta Basin, in the foothills of the Uinta Range and Tavaputs Plateau, and in the remote East Tavaputs Plateau.

The Ute tribe today consists of three bands: the Uintah (of Utah), the Whiteriver (moved from Colorado in 1880), and the Uncampahgre (moved from Colorado in 1882). Tribal headquarters are east of Roosevelt at Fort Duchesne, site of a U.S. Army base 1886–1912.

Nontribal members must keep to the main roads on the reservation and purchase permits for most activities. Camping is allowed at the backcountry lakes open to fishing; you'll need either a fishing or camping permit; boats need permits, too. Some lakes have boat ramps. Backcountry sites have outhouses and sometimes tables, but bring your own water. You'll need special permission to explore outside the permitted areas. Obtain permits at the Ute Indian Tribe Fish and Game Department (435/722-5511, www.utetribe.com) in Fort Duchesne, 1.5 miles south of U.S. 40.

Events

The July 4 **Northern Ute Indian Pow Wow and Rodeo** is the main annual event here; tribes from all over the West participate. Dances, rodeo action, crafts displays, and food booths entertain the crowds. Other powwows, rodeos, and dances happen at different times of the year.

ROOSEVELT

President Theodore Roosevelt opened the way for settlement of whites on the Uintah and Ouray Indian Reservation by a proclamation in 1902. Three years later, grateful homesteaders named two of their new towns in his honor—Theodore (later renamed Duchesne) and Roosevelt. Today Roosevelt (pop. 4,300) is the largest town in Duchesne County and a supply center for surrounding agricultural and oil businesses and for the Utes. Roosevelt offers a few places to stay and eat along the main highway (200 East and 200 North Streets downtown). The community is 30 miles west of Vernal and 146 miles east of Salt Lake City. Travelers can head north to Moon Lake and the High Uintas Wilderness. A scenic backcountry drive goes south to the many rock-art sites in Nine Mile Canyon (see the *East of Price* section).

The **U.B.I.C. (Uintah Basin in Celebration)** in early August is Roosevelt's biggest annual event, with parades, crafts shows, and entertainment.

Accommodations and Food

The **Frontier Motel** (75 South 200 East, 435/722-2201 or 800/248-1014, $55) has a swimming pool, hot tub, a pretty good restaurant, and some units with kitchenettes. **Best Western Inn** (2203 E. U.S. 40, 435/722-4644 or 800/528-1234, $90), one mile east of downtown, has a hot tub and outdoor pool. Next door, **JB's** is a reliable family-style restaurant.

Information and Services

At the **Duchesne County Area Chamber of Commerce** (50 E. 200 South 200, 435/722-4598, www.duschene.net, 8 A.M.–5 P.M. Mon.–Fri.), staff can tell you about points of interest in the area, events, and services. Ask at the **Roosevelt Ranger District office** (650 W. U.S. 40, 435/722-5018, 8 A.M.–5 P.M. Mon.–Fri.) of the Ashley National Forest about camping, fishing, hiking, and road conditions on the forestlands north of town including the High Uintas Wilderness.

The **post office** is at 81 South 300 East. **Uinta Basin Medical Center** is at 250 West 300 North (435/722-4691).

VICINITY OF ROOSEVELT

Guest Ranches and Resorts

A number of old-fashioned guest ranches operate in Ashley National Forest. The **U-Bar Wilderness Ranch** (435/645-7256 or 800/303-7256, www.rockymtnrec.com, $79 per person double occupancy includes meals) has been around since 1933, offering cabins, fly-fishing, horseback riding, and pack trips to those hankering to get away from it all. Lodging is in rustic one- or two-bedroom cabins or one cabin that can sleep 10. The ranch is 26 miles north of Roosevelt, up Hwy. 121 and Forest Route 118.

Anglers will love **LC Ranch** (14535 W. 4000 North, Altamont, 435/454-3750, www.lcranch.com, $75-125 for two people), just north of Altamont. The ranch was established in 1901 by an enterprising homesteader who decided to develop his holdings into a series of streams and ponds. Now a private reserve, the ranch contains 28 lakes and ponds filled with brookies, rainbow, and brown trout. Accommodations are in upscale cabins or larger lodges (a large lodge can sleep eight, $600), including one decorated with more than 30 trophy mounts.

A newer, exclusive resort in the area is **Falcon's Ledge** (P.O. Box 67, Altamont, UT 84001, 435/454-3737, www.falconsledge.com, $175 includes breakfast), an Orvis-endorsed lodge built to cater to fly fishers, upland game bird hunters, and falconers, though the luxury-level rooms and fine restaurant attract an increasing number of people who simply want to enjoy solitude and soft recreation. Rooms are located in a central lodge and are extremely comfortable. Breakfast is included, but other meals are by reservation only and are served family-style.

Ashley National Forest

Moon Lake is in the Uintas about 45 miles due north of Duchesne and 50 miles northwest of Roosevelt. Access roads are paved except for a seven-mile section crossing Native American lands. **Moon Lake Resort** (435/454-3142 summer, 970/731-9906 winter, www .moonlakeresort.com, $35-110) offers cabins of varying degree of rusticity (most have bathrooms) and boat rentals mid-May–mid-October. **Moon Lake Campground** (877/444-6777, www.recreation.gov, mid-May–Sept., $10) is lakeside at 8,100 feet.

Major access points to the High Uintas Wilderness near Roosevelt are (from west to east): Lake Fork at Moon Lake (three trails), Center Park at the head of Hells Canyon, Swift Creek on the Yellowstone River (two trails), Uinta Canyon on the Uinta River, and West Fork of Whiterocks River. In winter, snowmobilers use trails in the Snake John area north of Whiterocks.

Five campgrounds are located along the Yellowstone River on Forest Routes 119 and 124 northwest of Roosevelt; elevations range from 7,700 feet at **Yellowstone Campground** ($8) to 8,100 feet at **Swift Creek Campground** ($8); all have water and charge a fee from late May to the week after Labor Day.

Uinta Canyon ($5) and **Wandin** ($5) have no water and are along the Uinta River at an elevation of about 7,600 feet; take Hwy. 121 and Forest Route 118 north of Roosevelt.

The **Pole Creek (Elkhorn) Scenic Loop** on Forest Route 117 winds through canyons and atop ridges east of the Uinta River; some sections may be rough, though the drive is usually passable by cars with good clearance. **Pole Creek Campground** (877/444-6777, www .recreation.gov, $5), at 10,200 feet, is at the north end of the loop; no water.

DUCHESNE AND VICINITY

This small community (pop. about 1,500) at the confluence of the Duchesne and Strawberry Rivers is the seat of thinly settled Duchesne (pronounced doo-SHAYN) County, where ranching, farming, and the oil industry provide most of the employment. Main attractions for visitors are the High Uintas Wilderness and other sections of the Ashley National Forest, Starvation Lake, and fishing on the Duchesne and Strawberry Rivers. Although there is a motel and café in town, there are more accommodations down the road in Roosevelt.

Uinta Mountains

Forest Route 144 turns north from Stockmore off Hwy. 35, then follows the Duchesne River North Fork to **Aspen Grove Campground** (elev. 7,000 feet), **Hades Campground** (elev. 7,100 feet), and **Iron Mine Campground** (elev. 7,200 feet). All three campgrounds have water and charge a $10 fee mid-May–September; reserve sites at 877/444-6777 or www.recreation.gov. Forest Route 315 turns east from Defa's Ranch to **Grandview Trailhead,** an access point for the southwestern part of the High Uintas Wilderness; the grade is steep and rough, though cars with good clearance can make it in dry weather.

The **Rock Creek** area and **Upper Stillwater Reservoir** are reached by going north from Duchesne on Hwy. 87, turning north to Mountain Home, then west on Forest Route 134. The road is paved to the reservoir. **Yellow Pine Campground** nearby (elev. 7,600 feet) has developed sites with water and a dump station. **Upper Stillwater Campground** (elev. 7,900 feet) lies just south of Upper Stillwater Reservoir. Both have water and charge a $10 fee mid-May–September; reserve sites at 877/444-6777 or www.recreation.gov.

The **Duchesne Ranger District office** (85 W. Main, 435/738-2482, www.fs.fed.us/r4/ashley) of the Ashley National Forest has information on campgrounds, trailheads, and road conditions of this part of the Uintas.

Guest Ranch

The **Rock Creek Guest Ranch** (P.O. Box 510060, Mountain Home, 435/454-3332, www.rockcreekguestranch.net, $40–129) has both modern and rustic cabins, RV hookups ($13) and tent sites ($5), a store, a café, and horseback riding in a remote mountain setting 32 miles northwest of Altamont.

Starvation State Park

The large Starvation Reservoir (435/738-2326, http://stateparks.utah.gov, 800/322-3770 or www.reserveamerica.com reservations, $5 day use, $9–15 camping) sits among rolling hills of high-desert country four miles west of Duchesne. Water-skiing is the biggest summer activity, followed by fishing, sailboarding, and sailing. Anglers catch walleye (a state record was taken here), smallmouth bass, and some largemouth bass and German brown trout. The marina is open mid-April–Labor Day with boat rentals (fishing, personal watercraft, and ski boats) and a store. A developed campground with pull-through and tent sites with showers overlooks the water. This exposed location can be windy. Continue past the campground turnoff for a picnic area near a sand beach. A second developed campground is just past the picnic area. There are four primitive camping areas around the reservoir; other facilities include a paved boat ramp, a fish-cleaning station, and a dump station. The park is open all year. The main season, Memorial Day weekend–Labor Day, is sometimes extended up to a month earlier and later. The campground usually has vacancies except on major holiday weekends. Showers and restrooms close during the off-season, though outhouses are available. A paved four-mile road to the park turns off U.S. 40 just west of Duchesne.

Over the Mountains to Price

From Duchesne, U.S. 191 goes southwest 56 scenic miles over the West Tavaputs Plateau to Price. The route follows the Left Fork of Indian Canyon to a pass at an elevation of 9,100 feet, then descends through Willow Creek Canyon to the Price River. Snow may close the road in winter. **Avintaquin Campground** (elev. 8,800 feet, no water, $5) is reached by a short gravel road from just south of the pass; sites nestle in a fir and aspen forest. The Bamberger Monument, between the pass and Price Canyon, commemorates construction of the highway by state prisoners in 1919; Governor Simon Bamberger gave the workers reduced sentences and other benefits for their efforts.

Price

In the beginning, Price was a typical Mormon community. Ranchers and farmers had settled on the fertile land surrounding the Price River in 1879. Four years later, everything changed when the railroad came through. A flood of immigrants from all over the world arrived to work in the coal mines and other rapidly growing enterprises. (An informal census taken in a pool hall at nearby Helper in the 1930s found 32 different nationalities in the room.) Coal mining has had its ups and downs in the last 100 years but continues to be the largest industry in the area. Price (pop. about 8,000) is a good base for exploring the surrounding mountains and desert.

SIGHTS

College of Eastern Utah Prehistoric Museum

An excellent museum of natural and human history (155 E. Main, 435/613-5111 or 800/817-9949, 9 A.M.–6 P.M. daily Apr.–Sept., 9 A.M.–6 P.M. Mon.–Sat. Oct.–Mar., $5 adults, $4 seniors, $2 children 2–12), this is a must-stop for anyone interested in the prehistoric creatures and people that lived in Utah thousands of years ago. Dramatic dinosaur displays include the skeletons of a fierce flesh-eating allosaurus, a plant-eating camptosaurus (not to be fooled with, either), a camarasaurus, a chasmosaurus, a prosaurolophus, and a

DINOSAUR COUNTRY

© PAUL LEVY

Dinosaurs grapple outside the College of Eastern Utah Prehistoric Museum.

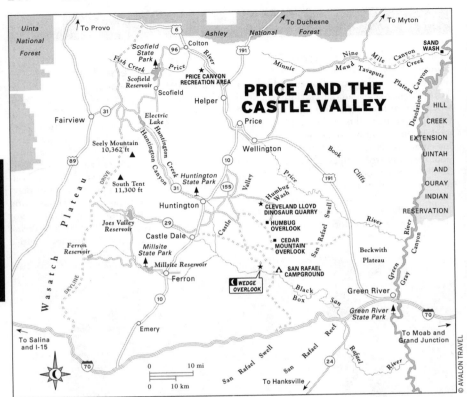

stegosaurus. See bones of the huge Huntington Canyon mammoth recently discovered nearby, the colorful gemstones of the mineralogy exhibits, and artifacts of the prehistoric Fremont and the modern Utes in the outstanding Native American collection. The power and mystery of prehistoric rock art is conveyed in a replica of the Barrier Canyon Mural. Contemporary art is on display in rotating exhibits. Kids can explore the hands-on displays in the Children's Room.

Price Mural

Artist Lynn Fausett captured the history of Price and Carbon County in a colorful mural four feet high and 200 feet long. It extends around all four walls in the foyer of the Price Municipal Building (200 E. Main, 8 a.m.–5 p.m. Mon.–Fri.). Look straight ahead for panels of the first settlers, Abram Powell and Caleb Rhodes. Follow the panels around to the right, past scenes of railroad workers, freight wagons, the first town hall in Price, religious leaders, the 1911 Fourth of July parade, and depictions of the coal-mining industry. A brochure available here gives details of each scene and identifies the self-portrait of the artist as a small boy. Fausett, a native of the area, used his own recollections and old photos for the project, which he worked on from 1938 to 1941. He also painted the Barrier Canyon Mural replica in the Prehistoric Museum and *The Pioneer Trek* at "This Is the Place" State Park near Salt Lake City.

EVENTS

A **PCRA Rodeo** provides plenty of action in early June at the Carbon County Fairgrounds. The **Greek Festival** in July features music, dancing, food, and tours of the Greek church. The **Carbon County Fair** is in August.

RECREATION

Washington Park (250 East 500 North, 435/637-7946) has a very popular outdoor Desert Wave Pool as well as an indoor pool, picnic areas, playground, volleyball, basketball, and horseshoe courts. Two historic log cabins dating from the 1880s and a fitness track are across to the north in **Pioneer Park.** A great playground, the **Basso Dino-Mine Adventure Park** (700 N. 1000 East) has dinosaur and mining themes and includes a skate park, a BMX track, and a basketball court along with the dinosaurs and mine-like mazes.

Carbon Country Club Golf Course (435/637-2388), four miles north of town on U.S. 6/191, has 18 holes.

Stop in at Decker's Bicycle (77 E. Main, 435/637-0086) for trail maps and advice about mountain biking Nine Mile Canyon or the San Rafael Swell.

ACCOMMODATIONS

Price has the Castle Valley's best selection of lodgings and reasonable prices, which makes it a great base for exploration of this part of Utah.

At the west end of Main Street is a shopping center complex that includes the **National 9 Price River Inn** (641 W. Price River Dr., 435/637-7000 or 800/524-9999, www.national 9price.com, $55 and up). Just to the north are the **Budget Host Inn** (145 N. Carbonville Rd., 435/637-2424 or 800/283-4678, $50 and up) and the local **Super 8** is at (180 North Hospital Dr., 435/637-8088 or 800/800-8000, $67 and up).

Two of Price's nicest motels sit on the east end of town near a clutch of fast-food restaurants and the local supermarket mall. The **Greenwell Inn** (655 E. Main, 435/637-3520 or 800/666-3520, www.greenwellinn.com, $68 and up) has a pool, exercise room, and restau-

rant. The **Best Western Carriage House Inn** (590 E. Main, 435/637-5660 or 800/528-1234, $76 and up) in Utah, has an indoor pool and hot tub.

FOOD

A number of cafés and diners along Main Street serve standard American fare, but two of the best local restaurants are a few miles out of town. Venture a few miles north to Helper to find the comfortable **Grogg's Pinnacle Brewing Co.** (1653 N. Carbonville Rd., 435/637-2924, lunch and dinner daily, $6–13), the local brewpub, with burgers and sandwiches to accompany the hand-crafted beers. Just southeast of Price, in Wellington, is the local favorite **Cowboy Kitchen** (31 E. Main, Wellington, 435/637-4223, breakfast, lunch and dinner daily, $10–25); although the exterior of the building is a little forbidding, it's worth going in for dinner.

In downtown Price, find Greek food at the **Greek Streak** (30 West 100 North, 435/637-1930, breakfast, lunch, and dinner Mon.–Sat., $6–16). **Farlaino's Cafe** (87 W. Main, 435/637-9217, breakfast and lunch Mon.–Sat., $5–10) serves Italian and American cooking.

INFORMATION AND SERVICES

Castle Country travel office (155 E. Main, 435/637-3009 or 800/842-0789, www.castle country.com) offers literature and ideas for travel in Price and elsewhere in Carbon and Emery Counties from a booth in the Prehistoric Museum. The **Manti-La Sal National Forest offices** (599 W. Price River Dr., 435/637-2817, www.fs.fed.us/r4/mantilasal, 8 A.M.–4:30 P.M. Mon.–Fri.), across from the Creekview Shopping Center, on the west edge of town, have information about recreation in the beautiful alpine country of the Wasatch Plateau to the west.

Staff at the **Bureau of Land Management** (125 South 600 West, 435/636-3600, www .blm.gov/utah/price) can tell you about exploring the San Rafael Swell, Cleveland-Lloyd Dinosaur Quarry, and Nine Mile Canyon, and about boating the Green River through Desolation, Gray, and Labyrinth Canyons.

DINOSAUR COUNTRY

The **post office** is at the corner of Carbon Avenue and 100 South (435/637-1638). **Castleview Hospital** (300 N. Hospital Drive, 435/637-4800) is on the west edge of town.

TRANSPORTATION

Amtrak (800/872-7245) trains stop in nearby Helper on their runs between Denver and Salt Lake City.

North of Price

North of Price, just as the highway enters a narrow canyon, is the town of Helper, which is a colorful mix of decrepitude, history, and art.

HELPER

In 1883, the Denver and Rio Grande Western Railroad began building a depot, roundhouse, and other facilities here for its new line. Trains headed up the long grade to Soldier Summit needed extra locomotives, or "helpers," based at the little railroad community, so the place became known as Helper. Miners later joined the railworkers, and the two groups still make up most of the current population of 2,500. The fine examples of early-20th-century commercial and residential buildings in downtown Helper have earned designation as a national historic site. The local economy has suffered downturns from layoffs in the railroad and coal industries, and this is reflected in the many vacant structures awaiting new owners.

The vacated structures have begun to attract artists who need inexpensive studio space, and an arts community has begun to take hold. The excellent **Helper Arts Festival,** held mid-August, showcases the local arts scene.

Western Mining and Railroad Museum

A venerable red caboose and examples of coal-mining machinery sit outside next to the museum in downtown Helper (296 S. Main,

Several of the old storefronts in Helper now house artists' studios.

© JUDY JEWELL

GHOST TOWNS

Many coal-mining communities have bloomed and died in canyons and hillsides surrounding Helper. Most have fared poorly since they were abandoned, yet their picturesque ruins can be worth seeking out. The mines and decaying buildings are dangerous and shouldn't be entered – security staff enforces no-trespassing rules. One former company town has survived intact. Kenilworth's residents bought their houses at low prices when the mines closed and have continued to live here; the large company store, however, now stands vacant. Follow Helper's Main Street a short way south, then turn left (east) 3.8 miles on paved Highway 157. A small *Driving Tour Guide* describes coal mines and town sites in Carbon and Emery Counties; it's sold at the museum in Helper.

Scenic Spring Canyon has some of the best and most easily visited ghost towns. The paved road begins as "Canyon Street" in east Helper (across U.S. 6/191 from downtown Helper). You'll see railroad grades, mines, and ruins along much of the road's 6.7 miles. Sagebrush hides most of the **Peerless** ghost-town site, 2.8 miles in. Only foundations and a few buildings survive from this community, which peaked in the 1920s and 1930s with a population of about 300, then died in the 1950s. A tramway brought coal down from the mine high on the hillside. **Spring Canyon** is a total ghost; only a loading platform remains of a community that had up to 1,000 people during the 1920s, 1930s, and 1940s. The site is near a junction 3.8 miles in; keep straight at the junction (the road to the right is still used by mining companies and is gated).

A large concrete loading facility on the right greets you on arrival at **Standardville,** 4.9 miles in. The formerly attractive, well-planned community had a population of 550 during its best years and set a standard for other mining towns. Mines nearby operated from 1912 until 1950. A ghostly two-story stone building, once the Liberty Fuel Company offices, marks the site of **Latuda,** 5.9 miles in. Several hundred people lived here from about 1920 to 1950; Latuda died completely in the late 1960s. Extensive ruins of the mine can be seen on the slopes to the left. Only foundations remain from **Rains,** once a town of 500, located 6.5 miles from Helper. A large stone ruin, once a store, stands at the site of **Mutual,** just beyond Rains. Most of the 250 or so residents lived to the north along a fork of Spring Canyon. You may have to park at the gate and walk a short distance on the road to Mutual.

435/472-3009, www.wmrrm.org, 10 A.M.– 5 P.M. Mon.–Sat. May–Sept., 11 A.M.–4 P.M. Tues.–Sat. Oct.–Apr., by donation). Inside, you'll see two elaborate model railroad sets and photos of old steam locomotives in action. A mine room has models of coal mines (all are underground in this area) and equipment worn by the miners. Other exhibits illustrate Utah's two great mine disasters—the 1900 Scofield tragedy, in which 200 men and boys died, and the 1924 Castle Gate explosion, which killed 173. Other bits of history include ghost-town memorabilia, a Butch Cassidy exhibit, and a dentist's office. The map room displays original maps showing hundreds of miles of tunnels. The brick building housing the museum dates from about 1914, when it was the Hotel Helper; from 1942 to 1982 it served as a YMCA for railroad men.

PRICE CANYON RECREATION AREA

This pleasant spot in the woods (435/636-3600, www.blm.gov/utah/price, water mid-May–mid-Oct., $8) makes a good stopping place for a picnic or a camp. From the turnoff 8.2 miles north of Helper, follow a narrow paved road three miles to the picnic area, a canyon overlook, and the campground (elev. 8,000 feet). **Bristlecone Ridge Trail** begins at the far end of the campground loop and winds through a forest of Gambel oak, ponderosa pine, and mountain mahogany to a ridgetop. Grand views from the top take in surrounding mountains and Price and Crandall Canyons below. The moderately difficult hike is about two miles round-trip with an elevation gain of 700 feet. Bristlecone pines and lots of chipmunks live on the ridge.

SCOFIELD STATE PARK

The large reservoir (435/448-9449, 800/322-3770 or www.reserveamerica.com reservations, $5 day use, $12–15 camping), popular with anglers, boaters, and water-skiers, lies in a broad mountain valley at an elevation of 7,600 feet. The main campground is on the east shore with a picnic area, showers, dump station, boat ramp, docks, and fish-cleaning station. Madsen Bay area at the north end, near the turnoff for Mountain View, has a campground, restrooms, fish-cleaning station, and dump station. The Mountain View area on the northwest side of the lake offers picnic and camping areas near a boat ramp and dock. The State Division of Parks and Recreation grooms snowmobile trails nearby at Pond-Town Canyon (on the west side of the lake four miles north of the town of Scofield) and Left Fork of Whiteriver (near Soldier Summit). Cross-country skiing in the area is good, too, though no facilities or trails have been developed. From Price, drive 23 miles north on U.S. 6, then turn left and follow Hwy. 96 for 13 miles. Other approaches are from Provo (66 miles) via Soldier Summit or from Hwy. 31 where it crosses the Wasatch Plateau to the south.

SCOFIELD

Two coal mines operate near this tiny mining town south of Scofield Reservoir. Production began in 1879 and peaked about 1920, when the town had a population of nearly 2,000. Utah's worst mining disaster took place nearby on May 1, 1900, at the Winter Quarters Mine, where about 200 men and boys perished in an explosion of coal dust. Weathered tombstones in the cemetery on the hill east of town still give testimony to the tragedy. A paved road continues south and west from Scofield to Hwy. 31 on the Wasatch Plateau.

FISH CREEK

The forest lands surrounding Scofield have plenty of places for dispersed camping. The **Fish Creek Trailhead**, west of the lake, is suitable for primitive camping. This is also the start of the 10-mile **Fish Creek National Recreation Trail**. From Scofield, go northwest 3.7 miles on a partly paved road, then turn left 1.5 miles at a fork up Fish Creek Valley. This last section of road is slippery when wet and may be too rough for cars at any time. The easy trail follows the creek through meadows and forests of aspen and evergreens. This is a good area to look for wildlife including moose, elk, mule deer, black bear, mountain lion, bobcat, and beaver. Anglers will find many places to cast a line; special fishing regulations (posted) apply in upper Fish Creek. The trail is good for both day and overnight hikes; Skyline Drive is 13 miles upstream.

East of Price

Aside from a few ranches and coal mines, the rugged canyon country of the West Tavaputs Plateau remains largely a wilderness. Two especially good areas to visit here are Nine Mile Canyon (accessible by car) and Desolation and Gray Canyons of the Green River (accessible by raft or kayak). Adventurous drivers with high-clearance vehicles can explore other places, too; ask the BLM staff in Price about the backcountry roads.

◀ NINE MILE CANYON BACKCOUNTRY BYWAY

A drive through this scenic canyon takes you back in time to when Fremont Indians lived and farmed here, about 900 years ago. Although their pit-house dwellings can be difficult for a nonarchaeologist to spot, the granaries and striking rock art stand out clearly. The canyon is especially noted for its abundant petroglyphs and smaller numbers of pictographs. You'll also see several ranches and the ghost town of Harper. In the late 1800s and early 1900s, these roads through Nine Mile Canyon formed the main highway between Vernal and the rest of Utah.

Today the distances and dusty roads may discourage the more casual traveler. However, if you're interested in rock art or ancient America, then Nine Mile Canyon is an extremely scenic and compelling back road. Although the road is frequently rough and dusty, normal family cars should be able to make the trip with no problem as long as the road is dry.

Nine Mile Canyon is actually more than 40 miles long; the origin of its misleading name is unclear. The drive is about 120 miles round-trip from Price and takes most of a day. From Price, drive 10 miles southeast (three miles past Wellington) on U.S. 6/191 and turn north on 2200 East (Soldier Creek Road) at a sign for Nine Mile Canyon. The road passes Soldier Creek Coal Mine after 13 miles (pavement ends), continues climbing to an aspen-forested pass, then drops into the canyon.

Nine Mile Canyon can also be reached from the north, from near Myton (on U.S. 40/191) in the Uinta Basin, via Wells Draw and Gate Canyon. Gate Canyon is the roughest section and may be impassable after storms. Turnoff for the northern approach from U.S. 191 is 1.5 miles west of Myton; the turn is not well marked, so watch for signs to Pleasant Valley and turn south at 5500 Road. In about two miles, bear right at an unmarked intersection. You'll know you're on the right road if it soon turns into a graveled corduroy roadbed. It's 26 miles from U.S. 191 to the bottom of Nine Mile Canyon.

Obtain a brochure and road-log for Nine Mile Canyon in Price at the Castle Country tourist office, the Prehistoric Museum, or the BLM offices. It describes the various rock-art sites, ancient villages, and historic relics.

DESOLATION AND GRAY CANYONS

The Green River leaves the Uinta Basin and slices deeply through the Tavaputs Plateau, emerging 95 miles downstream near the town

© SARAH BUTLER

along the Green River

Fremont rock-art along the Green River

sites. John Wesley Powell named the canyons in 1869, designating the lower 36 miles Gray Canyon. Boaters usually start at Sand Wash, the site of a ferry that operated here from the early 1920s to 1952; a 42-mile road (36 miles unpaved) south from Myton is the best way in. Another road turns east from Gate Canyon near Nine Mile Canyon. Some people save the long 200-mile car shuttle by flying from the town of Green River to an airstrip on a mesa top above Sand Wash. Swasey Rapids, north of the town of Green River, is the most common take-out point. The last part of Gray Canyon, between Nefertiti and Swasey Rapids, is a good day trip. Although not as difficult as Cataract Canyon, Desolation and Gray Canyons do have about 60 rapids and riffles navigable by raft or kayak. Some are Class III and require river-running experience. Contact the **BLM Price River Resource Area office** in Price (125 South 600 West, 435/636-0975, www .blm.gov/utah/price/riverinf.htm, 7:45 A.M.– 4:30 P.M. Mon.–Fri.) for information and the required permits. Commercial trips through the canyons are available; the BLM can give you names of the companies. The *Desolation River Guide,* by Bill Belknap, has maps and descriptions.

of Green River. River-runners enjoy the canyon scenery, hikes up side canyons, a chance to see wildlife, and visits to Fremont rock-art

The Castle Valley and North San Rafael Swell

High cliffs of the Wasatch Plateau rise fortress-like to the west above Castle Valley, which is traversed by Hwy. 10 between Price and I-70 to the south. The wide band of the 10,000-foot-high uplands wrings all the moisture out of east-flowing storm systems, creating a rain shadow. However, perennial streams flow down the rugged canyons, enabling farmers to transform the desert into verdant orchards and fields of crops. To the east is the isolated and relatively unexplored canyon country of the San Rafael Swell.

Mormon pioneers didn't settle this side of the Wasatch Plateau until the 1870s, long after valleys on the other side of the plateau had

been colonized. Water and good land began to run short by the time of the second generation of settlers, and many turned to jobs in nearby coal mines.

The barren mesas and badland formations, especially along the southern section of Hwy. 10, make for fine scenery. However, the real attraction of this area is the backcountry routes that lead to wild and undeveloped destinations. Unpaved roads lead west into the Wasatch Plateau, up steep canyons to lakes and pretty alpine country, to link up with Skyline Drive, or to cross the range to the Sanpete Valley and U.S. 89. Backcountry explorers can follow unpaved roads east to the San Rafael Swell, an

© PAUL LEVY

DINOSAUR COUNTRY

looking out over the San Rafael Swell

area of great dramatic beauty and unparalleled recreational opportunity that has somehow avoided the fame and throngs of the state's other canyon country. Destinations included in this near-wilderness are dinosaur fossil quarries and remote vista points and trailheads.

HUNTINGTON

This small town at the mouth of Huntington Canyon dates from 1878 and has a population of a little over 2,000. The town gained attention in August 2007 when a mine collapsed, trapping six miners; a few days later, three rescue workers were killed in another collapse.

Although Huntington is not exactly a tourist town, travelers can head west on paved Hwy. 31 and soon be in the cool forests and meadows of the Wasatch Plateau, or head east to the Cleveland-Lloyd Dinosaur Quarry and the San Rafael Swell.

Huntington State Park

The 250-acre Huntington Reservoir (435/687-2491 or 800/322-3770, www.reserveamerica

.com, $5 day use, $15 camping) is a popular destination for picnicking, camping, swimming, fishing, boating, and water-skiing. Lots of grass and shade trees and a swimming beach make the park especially enjoyable in summer. Anglers catch mostly largemouth bass and bluegill and some trout; crayfishing is good. The campground is open with showers March–October. Reservations are a good idea for summer weekends. In winter, the park is open for ice-skating and ice fishing. Located one mile north of town on Hwy. 10.

Huntington Canyon

Hwy. 31 turns west up the canyon from the north edge of town. The giant Huntington power plant looks out of place in the agrarian landscape of the lower canyon. Beyond the power plant, the canyon narrows as the road climbs higher and enters groves of spruce, fir, and aspen. **Forks of Huntington Canyon Campground** (435/384-2372, mid-May–mid-Sept., $10) sits in a side canyon among fir and spruce trees. The turnoff is on the left near milepost 30 (18 miles in from Hwy. 10); elevation is 7,600 feet. **Left Fork of Huntington Creek National Recreation Trail** begins at the end of the campground road and follows the creek up a pretty canyon. The trail offers easy walking and passes good trout-fishing spots; after four miles it comes to an open valley and connects with a jeep road.

Farther up the highway on the right, between mileposts 28 and 27 (20.5 miles in from Hwy. 10), **Old Folks Flat Campground** (435/384-2372 or 877/444-6777, www.recreation .gov, late May–early Sept., $10) has sites in a spruce and aspen forest. **Electric Lake** offers rainbow and cutthroat trout fishing; a boat ramp is at the upper (north) end. The turnoff is on the right near milepost 14 (34 miles in from Hwy. 10), then eight miles in. **Skyline Drive** lies near the top of the plateau amid expansive meadows and groves of fir and aspen. The junction for Skyline Drive to the south is on the left between mileposts 14 and 13; the turnoff for Skyline Drive to the north is five miles farther west along the highway. Roads branch off the northern section of Skyline Drive to Gooseberry Campground (1.5 miles), Flat Campground (4.5 miles), Electric Lake (six miles), and Scofield (17 miles). **Gooseberry Reservoir Campground** (435/283-4151 or 877/444-6777, www.recreation.gov, June–Oct., $5, no water) is near Lower Gooseberry Reservoir; take the north Skyline Drive turnoff and follow signs 1.5 miles to this scrubby open spot. Elevation is 8,400 feet. **Flat Canyon Campground** (435/283-4151 or 877/444-6777, www.recreation.gov, mid-June–mid-Sept., $8) also provides a good base for fishing lakes of the high country; campsites are reached by a 5.5-mile paved road from the north Skyline Drive turnoff; elevation is 8,800 feet. From the campground, Boulger Reservoir is a quarter mile away, Electric Lake is two miles, and Beaver Dam Reservoir is two miles.

Other forest roads branch off the highway to more reservoirs and scenic spots; see the Manti–La Sal Forest map available from the Sanpete, Ferron, and Price Ranger District offices. Hwy. 31 continues 10 miles down the other side of the plateau to Fairview on U.S. 89. Snowplows keep Hwy. 31 open in winter, though drivers must have snow tires or carry chains November–March. Snowmobilers can use groomed trails on the plateau.

CLEVELAND-LLOYD DINOSAUR QUARRY

You can learn more about dinosaurs and see their bones in an excavation here in the desert 22 miles east of Huntington or 30 miles south of Price via U.S. 6. Dinosaurs stalked this land about 147 million years ago, when it had a wetter and warmer climate. Mud in a lake bottom trapped some of the animals and preserved their bones. The mud layer, which later became rock of the Morrison Formation, has yielded more than 12,000 bones of at least 14 different dinosaur species at this site. Local ranchers discovered the bones and then interested the University of Utah, which started digs in 1928. Princeton University and Brigham Young University (which currently does excavations) also have participated in the quarry work.

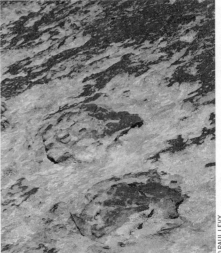

It helps to have a paleontologist tell you that these depressions in the sandstone are dinosaur tracks.

© PAUL LEVY

Visitors Center

The BLM has built a visitors center, quarry exhibits, a nature trail, and picnic sites here (435/636-3600, www.blm.gov/utah/price/quarry.htm, 10 A.M.–5 P.M. Fri.–Sat., noon–5 P.M. Sun. Mar.–Memorial Day and Labor Day–Oct., 10 A.M.–5 P.M. Mon.–Sat., noon–5 P.M. Sun. Memorial Day–Labor Day, $3 adults, $2 children 6–17). Inside the visitors center, you'll see exhibits on the dinosaur family tree, techniques of excavating and assembling dinosaur skeletons, and local flora and fauna. A fierce allosaurus skeleton cast gazes down on you. Related books, postcards, and posters can be purchased. The enclosed dinosaur quarry, about 100 yards behind the visitors center, contains excavation tools and exposed allosaurus, stegosaurus, camptosaurus, and camarasaurus bones. **Rock Walk Nature Trail** begins outside; a brochure available at the start outlines geology, dinosaurs, uranium mining, and ecology at numbered stops; allow 45 minutes.

The drive in is on graded dirt roads, though rains occasionally close them. From Price, drive south 13 miles on Hwy. 10 and turn left 17 miles on Hwy. 155 and follow the unpaved roads. From Huntington, go northeast two miles on Hwy. 10 and turn right 20 miles on Hwy. 155 and unpaved roads. Signs at the turn-offs from Hwy. 10 indicate the days and hours the quarry is open. If it's closed, there's nothing to see. Visitors are not allowed to collect dinosaur bones at the quarry or on other public lands; bones are of greater scientific value when researchers can examine them in place.

Humbug Overlook Driving Tour

A brochure available at the visitors center describes the plants and animals living in this desert country. The drive begins at the quarry and goes southeast seven miles to the rim of Humbug Canyon. Cars with good clearance can negotiate the road in dry weather. The **Jump Trail** winds from the viewpoint down to the canyon floor, about a half-mile one-way.

Look for hoodoos on the canyon walls. They are formed when water erodes rock material down to a hard cap rock. The resulting forma-tion often resembles a mushroom or a human head on a thin neck.

Cedar Mountain Driving Tour

The overlook atop Cedar Mountain has a great panorama to the south across the gently curved dome of the San Rafael Swell and the many canyons cutting into it. Distant ranges include the Wasatch Plateau (west), the Thousand Lake Mountains (southwest), the Henry Mountains (south), and the Book Cliffs (east). A picnic area is at the second overlook at the end of the drive. **Fossil Ledge Nature Trail** makes a quarter-mile loop from the picnic area. Distances to the second overlook are 39 miles from Price, 27 miles from Huntington, or 25 miles from Cleveland-Lloyd Dinosaur Quarry. A graded dirt road climbs about 2,000 feet in elevation through woodlands of juniper and piñon and ponderosa pine. Cars can easily drive the road in dry weather. A brochure describing points of interest along the way is available from the quarry visitors center or the BLM office in Price.

CASTLE DALE

Because they couldn't agree on which side of Cottonwood Creek to settle, two towns grew up here—Castle Dale (pop. about 1,600) on the north side and Orangeville (pop. about 1,300) on the south. Castle Dale has a good historical museum and is the seat of Emery County. A memorial in front of the courthouse honors the 27 miners who died nearby in the Wilberg Coal Mine fire on December 19, 1984.

Emery County Pioneer Museum

Period rooms in the Emery County Pioneer Museum (93 East 100 North, 435/381-5154, 10 A.M.–4 P.M. weekdays, 1–4 P.M. weekends; by donation) depict life in the early days of Castle Valley settlements: a schoolroom, lawyer's office, country store, and kitchen. Pioneer rooms have farm and coal-mining tools and memorabilia of one-time outlaw Matt Warner. An art gallery exhibits local works. The museum is in Castle Dale City Hall, one block north of the courthouse at 100 North and 100 East.

DINOSAUR COUNTRY

horses in the San Rafael Swell

Museum of the San Rafael

Exhibits at this museum (64 North 100 East, 435/381-5252, 10 A.M.–4 P.M. Mon.–Fri., noon–4 P.M. Sat., by donation), housed in a pretty building diagonally across the street from the courthouse, include a paleontology room with life-size skeletons of dinosaurs, such as a 22-foot allosaurus. The dinosaurs displayed include only those species that have been found in Emery County. There are also exhibits of the prehistoric Fremont and Anasazi peoples, including a rabbit-fur robe, pottery, baskets, tools, jewelry, and the famous Sitterud Bundle (a bowmaker's kit).

Events and Recreation

The **Castle Valley Pageant,** held in late July or early August, recounts the faith and trials of the pioneers who settled here; the pageant takes place on a hillside a short drive from town. The **Emery County Fair** is also in August; horse races are run in Ferron to the south, while the horse show, parade, and most exhibits are in Castle Dale.

The indoor **swimming pool** next to the city hall (one block north of the courthouse) is open May–September. The **city park,** be-

tween the courthouse and City Hall, has covered picnic tables. Castle Dale's **library** is next door to the city hall.

Accommodations and Food

The town's only motel is the **Village Inn** (375 E. Main, 435/381-2309, $45 and up). A bit fancier and much more personable is the **San Rafael B&B** (15 E. 100 North, 435/381-5689, www.sanrafaelbedandbreakfast.com, $65–110), where each of the theme rooms has its own private entrance and a refrigerator, microwave, and TV.

R Place Pizza (555 E. Main, 435/381-5080, lunch and dinner Mon.–Sat., $5–20) offers pizza, salads, and sandwiches.

THE HIGH COUNTRY WEST OF CASTLE DALE

Head northwest from town toward Joes Valley Reservoir on the paved road along Cottonwood Creek. After about 10 miles you'll reach a fork; an unpaved road turns right (north) along Cottonwood Creek to Upper Joes Valley (10 miles). The main road (Hwy. 29) enters Straight Canyon. Seely Creek below the dam in Straight Canyon has good fishing for German brown trout. Joes Valley Reservoir covers 1,170 acres in a large valley at the upper end of Straight Canyon, 16 miles from Castle Dale. Note that this is a popular ATV riding area.

Joes Valley Campground (435/384-2372 or 877/444-6777, www.recreation.gov, mid-May–Oct., $10) has two sections on the west shore of the reservoir; elevation is 7,100 feet. **Joes Valley Marina** (435/381-2628), about 20 miles west of Castle Dale, offers boat and ATV rentals and a small store; open mid-May–early November. Pavement ends after the turnoff for Joes Valley Campground. A forest road continues west and climbs 13 miles to Skyline Drive (elev. 10,200 feet) at the top of the Wasatch Plateau. The clay road surface is usually fine for cars in dry weather but treacherously slippery when wet for *any* vehicle. The road from Castle Dale to the reservoir is kept open in winter for ice fishing and snowmobile access.

North Dragon Road turns south between the two sections of Joes Valley Campground and goes about 15 miles to a spectacular overlook above Castle Dale; the San Rafael Swell and the distant Henry, La Sal, and Abajo Mountains can be seen on a clear day. The road is unpaved (high-clearance vehicles recommended).

EXPLORING THE SAN RAFAEL SWELL

About 65 million years ago, immense underground forces pushed rock layers into a dome about 80 miles long (north to south) and 30 miles wide. Erosion has exposed the colorful layers and cut deep canyons into this formation. I-70 divides the swell into roughly equal north and south halves. In the north, a 29-mile scenic drive passable by cars in dry weather branches off the road to Cedar Mountain and goes south past the Wedge Overlook, descends through Buckhorn Wash, crosses the San Rafael River, then winds across desert to I-70. For good maps and photos, visit www .sanrafaelswell.org.

◖ Wedge Overlook

An impressive panorama takes in surrounding mountains and canyons and the 1,000-foot sheer drop into the "Little Grand Canyon." Rain and snowmelt on the Wasatch Plateau feed tributaries of the San Rafael River, which has cut this deep canyon through the San Rafael Swell. Downstream from the Little Grand Canyon, the river plunges through narrow canyons of the Black Boxes and flows across the San Rafael Desert to join the Green River.

From Highway 10 at Castle Dale, head east on the well-maintained dirt Green River Cutoff Road for 13.7 miles to a four-way intersection. Turn south, stay on the main road 6.1 miles to the Wedge Overlook.

Floating the Little Grand Canyon

The 15-mile trip through this canyon provides one of the best ways to enjoy the scenery. The swift waters have a few riffles and small sand waves, but no rapids. Canoes, kayaks, and rafts can do the excursion in 5–6 hours with higher spring flows. An overnight trip will allow more time to explore side canyons. Best boating conditions occur during the spring runoff in May and June. Some people float through with inner tubes later in the summer. Life jackets should always be worn. No permits are needed for boating; the BLM in Price can advise on river flows and road conditions. Put-in is at Fuller's Bottom; the turnoff is near the one for the Wedge Overlook, then it's 5.4 miles to the river. Take-out is at the San Rafael Campground. Extremely dangerous rapids and waterfalls lie downstream from the campground in the Black Boxes; *don't* attempt these sections unless you really know what you're doing! Hikers can explore the canyons above and below the campground on day and overnight trips. Autumn has the best temperatures and lowest water levels; wear shoes suitable for wading.

San Rafael Campground

This small, primitive campground (435/636-3600, no water, no fee) at the San Rafael River makes a handy but bare-bones base for real a back-roads exploration of the San Rafael Swell. The road descends into the main canyon via pretty Buckhorn Wash (look for the pictographs here) and crosses the bridge to the camping area. The cottonwood trees at the campground mysteriously died, giving the area a bleak appearance.

From UT 10 at Castle Dale, head east on the well-maintained dirt Green River Cutoff Road for 13.7 miles to a four-way intersection. Continue 12 miles past the Wedge Overlook turnoff to the bridge and campground. From the campground, the road continues south 20 miles to I-70 at Ranch Exit 129.

FERRON

Millsite State Park and Ferron Reservoir are on a scenic road that connects Ferron (pop. about 1,570) with Skyline Drive. The **Ferron Ranger District office** (115 West Canyon Rd., 435/384-2372, 8 A.M.–noon and 12:30–4:30 P.M. Mon.–Fri.) can help you plan a trip to the Wasatch Plateau.

Canyon Road to Skyline Drive

Turn west on Canyon Road beside the Ferron Ranger District office for a trip to Millsite State Park and the high country of the Wasatch Plateau. **Millsite State Park** (435/687-2491 or 800/322-3770, www.reserveamerica.com, $5 day use, $15 camping) is four miles from town at an elevation of 6,200 feet. The 450-acre Millsite Reservoir is about twice the size of Huntington Reservoir and has the area's best sailing conditions and the most space for water-skiing. Anglers come to catch rainbow, cutthroat, and German brown trout. Ice fishing is done in win-

ter. The park has picnic grounds, campground with showers, boat ramp, and dock. Facilities, except for showers, stay open year-round.

Millsite Golf Course (435/384-2887), adjacent to the park, features nine challenging holes. Off-road vehicles are popular in the barren countryside near the reservoir.

Pavement ends past the state park, but a fairly good gravel road (narrow and winding in places) continues high into the mountains. Stop at **Ferron Canyon Overlook** (14 miles from town) for a panorama of Millsite Reservoir, the surrounding mountains and valleys, and the San Rafael Swell. Signs point out features and geology; elevation here is 8,200 feet. The road continues climbing to alpine country with pretty lakes and groves of fir and aspen.

Ferron Reservoir (28 miles from town) is the largest of the high-country lakes (57 acres) and has a campground (435/384-2372 or 877/444-6777, www.recreation.gov, mid-June–mid-Sept., $14); elevation is 9,400 feet. Skyline Drive is only two miles beyond Ferron Reservoir. Turn north on the drive to a fine view of the reservoir and canyon to the east and valleys near Manti to the west. The highest point on Skyline Drive, at 10,897 feet, is just 0.8 mile beyond the viewpoint. **Twelve Mile Flat Campground,** about 1.5 miles south of the Ferron road junction, is the only campground actually on Skyline Drive (435/283-4151 or 877/444-6777, www.recreation.gov, mid-June–mid-Sept., $7); elevation is 9,800 feet.

Green River and Vicinity

The town of Green River rests midway between two popular river-rafting areas. The Green River's Desolation and Gray Canyons are upstream, while Labyrinth and Stillwater Canyons lie downstream. Several river companies organize day and multiday trips through these areas.

GREEN RIVER

Green River (pop. about 950) is, except for a handful of motels and a lively tavern, largely

run down but the only real settlement on the stretch of I-70 between Salina and the Colorado border. Travelers can stop for a night or a meal here, take a trip on the Green River, or use the town as a base for exploring the scenic San Rafael Swell country nearby.

Green River is known for its melons. In summer, stop at roadside stands and partake of wondrous cantaloupe and watermelons. The blazing summer heat and ample irrigation water make such delicacies possible. **Melon Days** celebrates the harvest on the third weekend of September with a parade, city fair, music, canoe race, games, and free melons.

John Wesley Powell River History Museum

Stop by this fine museum (1765 E. Main, 435/564-3427, www.jwprhm.com, 8 A.M.– 8 P.M. daily in summer, 9 A.M.–5 P.M. daily fall–spring, $3 adults, $1 children 3–12) to learn about Powell's daring expeditions down the Green and Colorado Rivers in 1869 and 1871–1872. An excellent multimedia presentation about both rivers uses narratives from Powell's trips. Historic river boats on display include a replica of Powell's *Emma Dean.*

Floating Down Desolation and Gray Canyons

These canyons of the Green River cut through the Tavaputs Plateau, the vast and mostly untracked region between Roosevelt in the north and the town of Green River. Outfitters normally fly rafting parties into a remote airstrip at Sand Wash, south of Myton, and take 4–7 days to complete the 85-mile trip. Prices vary between outfitters. The river has a few Class III rapids, interspersed with flat water, making for a good family adventure. Expect to pay $800 for four days on the river, or up to $920 for a full week. Outfitters also offer day trips through the lower sections of the Gray Canyon, usually for around $50. Experienced kayakers or rafters can make the trip on their own; see the *Green River Scenic Drive* section for details.

For information on guided day or multiday Desolation and Gray Canyon trips, contact one of the following local companies: **Holiday Expeditions** (435/564-3273 or 800/624-6323, www.bikeraft.com, $930 five days, $995 six days) or **Moki-Mac River Expeditions** (100 Silliman Ln., 435/564-3361 or 800/284-7280, www.mokimac.com, $630 three days, $995 six days). Do-it-yourselfers can drive in from Price or Myton or arrange a flight to the put-in at Sand Wash with Green River Aviation (435/564-8383 or 877/597-5479, www.green

riverairport.com, $99 per person). Contact the Green River tourist office or the **BLM Price River Resource Area office** (600 Price River Dr., Price, UT 84501, 435/637-4591) for a complete list of licensed outfitters. You need both a permit and river-running experience to float the canyons on your own.

Canoeing Along Labyrinth and Stillwater Canyons

Labyrinth and Stillwater Canyons lie downstream from Green River, between the town of Green River and the river's confluence with the Colorado River in Canyonlands National Park. Primarily a canoeing or kayaking river, the Green at this point is calm and wide as it passes into increasingly deep, rust-colored canyons. This isn't a wilderness river, however, as regular power boats can also follow the river below town to the confluence with the Colorado River and head up the Colorado to Moab, 2–3 days and 186 river miles away.

Some guided canoe trips leave from Mineral Canyon and paddle 52 miles to the river's confluence; the remainder of the trip through the Colorado's Cataract Canyon is on raft (around $1,000 for a six-day trip). You'll find both guided and self-guided canoe trips available between Green River State Park just south of town and the Mineral Canyon boat launch. Depending on how fast you paddle it will be a three- or four-day trip. Prices for a guided trip start at about $500; canoe rentals are $17–20 a day, though the shuttle from Mineral Canyon back to Green River will cost you around $200–300 (for up to four people). For information on guided or independent canoe trips on the Green River, contact **Moki-Mac** (100 Silliman Ln., 435/564-3361 or 800/284-7280, www.mokimac.com) or **Red River Canoe Company** (1371 North U.S. 191, Moab, 435/259-7722 or 800/753-8216, www.redrivercanoe.com); **Tex's Riverways** (435/259-5101, www.texsriverways.com) offers rentals and shuttles.

Accommodations

Green River has a few older motels as well as newer chain motels to choose from; unless noted,

DINOSAUR COUNTRY

each of the following has a pool—a major consideration in this often sweltering desert valley.

One of the older places, the **Sleepy Hollow Motel** (94 E. Main, 435/564-8189, $45) is an attractive brick motel right in the center of town; it does not have a pool. The **Super 8** (1248 E. Main, 435/564-8888 or 800/888-8888, $60), out by I-70 Exit 162, is a good value, with spacious, comfortable rooms. The **Comfort Inn** (1065 E. Main, 435/564-3300, $71) operates a bit closer to town. The **Motel 6** (946 E. Main, 435/564-3436 or 800/466-8356, $45) is just two blocks from the river.

The nicest place to stay in town is the relatively expensive ◖ **Best Western River Terrace Motel** (880 E. Main, 435/564-3401 or 800/528-1234, www.bestwestern.com, $90), with very large, nicely furnished rooms, some of which overlook the Green River.

CAMPGROUNDS

Four campgrounds, all with showers, offer sites for tents and RVs year-round. **Green River State Park** (150 S. Green River Blvd., 435/564-3633 or 800/322-3770, www .reserveamerica.com, year-round, $5 day use, $15 camping) has a great setting near the river; it's shaded by large cottonwoods and has a boat ramp. **Shady Acres RV Park** (350 E. Main, 435/564-8290 or 800/537-8674, $20 tent, $27–36 hookups, $42 cabins) may be a bit too close to the noisy road for tent campers; open year-round with store, showers, and laundry. **United Campground** (910 E. Main, 435/564-8195, about $30 hookups) is set back a ways from the road; open year-round with a pool, store, showers, and laundry. **Green River KOA** (550 S. Green River Blvd., 435/564-3651, $20–28 tents, $33–45 hookups, $52–60 cabins) has campsites and cabins (bring sleeping bags).

Food

Other than motel restaurants and fast food, the one really notable place to eat in Green River is ◖ **Ray's Tavern** (25 S. Broadway,

Ray's Tavern is one of the few thriving businesses in downtown Green River, and it's a fun place to stop for a beer and a burger.

© PAUL LEVY

435/564-3511, diner nightly, $7–19). Ray's doesn't look like much from the outside, but inside you'll find a friendly welcome, tables made from tree trunks, and some of the best steaks, chops, and burgers in this part of the state. Don't expect haute cuisine, but the food is good and the atmosphere is truly Western; beer drinkers will be glad for the selection of regional microbrews after a long day navigating the river or driving desert roads.

Directly adjacent to the Best Western River Terrace Motel is a good restaurant, **The Tamarisk** (880 E. Main, 435/564-8109, breakfast, lunch, and dinner daily, $6–27) with riverfront views.

Services

The **post office** is on E. Main. **Green River Medical Center** (250 E. Main, 435/564-3434) offers services Monday–Friday 9 A.M.–5 P.M.

VICINITY OF GREEN RIVER
Crystal Geyser

With some luck, you'll catch the spectacle of this cold-water geyser on the bank of the Green River. The gusher shoots as high as 60 feet but only three or four times daily, so you may have to spend a half day here in order to see it. An eruption, typically lasting seven minutes, is powered by carbon dioxide and other gases. A 2,267-foot-deep petroleum test well drilled in 1935–1936 concentrated the geyser flow, but thick layers of old travertine deposits attest that mineral-laden springs have long been active at this site. Colorful newer travertine forms delicate terraces around the opening and down to the river. The orange and dark red of the minerals and algae make this a pretty spot, even if the geyser is only quietly gurgling.

Crystal Geyser is 10 miles south of town by road (boaters should look for the geyser deposits on the left about 4.5 river miles downstream from Green River). From downtown, drive east one mile on Main, turn left three miles on signed Frontage Road (near milepost 4), then turn right six miles on a narrow paved road just after going under a railroad overpass. The road goes under I-70, then is unpaved for

the last 4.5 miles; keep right at a fork near some power lines. Some washes have to be crossed, so the drive isn't recommended after rains. When the weather's fair, cars shouldn't have a problem. Buildings and antennas passed on the way belong to the Utah Launch Complex of White Sands Missile Range. From 1963 to 1979 several hundred Pershing and Athena rockets blasted off here for targets at White Sands, New Mexico, 400 miles away.

Green River Scenic Drive

Splendid cliffs of Gray Canyon enclose the Green River 10 miles north of town. An unpaved road winding 8.5 miles into the canyon allows drivers easy access to the scenery. Cars with good clearance can travel through the canyon in dry weather; when the clay road surface gets wet, don't attempt it in any vehicle.

From downtown Green River, head east on Main Street and turn north on Hastings Road (1200 East); it's the first paved road to the north past the bridge. After two miles the road follows the banks of the Green River a short way with views north to the castlelike cliffs of the Beckwith Plateau, through which the Green River has carved Gray Canyon. At 6.3 miles after turning off Main, make a right turn onto an unpaved road just before the paved road enters a ranch. The turn may have a small sign for Nefertiti. Follow the unpaved road 3.8 miles across a wash, then along the river to Swasey Beach and Rapids near the mouth of Gray Canyon. A primitive camping area under the cottonwoods is an inviting place to spend the night. The camping area has an outhouse; no drinking water or charge. A large sandy beach stretches along the shore just below the rapids.

The road becomes a bit rougher and narrows to a single lane in spots past Swasey Beach for the remaining 8.5 spectacular miles to Nefertiti. You'll see Price River Canyon entering Gray Canyon on the other side of the river two miles before Nefertiti. Look for petroglyphs near the end of the road. Hikers can explore many rugged side canyons or follow cattle trails a long distance upstream. Cowboys on horseback still work the range on the plateaus to the north much as they've always done. Cattle are driven on these trails to the high country in spring and brought back down in autumn.

Commercial **raft day trips** such as those offered by Moki-Mac (100 Silliman Ln., 435/564-3361 or 800/284-7280, www.mokimac.com, $59) provide a more relaxed way of enjoying this extremely remote part of Utah. River-runners enjoy half a dozen lively rapids on the section of river from the boat launch just above Nefertiti Rapid to the take-out at Swasey Beach.

You can also do it yourself. This makes a good day trip with rafts or kayaks; canoeists will find the white water very challenging. All boaters must wear life jackets and carry proper equipment (spare oar or paddle, extra life jacket, and bail bucket or pump). Campers will also need a portable toilet and, if planning a campfire, a firepan to contain the ashes. You won't need a permit, though the BLM has a register at the put-in.

SEGO CANYON AND GHOST TOWN

Prehistoric rock art and ruins of a coal-mining town lie within scenic canyons of the Book Cliffs just a short drive north from Thompson Springs and I-70.

Sego Canyon is a showcase of prehistoric rock art—it preserves rock drawings and images that are thousands of years old. The Barrier Canyon Style drawings may be 8,000 years old; the more recent Fremont Style images were created in the last thousand years. Compared to these ancient pictures, the Ute etchings are relatively recent; experts speculate that they may have been drawn in the 1800s, when Ute villages still lined Sego Canyon. Interestingly, the newer petroglyphs and pictographs are more representational than the older ones. The ancient Barrier Canyon figures are typically horned ghostlike beings that look like aliens from early Hollywood sci-fi thrillers. The Fre-

mont Style images depict stylized human figures made from geometric shapes; the crudest figures are the most recent. The Ute images are of buffaloes and hunters on horseback.

In the early 1900s, a local rancher discovered thick seams of high-quality coal here. A mining camp, served by the Ballard and Thompson Railroad, sprang to life at the site. Residents named their little town after Utah's state flower, the sego lily, which grew profusely in the canyons. Population peaked at about 500; families lived in fine houses or in rustic dugouts, while the bachelors stayed in a two-story boardinghouse. Production continued through water shortages, fires, and management troubles until the early 1950s, when the railroads switched to diesel locomotives and no longer needed Sego's coal. The town folded and was sold for salvage.

Visitors to the town can see the company store's stone walls, the frame boardinghouse, dugout houses, railroad grades, and foundations of coal-handling structures. Cars with good clearance can travel the road in dry weather; don't enter the canyons after recent rains or if storms threaten.

To reach Sego Canyon, take I-70 Thompson Exit 185 (25 miles east of Green River or five miles east of the U.S. 191 turnoff to Moab) and drive one mile north to Thompson. The small railroad community has a café and convenience store near I-70. Continue north across the tracks on a paved road, which becomes dirt after half a mile, into Thompson Canyon. At the first creek ford, 3.5 miles from town, look for petroglyphs and pictographs on cliffs to the left.

The ghost town lies one mile up Sego Canyon. Both the Sego and Thompson Canyon Roads lead deeper into the rugged Book Cliffs. Drivers with four-wheel drive and hikers can explore more of this land, seldom visited except in deer season.

ZION AND BRYCE

In the southwestern corner of Utah, the Mojave Desert, the Great Basin, and the Colorado Plateau meet to create a unique combination of climates and ecosystems. The lofty cliffs of the Colorado Plateau rise east of the desert country with some of the most spectacular scenery on earth—the grandeur and colors have to be seen to be believed. Great faults break the Colorado Plateau into a staircase of lesser plateaus across southern Utah and into northern Arizona. Angular features of cliffs and canyons dominate the landscape. Volcanic cones and lava flows have broken through the surface, some in geologically recent times. Elevations range from 2,350 feet at Beaver Dam Wash to 11,307 feet atop Brian Head Peak.

Here you'll find two of the nation's most popular national parks, Zion and Bryce Canyon, and an abundance of recreational opportunities. On the same spring day, you could hike through serpentine canyons or flower-filled meadows, hit the slopes at the Brian Head Ski Area, glide on cross-country skis across a high plateau, explore the desert, or play a leisurely round of golf. If you're looking for higher culture, Cedar City offers a well-respected summer Shakespeare festival; at Kanab, you can visit sets used for vintage movie and TV Westerns.

No matter what the season, you can nearly always find pleasant temperatures in some part of this region. Ever since Brigham Young built a winter house at St. George to escape the cold and snow, people have been coming to take advantage of the mild climate. Midwinter temperatures at St. George

© W. C. MCRAE

HIGHLIGHTS

⟮ Sunrise and Sunset Points: Although any one of the viewpoints along Bryce Canyon National Park's Rim Drive is spectacular, these two, linked by a half-mile stretch of the Rim Trail, are particularly stunning at their designated times of day. Each viewpoint gives rise to a trail into the hoodoos (page 268).

⟮ Best Friends Animal Sanctuary: Animal lovers should pull off the road north of Kanab to see this huge shelter (housing 1800 animals), which spreads across scenic Angel Canyon. Tours visit Dogtown (including a special old dogs' home), Cat World, Parrot's Landing, and the all-too-cute Bunny House (page 282).

⟮ Emerald Pools Trails: In Zion National Park, choose from one of three trails to the Lower, Middle, or Upper Emerald Pools. The highest pool is, of course, the most beautiful (page 297).

⟮ The Narrows: In Zion National Park, fit hikers who are also adept swimmers can gear up with the proper footwear and, possibly, a dry suit to hike up the high-walled canyon of the Virgin River...*in* the river (page 299).

⟮ St. George Dinosaur Discovery Site at Johnson Farm: The local eye doctor must have known there was something special about his land when he began peeling back the layers of rock. Before long he uncovered some of the best dinosaur tracks ever seen. They're preserved in this museum; just outside, excavation is ongoing (page 308).

⟮ Snow Canyon State Park: Camp here or come for a morning hike, when you'll share the trails through red-rock canyons and across lava flows with guests from the nearby spas. Snow Canyon is a lovely contrast to the city of St. George (page 315).

⟮ Utah Shakespearean Festival: Cedar City comes alive with this summer festival, which brings three Shakespearean plays as well as several non-Bard plays to town. The open-air theater-in-the-round is modeled on the original Globe Theatre (page 323).

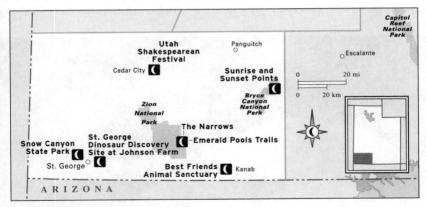

LOOK FOR ⟮ TO FIND RECOMMENDED SIGHTS, ACTIVITIES, DINING, AND LODGING.

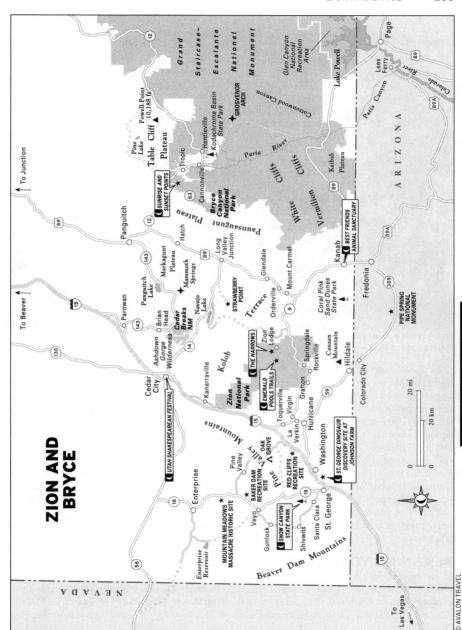

ZION AND BRYCE

ZION AND BRYCE

To Junction

To Beaver

To Las Vegas

NEVADA

ARIZONA

Grand   Staircase–   Escalante   National   Monument

Glen Canyon National Recreation Area

Lake Powell

Page

Lees Ferry

Colorado River

Cottonwood Canyon

Paria Canyon

Powell Point 10,188 ft

Pine Lake

Table Cliff Plateau

GROSVENOR ARCH

Henrieville

Kodachrome Basin State Park

Tropic

Cannonville

Paria   River

White   Cliffs

Vermilion   Cliffs

Kaibab Plateau

Panguitch

SUNRISE AND SUNSET POINTS

Bryce Canyon National Park

Paunsaugunt   Plateau

Hatch

Long Valley Junction

Glendale

Mount Carmel

Kanab

BEST FRIENDS ANIMAL SANCTUARY

Fredonia

Markagunt Plateau

Mammoth Springs

Navajo Lake

STRAWBERRY POINT

Cedar Breaks NM

Brian Head

Ashdown Gorge Wilderness

Parowan

Panguitch Lake

Terrace

Orderville

Coral Pink Sand Dunes State Park

PIPE SPRING NATIONAL MONUMENT

Cedar City

UTAH SHAKESPEAREAN FESTIVAL

Kanarraville

Kolob

Zion National Park

THE NARROWS

Zion Lodge

EMERALD POOLS TRAILS

Springdale

Rockville

Canaan Mountain

Hildale

Colorado City

Enterprise

Pine Valley

OAK GROVE

BAKER DAM RECREATION SITE

Pine Valley Mountains

Toquerville

La Verkin

Virgin

Grafton

Hurricane

Washington

RED CLIFFS RECREATION SITE

ST. GEORGE DINOSAUR DISCOVERY SITE AT JOHNSON FARM

MOUNTAIN MEADOWS MASSACRE HISTORIC SITE

Veyo

Gunlock

SNOW CANYON STATE PARK

Shivwits

Santa Clara

St. George

Beaver Dam Mountains

Enterprise Reservoir

20 mi

20 km

© AVALON TRAVEL

© EMILY ROTH

Not actually a canyon, Bryce Canyon is instead an eroded amphitheater at the edge of the Paunsaugunt Plateau.

ZION AND BRYCE

(elev. 2,880 feet) may drop below freezing at night, but days are typically in the middle to upper 50s with bright sunshine. Spring and autumn bring ideal weather. Summer, when the highs often top 100°F at the lower elevations, is the time to head for the mountains and high plateaus. The alpine meadows and cool forests of the Beaver Dam Mountains, Cedar Breaks National Monument, and Bryce Canyon National Park provide a welcome refuge from summer heat. Precipitation ranges widely from place to place and from year to year, but most falls in winter/early spring and late summer.

PLANNING YOUR TIME

If you have a week to spend in this corner of Utah, it makes sense to spend a couple of days exploring Zion National Park and another day or two at Bryce Canyon National Park. An ideal week in this part of Utah would begin near St. George, either camping at Snow Canyon State Park or finding the perfect balance of exertion and relaxation at one of the local spa resorts, then heading to Zion National Park for a couple of days of hiking. From Zion, head east and north to Bryce Canyon National Park, for another two days of exploring. Don't forget to venture outside the borders of the national park here to check out the great scenery and trails at nearby Kodachrome Basin State Park and Red Canyon. From the Bryce area, head west across the Markagunt Plateau (spend a summer night at the Cedar Breaks, or ski at Brian Head in winter) to Cedar City, where the summertime Shakespeare Festival makes a good end to the trip.

Guided van tours of many of southwestern Utah's grandest sights are available from **Southern Utah Scenic Tours** (435/867-8690 or 888/404-8687, www.utahscenic tours.com).

Bryce Canyon National Park

In Bryce Canyon (435/834-5322, www.nps .gov/brca, $25 per vehicle or $12 per bicyclist, pedestrian, or motorcyclist, good for seven days and unlimited shuttle use), a geologic fairyland of rock spires rises beneath the high cliffs of the Paunsaugunt Plateau. This intricate maze, eroded from a soft limestone, now glows with warm shades of reds, oranges, pinks, yellows, and creams. The rocks provide a continuous show of changing color through the day as the sun's rays and cloud shadows move across the landscape.

Looking at these rock formations is like looking at puffy clouds in the sky; it's easy to find images in the shapes of the rocks. Some see the natural rock sculptures as Gothic castles, others as Egyptian temples, subterranean worlds inhabited by dragons, or vast armies of a lost empire. The Paiute Indian tale of the Legend People relates how various animals and birds once lived in a beautiful city built for them by Coyote; when the Legend People began behaving badly toward Coyote, he transformed them all into stone.

Bryce Canyon isn't a canyon at all, but the largest of a series of massive amphitheaters cut into the Pink Cliffs. In Bryce Canyon National Park, you can gaze into the depths from viewpoints and trails on the plateau rim or hike down moderately steep trails and wind your way among the spires. A 17-mile scenic drive traces the length of the park and passes many overlooks and trailheads. Off-road, the nearly 36,000 acres of Bryce Canyon National Park offers many opportunities to explore spectacular rock features, dense forests, and expansive meadows.

The park's elevation ranges 6,600–9,100 feet, so it's usually much cooler here than at Utah's other national parks. Expect pleasantly warm days in summer, frosty nights in spring and autumn, and snow at almost any time of year. The visitors center, scenic drive, and a campground stay open throughout the year.

Allow a full day to see the visitors center exhibits, enjoy the viewpoints along the scenic drive, and take a few short walks. Photographers usually obtain best results early and late in the day when shadows set off the brightly colored rocks. Memorable sunsets and sunrises reward visitors who stay overnight. Moonlit nights reveal yet another spectacle.

From Bryce Junction (on U.S. 89, seven miles south of Panguitch), turn east 14 miles on Hwy. 12, then south three miles on Hwy. 63. Or, from Torrey (near Capitol Reef National Park), head west 103 miles on Hwy. 12, then turn south three miles (winter snows occasionally close this section). Both approaches have spectacular scenery.

"A HELL OF A PLACE TO LOSE A COW"

Mormon pioneer Ebenezer Bryce homesteaded near the town site of Tropic in 1875, but the work of scratching a living from the rugged land became too hard. He left five years later for more promising areas in Arizona. The name of the park commemorates his efforts. He is remembered as saying of the area, "Well, it's a hell of a place to lose a cow."

A later settler, Ruben "Ruby" Syrett, recognized the tourist potential of the area and opened the first small lodge near Sunset Point in 1919, then Ruby's Inn in 1924. Enthusiasm for the scenic beauty led to creation of Bryce Canyon National Monument in 1923. The name changed to Utah National Park in the following year, then took its current name in 1928. Tours organized by the Union Pacific Railroad, beginning in the late 1920s, made Bryce well known and easily visited.

The Hoodoos

The park's landscape originated about 60 million years ago as sediments in a large body of

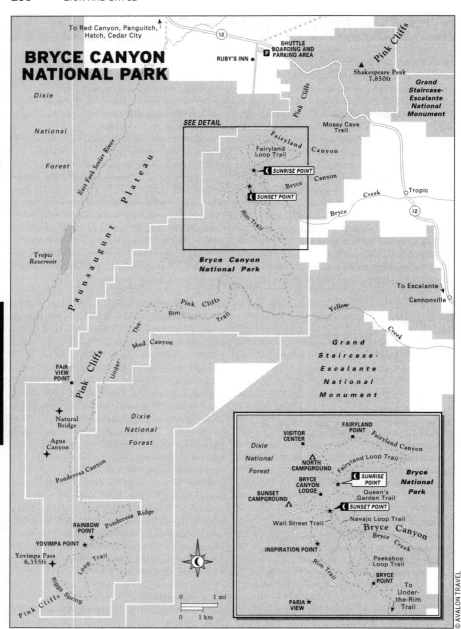

BRYCE CANYON NATIONAL PARK

To Red Canyon, Panguitch, Hatch, Cedar City

Dixie

National

Forest

East Fork Sevier River

Paunsaugunt Plateau

Tropic Reservoir

RUBY'S INN

SHUTTLE BOARDING AND PARKING AREA

Pink Cliffs

Shakespeare Peak 7,850ft

Grand Staircase-Escalante National Monument

SEE DETAIL

Fairyland

Fairyland Loop Trail

Canyon

Mossy Cave Trail

SUNRISE POINT

Bryce Canyon

SUNSET POINT

Rim Trail

Creek

Tropic

Bryce

Bryce Canyon National Park

To Escalante

Cannonville

Pink Cliffs Rim Trail

The

Mud Canyon

Under

FAIR VIEW POINT

Pink Cliffs

Natural Bridge

Agua Canyon

Ponderosa Canyon

Dixie

National

Forest

Yellow

Creek

Grand Staircase-Escalante National Monument

RAINBOW POINT

Ponderosa Ridge

YOVIMPA POINT

Yovimpa Pass 8,355ft

Loop Trail

Riggs Spring

Pink Cliffs

Dixie National Forest

VISITOR CENTER

FAIRYLAND POINT

Fairyland Canyon

Fairyland Loop Trail

NORTH CAMPGROUND

BRYCE CANYON LODGE

SUNRISE POINT

Queen's Garden Trail

SUNSET POINT

Bryce National Park

SUNSET CAMPGROUND

Wall Street Trail

Navajo Loop Trail

Bryce Canyon

Bryce Creek

INSPIRATION POINT

Rim Trail

Peekaboo Loop Trail

BRYCE POINT

To Under-the-Rim Trail

PARIA VIEW

0   1 mi

0   1 km

© AVALON TRAVEL

water—named Lake Flagstaff by geologists. Silt and calcium carbonate and other minerals settled on the lake bottom. These sediments consolidated and became the Claron Formation; a soft, silty limestone with some shale and sandstone. Lake Flagstaff had long since disappeared when the land began to rise as part of the Colorado Plateau uplift about 16 million years ago. Uneven pressures beneath the plateau caused it to break along fault lines into a series of smaller plateaus at different levels known as the "Grand Staircase." Bryce Canyon National Park occupies part of one of these plateaus—the Paunsaugunt.

The spectacular Pink Cliffs on the east edge contain the famous erosional features known as the "hoodoos," carved in the Claron Formation. Variations in hardness of the rock layers result in these strange features, which seem almost alive. Water flows through cracks, wearing away softer rock around hard, erosion-resistant caps. Finally, a cap becomes so undercut that the overhang allows water to drip down, leaving a "neck" of rock below the harder cap. Traces of iron and manganese provide the distinctive coloring.

The hoodoos continue to change—new ones form and old ones fade away. Despite appearances, wind plays little role in creation of the landscape; it's the freezing and thawing, snowmelt, and rainwater that dissolve weak layers, pry open cracks, and carve out the forms. The plateau cliffs, meanwhile, recede at a rate of about one foot every 50–65 years; look for trees on the rim that now overhang the abyss. Listen, and you might hear the sounds of pebbles falling away and rolling down the steep slopes.

Park Shuttle Bus

During the peak summer season (late May–Sept., 9 A.M.–6 P.M.), tour buses depart from the front of Ruby's Inn (just outside the park entrance) every 15 minutes or so, and stop at all the major viewpoints along the main amphitheater, as well as at the campgrounds, the visitors center, and Bryce Canyon Lodge. Passengers can take as long as they like at any viewpoint and catch a later bus. The shuttle

bus service also makes it easier for hikers, who don't need to worry about car shuttles between trailheads.

Use of the shuttle bus system is included in the cost of admission to the park, but it is not mandatory; you can still bring in your own vehicle. However, park officials note that there is generally one parking space for every four cars entering the park.

Visitors Center

From the turnoff on Hwy. 12, follow signs past Ruby's Inn to the park entrance; the visitors center (435/834-5322, 8 A.M.–8 P.M. May–Sept., 8 A.M.–6 P.M. Apr. and Oct., 8 A.M.–4:30 P.M. Nov.–Mar.) is a short distance farther on the right. Geologic exhibits illustrate how the land was formed and how it has changed. Historic displays interpret the Paiutes, early explorers, and the first settlers. Trees, flowers, and wildlife are identified. Rangers present a variety of naturalist programs, including short hikes, mid-May–early September; see the posted schedule. The staff sells travel and natural history books, maps of the park and adjacent Dixie National Forest, posters, postcards, slides, and film.

SCENIC DRIVE

From elevations of about 8,000 feet near the visitors center, the park's scenic drive gradually winds 1,100 feet higher to Rainbow Point. About midway you'll notice a change in the trees from largely ponderosa pine to spruce, fir, and aspen. On a clear day, you can enjoy vistas of more than 100 miles from many of the viewpoints. Because of parking shortages on the drive, trailers must be left at the visitors center or campsite. Visitors wishing to see all of the viewpoints should take a walk on the Rim Trail.

Note that even though we have presented the viewpoints in north-to-south order, when the park is bustling it's better to drive all the way to the southern end of the road and visit the viewpoints from south to north, thus avoiding left turns against traffic. (Of course, if you're just heading to one viewpoint or trailhead, it's fine to drive directly to it.)

Fairyland Point

To reach the turn-off (just inside the park boundary), go north 0.8 mile from the visitors center, then east one mile. Whimsical forms line Fairyland Canyon a short distance below. You can descend into the "fairyland" on the **Fairyland Loop Trail,** or follow the **Rim Trail** for other panoramas.

◖ Sunrise and Sunset Points

These overlooks are off to the left about one mile past the visitors center; they're connected by a half-mile paved section of the **Rim Trail.** Panoramas from each point take in large areas of Bryce Amphitheater and beyond. The lofty Aquarius and Table Cliff Plateaus rise along the skyline to the northeast; you can see the same colorful Claron Formation in cliffs that faulting has raised about 2,000 feet higher. A short walk down either the **Queen's Garden Trail** or the **Navajo Loop Trail** from Sunset Point will bring you close to Bryce's hoodoos and provide a totally different experience from what you get atop the rim.

© W. C. MCRAE

It's easy to imagine Sunrise Point's hoodoos as statues or fanciful characters.

Inspiration Point

It's well worth the 0.75-mile walk south along the **Rim Trail** from Sunset Point to see a fantastic maze of hoodoos in the "Silent City." (It's also accessible by car, from a spur road near the Bryce Point turn-off.) Weathering along vertical joints has cut many rows of narrow gullies, some more than 200 feet deep. It's a short but steep 0.2-mile walk up to Upper Inspiration Point.

Bryce Point

This overlook at the south end of Bryce Amphitheater has expansive views to the north and east. It's also the start for the **Rim, Peekaboo Loop,** and **Under-the-Rim trails.** From the turn-off two miles south of the visitors center, follow signs 2.1 miles in.

Paria View

Cliffs drop precipitously into the headwaters of Yellow Creek, a tributary of the Paria River. You can see a section of Under-the-Rim Trail winding up a hillside near the mouth of the amphitheater below. Distant views take in the Paria River Canyon, White Cliffs (of Navajo sandstone), and Navajo Mountain. The plateau rim in the park forms a drainage divide. Precipitation falling west of the rim flows gently into the East Fork of the Sevier River and the Great Basin; precipitation landing east of the rim rushes through deep canyons in the Pink Cliffs to the Paria River and on to the Colorado River and the Grand Canyon. Take the turn-off for Bryce Point, then keep right at the fork.

Farview Point

This sweeping panorama takes in a lot of geology. You'll see levels of the Grand Staircase that include the Aquarius and Table Cliff Plateaus to the northeast, Kaiparowits Plateau to the east, and White Cliffs to the southeast. Look beyond the White Cliffs to see a section of the Kaibab Plateau that forms the north rim of the Grand Canyon in Arizona. The overlook is on the left nine miles south of the visitors center.

Natural Bridge

This large feature lies just off the road on the left, 1.7 miles past Farview Point. The span is 54 feet wide and 95 feet high. Despite its name, this is an arch formed by weathering from rain and freezing, not by stream erosion like a true natural bridge. Once the opening reached ground level, runoff began to enlarge the hole and to dig a gully through it.

Agua and Ponderosa Canyons

You can admire sheer cliffs and hoodoos from the Agua Canyon overlook on the left, 1.4 miles past Natural Bridge. With a little imagination, you may be able to pick out the Hunter and the Rabbit below. Ponderosa Canyon overlook, on the left 1.8 miles farther, offers a panorama similar to that at Farview Point.

Yovimpa and Rainbow Points

The land drops away in rugged canyons and fine views at the end of the scenic drive, 17 miles south of the visitors center. At an elevation of 9,115 feet, this is the highest area of the park. Yovimpa and Rainbow Points lie only a short walk apart yet offer different vistas. The **Bristlecone Loop Trail** is an easy one-mile loop from Rainbow Point to ancient bristlecone pines along the rim. The **Riggs Spring Loop Trail** makes a good day hike; you can begin from either Yovimpa Point or Rainbow Point and descend into canyons in the southern area of the park. The **Under-the-Rim Trail** starts from Rainbow Point and winds 22.5 miles to Bryce Point; day hikers can make a 7.5-mile trip by using the Agua Canyon Connecting Trail and a car shuttle.

HIKING

Hikers enjoy close-up views of the wonderfully eroded features and gain a direct appreciation of Bryce's geology. Because almost all of the trails head down off the canyon's rim, they're moderately difficult, with many ups and downs, but the paths are well graded and signed. Hikers not accustomed to the 7,000- to 9,000-foot elevations will find the going relatively strenuous and should allow extra time. Be sure to carry water and drink frequently—staying well hydrated will give you more energy.

Wear a hat and sunscreen to protect against sunburn, which can be a problem at these elevations. Don't forget rain gear because storms can come up suddenly. Always carry water for day trips because only a few natural sources

ZION AND BRYCE

VISITING BRYCE CANYON IN WINTER

Though Bryce is most popular during the summer months, it is especially beautiful and other-worldly during the winter, when the rock formations are topped with snow. And, since Bryce is so high (the elevation ranges 8,000–9,000 feet), winter lasts a long time, often into spring break.

The main park roads and most viewpoints are plowed, and the Rim Trail is an excellent, easy snowshoe or cross-country ski route. **Paria Ski Trail** (five-mile loop) and **Fairyland Ski Trail** (2.5-mile loop) are marked for snowshoers and cross-country skiers. Snowshoes are loaned free of charge at the visitors center with deposit of a credit card whenever snow depth measures 18 inches or more at the visi-

tors center. Rent cross-country ski equipment just outside the park at Ruby's. Miles of snowmobile trails are groomed outside the park.

During the winter, most of the businesses around the park entrance shut down. The notable exception is Ruby's Inn, which is a wintertime hub of activity. During the winter months, rates drop precipitously – most rooms go for about $60 January–March.

Ruby's Inn hosts the Bryce Canyon Winter Festival during Presidents Day weekend in February. The three-day festival has free cross-country skiing and snowshoeing clinics, demos, and tours. This is also the time and place to pick up tips on ski archery and winter photography.

exist. Ask at the visitors center for current trail conditions and water sources; you can also pick up a free hiking map at the visitors center. Snow may block some trail sections in winter and early spring. Horses are permitted only on Peekaboo Loop. Pets must stay above the rim; they're allowed on the Rim Trail only between Sunset and Sunrise Points.

Special hazards you should be aware of include crumbly ledges and lightning strikes. People who have wandered off trails or gotten too close to the drop-offs have had to be pulled out by rope. Avoid cliffs and other exposed areas during electrical storms, which are most common in late summer.

Overnight hikers can obtain the required $5 backcountry permit at the visitors center (camping is allowed only on the Under-the-Rim and Riggs Spring Loop Trails). Backpack stoves must be used for cooking; wood fires are prohibited. Although there are several isolated springs in Bryce's backcountry, it's prudent to carry at least one gallon of water per person per day. Ask about the location and flow of springs when you register for the backcountry permit.

Don't expect much solitude during the summer on the popular Rim, Queen's Garden, Navajo Loop, and Peekaboo Loop Trails. Fairyland Loop Trail is less used, and the backcountry trails are almost never crowded. September and October are the choice hiking months—the weather is best and the crowds smallest, although nighttime temperatures in late October can dip well below freezing.

Rim Trail

This easy trail follows the edge of Bryce Amphitheater for 5.5 miles between Fairyland and Bryce Points; the elevation change is 540 feet. Most people walk just sections in leisurely strolls or use the trail to connect with five others. The half-mile section near the lodge between Sunrise and Sunset Points is paved and nearly level; other parts are gently rolling.

Fairyland Loop Trail

This trail winds in and out of colorful rock spires in the northern part of Bryce Amphitheater, a somewhat less-visited area one mile off the main park road. Although the trail is well graded, remember the 900-foot climb you'll make when you exit. You can take a loop hike of eight miles from either Fairyland Point or Sunrise Point by using a section of the **Rim Trail;** a car shuttle saves three hiking miles. The whole loop is too long for many visitors, who enjoy short trips down and back to see this "fairyland."

Queen's Garden Trail

A favorite of many people, this trail drops from Sunrise Point through impressive features in the middle of Bryce Amphitheater to a hoodoo resembling a portly Queen Victoria. The hike is 1.5 miles round-trip and has an elevation change of 320 feet, which you'll have to climb on the way back. This is the easiest excursion below the rim and takes about 1.5 hours. Queen's Garden Trail also makes a good loop hike with the **Navajo** and **Rim Trails;** most people who do the loop prefer to descend the steeper Navajo and climb out on Queen's Garden Trail for a 3.5-mile hike. Trails also connect with the **Peekaboo Loop Trail** and go to the town of Tropic.

Navajo Loop Trail

From Sunset Point, you'll drop 520 feet in three-quarters of a mile through a narrow canyon. At the bottom, the loop leads into deep, dark **Wall Street**—an even narrower canyon one-half mile long—then returns to the rim; the total distance is about 1.5 miles. Other destinations from the bottom of Navajo Trail are **Twin Bridges, Queen's Garden Trail, Peekaboo Loop Trail,** and the town of Tropic. The 1.5-mile trail to Tropic isn't as scenic as the other trails, but it does provide another way to enter or leave the park; ask at the visitors center or in Tropic for directions to the trailhead.

Peekaboo Loop Trail

This enchanting walk is full of surprises at every turn—and there are lots of turns! The

Hike down on Navajo Loop Trail to get up close and personal with the hoodoos.

trail is in the southern part of Bryce Amphitheater, which has some of the most striking rock features. You can start from Bryce Point (6.5 miles round-trip), from Sunset Point (5.5 miles round-trip via Navajo Trail), or from Sunrise Point (seven miles round-trip via Queen's Garden Trail). The loop itself is 3.5 miles long with many ups and downs and a few tunnels. The elevation change is 500–800 feet, depending on the trailhead you choose. This is the only trail in the park where horses are permitted; remember to give horseback travelers the right-of-way and, if possible, to step to higher ground when you allow them to pass.

Under-the-Rim Trail

The longest trail in the park winds 22.5 miles below the Pink Cliffs between Bryce Point in the north and Rainbow Point in the south. Allow at least two days to hike the entire trail; the elevation change is about 1,500 feet with many ups and downs. Four connecting trails from the scenic drive allow you to travel the Under-the-Rim Trail as a series of day hikes,

too. Another option is to combine the Under-the-Rim and **Riggs Spring Loop** trails for a total of 31.5 miles.

The **Hat Shop,** an area of delicate spires capped by erosion-resistant rock, makes a good day-hike destination; begin at Bryce Point and follow the Under-the-Rim Trail for about two miles. Most of this section is downhill (elevation change of 900 feet), which you'll have to climb on the way out.

Bristlecone Loop Trail

The easy one-mile loop begins from either Rainbow or Yovimpa Point and goes to viewpoints and ancient bristlecone pines along the rim. These hardy trees survive fierce storms and extremes of hot and cold that no other tree can. Some of the bristlecone pines here are 1,700 years old.

Riggs Spring Loop

One of the park's more challenging day hikes or a leisurely overnighter, this trail begins from Rainbow Point and descends into canyons in the southern area of the park. The loop is about nine miles long, with an elevation change of 1,625 feet. Of the three backcountry campgrounds along the trail, the Riggs Spring site is most conveniently located, about halfway around the loop. Great views of the hoodoos, lots of aspen trees, a couple of pretty meadows, and great views off to the east are some of the highlights of this hike. Day hikers may want to take a shortcut bypassing Riggs Spring, saving three-quarters of a mile.

Mossy Cave Trail

This easy trail is not on the main park road; it's just off Hwy. 12, northwest of Tropic, near the east edge of the park. Hike up Water Canyon to a cool alcove of dripping water and moss. Sheets of ice and icicles add beauty to the scene in winter. The hike is only one mile round-trip with a small elevation gain. A side trail, just before the cave, branches right a short distance to a little waterfall; look for several small arches in the colorful canyon walls above. Although the park lacks perennial natural streams, the stream

ZION AND BRYCE

in Water Canyon flows even during dry spells. Mormon pioneers labored three years to channel water from the East Fork of the Sevier River through a canal and down this wash to the town of Tropic. Without this irrigation, the town might not even exist. From the visitors center, return to Hwy. 12 and turn east 3.7 miles toward Escalante; the parking area is on the right just after a bridge (between mileposts 17 and 18). Rangers schedule guided walks to the cave and the waterfall during the main season.

MOUNTAIN BIKING

Although mountain biking is prohibited on trails inside the national park, just a few miles west of the park entrance Red Canyon's bike trails are spectacularly scenic and exhilarating to ride. See the *Vicinity of Bryce Canyon National Park* section for information on Red Canyon.

Ruby's Inn provides a shuttle service for Red Canyon mountain bikers.

HORSEBACK RIDING

If you'd like to get down among the hoodoos, but aren't sure you'll have the energy to hike back up to the rim, consider letting a horse help you along. **Canyon Trail Rides** (Bryce Canyon Lodge, 435/679-8665, www.canyonrides.com), a park concessionaire, offers guided rides near Sunrise Point, and both two-hour ($40) and half-day ($65) trips are offered. Both rides descend to the floor of the canyon; the longer ride follows the Peekaboo Loop Trail. Riders must be at least seven years old, and no more than 220 pounds; the horses and wranglers are accustomed to novices.

TOURS

The most basic tour of the park, which comes with the price of admission, is a ride on the park shuttle bus (see the *Park Shuttle Bus* section). Shuttle buses run every 12 minutes, and the trip through the park takes 50 minutes. Of course, the beauty of the shuttle is that you can get off at any stop, hike for a while, then catch another bus. Shuttle season runs Memorial Day–Labor Day.

Beyond a shuttle ride, **Ruby's Inn,** a hotel, restaurant, and recreation complex at the park entrance, is a good place to take measure of the opportunities for organized recreation and sightseeing excursions around Bryce Canyon. The lobby is filled with outfitters who are anxious to take you out on the trail; you'll find each of the following there, along with other vendors who organize hayrides, barn dances, and chuck-wagon dinners. **Ruby's Horseback Rides** (435/834-5341 or 866/782-0002, www.horserides.net, Apr.–Oct.) has horseback riding near Bryce Canyon. There's a choice of half ($65) and whole ($100 including lunch) day trips, as well as a 1.5-hour trip ($45). Short rides (as well as half- and full-day trips) are offered by **Scenic Rim Trail Rides** (435/679-8761 or 800/679-5859, www.brycecanyon horseback.com), which also operates out of Ruby's. An hour-long ride is $30. Horseback rides are also offered by a concessionaire inside the park, **Canyon Trail Rides** (Bryce Canyon Lodge, 435/679-8665, www.canyonrides.com); a 2-hour ride ($40) goes to the canyon floor. During the summer, Ruby's also sponsors a rodeo every Wednesday through Saturday at 7 P.M. across from the inn ($9 adults, $6 children 3–12).

You can also explore the area around Bryce Canyon on a noisier steed. Guided all-terrain-vehicle (ATV) tours of Red Canyon are offered by **Great Western ATV** (866/866-6616, $35 for a one-hour trip).

If you'd like to get a look at Bryce and the surrounding area from the air, you can choose to take a scenic flight-seeing tour from **Bryce Canyon Airlines** (Ruby's Inn, 435/834-8060), which offers both plane and helicopter tours. There's quite a range of options, but a 35-minute airplane tour costs $139 per person (two-fare minimum) and gives a good look at the surroundings.

ACCOMMODATIONS

Travelers may have a hard time finding accommodations and campsites April–October in both the park and nearby areas. Advance reservations at lodges, motels, and the park campground are a good idea; otherwise, plan to arrive by late morning. Bryce Canyon Lodge is the only lodge in the park itself, and you'll generally need to make reservations months in advance to get a room in this historic landmark. (But it doesn't hurt to ask about vacancies.) Other motels are clustered near the park entrance road, but many do not offer much for the money. The quality of lodgings are somewhat better in Tropic, 11 miles east on Hwy. 12 and Panguitch, 25 miles to the northwest.

One of the park's two large campgrounds has 32 sites available by reservation (877/444-6777, www.recreation.gov, $10 per night, plus a $10 reservation fee). The rest of the sites are first come, first served; arrive by noon in the main season for a better chance of finding a spot.

About $50

During the winter, it's easy to find inexpensive accommodations in this area; even rooms at Ruby's Inn start at about $60. Several motels are clustered on Hwy. 12, right outside the park boundary. Many of these have seen a lot of use over the years, usually without a lot of attendant upkeep. **Foster's Motel** (1150 Hwy. 12, 435/834-5227 or 800/372-4750, www.fostersmotel.com, $50) has plain-vanilla motel rooms best suited for budget travelers who don't want to camp and don't plan to spend a lot of time in their room. It's located four miles west of the park entrance in a small complex with a restaurant and a supermarket.

$50-100

One of the newest hotels, and a good value for the area, is the **Bryce View Lodge** (991 S. Hwy. 63, 888/279-2304 or 435/834-5180, www.bryceviewlodge.com, $78 and up), which has rooms in handsome buildings near the park entrance, across the road from Ruby's Inn. (It's actually owned by Ruby's.)

Six miles west of the park turn-off, **Bryce Canyon Pines Motel** (Hwy. 12, Milepost 10, 435/834-5441 or 800/892-7923, www.bryce canyonmotel.com, $75–90) is an older motel with both motel rooms and cottages, a seasonal

covered pool, horseback rides, an RV park, and a restaurant open daily for breakfast, lunch, and dinner early April–late October.

Over $100

Set among ponderosa pines a short walk from the rim, **Bryce Canyon Lodge** (435/834-5361 for same-day reservations or 888/297-2757, www.brycecanyonlodge.com, Apr.–Oct., $115–140) was built in 1923 by a division of the Union Pacific Railway; a spur line once terminated at the front entrance. The lodge has lots of charm and is listed on the National Register of Historic Places. It also has by far the best location of any Bryce-area accommodation; it's the only lodging in the park itself.

Activities at the lodge include horseback rides, park tours, evening entertainment, and ranger talks; a gift shop sells souvenirs, while food can be found at both a restaurant and a snack bar. Try to make reservations as far in advance as possible.

The sprawling **Best Western Ruby's Inn** (435/834-5341 or 800/468-8660, www.rubysinn.com, $130 and up, winter rates are about half of high-season rates) offers many year-round services on Hwy. 63 just north of the park boundary. The hotel features an indoor pool and a hot tub and all the bustling activity you could ever want. Kitchenettes and family rooms are also available; pets are okay. Ruby's Inn is more than just a place to stay, however. This is one of the area's major centers for all manner of recreational outfitters, dining, entertainment, and shopping. Many tour bus groups bed down here. Although it is kind of a zoo, the quality of the rooms at Ruby's is generally higher than what you'll find at other lodgings in the immediate area. If you want something more sumptuous and relaxing, consider staying at a B&B in nearby Tropic.

Campgrounds

The park's two campgrounds both have water and some pull-through spaces. Reservations are accepted at North Campground; make them at least two days in advance (877/444-6777, www.recreation.gov, $10 per night, plus a $10

ZION AND BRYCE

reservation fee). Otherwise, try to arrive early for a space during the busy summer season because both campgrounds usually fill by 1 or 2 P.M. The **North Campground** is on the left just past the visitors center. The best sites here are just a few yards downhill from the Rim Trail, with easy hiking access to other park trails. The **Sunset Campground** is about 2.5 miles farther on the right, across the road from Sunset Point. Sunset has campsites accessible to people with disabilities.

Basic groceries, camping supplies, and coin-operated showers and a laundry room are available from mid-April through late September at the **General Store,** between North Campground and Sunrise Point. During the rest of the year, you can go outside the park to Ruby's Inn for these services.

The Dixie National Forest has three Forest Service **campgrounds** located in scenic settings among ponderosa pines. They'll often have room when campgrounds in the park are full. Sites can be reserved at Pine Lake, King Creek, and Red Canyon campgrounds (877/444-6777, www.recreation.gov, $9–18, water available). The **Pine Lake Campground** lies at 7,700 feet just east of its namesake lake in a forest of ponderosa pine, spruce, and juniper. Sites are open mid-May–mid-September. From the highway junction north of the park, head northeast 11 miles on Hwy. 63 (gravel), then turn southeast six miles.

King Creek Campground is located on the west shore of Tropic Reservoir, which has a boat ramp and fair trout fishing. Sites are at 8,000 feet and are usually open May–late September. Head seven miles south of Hwy. 12 down the gravel East Fork Sevier River Road, located 2.8 miles west of the park turn-off. **Red Canyon Campground** is just off Hwy. 12 four miles east of U.S. 89. It's located at 7,400 feet, below brilliantly colored cliffs, and stays open late May–late September. Contact the Powell Ranger District office in Panguitch (435/676-9300) for more information on Kings and Red Canyon Campgrounds. Contact the Escalante Ranger District office in Escalante (435/826-5400) for information on Pine Lake.

A little farther away is beautiful **Kodachrome State Park.** From Bryce, take Hwy. 12 east to Cannonville, then head south to the park. (See *The Escalante Region* chapter for details.)

Private campgrounds in the area are $20 and up per night. **Ruby's Inn Campground** (435/834-5301, early Apr.–late Oct.) is at the park junction and has spaces for tents ($20) and RVs ($28–31); showers and a laundry room are open year-round. They've also got a few tepees (starting at $28) and bunkhouse-style cabins ($50, no bedding provided). All of the considerable facilities at Ruby's are available to camping patrons. The **Bryce Canyon Pines Campground** (435/834-5441 or 800/892-7923), four miles west of the park entrance, has an indoor pool, game room, groceries, and shaded sites.

FOOD

The dining room at the **Bryce Canyon Lodge** (435/834-5361, breakfast, lunch, and dinner in season, $12–22) is atmospheric and offers food that's as good as you're going to find in the area. Reservations are advised for dinner. For lunch, the snack bar is a good bet in nice weather; the only seating is outside on the patio or in the hotel lobby. With 12 hours advance notice, you can order a box lunch from the dining room.

If you really want a high-volume dining experience, Ruby's Inn **Cowboy Buffet and Steak Room** (435/834-5341, breakfast, lunch, and dinner daily, $10–25) is an incredibly busy place. It's also one of Bryce Canyon's better restaurants. Casual lunch and dinner fare is served in the inn's snack bar, the **Canyon Diner,** April–October.

Bryce Canyon Resort (435/834-5351 or 800/834-0043, breakfast, lunch, and dinner daily, $4–20), near the turn-off for the park, has an on-site restaurant that features steak and barbecue.

Two long-established restaurants west of the park entrance have a low-key, non-corporate atmosphere and pretty good food. The small family-run restaurant attached to **Bryce Canyon Pines** (Hwy. 12, Milepost 10,

435/834-5441 or 800/892-7923, breakfast, lunch, and dinner daily, $3–20) is a homey place to stop for burgers, soup ($3.25), or sandwiches. Two miles west of the park turn-off is **Foster's** (1150 Hwy. 12, 435/834-5227, breakfast, lunch, and dinner daily, $4–20), with steaks and old-fashioned diner food.

SERVICES

The **general store** at Ruby's has a large stock of groceries, camping and fishing supplies, film and processing, Native American crafts, books,

and other souvenirs. The **Bryce post office** is at the store, too. Horseback rides, helicopter tours, and airplane rides are arranged in the lobby. In winter, cross-country skiers can rent gear and use trails located near the inn as well as in the park. Snowmobile trails are available (snowmobiles may not be used within the park). Western-fronted shops across from Ruby's Inn offer trail rides, chuckwagon dinners, mountain-bike rentals, souvenirs, and a petting farm. **Rodeos** take place in the nearby arena nightly Monday–Saturday in-season.

Vicinity of Bryce Canyon National Park

Sometimes the bustle at Bryce's rim and at the large commercial developments right at the entrance to the park can be a little off-putting. It's easy to escape the crowds by heading just a few miles west on scenic Hwy. 12.

RED CANYON

The drive on Hwy. 12 between U.S. 89 and the turn-off for Bryce Canyon National Park passes through this well-named canyon. Because Red Canyon is not part of Bryce, many of the trails here are open to mountain biking and ATV riding. In fact, this canyon has become very popular as other Utah mountain-biking destinations become crowded.

Staff members at the **Red Canyon Visitors Center** (Hwy. 12 between Mileposts 3 and 4, 435/676-2676, 9 A.M.–6 P.M. daily Memorial Day–Labor Day, 9 A.M.–6 P.M. Fri.–Mon. spring and fall) can tell you about the trails and scenic backcountry roads that wind through the area. Books and maps are available here. (For details about Red Canyon Campground, see the *Campgrounds* section under *Accommodations,* earlier in this chapter.)

Hiking

The U.S. Forest Service maintains many scenic hiking trails that wind back from the highway to give you a closer look at the geology. The following are open to hikers only. **Pink**

Ledges Trail, the easiest and most popular, loops one mile past intriguing erosional features from the Red Canyon Visitors Center. Signs identify some of the trees and plants; the elevation gain is 100 feet. The **Birdseye Trail** winds through formations and connects the visitors center with a parking area on Hwy. 12 just inside the forest boundary, 0.8 mile away. **Buckhorn Trail** begins from site number 23 in Red Canyon Campground and climbs one mile for views of erosional forms and Red Canyon; the campground is on the south side of Hwy. 12 between mileposts 3 and 4. The **Tunnel Trail** ascends 300 feet in 0.7 mile for fine views of the canyon. The trail begins from a pullout on the south side of Hwy. 12 just west of a pair of tunnels, crosses the streambed, then climbs a ridge to viewpoints on the top. Ask at the visitors center for other good area trails worth exploring.

Biking

A rather wonderful paved bike trail parallels Hwy. 12 for five miles through Red Canyon. Parking lots are located at either end of the trail, at the Thunder Mountain Trailhead and Coyote Hollow Road.

True mountain bikers will eschew the pavement and head to **Casto Canyon Trail,** a 5.5-mile one-way trail that winds through a variety of red-rock formations and forest. This ride

ZION AND BRYCE

starts west of the visitors center, about two miles east of Hwy. 89. Turn north from Hwy. 12 onto Forest Road 118, and continue about three miles to the Casto Canyon parking lot. For part of the way, the trail is shared with ATVs, but then the bike trail splits off to the right. The usual turn-around point is at Sanford Road.

This ride can be linked with other trails to form a 17-mile one-way test of biking skills and endurance, with the route starting and ending along Hwy. 12. If you don't have a shuttle vehicle at each of the trailheads, you'll need to peddle back another eight miles along the paved roadside trail to retrieve your vehicle. Start at Tom Best Road, just east of Red Canyon. You'll climb through forest, turning onto Berry Spring Creek Road and then Cabin Hollow Road. Once the trail heads into Casto Canyon, you'll have five downhill miles of wonderful red-rock scenery. When you reach the Casto Canyon Trailhead, you can choose to return to Hwy. 12, or you can pedal out to Hwy. 89 and Panguitch. Much of the trail is strenuous, and you'll need to take water along because there's no source along the way. There are several side trails to make this into a shorter ride; stop by the visitors center for more information.

PAUNSAGAUNT WILDLIFE MUSEUM

The Paunsagaunt Wildlife Museum (1945 W. Hwy. 12, 435/834-5555 summer, 702/877-8664 winter, www.brycecanyonwildlifemuseum .com, 9 A.M.–10 P.M. daily April 1–Nov. 15, $8 adults, $5 children 6–12), formerly located in the town of Panguitch, is housed in a large new building just west of the turnoff to Bryce Canyon. This taxidermy collection depicts more than 450 animals from around the world displayed in dioramas resembling their natural habitats. It's actually quite well done, and kids seem to love it. There's also a good collection of Native American artifacts and a beautiful butterfly display.

POWELL POINT

Even in a state with many superb viewpoints, Powell Point (elev. 10,188 feet) is outstanding.

Yet surprisingly few people know about this lofty perch at the southern tip of the Table Cliff Plateau, a southwestern extension of the Aquarius Plateau. Its light-colored cliffs stand about 15 air miles northeast of Sunset Point in Bryce Canyon National Park. Getting to Powell Point involves a bit of adventure. You can drive a car with good clearance within 4.3 miles of the point; high-clearance vehicles can go to within 0.6 mile. From the highway junction north of the national park, drive northeast 11 miles on Hwy. 63 (gravel), turn southeast six miles to Pine Lake, continue east six miles on Forest Route 132 up onto the plateau, then look for the one-lane dirt road on the right to Powell Point; high-clearance vehicles can turn in 3.7 miles to the Powell Point Trailhead. If you're not equipped for driving this rough road, you'll still find it good for hiking or mountain biking. The road ends where the ridge becomes too narrow for it; a clearing here is fine for camping (no facilities).

A foot trail continues 0.6 mile to the very end of Powell Point. The route passes through an extremely weather-beaten and picturesque forest of bristlecone and limber pine. Panoramic views begin well before trail's end; at the point itself it feels as though you're at the end of the world. Much of southern Utah and northern Arizona stretches out below to the far horizon. The colorful cliffs of the Claron Formation lie directly underfoot; take care near the crumbly cliff edges. Avoid Powell Point if thunderstorms threaten. (Note the many lightning scars on trees here!) The **Escalante Ranger District office** (755 W. Main St., Escalante, 435/826-5400, 8:30 A.M.–4:30 P.M. Mon.–Fri.) may have current road conditions to Powell Point.

TROPIC

Mormon pioneer Ebenezer Bryce homesteaded near the town site of Tropic in 1875, but the work of scratching a living from the rugged land became too hard. He left five years later for more promising areas in Arizona. The name of the park commemorates his efforts. He is remembered as saying of the area, "Well, it's a hell of a place to lose a cow." Other pioneers settled six villages near the upper Paria River between 1876 and 1891. The towns of Tropic, Cannonville, and Henrieville still survive. Tropic lies just 11 miles east of Bryce Canyon National Park, and is visible from many of the park's viewpoints. Travelers think of Tropic primarily for its cache of motels lining Main Street (Hwy. 12), but several pleasant B&Bs also grace the town. A **log cabin** built by Ebenezer Bryce has been moved to a site beside the Bryce Pioneer Village Motel; ask to see the cabin's small collection of pioneer and Indian artifacts. A **tourist booth** (11 A.M.–7 P.M., early May–late Oct.) is in the center of town.

Accommodations

$50-100

Aside from a couple of nice B&Bs, the best place to stay in Tropic is in the **Bryce Country Cabins** (80 S. Main St., 888/679-8643 or 435/679-8643, www.brycecountrycabins.com, $75). The cabins overlook a meadow, and each has a private bath. On the south end of town, the **Bryce Pioneer Village Motel** (80 S. Main, 435/679-8546 or 800/222-0381, www.bpvillage.com, $55 and up) has typical budget-level rooms and several cabins (one with kitchen); there's also a campground with sites for tents and RVs.

Up on a bluff on the outskirts of town, the **Buffalo Sage B&B** (980 N. Hwy. 12, 435/679-8443 or 866/232-5711, www.buffalosage.com, $95) has great views and rooms decorated in an upscale Southwestern style. At the other end of town, the **Bullberry Inn B&B** (435/679-8820 or 800/249-8126, www.bullberryinn.com, $105) has wraparound porches and guest rooms with private baths and rustic-style furniture.

At the **Bryce Canyon Inn** (21 N. Main, 435/679-8502 or 800/592-1468, www.brycecanyoninn.com, March–Oct., $60 motel rooms, $85 cabins), the tidy new cabins are nicely furnished and one of the more appealing options in the Bryce neighborhood.

America's Best Value Bryce Valley Inn

(199 N. Hwy. 12, 435/679-8811 or 800/442-1890, www.brycevalleyinn.com, $85) has conventional motel rooms in an attractive wood-fronted, Western-look motel with an adjoining restaurant. Pets are permitted, but are charged an extra fee.

OVER $100

The **Stone Canyon Inn** (435/679-8611 or 866/489-4680, www.stonecanyoninn.com, $110–175 rooms, $295 cottages), just west of Tropic with views of Bryce, has comfortable, uncluttered rooms. Stone Canyon also has brand-new two-bedroom "cabin cottages," which can be divided to provide smaller units. The owners are happy to point you toward their favorite trails. At **Bryce Canyon Livery B&B** (660 W. 50 South, 888/889-8910 or 435/679-8780, www.brycecanyonbandb.com, $105) every room has a private bath; several have balconies with views of Bryce Canyon.

CAMPGROUNDS

In town, you can find RV camping at **Bryce Pioneer Village Motel** (80 S. Main, 435/679-8546 or 800/222-0381, www.bpvillage.com, $12 tent, $18 hookup). Head east to Cannonville for a KOA (175 N. Red Rock Dr., 435/679-8988 or 888/562-4710, www.koa.com, $22 tent, $32 hookup), or continue south from Cannonville to Kodachrome Basin State Park (see *The Escalante Region* chapter for details on this lovely park).

Food

There are a few adequate restaurants in town. **Clarke's** (141 N. Main, 435/679-8633, breakfast, lunch, and dinner daily, $10–20) is an all-around place that serves Mexican food, pasta, and steaks. **Bryce Pioneer Village Motel** (80 S. Main, 435/679-8546 or 800/222-0381, dinner some nights, 6–9 P.M., $13–16, call for reservation) has a restaurant specializing in Dutch-oven cooking. Because it's only open when they have 20 or more confirmed customers, it's critical to call ahead.

ZION AND BRYCE

Along U.S. 89: Panguitch to Kanab

If you're driving between Bryce and Zion, you'll probably follow this route, at least as far as Mount Carmel Junction. Head farther south to Kanab to find a wide selection of mostly inexpensive lodgings, and access to the southwestern part of Grand Staircase–Escalante National Monument.

PANGUITCH

Pioneers arrived here in 1864, but hostile Utes forced evacuation just two years later. A second attempt by settlers in 1871 succeeded, and Panguitch (Big Fish) is now the largest town in the area.

Panguitch is one of the more pleasant towns in this part of Utah, with an abundance of reasonably priced motels and a couple of good places to eat. It's also a good hub for exploring the many scenic highlights of the Escalante region.

The early 20th-century commercial buildings downtown have some of their original facades. On side streets you can see sturdy brick houses built by the early settlers. Stop by the **Daughters of Utah Pioneers Museum** (125 E. Center St., 4–8 P.M. Mon.–Sat. Memorial Day–Labor Day) in the old bishop's storehouse to see historic exhibits of Panguitch. During the off-season, the museum is open by appointment; phone numbers of volunteers are on the door.

Travelers in the area during the second weekend in June should try to swing by for the annual **Quilt Walk,** an all-out festival with historic home tours, quilting classes, and lots of food. The Quilt Walk commemorates a group of seven pioneers who trudged through snow to bring food back to starving townspeople—they spread quilts on the deep, soft snow and walked on them in order not to sink.

Panguitch has a small, old-fashioned downtown with classic red-brick storefronts.

© PAUL LEVY

The **city park** on the north edge of town has picnic tables, a playground, tennis courts, and a tourist information cabin. A **swimming pool** is by the high school (250 E. Center, 435/676-2259).

Accommodations

ABOUT $50
Panguitch is the best place in greater Bryce Canyon to find a budget motel room. Of these, the **Color Country Motel** (526 N. Main St., 435/676-2386 or 800/225-6518, www.color countrymotel.com, $52) is the most attractive, with an outdoor pool and clean, well-maintained rooms.

$50-100
A good mid-range pick is the **Canyon Lodge** (210 N. Main St., 435/676-8292 or 800/440-8292, www.color-country.net, $75). The **Panguitch Inn** (50 N. Main St., 435/676-8871 or 800/331-7407, www.panguitchinn .com, $75) is an old downtown hotel open April through October.

Along U.S. 89, the **New Western** (180 E. Center St., 435/676-8876 or 800/528-1234, $75) has a swimming pool and hot tub, plus laundry facilities. Some rooms are in an older building—you may want to assess room quality and noise level before handing over your credit card.

The **Adobe Sands** (390 N. Main St., 435/676-8874 or 800/497-9261, $75) is a perfectly acceptable standard motel, open May through October.

Stay in one of the landmark red-brick homes: The tidy **Red Brick Inn of Panguitch B&B** (161 N. 100 West, 435/676-2141 or 866/733-2745, www.redbrickinnutah.com, $89 and up) has distinctive barn-like architecture and includes cozy bedrooms and a three-bedroom apartment. If you like B&Bs, this is definitely the best place in town to stay.

If you'd rather go with a standard motel room, the **Marianna Inn Motel** (699 N. Main St., 435/676-8844 or 800/331-7407, $85) is an attractive place that allows pets.

CAMPGROUNDS
Open year-round, **Hitch-N-Post Campground** (420 N. Main, 435/676-2436, year-round, $15 tent, $25 RV) offers spaces for tents and RVs and has showers and a laundry room. The **Big Fish KOA Campground** (555 S. Main, 435/676-2225, mid-Apr.–mid-Oct., $24 tents, $30 RVs, $49 cabins) on the road to Panguitch Lake includes a pool, recreation room, laundry, and showers. The closest public campground is on Hwy. 12 in Red Canyon.

Food
The culinary high point of a visit to Panguitch will likely be the mesquite-grilled meats at **Cowboy's Smokehouse Bar-B-Q** (95 N. Main St., 435/676-8030, lunch and dinner Mon.–Sat. mid-March–mid-Oct., $10–17), where live country music and Western atmosphere is a regular on the menu. Then again, it may be a traditional Utah scone from **Grandma Tina's** (523 N. Main St., 435/676-2377, breakfast, lunch, and dinner daily in summer, lunch and early dinner Thurs.–Sun. in winter, $7–21). The scones are deep fried and are very tasty, like not-too-sweet doughnuts. For dinner, Tina's serves Italian favorites, with several vegetarian options. Both places serve beer and wine, and you'll find it hard to spend more than $20 on dinner in Panguitch.

Believe it or not, there's a tavern in Panguitch! The **Trails End Saloon** (535 N. Main St., 435/676-2235, open evenings and summer weekend afternoons) serves beer (including local microbrews) and wine coolers. During the summer, there's often live music on weekend evenings.

Information and Services
Contact the **Garfield County Travel Council** (55 S. Main St., 435/676-1160 or 800/444-6689, www.brycecanyoncountry.com) for information on Panguitch and the nearby area. The **Powell Ranger District office** (225 E. Center, 435/676-9300, 8 A.M.–4:30 P.M. Mon.–Fri.) of the Dixie National Forest has information on campgrounds, hiking trails, fishing,

and scenic drives in the forest and canyons surrounding Bryce Canyon National Park.

The **post office** is at 65 North 100 West. **Garfield Memorial Hospital** is at 200 North 400 East, and can be reached at 435/676-8811 (hospital) or 435/676-8842 (clinic). It's the main hospital in this part of the state.

HATCH

At this small town in the upper Sevier River Valley, colorful cliffs of the Paunsaugunt Plateau contrast with the blue sky to the east. There are several basic motels in town, including the **Riverside Motel and Campground** (594 U.S. 89, 435/735-4223 or 800/824-5651, $55–85 motel room, $26 RV hookup), which is just north of town and offers a store, laundry, showers and trout fishing in the Sevier River. It's a handy stopping place between Zion and Bryce.

LONG VALLEY

U.S. 89 follows the East Fork of the Virgin River past a series of small Mormon towns north of Kanab: Long Valley Junction, Glendale, Orderville, and Mount Carmel. Nearly all travelers visiting the national parks of the region will pass through this forested valley. Most of the towns in Long Valley offer a handful of motels, B&Bs, campgrounds, and restaurants.

At Mount Carmel Junction, Hwy. 9 turns west from U.S. 89 to Zion National Park.

Accommodations

GLENDALE

The historic **Smith Hotel** (295 N. Main St., Glendale, 435/648-2156 or 800/528-3558, www.historicsmithhotel.com, $44–80) dates from 1927 and has been restored as a bed-and-breakfast; all rooms have baths.

The sweet **Windwhisper Cabins** (Hwy. 89, two miles north of Glendale, 435/648-2162 or 435/632-8410, www.windwhisperbb.com, $89–119) include a B&B-style breakfast.

MOUNT CARMEL

The **Arrowhead Country Inn** (2155 S.

THE UNITED ORDER OF ENOCH

The United Order of Enoch was an attempt by Brigham Young to remedy several ills caused by an economic boom in the church community. The arrival of the railroad had brought some forms of prosperity to the Mormons, especially in allowing the development of mining. But the railroad also brought in a rougher class of folk who had no intention of emulating the quiet, industrious lifestyle of the Mormons, and it allowed the import of commercially produced goods at cheaper prices than could be had locally. Both factors spelled trouble for a church seeking self-sufficiency.

As Joseph Smith had envisioned in his Law of Consecration, the United Order was proposed as a policy of communal living in which members would commit all their privately owned goods toward a common end. Many members had surrendered their property in the early days of the church, but in troubled times the church found in the east had thwarted the success of true communal villages. In the 1870s, church leaders felt time had come.

When Brigham Young reactivated the United Order, it took life in several forms. The earliest and one of the most successful was the Brigham City Cooperative (BCC), started by Lorenzo Snow in 1864. BCC was a cooperative general store that met with great success, expanding over the years to 40 departments. The store was run on investments by voluntary members who received dividends based on their contributions. So successful was this venture that its business was barely touched by the Panic of 1873.

Branches of the order offered full communal living in which members ate in a communal dining hall, wore uniform clothing, and worked in community-owned facilities. In such a commune, all private possessions were surrendered upon membership. The most successful commune of this type may have been

State St., 435/648-2569 or 888/821-1670, $79–179) at White Cliffs Ranch has four attractive rooms in a ranch home and several private cabins surrounded by meadows and grassland. You'll enjoy the swimming pool, hot tub, and pool table. The B&B-style breakfasts are excellent, and the inn's restaurant is open for dinner Friday–Sunday April–December.

MOUNT CARMEL JUNCTION AND VICINITY

Clean basic rooms in Mount Carmel Junction are available at the **Golden Hills Motel** (U.S. 89 at Hwy. 9, 435/648-2268 or 800/648-2268, www.goldenhillsmotel.com, $38–52). The on-site restaurant serves breakfast, lunch, and dinner daily.

Also in Mount Carmel Junction, **Best Thunderbird Resort** (435/648-2203, www .bestwestern.com, $92 and up) features a good restaurant, nine-hole golf course, a pool, and large attractive rooms with balconies.

West of Mount Carmel Junction, just a few miles east of Zion National Park, are the very appealing cabins of the **Zion Mountain Resort** (E. Hwy. 9, 435/648-2555 or 866/648-2555, www.zionmountainresort .com, $120 and up weekdays, $145 and up weekends). The cabins have anywhere from one bedroom with microwave and fridge to two bedrooms with kitchens. The setting is great, with expansive views and a decent on-site restaurant. Rates drop by about $40 in the off-season.

CAMPGROUNDS

Glendale KOA (435/648-2490, May–Sept., $20 tent, $25–30 RV, $40 cabin), five miles north of Glendale, has a pool, a store, horseback rides, laundry, and showers. **Bauer's Canyon Ranch RV Camp** (on Hwy. 89 in Glendale, 435/648-2564, Mar.–Oct., $20 tent, $25–30 RV) offers hot showers and laundry facilities.

ZION AND BRYCE

Orderville, where travel-weary settlers went about living the United Order in its most idealistic form.

Orderville's effort was largely a success, but citizens from surrounding communities openly scoffed at the spartan life of the commune. Mormon children were gradually swayed by the taunts of their peers, which led to a "trouser rebellion." One story tells of a Mormon youth who sought permission and money to buy pants more fashionable than the standard communal issue. When he was denied on the grounds that his present pair was still serviceable, he took to work, earned the money himself, and promptly purchased a pair in the fashionable store-bought style. He was taken before the commune's elected board, which lauded his enterprise but decreed that every youth had to have the new pants or no one would. It was considered wasteful to replace pants that were still wearable, so youngsters were soon busy at the community grindstone wearing out the seats of their britches.

Younger members of the Orderville commune also suffered in that, unlike their elders, they didn't receive shares in the community when relinquishing their property. They were paid only a wage with no dividends – $0.75 a day until they reached 18, $1.50 thereafter. Eventually, the younger population trickled away, seeking higher-paying jobs in the surrounding area.

Most communal attempts, though, lasted less than a year, crippled primarily by human nature. Wealthy residents didn't wish to relinquish their property, dissatisfaction with the distribution of goods was common, and residents were often lured away by employment and business opportunities outside the commune. The Orderville community lasted 11 years, during which time its communal property nearly quadrupled in value. In that, it can be considered something of a success.

Kanab and Vicinity

Striking scenery surrounds this small town in Utah's far south. The Vermilion Cliffs to the west and east glow with a fiery intensity at sunrise and sunset. Streams have cut splendid canyons into surrounding plateaus. The Paiute Indians knew the spot as *Kanab*, meaning "place of the willows," which still grow along Kanab Creek. Mormon pioneers arrived in the mid-1860s and tried to farm along the unpredictable creek. Irrigation difficulties culminated in the massive floods of 1883, which in just two days gouged a section of creek bed 40 feet below its previous level. Ranching proved better suited to this rugged and arid land.

Hollywood discovered this dramatic scenery in the 1920s and has filmed more than 150 movies and TV series here since. Famous films shot hereabouts include movies as different as *My Friend Flicka, The Lone Ranger,* and *The Greatest Story Ever Told.* The TV series *Gunsmoke* and *F Troop* were shot locally. Film crews have constructed several Western sets near Kanab, but most lie on private land and are difficult to visit. The Paria set east of town, however, is on BLM land and open to the public.

If, while exploring Kanab, you see what looks like a family reunion, it might be just a man and his wives from the nearby polygamist settlements of Colorado City or Hildale. Visitors may also want to note that in 2006, the Kanab mayor and city council passed a resolution declaring, "We envision a local culture that upholds the marriage of a woman to a man, and a man to a woman, as ordained of God . . .We see our homes as open to a full quiver of children, the source of family continuity and social growth. We envision young women growing into wives, homemakers, and mothers; and we see young men growing into husbands, home-builders, and fathers."

While most park visitors see Kanab (pop. 5,500) as a handy stopover on trips to Bryce, Zion, and Grand Canyon National Parks and the southern reaches of Grand Staircase–Escalante National Monument, there are a few interesting sites around town that may warrant more than a sleep, eat, dash-out-of-town visit.

SIGHTS
◖ Best Friends Animal Sanctuary
Located in Angel Canyon just north of Kanab, this is one of the more unusual destinations in Utah. The scenic canyon was formerly the set for several Western movies and TV shows (including *The Outlaw Josie Wales* and *Rin Tin Tin*), and several of the sets are still standing. However, the canyon is now home to Best Friends Animal Sanctuary (5001 Angel Canyon Rd.), the largest no-kill animal shelter in the country. Best Friends takes in unwanted or abused "companion animals"—pets, farm animals, or other abandoned or neglected creatures—and gives them a permanent home on the preserve's 350 acres. Most animals are rehabilitated and are given new homes. Around 1,800 animals live at the sanctuary at any given time.

Ninety-minute tours of the facility are offered several times a day. Call 435/644-2001 for reservations. Donations are gladly accepted. The tour also visits some of the movie sets and features a short talk on the natural history of the canyon.

Squaw Trail
This well-graded trail provides a close look at the geology, plantlife, and animals of the Vermilion Cliffs just north of town. Allow about an hour on the moderately difficult trail to reach the first overlook (two miles round-trip with a 400-foot elevation gain) or 90 minutes to go all the way up (three miles round-trip with an 800-foot elevation gain). Views to the south take in Kanab, Fredonia, Kanab Canyon, and the vast Kaibab Plateau. At the top, look north to see the White, Gray, and Pink Cliffs of the Grand Staircase. The trailhead is at the north end of 100 East near the city park. Pick up a trail guide at the information center (brochures may also be available at the

trailhead or BLM office). Bring water. Try to get a very early start in summer.

Moqui Cave

This natural cave (five miles north of Kanab on U.S. 89, 435/644-8525, www.moquicave .com, 9 A.M.–7 P.M. Mon.–Sat. Memorial Day–Labor Day, 10 A.M.–4 P.M. Mon.–Sat. off-season, $4.50 adults, $4 seniors, $3 ages 13–17, $2.50 ages 6–12) has been turned into a tourist attraction with a large collection of Indian artifacts. Most of the arrowheads, pottery, sandals, and burial items on display have been excavated locally. A diorama re-creates an Anasazi ruin located five miles away in Cottonwood Wash. Fossils, rocks, and minerals are exhibited too, including what's claimed to be one of the largest fluorescent mineral displays in the country. The collections and a gift shop lie within a spacious cave that stays pleasantly cool even in the hottest weather.

Kanab Heritage House

This 1895 Queen Anne–style Victorian house (corner of Main and 100 South, 1–5 P.M. Mon.– Fri. in summer, free) reflects the prosperity of two of Kanab's early Mormon residents. Henry Bowman built it, but he lived here only two years before going on a mission. He sold the property to Thomas Chamberlain, who led a busy life serving as a leader in the Mormons' United Order and caring for his six wives and 55 children. (There's a family photo in the sitting room.) A guide will show you around the house and explain its architectural details. The town had no stores when the house was built, so each family grew its own vegetables and fruit. The grape arbor, berry bushes, and trees here represent those grown during pioneer times; fruit is free for the picking to visitors.

Frontier Movie Town

The owners assembled this movie-set replica (297 W. Center St., 435/644-5337, 9 A.M.– 11 P.M. Apr.–Oct., free) in Kanab to show tourists a bit of Hollywood's Old West. Some of the buildings have seen actual use in past movies and TV shows. Many small exhibits display Western and movie memorabilia; there's a selection of Western costumes available if you feel like getting gussied up as a cowboy or showgirl. A gift shop, a saloon, and chuckwagon dinners bring in the money.

ENTERTAINMENT AND EVENTS

In summer, free musical concerts are held at the city park gazebo, at the center of town. Wednesdays bring an ongoing local talent show. The GSENM office (435/644-4680, www.ut.blm.gov/monument) sponsors regular ranger talks through the spring. A unique Kanab event is the **Greyhound Gathering** (mid-May of most years, 435/644-2903, www .greyhoundgang.com), when hundreds of greyhound owners converge on the town. Events include a parade, a race, and a howl-in. The Greyhound Gang, a nonprofit organization dedicated to the rescue, rehabilitation, and adoption of ex-racing greyhounds, hosts this unlikely festival.

SHOPPING

Find a good selection of books, camping gear, and clothing, along with a little coffee bar at **Willow Canyon Outdoor** (263 S. 100 East, 435/644-8884, 7:30 A.M.–dusk). **Terry's Cameras** (19 W. Center, 435/644-5981, 9:30 A.M.–4:30 P.M. Mon.–Fri., 9:30 A.M.–noon Sat.) supplies film and camera needs (including repairs for film cameras) beyond what you would expect in a town of this size. The shop almost qualifies as an antique camera museum.

Denny's Wigwam (78 E. Center, 435/644-2452, 8:30 A.M.–10 P.M. daily, shorter hours in winter) is a landmark Old West trading post with a broad selection of Western jewelry, cowboy hats and boots, and souvenirs.

ACCOMMODATIONS

Most of the lodgings in Kanab are in modest family-run motels. Reservations are a good idea during the busy summer months. All of the motels and campgrounds are on U.S. 89, which follows 300 West, Center, 100 East, and 300 South through town.

Under $50

The **Quail Park Lodge** (125 U.S. 89 North, 435/644-5094 or 866/702-8099, www.quail parklodge.com, $45 and up) has a pool and accepts pets. It's one of the nicer budget motels in town. The **Bob-Bon Inn** (236 U.S. 89 North, 435/644-5094, $45 and up) is a renovated family-run motel. The **Sun-N-Sand Motel** (347 S. 100 East, 435/644-5050 or 800/654-1868, $42 and up) has a pool, spa, and kitchenettes.

$50-100

One place in Kanab that varies from the usual motor-court formula is the **Parry Lodge** (89 E. Center, 435/644-2601 or 800/748-4104, $57 and up). Built during Kanab's heyday as a movie-making center, the Parry Lodge was where the stars stayed; 60 years later, this is still a pleasantly old-fashioned place to spend the night. At the very least, you'll want to stroll through the lobby, where lots of photos of celebrities who once stayed here are displayed. There are several two-bedroom units, a pool, and a restaurant.

A good mid-range choice is the **Four Seasons Motel** (36 N. 300 West, 435/644-2635, $60 and up), which has a pool and accepts pets. Another good bet is **Aiken's Lodge** (79 W. Center, 435/644-2625 or 800/790-0380, www.aikenslodge.com, $65), also with a pool. It's closed in January and February.

The rooms at **Best Western Red Hills Motel** (125 W. Center, 435/644-2675 or 800/830-2675, www.bestwesternredhills.com, $90 and up) are a step up in comfort from Kanab's lower-priced digs. It has a pool and is within a short walk of restaurants. Rates drop substantially during summer, fall, and winter.

North of Kanab, at Mount Carmel Junction, is another Best Western. The **Best Thunderbird Resort** (435/648-2203, www .bestwestern.com, $92 and up) is convenient if you're heading to Zion or Bryce Canyon National Parks.

Over $100

Especially nice if you're traveling with a group are the **Kanab Garden Cottages** (various lo-

cations, 435/644-2020, www.kanabcottages .com, $150 and up, three-night minimum). The three houses can easily sleep five or six people, are all within walking distance of town, and are pet-friendly.

Campgrounds

The campground at **Coral Pink Sand Dunes State Park** (435/648-2800, 800/322-3770 for reservations, www.stateparks.utah.gov, $5 per vehicle day use, $15 per vehicle camping) is a pleasant, shady spot, but it can hum with ATV traffic.

On the north edge of the dunes, just north of the state park, the BLM maintains **Ponderosa Grove Campground** (435/644-4600, www .ut.blm.gov/kanab_fo, $5, no water). From Kanab, head eight miles north on U.S. 89, turn west on Hancock Road (between Mileposts 72 and 73), and continue 7.3 miles to the campground.

The **Kanab RV Corral** (483 S. 100 East, 435/644-5330, year-round, $28) has RV sites (no tents) with hot showers, a pool, and laundry service. The **Hitch'n Post RV Park** (196 E. 300 South, 435/644-2142 or 800/458-3516, year-round, $16 tent, $20 and up RV) has sites for both RVs and tents, and has showers.

FOOD

Find the best food in town at ◖ **Rocking V Café** (97 W. Center, 435/644-8001, lunch and dinner daily, $14–27). The setting is casual and the food has a modern Southwest flair. Rocking V, which caters to both vegans and steak-lovers, pays homage to the "slow food" movement and makes everything from scratch. Be sure to check out the art gallery upstairs.

Drop by **Laid-Back Larry's** (98 S. 100 East, 435/644-3636, 7 A.M.–4 P.M. Mon.– Fri., 8 A.M.–4 P.M. Sat.–Sun.) for espresso or a smoothie. True to its name, this place has a tropical beach-hut ambiance. The **Vermilion Café** (4 E. Center, 435/644-3886, breakfast, lunch, and dinner daily Apr.–Oct., breakfast and lunch daily Nov.–Mar., $2–10) is another good place for espresso drinks, pastries, and deli sandwiches.

If you're hankering for a good spinach enchilada or other Mexican food, settle into the friendly **Nedra's Too** (300 S. 100 East, 435/644-2030, lunch and dinner daily, $8–10).

Travelers setting out into the desert from Kanab should note that this is the best place for many miles around to stock up on groceries. **Honey's Food Jubilee** (260 E. 300 South, 435/644-5877, 8 A.M.–9 P.M.) is a good grocery store on the way out of town to the east.

INFORMATION AND SERVICES

Staff members at the **information center** (78 S. 100 East, 435/644-5033, www.kane utah.com, Mon.–Sat. 8 A.M.–8 P.M.) offer literature and advice for services in Kanab and travel in Kane County. The **Grand Staircase-Escalante National Monument** has a visitors center on the east edge of town (745 East Hwy. 89, Kanab, 435/644-4680, 8 A.M.–5 P.M. daily mid-Mar.–mid-Nov., Mon.–Fri. 8 A.M.–4:30 P.M. mid-Nov.–mid-Mar.).

CORAL PINK SAND DUNES STATE PARK

Churning air currents funneled by surrounding mountains have deposited huge sand dunes in this valley west of Kanab. The ever-changing dunes reach heights of several hundred feet and cover about 2,000 of the park's 3,700 acres. Different areas in the park (435/648-2800, 800/322-3770 reservations, www.stateparks.utah.gov, $5 per vehicle day use, $15 per vehicle camping) have been set aside for hiking, off-road vehicles, and a campground.

From Kanab, the shortest drive is to go north eight miles on U.S. 89 (between Mileposts 72 and 73), turn left 9.3 miles on the paved Hancock Road to its end, then turn left (south) one mile on a paved road into the park. From the north, you can follow U.S. 89 3.5 miles south of Mount Carmel Junction, then turn right (south) 11 miles on a paved road. The back road from Cane Beds in Arizona has about 16 miles of gravel and dirt with some sandy spots; ask a park ranger for current conditions.

The canyon country surrounding the park has good opportunities for hiking and off-road-vehicle travel; the BLM office in Kanab can supply maps and information. Drivers with four-wheel drive vehicles can turn south on Sand Springs Road (1.5 miles east of Ponderosa Grove Campground) and go one mile to Sand Springs and another four miles to the South Fork Indian Canyon Pictograph Site in a pretty canyon. Visitors may not enter the Kaibab-Paiute Indian Reservation, which is south across the Arizona state line, from this side.

Zion National Park

Zion National Park (435/772-3256, www.nps .gov/zion, $25 per vehicle, $12 per person for pedestrians, bicyclists, and motorcyclists) is a magnificent park, with stunning, soaring scenery. The story here is really just all about rocks and water. Little trickles of water, percolating through massive chunks of sandstone, have created both dramatic canyons and markedly un-desertlike habitats, enabling an incredible variety of plants to find niches here.

When you visit Zion, the first thing to catch your attention will be the sheer cliffs and great monoliths of Zion Canyon reaching high into the heavens. Energetic streams and other forces of erosion created this land of finely sculptured rock. The large park spreads across 147,000 acres and contains eight geologic formations and four major vegetation zones. Elevations range from 3,666 feet in lower Coalpits Wash to 8,726 feet atop Horse Ranch Mountain.

The highlight for most visitors is Zion Canyon, which is approximately 2,400 feet deep. The Zion Canyon visitors center, at the mouth of Zion Canyon, is on Hwy. 9 about midway between I-15 and U.S. 89. It's 43 miles northeast of St. George, 60 miles south of Cedar

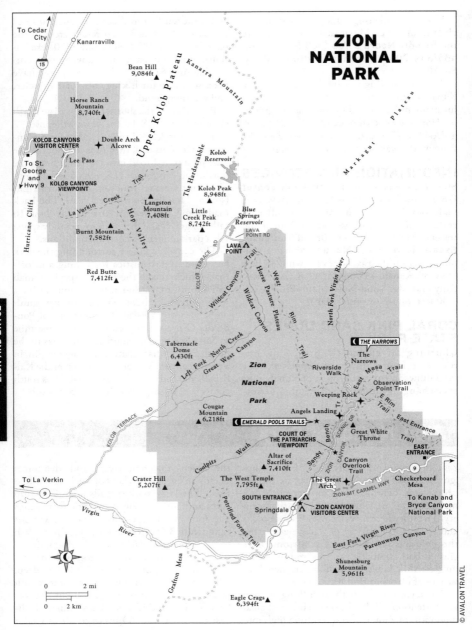

ZION NATIONAL PARK

To Cedar City

Kanarraville

Bean Hill
9,084ft

Upper Kolob Plateau

Kanarra Mountain

Markagut Plateau

Horse Ranch
Mountain
8,740ft

KOLOB CANYONS
VISITOR CENTER

Double Arch
Alcove

The Hardscrabble

Kolob
Reservoir

To St.
George
and
Hwy 9

Lee Pass

KOLOB CANYONS
VIEWPOINT

Kolob Creek Trail

Langston
Mountain
7,408ft

Kolob Peak
8,948ft

La Verkin Creek

Little
Creek Peak
8,742ft

Blue
Springs
Reservoir

Hop Valley

LAVA
POINT RD

Hurricane Cliffs

Burnt Mountain
7,582ft

KOLOB TERRACE RD

LAVA
POINT

Red Butte
7,412ft

Wildcat Canyon Trail

Wildcat Canyon

West Rim Trail

Horse Pasture Plateau

North Fork Virgin River

Tabernacle
Dome
6,430ft

Left Fork North Creek

Great West Canyon

Zion

National

Park

THE NARROWS

The
Narrows

Riverside
Walk

East Mesa Trail

Observation
Point Trail

Cougar
Mountain
6,218ft

Weeping Rock

Angels Landing

EMERALD POOLS TRAILS

E Rim Trail

Great White
Throne

East Rim Trail

East Entrance

KOLOB TERRACE RD

COURT OF
THE PATRIARCHS
VIEWPOINT

Coalpits Wash

Altar of
Sacrifice
7,410ft

Sandy

ZION CANYON SCENIC DR

Canyon
Overlook
Trail

EAST
ENTRANCE

To La Verkin

Crater Hill

The West Temple
7,795ft

The Great
Arch

ZION-MT CARMEL HWY

Checkerboard
Mesa

Virgin River

Petrified Forest Trail

SOUTH ENTRANCE

Springdale

ZION CANYON
VISITORS CENTER

To Kanab and
Bryce Canyon
National Park

East Fork Virgin River

Parunuweap Canyon

Grafton Mesa

Shunesburg
Mountain
5,961ft

0   2 mi

0   2 km

Eagle Crags
6,394ft

© PAUL LEVY

The Three Patriarchs are a trio of landmark mountains in Zion National Park.

ZION AND BRYCE

City, 41 miles northwest of Kanab, and 86 miles southwest of Bryce Canyon National Park. Large RVs and bicycles must heed special regulations for the long tunnel on the Zion–Mount Carmel Highway (see the sidebar *The Zion–Mount Carmel Tunnel*). Visitors short on time usually drop in at the visitors center, travel the Zion Canyon Scenic Drive, and take short walks on Weeping Rock or Riverside Walk Trails. A stay of two days or longer is better to take in more of the grand scenery and hike other inviting trails.

Zion Canyon Scenic Drive winds through the canyon along the North Fork of the Virgin River past some of the most spectacular scenery in the park. (During the spring, summer, and early fall, a shuttle bus ferries visitors along this route.) Hiking trails branch off to lofty viewpoints and narrow side canyons. Adventurous souls can continue on foot past the road's end into the eerie depths of the Virgin River Narrows in upper Zion Canyon.

The spectacular Zion–Mount Carmel Highway, with its switchbacks and tunnels, provides access to the canyons and high plateaus east of Zion Canyon. Two other roads enter the rugged Kolob section northwest of Zion Canyon. The *Kolob,* a Mormon name meaning "the brightest star, next to the seat of God," includes wilderness areas rarely visited by humans. Kolob Canyons Road, in the extreme northwestern section of the park, begins just off I-15 Exit 40 at the **Kolob Canyons Visitors Center** and climbs to an overlook for great views of the Finger Canyons of the Kolob; the drive is 10 miles round-trip. Motorists with more time may also want to drive the Kolob Terrace Road to Lava Point for another perspective of the park; this drive is about 44 miles round-trip from Virgin (on Hwy. 9) and has some unpaved sections.

Zion's grandeur extends all through the year. Even rainy days can be memorable as countless waterfalls plunge from every crevice in the cliffs above. Spring and autumn are the choice seasons for the most pleasant temperatures and the best chances of seeing wildlife and wildflowers. About mid-October–early November,

THE ROCKS OF ZION

The rock layers at Zion began as sediments of oceans, rivers, lakes, or sand dunes deposited 65-240 million years ago. The soaring Navajo sandstone cliffs that form such distinctive features as the Great White Throne and the Three Patriarchs were originally immense sand dunes. Look for the slanting lines in these rock walls, which result from shifting winds as the sand dunes formed. Calcium carbonate in the sand piles acted as a glue to turn the dunes into rock, and it's also responsible for the white color of many of the rocks. The reddish rocks are also Navajo sandstone, but they've been stained by iron oxides — essentially rust.

Kayenta shale is the other main rock you'll see in Zion. For an up-close look, check out the streambed at Middle Emerald Pool. The rippled gray rock is Kayenta shale. This shale, which lies beneath Navajo sandstone, is much less permeable than the sandstone. Water can easily trickle through the relatively porous sandstone, but when it hits the impermeable Kayenta shale, it runs along the top surface of the rock and seeps out on the side of the nearest rock face. Weeping Rock, with its lush cliffside springs, is a good place to see the junction between Navajo sandstone and Kayenta shale.

A gradual uplift of the Colorado Plateau, which continues today, has caused the formerly lazy rivers on its surface to pick up speed and knife through the rock layers. You can really appreciate these erosive powers during flash floods, when the North Fork of the Virgin River or other streams roar through their canyons. Erosion of some of the Virgin River's tributaries couldn't keep up with the main channel, and they were left as "hanging valleys" on the canyon walls. A good example is Hidden Canyon, which is reached by trail in Zion Canyon.

Faulting has broken the Colorado Plateau into a series of smaller plateaus. At Zion you are on the Kolob Terrace of the Markagunt Plateau, whose rock layers are younger than those of the Kaibab Plateau at Grand Canyon National Park and older than those exposed on the Paunsaugunt Plateau at Bryce Canyon National Park.

Although some erosive forces, like flash floods, are dramatic, the subtle freezing and thawing of water and the slow action of tree roots are responsible for most of the changes. Water seeps into the Navajo sandstone, accumulating especially in the long, vertical cracks in the cliffs. The dramatic temperature changes, especially in the spring and fall, cause regular freezing and thawing, slowly enlarging the cracks and setting the stage for more dramatic rockfalls. Erosion and rockfall continue to shape Zion Canyon. In 1995 a huge rockslide blocked Zion Canyon Scenic Drive and left hundreds of people trapped at the lodge for several days until crews were able to clear a path.

---

cottonwoods and other trees and plants blaze with color. Summer temperatures in the canyons can be uncomfortably hot, with highs hovering above 100°F. It's also the busiest season. In winter, nighttime temperatures drop to near freezing and weather tends to be unpredictable, with bright sunshine one day and freezing rain the next. Snow-covered slopes contrast with colorful rocks. Snow may block some of the high-country trails and the road to Lava Point, but the rest of the park is open and accessible year-round.

Zion National Park is 43 miles northeast of St. George, 60 miles south of Cedar City, 41 miles northwest of Kanab, and 86 miles southwest of Bryce Canyon National Park. There are two entrances to the main section of the park: from Springdale you enter the south end of Zion Canyon, right near the visitors center and the Zion Canyon shuttle buses; from the east, you come in on the Zion–Mount Carmel Highway, pass through a long tunnel, then pop into Zion Canyon a couple of miles north of the visitors center. There's a separate entrance for the Kolob Canyons area, in the park's northwest corner. A far-less-traveled part of the park is accessed by the Kolob Terraces Road, which heads north from Hwy. 9 at the tiny town of Virgin and goes to backcountry sites. (There's no entrance station on this road.)

Large RVs and bicycles must heed special regulations for the long tunnel on the Zion–Mount Carmel Highway. (See the sidebar *The Zion–Mount Carmel Tunnel* for vehicle size restrictions in the tunnel.)

Kolob Canyons Road, in the extreme northwestern section of the park, begins just off I-15 Exit 40 at the **Kolob Canyons Visitors Center** and climbs to an overlook for great views of the Finger Canyons of the Kolob; the drive is 10 miles round-trip.

HISTORY

As early as A.D. 285, the Kayenta-Virgin branch of the Anasazi built small villages of sunken pit houses in what's now the park. Their culture gradually developed over the centuries with improved agriculture and crafts until they left the region in about 1200. Next came the Kaibab band of Southern Paiutes, who spent part of the year here on seasonal migrations. The Paiutes relied heavily on wild seeds for food, supplemented by hunting and some agriculture. White settlers and their livestock depleted the range and wildlife so much that the Paiutes had to abandon this old lifestyle.

Mormon pioneers pushed up the Virgin River Valley in 1859 and founded Grafton, the first of a series of towns south of the present-day park. In 1863, the Isaac Behunin family began farming in Zion Canyon and built a one-room cabin near where Zion Lodge now stands. Other families settled and farmed the canyon until the area was established as a national monument. The canyon's naming is credited to Isaac Behunin, who believed this spot to be a refuge from religious persecution. When Brigham Young later visited the canyon, however, he found tobacco and wine in use and declared the place "not Zion"—which some dutiful followers then began calling

it. A scientific expedition led by John Wesley Powell in 1872 helped make the wonders known to the outside world. Efforts by Stephen T. Mather, first director of the National Park Service, and others led to designation of Mukuntuweap (Straight Canyon) National Monument in 1909 and the establishment of Zion National Park in 1919.

PARK SHUTTLE BUS

By the late 1990s, visitors to Zion remembered the traffic nearly as vividly as they remembered the Great White Throne; throughout much of the summer, the canyon road was simply a parking lot for enormous RVs. To relieve the congestion, the National Park Service has instituted an April–October shuttle bus service through the canyon.

There are two bus lines: One line travels between Springdale and the park entrance, stopping within a short walk of every Springdale motel and near several large visitor parking lots; the other bus line starts just inside the park entrance at the visitors center and runs the length of Zion Canyon Road, stopping at scenic overlooks, trailheads, and Zion Lodge. Lodge guests may obtain a pass authorizing them to drive to the lodge, but in general, private vehicles are no longer allowed to drive up Zion Canyon.

This is less of a pain than it might seem. It's still fine to drive to the campgrounds; in fact, the road between the park entrance and the Zion–Mount Carmel Highway junction is open to all vehicles. Buses run frequently, so there's rarely much of a wait, and most of the bus drivers are friendly and well-informed, offering an engaging commentary on the sights that they pass (even pointing out rock climbers on the canyon's big walls).

If you get to Zion before 10 A.M. or after 3 P.M., there may be parking spaces available in the visitors center lot. Midday visitors should just park in Springdale (at your motel or in a public lot) and catch a shuttle bus to the park entrance.

Riding the bus is free; its cost of operation is included in the park admission fee. Buses run as often as every six minutes 5:30 A.M.–11 P.M. (less frequently early in the morning and in the evening). No pets are allowed on the buses. November–March, private vehicles are allowed on all roads, and the buses are out of service.

Zion Canyon Scenic Drive is a six-mile road that follows the North Fork of the Virgin River upstream. Impressive natural formations along the way include the Three Patriarchs, Mountain of the Sun, Lady Mountain, Great White Throne, Angels Landing, and Weeping Rock. The bus stops at eight points of interest along the way; you can get on and off the bus as often as you wish at these stops. The road ends at Temple of Sinawava and the beginning of the Riverside Walk Trail.

TOURS

With the exception of ranger-led hikes, Zion Canyon Field Institute classes, the horseback rides from Zion Lodge, and the running commentary from the more loquacious shuttle bus drivers, Zion is a do-it-yourself park. Outfitters are not permitted to lead trips within the park. If you'd like a guided tour outside park boundaries, there are several outfitters in Springdale that lead biking, canyoneering, and climbing trips (see the *Springdale and Vicinity* section).

The **Zion Canyon Field Institute** (435/772-3264, www.zionpark.org) is authorized to run educational programs in the park. These programs range from animal tracking to photography to archaeology.

ZION CANYON

During the busy spring, summer, and fall seasons, you'll be traveling up and down Zion Canyon in a shuttle bus. Most visitors find this to be an easy and enjoyable way to visit the following sites.

Zion Canyon Visitors Center

The park's sprawling visitors center (8 A.M.–7 P.M. daily in summer, 8 A.M.–6 P.M. daily in spring and fall, 8 A.M.–5 P.M. daily in winter), between Watchman and South campgrounds,

is a hub of activity. The plaza outside the building features several interpretive plaques, including some pointing out environmentally sensitive design features of the visitors center. Inside, a large area is devoted to backcountry information; staff members can answer your questions about various trails, give you updates on the weather forecast, and help you arrange a shuttle to remote trailheads.

The busiest part of the visitors center is its bookstore, which is stocked with an excellent selection of books covering natural history, human history, and regional travel. Topographic and geologic maps, posters, slides, postcards, and film are sold here, too.

The best way by far to get a feel for Zion's impressive geology and variety of habitats is to take a hike with a park ranger. Many nature programs and hikes are offered late March–November; check the posted schedule. From Memorial Day to Labor Day, children's programs are held at Zion Nature Center near South Campground; ask at the visitors center for details. A Backcountry Shuttle Board allows hikers to coordinate transportation between trailheads.

Zion Nature Center

At the northern end of South Campground, this recently refurbished building houses programs for kids, including Junior Ranger activities for ages 6–12. Morning-long outdoor activities for kids run 9–11:30 A.M. daily Memorial Day–Labor Day (arrive 30 minutes early to register). The entire family can participate in afternoon activities, 1:30–3 P.M. daily Memorial Day–Labor Day. Programs focus on natural history topics such as insects and bats in the park.

Museum of Human History

The old park visitors center has been retooled as a museum (8 A.M.–7 P.M. daily in summer, 10 A.M.–6 P.M. daily in spring and fall, 10 A.M.–5 P.M. daily in winter) of southern Utah's cultural history, with a schmaltzy film introducing the park, and fairly bare-bones exhibits focusing on Native American and Mor-

FLORA AND FAUNA OF ZION

Many different plant and animal communities live in the rugged terrain of deep canyons and high plateaus. Because the park lies near the meeting place of the Colorado Plateau, the Great Basin, and the Mojave Desert, species representative of all three regions can be found here.

Only desert plants can endure the long, dry spells and high temperatures found at Zion's lower elevations; they include cacti (prickly pear, cholla, and hedgehog), blackbrush, creosote bush, honey mesquite, and purple sage. Cacti and yucca are common throughout the park. Pygmy forests of piñon pine, Utah juniper, live oak, mountain mahogany, and clif-frose grow between about 3,900–5,600 feet.

Once you get above the canyon floor, Zion's plants are not so different from what you'd find in the Pacific Northwest. Trees such as ponderosa pine and Douglas fir can thrive here thanks to the moisture they draw from the Navajo sandstone. White fir and aspen are also common on high, cool plateaus. Permanent springs and streams support a profusion of greenery such as cottonwood, box elder, willow, red birch, horsetail, and ferns. Watch out for poison ivy in moist, shady areas.

Colorful wildflowers pop out of the ground – indeed even out of the rocks – at all elevations from spring through autumn. In early spring, look for the Zion shooting star, a plant in the primrose family found only in Zion. Here, its nodding pink flowers are easily spotted along the Emerald Pools trails and at Weeping Rock. You're also likely to see desert phlox, a low plant covered with pink flowers, and, by mid-May, golden columbine.

Mule deer are common throughout the park. Also common is a type of beaver called a "bank beaver," which lives along the banks of the Virgin River rather than in log lodges, which would be too frequently swept away by flash floods. (Even though these beavers don't build log lodges, they still gnaw like crazy on trees – look near the base of riverside trees near Zion Lodge for their work.) Other wildlife includes elk, mountain lion, bobcat, black bear, bighorn sheep (reintroduced), coyote, gray fox, porcupine, ringtail cat, black-tailed jackrabbit, rock squirrel, cliff chipmunk, beaver, and many species of mice and bats.

Birders have spotted more than 270 species in and near the park, but most common are red-tailed hawk, turkey vulture, quail, mallard, great horned owl, hairy woodpecker, raven, scrub jay, black-headed grosbeak, blue-gray gnatcatcher, canyon wren, Virginia's warbler, white-throated swift, and broad-tailed hummingbird. Zion's high cliffs are good places to look for peregrine falcons; try spotting them from the cliffside at Angel's Rest trail.

Hikers and campers will undoubtedly see northern sagebrush lizards, and hikers need to watch for western rattlesnakes, although these relatively rare reptiles are unlikely to attack unless provoked.

Cactus flowers are brilliant and short-lived.

© PAUL LEVY

---

mon history. It's at the first shuttle stop after the visitors center. This is a good place to visit when you're too tired to hike any farther, or if the weather forces you to seek shelter.

Court of the Patriarchs Viewpoint

A short trail from the parking area leads to the viewpoint. The Three Patriarchs, a trio of peaks to the west, overlook Birch Creek; they are (from left to right) Abraham, Isaac, and Jacob. Mount Moroni, the reddish peak on the far right, partly blocks the view of Jacob. Although the official viewpoint is a beautiful place to relax and enjoy the view, you'll get an even better view if you cross the road and head about half a mile up Sand Bench Trail.

Zion Lodge

Rustic Zion Lodge, with its big front lawn, spacious lobby (with free but incredibly slow Internet access), snack bar, restaurant, and restrooms, is a natural stop for most park visitors. You don't need to be a guest at the lodge to enjoy the ambiance of its public areas.

Cross the road from the lodge to catch the Emerald Pools trail, or walk a half-mile north from the Zion Lodge shuttle stop to reach the Grotto.

The Grotto

The Grotto is a popular place for a picnic. From here, a trail leads back to the lodge and, across the road, the Kayenta Trail links up with the Emerald Pools trails.

Visible from several points along Zion

NAVAJO SANDSTONE

Take a look anywhere along Zion Canyon, and you'll see 1,600–2,200-foot cliffs of Navajo sandstone. The big walls of Zion were formed from sand dunes deposited during a hot, dry period about 200 million years ago. Shifting winds blew the sand from one direction, then another – a careful inspection of the sandstone layer reveals the diagonal lines resulting from this "cross-bedding." Recent studies by researchers at the University of Nebraska, Lincoln, printed in *Nature* magazine, conclude that the vast dunes of southern Utah were formed when the landmass on which they sit was about 15 degrees north of the equator,

about the same location as today's Honduras. The shift patterns apparent in the sandstone – the slanting striations easily seen in cliff faces – were caused in part by intense monsoon rains, which served to compact and move the dunes each rainy season.

Eventually, a shallow sea washed over the dunes. Lapping waves left shells behind, and, as the shells dissolved, their lime seeped down into the sand and cemented it into sandstone. After the Colorado Plateau lifted, rivers cut deeply through the sandstone layer. The formation's lower layers are stained red from iron oxides.

© PAUL LEVY

The Great White Throne is a gleaming hunk of Navajo sandstone.

Canyon Drive is the **Great White Throne.** Topping out at 6,744 feet, this bulky chunk of Navajo Sandstone has become, along with the Three Patriarchs, emblematic of the park. Ride the shuttle in the evening to watch the rock change color as the setting sun lights it up.

Weeping Rock

Several trails, including the short and easy Weeping Rock Trail, start here. Weeping Rock is home to hanging gardens and many moisture-loving plants, including the striking Zion shooting star. The rock "weeps" because this is a junction between porous Navajo sandstone and denser Kayenta shale. Water trickles down through the sandstone, and, when it can't penetrate the shale, moves laterally to the face of the cliff.

While you're at Weeping Rock, scan the cliffs for remains of cables and rigging that were used to lower timber from the top of the rim down to the canyon floor. During the early 1900s, this wood was used to build pioneer settlements in the area.

Big Bend

Look up! This is where you're likely to see rock climbers on the towering walls. Because outfitters aren't allowed to bring groups into the park, these climbers presumably are quite experienced and know what they're doing up there.

Temple of Sinawava

The last shuttle stop is at this canyon, where 2,000-foot-tall rock walls reach up from the sides of the Virgin River. There's not really enough room for the road to continue farther up the canyon, but it's plenty spacious for a fine paved walking path. The Riverside Walk heads a mile upstream to the Virgin Narrows, a place where the canyon becomes too narrow for even a sidewalk to squeeze through. You may see people hiking up The Narrows (in the river) from the end of the Riverside Walk. Don't join them unless you're properly outfitted.

EAST OF ZION CANYON

The east section of the park is a land of sandstone slickrock, hoodoos, and narrow canyons.

THE ZION-
MT. CARMEL TUNNEL

If your vehicle is 7 feet 10 inches wide, 11 feet 4 inches tall, or larger, you will need a traffic-control escort through the narrow, mile-long Zion-Mt. Carmel Tunnel. Vehicles this size are too large to stay in their lane while traveling through the tunnel, which was built in the 1920s, when autos were not only small, but few and far between. Nearly all RVs, buses, trailers, fifth-wheels, and some camper shells will require an "escort."

Visitors requiring an escort must pay a $15 fee per vehicle in addition to the entrance fee. Pay this fee at either park entrance before proceeding to the tunnel. The fee is good for two trips through the tunnel for the same vehicle during a seven-day period.

Though the park service persists in using the term "escort," you're really on your own through the tunnel. Rather than providing an escort vehicle, park staff will stop oncoming traffic, allowing you enough time to drive down the middle of the tunnel. From April 1 through late October, traffic-control staff is present at the tunnel 8 A.M.-8 P.M. daily. During the winter season, oversized vehicle passage must be arranged at the entrance stations, Zion Canyon Visitors Center, Zion Lodge, or by phoning 435/772-3256.

Bicycles and pedestrians are not allowed in the tunnel.

You can see much of the dramatic scenery along the Zion–Mount Carmel Highway (Hwy. 9) between the East Entrance Station and Zion Canyon. Most of this region invites exploration on your own. Try hiking a canyon or heading up a slickrock slope (the pass between Crazy Quilt and Checkerboard Mesas is one possibility). Highlights on the plateau include views of the White Cliffs and Checkerboard Mesa (both near the East Entrance Station) and a hike on the Canyon Overlook Trail (it begins

ZION AND BRYCE

just east of the long tunnel). Checkerboard Mesa's distinctive pattern is caused by a combination of vertical fractures and horizontal bedding planes, both accentuated by weathering. The highway's spectacular descent into Zion Canyon goes first through a 530-foot tunnel, then a 5,600-foot tunnel, followed by a series of six switchbacks to the canyon floor. See the sidebar *The Zion–Mount Carmel Tunnel* for vehicle size restrictions in the tunnel.

KOLOB CANYONS

North and west of Zion Canyon lies the remote backcountry of the Kolob. This area became a second Zion National Monument in 1937, then was added to Zion National Park in 1956. You'll see all but one of the rock formations present in the park and evidence of past volcanic eruptions. Two roads lead into the Kolob. The paved five-mile Kolob Canyons Road begins at the Kolob Canyons Visitors Center just off I-15 and ends at an overlook and picnic area; it's open year-round. Kolob Terrace Road is paved from the town of Virgin (15 miles west on Hwy. 9 from the South Entrance Station) to the turnoff for Lava Point; snow usually blocks the way in winter.

Kolob Canyons Visitors Center

Although it is small and has just a handful of exhibits, this visitors center (435/586-9548, 8 A.M.–4:30 P.M. daily, until 5 P.M. in summer) is a good place to stop for information on exploring the Kolob region. Hikers can learn current trail conditions and obtain the permits required for overnight trips and Zion Narrows day trips. Books, topographic and geologic maps, posters, postcards, slides, and film are sold. The visitors center and the start of Kolob Canyons Road lie just off I-15 Exit 40.

Kolob Canyons Road

This five-mile scenic drive winds past the dramatic Finger Canyons of the Kolob to Kolob Canyons Viewpoint and a picnic area at the end of the road. The road is paved and has many pullouts where you can stop to admire the scenery. The first part of the drive follows

the 200-mile-long Hurricane Fault that forms the west edge of the Markagunt Plateau. Look for the tilted rock layers deformed by friction as the plateau rose nearly one mile. **Taylor Creek Trail,** which begins two miles past the visitors center, provides a close look at the canyons (see the *Hikes in Kolob Canyons* section). Lee Pass, four miles beyond the visitors center, was named after John D. Lee of the infamous Mountain Meadows Massacre; he's believed to have lived nearby for a short time after the massacre. **La Verkin Creek Trail** begins at Lee Pass Trailhead for trips to Kolob Arch and beyond. Signs at the end of the road identify the points, buttes, mesa, and mountains. The salmon-colored Navajo sandstone cliffs glow a deep red at sunset. **Timber Creek Overlook Trail** begins from the picnic area at road's end and climbs one-half mile to the overlook (elev. 6,369 feet); views encompass the Pine Valley Mountains, Zion Canyons, and distant Mount Trumbull.

KOLOB TERRACE

The Kolob Terrace section of the park is a high plateau roughly parallel to and west of Zion Canyon. From the town of Virgin, the road runs north through ranch land and up a narrow tongue of land, with drop-offs on either side, then widens into a high plateau. The Hurricane Cliffs rise from the gorge to the west, and the back side of Zion Canyon's big walls are to the east. The road passes in and out of the park and terminates at Kolob Reservoir, which is not in the park, but is a popular boating and fishing destination. This section of the park is much higher than Zion Canyon, so it's a good place to explore when the canyon swelters in the summertime. It's also much less crowded than the busy canyon.

Lava Point

The panorama from Lava Point (elevation 7,890 feet) takes in the Cedar Breaks area to the north, the Pink Cliffs to the northeast, Zion Canyon Narrows and tributaries to the east, the Sentinel and other monoliths of Zion Canyon to the southeast, and Mount Trumbull on the Arizona

In the Kolob Terrace hikers can see the backside of Zion Canyon.

Strip to the south. Signs help identify features. Lava Point, which sits atop a lava flow, is a good place to cool off in summer—temperatures are about 20°F cooler than in Zion Canyon. Aspen, ponderosa pine, Gambel oak, and white fir grow here. A small, primitive **campground** near the point offers sites during warmer months; no water and no fee. From Virgin, take the Kolob Terrace Road about 21 miles north to the Lava Point turnoff; the viewpoint is 1.8 miles farther on a well-marked spur road.

Kolob Reservoir

This high-country lake north of Lava Point has good fishing for rainbow trout. An unpaved boat ramp is at the south end near the dam. People sometimes camp along the shore, although there are no facilities. Most of the surrounding land is private. To reach the reservoir, continue north 3.5 miles on Kolob Terrace Road from the Lava Point turn-off. The fair-weather road can also be followed past the

reservoir to the Cedar City area. Blue Springs Reservoir, near the turn-off for Lava Point, is closed to the public.

HIKES IN ZION CANYON

The trails in Zion Canyon provide perspectives of the park that are not available from the roads. Many of the hiking trails require long ascents but aren't too difficult at a leisurely pace. Carry water on all but the shortest walks. Descriptions of the following trails are given in order from the mouth of Zion Canyon to the Virgin River Narrows.

Experienced hikers can do countless off-trail routes in the canyons and plateaus surrounding Zion Canyon; rangers can suggest areas. Rappelling and other climbing skills may be needed to negotiate drops in some of the more remote canyons. Groups cannot exceed 12 hikers per trail or drainage. Overnight hikers must obtain backcountry permits ($5) from either the Zion Canyon or Kolob

Canyons Visitors Center. Some areas of the park—mainly those near roads and major trails—are closed to overnight use. Zion Lodge offers shuttle services for hikers, or you can check the Backcountry Shuttle Board at the visitors center.

Pa'rus Trail
SHUTTLE STOPS: VISITORS CENTER AND CANYON JUNCTION
This two-mile paved trail runs from the South Campground to the Canyon Junction shuttle bus stop. For most of its distance, it skirts alongside the Virgin River and makes for a nice early morning or evening stroll. Listen for the trilling song of the canyon wren, then try to spot the small bird in the bushes. The accessible Pa'rus Trail is the only trail in the park that's open to bicycles and pets.

Watchman Trail
SHUTTLE STOP: VISITORS CENTER
From a trailhead north of Watchman Campground, the trail climbs 370 feet to a bench below Watchman Peak, the prominent mountain southeast of the visitors center. Views encompass lower Zion Canyon and the town of Springdale. The well-graded trail follows a side canyon past some springs, then ascends to the overlook; the distance is 2.4 miles round-trip and takes about two hours. Trees and plants line the way. In summer, it's best to get an early start. Rangers lead nature walks during the main season.

Court of the Patriarchs Viewpoint
SHUTTLE STOP: COURT OF THE PATRIARCHS
A short trail from the parking area leads to the viewpoint. The Three Patriarchs overlook Birch Creek; they are (from left to right) Abraham, Isaac, and Jacob. Mount Moroni, the reddish peak on the far right, partly blocks the view of Jacob. Although the official viewpoint is a beautiful place to relax and enjoy the view, you can get an even better view by crossing the road and heading about one-half mile up the Sand Bench Trail.

ZION CANYON FIELD INSTITUTE

Delve a little more deeply into Zion's natural and human history by taking a workshop with the Zion Canyon Field Institute. Workshops run 1-3 days and focus on such topics as bighorn sheep, bats, photography, native plants, nature sketching, and backcountry skills. Some of the workshops are service projects, which give participants the chance to learn about Zion while working on a project that benefits the park. These service projects are far more interesting than many service projects, and include such workshops as participating in an archaeological survey or studying the abundance and distribution of mountain lions in the park.

The Field Institute's programs are very reasonably priced, about $50 for a one-day workshop. For details on upcoming workshops, call 435/772-3264 or 800/635-3959 or check the schedule at www.zionpark.org.

Sand Bench Trail
SHUTTLE STOPS: COURT OF THE PATRIARCHS AND ZION LODGE
This easy loop has good views of the Three Patriarchs, the Streaked Wall, and other monuments of lower Zion Canyon. The trail is 1.7 miles long with a 500-foot elevation gain; allow about three hours. During the main season, Zion Lodge organizes three-hour horseback rides on the trail. (The horses churn up dust and leave an uneven surface, though, so hikers usually prefer to go elsewhere.) The trail soon leaves the riparian forest along Birch Creek and climbs onto the dry benchland. Piñon pine, juniper, sand sage, yucca, prickly pear cactus, and other high-desert plants and animals live here. Hikers can get off the shuttle at the Court of the Patriarchs Viewpoint, walk across the scenic drive, then follow a service road to the footbridge and trailhead. A 1.2-mile trail along the river connects the trailhead with

Zion Lodge. In warmer months, try to hike in early morning or late afternoon.

🄲 Emerald Pools Trails
SHUTTLE STOP: ZION LODGE

Three spring-fed pools, small waterfalls, and views of Zion Canyon make this climb worthwhile. You have a choice of three trails. The easiest is the paved trail to the Lower Pool; cross the footbridge near Zion Lodge and turn right 0.6 mile. The Middle Pool can be reached by continuing 0.2 mile on this trail or by taking a totally different trail from the footbridge at Zion Lodge (after crossing the bridge, turn left, then right up the trail). Together these trails make a 1.8-mile round-trip loop. A third trail begins at the Grotto Picnic Area, crosses a footbridge, and turns left 0.7 mile; the trail forks left to the Lower Pool and right to the Middle Pool. A steep 0.4-mile trail leads from the Middle Pool to Upper Emerald Pool. This magical spot has a white-sand beach and towering cliffs rising above. Allow 1–3 hours to visit the pools, and don't expect to find solitude; these relatively easy trails are quite popular.

West Rim Trail
SHUTTLE STOP: THE GROTTO

This strenuous trail leads to some of the best views of Zion Canyon. Backpackers can continue on the West Rim Trail to Lava Point and other destinations in the Kolob region. Start from Grotto Picnic Area (elev. 4,300 feet) and cross the footbridge, then turn right along the river. The trail climbs the slopes and enters the cool and shady depths of Refrigerator Canyon. Walter's Wiggles, a series of 21 closely spaced switchbacks, wind up to Scout Lookout and a trail junction—four miles round-trip and a 1,050-foot elevation gain. Scout Lookout has fine views of Zion Canyon. The trail is paved and well graded to this point. Turn right one-half mile at the junction to reach the summit of Angels Landing.

Angels Landing rises as a sheer-walled monolith 1,500 feet above the North Fork of the Virgin River. Although the trail to the summit is rough, chains provide security in the more exposed places. The climb is safe with care and good weather, but don't go if the trail is covered with snow or ice or if thunderstorms threaten. Children must be closely supervised, and people who are afraid of heights should skip this trail. Once on top, you'll see why Angels Landing got its name—the panorama makes all the effort worthwhile. Average hiking time for the round-trip between Grotto Picnic Area and Angels Landing is four hours, best hiked during the cooler morning hours.

Energetic hikers can continue 4.8 miles on the main trail from Scout Lookout to West Rim Viewpoint, which overlooks the Right Fork of North Creek. This strenuous 12.8-mile round-trip from Grotto Picnic Area has a 3,070-foot elevation gain. West Rim Trail continues through Zion's backcountry to Lava Point (elev. 7,890 feet), where there's a primitive campground. A car shuttle and one or more days are needed to hike the 13.3 miles (one-way) from Grotto Picnic Area. You'll have an easier hike by starting at Lava Point and hiking down to the picnic area; even so, be prepared for a *long* day hike. The trail has little or no water in some seasons.

Weeping Rock Trail
SHUTTLE STOP: WEEPING ROCK

A favorite with visitors, this easy trail winds past lush vegetation and wildflowers to a series of cliffside springs above an overhang. Thousands of water droplets glisten in the afternoon sun. The springs emerge where water seeping through more than 2,000 feet of Navajo sandstone meets a layer of impervious shale. The paved trail is a half-mile round-trip with a 100-foot elevation gain. Signs along the way identify some of the trees and plants.

Observation Point Trail
SHUTTLE STOP: WEEPING ROCK

This strenuous trail climbs 2,150 feet in 3.6 highly scenic miles to Observation Point (elev. 6,507 feet) on the edge of Zion Canyon. Allow about six hours for the round-trip. Trails branch off along the way to Hidden Canyon, upper

© EMILY ROTH

Branch off from the Observation Point Trail to explore narrow Echo Canyon.

Echo Canyon, East Entrance, East Mesa, and other destinations. The first of many switchbacks begins a short way up from the trailhead at Weeping Rock parking area. The junction for Hidden Canyon Trail appears after 0.8 mile. Several switchbacks later, the trail enters sinuous Echo Canyon. This incredibly narrow chasm can be explored for short distances upstream and downstream to deep pools and pour-offs. **Echo Canyon Trail** branches to the right at about the halfway point; this rough trail continues farther up the canyon and connects with trails to Cable Mountain, Deertrap Mountain, and the East Entrance Station (on Zion–Mount Carmel Highway). The East Rim Trail then climbs slickrock slopes above Echo Canyon with many fine views. Parts of the trail are cut right into the cliffs (work was done in the 1930s by the Civilian Conservation Corps). You'll reach the rim at last after three miles of steady climbing. Then it's an easy 0.6 mile through a forest of piñon pine, juniper, Gambel oak, manzanita, sage, and some ponderosa pine to Observation Point. Impressive views

take in Zion Canyon below and mountains and mesas all around. The **East Mesa Trail** turns right about 0.3 mile before Observation Point and follows the plateau northeast to a dirt road outside the park.

Hidden Canyon
SHUTTLE STOP: WEEPING ROCK
See if you can spot the entrance to Hidden Canyon from below. Inside the narrow canyon await small sandstone caves, a little natural arch, and diverse plantlife. The high walls, rarely more than 65 feet apart, block sunlight except for a short time at midday. Hiking distance on the moderately difficult trail is about three miles round-trip between the Weeping Rock parking area and the lower canyon; follow the East Rim Trail 0.8 mile, then turn right 0.7 mile on Hidden Canyon Trail to the canyon entrance. Footing can be a bit difficult in places because of loose sand, but chains provide handholds on the more exposed sections. Steps chopped into the rock just inside Hidden Canyon help bypass some deep pools. Allow 3–4 hours for the round-trip; the elevation change is about 1,000 feet. After heavy rains and spring runoff, the creek forms a small waterfall at the canyon entrance. The canyon is about one mile long and mostly easy walking, although the trail fades away. Look for the arch on the right about one-half mile up the canyon.

Riverside Walk
SHUTTLE STOP: TEMPLE OF SINAWAVA
This is one of the most popular hikes in the park and, except for the Pa'rus, it's the easiest. The nearly level paved trail begins at the end of Zion Canyon Scenic Drive and winds one mile upstream along the river to the Virgin River Narrows. Allow about two hours to take in the scenery—it's a good place to see Zion's lovely hanging gardens. Countless springs and seeps on the canyon walls support luxuriant plant growth and swamps. Most of the springs occur at the contact between the porous Navajo sandstone and the less permeable Kayenta Formation below. The water and vegetation attract

© W. C. MCRAE

At the end of Riverside Walk, the trail continues into the Virgin River itself.

abundant wildlife; keep an eye out for birds and animals and their tracks. At trail's end, the canyon is wide enough for only the river. Hikers continuing upstream must wade and sometimes even swim. Late morning is the best time for photography. In autumn, cottonwoods and maples display bright splashes of color.

◖ The Narrows
SHUTTLE STOP: TEMPLE OF SINAWAVA
Upper Zion Canyon is probably the most famous backcountry area in the park, yet it's also one of the most strenuous. There's no trail and you'll be wading much of the time in the river, which is usually knee- to chest-deep. In places, the high, fluted walls of the upper North Fork of the Virgin River are only 20 feet apart, and very little sunlight penetrates the depths. Mysterious side canyons beckon.

Hikers should be well prepared and in good condition—river hiking is more tiring than that over dry land. The major hazards are flash floods and hypothermia. Finding the right time to go through can be tricky: spring runoff is too

high, summer thunderstorms bring hazardous flash floods, and winter is too cold. That leaves just part of early summer (mid-June–mid-July) and early autumn (mid-Sept.–mid-Oct.) as the best bets. You can get through the entire 16-mile (one-way) Narrows in about 12 hours, although two days is best to enjoy the beauty of the place. Children under 12 shouldn't attempt hiking the entire canyon.

Don't be tempted to wear river sandals or sneakers up the Narrows; it's easy to twist an ankle on the slippery rocks. If you have a pair of hiking boots that you don't mind drenching, they'll work, but an even better solution is available from the Zion Adventure Company (36 Lion Blvd., Springdale, 435/772-0990, www.zionadventures.com) and other Springdale outfitters. They rent specially designed river-hiking boots, along with neoprene socks, walking sticks, and, in cool weather, dry suits. They also provide a valuable orientation to hiking The Narrows. Boots, socks, and sticks rent for $17 per day, $26 for two days; with a dry suit the package costs $39 per day, $59 for two days.

Talk with rangers at the Zion Canyon Visitors Center before starting a trip; they also have a handout with useful information on planning a Narrows hike. You'll need a permit for hikes all the way through The Narrows—even on a day-trip. No permit is needed if you're just going partway in and back in one day, although you must first check conditions and the weather forecast with rangers. Permits are required for overnight hikes; get them from the backcountry desk at the visitors center the day before you plan to hike or the morning of your hike (8 A.M.–noon). You will also be issued a plastic bag that's been specially designed to collect human waste. Only one-night stays are allowed. No camping is permitted below Big Springs. Group size for hiking and camping is limited to 12 along the *entire* route.

A downstream hike saves not only climbing but also the work of fighting the river currents. In fact, the length of The Narrows should only be hiked downstream. The upper trailhead is near Chamberlain's Ranch, reached by an

ZION AND BRYCE

18-mile dirt road that turns north from Hwy. 9 east of the park. The lower trailhead is at the end of the Zion Canyon Scenic Drive. The elevation change is 1,280 feet.

A good half-day trip begins at the end of the Riverside Walk and follows The Narrows 1.5 miles (about two hours) upstream to Orderville Canyon, then back the same way. Orderville Canyon makes a good destination in itself; you can hike quite a ways up from Zion Canyon.

During the summer, Zion Rock and Mountain Guides (1458 Zion Park Blvd, 435/772-3303) offers a daily shuttle to Chamberlain's Ranch, leaving at 6 A.M. Make shuttle reservations between 9 A.M.–6 P.M. on the day before you want to ride. The fee is $28 per person, with a small discount if you rent gear from them. Zion Adventure Company (435/772-0990) has a similar service.

HIKES EAST OF ZION CANYON
Canyon Overlook Trail
You can't take the shuttle bus to this fun hike; it starts on the road east of Zion Canyon and features great views from the heights without the stiff climbs found on most other Zion trails. Allow about one hour for the one-mile round-trip; elevation gain is 163 feet. A booklet available at the start or at the Zion Canyon Visitors Center describes the geology, plantlife, and clues to the presence of wildlife. The trail winds in and out along the ledges of Pine Creek Canyon, which opens into a great valley. Panoramas at trail's end take in lower Zion Canyon in the distance. A sign at the viewpoint identifies Bridge Mountain, Streaked Wall, East Temple, and other features. The Great Arch of Zion—termed a "blind arch" because it's open on only one side—lies below; the arch is 580 feet high, 720 feet long, and 90 feet deep. The Canyon Overlook Trail begins across from the parking area just east of the longer (west) tunnel on the Zion–Mount Carmel Highway.

HIKES IN THE SOUTHWEST DESERT
Huber Wash
From the parking area on Hwy. 9, this trail heads 2.5 miles up Huber Wash, through painted desert and canyons. One of the highlights of hiking in this area, besides the desert scenery, is the abundance of petrified wood. There's even a logjam of petrified wood at the 2.5-mile mark, where the trail ends in a box canyon, decked with a hanging garden. If you're up to a tricky climb over the petrified logjam, you can climb up and catch the Chinle Trail, then hike five miles back to the road on that trail. The Chinle Trail emerges onto Hwy. 9 about 2.5 miles east of the Huber Wash Trailhead.

During the summer, this area of the park can be extremely hot, and in the early spring, it's often too muddy to hike. Thus, this is the ideal autumn hike. Even then, it'll be quite warm. Remember to bring plenty of water.

The Huber Wash Trailhead is about six miles west of the park entrance on Hwy. 9, near a power substation. Because the trail starts outside the park, it's not necessary to pay the park entrance fee if all you want to do is hike in this area.

HIKES IN KOLOB CANYONS
Taylor Creek Trail
This is an excellent day hike from Kolob Canyons Road. The easy-to-moderate trail begins on the left two miles from the Kolob Canyons Visitors Center and heads upstream into the canyon of the Middle Fork of Taylor Creek. Double Arch Alcove is 2.7 miles from the trailhead; a dry fall 0.2 mile farther blocks the way (water flows over it during spring runoff and after rains). A giant rockfall occurred here in June 1990. From this trail you can also explore the North Fork of Taylor Creek. A separate trail along the **South Fork of Taylor Creek** leaves the drive at a bend 3.1 miles from the visitors center, then goes 1.2 miles upstream beneath steep canyon walls.

Kolob Arch
Kolob Arch vies with Landscape Arch in Arches National Park as the world's longest natural rock span. Differences in measurement techniques have resulted in a controversy regarding

ZION AND BRYCE

which is longer: Kolob Arch's span has been measured variously at 292–310 feet, while Landscape Arch's measures at 291–306 feet. Kolob probably takes the prize because its 310-foot measurement was done with an accurate electronic method. Kolob's height is 330 feet and its vertical thickness is 80 feet. The arch makes a fine destination for a backpacking trip. Spring and autumn are the best seasons to go; summer temperatures rise into the 90s and winter snows make the trails hard to follow.

You have a choice of two moderately difficult trails. **La Verkin Creek Trail** begins at Lee Pass (elev. 6,080 feet) on Kolob Canyons Scenic Drive, four miles beyond the visitors center. The trail drops into Timber Creek (intermittent flow), crosses over hills to La Verkin Creek (flows year-round, some springs, too), then turns up side canyons to the arch. The 14-mile round-trip can be done as a long day trip, but you'll enjoy the best lighting for photos at the arch if you camp in the area and see it the following morning. Carry plenty of water for the return trip; the 800-foot climb to the trailhead can be hot and tiring.

You can also hike to Kolob Arch on the **Hop Valley Trail,** reached from Kolob Terrace Road. The Hop Valley Trail is seven miles one-way to Kolob Arch with an elevation drop of 1,050 feet; water is available in Hop Valley and La Verkin Creek. You may have to do some wading in the creek, and the trail crosses private land (don't camp there).

HIKES FROM LAVA POINT

Two trails—West Rim and Wildcat Canyon—begin from Lava Point Trailhead in the remote West Rim area of the park. You can reach the trailhead via the Kolob Terrace Road or by hiking the one-mile **Barney's Trail** from site 2 in the Lava Point campground.

The **West Rim Trail** goes southeast to Zion Canyon, 13.3 miles one-way with an elevation drop of 3,600 feet (3,000 of them in the last six miles). Water can normally be found along the way at Sawmill, Potato Hollow, and Cabin Springs.

The **Wildcat Canyon Trail** heads southwest

five miles to a trailhead on Kolob Terrace Road (16 miles north of Virgin); the elevation drop is 450 feet. This trail lacks a reliable water source. You can continue north and west toward Kolob Arch by taking the four-mile **Connector Trail** to **Hop Valley Trail.**

Snow blocks the road to Lava Point for much of the year; the usual season is May or June to early November. Check road conditions with the Zion Canyon or Kolob Canyon Visitors Center. From the South Entrance Station in Zion Canyon, drive west 15 miles on Hwy. 9 to Virgin, turn north 21 miles on Kolob Terrace Road (signed Kolob Reservoir), then turn right 1.8 miles to Lava Point.

A special hike for strong swimmers is the **Left Fork of North Creek,** a.k.a. **"The Subway."** This challenging nine-mile day hike involves, at the very least, lots of route-finding and many stream crossings.

Like The Narrows, the Left Fork can be hiked either partway up, then back down (starting and ending at the Left Fork Trailhead) or, with a shuttle, from an upper trailhead at the Wildcat Canyon Trailhead downstream to the Left Fork Trailhead. The "top-to-bottom" route requires rappelling skills and at least 60 feet of climbing rope or webbing. It also involves swimming through several deep sections of very cold water.

Even though it is in a day-use-only zone, the Park Service requires a special permit, which, unlike other Zion backcountry permits, is available ahead of time through a somewhat convoluted lottery process. Prospective hikers should visit the park's website (www.nps.gov/zion), click on the "Backcountry Information" link, then click the "Reservations and Permits," followed by "Subway and Mystery Canyon Reservations." From there you will be introduced to the complicated lottery system of applying for a permit to hike the Subway. Lotteries are run monthly for hiking dates several months in the future. Each lottery entry costs $5, and each individual hiker can apply only once per month. If you're planning this hike at the last minute, try calling 435/772-0170 to see if there are any openings.

ZION AND BRYCE

The Left Fork trailhead is on Kolob Terrace Road 8.1 miles north of Virgin.

BIKING

One of the fringe benefits of the Zion Canyon shuttle bus is the great bicycling that's resulted from the lack of automobile traffic. It used to be way too scary to bike along the narrow, traffic-choked Zion Canyon Scenic Drive, but now it's a joy.

On the stretch of road where cars are permitted—between the visitors center and Canyon Junction (where the Zion–Mount Carmel Highway meets Zion Canyon Scenic Drive)—the two-mile, paved Pa'rus Trail is open to bikers as well as pedestrians, and makes for easy, stress-free pedaling.

If you decide you've had enough cycling, every shuttle bus has a rack that can hold two bicycles. Bike parking is plentiful at the visitors center, Zion Lodge, and most trailheads.

Outside the Zion Canyon area, Kolob Terrace Road is a good place to stretch your legs; it's 22 miles to Kolob Reservoir.

There's really no place to mountain bike within the park, but there are good mountain-biking spots, including places to practice slickrock riding, just outside the park boundaries. It's best to stop by one of the local bike shops for advice and a map of your chosen destination.

Bike rentals and maps are available in Springdale at Bike Zion (1458 Zion Park Blvd., 435/772-3303, www.bikingzion.com) and at Zion Cycles (868 Zion Park Blvd., 435/772-0400).

ROCK CLIMBING

Rock-climbers come to scale the high Navajo sandstone cliffs; after Yosemite, Zion is the nation's most popular big-wall climbing area. However, Zion's sandstone is far more fragile than Yosemite's granite, and has a tendency to crumble and flake, especially when wet. Beginners should avoid these walls—experience with crack climbing is a must.

For route descriptions, pick up a copy of *Desert Rock,* by Eric Bjørnstad, or *Rock*

Horse and mule rides leave from Zion Lodge and travel along the Sand Bench Trail.

© PAUL LEVY

Climbing Utah, by Stewart M. Green. Both books are sold at the visitors center bookstore. The backcountry desk in the visitors center also has a notebook full of route descriptions supplied by past climbers. Check here to make sure your climbing area is open—some are closed to protect nesting peregrine falcons—and remember to bring a pair of binoculars to scout climbing routes from the canyon floor.

If you aren't prepared to tackle the 2,000-foot-high canyon walls, you may want to check out a couple of bouldering sites, both quite close to the south entrance of the park. One huge boulder is 40 yards west of the park entrance; the other is a large slab with a crack, located 0.5 mile north of the entrance.

During the summer, it can be intensely hot on unshaded walls. The best months for climbing are March–May and September–early November.

If watching the climbers at Zion gives you a hankering to scale a wall, the Zion Adventure Company in Springdale (36 Lion Blvd., 435/772-1001, www.zionadventures.com) runs half-day and daylong climbing clinics for beginning and experienced climbers. Similar offerings are provided by Zion Rock and Mountain Guides (1458 Zion Park Blvd., 435/772-3303, www.zionrockguides.com). Because no outfitters are permitted to operate inside the park, these classes are held near St. George.

HORSEBACK RIDING

Trail rides on horses and mules leave from the corral near Zion Lodge (435/772-3810) and head down the Virgin River. A one-hour trip ($30) goes to the Court of the Patriarchs, and a half-day ride ($65) follows the Sand Bench Trail. Riders must be at least seven years old for the short ride, and 10 for the half-day ride, and weigh no more than 220 pounds.

ACCOMMODATIONS AND FOOD

Within the park, lodging is limited to Zion Lodge and the two park campgrounds. Look to Springdale or the East Entrance of the park for more options.

Zion Lodge

This rustic lodge (435/772-7700 or 888/297-2757, www.zionlodge.com, $151 room, $161 cabin) sits in the heart of Zion Canyon, three miles up Zion Canyon Scenic Drive. Zion Lodge provides the only accommodations and food options within the park. It's open year-round; reservations for rooms can be made up to 13 months in advance. During high season, all rooms are booked months in advance.

The lodge restaurant offers a southwestern and Mexican-influenced menu daily for breakfast, lunch, and dinner (435/772-7760, dinner reservations required, most dinner entrées around $15). A snack bar serves decent fast food, including salads (closes in winter).

The lodge also has evening programs, a post office (open Mon.–Sat.), and a gift shop.

Zion Canyon Campgrounds

Campgrounds in the park often fill up on Easter and other major holidays. During the summer, they're often full by early afternoon, so it's best to arrive early in the day. The **South** and **Watchman Campgrounds,** both just inside the South Entrance, have sites for $16 with water but no showers. Watchman has some sites with electrical hookups for $18; prime riverside spots are $20. Reservations can be made in advance for some sites at Watchman Campground (877/444-6777, www.recreation.gov). One of the campgrounds stays open in winter.

South Campground is a bit smaller and than Watchman, with a few choice walk-in sites and easy access to the Pa'rus Trail, but tenters shouldn't eschew Watchman; loops C and D are for tents, and these sites are more spacious than those at South. Some of the pioneers' fruit trees in the campgrounds are still producing; you're free to pick your own.

Private campgrounds lie just outside the park in Springdale and just east of the park's east entrance.

It should be noted that camping in Zion's two big campgrounds can be pretty laid back; indeed, it can be luxurious. Campers have easy access, via the park's free shuttles, to good restaurants in Springdale. It's also simple enough to find showers in Springdale; just outside the park, the privately owned Zion Canyon Campground has showers ($4).

Other Campgrounds
Up the Kolob Terrace Road, find Lava Point Campground (see *Lava Point* under *Kolob Terrace* section). The **Red Ledge Campground** (435/586-9150, $24 tent or RV), in Kanarraville, is the closest commercial campground to the Kolob Canyons area (there's no camp-

ground in this area of the park); go two miles north on I-15, take Exit 42, and continue 4.5 miles into downtown Kanarraville. The campground is open year-round with tent and RV sites, cabins, a store, showers, and a laundry room. The tiny agricultural community here was named after a local Paiute chief. A low ridge south of town marks the southern limit of prehistoric Lake Bonneville. Hikers can explore trails in Spring and Kanarra Canyons within the **Spring Canyon Wilderness Study Area** just east of town.

Vicinity of Zion National Park

Just past the mouth of Zion Canyon, near the park's south entrance, are several small towns with good—even appealing—services for travelers. Springdale has the widest range of services, including excellent lodgings and restaurants; Rockville has a few B&Bs; and Hurricane is a hub for less-expensive chain motels.

SPRINGDALE AND VICINITY
Mormons settled this tiny town (pop. about 500) in 1862, but with its location just outside the park's south entrance, Springdale is geared more toward serving park visitors than the typical Mormon settlement. Its many high-quality motels and B&Bs, as well as frequent shuttle bus service into the park, make Springdale an appealing base for a visit to Zion. Farther down the road toward Hurricane are the little towns of Rockville and Virgin, both of which are quickly becoming B&B suburbs of Springdale.

Zion Canyon Giant Screen Theatre
You *know* you should be in the park itself, not looking at movies of it on a six-story-tall screen (145 Zion Park Blvd., 435/772-2400 or 888/256-3456, films start on the hour, 11 A.M.–8 P.M. in summer, winter hours vary, $8 adults, $5.50 children under 12). But, assuming you've been out hiking all day and need a little rest, come here to meet the Ana-

sazi, watch Spanish explorers seek golden treasure, witness the hardships of pioneer settlers, enter remote slot canyons, and join rock-climbers hundreds of feet up vertical cliff faces. The feature program is *Treasure of the Gods,* but there's nearly always a big-screen version of a Hollywood movie showing as well (don't expect to see current hits; all the movies are a few years old).

O. C. Tanner Amphitheater
The summer highlight at this open-air theater (435/652-7994) is a series of musical concerts held on Saturday evenings throughout the summer. The amphitheater is located just outside the park entrance.

Outfitters
Several good outfitters have shops in Springdale, just outside the park. Here you can buy all manner of gear and outdoor clothing. You can also pick up canyoneering skills, take a guided mountain bike ride (outside the park, of course), or learn to climb big sandstone walls.

Campers who left that crucial piece of equipment at home should visit **Zion Outdoors** (868 Zion Park Blvd., 435/772-0630), as should anybody who needs to spruce up their wardrobe with some stylish outdoor clothing.

Zion Cycles (868 Zion Park Blvd., 435/772-0400, www.zioncycles.com) and **Bike Zion**

(1458 Zion Park Blvd., 435/772-3303, www.bikingzion.com) both offer rentals of all sorts of bikes, from kids' bikes ($10 for a half-day rental) to road bikes ($25 half day) to full-suspension mountain bikes ($35 half day).

Canyoneering supplies, including gear to hike the Narrows or the Subway, are available from **Zion Adventure Company** (36 Lion Blvd., 435/772-1001, www.zionadventures.com) and **Zion Rock and Mountain Guides** (1458 Zion Park Blvd., 435/772-3303, www.zionrockguides.com).

Accommodations

$50-100

The least expensive lodgings in Springdale are the motel rooms at the **Terrace Brook Lodge** (990 Zion Park Blvd., 435/772-3237, http://terracebrooklodge.com, $60 and up) and the **El Rio Lodge** (995 Zion Park Blvd., 888/772-3205 or 435/772-3205, www.elriolodge.com, $52 and up), which offers rooms in a green, shady location with a sundeck. Both are about a mile from the park entrance. If you want to be closer to the park entrance, **Zion Canyon Campground** (479 Zion Park Blvd., 435/772-3237, www.zioncanyoncampground.com, $65 and up) has motel rooms as well as tent and RV sites. The **Canyon Ranch Motel** (668 Zion Park Blvd., 435/772-3357 or 866/946-6276, www.canyonranchmotel.com, $64 and up) is another good value, with small units—some with kitchenettes—scattered around a grassy, shaded lawn.

The hosts at the **Bunkhouse at Zion B&B** (149 E. Main St., Rockville, 435/772-3393, www.bunkhouseatzion.com, $55–80) are dedicated to living sustainably, and they bring this ethic into their two-room B&B. The views are remarkable from this quiet spot in Rockville.

The **Driftwood Lodge** (1515 Zion Park Blvd., 435/772-3262 or 800/528-1234, www.driftwoodlodgeandsuites.com, $72 and up) has a pool and a spa, and is a step up from the budget motels. Another mid-range choice is the **Zion Park Motel** (865 Zion Park Blvd., 435/772-3251, www.zionparkmotel.com, $79) with clean basic rooms and a small pool.

In Springdale, **Under the Eaves B&B** (980 Zion Park Blvd., 435/772-3457, www.under-the-eaves.com, $80 and up) features homey guest rooms, two with shared bath, in a vintage home. It's also possible to pay a bit more for a gorgeous kitchenette suite. Children over seven are welcome.

Down the road in Rockville, **Rockville Rose Inn** (125 E. Main St., Rockville, 435/772-0800, www.rockvillerose.com, $75–100) has rooms in a large Victorian set back from the road.

OVER $100

◖ **Flanigan's Inn** (428 Zion Park Blvd., 435/772-3244 or 800/765-7787, www.flanigans.com, $109 and up) is a quiet and convenient place to stay. Rooms are set back off the main drag and face onto a pretty courtyard. Up on the hill behind the inn, a labyrinth provides an opportunity to take a meditative walk in a stunning setting. An excellent restaurant, a pool, and spa services make this an inviting place to spend several days.

Probably the most elegant place to stay in Springdale is the ◖ **Desert Pearl Inn** (707 Zion Park Blvd., 888/828-0898 or 435/772-8888, www.desertpearl.com, $143 and up), a very handsome lodgelike hotel perched above the Virgin River. (Some rooms have views of the river; others face the pool.) Much of the wood used for the beams and the finish moldings was salvaged from a railroad trestle made of century-old Oregon fir and redwood that once spanned the north end of the Great Salt Lake. The rooms are all large and beautifully furnished, with a modern look.

Another attractive newer motel is **Best Western Zion Park Inn** (1215 Zion Park Blvd., 435/772-3200 or 800/934-7275, www.zionparkinn.com, $115 and up), part of a complex with a good restaurant, a swimming pool, a gift shop, and some of the nicest rooms in Springdale. In addition to regular rooms, there are also various suites and kitchen units available.

Just outside the south gates to Zion, the ◖ **Cliffrose Lodge** (281 Zion Park Blvd.,

435/772-3234 or 800/243-8824, www.cliff roselodge.com, $139 and up) sits in five acres of lovely, well-landscaped gardens with riverfront access. The rooms are equally nice, and there's a pool and a laundry room. The Cliffrose is favored by many longtime Zion fans.

For a place with a bit of personality (or perhaps, more accurately, with multiple personalities), try the **Novel House Inn at Zion** (73 Paradise Rd., 435/772-3650 or 800/711-8400, www.novelhouse.com, $129–149), a B&B with 10 guest rooms, each decorated with a literary theme and named after an author (including Mark Twain, Rudyard Kipling, and Louis L'Amour). All rooms have private baths and great views, and the B&B is tucked off the main drag.

Red Rock Inn (998 Zion Park Blvd., 435/772-3139, www.redrockinn.com, $112 and up) offers accommodations in newly constructed individual cabins, all with canyon views. Full-breakfast baskets are delivered to your door.

CAMPGROUNDS

The **Zion Canyon Campground** (479 Zion Park Blvd., 435/772-3237, $22 tent, $27 RV) offers cabins, new motel rooms, tent sites (no dogs allowed in tent sites), and RV sites. Though the sites are pretty close together, a few are situated right on the bank of the Virgin River. Facilities include a store, pizza parlor, game room, laundry room, and showers.

Food

Just outside the park entrance, near the Springdale shuttle stop, **Sol Foods** (95 Zion Park Blvd., 435/772-0277, 7 A.M.–10 P.M. daily, $6.50–9) is a short walk from either park campground and a good place for a salad or sandwich. There's also a computer with Internet access.

Mean Bean Coffee (932 Zion Park Blvd., 435/772-0654, 6:30 A.M.–afternoon daily) is the hip place to hang in the morning. Besides coffee drinks, they serve breakfast burritos and a few pastries. For a more substantial meal, head across the way to **Oscar's Café** (948 Zion

Park Blvd., 435/772-3232, 8 A.M.–two hours after sunset daily, $8–17) where you can get a good burger or a Mexican-influenced breakfast or lunch. The patio here is set back off the main road and is especially pleasant.

An old gas station has become the **(Whiptail Grill** (445 Zion Park Blvd., 435/772-0283, lunch and early dinner daily, $8–13), a casual spot serving innovative homemade food such as spaghetti-squash enchiladas. There's very little seating inside, so plan to eat at the outdoor tables or take your meal to go.

Also good, and reasonably priced, is **Zion Pizza and Noodle** (868 Zion Park Blvd., 435/772-3815, dinner nightly, $9–20), housed in an old church and serving a good selection of microbrews. The American-style menu at the **Bumbleberry Inn** (897 Zion Park Blvd., 435/772-3224, breakfast, lunch, and dinner Mon.–Sat., $5–20) includes bumbleberry pies (just ask them what a bumbleberry is) and pancakes.

The following restaurants all offer full liquor service: The **(Spotted Dog Café** (at Flanigan's Inn, 428 Zion Park Blvd., 435/772-3244, breakfast, lunch, and dinner daily, $12–24) is one of Springdale's top restaurants; it has varied Southwestern and traditional American offerings, including a surprisingly good pumpkin-seed pizza. Be sure to order a salad with (or for) your dinner—the house salad is superb. If you want to eat outside, try to get a table on the back patio, which is quieter and more intimate than the dining area out front.

The other really good place for dinner in Springdale is the **(Bit and Spur Restaurant** (1212 Zion Park Blvd., 435/772-3498, dinner nightly, $10–25, reservations recommended during busy season), a lively Mexican place with a menu that goes far beyond the usual south-of-the-border concoctions. (Keep your fingers crossed that sweet-potato tamales will be the evening's special.)

Across the street from the Bit and Spur, the **Switchback Grille** (1215 Zion Park Blvd., 435/772-3200, breakfast, lunch, and dinner daily, $14–25) offers steaks, wood-fired pizza, rotisserie chicken, and seafood in a pleasantly bland atmosphere. There's patio seating in good weather.

Information and Services

People traveling with their dogs are in a bit of a dilemma when it comes to visiting Zion. No pets are allowed on the trails (except the Pa'rus Trail) or in the shuttle buses, and it's absolutely unconscionable to leave a dog inside a car here in the warmer months. Fortunately, the **Doggy Dude Ranch** (800 E. Main St./Hwy. 9, Rockville, 435/772-3105, www .doggyduderanch.com) provides conscientious daytime and overnight pet care.

The **Zion Canyon Medical Clinic** (120 Lion Blvd., 435/772-3226) provides urgent-care services. The **post office** is in the center of town on Zion Park Boulevard (435/772-3950). You may also want to check out the art galleries along Zion Park Boulevard; some of them have high-quality merchandise.

GRAFTON

Grafton is one of the best-preserved and most picturesque ghost towns in Utah. Mormon families founded Grafton in 1859 near the Virgin River at a spot one mile downstream from the present site, but a big flood two years later convinced them to move here. Hostilities with the Paiutes during the Black Hawk War forced residents to depart again for safer areas from 1866 to 1868. Floods and irrigation difficulties made life hard even in the best of times, and the population declined in the early 1900s until only ghosts remained.

Moviemakers discovered Grafton and used it for *Butch Cassidy and the Sundance Kid,* among other films. You may notice a few fiberglass chimneys and other "improvements." A schoolhouse, store, houses, cabins, and outbuildings still stand. One story goes that the Mormon bishop lived in the large two-story house with wife number one while wife number two had to settle for the rough cabin across the road—probably not an amicable situation! Grafton's cemetery is worth a visit, too; it's on the left at a turn 0.3 mile before the town site. A monument commemorates three settlers

killed by Native Americans in 1866. Many of Grafton's families now live in nearby Rockville; they tend the cemetery and look after the old buildings. From Springdale, follow Hwy. 9 southwest two miles to Rockville and turn south 3.5 miles on Bridge Road (200 East). The last 2.6 miles are unpaved but should be okay for cars in dry weather; keep right at a road junction 1.6 miles past Rockville.

CANAAN MOUNTAIN

The rocky hills south of Springdale and Rockville offer fine scenery for back-road drives or hikes. The **Smithsonian Butte National Back Country Byway,** a nine-mile dirt road from the Grafton road, climbs into the scenic high country south of the Virgin River and continues to Hwy. 59 (near milepost 8) between Hurricane and Hildale on the other side; follow the directions to Grafton but turn left at the road junction 1.6 miles past Rockville. Panoramas take in Zion National Park, Smithsonian Butte, Canaan Mountain, and the rugged countryside all around. You can also find good places to hike or camp along the way. Cars with good clearance can usually make this trip if the road is dry.

Canaan Mountain (elev. 7,200 feet), a wilderness study area south of Springdale, rises more than 2,000 feet above the surrounding land. The summit is a plateau of rolling slickrock, pinnacles, balanced rocks, and deep fractures similar to the plateaus of Zion National Park. High cliffs on three sides give you the feeling of being on an island in the sky. **Eagle Crags Trailhead** (elev. 4,400 feet) near Rockville provides access from the north past the Eagle Crags, a group of towering sandstone monoliths. **Squirrel Canyon Trailhead** (elev. 5,100 feet) near Hildale is the starting point for hikes from the south via Water or Squirrel Canyon. This is pretty wild country, and it's best to head in with maps, compass, and the ability to use both. See the USGS 7.5-minute topo maps Springdale West, Springdale East, Smithsonian Butte, and Hildale. Contact the BLM office in St. George (435/688-3200, www.ut.blm.gov/stgeorge_ fo/sgfocanaan.html) for more details.

ZION AND BRYCE

HURRICANE AND VICINITY

Legend has it that in the early 1860s a group of pioneers was descending the steep cliffs above the present town site when a strong wind came up; Erastus Snow compared it with a hurricane and named the place Hurricane Hill. (By the way, locals pronounce the town's name as HUR-uh-kun.) A canal to bring water from the Virgin River to Hurricane Bench took 11 years of hard work to build, beginning in 1893, but it allowed farming in the area for the first time. Settlers founded the town in 1906. Many retirees and winter visitors live here now.

Enjoy the small but select collection of pioneer and Native American artifacts on display at the **Hurricane Valley Heritage Park and Museum** (35 W. State St., 435/635-3245, 9 A.M.–5 P.M. Mon.–Sat.).

Recreation

Inner Light Yoga Center (134 S. Main, 435/635-3981) offers several classes a week.

Sky Mountain Golf Course (1030 North 2600 West, 435/635-7888, from $16 for 18 holes) is one of the state's most highly regarded public golf courses, with some of the most reasonable greens fees. The setting is spectacular, with the Hurricane Cliffs looming behind; volcanic outcrops jut up through the fairways, making for unique natural obstacles. This par-72 course has 18 holes; facilities include a clubhouse with full rental options.

Accommodations

Hurricane has a scattering of inexpensive chain motels. It's a good place to stay if you're looking to save a few bucks, but if you value luxury (or even a comfy mattress and a quiet room), there are better, though more expensive, choices in Springdale. Even the nicest place in this modest town is not a budget-breaker, but it's not fancy, either: the **Comfort Inn** (43 N. 2600 W., 435/635-3500 or 800/635-3577, $50–65) has a pool and hot tub. **Travelodge Zion** (280 W. State, 435/635-4647, www.travelodgezion .com, $44) has an outdoor pool and a hot tub. The **Days Inn** (40 North 2600 West, 435/635-0500 or 800/325-2525, www.daysinn.com,

$40–60) has an indoor pool and complimentary continental breakfast.

CAMPGROUNDS

The best bet for tent campers is **Quail Creek State Park** (472 N 5300 W, 435/879-2378, http://stateparks.utah.gov, $12 camping fee), 6.5 miles west of town, then two miles north, it's on a reservoir with swimming access. **Zion's Gate RV Resort** (150 N 3700 W, 435/635-2320 or 800/447-2239), 4.5 miles west of town, is open year-round with a nine-hole golf course, indoor pool, tennis courts, recreation room, and showers; a restaurant, bowling alley, water slide, and mini golf course are across the street.

Food

Turn off busy State Street and away from its chain restaurants to find **Main St. Cafe** (138 S. Main, 435/635-9086, breakfast and lunch Tues.–Sat., $6–9). Here you'll find good food served either inside, in a gallery-like space, or outside, on quiet Main Street.

DINOSAUR TRACKWAYS

Back in the Early Jurassic, when the supercontinent of Pangaea was just beginning to break up, lakes covered this part of present-day Utah, and dinosaurs were becoming the earth's dominant vertebrates. Two sites southeast of St. George preserve dinosaur tracks from this era. Of the two, the more recently discovered site at Johnson Farm is more impressive and much easier to get to; indeed, it's been called one of the world's ten best dinosaur track sites. The Fort Pearce site is good if you're hankering for some back-road travel and scouting dino tracks and petroglyphs in remote washes.

◖ St. George Dinosaur Discovery Site at Johnson Farm

Tracks at the Johnson Farm site (2180 E. Riverside Dr., 435/574-3466, www.dinotrax.com, 10 A.M.–6 P.M. Mon.–Sat., $3 adults, $2 children 3–11) were discovered in 2000 by a retired optometrist. Since then, a vast number of tracks, including those of three species of theropods (meat-eating dinosaurs), and important "trace fossils" of pond scum, plants, invertebrates, and fish have also been uncovered.

Excavation work is ongoing, but a new visitors center provides a good look at some of the most exciting finds, including a wall-sized slab of rock with footprints going to and fro. Also quite remarkable are the "swim tracks," which settled a long-standing argument over whether or not dinosaurs actually swam.

The track site is on the outskirts of St. George, about two miles south of Exit 10 from I-15.

Fort Pearce Dinosaur Tracks

A scenic back-road drive through the desert between St. George and Hurricane passes the ruins of Fort Pearce and more dinosaur tracks. Much of the road is unpaved and has rough and sandy spots, but it's usually suitable for cautious drivers in dry weather.

This group of tracks documents the passage of at least two different dinosaur species more than 200 million years ago. The well-preserved tracks, in the Moenave Formation, were made by a 20-foot-long herbivore weighing an estimated 8–10 tons and by a carnivore half as long. No remains of the dinosaurs themselves have been found here.

In 1861, ranchers arrived in Warner Valley to run cattle on the desert grasslands. Four years later, however, Indian troubles threatened to drive the settlers out. The Black Hawk War and periodic raids by Navajo Indians made life precarious. Springs in Fort Pearce Wash—the only reliable water for many miles—proved the key to domination of the region. In December 1866, work began on a fort overlooking the springs. The stone walls stood about eight feet high and were more than 30 feet long. No roof was ever added. Much of the fort and the adjacent corral (built in 1869) have survived to the present. Local cattlemen still use the springs for their herds. Petroglyphs can be seen in various places along the wash, including a quarter mile downstream from the fort along ledges on the north side of the wash.

To reach this somewhat remote site from St. George, head south on River Road, cross the Virgin River Bridge, and turn left on 1450 South. Continue on main road and keep bearing east through several 90-degree left and right turns. Turn left (east) onto a dirt road at the Fort Pearce sign and continue 5.6 miles to a road that branches right along a small wash to the Fort Pearce parking lot. The dinosaur tracks are in a wash about two miles farther down the road from Fort Pearce; the parking area is marked by a sign.

St. George

Southern Utah's largest town lies between lazy bends of the Virgin River on one side and rocky hills of red sandstone on the other. Although it has gained a reputation as a retirement haven (thanks in large part to its warm winter climate and its plethora of golf courses), it is not particularly appealing to most travelers. In order to appreciate St. George, it may be necessary to visit its outskirts, where Snow Canyon State Park and a couple of spas can be found.

In 1861, more than 300 Mormon families in the Salt Lake City area answered the call to go south to start the Cotton Mission, of which St. George became the center (hence the frequently used term "Dixie" to describe the area). The settlers overcame great difficulties to farm and to build an attractive city in this remote desert. Brigham Young chose the city's name to honor George A. Smith, who had served as head of the Southern (Iron) Mission during the 1850s. (The title "Saint" means simply that he was a Mormon—a Latter-day Saint.) Visits to some of the historic sites will add to your appreciation of the city's past; ask for the brochure *St. George Historic Walking Tour* at the chamber of commerce. The warm climate, dramatic setting, and many year-round recreation opportunities have helped

ZION AND BRYCE ·

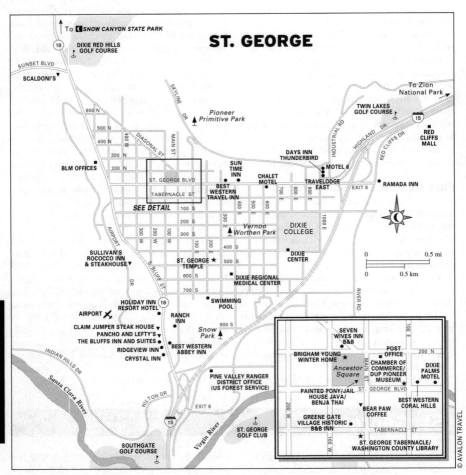

make St. George (pop. about 50,000) the fastest-growing city in the state. Local boosters claim that this is where Utah's summer sun spends the winter.

SIGHTS
St. George Temple
Visible for miles, the city's gleaming white temple (250 East 400 South, at the corner of 200 South, 435/673-5181) rises from landscaped grounds in the center of St. George. In 1871, enthusiastic Mormons from all over the territory gathered to erect the temple. Dedicated on April 6, 1877, the structure was the church's first sacred house of worship in the West. The St. George Temple is the oldest active Mormon temple in the world. It's constructed of stuccoed stone in a castellated Gothic Revival style; a cupola with a weather vane caps the structure. Sacred ceremonies take place inside, so no tours are offered, but you're welcome to visit the grounds to admire the architecture. The

temple is especially impressive at night when it's lit up against the black sky. A visitors center (9 A.M.–9 P.M.) on the northeast corner of the grounds has short films and videos introducing the LDS Church.

St. George Tabernacle

When Brigham Young visited the Cotton Mission after its first year, he found the community afflicted with difficulties and low morale. Soon after, he ordered construction of a tabernacle (18 S. Main St., 435/673-5181, 9 A.M.–6 P.M. daily in summer, 9 A.M.–5 P.M. daily in winter) to help rally the members. The task, paid for with tithes, took 13 years to complete. Builders used local red sandstone for the walls and placed a slender white steeple on the roof, reminiscent of a New England church.

Brigham Young Winter Home

Late in life, Brigham Young sought relief from arthritis and other aches and pains by spending winters in Dixie's mild climate. This also gave him an opportunity to supervise more closely the affairs of the church here, especially construction of the temple. A telegraph line connected Young's house (67 West 200 North, 435/673-5181, 9 A.M.–7 P.M. daily in summer, 9 A.M.–5 P.M. in winter) with Salt Lake City. He moved here late in 1873 and returned each winter until his death in 1877. The carefully restored adobe house contains furnishings of the era, including some that belonged to Young. Fruit and mulberry trees grow in the yard; mulberry leaves once fed the silkworms of the short-lived pioneer industry. Free tours begin at Young's office on the east side of the house.

Jacob Hamblin Home

No one did more to extend the Mormons' southern settlements and keep peace with the Native Americans than Jacob Hamblin. He came west in 1850 with four children (his first wife refused to come) and settled in the Tooele area with wife number two. At Brigham Young's request, Hamblin moved south in 1856 and helped build the Santa Clara Fort. He built the present sandstone house (Santa Clara Blvd. and Hamblin Drive, 435/673-5181, 9 A.M.–7 P.M. daily in summer, 9 A.M.–5 P.M. in winter) in the village of Santa Clara, four miles northwest of St. George, after floods washed away the fort in 1862. Almost always on the move serving on missions, Hamblin had little time for home life. He moved to Kanab in 1870, then to Arizona and New Mexico. Even so, he had four wives and managed to father 24 children. The kitchen, work areas, and living rooms provide a good idea of what pioneer life was like. Free tours offer a view of the house and tell of activities that once took place here.

Daughters of Utah Pioneers Museum

This museum (145 North 100 East, 435/628-7274, 10 A.M.–5 P.M. Mon.–Sat., by donation), behind the old county courthouse, is staffed by the Daughters of Utah Pioneers. Drop in to see hundreds of pioneer portraits and the tools and clothing used by early settlers. The spinning wheels and looms on display served in the mission's cotton and silk industries.

St. George Art Museum

This relatively new museum (47 East 200 North, 435/627-4525, http://sgcity.org/artmuseum, 10 A.M.–5 P.M. Mon.–Sat., $2 adults, $1 children 3–11), housed in a renovated beet-seed warehouse, is worth a visit both for its exhibits and its design. It's also a good place to get out of the sun for a couple of hours on a sweltering summer afternoon. The permanent collection has a strong regional emphasis; visiting shows often feature contemporary Western art.

ENTERTAINMENT AND EVENTS

Major annual events in St. George include the **Dixie Invitational Art Show** (435/652-7500), which hosts regional artists in February; it begins President's Day weekend at the Fine Arts Building on Dixie College campus.

September brings the **Lions Dixie PRCA Round-Up Rodeo.** In October, the **Huntsman World Senior Games** (800/562-1268) presents

ZION AND BRYCE

a wide variety of Olympic-type competitions for seniors; you'll be amazed at the enthusiasm and abilities. Also in October, the **St. George Marathon** (435/634-5850) attracts about 4,000 runners from all over the United States.

RECREATION

Golf

With 10 golf courses in the area, St. George enjoys a reputation as Utah's winter golf capital. Red sandstone cliffs serve as the backdrop for **Dixie Red Hills** (1250 N. 645 West, 435/634-5852) on the northwest edge of town, a nine-hole, par-34 municipal course. **Green Spring Golf Course** (588 N. Green Spring Dr., 435/673-7888), just west of I-15 Washington Exit 10, has 18 holes (par 71) and a reputation as one of the finest courses in Utah.

Professionals favor the cleverly designed **Sunbrook Golf Course** (2366 Sunbrook Dr., 435/634-5866) off Dixie Downs Road, between Green Valley and Santa Clara: 27 holes, par 72. The **St. George Golf Club** (2190 S. 1400 East, 435/634-5854) has a popular 18-hole, par-73 course south of town in Bloomington Hills. The **Southgate Golf Course** (1975 S. Tonaquint Dr., 435/628-0000), on the southwest edge of town, has 18 holes. The adjacent **Southgate Game Improvement Center** (435/674-7728) can provide golfers with computerized golf-swing analyses plus plenty of indoor practice space and lots of balls. **Entrada** (2511 W. Entrada Trail, 435/674-7500) is a newer 18-hole private course that's fast on its way to becoming St. George's most respected. The Johnny Miller–designed course is located northwest of St. George at beautiful Snow Canyon and incorporates natural lava flows, rolling dunes, and *arroyos* (dry river beds) into its design. The 18-hole, par-72 **Sky Mountain** (1030 N. 2600 W., 435/635-7888) is located northeast of St. George in nearby Hurricane.

Spas

St. George is home to two large spa resorts and recreation centers in gorgeous natural settings. The **Green Valley Spa** (1871 West Canyon View Dr., 435/628-8060 or 800/237-1068, www.greenvalleyspa.com, $112 and up per person, double occupancy, for room only, $564 and up per person per night for a package with all meals and lots of treatments and activities) is a fitness, sports, health, and beauty spa with all-inclusive rates. Facilities include three pools, racquetball courts, a fully equipped gym with an array of fitness, yoga, and meditation classes as well as tennis instruction, golf privileges, plus hiking and climbing in neighboring canyons. There's also a whole catalog of beauty and rejuvenation treatments (which may be included in a package deal or tacked on at extra cost), ranging from massage, wraps, and aromatherapy to more spiritual renewals such as personal meditation guidance. Rooms flank a park-like pool and garden area. Three spa meals daily are served; they're included in the cost of most packages. Rates vary widely; summer is the least expensive time to visit.

Slightly less swanky, the **Red Mountain Spa** (202 N. Snow Canyon Rd., 800/407-3002, www.redmountainspa.com, $240 and up per person per day, double occupancy) focuses even more intently on outdoor adventure and fitness. Facilities include numerous swimming and soaking pools, a fitness center and gym, tennis courts, a salon, a spa, conference rooms, plus access to lots of hiking and biking trails. Prices include all meals, lodging, and use of most spa facilities and recreation. Special deals are often available online. Spa services, including massage, facials, body polishing, and aromatherapy, cost extra.

Other Recreation

Vernon Worthen Park (400 East and 200 South) offers shaded picnic tables, a playground, and tennis courts. **J. C. Snow Park** (400 East and 900 South) has picnic tables and a playground (but little shade). **Pioneer Primitive Park** overlooks the city from the north; in desert country just off Skyline Drive, it has a few picnic tables. The outdoor public **swimming pool** (250 East 700 South, 435/634-5867, Memorial Day–Labor Day) features a hydro slide. **Tennis** players may use the public courts at Dixie College and Vernon Worthen Park.

ACCOMMODATIONS

St. George offers many places to stay and eat. Motel prices stay about the same year-round, although they may drop if business is slow in summer. Considering the popularity of this destination, prices are reasonable. Golfers should ask about golf-and-lodging packages. You'll find most lodgings along the busy I-15 business route of St. George Boulevard (Exit 8) and Bluff Street (Exit 6). As for food, you'll find almost every fast-food place known to humanity just off the interstate on St. George Boulevard.

Under $50

Many of St. George's less expensive lodging choices operate at Exit 8 off I-15 or on St. George Boulevard as it heads west to downtown. Right at the freeway exchange you'll find **Motel 6** (205 N. 1000 East, 435/628-7979 or 800/466-8356, $41–59), with a pool; pets are okay.

Near downtown, the **Chalet Motel** (664 E. St. George Blvd., 435/628-6272, $30–60) offers some efficiency kitchens, two three-bed rooms, and a pool. **Dixie Palms Motel** (185 East St. George Blvd., 435/673-3531, $30–50) is a classic old-fashioned courtyard motel on the main strip right downtown with an outdoor pool and fridges and microwaves in the rooms. The **Sun Time Inn** (420 E. St. George Blvd., 435/673-6181 or 800/237-6253, $35–60, higher in winter) has kitchenettes and a pool.

Near Exit 6 off I-15, the **Ridgeview Inn** (1230 S. Bluff St., 435/628-5234 or 800/275-3494, $40–50) offers a pool and a spa.

$50-100

The **Days Inn Thunderbird** (150 N. 1000 East, 435/673-6123 or 800/527-6543, $50 and up) has a pool, hot tub, sauna, fitness center, free continental breakfast, and pets are okay.

In the downtown area, the Spanish-style **Best Western Travel Inn** (316 E. St. George Blvd., 435/673-3541 or 800/528-1234, $65–83) is a relatively small motel with an outdoor pool and an indoor spa.

Leave the freeway at Exit 6 off I-15 to find another selection of motels. Most rooms at **The Bluffs Inn and Suites** (1140 S. Bluff St., 435/628-6699 or 800/832-5833, $50–90) are suites with efficiency kitchens. Facilities include a pool and a spa; pets are okay.

Close to downtown is one of St. George's best: the **Best Western Coral Hills** (125 E. St. George Blvd., 435/673-4844 or 800/542-7733, www.coralhills.com, $80–120), a very attractive property with indoor and outdoor pools and two spas, an exercise room, and a complimentary continental breakfast.

Leave the I-15 freeway at Exit 6 to find another bevy of motels. The **Holiday Inn Resort Hotel and Convention Center** (850 S. Bluff St., 435/628-4235 or 800/457-9800, www.histgeorgeutah.com, $80 and up) is a large complex with a "Holidome" complete with indoor and outdoor pools, whirlpool, recreation/fitness facilities, tennis court, and putting green. At the **Best Western Abbey Inn** (1129 S. Bluff St., 888/222-3946 or 435/652-1234, www.bwabbeyinn.com, $85–95), all rooms have microwaves and refrigerators. There's an outdoor pool, an indoor spa, recreation/fitness facilities, and a free hot breakfast. Both of these lodgings are near Exit 6 off I-15.

Just across from Brigham Young's winter home, the **Seven Wives Inn Bed and Breakfast** (217 N. 100 West, 435/628-3737 or 800/600-3737, www.sevenwivesinn.com, $90 and up) offers rooms in two historic homes (including one that served as a safe house for polygamists after the practice was banned in the 1880s) and a cute cottage. All guest rooms have private baths and are decorated with antiques. Children and pets are welcome; there's an outdoor pool, and in-room massages are available.

You'll find an entire compound of pioneer-era homes at the **Greene Gate Village Historic Bed and Breakfast Inn** (76 W. Tabernacle, 435/628-6999 or 800/350-6999, www.greengatevillage.com, $89 and up). Nine beautifully restored homes offer a variety of lodging options—groups or families can rent an entire home. Many rooms come with kitchens and private baths, some with private whirlpools. There's also a pool shared by all guests. Children are welcome.

East of the Exit 8 interchange, right beside the Factory Outlet Mall, is the **Ramada Inn** (1440 E. St. George Blvd., 435/628-2828 or 800/713-9435, $75–89). Facilities include an outdoor pool and a hot tub; a complimentary continental breakfast is also included.

Over $100

The **Crystal Inn** (1450 S. Hilton Inn Dr., 435/688-7477 or 800/662-2525, www.crystal inns.com, $115) is located on a golf course and has beautiful public areas and nicely appointed guest rooms. Facilities include a pool, a sauna, and private tennis courts.

Campgrounds

The best camping in the area is at **Snow Canyon State Park** (435/628-2255 or 800/322-3770, www.reserveamerica.com, reservations necessary in spring, $15 without hookups, $18 with hookups). Sites are in a pretty canyon and include showers. From downtown St. George, go 12 miles north on Hwy. 18, then left two miles.

The BLM's **Red Cliffs Recreation Site** (1 mi. west of I-15 at Leeds, 435/688-3200, $8) is north of town off I-15, Exit 16 when coming from the south, Exit 23 when approaching from the north. Quail Creek State Park shares the same exit, but Red Cliffs is a little more scenic and has trails.

Right in St. George, **McArthur's Temple View RV Resort** (975 S. Main, 435/673-6400 or 800/776-6410, $29 tent, $39 RV) is located near the temple district and has a pool, laundry room, and showers. East of town, near Exit 8 off I-15, is **Settlers RV Park** (1333 E. 100 South, 435/628-1624, $19–28 RV), with a pool and showers. The park accepts RVs only.

FOOD

For a major recreation and retirement center, St. George is curiously lacking in unique places to eat. Almost every chain restaurant can be found here, but don't expect a bevy of local fine-dining houses. You'll also find it bizarrely difficult to find restaurants that stay open late; even in high season, most restaurants close by 9 P.M.

The best place to head for lunch or dinner is Ancestor's Square, a trendy shopping development at the intersection of St. George Boulevard and Main Street. **Painted Pony** (435/634-1700, lunch and dinner Mon.–Sat., dinner Sun., $21–31) puts Southwestern and, in some cases, Asian touches on American standards; try salmon rolls with a carrot orange sauce or, for lunch, a pulled pork sandwich with poblano aioli ($9). Downstairs from the Painted Pony is another pretty good restaurant, **Benja Thai and Sushi** (435/628-9538, lunch and dinner Tues.–Sat., $10–12), one of the very few Thai restaurants in southern Utah. Also in Ancestor's Square is the tiny **Jail House Java** (435/668-1819, 8 A.M.–6 P.M. Mon.–Sat.).

Just across St. George Boulevard, **Bear Paw Coffee** (75 N. Main St., 435/634-0126, breakfast and lunch daily, $5–11) is another of the few places in town to hang out and drink coffee. Breakfasts are large and delicious.

For formal dining and spectacular views, head west toward the airport for **Sullivan's Rococo Inn and Steak House** (511 Airport Rd., 435/628-3671, lunch and dinner daily, $15–28), where prime rib, steak, and seafood are the specialties. The best Italian food in town is at **Scaldoni's Gourmet Grill** (Phoenix Plaza Mall, 929 W. Sunset Blvd., 435/674-1300, lunch Mon.–Fri., dinner nightly, $10–28), with some delicious pasta dishes (including the rich Bolognese) and a variety of meat and seafood entrées.

INFORMATION AND SERVICES

The **St. George Chamber of Commerce** (97 E. St. George Blvd., 435/628-1658, www .stgeorgechamber.com, Mon.–Fri. 9 A.M.– 5 P.M., Sat. 9 A.M.–1 P.M.), in the old county courthouse (built 1866–1876), can tell you about the sights, events, and services of southwestern Utah; it has brochures of accommodations, restaurants, a historic walking tour, and area ghost towns. Another good online source of information is www.utahsdixie.com.

For recreation, see the **Pine Valley Ranger District office** (196 E. Tabernacle, 435/688-3246, www.fs.fed.us/r4/dixie, Mon.–Fri. 8 A.M.–5 P.M.) for information on fishing, hiking, and camping in the Dixie National Forest north of town. Maps of the forest and Pine Valley Wilderness are available. The **Bureau of Land Management** (345 E. Riverside, 435/688-3200, www.ut.blm.gov/stgeorge_fo/, 8 A.M.–4:30 P.M. Mon.–Fri.) oversees vast lands in Utah's southwest corner and the Arizona Strip.

The **post office** is at 180 North Main (435/673-3312). The **Dixie Regional Medical Center** provides hospital care (544 S. 400 East, 435/688-4000).

TRANSPORTATION

United and **Delta** (represented by SkyWest) both fly into the St. George Municipal Airport (SGU, 317 S. Donlee Dr., 435/634-5822). Several of the usual rental-car companies operate at the St. George airport: **Budget** (435/673-6825 or 800/527-0700), **Avis** (435/627-2002 or 800/230-4898), and **Hertz** (435/652-9941 or 800/654-3131).

SkyWest Airlines, in partnership with Delta, has several daily direct flights to Salt Lake City and Las Vegas. United Express flies to Los Angeles. It's an easy drive from Las Vegas to St. George, so travelers may want to consider flying into Vegas and renting a car there.

Greyhound buses (435/673-2933) depart from McDonald's (1235 South Bluff Street) for Salt Lake City, Denver, Las Vegas, and other destinations. The **St. George Shuttle** (435/628-8320 or 800/933-8320, www.stgshuttle.com) will take you to Las Vegas in a 15-passenger van for $30. Trips depart from the Shuttle Lodge Inn (915 South Bluff Street).

Vicinity of St. George

Some good scenic drives begin at St. George. Whether you're short on time or have all day, a good choice is the 24-mile loop through Snow Canyon State Park via Hwy. 18, the park road (Hwy. 300), and Santa Clara. The old highway to Littlefield, Arizona, makes a 67-mile loop with I-15; this route follows former U.S. 91 through the pioneer settlement of Santa Clara and the sparsely settled Shivwits Reservation and over a 4,600-foot pass in the Beaver Dam Mountains to Littlefield; the I-15 section goes through the spectacular Virgin River Gorge upstream from Littlefield. In summer, the cool forests of the Pine Valley Mountains, 37 miles northwest of town, are an especially attractive destination: You can make a 130-mile drive with many possible side trips by circling the mountains on Hwy. 18, Hwy. 56, and I-15. Zion National Park, with its grandeur and color, is about 40 miles northeast of St. George. Adventurous motorists may want to try some of the unpaved roads through the desert east and west of St. George.

◖ SNOW CANYON STATE PARK

North of St. George, Snow Canyon State Park (435/628-2255, 800/322-3770 or www.reserveamerica.com for camping reservations, $5 day-use fee per vehicle, $15–18 camping fee) is a great place to explore and enjoy the desert scenery. Red-rock canyons, sand dunes, volcanoes, and lava flows have formed an incredible landscape. Walls of Navajo sandstone 50–750 feet high enclose five-mile-long Snow Canyon. Hiking trails lead into the backcountry for a closer look at the geology, flora, and fauna. Common plants are barrel, cholla, and prickly pear cacti, yucca, Mormon tea, shrub live oak, cliffrose, and cottonwood. Delicate wildflowers bloom mostly in the spring and autumn, following the wet seasons, but cactus and the sacred datura can flower in the heat of summer. Wildlife includes sidewinder and Great Basin rattlesnakes, Gila monster, desert tortoise, kangaroo rat, squirrel,

ZION AND BRYCE

© PAUL LEVY

Snow Canyon State Park trails are convenient to St. George spa-goers.

cottontail, kit fox, coyote, and mule deer. You may find some Native American rock art, arrowheads, bits of pottery, and ruins. Many of the place-names in the park honor Mormon pioneers. Snow Canyon was named for Lorenzo and Erastus Snow—not for the rare snowfalls. Cooler months have the best weather; summers are too hot for comfortable hiking except in early morning.

Hwy. 18 leads past an overlook on the rim of Snow Canyon and to the paved park road (Hwy. 300) that drops into the canyon and follows it to its mouth and the small town of Ivins. Snow Canyon is about 12 miles northwest of St. George. It's reached either by Hwy. 18—the faster way—or via Santa Clara and Ivins.

Hiking

The **Hidden Piñon Trail** (also signed as Nature Trail) begins across the road from the campground entrance, then weaves among sandstone hills and lava flows to the Varnish Mountain Overlook above Snow Canyon. At the over-look, desert varnish on sandstone has turned the rock jet black. The easy trail is 1.5 miles round-trip and has a small elevation gain; some sections cross rough rocks and deep sand. It's an easy scramble from the overlook area to the canyon floor below. **West Canyon Trail** is the longest in the park; it begins near the stables (0.7 mile south of the campground) and goes northwest along an old road up Snow Canyon to West Canyon. (You can also take cross-country hikes into other canyons passed on the way.) The trail is seven miles round-trip with a small elevation gain. **Lava Tubes Trail** winds across a lava field to an area of lava caves (one mile round-trip). The caves formed when molten lava broke out of the partly cooled flow and left rooms and tunnels behind. Artifacts indicate that Native Americans took shelter in the chambers. The trailhead is 1.5 miles north of the campground. The steep and strenuous **Volcano Trail** ascends a cinder cone northeast of Snow Canyon. The 1,000-year-old volcano is on the east side of Hwy. 18 one mile north of the turnoff for Snow Canyon. Near the park entrance, the 0.5-mile **Jenny's Trail** leads to a slot canyon; this trail is closed April–May.

TUACAHN AMPHITHEATER

Tuacahn (1100 Tuacahn Drive, 800/746-9882, www.tuacahn.org, shows Mon.–Sat. mid-June–mid-Oct., $28–44 adults, $20–36 children, $21–44 seniors or AAA discount) is an outdoor amphitheater that seats 1,900 among 1,500-foot-high red-rock cliffs northwest of St. George. Tuacahn offers a four-show summer theater season called "Broadway in the Desert." Recent performances have included *My Fair Lady* and *Little Shop of Horrors*. Between Thanksgiving and Christmas, Tuacan hosts a free Festival of Lights, with a Nativity reenactment. Pre-show dinner ($11 adults, $8 children) is available before each production, as are backstage tours ($5 adults, $3 children). The amphitheater is northwest of St. George near the south entrance to Snow Canyon State Park.

VEYO AND VICINITY
Veyo Resort

Warm-water springs feed a swimming pool in this pretty spot. The family resort here (435/574-2744, www.veyopool.com, 11 A.M.–8 P.M. daily Apr.–Sept., $6 adults, $4 children under 14) has picnic tables and a snack bar.

The resort has also developed a private rock-climbing area called **Crawdad Canyon.** For a $5 fee, climbers can scale the 80-foot basalt cliffs, with more than 180 bolted sport climbing routes ranging from 5.6 to 5.13. Climbers (and other visitors) can also camp here ($10 hike-in, $20 drive-in).

Take the Veyo Pool Resort Road from Hwy. 18 southeast of town. The little village of Veyo lies along the Santa Clara River 19 miles northwest of St. George.

Gunlock Lake State Park

The 266-acre reservoir is set among red and gray hills 10 miles southwest of Veyo. A parking area, docks, and paved boat ramp lie just off the road near the dam. The red-sand beach across the lake can be reached by boat or by a short walk across the dam. Largemouth bass, channel catfish, bluegill, and the odd trout swim in the waters. Open all year; no water or charge. Check with Snow Canyon State Park (P.O. Box 140, Santa Clara, UT 84765, 435/628-2255) for current info. Gunlock Lake can be reached from St. George via Veyo or by the slightly shorter route through Santa Clara.

Baker Dam Recreation Site

This 50-acre reservoir on BLM land is on the Santa Clara River upstream from Veyo. Anglers come for the rainbow and brown trout. An established campground is just before the dam; drive across the dam to undeveloped camping areas and a boat ramp. Open year-round; no water or charge. Go north four miles on Hwy. 18 from Veyo, then turn right a half mile on a paved road (between mileposts 24 and 25).

HIGHWAY 18 NORTH TO ENTERPRISE
Mountain Meadows Massacre Historic Site

A short trip from Hwy. 18 west of the Pine Valley Mountains leads to the site of one of the darkest chapters of Mormon history. The pleasant valley had been a popular rest stop for pioneers about to cross the hot desert country to the west. In 1857, a California-bound wagon train whose members had already experienced trouble with Mormons of the region was attacked by an alliance of Mormons and local Native Americans. About 120 people in the wagon train died in the massacre. Only some small children too young to tell the story were spared. The closely knit Mormon community tried to cover up the incident and hindered federal attempts to apprehend the killers. Only John D. Lee, who was in charge of Indian affairs in southern Utah at the time, was ever brought to justice. After nearly 20 years and two trials, authorities took him back to this spot to be executed by firing squad. Many details of the massacre remain unknown. The major causes seem to have been a Mormon fear of invasion, aggressive Mormons and Native

Americans, and poor communications between the Mormon leadership in Salt Lake City and southern Utah. A monument now marks the site of the tragedy; turn west one mile on a paved road from Hwy. 18 between mileposts 31 and 32.

Enterprise Reservoirs

Rainbow trout lurk in the lower and upper reservoirs. Larger Upper Enterprise Reservoir has a paved boat ramp and easier access. Nearby **Honeycomb Rocks Campground** (elev. 5,700 feet) has water and a camping fee roughly Memorial Day–October. Its name describes the outcrops of porous volcanic rock. The open country here supports mostly grass, sage, and some ponderosa pine and Gambel oak. Drive to the town of Enterprise, 41 miles northwest of St. George (47 miles west of Cedar City), then follow paved roads 11.5 miles west and south.

Pine Valley Mountains

A massive body of magma uncovered by erosion makes up the Pine Valley Mountains. Signal Peak (elev. 10,365 feet) tops the range, much of which has been designated the Pine Valley Mountain Wilderness Area.

In 1856, pioneers established the town of Pine Valley (elev. 6,800 feet) to harvest the extensive forests and raise livestock. Lumber from Pine Valley helped build many southern Utah settlements and even went into Salt Lake City's great tabernacle organ. The town's picturesque white chapel was built in 1868 by Ebenezer Bryce, who later homesteaded at what's now Bryce Canyon National Park. Right near the chapel, the **Pine Valley Heritage Center** (100 E. Main St., 435/574-2463, 10 A.M.–P.M. Mon.–Sat. Memorial Day–Labor Day) is run by the Forest Service and dispenses visitor information and sells books and maps.

Pine Valley Recreation Area

Continue three miles on the paved road past Pine Valley to the picnic areas, campgrounds, and trails in Dixie National Forest. At Pine Valley Reservoir, 2.3 miles up on the right, you can fish for rainbow and some brook trout; fishing is fair in the Santa Clara River up- and downstream from the reservoir. About a half mile past the reservoir are several large streamside picnic areas and **Pines Campground.** Continue straight for **Blue Springs** (reservations available, 877/444-6777, www

.recreation.gov) and **South and North Juniper Campgrounds** and for **Whipple Trailhead.** Each campground has water and a $12 fee during the May–mid-September season. Elevation is 6,800 feet. All campsites fill up most days in summer; try to arrive early or reserve a site at Blue Springs.

Pine Valley Wilderness

The 50,000-acre wilderness has the best scenery of the Pine Valley Mountains, but it can be seen only on foot or horseback. A network of trails from all directions leads into the wilderness. The road from Pine Valley provides access to the **Whipple Trailhead** and **Brown's Point Trailhead** on the east side of the wilderness area. Trails are usually open mid-June into October. **Summit Trail** is the longest (35 miles one-way) and connects with many other trails. Several loops are possible, though most are too long for day hikes. **Whipple National Recreation Trail** is one of the most popular for both day- and overnight trips; it ascends 2,100 feet in six miles to Summit Trail. **Brown's Point Trail** also climbs to Summit Trail, but in four miles. Strong hikers can use the Brown's Point and Summit Trails to reach the top of Signal Peak on a day hike; the last part of the climb is a rock-scramble. Generally, the trails from Pine Valley are signed and easy to follow; trails in other areas may not be maintained. Take topo maps and a compass if you're going for more than a short stroll. The Pine Valley

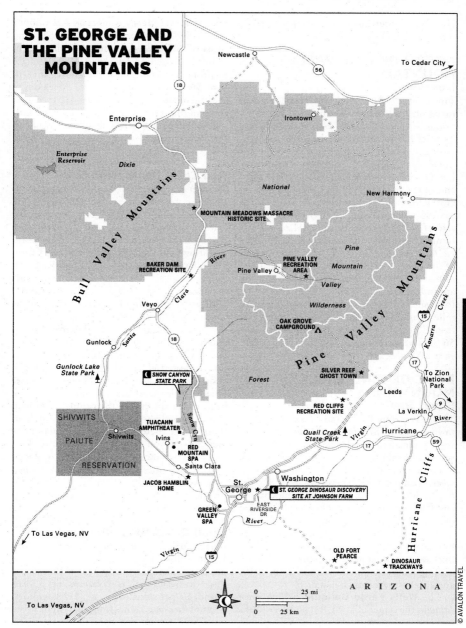

ST. GEORGE AND THE PINE VALLEY MOUNTAINS

Newcastle

To Cedar City

56

18

Enterprise

Irontown

Enterprise Reservoir

Dixie

New Harmony

★ MOUNTAIN MEADOWS MASSACRE HISTORIC SITE

National

Pine

Valley

Mountains

Bull Valley Mountains

BAKER DAM RECREATION SITE ★

River

Pine Valley

PINE VALLEY RECREATION AREA ★

Mountain

Valley

Wilderness

Veyo

Clara

OAK GROVE CAMPGROUND

Pine Valley

Gunlock

Santa

18

15

Kanarra Creek

Gunlock Lake State Park

SILVER REEF GHOST TOWN ★

Forest

17

To Zion National Park

SNOW CANYON STATE PARK

Leeds

9

SHIVWITS

TUACAHN AMPHITHEATER

RED CLIFFS RECREATION SITE ★

La Verkin

River

PAIUTE

Shivwits

Ivins

Snow Cyn

RED MOUNTAIN SPA

Quail Creek State Park

Virgin

Hurricane

RESERVATION

Santa Clara

17

59

JACOB HAMBLIN HOME ★

St. George ★

Washington

ST. GEORGE DINOSAUR DISCOVERY SITE AT JOHNSON FARM

GREEN VALLEY SPA

EAST RIVERSIDE DR

River

Virgin

Hurricane Cliffs

To Las Vegas, NV

OLD FORT PEARCE ★

DINOSAUR ★ TRACKWAYS

Virgin

15

A R I Z O N A

To Las Vegas, NV

0   25 mi

0   25 km

ZION AND BRYCE

© AVALON TRAVEL

Heritage Center has a recreation map that shows trails and trailheads.

NORTH OF PINE VALLEY MOUNTAINS
Irontown

This is one of Utah's best-preserved 19th-century iron smelter sites. The original Iron Mission near Cedar City had poor success during its brief life in the 1850s. In 1870, though, more extensive ore deposits farther west at this site encouraged another attempt at iron-making. Daily production rose to nearly five tons, and a town of several hundred workers grew up around the smelter. Profits began to decline in the 1880s when cheaper iron from the eastern states flooded in. The town soon died, though mining has since continued on and off in the vicinity. A brick chimney, stone foundations of the smelter, and a beehive-shaped charcoal kiln show the layout of the operation. Look around in the sagebrush for remnants of the town site and pieces of slag and iron. Drive 16 miles west from Cedar City or 30 miles east from Enterprise to the signed turnoff on Hwy. 56 (just west of milepost 41), then turn southwest 2.7 miles.

EAST OF PINE VALLEY MOUNTAINS
Silver Reef

This is probably Utah's most accessible ghost town. In about 1870, prospectors found rich silver deposits in the sandstone here, much to the surprise of mining experts who thought such a combination impossible. The town grew up several years later and boomed 1878–1882. The population peaked at 1,500 and included a sizable Chinese community. Then a combination of lower silver prices, declining yields, and water in the mines forced the operations to close one by one, the last in 1891. Other attempts at mining have since been made from time to time, including some uranium production in the 1950s and 1960s, but the town had died.

The **Wells Fargo Building,** which once stood in the center of town, is now Silver Reef's main attraction. Built of stone in 1877, it looks as solid as ever. **Jerry Anderson Art Gallery** (435/879-2254, 9 A.M.–5 P.M. Mon.–Sat.) and the small **Silver Reef Museum** occupy the interior. Encroaching modern houses detract a bit from the setting, but the ghosts are still here. Stone walls and foundations peek out of the sagebrush. A short walk on the road past the building takes you to the ruins and tailings of the mills that once shook the town with their racket. Take I-15 Leeds Exit 22 or 23 and follow signs 1.3 miles on a paved road.

Red Cliffs Recreation Site

Weather-sculpted cliffs of reddish-orange sandstone rise above this pretty spot (435/688-3200, www.ut.blm.gov/stgeorge_fo/sgfored_cliffs.html, $2 per vehicle day use, $8 camping). The seasonal Quail Creek emerges from a canyon, flows through the middle of the campground, then goes on to Quail Creek Reservoir two miles away. The campground and picnic area (elev. 3,240 feet) are open year-round with water; camping is most pleasant in the spring and fall. **Desert Trail** starts on the left near the beginning of the campground loop and follows the creek a half mile into the canyon. Idyllic pools and graceful rock formations line the way. You'll need to do some wading to continue upstream past trail's end. A shorter (quarter-mile round-trip) but more rugged trail begins near the end of the campground loop and crosses slickrock to Silver Reef Lookout Point. Here there's a good panorama of the area, though you can't actually see Silver Reef ghost town. Take I-15 Leeds Exit 22 or 23, go south three miles on the frontage road, then turn west 1.7 miles on a paved road. Long trailers and low-clearance cars may drag on dips at stream crossings.

Quail Creek State Park

Barren rock hills surround the 590-acre reservoir at this busy park (435/879-2378, www.utah.com/stateparks, 800/322-3770 or www.reserveamerica.com reservations, open year-round, $7 per vehicle day use, $12 camping). Most of the water comes from the Virgin River, but Quail Creek also contributes its share.

Curiously, the reservoir has two dams to hold back the waters. The state park on the west shore offers a campground (water but no showers or hookups), swimming beach, paved boat ramp, and docks. Anglers come for the largemouth bass, rainbow trout, catfish, and bluegill. Other popular activities include water-skiing, personal watercrafting, and sailboarding. If coming from the north, take I-15 Leeds Exit 23 and follow the frontage road south 3.4 miles, then turn left 1.5 miles; from the south, take I-15 Hurricane Exit 16, go east 2.6 miles on Hwy. 9, then north two miles on a paved road.

Oak Grove Campground

On the east side of the Pine Valley Mountains, Oak Grove (435/688-3246, www.fs.fed.us/r4/ Dixie, May 1–Oct. 2, $5, no reservations, piped water) is in a forest of Gambel and shrub live oak, ponderosa pine, and some spruce. **Oak Grove Trail** winds three miles from this small campground (elev. 6,800 feet) to Summit Trail in the Pine Valley Mountain Wilderness. Take I-15 Leeds Exit 22 or 23 and go northwest nine miles. The unpaved road may be rough, especially late in the season; it's usually passable by cars but isn't recommended for trailers.

Cedar City

Cedar City (pop. around 24,000), known for its scenic setting and its summertime Utah Shakespearean Festival, is a handy base for exploring a good chunk of southern Utah. Just east of town rise the high cliffs of the Markagunt Plateau—a land of panoramic views, colorful rock formations, desolate lava flows, extensive forests, and flower-filled meadows. Also on the Markagunt Plateau is the Cedar Breaks National Monument, an immense amphitheater eroded into the vividly hued underlying rock.

Within an easy day's drive are Zion National Park to the south and Bryce Canyon National Park and Grand Staircase–Escalante National Monument to the east. Cedar City is just east of I-15, 52 miles northeast of St. George and 253 miles southwest of Salt Lake City; take I-15 Exit 57, 59, or 62.

SIGHTS
Iron Mission State Park Museum

This large museum (589 N. Main, 435/586-9290, 9 a.m.–6 p.m. daily in summer, 9 a.m.–5 p.m. Mon.–Sat. in winter, closed major holidays, $3 per person or $6 per vehicle) dedicates itself to the history of the cultures that have lived in and developed Iron County, and to pioneer efforts to mine and process iron. Cedar City began as a mission in 1851 to supply the Mormon settlements with much-

needed iron products. Church leaders, upon hearing of promising iron ore and coal deposits, decided to launch the first major colonizing effort since the settlement of the Salt Lake area. Hard winters, crop failures, floods, shortages of skilled workmen, and cheaper imported iron nearly doomed the whole project. Only a small amount of iron was produced, and operations ceased in 1858. Sizable quantities of iron ore did exist, though; large-scale mining west of Cedar City began in the 1920s, peaked in 1957, and has tapered off in recent years.

Exhibits at the museum illustrate the Iron Mission's early hardships and the first iron production on September 30, 1852. Past members of the Iron Mission cast the old community bell on display. A diverse array of carriages is the museum's main attraction. You'll see everything from a bullet-scarred Overland stagecoach to an elegant Clarence carriage. All the sleighs, utility wagons, hearses, and many other forms of 19th-century transport have been meticulously restored. Also displayed are artifacts of prehistoric and modern tribes. Pioneer memorabilia include clothing, furniture, saddles, and a bathtub. A large collection of horse-drawn farm machinery sits out back.

Rock Church
Depression-era residents needed a new LDS

ZION AND BRYCE

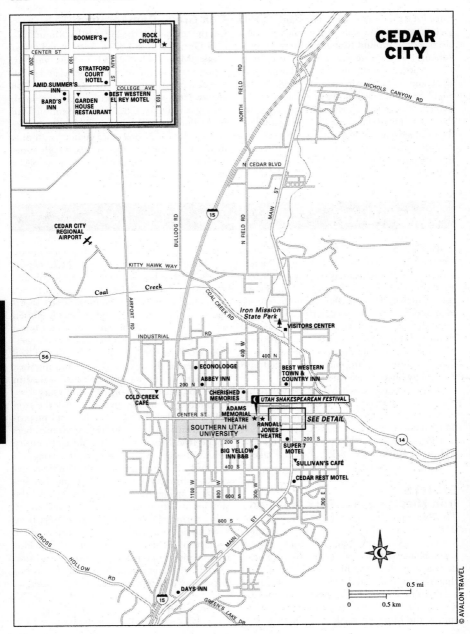

CEDAR CITY

BOOMER'S
ROCK CHURCH
CENTER ST
STRATFORD COURT HOTEL
AMID SUMMER'S INN
COLLEGE AVE
BARD'S INN
GARDEN HOUSE RESTAURANT
BEST WESTERN EL REY MOTEL
200 W
180 W
MAIN ST
100 E

NICHOLS CANYON RD

NORTH FIELD RD

N CEDAR BLVD

MAIN ST

15

BULLDOG RD

N FIELD RD

CEDAR CITY REGIONAL AIRPORT

KITTY HAWK WAY

Coal Creek

AIRPORT RD

COAL CREEK RD

Iron Mission State Park

VISITORS CENTER

INDUSTRIAL RD

400 W

400 N

56

ECONOLODGE

ABBEY INN

BEST WESTERN TOWN & COUNTRY INN

290 N

COLD CREEK CAFE

CHERISHED MEMORIES

UTAH SHAKESPEAREAN FESTIVAL

CENTER ST

ADAMS MEMORIAL THEATRE

RANDALL JONES THEATRE

SEE DETAIL

SOUTHERN UTAH UNIVERSITY

14

200 S

200 S

BIG YELLOW INN B&B

SUPER 7 MOTEL

400 S

SULLIVAN'S CAFÉ

CEDAR REST MOTEL

1100 W

800 W

600 S

300 W

800 S

MAIN ST

CROSS HOLLOW RD

DAYS INN

15

GREEN'S LAKE DR

0   0.5 mi

0   0.5 km

© AVALON TRAVEL

Church building but lacked the money to build one. Undaunted, they set to work using local materials and came up with this beautiful structure (75 E. Center, 435/586-6759, tours 1–6 P.M. Thurs.–Sat., free) composed of many different types of rocks. Skilled craftspeople made the metal lamps, carpets, Western red cedar pews, and most other furnishings.

Southern Utah University

The towns of southern Utah eagerly sought a branch of the state's teacher training school after it had been authorized in 1897 by the Utah legislature. A committee awarded the school to Cedar City, and classes began the same year in a borrowed church building. Some people say that Cedar City was chosen because it was the only one of the candidate towns without a saloon or pool hall. This satellite school inevitably became a four-year university with 6,000 students and today offers major fields of study in education, arts and letters, science, and business. The attractively landscaped campus (435/586-7700, www.suu.edu) occupies 104 acres just west of downtown. The Utah Shakespearean Festival is the main summer event on campus.

Braithwaite Fine Arts Gallery (435/586-5432, noon–7 P.M. Tues.–Sat.) presents changing exhibits in the Braithwaite Fine Arts Center, one block north of the intersection of 200 South and 400 West.

EVENTS

◖ Utah Shakespearean Festival

Cedar City's lively festival (435/586-7880 general info, 435/586-7878 or 800/752-9849 box office, www.bard.org) presents three Shakespearean plays each season, choosing from both well-known and rarely performed works. Most of the action centers on the Adams Shakespeare Theatre, an open-air theater-in-the-round, which is closely designed after the original Globe Theatre from Elizabethan London. The indoor Randall Jones Theatre presents the "Best of the Rest"—works by other great playwrights such as Chekhov, George Bernard Shaw, and Arthur Miller. A total of nine plays are staged each season late June–mid-October.

Costumed actors stage the popular free Greenshow each evening (7 P.M. Mon.–Sat.) before the performances with a variety of Elizabethan comedy skits, Punch and Judy shows, period dances, music, juggling, and other good-natured 16th-century fun. Backstage tours of the costume shop, makeup room, and stage show you how the festival works. At literary seminars each morning, actors and Shakespearean scholars discuss the previous night's play. Production seminars, held daily except Sunday, take a close look at acting, costumes, stage props, special effects, and other details of play production.

The Greenshow and seminars are free, but you'll have to pay for most other events. Tickets cost $20–48, and it's wise to purchase them well in advance; however, last-minute theater-goers usually can find tickets to *something.*

The theaters are on the Southern Utah University campus, near the corner of Center and 300 West. Rain occasionally dampens the performances (the Elizabethan theater is open to the sky), and plays may move to a conventional theater next door, where the box office is located.

Other Events

Other events and festivals include the **Cedar City Cowboy Gathering** in March. The highlights are the great music and the readings by cowboy poets; there's also a display of Western art.

Paiutes have lived here since before pioneer days. Sponsorship by the Mormon community allowed them to remain when the federal government forced most other tribes in the state to move onto reservations. There's a Paiute village in the northeastern part of Cedar City, and the tribe sponsors the mid-June **Paiute Restoration Gathering** (440 Paiute Dr., 435/586-1112), with a parade, dances, traditional games, native food, and a beauty pageant the second weekend in June. Mid-June brings **Groovefest** (435/867-9800, www.groovefestutah.com), a festival celebrating American roots music.

Utah athletes compete in the **Utah Summer Games** during late June; events, patterned after the Olympic games, begin with a torch relay and include track and field, 10K and marathon runs, cycling, boxing, wrestling, basketball, tennis, soccer, karate, and swimming.

Everyone dresses up in period clothing in July for the **Utah Midsummer Renaissance Faire** (435/586-3711, www.umrf.net), with 16th-century entertainment, crafts, and food. **Pioneer Day** honors Utah's early settlers with a parade and games in town on July 24.

The season ends in November, when Cedar City celebrates its birthday on the 11th with games and pioneer crafts in **Iron Mission Days** (435/586-9290).

RECREATION

The main **city park** has picnic tables, a playground, and horseshoe courts at Main and 200 North. The **municipal swimming pools** (400 Harding Ave./400 West 100 North, 435/586-2869) have indoor and outdoor areas and a hydrotube. Look for **tennis courts** at Canyon Park (on Hwy. 14, three blocks east of Main). From this park the new, paved Coal Creek walking and biking trail leads four miles up the desert canyon.

Southern Utah University sports facilities (600 West 200 South, 435/586-7815) open to the public include an indoor swimming pool, tennis and racquetball courts, and gym.

ACCOMMODATIONS

During the Shakespeare Festival, Cedar City is a popular destination, so it's best to reserve a room at least a day or two in advance during the summer. There are two major concentrations of motels. A half-dozen large chain hotels cluster around the I-15 exits, together with lots of fast-food restaurants and strip malls. Downtown, along Main Street, are even more motels, ranging from classy new places to budget motels. You can easily walk from most of the downtown motels to the Shakespeare Festival. Most of Cedar City's B&Bs are also within a stroll of the festival grounds.

Note that the following prices are for the high summer festival season. Outside of high season, expect rates to drop by about a third.

Under $50

Cedar City has few mom-and-pop budget motels. Downtown, the **Super 7 Motel** (190 S. Main, 435/586-6566, $35 and up) has a bit of a budget ambiance, but is a good deal.

$50–100

Along Main Street in downtown Cedar City, the **Cedar Rest Motel** (479 S. Main, 435/586-9471, $55 and up) is one of the best values in town; it offers free breakfasts and small pets are okay.

At I-15 Exit 57, the **Days Inn** (1204 S. Main, 888/556-5637 or 435/867-8877, $64 and up) is a well-kept place with an indoor pool and complimentary continental breakfast.

At I-15 Exit 52, the **Econolodge** (333 N. 1100 West, 435/867-4700 or 888/326-6613 , $59 and up) is a newer motel with an outdoor pool and a hot tub.

One of the best places to stay in Cedar City is the **Stratford Court Hotel** (18 S. Main, 435/586-2433 or 877/688-8884, www.stratford courthotel.com, $79 and up). This nice hotel has an outdoor pool, free passes to a local gym, and a complimentary continental breakfast. The on-site restaurant is one of the better places in town.

Another good choice is the **Abbey Inn** (940 W. 200 North, 435/586-9966 or 800/325-5411, www.abbeyinncedar.com, $83 and up), with recently redone rooms, an indoor pool, and a good free breakfast.

The **Best Western El Rey Inn** (80 S. Main, 435/586-6518 or 800/528-1234, www.bwelrey .com, $79 and up) offers suites, a restaurant, pool, sauna, and spa.

Bed-and-breakfast inns and Shakespeare seem to go hand-in-hand. The **Bard's Inn Bed and Breakfast** (150 S. 100 West, 435/586-6612, www.bardsbandb.com, $85 and up), two blocks from the Shakespearean Festival, has seven guest rooms, all with private bath, plus there's a two-bedroom cottage. It's open during festival season only. Right next door, the antiques-filled **Amid Summer's Inn** (140 S. 100 West, 435/867-4691, www.amid summersinn, $99 and up) has five sumptuously decorated rooms, including one suite, all with private bathrooms in a restored 1930s cottage. Also near the Shakespeare Festival, at the edge of the Southern Utah University campus, the **Ⓒ Big Yellow Inn** (234 S. 300 West, 435/586-0960, www.bigyellowinn.com, $79 and up) is easy to spot; rooms are packed full of antiques, and have high-speed Internet hookups. Several rooms are actually in a house directly across the street from the main inn. **Cherished Memories** (170 N. 400 West, 888/867-6498 or 435/867-6498, www.cherishedmemoriesbnb .com, $105) is an antiques-furnished Victorian home with four guest rooms, located two blocks from the Shakespearean Festival.

For a more rural touch, the **Willow Glen Inn Bed & Breakfast** (3308 N. Bulldog Rd., 435/586-3275, www.willowgleninn.com, $67–195) has 10 units in four separate buildings, including an old "pony barn," located on a 10-acre farm five miles north of downtown Cedar City, I-15 Exit 62.

Campgrounds

East of Cedar City on Hwy. 14 are a handful of campgrounds in the Dixie National Forest. The closest, **Cedar Canyon** (635/865-3200, www.fs.fed.us/r4/dixie), is 12 miles from town in a pretty canyon along Cow Creek. It's at 8,100 feet and open with water early June–mid-September.

Cedar City KOA (1121 N. Main, 435/586-9872 or 800/562-9873) is open year-round with cabins, showers, a playground, and a pool, and can accommodate tents as well as RVs. **Country Aire RV Park** (1700 N. Main, 435/586-2550) is open year-round with showers and a pool.

FOOD

Family restaurants dominate Cedar City's cuisine. **Sullivan's Cafe** (301 S. Main, 435/586-6761, breakfast, lunch, and dinner daily, $5–13) is a favorite for casual family dining.

At the **Ⓒ Pastry Pub** (86 W. Center, 435/867-1400, lunch and dinner daily, open late in theater season, $6–12) you'll find pastries, good sandwiches, and coffee.

The following fine-dining restaurants each serve wine and cocktails. The **Garden House Restaurant** (164 S. 100 West, 435/586-6110, lunch and dinner Mon.–Sat. in summer, call for hours off season, $8–20) is housed in a charming cottage off the main drag with fine dining (try the trout quesadilla for lunch, $9). Don't worry when you see that **Cold Creek Cafe** (1575 W. 200 North, 435/586-1700, breakfast, lunch, and dinner daily, $8–25) is attached to a hotel; it's one of the best restaurants in town.

East of Cedar City on Hwy. 14 is a dramatic desert canyon with two of the area's finest restaurants; both open for dinner only. The steakhouse atmosphere is casual and welcoming at **Rusty's Ranch House** (2275 E. Hwy. 14, 435/586-3839, dinner Mon.–Sat., $12–28), two miles east of town on Hwy. 14, serving good steak and seafood dinners in a dramatic canyon setting. Two miles farther up the same road is the Western-style **Milt's Stage Stop** (3560 E. Hwy. 14, 435/586-9344, dinner nightly, $12–25), serving steak, prime rib, and seafood.

INFORMATION AND SERVICES

The **Iron County Visitors Center** (581 N. Main, 435/586-5124 or 800/354-4849, www .scenicsouthernutah.com, 9 A.M.–5 P.M. Mon.–Fri., 9 A.M.–1 P.M. Sat.) is a big, new place just south of the Iron Mission State Park, with a raft of information and free Internet access. The **Cedar City Ranger District office** of Dixie National Forest (1789 Wedgewood Ln., 435/865-3700, 8:30 A.M.–4:30 P.M. Mon.–Fri.) has information on recreation and travel on the Markagunt Plateau.

The **BLM's Cedar City District office** (176 East DL Sargeant Dr., 435/586-2401, Mon.–Fri. 7:45 A.M.–4:30 P.M.) is just off Main Street, on the north edge of town.

The **Mountain West Bookstore** (77 N. Main, 435/586-3828, 10 A.M.–6 P.M. Mon.–Sat.) offers a selection of Utah history, travel, general reading, and LDS titles.

Valley View Medical Center (595 South 75 East, 435/586-6587) provides hospital care. The **post office** is at 333 N. Main (435/586-6701).

TRANSPORTATION
America West (800/235-9292, www.usairways .com) has flights between the Cedar City Municipal Airport and Salt Lake City (800/453-9417). Rent a car from **Enterprise** (435/865-1435) or Avis (435/867-9898) at the airport.

PAROWAN
Although just a small town, Parowan (pop. 2,565) is southern Utah's oldest community and the seat of Iron County. Hwy. 143 turns south from downtown to the Brian Head Ski Area, Cedar Breaks National Monument, and other scenic areas on the Markagunt Plateau. To the west lies Utah's desert country. Accommodations in town offer a less expensive alternative to those in Brian Head. The **Iron County Fair** (435/477-8380) presents a parade, rodeos, horse races, exhibits, and entertainment during the Labor Day holiday. Stop by the **Parowan visitors center** (73 N. Main, 435/477-8190, 10 A.M.–4 P.M. Mon.–Fri.). Parowan is 18 miles northeast of Cedar City and 14 miles north of Brian Head; take I-15 Exits 75 or 78.

Parowan Gap Petroglyphs
Native Americans have pecked many designs into the rocks at this pass 10.5 miles northwest of Parowan. The common route for Native Americans and wildlife hunting the Red Hills crossed this gap, and it may have served as an important site for hunting rituals. The rock art's meaning hasn't been deciphered but it probably represents the thoughts of many different tribes over the past 1,000 or more years. Geometric designs, snakes, lizards, mountain sheep, bear claws, and human figures are all still recognizable. You can get here on a good gravel road from Parowan by going north on Main and turning left 10.5 miles on the last street (400 North). Or, from Cedar City, go north on Main (or take I-15 Exit 62), follow signs for Hwy. 130 north 13.5 miles, then turn right 2.5 miles on a good gravel road (near milepost 19). You'll find an interpretive brochure and map at the BLM offices in Cedar City.

Accommodations
There's not a lot to choose from in Parowan. The **Days Inn** (625 W. 200 South, 435/477-3326 or 888/530-3138, $45–65) has new rooms and an on-site restaurant.

Splurge at the nicely restored **Victorian Rose Country Inn** (7 N. Main, 435/477-1555, http://victorianrosecountryinn.com, $80–150).

Tent campers should head a few miles out of town to the Markagunt Plateau.

Food
Right downtown is the homey **Parowan Cafe** (33 N. Main, 435/477-3593, breakfast, lunch, and dinner daily, $6–15). **Pizza Barn** (595 West 200 South, 435/477-8240, dinner nightly, $8–20) serves pasta and salads as well as pizza.

The Markagunt Plateau

Markagunt is a Native American name for "highland of trees." The large, high plateau—much of the land is between 9,000 and 11,000 feet in elevation—consists mostly of gently rolling country, forests, and lakes. Black tongues of barren lava extend across some parts of the landscape. Cliffs at Cedar Breaks National Monument are the best-known feature of the plateau, but the land also drops away in the colorful pink cliffs farther southeast.

Two Scenic Byways cross this highly scenic area. Hwy. 14 climbs up a very dramatic cliff-lined canyon from Cedar City, reaching vista points over Zion National Park before dropping onto Long Valley Junction on Hwy. 89. Hwy. 143 departs from Parowan, climbing steeply up to lofty Brian Head with its ski and recreation area, past Panguitch Lake, and down to Panguitch in the Sevier Valley.

Popular activities on the Markagunt include fishing, hiking, mountain biking, downhill and cross-country skiing, and snowmobiling. Contact the Cedar City Ranger District (1789 Wedgewood Ln., 435/865-3700, www.fs.fed .us/r4/dixie) of the Dixie National Forest for information. In summer, volunteers or foresters staff the visitors center (435/682-2432) on Hwy. 14 opposite the Duck Creek Campground turnoff.

MARKAGUNT SCENIC BYWAY

Starting at Cedar City's eastern boundary, Markagunt Scenic Byway (Hwy. 14) plunges into a narrow canyon flanked by steep rock walls before climbing up to the top of the Markagunt Plateau. This is a very scenic route, passing dramatic rock cliffs and pink rock hoodoos that echo the formations at Zion and Bryce Canyon National Parks, but it's also a slow drive, especially if you get caught behind a lumbering RV. The route also passes a number of wooded campgrounds and small mountain resorts, which are especially popular with snowmobilers and ATV riders (though cross-country skiing and mountain biking are tolerated). Due to their elevations—mostly 8,000–9,000 feet—these high mountain getaways are popular when the temperatures in the desert basin towns begin to bake. The route ends at the Long Valley Junction, at Hwy. 89, 41 miles from Cedar City.

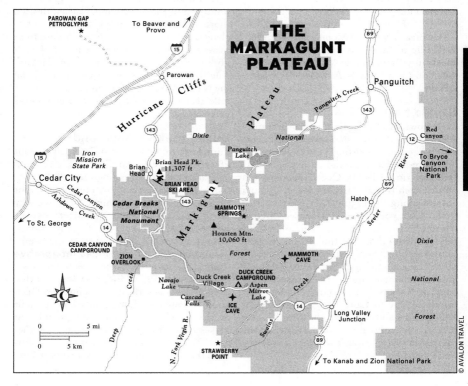

Zion Overlook

A sweeping panorama takes in the deep canyons and monuments of Zion National Park to the south. Zion Overlook is 16.5 miles east of Cedar City on the south side of the road.

Bristlecone Pine Trail

This easy half-mile loop, graded for wheelchair access, leads to the rim of the Markagunt Plateau and excellent views. A dense spruce and fir forest opens up near the rim, where storm-battered limber and bristlecone pines cling precariously near the edge. You can identify the bristlecone pines by their short-needled, "bottlebrush" branches. The trailhead is 17 miles east of Cedar City on the south side of Hwy. 14.

Highway 148 Junction

Eighteen miles east of Cedar City is the junction with Hwy. 148, which leads north to Cedar Breaks National Monument. The route climbs up to elevations well over 10,000 feet and is usually open late May–mid-October. (See the *Cedar Breaks National Monument* section.)

Navajo Lake

Lava flows dammed this unusual 3.5-mile-long lake, which has no surface outlet. Instead, water drains through sinkholes in the limestone underneath and emerges as Cascade Falls (in the Pacific Ocean drainage) and Duck Creek (Great Basin drainage). From a pullout along the highway 24 miles east of Cedar City, you can sometimes see three of the sinkholes at the east end; a dam prevents the lake from draining into them. Anglers catch rainbow trout and occasionally some eastern brook and brown trout; ice fishing is possible in winter. You can hand-launch small boats at Navajo Campground or from boat ramps at Navajo Lake Lodge and Behmer Lodge and Landing. Take the Navajo Lake turnoff, 25.5 miles east of Cedar City, for the campgrounds, marina, and lodge along the south shore.

Virgin River Rim Trailhead

This trail stretches about 38 miles along the rim between Deer Haven Group Campground and Strawberry Point. Beautiful panoramas of Zion National Park and the headwaters of the Virgin River reward trail users. You can also reach it at Te-Ah Campground, from Navajo Lake via short (one-half to three-quarter mile) spur trails and at the start of the Cascade Falls National Recreation Trail. The entire length is open to hikers and mountain bikers. Off-highway vehicles can use the section from Deer Haven to Te-Ah Campground.

Cascade Falls National Recreation Trail

Splendid views and a waterfall make this an exciting trip. The easy trail is 1.1 miles round-trip with some ups and downs. It begins at the south rim of the Markagunt Plateau, drops a short way down the Pink Cliffs, then winds along the cliffs to the falls. The falls gush from a cave and bounce their way down to the North Fork of the Virgin River and Zion Canyon. The flow peaks during spring runoff. Take the Navajo Lake turnoff from Hwy. 14, go 0.3 mile, then turn left three miles on a gravel road to its end.

Duck Creek Campground

Turn north from Hwy. 14 at Duck Lake, about 28 miles east of Cedar City. The creek and lake adjacent to the campground (877/444-6777, www.recreation.gov, mid-June–Labor Day, $12) offer trout fishing. You'll see why Duck Lake got its name. A **visitors center** (435/682-2432, 10 A.M.–5 P.M. daily in summer) is across the highway from the campground turnoff. **Singing Pines Interpretive Trail,** just east of the visitors center, makes a half-mile loop and **Old Ranger Interpretive Trail** makes a one-third-mile loop from Duck Creek Campground; look for a large pullout on the left where the main campground road makes a curve to the right (near the amphitheater). Pick up information sheets for both trails from the visitors center. The **Lost Hunter Trail** makes a three-mile loop from the same trailhead in Duck Creek Campground to the top of Duck Creek Bench; elevation gain is about 600 feet with many fine views.

Ice Cave

Cool off inside this small cave, where the lava rock insulates ice throughout the summer. The road may be too rough for cars—ask conditions at the visitors center. Turn south on the dirt road beside the visitors center, keep left at the fork 0.2 mile in, keep right at another fork 0.8 mile farther, and continue 0.4 mile to the cave at the end of the road; signs mark the way.

Aspen Mirror Lake

Trout and scenic beauty attract visitors to this pretty reservoir. The turnoff is on the north side of Hwy. 14 about midway between Duck Creek Campground and Duck Creek Village. Park, then walk the level trail about one-quarter mile.

Duck Creek Village

Hollywood has used this area since the 1940s to film such productions as *How the West Was Won, My Friend Flicka,* and the *Daniel Boone* TV series. This handsome village—a collection of lodges, cabins, and log-built homes—lies at the edge of a large meadow (elev. 8,400 feet) about 30 miles east of Cedar City. The surrounding countryside is excellent for snowmobiling, a popular winter sport here. A big snowmobile race takes place on the weekend closest to Valentine's Day. Cross-country skiing is good, too, on meadow, forest, and bowl terrain. The snow season lasts about late November–late March. Blue Pine Tours, at Pinewoods Resort (800/848-2525), offers snowmobile and ATV tours and rentals.

Strawberry Point

A magnificent panorama takes in countless ridges, canyons, and mountains south of the Markagunt Plateau. You can spot Zion National Park and even the Arizona Strip from this lofty perch (elev. 9,016 feet). Erosion has cut delicate pinnacles and narrow canyons into the Pink Cliffs on either side below the viewpoint. Turn south from Hwy. 14 between mileposts 32 and 33 (32.5 miles east of Cedar City) onto a gravel road and go nine miles to its end. A 500-foot path continues to Strawberry Point. Take care near the edge—the rock is crumbly and there are no guardrails.

Accommodations

In Duck Creek Village, **Meadow View Lodge** (Hwy. 14, 435/682-2495 or 877/384-0361, www.meadowviewlodge.com, $135) rents cabins all year. They also rent snowmobiles and ATVs. **Falcon's Nest** (60 Movie Ranch Rd., 435/682-2556, www.falconsnestcabins.com, year-round, $80–115) offers A-frame cabins with kitchens; two-night minimum on weekends (three nights on holidays). **Pinewoods Resort** (121 Duck Creek Ridge Rd., 435/682-2512 or 800/848-2525, www .pinewoodsresort.com, $65–125) offers accommodations ranging from motel rooms to a house that sleeps up to twelve. The resort also has a coffee shop and a sit-down restaurant. **Duck Creek Village Inn** (Duck Creek Village, 435/682-2565, www.duckcreekvillageinn.com, $85–90 lodge room, $170 cabin) has similar accommodations.

CAMPGROUNDS

All of the campgrounds in the area have water and a few sites for reservation (877/444-6777, www.recreation.gov, early June–Labor Day, $12). Sites in the **Cedar Canyon Campground** lie at 8,100 feet elevation along Crow Creek among aspen, fir, and spruce in a pretty canyon setting 12 miles east of Cedar City on Hwy. 14.

The U.S. Forest Service (Cedar City Ranger District of Dixie National Forest, 1789 Wedgewood Ln., 435/865-3700, $12) maintains **Spruces** and **Navajo Campgrounds** along the lake and **Te-Ah Campground** 1.5 miles west; expect cool nights at the 9,200-foot elevation. Aspen, spruce, and fir grow along the lake.

ZION AND BRYCE

Duck Creek Campground is north from Hwy. 14 at Duck Lake (elev. 8,600 feet).

BRIAN HEAD-PANGUITCH LAKE SCENIC BYWAY 143

Beginning in Parowan, Hwy. 143 very quickly climbs up to nearly 10,000 feet, ascending some of the steepest paved roads in Utah in the process (some of the grades here are 13 percent). The terrain changes from arid desert to pine forests to alpine aspen forests in just 14 miles.

At an elevation of 9,850 feet, Brian Head is the highest municipality in Utah, with a year-round population of about 100. Winter skiers like Brian Head for its abundant snow, challenging terrain, and good accommodations. Summer visitors come to enjoy the high country and to plunge down the slopes on mountain bikes. The beautiful colors of Cedar Breaks National Monument lie just a few miles south. Panguitch Lake, to the east, receives high ratings for its excellent trout fishing.

Brian Head Peak

You can drive all the way to Brian Head's 11,307-foot summit by car when the road is dry, usually July–October. Panoramas from the top take in much of southwestern Utah and beyond into Nevada and Arizona. Sheep graze the grassy slopes below. From Brian Head, follow the highway about two miles south, then turn left (northeast) three miles on a gravel road to the summit. The stone shelter here was built by the Civilian Conservation Corps in the 1930s.

Brian Head Resort

Brian Head Resort (435/677-2035, www.brian head.com, $45 adults full day, $52 holiday, $32 children 12 and under and seniors full day, $37 holiday) comes alive during the skiing season, late November–late April. While it's not Utah's most exciting ski area, it's a good place to bring a family, and new lifts and a skier bridge make it easy to get between the two mountains comprising the main ski areas: Navajo Peak, good for beginners and families, and Giant Steps,

with more advanced runs. Lifts carry skiers up to elevations of 10,920 feet; the resort has 63 runs and 600 skiable acres, with a vertical drop of 1,320 feet from the lift and 1,707 feet from the top of Brian Head peak. Forty percent of the terrain is rated beginner, 40 percent intermediate, and 20 percent advanced. The resort also features three terrain parks for all abilities, and a tubing area.

MOUNTAIN BIKING

Brian Head's second season is during the summer and fall, roughly June–October, when the area comes alive with mountain bikers taking advantage of great terrain and discounted accommodations. Brian Head Resort opens itself to bikers as a mountain-bike park, complete with chairlift ($20) and trailhead shuttle services, bike wash, rentals, and repair services. They supply free maps (preview the routes and print maps from www.brianhead. com). Thrifty bikers can come away with some really good deals by shopping area hotels for mountain-bike lodging packages, which combine a few days of lodging with lift tickets, shuttle service, and sometimes even food and bike rentals. Bike-oriented summertime events in Brian Head include a late-July bike festival and mountain-bike races in August, September, and March. Mountain-bike rentals are available from Brian Head Resort (435/677-3101).

Panguitch Lake and Vicinity

This 1,250-acre reservoir sits in a volcanic basin surrounded by forests and barren lava flows. The cool waters have a reputation for outstanding trout fishing, especially for rainbow. Resorts line the lakeshore; many are venerable older fishing lodges with basic lodging in free-standing cabins; a couple are more upscale. Panguitch Lake is increasingly popular as a site for resort homes, as a glance at the dirt-moving equipment and piles of building supplies makes apparent.

Panguitch Lake lies along Hwy. 143 about 16 miles southwest of Panguitch and 14 miles northeast of Cedar Breaks National Monument. The lake has public boat ramps on the south and north shores.

Mammoth Springs

Moss and luxuriant streamside vegetation surround the crystal-clear spring waters at this beautiful spot. Mammoth Springs is about 5.5 miles south of Panguitch Lake. The last two miles are on gravel Forest Route 068. See the Dixie National Forest map (available at the Pine Valley and Cedar City Ranger District offices). A footbridge leads across the stream to the springs.

Mammoth Cave

Step a few feet underground to explore the inside of a lava flow. When this mass of lava began to cool, the molten interior burst through the surface and drained out through a network of tunnels. A cave-in revealed this section of tunnel, which has two levels. One of them you can follow through to another opening. The lower tunnel (with the large entrance) goes back about a quarter mile. To explore beyond that or to check out other sections, you'll have to stoop or crawl. Bring at least two reliable, powerful flashlights; the caves are very dark. Mammoth Cave is about 14 miles south of Panguitch Lake. Roads also lead in from Duck Creek on Hwy. 14 and Hatch on U.S. 89. You'll need a good map to navigate the back roads, though there are some signs for Mammoth Cave.

Accommodations

Lodgings and campgrounds along Hwy. 143 are concentrated around Panguitch Lake, and there are a number of accommodations that serve Brian Head.

PANGUITCH LAKE

On the west shore of Panguitch Lake, the **Rustic Lodge** (186 S. West Shore Rd., 435/676-2627 or 800/427-8345, www.rusticlodge.com, summer only, $69–89) offers handsome kitchen-equipped cabins in a forested glen. Unfortunately, the resort is not directly on the lake (the lodge and cabins face onto a pasture) but this is otherwise a very pleasant place to stay. Campsites and boat rentals are available also.

Bear Paw Lakeview Resort (905 S. Hwy. 143, 435/676-2650 or 888/553-8439, www.bearpawfishingresort.com, early May–mid-Nov., $69–76) is on the east shore of Panguitch Lake and has lakeview cabins and a clientele composed mostly of anglers. There's also a small store, on-site restaurant, post office, and boat rentals.

Blue Springs Lodge (225 N. Shore Rd., 435/676-2277 or 800/987-5634, www.bluespringslodge.com, $85 and up) is also a ways from the lake—right on Hwy. 143—and comprises modern log cabins with kitchens.

BRIAN HEAD

Rates at Brian Head are steep during the ski season, though not nearly as high as at fancier ski resorts, and most places offer skiers package discounts. Several reservations services can help you book a condo: try **Brian Head Resort Reservation Service** (435/677-2042 or 800/845-9781, www.brianheadtown.com). **Brian Head Condo Reservations** (435/677-2045 or 800/722-4742, www.brianheadcondoreservations.com) offers units near both the Giant Steps and Navajo Mountain lifts in five large condo developments. Most units come with two bedrooms and two baths, full kitchen, plus a wood-burning fireplace. Prices for small studio condos start at about $100 (double) in summer; during the ski season expect to pay at least $125.

The most upscale lodging choice in Brian Head is **Cedar Breaks Lodge** (223 Hunter Ridge Rd., 435/667-3000 or 888/282-3327, www.cedarbreakslodge.com, $70–230 in summer, $115–360 in winter) at the base of Navajo Peak on the north (lower) side of town. All rooms come with jetted tubs, a refrigerator, in-room coffee, and cable TV; kitchens are available in some rooms. There's also an indoor pool, two hot tubs, a steam room, sauna, day spa, and fitness center. Lodging choices range from hotel rooms to three-bedroom suites.

CAMPGROUNDS

The U.S. Forest Service has three campgrounds at Panguitch Lake. **Panguitch Lake North Campground** (435/865-3200 or 877/444-6777, www.recreation.gov, June–Sept., $10), on the southwest side of the lake, has developed sites in a ponderosa pine forest at an elevation of 8,400 feet. **Panguitch Lake South Campground** (435/865-3200, no reservations, June–Sept., $8) across the highway, is more suited for small rigs and tents. **White Bridge Campground** (435/865-3200 or 877/444-6777, www.recreation.gov, June–Sept., $10), elevation 7,900 feet, lies among cottonwoods and junipers along Panguitch Creek four miles northeast of the lake.

Panguitch Lake General Store and RV Park (53 W Hwy. 143, 435/676-2464) has an RV park with a few hookup sites for self-contained RVs. The store is open year-round and sells groceries, gas, gifts, and fishing supplies.

Food

At the Brian Head Mall, **Bump and Grind** (259 S. State Hwy. 143, 435/677-3111, lunch daily, $5–10) serves coffee and deli items. Typical ski-area grills operate in both the Navajo and Giant Steps Lodges.

At Cedar Breaks Lodge, there are a couple dining rooms. The **Cedar Breaks Café** (435/667-3000, breakfast and dinner daily, $6–16) is the most casual, while the **Double Black Diamond Steak House** (435/677-4242, dinner Fri.–Sat., $11–26, reservations recommended) serves Western-style fine dining.

Information

General information is available from **Brian Head Chamber of Commerce** (435/677-2810, www.brianheadutah.com).

CEDAR BREAKS NATIONAL MONUMENT

Erosion on the west edge of the Markagunt Plateau has carved a giant amphitheater 2,500 feet deep and more than three miles across. A fairyland of forms and colors appears below the rim. Ridges and pinnacles extend like buttresses from the steep cliffs. Cottony patches of clouds often drift through the craggy landscape. Traces of iron, manganese, and other minerals have tinted the normally white limestone a rainbow of warm hues. The intense colors blaze during sunsets and glow even on a cloudy day. Rock layers look much like those at Bryce Canyon National Park and, in fact, are the same Claron Formation, but here they're 2,000 feet higher. Elevations range from 10,662 feet at the rim's highest point to 8,100 feet at Ashdown Creek below. In the distance beyond the amphitheater, you can see Cedar City and the desert's valleys and ranges. Dense forests broken by large alpine meadows cover the rolling plateau country away from the rim. More than 150 species of wildflowers brighten the meadows during summer; the colorful display peaks during the last two weeks in July.

A five-mile scenic drive leads past four spectacular overlooks, each with a different perspective. Avoid overlooks and other exposed areas during thunderstorms, which are common on summer afternoons. Heavy snows close the road most of the year. You can drive in only from about late May until the first big snowstorm of autumn, usually sometime in October. Winter visitors can come in on snowmobiles (unplowed roads only), skis, or snowshoes from Brian Head (two miles north of the monument) or from Hwy. 14 (2.5 miles south). Cedar Breaks National Monument is 24 miles east of Cedar City, 17 miles south of Parowan, 30 miles southwest of Panguitch, and 27 miles northwest of Long Valley Junction. The nearest accommodations and restaurants are two miles north in Brian Head.

Visitors Center and Campground

A log cabin visitors center (435/586-0787 summer, 435/586-0787 winter, www.nps.gov/cebr, daily 8 A.M.–6 P.M. June 1–mid-Oct., $4 per vehicle park-entrance fee) includes exhibits, an information desk, and a bookstore. The exhibits provide a good introduction to the Markagunt Plateau and identify local rocks, wildflowers, trees, animals, and birds. Staff members offer nature walks, geology talks, and campfire programs; see the schedules posted in the visitors center and at the campground. An entrance fee of $4 per vehicle is collected near the visitors center; there's no charge if you're just driving through the monument without stopping. The small campground to the east has water and a $14 fee; camping is first come, first served. The campground is open about mid-June–late September. (If you plan to visit in June or September, it's best to call ahead to check the campground's status; some years its season is remarkably short.) There's a picnic area near the campground.

Hiking

Two easy trails near the rim give an added appreciation of the geology and forests here. Allow extra time while on foot—it's easy to get out of breath at these high elevations. Regulations prohibit pets on the trails. **Spectra Point/Wasatch Rampart Trail** begins at the visitors center, then follows the rim along the south edge of the amphitheater to an overlook. The hike is four miles round-trip with some ups and downs. Weather-beaten bristlecone pines grow at Spectra Point, about halfway down the trail.

Alpine Pond Trail forms a two-mile loop that drops below the rim into one of the few densely wooded areas of the amphitheater. The trail winds through enchanting forests of aspen, subalpine fir, and Engelmann spruce. You can cut the hiking distance in half with a car shuttle between the two trailheads or by taking a connector trail that joins the upper and lower parts of the loop near Alpine Pond. Begin from either Chessmen Ridge Overlook or the trailhead pullout 1.1 miles farther north. A trail guide is available at the start or at the visitors center.

ZION AND BRYCE

THE ESCALANTE REGION

The south-central region of Utah is domi-nated by three vast tracts of public land, the Grand Staircase–Escalante National Monu-ment (GSENM), Capitol Reef National Park, and the Glen Canyon National Recreation Area, at the heart of which lies Lake Powell. While these public lands are not as famous as the brand-name national parks of southern Utah, they have much to offer travelers—par-ticularly those people who love backcountry and solitude.

GSENM represents a unique combination of archaeological, historical, paleontological, geo-logical, and biological wonders. Capitol Reef National Park is for the connoisseur of Utah backcountry—it may not be the first park you plan to visit, but it's the one that you will focus

on as you hone your enthusiasm for the desert outback. Glen Canyon National Recreation Area encompasses the rugged canyons leading to the Colorado River's Glen Canyon, which was once considered the equal of the Grand Canyon for drama and beauty. The canyon is now trapped beneath the waters of Lake Pow-ell, a magnet for boating and water sports.

PLANNING YOUR TIME

Even the most casual travelers with a few hours to spare can enjoy traveling through this fan-tastic landscape of desert and rock. Hwy. 12, which begins near Bryce Canyon National Park and continues along the wild canyon and slickrock country of the Grand Staircase–Escalante National Monument, is one of the

HIGHLIGHTS

[Kodachrome Basin State Park: Strange-looking rock pillars are the attraction at this state park on the northwestern edge of Grand Staircase-Escalante National Monument. Hiking trails and a campground make this a good base for exploring the monument's Cottonwood Canyon Road (page 343).

[The Million-Dollar Road: Although Highway 12 is spectacular for its entire length – from the Red Rocks west of Bryce Canyon National Park to Torrey, near Capitol Reef – this stretch of the highway between Escalante and Boulder was a real feat of engineering when it was built in 1935. Acrophobics should bring blinders (page 347).

[Dry Fork of Coyote Gulch: This hike down into sinuous slot canyons requires a little bit of driving along the rugged Hole-in-the-Rock Road, but unlike many spectacular Escalante canyon hikes, it's a moderate day hike (page 355).

[Hikes in the Calf Creek Recreation Area: If your car won't make it down bumpy dirt roads of the Grand Staircase-Escalante National Monument, don't worry. Good hikes are just off Highway 12 in the Calf Creek Recreation Area. Lower Calf Creek Falls is a classic (page 356).

[Capitol Gorge: At the southern end of the Capitol Reef National Park Scenic Drive, hike up the sandy wash into Capitol Gorge, where you'll find petroglyphs and incised names of Mormon pioneers. Go up a side trail to explore waterpockets, natural water-collecting depressions in the rocks (page 370).

[Goblin Valley State Park: Whether or not you find them spooky, the rock formations

at this state park north of Hanksville are fun to explore. Take time to walk around the goblin-like spires and rocks along the trails (page 382).

[Lake Powell: Love it or hate it, Lake Powell is worth a look. The lake is an artificial reservoir covering Glen Canyon, once one of the southwest's most beautiful river canyons. In especially dry years, when the reservoir is drawn down, parts of Glen Canyon reemerge (page 384).

LOOK FOR **[** TO FIND RECOMMENDED SIGHTS, ACTIVITIES, DINING, AND LODGING.

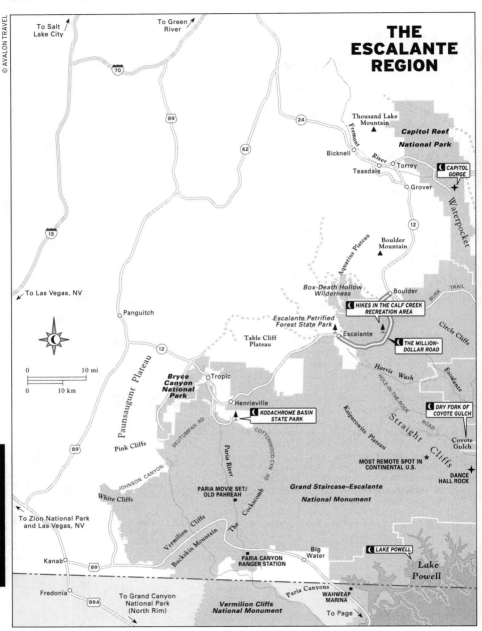

© AVALON TRAVEL

THE ESCALANTE REGION

THE ESCALANTE REGION

To Salt Lake City

To Green River

70

89

24

Thousand Lake Mountain

Capitol Reef National Park

Bicknell

Fremont River

Torrey

CAPITOL GORGE

Teasdale

Grover

15

62

Waterpocket

12

Aquarius Plateau

Boulder Mountain

To Las Vegas, NV

Box-Death Hollow Wilderness

Boulder

BURR TRAIL

Panguitch

HIKES IN THE CALF CREEK RECREATION AREA

Circle Cliffs

Escalante Petrified Forest State Park

Escalante

Table Cliff Plateau

THE MILLION-DOLLAR ROAD

Escalante

0   10 mi

0   10 km

12

Harris Wash

HOLE-IN-THE-ROCK

Bryce Canyon National Park

Tropic

Paunsaugunt Plateau

Henrieville

KODACHROME BASIN STATE PARK

Kaiparowits Plateau

Straight Cliffs

DRY FORK OF COYOTE GULCH

ROAD

Coyote Gulch

89

Pink Cliffs

SKUTUMPAH RD

Paria River

COTTONWOOD CYN RD

MOST REMOTE SPOT IN CONTINENTAL U.S.

DANCE HALL ROCK

JOHNSON CANYON

White Cliffs

PARIA MOVIE SET/ OLD PAHREAH

The Cockscomb

Grand Staircase–Escalante National Monument

To Zion National Park and Las Vegas, NV

Vermilion Cliffs

Buckskin Mountain

The Cockscomb

Big Water

LAKE POWELL

Kanab

89

PARIA CANYON RANGER STATION

Lake Powell

Fredonia

89A

To Grand Canyon National Park (North Rim)

Paria Canyons

WAHWEAP MARINA

Vermilion Cliffs National Monument

To Page

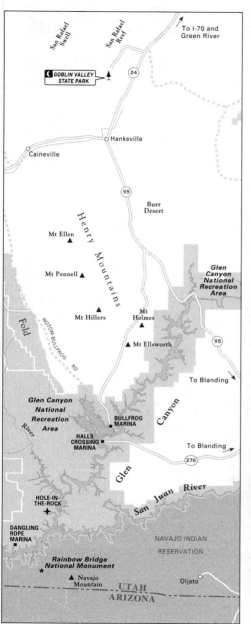

most scenic roads in Utah. It's also worth spending a night along the road in Boulder, home of the Boulder Mountain Lodge and famed Hell's Backbone Grill.

If you have more time, plan to spend a couple of days exploring Grand Staircase–Escalante National Monument: perhaps a hike to Lower Calf Creek Falls and a day trip down Hole-in-the-Rock Road, with explorations of Devil's Garden and the slot canyons in the Dry Fork of Coyote Gulch.

Allow at least a day to hike in Capitol Reef, which has many good day hikes, including the hike to waterpockets in Capitol Gorge.

In the Glen Canyon National Recreation Area, the ultimate vacation is to rent a houseboat on Lake Powell, but if you're not ready to make that commitment, consider a ferryboat ride across the reservoir between Hall's Crossing and Bullfrog.

hiking through Grand Staircase-Escalante National Monument

Grand Staircase-Escalante National Monument

The 1.9-million-acre Grand Staircase–Escalante National Monument (GSENM, 435/644-4600, www.ut.blm.gov/monument) contains a vast and wonderfully scenic collection of slickrock canyonlands and desert, prehistoric village sites, Old West ranch land, arid plateaus, and miles of back roads linking stone arches, mesas, and abstract rock formations. The monument even preserves a historic movie set (think vintage Westerns).

The monument contains essentially three separate districts: On the eastern third are the narrow wilderness canyons of the Escalante River and its tributaries. In the center of the monument is a vast swath of arid rangeland and canyons called the Kairparowits Plateau, with few developed destinations—before use of all-terrain vehicles (ATVs), dune buggies, and dirt bikes was limited, these canyons and bluffs were a popular playground for off-road enthusiasts. The western third of the monument edges up against the Grey, White, and Pink Cliffs of the Grand Staircase. These thinly treed uplands are laced with former Forest Service roads. The GSENM is the largest land grouping designated as a national monument in the lower 48 states.

There's little dispute that the **Escalante Canyons** are the primary reason people visit the monument. The river and its tributaries cut deep and winding slot canyons through massive slickrock formations, and hiking these canyon bottoms is an extremely popular adventure. A multi-day trek is a rite of passage for many devoted hikers, but you don't have to be a hardened backcountry trekker to enjoy this landscape: Two backcountry roads wind through the area, and some day hikes are possible.

The other districts offer less well-defined opportunities for adventure. Backcountry drivers and long-distance mountain bikers will find mile after mile of desert and canyon to explore. **Grosvenor Arch,** with double windows, is a popular back-road destination. At the southern edge of the park, along the Arizona border, is another rugged canyon system that's popular with long-distance hikers. The **Paria River Canyon** is even more remote than the Escalante, and hiking these slot canyons requires experience and preparation.

There is currently no entrance fee for visiting the monument. Free permits are required for all overnight backcountry camping or backpacking. There is a fee to camp in the monument's three developed campgrounds.

Hikers in the Paria Wilderness area are required to buy a permit (this includes Paria Canyon and Coyote Buttes), as are hikers at the Calf Creek Recreation Area.

Only two paved roads pass through the monument, both in an east–west trajectory. Hwy. 12, on the northern border of the park, links Bryce Canyon and Capitol Reef National Parks with access to the Escalante canyons. This is one of the most scenic roads in Utah—in fact, *Car and Driver* magazine rates this route as one of the 10 most scenic in all of the United States. Its innumerable swallow-your-gum vistas and geologic curiosities will keep you on the edge of your seat.

U.S. 89, which travels along the southern edge of the monument between Kanab and Lake Powell, is no scenery slouch either. It is also the access road for the North Rim of the Grand Canyon in Arizona. Three fair-weather dirt roads, each with a network of side roads and trails, cut through the rugged heart of the monument, linking the two paved roads. Before heading out on these back roads, check with a visitors center for conditions; high-clearance vehicles are recommended.

History

Anasazi and Fremont people lived in the Escalante area about A.D. 1050–1200. You can spot their petroglyphs, pictographs, artifacts, storage rooms, and village sites while you're hiking in the canyons of the Escalante River and its tributaries. High alcoves in canyon walls protect small stone granaries; check the

THE POLITICS OF ESTABLISHING
THE NATIONAL MONUMENT

In September 1996, President Bill Clinton declared 1.9 million acres of south-central Utah a national monument, ending a decades-old debate about preserving the wilderness canyons in this part of the Southwest. The federal government's move sought to prevent the establishment of coal mines in the area, which had been planned by a Dutch resource-extraction consortium. The monument was formed by combining existing public land into a single administrative unit: The land now preserved as Grand Staircase–Escalante National Monument consists of land formerly supervised by the Bureau of Land Management (BLM), the Forest Service, and the state of Utah. The responsibility for administering the new monument was assigned to the BLM.

Preservation of the canyons as a national monument angered the Republican Utah legislative delegation and many others in this deeply conservative state. They were angry that they were not consulted about the formation of the monument, and they argued that the federal government should not interfere with local agriculture and the existing community. The move pleased environmentalists and backcountry recreationists, however, who feared that the existence of a mining operation, no matter how environmentally sound,

would destroy the area's unique scenic splendor and ancient Anasazi art and ruins.

Feelings pro and con about the monument can still run deep around Escalante and southern Utah, but a whole new breed of business is springing up to address the needs of the tourists and recreationists who flock here. For people who have adapted to the changing economic and environmental forces, hostility to the monument and the crowds it attracts is subsiding, though certain issues, especially concerning the size of the monument and activities permitted within its boundaries, are still being litigated, and may be for years.

The irony in all of this is that so far, in terms of land usage, very little has changed for either the farmers and ranchers who have leased these federal lands for generations or for the hikers and bikers who want to explore the wilds of this canyon country. The BLM has moved slowly to reassess access to the land and is trying to preserve the land's tradition as a multiuse area (with ranchers retaining grazing leases on federal land). Certain restrictions are in place, but these mostly affect the use of all-terrain vehicles (ATVs) and non-street-legal vehicles (off-road vehicles, dune buggies, and certain kinds of dirt bikes).

---

floors of sandstone caves for things left behind—pieces of pottery, arrowheads, mats, sandals, and corncobs. (Federal laws prohibit removal of artifacts; please leave *everything* for the next person to enjoy.) You can visit an excavated Anasazi village, along with a modern replica of the original, 27 miles east in Boulder.

Southern Paiute arrived in the 1500s and stayed until white settlers took over. The nomadic Paiute had few possessions and left little behind despite their long stay. Mormon colonists didn't learn about the Escalante region until 1866, when Captain James Andrus led his cavalry east from Kanab in pursuit of Paiutes. Reports of the expedition described the

upper Escalante, which was named Potato Valley after the wild tubers growing there.

Major John Wesley Powell's expedition down the Green and Colorado Rivers in 1869 had failed to recognize the mouth of the Escalante River; it seemed too shallow and narrow for a major tributary. In 1872, a detachment of Powell's second expedition led by Almon H. Thompson and Frederick S. Dellenbaugh stumbled across the Escalante on an overland journey. After some confusion they realized that an entire new river had been found, and they named it for Spanish explorer and priest Silvestre Valez de Escalante. The elusive river was the last to be discovered in the contiguous

United States. Mormon ranchers and farmers arrived in the upper valleys of the Escalante in 1876 from Panguitch and other towns to the west, not as part of a church-directed mission but simply in search of new and better lands.

The sleepy town of Escalante served the needs of local farmers and ranchers for nearly a century, until 1996 when President Bill Clinton created the Grand Staircase–Escalante National Monument out of existing state and federal lands. The resulting political flap and hardening local sentiments against outsiders and environmentalists have not eased the creation of an eco-tourism Eden in this desert backcountry.

Visitors Centers

The administrative headquarters of GSENM (190 E. Center St., 435/644-4300, www.ut.blm .gov/monument, 7:30 A.M.–5:30 P.M. daily Mar. 15–Nov. 15, 8 A.M.–4:30 P.M. Mon.–Fri. Nov. 15–Mar. 15) is in Kanab, about 15 miles from the southwestern edge of the monument, but the regional visitors centers, listed below, are the best places to contact for practical travel information.

Escalante Interagency Visitors Center (755 West Main, Escalante, 435/826-5499, 7:30 A.M.–5:30 P.M. daily mid-Mar.–mid-Nov., Mon.–Fri. 8 A.M.–4:30 P.M. mid-Nov.–mid-Mar.) is housed in a sprawling building at the west end of the town of Escalante. Staff here are very knowledgeable and helpful, and exhibits focus on the monument's ecology and biological diversity.

Kanab Visitors Center (745 East Hwy. 89, Kanab, 435/644-4680, 8 A.M.–5 P.M. daily mid-Mar.–mid-Nov., Mon.–Fri. 8 A.M.– 4:30 P.M. mid-Nov.–mid-Mar.) is the place to stop if you're planning to drive Cottonwood or Johnson Canyon/Skutumpah Roads from the south. Staff can give you updates on the road conditions and suggest driving and hiking strategies. Exhibits at this visitor center concentrate on geology and archaeology.

Cannonville Visitors Center (10 Center St., Cannonville, 435/826-5640, 8 A.M.–4:30 P.M. daily mid-Mar.–mid-Nov.) is an attractive

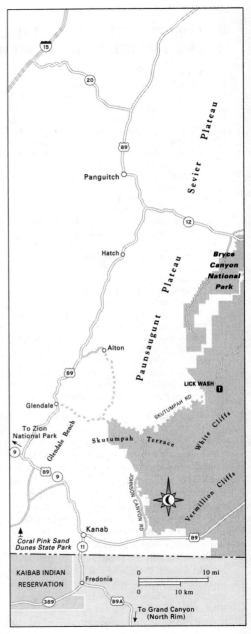

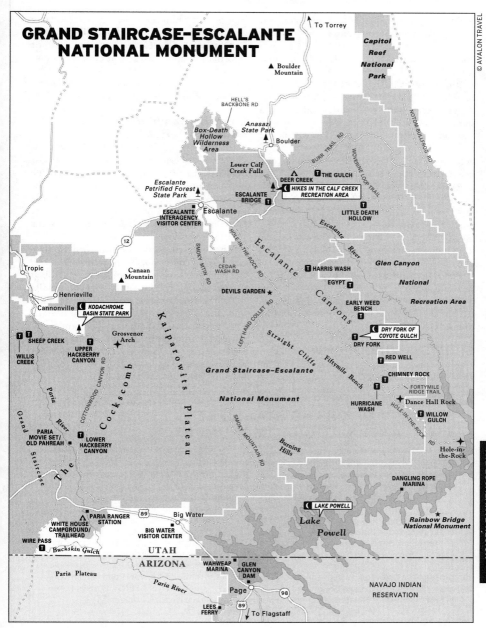

GRAND STAIRCASE-ESCALANTE NATIONAL MONUMENT

To Torrey

Capitol Reef National Park

Boulder Mountain

HELL'S BACKBONE RD

Box-Death Hollow Wilderness Area

Anasazi State Park

Boulder

BURR TRAIL RD

NOTOM-BULLFROG RD

WOLVERINE LOOP TRAIL

Lower Calf Creek Falls

Escalante Petrified Forest State Park

DEER CREEK

THE GULCH

HIKES IN THE CALF CREEK RECREATION AREA

ESCALANTE BRIDGE

Escalante

LITTLE DEATH HOLLOW

ESCALANTE INTERAGENCY VISITOR CENTER

Escalante River

12

Tropic

SMOKY MTN. RD

HOLE-IN-THE-ROCK RD

Canaan Mountain

CEDAR WASH RD

Escalante

HARRIS WASH

Glen Canyon

Henrieville

DEVILS GARDEN

EGYPT

National

Cannonville

KODACHROME BASIN STATE PARK

Canyons

EARLY WEED BENCH

Recreation Area

DRY FORK OF COYOTE GULCH

Grosvenor Arch

LEFT HAND COLLET RD

Straight Cliffs

DRY FORK

SHEEP CREEK

Kaiparowits Plateau

RED WELL

WILLIS CREEK

UPPER HACKBERRY CANYON

Fiftymile Bench

CHIMNEY ROCK

Cottonwood Canyon RD

Grand Staircase-Escalante

FORTYMILE RIDGE TRAIL

Paria

Cockscomb

National Monument

SMOKY MOUNTAIN RD

HURRICANE WASH

Dance Hall Rock

HOLE-IN-THE-ROCK RD

Grand Staircase

Paria River

PARIA MOVIE SET/ OLD PAHREAH

LOWER HACKBERRY CANYON

Burning Hills

WILLOW GULCH

Hole-in-the-Rock

The

DANGLING ROPE MARINA

PARIA RANGER STATION

89

Big Water

Lake Powell

LAKE POWELL

Rainbow Bridge National Monument

WHITE HOUSE CAMPGROUND/ TRAILHEAD

BIG WATER VISITOR CENTER

WIRE PASS

Buckskin Gulch

UTAH

ARIZONA

WAHWEAP MARINA

GLEN CANYON DAM

Paria Plateau

Paria River

Page

98

NAVAJO INDIAN RESERVATION

LEES FERRY

89

To Flagstaff

© AVALON TRAVEL

THE ESCALANTE REGION

building at the north end of Cottonwood and Johnson Canyon/Skutumpah Roads. Even if the office is closed, stop by to look at the outdoor exhibits, which depict the different cultures that have lived in the area.

Big Water Visitors Center (100 Upper Revolution Way, Big Water, 435/675-3200, 8 A.M.–5 P.M. daily mid-Mar.–mid-Nov.), a spiral-shaped building designed to resemble an ammonite, is home to a small but distinctive collection of dinosaur bones and a wild mural depicting Late Cretaceous life in the area. Stop here to learn about local paleontology.

Anasazi State Park (460 N. Hwy. 12, Boulder, 435/335-7382, www.stateparks .utah.gov, 9 A.M.–5 P.M. daily mid-Mar.–mid-Nov., $3 per person to visit park) has a ranger on duty at an information desk inside the museum. The museum itself is worth a visit, so don't be stingy with your three bucks!

Paria Contact Station (Hwy. 89, 44 miles east of Kanab, no phone, 8:30 A.M.–4:15 P.M. daily Mar. 15–Nov. 15) is a small visitors center, but an important stop for anyone planning to hike Paria Canyon.

SIGHTS ALONG HIGHWAY 12

This tour proceeds west–east, from Bryce Canyon National Park and Tropic along the north edge of the monument to the towns of Escalante and Boulder. Stop at the **Cannonville Visitors Center** (see *Visitors Centers* in this section) for information about back-road conditions and hikes in this part of the monument. Two backcountry roads depart from Cannonville and lead to remote corners of the monument.

Johnson Canyon/ Skutumpah Road

The northern end of this route is in Cannonville; its southern terminus is at U.S. 89 just east of Kanab (46 miles one-way). From the northernmost stretch of this road, Bryce Canyon rises to the west; about six miles from the southern end, and off to the east on private land (look from the road, don't trespass), is the set from the TV show *Gunsmoke*.

The unpaved portions of the road are usually in good condition, except after rains, when the bentonite soils that comprise the roadbed turn to goo. In good weather, cars can usually make the journey. The road follows the Pink and White Cliff terraces of the Grand Staircase, with access to some excellent and comparatively undersubscribed-to hiking trails. Several steep slot canyons make for excellent canyoneering. The lower 16 miles of Johnson Canyon Road are paved.

GEOLOGY OF GRAND STAIRCASE-ESCALANTE NATIONAL MONUMENT

This desert landscape once sat at the verge of a vast inland sea. About 300 million years ago, sandy dunes rose hundreds of feet above the waves, then sank below sea level and were covered by water. Thick layers of sediment built up one on top of the other, turning the sand dunes to stone. During the last 50 million years, powerful forces within the earth slowly pushed the entire region one mile upward. The ancestral Colorado River began to carve the deep gorges seen today near Glen Canyon. In turn, the tributaries of the Colorado, such as the Escalante, were also forced to trench deeper and deeper in order to drain their watershed.

The most characteristic rocks in the monument are the ancient dunes, turned to stone called slickrock, which make up many of the sheer canyon cliffs, arches, and spires of the region. Delicate cross-bedded lines of the former dunes add grace to these features. Forces within the restless plateau have also buckled and folded rock layers into great reefs as long as 100 miles. Weathering then carved them into rainbow-hued rock monuments. The aptly named Cockscomb, visible from Cottonwood Canyon Road, which cuts through the center of GSENM, is an example of these massive rock wrinkles.

Cottonwood Canyon Scenic Back Road

This 46-mile route also connects Cannonville with U.S. 89, but passes through quite different terrain and landscapes. One of the most scenic backcountry routes in the monument, the Cottonwood Canyon road not only offers access to dramatic Grosvenor Arch, but it also passes along the Cockscomb, a soaring buckle of rock that divides the Grand Staircase and the Kairparowits Plateau. Cottonwood Creek, which this road parallels, is a normally dry streambed that cuts through the angular rock beds of the Cockscomb. Several excellent hikes lead into the canyons and narrows, where Paria River, Hackberry Canyon, and Cottonwood Creek all meet, about 20 miles south of Cannonville.

Check at the Cannonville or Big Water visitors centers for information about road conditions. Although the road is sometimes passable for cars, several road crossings are susceptible to washouts after rainstorms, and the northern portion is impassable even to four-wheel drive vehicles when wet because of the extremely unctuous nature of the roadbed. Check conditions before setting out if you plan to go beyond Grosvenor Arch.

© JUDY JEWELL

Kodachrome Basin State Park

◖ Kodachrome Basin State Park

Visitors come to Kodachrome Basin State Park (435/679-8562, www.stateparks.utah.gov, $6 day use, $15 camping), located in a basin southeast of Bryce, to see not only colorful cliffs but also strange-looking rock pillars that occur nowhere else in the world. Sixty-seven rock pillars (here called "sand pipes"), found in and near the park, range in height from six to nearly 170 feet. One theory of their origin is that earthquakes caused sediments deep underground to be churned up by water under high pressure. The particles of calcite, quartz, feldspar, and clay in the sand pipes came from underlying rock formations, and the pipes appeared when the surrounding rock eroded away. Most of the other rocks visible in the park are Entrada sandstone: The lower orange layer is the Gunsight Butte Member, and the white layer with orange bands is the Cannonville Member.

Signs name some of the rock features. "Big Stoney," the phallus-shaped sand pipe overlooking the campground, is so explicit that it doesn't need a sign! The article "Motoring into Escalante Land" by Jack Breed, in the September 1949 issue of *National Geographic,* brought attention to the scenery and renamed the area "Kodachrome Flat," for the then-experimental Kodak film used by the expedition. The state park is a worthwhile stop, both as a day trip to see the geology and as a pleasant spot to camp. The park also offers several good half-day hiking trails and a host of shorter hikes.

To reach the park, drive to Cannonville and follow signs for nine miles along paved Cottonwood Canyon Road. Adventurous drivers can also approach the park from U.S. 89 to the south via Cottonwood Canyon Road (35 miles) or Skutumpah Road through Bull Valley Gorge and Johnson Canyon (48 miles). These routes may be impassable in wet weather but are generally okay in dry weather for cars with good clearance.

You can arrange horseback rides at **Trailhead**

THE ESCALANTE REGION

Station (435/679-8787, www.brycecanyoninn
.com), a small store in the park that sells groceries and camping supplies early April–late
October. They also rent several cabins ($75);
call ahead or reserve online.

The state park's **campground** (435/679-
8562, 800/322-3770 or www.reserveamerica
.com reservations) sits in a natural amphitheater at an elevation of 5,800 feet. It's open all
year and has restrooms, showers, and a dump
station. During the winter, restrooms and
showers may close, but pit toilets are available.
The campground usually has room except on
summer holidays.

Grosvenor Arch

Just one mile off Cottonwood Canyon Road,
a side road leads to the magnificent Grosvenor Arch. It takes a little bit of effort to get
here (the 10-mile dirt road from the turnoff to
Kodachrome State to the arch can be bumpy
and, in wet weather, should be avoided), so a
visit to the arch can take on the qualities of a
pilgrimage. There are actually two arches here,

© JUDY JEWELL

THE ESCALANTE REGION

Though Grosvenor Arch is spectacular,
bad weather frequently closes the unpaved
access road.

which is a pretty rare occurrence for such ero-
sion-formed arches; their position, jutting like
flying buttresses out of a soaring cliff, is also
quite stunning. The larger of the two openings
is 99 feet across. A 1949 National Geographic
Society expedition named the double arch in
honor of the society's president. The turn-off
is 10 miles from the state park turn-off and 29
miles from U.S. 89.

Escalante Petrified Forest State Park

This pleasant park (435/826-4466, www
.stateparks.utah.gov, $5 day use, $15 camping),
just northwest of the town of Escalante, offers
camping, boating, fishing, picnicking, hiking,
a visitors center with displays of petrified wood
and dinosaur bones, and a chance to see petrified wood along trails. Rivers of 140 million
years ago carried trees to the site of present-day
Escalante and buried them in sand and gravel.
Burial prevented decay as crystals of silicon dioxide gradually replaced the wood cells. Mineral impurities added a rainbow of colors to the
trees as they turned to stone. Weathering has
exposed this petrified wood and the water-worn
pebbles and sand of the Morrison Formation.
For a look at some colorful petrified wood, follow the **Petrified Forest Trail** from the campground up a hillside wooded with piñon pine
and juniper. At the top of the 240-foot-high
ridge, continue on a loop trail to the petrified
wood; allow 45–60 minutes for the one-mile
round-trip hike. The steep **Rainbow Loop Trail**
(0.75 mile) branches off the Petrified Forest
Trail to more areas of petrified wood.

The **campground** (800/322-3770, www
.reserveamerica.com) stays open all year and
offers drinking water and showers but no
hookups. The adjacent 139-acre Wide Hollow
Reservoir offers fishing, boating, and bird-
watching. Canoe rentals are $5 per hour, or
$10 for 4 hours. The park is 1.5 miles west of
Escalante on Hwy. 12, then 0.7 mile north on
a gravel road.

Escalante

The town of Escalante, 38 miles east of Bryce

Canyon and 23 miles south of Boulder, has all services and is the headquarters for explorations of the Escalante River canyons. The Escalante Interagency Office (755 W. Main St., 435/826-5499, 7:30 A.M.–5:30 P.M. daily mid-Mar.–mid-Nov., 8 A.M.–4:30 P.M. Mon.–Fri. mid-Nov.–mid-Mar.) provides information on local hikes and road conditions.

Smokey Mountain Road

From Escalante, it's 78 miles south to Hwy. 89 at Big Water, just shy of Lake Powell, along Smokey Mountain Road. This road is rougher than other cross-monument roads. Be sure to check on conditions before setting out; four-wheel drive vehicles are required. As this route passes across the Kaiparowits Plateau, the landscape is bleak and arid. Then, the road drops precipitously down onto a bench where side roads lead through badlands to Lake Powell beaches. Big Water is 19 miles from Page, Arizona, and 57 miles from Kanab.

Hole-in-the-Rock Road

The building of this road by determined Mormons was one of the great epics in the colonization of the West. Church leaders organized the Hole-in-the-Rock Expedition to settle the wild lands around the San Juan River of southeastern Utah, believing that a Mormon presence would aid in ministering to the Indians there and prevent non-Mormons from moving in. In 1878, the Parowan Stake issued the first call for a colonizing mission to the San Juan, even before a site had been selected.

Preparations and surveys took place the following year as the 236 men, women, and children received their calls. Food, seed, farming and building tools, 200 horses, and more than 1,000 head of cattle would be taken along. Planners ruled out lengthy routes through northern Arizona or eastern Utah in favor of a straight shot via Escalante that would cut the distance in half. The expedition set off in the autumn of 1879, convinced that they were part of a divine mission.

Yet hints of trouble to come filtered back from the group as they discovered the Colorado River crossing to be far more difficult than first believed. Lack of springs along the way added to their worries. From their start at Escalante, road builders progressed rapidly for the first 50 miles, then slowly over rugged slickrock for the final six miles to Hole-in-the-Rock. A sheer 45-foot drop below this narrow notch was followed by almost a mile of extremely steep slickrock to the Colorado River. The route looked impossible, but three crews of workers armed with picks and blasting powder worked simultaneously to widen the notch and construct a precarious wagon road down to the river and up the cliffs on the other side.

The job took six weeks. Miraculously, all of the people, animals, and wagons made it down and were ferried across the Colorado River without a serious accident. Canyons and other obstacles continued to block the way as the weary group pressed on. Only after six months of exhausting travel did they stop at the present-day site of Bluff on the San Juan River.

Today, on a journey from Escalante, you can experience a bit of the same adventure the pioneers knew. Except for scattered signs of ranching, the land remains unchanged. If the road is dry, vehicles with good clearance can drive to within a short distance of Hole-in-the-Rock. The rough conditions encountered past Dance Hall Rock require more clearance than most cars allow. Bring sufficient gas, food, and water for the entire 126-mile round-trip from Escalante.

The turn-off from Hwy. 12 is five miles east of Escalante. In addition to rewarding you with scenic views, Hole-in-the-Rock Road passes many side drainages of the Escalante River to the east and some remote country of the Kaiparowits Plateau high above to the west. Staff at the information center just west of Escalante can give current road conditions and suggest hikes.

Metate Arch and other rock sculptures decorate **Devil's Garden,** 12.5 miles down Hole-in-the-Rock Road. Turn west 0.3 mile at the sign to the parking area because you can't really see the "garden" from the road. Red- and cream-colored sandstone formations sit atop pedestals or tilt at crazy angles. Delicate bedding lines run through the rocks. There are no

THE ESCALANTE REGION

trails or markers—just wander about at your whim. The Bureau of Land Management has provided picnic tables, grills, and outhouses for day use. No overnight camping is permitted at Devil's Garden.

Dance Hall Rock (38 miles down Hole-in-the-Rock Road) jumped to the fiddle music and lively steps of the expedition members in 1879. Its natural amphitheater has a relatively smooth floor and made a perfect gathering spot when the Hole-in-the-Rock group had to wait three weeks at nearby Fortymile Spring for roadwork to be completed ahead. Dance Hall Rock is an enjoyable place to explore and only a short walk from the parking area. Solution holes, left from water dissolving in the rock, pockmark the sandstone structure.

At road's end (57 miles from Hwy. 12), continue on foot across slickrock to the notch and views of the blue waters of Lake Powell below. Rockslides have made the descent impossible for vehicles, but hikers can scramble down to the lake and back in about one hour. The elevation change is 600 feet. The half-mile round-trip is strenuous. After a steep descent over boulders, look for steps of Uncle Ben's Dugway at the base of the notch. Below here the grade is gentler. Drill holes in the rock once held oak stakes against which logs, brush, and earth supported the outer wagon wheels. The inner wheels followed a narrow rut 4–6 inches deep. About two-thirds of the route down is now under water, although the most impressive roadwork can still be seen.

Hundred Hands Pictograph

Be sure to pull off Hwy. 12 at the **Boynton Overlook** and scan the walls on the far side of the Escalante River for the Hundred Hands pictograph. (Binoculars help immensely.) For a closer look, hike up from the parking lot just at the bottom of the hill, at the Escalante River crossing. Rather than hike along the river, go up above the house (don't stray onto fenced-in private property), scramble up the face of the first cliff, and follow faint trails and rock cairns across the bench. (It's easiest if you've located the pictographs first from the overlook.)

The Hundred Hands are high up on a cliff face that's larger than the one you scrambled up. Follow the cliff to the right, where pictographs of goats are lower on the wall.

Back down at river level, head downstream a few hundred yards and look up to the left to see the Anasazi ruins known as the "Moki house."

Calf Creek Recreation Area

This stunning canyon and park offer the most accessible glimpse of what Escalante Canyon country is all about. The trailhead to 126-foot **Lower Calf Creek Falls** is here, and you should definitely make plans for the half-day hike, especially if you have no time for further exploration of this magical landscape. Otherwise, stop here to picnic in the shade of willows and cottonwoods. This is also the most convenient and attractive **campsite** (Escalante Interagency Office, 755 W. Main St., 435/826-5499, $7) for dozens of miles. The 13 campsites have water, fire pits, and picnic tables.

Lower Calf Creek Falls

© JUDY JEWELL

◖ The Million-Dollar Road

Hwy. 12 between Escalante and Boulder was completed in 1935 by workers from the Civilian Conservation Corps. The cost was a budget-busting $1 million. Before then, mules carried supplies and mail across this wilderness of slickrock and narrow canyons. The section of Hwy. 12 between Calf Creek and Boulder is extraordinarily scenic—even jaded travelers used to the wonders of Utah will have to pull over and ogle the views from the **Hog's Back,** where the road crests a fin of rock above the canyons of the Escalante. Be here for sunset on a clear evening and you'll have a memory to carry for the rest of your life.

Boulder

Boulder is a tiny community in a lovely location at the base of Boulder Mountain, where the alpine air mixes with the desert breezes. The single best lodging choice in the Escalante region—the Boulder Mountain Lodge—is here, so plan accordingly (see *Accommodations* later in this section for more information).

Anasazi State Park

At this excellent state park (Hwy. 12 one mile north of Boulder, 435/335-7308, www.state parks.utah.gov, 8 A.M.–6 P.M. daily, $3 per person), museum exhibits, an excavated village site, and a pueblo replica provide a look into the life of these ancient people. The Anasazi stayed here for 50–75 years sometime between A.D. 1050 and 1200. They grew corn, beans, and squash in fields nearby. The village population peaked at about 200, with an estimated 40–50 dwellings. Why the Anasazi left or where they went isn't known for sure, but a fire swept through much of the village before the Anasazi abandoned it. Perhaps they burned the village on purpose, knowing they would move on. University of Utah students and faculty excavated the village, known as the Coombs Site, in 1958 and 1959. You can view pottery, axe heads, arrow points, and other tools found at the site in the museum, along with delicate items like sandals and basketry that came from more protected sites elsewhere. A diorama shows how the village might have appeared in its heyday. You can

© W. C. MCRAE

Anasazi State Park features excavated Anasazi structures.

see video programs on the Anasazi and modern tribes upon request.

The self-guided tour of the ruins begins behind the museum, which is located on Hwy. 12, 28 miles northeast of Escalante and 38 miles south of Torrey. You'll see a whole range of Anasazi building styles—a pit house, masonry walls, *jacal* walls (mud reinforced by sticks), and combinations of masonry and jacal. Replicas of habitation and storage rooms behind the museum show complete construction details.

Burr Trail Road

Burr Trail Road, originally a cattle trail blazed by stockman John Atlantic Burr, extends from the town of Boulder on Hwy. 12 to the Notom-Bullfrog Road, which runs between Hwy. 24 near the eastern entrance to Capitol Reef National Park and Bullfrog Marina on Lake Powell, off Hwy. 276. Starting at Boulder, the road is paved until the boundary between GSENM and Capitol Reef National Park (31 miles), where the route traverses the Circle Cliffs, as well as spectacular canyon areas such as Long Canyon and the Gulch. As the route meets Waterpocket Fold, in Capitol Reef National Park, a breathtaking set of switchbacks rise some 800 feet in just half a mile. These switchbacks are not considered suitable for RVs or vehicles towing trailers. The unpaved sections of the road may be impassable in poor weather. Visitors should inquire about road and weather conditions before setting out. Also inquire about hiking trails that depart from side roads.

Burr Trail Road joins Notom-Bullfrog Road just before it exits Capitol Reef National Park. For information on Notom-Bullfrog Road, see the *Capitol Reef National Park* section later in this chapter.

SIGHTS ALONG U.S. 89

This tour proceeds from Kanab to the Utah–Arizona border. From Kanab to Page, Arizona, at the Colorado River's Glen Canyon Dam, is 80 miles.

Johnson Canyon Road

Eight miles east of Kanab, Johnson Canyon Road heads north along the western border of the monument before joining Skutumpah Road and Glendale Bench Road. This road system links up with several more remote backcountry roads in the monument, and eventually leads to Cannonville along Hwy. 12. From U.S. 89, Johnson Canyon Road is paved for its initial miles. The road passes an abandoned movie set, where the TV series *Gunsmoke* was sometimes filmed. The road then climbs up through the scenic Vermilion and then White Cliffs of the Grand Staircase. The road eventually passes over Skutumpah Terrace, a rather featureless plateau covered with scrub.

Pariah Townsite Road

This road has several names, including Paria Valley Road. It turns north off U.S. 89 at Milepost 31. The five-mile dirt road is passable to cars when dry. It passes some towering and colorful canyons and mesas, among which the remains of a **1930s Western movie set** are slowly decaying. From the parking area, walking trails lead to the abandoned bleached wood buildings, which make for great photo opportunities against the rugged backdrop. Farther along the road, as it approaches the Paria River, are the remains of Pareah, although there's not much left of this ghost town.

Paria Canyon

Paria Canyon—a set of magnificent slot canyons that drain from Utah down through northern Arizona to the Grand Canyon—is the focus of popular multi-day canyoneering expeditions. Paria Canyon and 293,000 acres of surrounding desert grasslands are now protected as **Vermilion Cliffs National Monument.** Although the monument spreads south from the Utah–Arizona border, access to the monument's most famous sites is through back roads in Utah. In addition to the long Paria Canyon backpacking route, some shorter but strenuous day hikes explore this area (see *Recreation* later in this section). For more information, contact the Kanab Visitors Center (745 East Hwy. 89, Kanab, 435/644-4680, 8 A.M.–5 P.M. daily mid-Mar.–mid-Nov., Mon.–Fri.

8 A.M.–4:30 P.M. mid-Nov.–mid-Mar.) or stop at the Paria Contact Station, near Milepost 21 on U.S. 89.

Cottonwood Canyon Road

A few miles east of the ranger station, Cottonwood Canyon Road leads north. The unpaved road's lower portions, usually passable with a car in dry weather, pass through scenic landscapes as the road pushes north. The route climbs up across a barren plateau before dropping down onto the Paria River. Several good hikes lead from roadside trailheads into steep side canyons. The route continues north along the Cockscomb, a long wrinkle of rock ridges that run north and south across the desert. At the northern end of this route are Grosvenor Arch, Kodachrome State Park, and Hwy. 12 (46 miles).

Big Water and Smoky Mountain Road

At the little crossroads of **Big Water,** GSENM has built a new visitors center (100 Upper Revolution Way, Big Water, 435/675-3200, 8 A.M.–5 P.M. daily mid-Mar.–mid-Nov.) to serve the needs of travelers to the monument and to Glen Canyon National Recreation Area (NRA), which is immediately adjacent to this area. The visitor center is definitely worth a stop—it houses bones from a 75-million-year-old, 30-foot-long duck-billed dinosaur. Especially impressive are the backbone bearing toothmarks from a tyrannosaur and the 13-foot-long dino tail.

Joining Hwy. 89 at Big Water is **Smoky Mountain Road.** This long and rugged road links Big Water to Hwy. 12 at Escalante, 78 miles north. The southern portions of the route pass through Glen Canyon NRA, and side roads lead to remote beaches and flooded canyons. The original *Planet of the Apes* was shot here, before the area was inundated by Lake Powell.

From Big Water, it's 19 miles to Page, Arizona, on U.S. 89.

HIKING

The monument preserves some of the best long-distance hiking trails in the American Southwest. Since the monument was established and the consequent increase in tourism, shorter day hikes have also been developed to serve travelers who want to sample the wonderful slot canyons and backcountry of this vast desert landscape without venturing too far afield.

Be sure to check at local visitors centers for road and trail conditions, and to get up-to-date maps. Many of the following hikes require extensive travel on backcountry roads, which can be impassable after rains and rough the rest of the time. In summer, these trails are hot and exposed: Always carry plenty of water and sunscreen and wear a hat.

Hiking the **Escalante River Canyon** is recognized worldwide as one of the great

WALKING SOFTLY

Only great care and awareness can preserve the pristine canyons of the Escalante. You can help if you pack out all trash, avoid trampling on the fragile cryptobiotic soils (dark areas of symbiotic algae and fungus on the sand), travel in groups of 12 or fewer, don't disturb Native American artifacts, and protect wildlife by leaving your dogs at home. Most important, pack out human waste in areas where that's required, or bury it well away from water sources, trails, and camping areas; unless there's a fire hazard, burn toilet paper to aid decomposition. Campfires in developed or designated campgrounds are allowed only in fire grates, fire pits, or fire pans. Wood collection in these areas is not permitted. The use of backpacker stoves is recommended by the National Parks Service and the Bureau of Land Management. Visitors are encouraged to maximize efforts to "leave no trace" of their passage in the area.

Leave No Trace, Inc. (www.lnt.org) is a national organization dedicated to awareness, appreciation, and respect for our wildlands. The organization also promotes education of environmentally responsible outdoor recreation.

THE ESCALANTE REGION

© PAUL LEVY

Navigation is not always simple across slickrock; map-reading skills come in handy.

wilderness treks. Most people devote 4–6 days to exploring these slickrock canyons, which involve frequent scrambling (if not rock climbing), stream fording (if not swimming), and exhausting detours around rockfalls and logjams. Some day hikes are possible along the Escalante River drainage. Hikers without a week to spare can sample the landscape along the Dry Fork Coyote Gulch trail, which links two fascinating and beautifully constricted slot canyons.

Paria Canyon is another famed long-distance slickrock canyon hike that covers 37 miles between the border of Utah and the edge of the Colorado River's Marble Canyon. Several long day hikes leave from trailheads on the Paria Plateau, along the border with Arizona.

Other areas with developed hiking trails include the Skutumpah Road area and Cottonwood Canyon, in the center of the park. Otherwise, hiking in the monument is mostly on unmarked routes. Although the park is developing more day-hiking options, the rangers also encourage hardy adventurers to consider extended hikes across the rugged and primitive outback, beyond the busy canyon corridors. Call one of the visitors centers and ask for help from the rangers to plan a hiking adventure where there are no trails.

HIKES ALONG JOHNSON CANYON/SKUTUMPAH ROAD

The northern portions of this road pass through the White Cliffs area of the Grand Staircase, and several steep and narrow canyons are trenched into these terraces. Rough hiking trails explore these slot canyons. The **Willis Creek Narrows** trailhead is nine miles south of Cannonville along Skutumpah Road. The relatively easy trail follows a small stream as it etches a deep and narrow gorge through the Navajo sandstone. From the parking area, where Skutumpah Road crosses Willis Wash, walk downstream along the wash. Follow the streambed, which quickly descends between slickrock walls. The canyon is at times no more than 6–10 feet across, while the walls rise up 200–300 feet. The trail follows the (usually dry) streambed through the canyon for nearly 2.5 miles. To return, backtrack up the canyon.

Approximately 1.5 miles farther south on Skutumpah Road, a narrow bridge vaults over **Bull Valley Gorge.** Like the Willis Creek Narrows, this is a steep and narrow cleft in the slickrock; however, scrambling along the canyon bottom is a greater challenge, part of the reward for which is viewing a wrecked automobile wedged between the canyon walls. From the bridge, walk upstream along a faint trail on the north side of the crevice until the walls are low enough to scramble down. From here, the canyon deepens quickly, and you'll have to negotiate several dry falls along the way (a rope will come in handy). When you reach the area below the bridge, look up to see a 1950s-model pickup truck trapped between the canyon walls. Three men died in this 1954 mishap; their bodies were recovered, but the pickup was left in place. The canyon continues another mile from this point; there is no loop trail out of the canyon, so turn back when you've seen enough.

Twenty miles south of Cannonville, Skutumpah Road crosses **Lick Wash,** from which trails lead downstream into slot canyons to a remote *arroyo* (dry river bed) surrounded by rock-topped mesas. One of these lofty perches contains a preserve of now-rare native grasses. Although this area can be reached on a day hike, this is also a good place to base a multiday camping trip. The trail starts just below the road crossing on Lick Wash and follows the usually dry streambed as it plunges down into a narrow slot canyon. The canyon bottom is mostly level and easy to hike. After one mile, the canyon begins to widen, and after four miles Lick Wash joins Park Wash, a larger desert canyon.

Looming above this canyon junction are mesas topped with deep sandstone terraces that are part of the White Cliffs of the Grand Staircase. Rising to the east is **No Mans Mesa,** skirted on all sides by steep-sided cliffs. The 1,788 acres atop the mesa were grazed by goats for six months in the 1920s, but before or since then has never been grazed by herbivores. This pristine grassland is protected by the BLM as an Area of Critical Environmental Concern. Hardy hikers can scramble up a steep trail—used by the aforementioned goats—to visit this wilderness preserve. The ascent of No Mans Mesa is best considered an overnight trip from the Lick Wash trailhead.

HIKES ALONG COTTONWOOD CANYON ROAD

The northerly portions of this route pass by **Kodachrome Basin State Park,** with a fine

selection of hiking trails through colorful rock formations. The short **Nature Trail** introduces the park's ecology. The **Panorama Trail** loops through a highly scenic valley with sand pipes and colorful rocks; the easy trail is three miles round-trip and takes about two hours. **Angel's Palace Trail** begins just east of the group campground and makes a three-quarter-mile loop with fine views; the elevation gain is about 300 feet. The **Grand Parade Trail** makes a 1.5-mile loop with good views of rock pinnacles; begin from the concession stand or group campground. **Eagles View Trail,** a historic cattle trail, climbs nearly 1,000 feet up steep cliffs above the campground, then drops into Henrieville, two miles away; the highest overlook is a steep half-mile ascent from the campground. **Shakespeare Arch Trail** is a half-mile round-trip hike to a natural arch; access the trailhead by a signed dirt road.

Continue south on Cottonwood Canyon Road for 7.5 miles from the state park to the crossing of Round Valley Draw. From

© JUDY JEWELL

Discovered in 1976, Shakespeare Arch is at the end of an easy hike.

THE ESCALANTE REGION

easy hiking through a dry wash off
Cottonwood Canyon Road

here, turn south on BLM Road 422 toward **Hackberry Canyon.** Hikers can travel the 22-mile length of this scenic canyon in three days or make day hikes from either end of the trail. The lower canyon meets Cottonwood Canyon at an elevation of 4,700 feet just above the mouth of the Paria River. Cottonwood Canyon Road provides access to both ends. A small spring-fed stream flows down the lower half of Hackberry. Many side canyons invite exploration. One of them, Sam Pollock Canyon, is on the west about 4.5 miles upstream from the junction of Hackberry and Cottonwood Canyons; follow it 1.75 miles up to **Sam Pollock Arch** (60 feet high and 70 feet wide). Available topographic maps include the metric 1:100,000 Smoky Mountain or the 7.5-minute Slickrock Bench and Calico Peak.

The confluence of the Paria, Hackberry, and Cottonwood Canyons provide the backdrop to an excellent, although strenuous, day hike. The **Box of the Paria River** involves some steep climbs up rocky slopes as it traverses a tongue of slickrock between the mouth of the Hackberry and Paria Canyons. The route then follows the Paria River through its "box" or cliff-sided canyon in The Cockscomb formation. The trail returns to the trailhead by following Cottonwood Canyon upstream to the trailhead. The round-trip hike is about seven miles long. Inquire at visitors centers for maps and about conditions.

Although not as well known as the lower canyon, the **upper Paria River Canyon** has some beautiful scenery and offers many side canyons to explore, too. The Paria lies west of both Hackberry and Cottonwood Canyons. Access to the upper end is from the Skutumpah or Cottonwood Canyon Road near Kodachrome Basin State Park (elev. about 5,900 feet). The usual lower entry is from near Pahreah ghost town (elev. 4,720 feet); turn north six miles from U.S. 89 between mileposts 30 and 31 and continue past the Pahreah movie set to road's end. (The clay road surface is very slippery when wet but is okay for cars when dry.) The upper canyon is about 25 miles long, and the hike takes 3–4 days (allowing some time to explore side canyons). You can find water at springs along the main canyon and in many side canyons (purify first); try not to use water from the river itself as it may contain chemical pollution. Topo maps are the metric 1:100,000 Kanab and Smoky Mountain or the 7.5-minute Cannonville, Bull Valley Gorge, Deer Range Point, and Calico Peak.

HIKES ALONG THE ESCALANTE RIVER

The maze of canyons that drain the Escalante River presents exceptional hiking opportunities. You'll find everything from easy day hikes to challenging backpacking treks. The Escalante's canyon begins just downstream from the town of Escalante and ends at Lake Powell about 85 miles beyond. In all this distance, only one road (Hwy. 12) bridges the river. Many side canyons provide additional access to the Escalante, and most are as beautiful as the main gorge. The river system covers such a large area that you can find solitude even in spring, the busiest hiking season.

The many eastern canyons remain virtually untouched.

The Escalante canyons preserve some of the quiet beauty once found in Glen Canyon, which is now lost under the waters of Lake Powell. Prehistoric Anasazi and Fremont cultures have left ruins, petroglyphs, pictographs, and artifacts in many locations. These archaeological resources are protected by federal law. *Please don't collect or disturb them.*

Before setting out, visit the rangers at the information center on the west edge of Escalante for the required free permit to backpack overnight in GSENM, and to check on the latest trail and road conditions before setting out. Restrictions on group size may be in force on some of the more popular trails. You can also obtain topographic maps and literature that show trailheads, mileages, and other information that may be useful in planning trips. Some of the more popular trailheads have self-registration stations for permits.

The best times for a visit are early March–early June and mid-September–early November. Summertime trips are possible, too, but be prepared for higher temperatures and greater flash-flood danger in narrow canyons. Travel along the Escalante River involves frequent crossings, and there's always water in the main canyon, usually ankle- to knee-deep. Pools in the "Narrows" section between Scorpion Gulch and Stevens Canyon can be up to chest-deep in spots (which you can bypass), but that's the exception. All this wading can destroy leather boots, so it's best to wear canvas shoes or boots. High-topped boots, available at surplus stores, work well and prevent gravel from getting inside. Occasional springs, some tributaries, and the river itself provide drinking water. Always purify it first; the BLM warns of the unpleasant disease giardiasis, which is caused by an invisible protozoan. Don't forget insect repellent—mosquitos and deer flies seek out hikers in late spring and summer.

Escalante Canyon Trailheads

The many approaches to the area allow all sorts of trips. Besides the road access at Escalante and the Hwy. 12 bridge, hikers can reach the Escalante River through western side canyons from Hole-in-the-Rock Road or eastern side canyons from Burr Trail Road. The western-canyon trailheads on Hole-in-the-Rock Road can be more easily reached by car, thus facilitating vehicle shuttles. To reach eastern-canyon trailheads, with the exceptions of Deer Creek and the Gulch on Burr Trail Road, you'll need lots of time and, if the road is wet, a four-wheel drive vehicle. Carry water for these more remote canyons; with the exception of Deer Creek, they're usually dry.

Town of Escalante to Highway 12 Bridge
15 MILES

This first section of canyon offers easy walking and stunning canyon scenery. Tributaries and sandstone caves invite exploration. You'll find good camping areas all along. Usually the river here is only ankle deep. Either enter Escalante River at the bridge next to the sawmill, or go one mile east of town on Hwy. 12 and turn north past the cemetery (visible from highway) and town dump. Almost immediately, the river knifes its way through the massive cliffs of the Escalante Monocline, leaving the broad valley of the upper river behind. Although there is no maintained trail along this stretch of the east-flowing river, it's relatively easy to pick your way along the riverbank.

Death Hollow, which is far prettier than the name suggests, comes in to the Escalante from the north after 7.5 miles. Several good swimming holes carved in rock lie a short hike upstream from the Escalante; watch for poison ivy among the greenery. Continue farther up Death Hollow to see more pools, little waterfalls, and outstanding canyon scenery. You can bypass some pools, but some you'll have to swim—bring a little inflatable boat, air mattress, or waterproof bag to ferry packs.

Sand Creek, on the Escalante's north side 4.5 miles downstream from Death Hollow, is also worth exploring; deep pools begin a short way up from the mouth. After another one-half mile down the Escalante, a natural arch

THE ESCALANTE REGION

appears high on the canyon wall. Then the Escalante Natural Bridge comes into view about one-half mile farther, just two miles from the Hwy. 12 bridge. In fact, Escalante Natural Bridge makes a good day-hike destination upstream from the highway.

Highway 12 Bridge to Harris Wash
26.5 MILES
This is where many long-distance trekkers begin their exploration of the Escalante canyons. In this section, the Escalante Canyon offers a varied show: In places the walls close in to make constricted narrows, at other places they step back to form great valleys. Side canyons filled with lush greenery and sparkling streams contrast with dry washes of desert, yet all can be fun to explore. A good hike of 4–6 days begins at the highway bridge, goes down the Escalante to Harris Wash, then up Harris to a trailhead off Hole-in-the-Rock Road (37 miles total).

From the Hwy. 12 bridge parking area, a trail leads to the river. Canyon access goes through private property; cross the river at the posted signs to avoid barking dogs at the ranch just downstream. **Phipps Wash** comes in from the south (right side) after 1.5 miles and several more river crossings. Turn up its wide mouth one-half mile to see Maverick Bridge in a drainage to the right. To reach Phipps Arch, continue another three-quarters of a mile up the main wash, turn left into a box canyon, and scramble up the left side (see the 7.5-minute Calf Creek topo map).

Bowington (Boynton) Arch is an attraction of a north side canyon known locally as Deer Creek. Look for this small canyon on the left one mile beyond Phipps Wash; turn up it one mile past three deep pools and then turn left a short way into a tributary canyon. In 1878, gunfire resolved a quarrel between local ranchers John Boynton and Washington Phipps. Phipps was killed, but both their names live on.

Waters of **Boulder Creek** come rushing into the Escalante from the north in the next major side canyon, 5.75 miles below the Hwy. 12

bridge. The creek, along with its Dry Hollow and Deer Creek tributaries, provides good canyon walking; deep areas may require swimming or climbing up on the plateau. (You could also start down Deer Creek from Burr Trail Road where they meet, 6.5 miles southeast of Boulder at a primitive BLM campground; starting at the campground, follow Deer Creek 7.5 miles to Boulder Creek, then 3.5 miles down Boulder to the Escalante.) Deer and Boulder Creeks have water year-round.

High, sheer walls of Navajo sandstone constrict the Escalante River in a narrow channel below Boulder Creek, but the canyon widens again above **The Gulch** tributary, 14 miles below the highway bridge. Hikers can head up The Gulch on a day hike.

Alternatively, descend The Gulch from Burr Trail Road to join the Escalante Canyon at this point (The Gulch trailhead is 10.8 miles southeast of Boulder). The hike from the road down to the Escalante is 12.5 miles, but there's one difficult spot: A 12-foot waterfall in a section of narrows about halfway down has to be bypassed. When Rudi Lambrechtse, author of *Hiking the Escalante,* tried friction climbing around the falls and the pool at their base, he fell 12 feet and broke his foot. That meant a painful three-day hobble out. Instead of taking the risk, Rudi recommends backtracking about 300 feet from the falls and friction climbing out from a small alcove in the west wall (look for a cairn on the ledge above). Climb up Brigham Tea Bench, walk south, then look for cairns leading back east to the narrows, and descend to the streambed (a rope helps to lower packs in a small chimney section).

Most springs along the Escalante are difficult to spot. One that's easy to find is in the first south bend after the Gulch; water comes straight out of the rock a few feet above the river. The Escalante Canyon becomes wider as the river lazily meanders along. Hikers can cut off some of the bends by walking in the open desert between canyon walls and riverside willow thickets. A bend cut off by the river itself loops to the north just before **Horse Canyon,** three miles below the Gulch. Along with its tributaries **Death Hollow** and **Wolverine Creek,** Horse Canyon drains the Circle Cliffs to the northeast. Floods in these mostly dry streambeds wash down pieces of black petrified wood. (Vehicles with good clearance can reach the upper sections of all three canyons from a loop road off Burr Trail Road.) Horse and Wolverine Creek Canyons offer good easy-to-moderate hiking, but if you really want a challenge, try Death Hollow (sometimes called "Little Death Hollow" to distinguish it from the larger one near Hell's Backbone Road). Starting from the Escalante River, go about two miles up Horse Canyon and turn right into Death Hollow; rugged scrambling over boulders takes you back into a long section of twisting narrows. Carry water for Upper Horse Canyon and its tributaries; Lower Horse Canyon usually has water.

About 3.5 miles down the Escalante from Horse Canyon, you enter Glen Canyon NRA and come to Sheffield Bend, a large, grassy field on the right. Only a chimney remains from Sam Sheffield's old homestead. Two grand amphitheaters lie beyond the clearing and up a stiff climb in loose sand. Over the next 5.5 river miles to Silver Falls Creek, you'll pass long bends, dry side canyons, and a huge slope of sand on the right canyon wall. Don't look for any silver waterfalls in **Silver Falls Creek**—the name comes from streaks of shiny desert varnish on the cliffs. You can approach Upper Silver Falls Creek by a rough road from Burr Trail Road, but a car shuttle between here and any of the trailheads on the west side of the Escalante River would take all day. Most hikers visit this drainage on a day hike from the river. Carry water with you.

When the Hole-in-the-Rock route proved so difficult, pioneers figured there had to be a better way to the San Juan Mission. Their new wagon road descended Harris Wash to the Escalante River, climbed part of Silver Falls Creek, crossed the Circle Cliffs, descended Muley Twist Canyon in the Waterpocket Fold, then followed Hall's Creek to Hall's Crossing on the Colorado River. Charles Hall operated a ferry there 1881–1884. Old maps show a jeep road through Harris Wash and Silver Falls Creek Canyons, used before the National Park Service closed off the Glen Canyon NRA section. Harris Wash lies just one-half mile downstream and across the Escalante from Silver Falls Creek.

Harris Wash
10.25 MILES ONE-WAY FROM TRAILHEAD TO RIVER

Clear, shallow water glides down this gem of a canyon. High cliffs streaked with desert varnish are deeply undercut and support lush hanging gardens. Harris Wash provides a beautiful route to the Escalante River, but it can also be a destination in itself; tributaries and caves invite exploration along the way. The sand and gravel streambed makes for easy walking. Reach the trailhead from Hwy. 12 by turning south 10.8 miles on Hole-in-the-Rock Road, then left 6.3 miles on a dirt road (keep left at the fork near the end). Don't be dismayed by the drab appearance of upper Harris Wash. The canyon and creek appear a few miles downstream.

◖ Dry Fork of Coyote Gulch

Twenty-six miles south on the Hole-in-the-Rock Road is a series of narrow, scenic, and exciting-to-explore slot canyons reached by a moderate day hike. The canyons feed into the Dry Fork of Coyote Gulch, reached from the Dry Fork trailhead. These three enchanting canyons are named **Peek-a-boo, Spooky,** and **Brimstone.** Exploring these slot canyons requires basic canyoneering or scrambling skills. From the trailhead parking lot, follow cairns down into the sandy bottom of Dry Fork Coyote Gulch. The slot canyons all enter the gulch from the north; watch for cairns and trails because the openings can be difficult to notice. The slots sometimes contain deep pools of water; chokestones and pour-offs can make access difficult. No loop trail links the three slot canyons; follow each until the canyon becomes to narrow to continue, then come back out. To make a full circuit of these canyons requires about 3.5 miles of hiking.

THE ESCALANTE REGION

© PAUL LEVY

It takes a little scrambling to enter Peek-a-boo Canyon.

Coyote Gulch

Coyote Gulch has received more publicity than other areas of the Escalante, and you're more likely to meet other hikers here. Two arches, a natural bridge, graceful sculpturing of the streambed and canyon walls, deep undercuts, and a cascading creek make a visit well worthwhile. The best route in starts where Hole-in-the-Rock Road crosses Hurricane Wash, 34.7 miles south of Hwy. 12. It's 12.5 miles one-way from the trailhead to the river, and the hike is moderately strenuous. For the first mile, you follow the dry, sandy wash without even a hint of being in a canyon. Water doesn't appear for three more miles. You'll reach Coyote Gulch, which has water, 5.25 miles from the trailhead. Another way into Coyote Gulch begins at the Red Well Trailhead; it's 31.5 miles south on Hole-in-the-Rock Road, then 1.5 miles east (keep left at the fork). A start from Red Well adds three-quarters of a mile more to the hike than the Hurricane Wash route, but it is also less crowded.

In some seasons, Lake Powell comes within one mile of Coyote Gulch and occasionally floods the canyon mouth. Coyote can stay flooded for several weeks, depending on the release flow of Glen Canyon Dam and water volume coming in. The river and lake don't have a pretty meeting place—quicksand and dead trees are found here. Logjams make it difficult to travel in from the lake by boat.

◖ HIKES IN THE CALF CREEK RECREATION AREA

The hike to **Lower Calf Creek Falls** is, for many people, the highlight of their first trip to the Escalante area. It's the dazzling enticement that brings people back for longer and more remote hiking trips. From the trailhead and park just off Hwy. 12, the trail winds between high cliffs of Navajo sandstone streaked with desert varnish, where you'll see beaver ponds, Native American ruins and pictographs, and the misty 126-foot-high Lower Calf Creek Falls. A brochure available at the trailhead next to the campground identifies many of the desert and riparian plant species along the way. Round-trip is 5.5 miles with only a slight gain in elevation; bring water and perhaps a lunch. Summer temperatures can soar, but the falls and the crystal-clear pool beneath stay cool. Sheer cliffs block travel farther upstream.

Calf Creek Campground, near the road, has 13 sites with drinking water early April–late October ($7). Reserve group sites through the Escalante visitors center.

HIKES IN PARIA CANYON/ VERMILION CLIFFS

The wild and twisting canyons of the Paria River and its tributaries offer a memorable experience for experienced hikers. Silt-laden waters have sculpted the colorful canyon walls, revealing 200 million years of geologic history. *Paria* means "muddy water" in the Paiute language. You enter the 2,000-foot-deep gorge of the Paria in southern Utah, then hike 37 miles downstream to Lee's Ferry in Arizona, where the Paria empties into the Colorado River. A handful of shorter but rugged day hikes lead to superb scenery and geologic curiosities.

Ancient petroglyphs and campsites show that Pueblo Indians traveled the Paria more than 700 years ago. They hunted mule deer and bighorn sheep while using the broad, lower end of the canyon to grow corn, beans, and squash. The Dominguez-Escalante Expedition stopped at the mouth of the Paria in 1776, and these were the first white men to see the river. John D. Lee and three companions traveled through the canyon in 1871 to bring a herd of cattle from the Pahreah settlement to Lee's Ferry. After Lee began a Colorado River ferry service in 1872, he and others farmed the lower Paria Canyon. Prospectors came here to search for gold, uranium, and other minerals, but much of the canyon remained unexplored. In the late 1960s, the BLM organized a small expedition whose research led to protection of the canyon as a primitive area. The Arizona Wilderness Act of 1984 designated Paria Canyon a wilderness, along with parts of the Paria Plateau and Vermilion Cliffs. In 2000, Vermilion Cliffs National Monument was created. For more information, check out the website at www.az.blm.gov/vermilion/vermilion.htm.

The **BLM Paria Canyon Ranger Station** is in Utah, 43 miles east of Kanab on U.S. 89 near milepost 21. It's on the south side of the highway, just east of the Paria River. Permits are required for hiking in the Paria Canyon and to visit other sites in Vermilion Cliffs National Monument.

Paria Canyon

Allow 4–6 days to hike Paria Canyon because of the many river crossings and because you'll want to make side trips up some of the tributary canyons. The hike is considered moderately difficult. Hikers should have enough backpacking experience to be self-sufficient, because help may be days away. Flash floods can race through the canyon, especially July–September. Rangers close the Paria if they think a danger exists. Because the upper end has the narrowest passages (between miles 4.2 and 9.0), rangers require that all hikers start here in order to have up-to-date weather information.

The actual trailhead is two miles south of the ranger station on a dirt road near a campground and old homestead site called White House Ruins. The exit trailhead is in Arizona at Lonely Dell Ranch of Lee's Ferry, 44 miles southwest of Page via U.S. 89 and 89A (or 98 miles southeast of Kanab on U.S. 89A).

You must register at a trailhead or the Kanab BLM office (318 N. 100 East, Kanab, UT, 435/644-2672, 8 A.M.–4:30 P.M. Mon.–Fri. year-round). Permits to hike the canyon are $5 per day per person; backpackers should get a permit at the ranger station, but day hikers can just register and pay the fee at the trailhead. The visitors center and the office both provide weather forecasts and brochures with map and hiking information. The visitors center always has the weather forecast posted at an outdoor information kiosk.

The hike requires a 150-mile round-trip car shuttle. For a list of shuttle services, check the BLM website or ask at the Arizona Strip Interpretive Association (345 E. Riverside Dr., St. George, UT, 435/688-3246), Paria Contact Station, or Kanab Field Office. Expect to pay about $100 for this service.

All visitors need to take special care to minimize their impact on this beautiful canyon. Check the BLM *Visitor Use Regulations* for the Paria before you go. Regulations include no campfires in the Paria and its tributaries, a pack-in/pack-out policy, and that latrines be made at least 100 feet away from river and campsite locations. Also, remember to take some plastic bags to carry out toilet paper; the stuff lasts years and years in this desert climate. You don't want to haunt future hikers with TP flowers!

The Paria ranger recommends a group size maximum of six; regulations specify a 10-person limit. No more than 20 people per day can enter the canyon for overnight trips. The best times to travel along the Paria are about mid-March–June and October–November. May, especially Memorial Day weekend, tends to be crowded. Winter hikers often complain of painfully cold feet. Wear (or bring) shoes suitable for frequent wading. You can get good drinking water from springs along the way

THE ESCALANTE REGION

(see the BLM hiking brochure for locations); it's best not to use the river water because of possible chemical pollution from farms and ranches upstream. Normally the river's only ankle-deep, but in spring or after rainy spells, it can become waist-deep. During thunderstorms, levels can rise to more than 20 feet deep in the Paria Narrows, so heed weather warnings! Quicksand, which is most prevalent after flooding, is more a nuisance than a danger—usually it's just knee-deep. Many hikers carry a walking stick to probe the opaque waters for good crossing places.

Wrather Canyon Arch

One of Arizona's largest natural arches lies about one mile up this side canyon of the Paria. The massive structure has a 200-foot span. Turn right (southwest) at mile 20.6 on the Paria hike. (The mouth of Wrather Canyon and other points along the Paria are unsigned; follow your map.)

Buckskin Gulch and Wire Pass

Buckskin Pass is an amazing tributary of the Paria, with convoluted walls reaching hundreds of feet high. Yet the canyon narrows to as little as four feet in width. In places the walls block out so much light that it's like walking in a cave. Be *very* careful to avoid times of flash-flood danger. Hiking this 20-mile-long gulch can be strenuous, with rough terrain, deep pools of water, and log- and rock jams that may require the use of ropes. Conditions vary considerably from one year to the next.

Day hikers can get a taste of this incredible canyon country by driving to Wire Pass Trailhead, 8.5 bumpy miles down BLM Road 700 (also called Rock House Valley Rd.), between mileposts 25 and 26, about 37 miles east of Kanab. From the trailhead, a relatively easy trail leads into **Wire Pass,** a narrow side canyon that joins Buckskin Gulch. The 3.5-mile in-and-out round-trip travels the length of Wire Pass to its confluence with Buckskin Gulch. From here, you can explore this exceptionally narrow canyon or follow Buckskin Gulch to its appointment with Paria Canyon (12.5 miles).

For the full experience of Buckskin Gulch, long-distance hikers can begin at Buckskin Gulch Trailhead, 4.5 miles south of U.S. 89 off BLM Road 700. From here, it's 16.3 miles (one-way) to Paria Canyon. Hikers can continue down the Paria or turn upstream and hike six miles to exit at the White House trailhead near the ranger station. Hiking this gulch can be strenuous, with rough terrain, deep pools of water, and log- and rock jams that may require the use of ropes. Conditions vary considerably from one year to the next. Regulations mandate packing your waste out of this area.

Hiking permits are $5 per day per person; backpackers should get a permit at the ranger station, but day hikers can just register and pay the fee at the trailhead.

Coyote Buttes

You've probably seen photos of these dramatic rock formations: towering sand dunes frozen into rock. These much-photographed buttes are located on the Paria Plateau, just south of Wire Pass. Access is strictly controlled, and you can only enter the area with advanced reservation and by permit. The number of people allowed into the area is also strictly limited; however, the permit process, fees, and restrictions are exactly the same as for Paria Canyon. See the Vermilion Cliffs Monument website for information (www.az.blm.gov/vermilion/vermilion.htm).

The BLM has divided the area into Coyote North and Coyote South, with a limit of 10 people per day in each. No dogs are allowed. The Wave—the most photographed of the buttes—is in Coyote North, so this region is the most popular (and easiest to reach from Wire Pass Trailhead—see previous entry); BLM staff will give you a map and directions when you get your permit. After the trailhead, you're on your own because the wilderness lacks signs. Permits are more difficult to obtain in spring and autumn—the best times to visit—and on weekends. The fragile sandstone can break if climbed on, so it's important to stay on existing hiking routes and wear soft-soled footwear.

MOUNTAIN BIKING

Mountain bikes are allowed on all roads in the monument, but not on hiking trails. Mountain bikers are not allowed to travel cross-country off roads, or to make their own routes across slickrock; however, there are hundreds of miles of primitive road in the monument, with dozens of loop routes available for cyclists on multi-day trips. In addition to following the scenic **Burr Trail** from Boulder to Waterpocket Fold in Capitol Reef National Park, cyclists can loop off this route and follow the Circle Cliffs/Wolverine Trail. This 45-mile loop traverses the headwaters of several massive canyons as they plunge to meet the Escalante River.

Hole-in-the-Rock Road is mostly a one-way-in, one-way-out affair, but cyclists can follow side roads to hiking trailheads and big vistas over the Escalante canyons. Popular side roads include a 10-mile round-trip road to the area known as Egypt, and the Fifty Mile Bench Road, a 27-mile loop from Hole-in-the-Rock Road that explores the terrain above Glen Canyon. Left Hand Collet Road, a rough jeep trail that a mountain bike can bounce through easily enough, links Hole-in-the-Rock Road with the Smoky Mountain Road system, with links to both Escalante in the north and Big Water in the south.

Other popular routes in the **Big Water area** include the Nipple Butte loop and the steep loop around Smoky Butte and Smoky Hollow, with views over Lake Powell. **Cottonwood Canyon Road,** which runs between U.S. 89 and Cannonville, is another long back road with access to a network of less-traveled trails.

Request more information on mountain biking from the visitors centers. They have handouts and maps and can help cyclists plan backcountry bike adventures. This country is remote and primitive, so cyclists must carry everything they are likely to need. Also, there are no clean water sources in the monument, so cyclists must transport all drinking water or be prepared to purify it.

RAFTING

Most of the year, shallow water and rocks make boat travel impossible on the Escalante River, but for two or three weeks during spring run-off, which peaks in early April and late May, river levels rise high enough to be passable. (In some years there may not be enough water in any season.) Contact the information center in Escalante for ideas on when to hit the river at its highest. Shallow draft and maneuverability are essential, so inflatable canoes or kayaks work best (also because they are easier to carry out at trip's end or if water levels drop too low for floating). Not recommended are rafts (too wide and bulky) and hard-shelled kayaks and canoes (they get banged up on the many rocks). The usual launch is the Hwy. 12 bridge; Coyote Gulch—a 13-mile hike—is a good spot to get out, as are Crack in the Wall (a 2.75-mile hike on steep sand from the junction of Coyote and Escalante Canyons to Forty-Mile Ridge Trailhead; four-wheel drive needed; a rope is required to negotiate the vessel from the canyon rim) and Hole-in-the-Rock (a 600-foot ascent over boulders; rope suggested). You could also arrange for a friend to pick you up by boat from Halls Crossing or Bullfrog Marina. River boaters must obtain a free backcountry permit from either the BLM or the National Park Service.

FOUR-WHEEL DRIVE EXPLORATION

Without a mountain bike or a pair of hiking boots, the best way to explore the backcountry of GSENM is with a four-wheel drive high-clearance vehicle; however, the scale of the monument, the primitive quality of many of the roads, and the extreme weather conditions common in the desert mean that you shouldn't head into the backcountry unless you are confident in your skills as a mechanic and driver. Choose roads that match your vehicle's capacity and your driving ability, and you should be okay. Some roads that appear on maps are slowly going back to nature: Rather than close some roads, park officials are letting the desert reclaim them. Other roads are being closed, so it's best to check on access and road conditions before setting out. Remember that many of the roads in the monument are *very* slow going. If you've got somewhere to be in a hurry, these corrugated, boulder-dodging roads may not get you there in time. Be sure to take plenty of water—not only for drinking, but also for overheated radiators. It's also wise to carry wooden planks or old carpet scraps for help in gaining traction should your wheels be mired in the sand.

TOURS AND EXCURSIONS

For **guided tours** of the Escalante canyons, contact **Utah Canyons Outback Adventures** (325 W. Main St, 435/826-4967 or 877/777-7988, www.utahcanyons.com). Trips focus on day hikes ($80 for a full day), with popular trips going to slot canyons and scenic Phipps Arch. They also offer hiker shuttles and run a good gear shop in the salmon-colored building in downtown Escalante.

The guides at **Excursions of Escalante** (125 E. Main St., Escalante, 800/839-7567, www.excursionsofescalante.com) lead trips into more remote canyons, including some that require some technical canyoneering to explore and some multi-day backpacking trips. A day of basic canyoneering costs $135, including instruction.

Many local outfitters use pack animals. With **Escape Goats** (435/826-4652, www.utahpackgoats.com), you'll hike with goats (and a friendly, goat-loving human guide) into canyons. This is a good bet for families with kids.

Hike into the canyon backcountry (let horses pack your gear) and spend a few days exploring with **Escalante Canyon Outfitters** (888/326-4453 or 435/335-7311, www.ecohike.com). Four-day trips run just over $1,200.

Red Rock 'n Llamas (877/955-2627 or 435/559-7325, www.redrocknllamas.com) offers a variety of fully outfitted hiking adventures in the Escalante area. Llamas will carry most of the gear, leaving you to explore in comfort. Most trips are for three or four nights and cost $800–900.

The Boulder-based **Earth Tours** (435/691-1241, www.earth-tours.com) offers half-day ($50 per person) to six-day (price varies according to number of guests) tours of the area. Most trips are led by a geologist with a wide-ranging interest in natural history; lodging for the longer trips is at the luxurious Boulder Mountain Lodge.

Escalante

Escalante (elevation 5,813 feet) is a natural hub for exploration of GSENM. Even if you don't have the time or the inclination to explore the rugged canyon country that the monument protects, you'll discover incredible scenery just by traveling Hwy. 12 through Escalante country.

At first glance, Escalante looks like a town that time has passed by. Only 744 people live here, in addition to the resident cows, horses, and chickens that you'll meet just one block off Main Street. Yet this little community is the biggest place for more than 60 miles around and a center for ranchers and travelers. Escalante has the neatly laid-out streets and trim little houses typical of Mormon settlements.

One caveat: Drive slowly through town! The local police officer seems to have a refined eye for out-of-towners exceeding the speed limit.

ACCOMMODATIONS

Accommodations in Escalante range from simple to luxurious, but they all must add a hefty 12.5 percent room tax to the fees listed here.

Under $50

The seven small but comfy log cabins at **Escalante Outfitters** (310 W. Main St., 435/826-4266, www.escalanteoutfitters.com, $45) share men's and women's bathhouses and a common grassy area. Tucked behind the store (which also houses a casual pizza and espresso restaurant and a tiny liquor store), these cabins are convenient to all the action the town has to offer, including wireless Internet access. If you'd rather sleep in your own tent, camping is permitted on the lawn ($14), which is sheltered from the street. Dogs are permitted for a

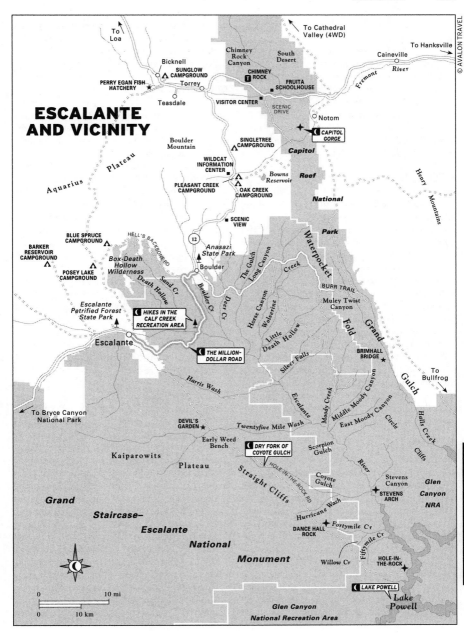

ESCALANTE
AND VICINITY

small fee in the cabins and are free if they stay in your tent.

The following are basic but perfectly acceptable: The **Moqui Motel** (480 W. Main, 435/826-4210, www.go-utah.com/moqui-motel, $30–50) has rooms and some kitchenettes and an RV park ($15 with hookups, no tents). The **Padre Motel** (20 E. Main, 435/826-4276, www.padremotel.com, Mar.–Nov., $30–75) has standard rooms as well as five mini-suites with two bedrooms each.

$50-100

Just a shade more expensive than the rock-bottom places is the **Circle D Motel** (475 W. Main, 435/826-4297, www.utahcanyons.com/circled.htm, $60), which reaches out to bicyclists and hikers. Pets are welcome in some rooms. In the winter, rates drop to as low as $30.

Another pleasant and modern establishment is **Rainbow Country B&B** (586 E. 300 South, 435/826-4567 or 800/252-8824, www.bnbescalante.com, $59–89), with four guest rooms sharing 2.5 baths; guests have the use of a hot tub, a pool table, and a TV lounge.

The **Prospector Inn** (380 W. Main, 435/826-4653, www.prospectorinn.com, $62) is Escalante's largest and most modern motel; there's a restaurant and lounge on the premises. If you usually stay at Best Westerns or comparable motels, this is the only standard motel in town you'll find even close to that quality.

Over $100

Head east from Escalante on Hwy. 12 to the landmark **Kiva Koffeehouse** (milepost 73.86 on Hwy. 12, 435/826-4550, www.kivakoffeehouse.com, $160 includes breakfast), a quirky hilltop restaurant located just east of the Boynton Overlook high above the Escalante River. The two spacious and beautifully decorated rooms each include a remarkable view of the surrounding country. The comfortable rooms with their grand views, fireplaces, and the big, deep, jetted bathtubs all make this a wonderful place to relax after a day of exploring, and the absence of TV and telephone make

it all the better. The Kiva is just above the spot where the Escalante River crosses Hwy. 12, and is a good base for hikers.

Right in the center of town, but tucked back from the main drag, rooms at **Escalante's Grand Staircase B&B** (280 W. Main, 435/826-4890 or 866/826-4890, www.escalantebnb.com, $135) are some of the nicest in the area. Rooms are individually decorated—several have rather bold murals—and are separate from the main house.

Another downtown Escalante B&B is **Canyons B&B** (120 E. Main, 435/826-4747 or 866/526-9667, www.canyonsbnb.com, $105–115, Mar.–Nov.), where a modern "bunkhouse" has been built behind an old farmhouse. There's nothing rustic about the three guest rooms; all are attractively decorated and equipped with TV, telephones, and wireless Internet access.

If you're traveling with a family or group of friends, consider renting the architecturally striking, solar-heated **LaLuz Desert Retreat** (888/305-4705, www.laluz.net, $150 and up), located in a private setting just south of town. Two houses, designed in the "Usonian" tradition of Frank Lloyd Wright, are available. Each house sleeps up to six.

Campgrounds

Escalante Petrified Forest State Park (435/826-4466, www.stateparks.utah.gov, reservations at 800/322-3770, www.reserveamerica.com, $15 camping, year-round) just northwest of the town of Escalante is conveniently located and full of attractions of its own, including most notably trails passing big chunks of petrified wood. Drinking water and showers are available, but the park has no hookups.

In town, you can stay at **Broken Bow RV Camp** (495 W. Main St., 888/241-8785 or 435/826-4959, $21 and up), which has simple cabins and sites for tents and RVs, plus showers and laundry services. It's closed in winter.

Calf Creek Recreation Area lies in a pretty canyon 15.5 miles east of Escalante on Hwy.

12; sites run $10 and are open early April–late October; you can reserve group sites through the BLM office. **Calf Creek Falls Trail** (5.5 miles round-trip) begins at the campground and follows the creek upstream to the 126-foot-high falls.

Campgrounds at **Posey Lake** (16 miles north, $8) and **Blue Spruce** (19 miles north, $7) sit atop the Aquarius Plateau in Dixie National Forest (435/826-5400). Sites open around Memorial Day weekend and close in mid-September. Take Hell's Backbone Road (dirt) from the east edge of town.

FOOD

The **Esca-Latte Coffee Shop and Pizza Parlor** (310 W. Main St, 435/826-4266, breakfast, lunch, and dinner daily, $2–21), part of Escalante Outfitters, is a reliable place to eat in this little town. It serves espresso, handmade pizza ($17–21), and microbrew beer. The smoked trout plate ($9) is a special treat here. The cafe has a couple of computers where customers can check email.

The **Trailhead Café** (125 E. Main, 435/826-4714, 11:30 A.M.–4 P.M. Wed.–Mon. Apr.–Nov., $5–10) has the best burgers in town. For sandwiches or the town's best Mexican food, stop in at **Georgie's** (190 W. Main, 435/826-4784, lunch and dinner Tues.–Sat., less than $10).

Other dining spots are more traditional small-town restaurants. The **Golden Loop Cafe** (39 W. Main, 435/826-4433, breakfast, lunch, and dinner daily, $5–12) is a typical Main Street diner with plenty of local color and homemade food.

East of town, **Kiva Koffeehouse** (Milepost 73.86 on Hwy. 12, 435/826-4550, 8:30 A.M.–4:30 P.M. Wed.–Mon., $2–10) is worth a stop, both for a latte and for lunch (delicious food, much of it organic), and for a look at the view.

INFORMATION AND SERVICES

The Escalante Interagency office (755 West Main, 435/826-5499, 8 A.M.–5 P.M. Mon.–Fri.

daily early Mar.–late Oct.), on the west edge of town, has an **information center** for visitors to Forest Service, BLM, and National Park Service areas around Escalante; this is also one of the best spots for information on GSENM. Hikers or bikers headed for overnight trips in the monument system can obtain permits at the information center.

Kazan Memorial Clinic (65 N. Center Street, 435/826-4374) offers medical care on Mondays, Wednesdays, and Fridays. The nearest hospital is 70 miles away, in Panguitch.

HELL'S BACKBONE

This scenic 38-mile drive climbs high into the forests north of Escalante with excellent views of Death Hollow and Sand Creek Canyons and the distant Navajo, Fiftymile, and Henry Mountains.

Hell's Backbone Road reaches an elevation of 9,200 feet on the slopes of Roger Peak before descending to Hell's Backbone, 25 miles from town. Mule teams used this narrow ridge, with precipitous canyons on either side, as a route to Boulder until the 1930s. At that time, a bridge built by the Civilian Conservation Corps allowed the first vehicles to make the trip. You can still see the old mule path below the bridge. After 38 miles, the road ends at Hwy. 12; turn right 24 miles to return to Escalante or turn left three miles to Boulder. Cars can usually manage the gravel and dirt Hell's Backbone Road when it's dry. Snows and snowmelt, however, block the way until about late May. Check with the Interagency office in Escalante for current conditions. Trails and rough dirt roads lead deeper into the backcountry to more vistas and fishing lakes.

Posey Lake Campground (elevation 8,700 feet) offers sites amid aspen and ponderosa pines and is open with drinking water Memorial Day weekend–September ($8). Rainbow and brook trout swim in the adjacent lake. A hiking trail (two miles round-trip) begins near space number 14 and climbs 400 feet to an old fire-lookout tower, with good views of the lake and surrounding country. Posey Lake is

14 miles north of Escalante, then two miles west on a side road.

Blue Spruce Campground (elevation 7,860 feet) is another pretty spot, but it has only six sites. Anglers can try for pan-sized trout in a nearby stream. The campground, surrounded by blue spruce, aspen, and ponderosa pine, has drinking water Memorial Day weekend–mid-September ($7); go north 19 miles from town, then turn left and drive half a mile.

Boulder

About 180 people live in this farming community at the base of Boulder Mountain. Ranchers began drifting in during the late 1870s, although not with the intent that they'd form a town. By the mid-1890s, Boulder had established itself as a ranching and dairy center. Remote and hemmed in by canyons and mountains, Boulder remained one of the last communities in the country to rely on pack trains for transportation. Motor vehicles couldn't drive in until the 1930s. Today Boulder is worth a visit to see an excavated Anasazi village and the spectacular scenery along the way. Take paved Hwy. 12, either through the canyon and slickrock country from Escalante or over the Aquarius Plateau from Torrey (near Capitol Reef National Park). Burr Trail Road connects Boulder with Capitol Reef National Park's southern district via Waterpocket Fold and Circle Cliffs. A fourth way in is from Escalante on the dirt Hell's Backbone Road, which comes out three miles west of Boulder at Hwy. 12.

ACCOMMODATIONS

You wouldn't expect to find one of Utah's nicest places to stay in tiny Boulder, but the **(Boulder Mountain Lodge,** (435/355-7460 or 800/556-3446, www.boulder-utah.com, $72 and up in winter, $97 and up high season), along Hwy. 12 right in town, offers the kinds of facilities and setting that make this one of the few destination lodgings in the state. The lodge's buildings are grouped around the edge of a private, 15-acre pond that serves as an ad hoc wildlife refuge. You can sit on the deck or wander paths along the pond, watching and listening to the amazing variety of birds that make this spot their home. The guest rooms and suites are in a handsome and modern Western-style lodge facing the pond; rooms are nicely decorated with quality furniture and beddings, and there's a central Great Room with a fireplace and library and a large outdoor hot tub. One of Utah's best restaurants, Hell's Backbone Grill, is on the premises.

More modest accommodations are available at **Pole's Place** (435/335-7422 or 800/730-7422, www.boulderutah.com/polesplace, closed in winter), across the road from the state park. It has a well-maintained motel, café, and gift shop. The **Hills and Hollows Mini-Mart** (on hill above Hwy. 12, 435/335-7349) rents bunkhouse cabins for $24 a night.

Campgrounds

The best bet for tent campers is **Deer Creek Campground** ($4), 6.5 miles from Boulder on Burr Trail Road. During the summer, another alternative is to head north on Hwy. 12 up Boulder Mountain to a cluster of Forest Service campgrounds (see the *Around Boulder* section).

Guest Ranches

Cowboy up at the **Boulder Mountain Ranch** (435/355-7480, www.boulderutah.com/bmr, $62–84), seven miles from Boulder on Hell's Backbone Road. Guests have a choice of simple B&B accommodations in the lodge or free-standing cabins, horseback riding, or multi-day horse-packing trips. There are also two- to five-day riding and lodging packages based out of the ranch.

FOOD

The restaurant at the Boulder Mountain Lodge restaurant, the **(Hell's Backbone**

Hell's Backbone Grill in tiny and remote Boulder offers some of the finest dining in Utah.

Grill (435/355-7460 or 800/556-3446, $12–26) has gained something of a cult following across the West. Run by two American Buddhist women, the restaurant's menu changes with the seasons, but you can count on finding fresh fish, chipotle-rubbed meat, outstanding meatloaf, tasty *posole,* and excellent desserts. For simpler but good fare, the **Burr Trail Cafe** (435/335-7432, lunch and dinner, Memorial Day weekend–autumn, $8–15) is at the intersection of Hwy. 12 and Burr Trail Road.

INFORMATION AND SERVICES
A good stop for **visitor information** is the Anasazi State Park Museum, where there's an info desk for GSENM. The two gas stations in Boulder sell groceries and snack food; at Hills and Hollows Mini-Mart, you'll actually find provisions like soy milk and organic cashews.

BOULDER MOUNTAIN SCENIC DRIVE
Utah 12 climbs high into forests of ponderosa pine, aspen, and fir on Boulder Mountain be-

tween the towns of Boulder and Torrey. Travel in winter is usually possible, although heavy snows can close the road. Viewpoints along the drive offer sweeping panoramas of Escalante Canyon country, Circle Cliffs, Waterpocket Fold, and the Henry Mountains. Hikers and anglers can explore the alpine country of Boulder Mountain and seek out the 90 or so trout-filled lakes. The Great Western Trail, which was built with ATVers in mind, runs over Boulder Mountain to the west of the highway. The Dixie National Forest map (Escalante and Teasdale Ranger District offices) shows the back roads, trails, and lakes.

The U.S. Forest Service has three developed campgrounds about midway along this scenic drive: **Oak Creek** (18 miles from Boulder, elev. 8,800 feet), **Pleasant Creek** (19 miles from Boulder, elev. 8,600 feet), and **Singletree** (the largest of the three and the best pick for larger RVs, 24 miles from Boulder, elev. 8,200 feet). The season (with water) lasts about late May–mid-September; sites cost $9–10. Campgrounds may also be open in spring and autumn without water. **Lower Bowns Reservoir** (elev. 7,000 feet) has primitive camping (no water or fee) and fishing for rainbow and cutthroat trout; turn east five miles on a rough dirt road (not recommended for cars) just south of Pleasant Creek Campground.

Contact the the **Escalante Ranger District office** (755 W. Main, Escalante, 435/826-5400, 8:30 A.M.–4:30 P.M. Mon.–Fri.) for information about camping or recreation on Boulder Mountain.

Capitol Reef National Park

Wonderfully sculptured rock layers in a rainbow of colors put on a fine show here. Although you'll find these same rocks throughout much of the Four Corners region, their artistic variety has no equal outside Capitol Reef National Park (435/425-3791, www.nps.gov/care, $5 per vehicle). About 70 million years ago, gigantic forces within the earth began to uplift, squeeze, and fold more than a dozen rock formations into the central feature of the park today—Waterpocket Fold, so named for the many small pools of water trapped by the tilted strata. Erosion has since carved spires, graceful curves, canyons, and arches. Waterpocket Fold extends 100 miles between Thousand Lake Mountain in the north and Lake Powell in the south. The most spectacular cliffs and rock formations of Waterpocket Fold form Capitol Reef, located north of Pleasant Creek and curving northwest across the Fremont River toward Thousand Lake Mountain. The reef was named by explorers who found Waterpocket Fold a barrier to travel and likened it to a reef blocking passage on the ocean. The rounded sandstone hills reminded them of the Capitol Dome in Washington, D.C., hence the name Capitol Reef.

Roads and hiking trails in the park provide access to the colorful rock layers and to the plants and wildlife that live here. Remnants exist of the area's long human history—petroglyphs and storage bins of the prehistoric Fremont, a schoolhouse and other structures built by Mormon pioneers, and several small uranium mines of the 20th century. Legends tell of Butch Cassidy and other outlaw members of the "Wild Bunch" who hid out in these remote canyons in the 1890s.

Even travelers short on time will enjoy a quick look at visitors center exhibits and a drive on Hwy. 24 through an impressive cross section of Capitol Reef cut by the Fremont River. You can see more of the park on the scenic drive, a narrow paved road that heads south from the visitors center. The drive passes beneath spectacular cliffs of the reef and enters scenic Grand Wash and Capitol Gorge Canyons; allow at least 90 minutes for the 21-mile round-trip (plus side trips). The fair-weather Notom-Bullfrog Road (paved as far as Notom) heads south along the other side of the reef for almost 80 miles with fine views of Waterpocket Fold. Burr Trail Road (dirt inside the park) in the south actually climbs over the fold in a steep set of switchbacks, connecting Notom Road with Boulder. Only drivers with high-clearance vehicles can explore Cathedral Valley in the park's northern district. All of these roads provide access to viewpoints and hiking trails.

Visitors Center

Start with a good 10-minute slideshow, which is shown on request, introducing Capitol Reef's natural wonders and history. In the main room of the visitors center (435/425-3791, 8 A.M.–7 P.M. daily June–Sept., 8 A.M.–4:30 P.M. daily the rest of the year), a giant relief map offers a bird's-eye view of the entire park. Rock samples and diagrams illustrate seven of the park's geologic formations, and photos identify local plants and birds. Prehistoric Fremont Indian artifacts on display include petroglyph replicas, sheepskin moccasins, pottery, basketry, stone knives, spear and arrow points, and bone

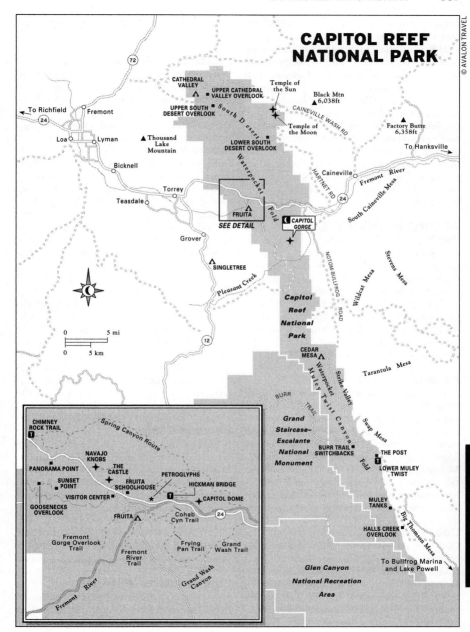

© AVALON TRAVEL

CAPITOL REEF NATIONAL PARK

72

To Richfield
24

Loa

Lyman

Fremont

CATHEDRAL
VALLEY

UPPER CATHEDRAL
VALLEY OVERLOOK

UPPER SOUTH
DESERT OVERLOOK

South Desert

Thousand
Lake
Mountain

LOWER SOUTH
DESERT OVERLOOK

Waterpocket Fold

Temple of
the Sun

Black Mtn
6,038ft

CAINEVILLE WASH RD

Temple of
the Moon

HARTNET RD

Factory Butte
6,358ft

To Hanksville

Bicknell

Torrey

Teasdale

FRUITA

SEE DETAIL

Grover

Caineville

Fremont River

24

CAPITOL
GORGE

South Caineville Mesa

SINGLETREE

Pleasant Creek

Capitol
Reef
National
Park

NOTOM-BULLFROG ROAD

Stevens Mesa

Wildcat Mesa

0   5 mi

0   5 km

12

CEDAR
MESA

Tarantula Mesa

Muley Twist Canyon

Strike Valley

Waterpocket Fold

BURR
TRAIL

Grand
Staircase-
Escalante
National
Monument

BURR TRAIL
SWITCHBACKS

THE POST

LOWER MULEY
TWIST

Swap Mesa

MULEY
TANKS

HALLS CREEK
OVERLOOK

Big Thomson Mesa

To Bullfrog Marina
and Lake Powell

Glen Canyon
National Recreation
Area

THE ESCALANTE REGION

Detail inset

CHIMNEY
ROCK TRAIL

Spring Canyon Route

NAVAJO
KNOBS

PANORAMA POINT

THE
CASTLE

PETROGLYPHS

SUNSET
POINT

FRUITA
SCHOOLHOUSE

HICKMAN BRIDGE

VISITOR CENTER

CAPITOL DOME

GOOSENECKS
OVERLOOK

FRUITA

Cohab
Cyn Trail

24

Fremont
Gorge Overlook
Trail

Fremont
River
Trail

Frying
Pan Trail

Grand
Wash Trail

Grand Wash Canyon

Fremont River

jewelry. Other historic exhibits outline exploration and early Mormon settlement.

Hikers can pick up a map of trails that are near the visitors center and of longer routes in the southern park areas; naturalists will want the checklists of plants, birds, mammals, and other wildlife, while history buffs can learn more about the area's settlement and the founding of the park. Rangers offer nature walks, campfire programs, and other special events from Easter to mid-October; the bulletin board outside the visitors center lists what's on. The visitors center is on Hwy. 24 at the turn-off for Fruita Campground and the Scenic Drive.

ALONG HIGHWAY 24

From the west, Hwy. 24 drops from the broad mountain valley near Torrey onto Sulphur Creek, with dramatic rock formations soaring into the horizon. A huge amphitheater of stone rings the basin, with formations such as Twin Rocks, Chimney Rock, and the Castle glowing in deep red and yellow tones. Ahead, the canyon narrows as the Fremont River slips between the cliffs to carve its chasm through Waterpocket Fold.

Panorama Point

Take in the incredible view from Panorama Point, 2.5 miles west of the visitors center on the south side of the highway. Follow signs south for 0.15 mile to Panorama Point and views of Capitol Reef and the distant Henry Mountains to the east and looming Boulder Mountain to the west. The large black basalt boulders were swept down from Boulder Mountain to the reef as part of giant debris flows between 8,000 and 200,000 years ago.

Goosenecks

Continue past Panorama Point one mile on a gravel road to the Goosenecks of Sulphur Creek. A short trail leads to Goosenecks Overlook on the rim (elev. 6,400 feet) for dizzying views of the creek below. Canyon walls display shades of yellow, green, brown, and red. Another easy trail leads a third of a mile to **Sunset**

Point and panoramic views of the Capitol Reef cliffs and the distant Henry Mountains.

Fruita Schoolhouse

Remnants of the pioneer community of Fruita stretch along the narrow Fremont River Canyon. The Fruita Schoolhouse is just east of the visitors center on the north side of the highway. Early settlers completed this one-room log structure in 1896. Teachers struggled at times with rowdy students, but the kids learned their three Rs in grades one through eight. Mormon Church meetings, dances, town meetings, elections, and other community gatherings took place here. A lack of students caused the school's closing in 1941. Rangers are on duty some days in summer (ask at the visitors center). At other times, you can peer inside the windows and listen to a recording of a former teacher recalling what school life was like.

Fremont Petroglyphs

Farther down the canyon, 1.2 miles east of the visitors center on the north side of the highway, are several panels of Fremont petroglyphs (watch for road signs). Several human figures with headdresses and mountain sheep decorate the cliff. You can see more petroglyphs by walking to the left and right along the cliff face. Stay on the trail and *do not* climb the talus slope.

Behunin Cabin

Behunin Cabin is located 6.2 miles east of the visitors center on the south side of the highway. Elijah Cutlar Behunin used blocks of sandstone to build this cabin in about 1882. For several years, Behunin, his wife, and 11 of their 13 children shared this sturdy but quite small cabin. (The kids slept outside.) He moved on, though, when floods made life too difficult. Small openings allow a look inside the dirt-floored structure, but no furnishings remain.

Fremont River Waterfall

Near the end of the narrow sandstone canyon, a small waterfall in the Fremont River attracts photographers and impromptu swimming

THE ORCHARDS OF CAPITOL REEF

Capitol Reef remained one of the last places in the West to be discovered by white settlers. First reports came in 1866 from a detachment of Mormon militia pursuing renegade Utes. In 1872, Professor Almon H. Thompson of the Powell Expedition led the first scientific exploration in the fold country and named several park features along the group's Pleasant Creek route. Mormons, expanding their network of settlements, arrived in the upper Fremont Valley in the late 1870s and spread downriver to Hanksville. Junction (renamed Fruita in 1902) and nearby Pleasant Creek (Sleeping Rainbow/Floral Ranch) were settled about 1880.

Floods, isolation, and transport difficulties forced many families to move on, especially downstream from Capitol Reef. Irrigation and hard work paid off with prosperous fruit orchards and the sobriquet "the Eden of Wayne County." The aptly named Fruita averaged about 10 families who grew alfalfa, sorghum (for syrup), vegetables, and a wide variety of fruit. Getting the produce to market required long and difficult journeys by wagon. The region remained one of the most isolated in Utah until after World War II.

Although Fruita's citizens have departed, the National Park Service still maintains the old orchards. The orchards are lovely in late April, when the trees are in bloom beneath the towering canyon walls. Visitors are welcome to pick and carry away the cherries, apricots, peaches, pears, and apples during harvest seasons. Harvest times begin in late June or early July and end in October. You'll be charged about the same as in commercial pick-your-own orchards. You may also wander through any orchard and eat all you want on the spot before and during the designated picking season (no charge).

parties. The river twists through a narrow human-made crack in the rock before making its final plunge into a pool below. A sign warns of hazardous footing above the falls. Take the sandy path from the parking area to where you can safely view the falls from below. Use extreme caution if you intend to cool off in the pool at the base of the waterfall because the undertow is strong and dangerous. Parking is 6.9 miles east of the visitors center on the north side of the highway.

THE SCENIC DRIVE

Turn south from Hwy. 24 at the visitors center to experience some of the reef's best scenery and to learn more about its geology. An illustrated pamphlet, available on the drive or in the visitors center, has keyed references to numbered stops along the 25-mile (round-trip) drive. Descriptions identify rock layers and explain how they were formed. A quick tour requires about 1.5 hours, but several hiking trails may tempt you to extend your stay. The scenic drive is paved, although side roads have gravel surfaces.

Fruita

You'll first pass orchards and several of Fruita's buildings. A **blacksmith shop** (0.7 miles from the visitors center on the right) displays tools, harnesses, farm machinery, and Fruita's first tractor. The tractor didn't arrive until 1940—long after the rest of the country had modernized. In a recording, a rancher tells about living and working in Fruita.

The **Historic Gifford Homestead,** one mile south on the Scenic Drive, is typical of rural Utah farmhouses of the early 1900s. Cultural demonstrations and handmade items are available. A picnic area is just beyond; with fruit trees and grass, this is a pretty spot for lunch. A short trail crosses orchards and the Fremont River to the Fruita schoolhouse.

Grand Wash

The Scenic Drive leaves the Fremont River valley and climbs up a desert slope, with the rock walls of the Waterpocket Fold rising to the

THE ESCALANTE REGION

east. Turn east into Grand Wash, a dry channel etched through the sandstone. A dirt road follows the twisting gulch one mile, with sheer rock walls rising along the sandy stream bed. At the road's end, an easy hiking trail follows the wash 2.5 miles to its mouth along Hwy. 24.

Past Slickrock Divide, the rock lining the reef deepens into a ruby red and forms itself into odd columns and spires that resemble statuary. Called the **Egyptian Temple,** this is one of the most striking and colorful areas along the road.

◖ Capitol Gorge

Capitol Gorge is the end of the Scenic Drive, 10.7 miles from the visitors center. Capitol Gorge is a dry canyon through Capitol Reef much like Grand Wash. Believe it or not, the narrow, twisting Capitol Gorge was the route of the main state highway through south-central Utah for 80 years! Mormon pioneers laboriously cleared a path so wagons could go through, a task they repeated every time flash floods rolled in a new set of boulders. Cars

Capitol Gorge is one of only five canyons that cuts through Waterpocket Fold.

© W. C. MCRAE

THE ESCALANTE REGION

bounced their way down the canyon until 1962, when Hwy. 24 opened, but few traces of the old road remain today. Walking is easy along the gravel riverbed, but don't enter if storms threaten. An easy one-mile saunter down the gorge will take day hikers past **petroglyphs** and a "register" rock where pioneers carved their names. For other Capitol Gorge hikes, see the following sections.

Pleasant Creek Road

Turn right 8.3 miles from the visitors center, where the Scenic Drive curves east toward Capitol Gorge onto Pleasant Creek Road, which continues south below the face of the reef. After three miles, the sometimes rough dirt road passes Sleeping Rainbow/Floral Ranch (closed to the public) and ends at Pleasant Creek. A rugged four-wheel drive road continues on the other side but is much too rough for cars. Floral Ranch dates back to Capitol Reef's early years of settlement. In 1939 it became the Sleeping Rainbow Guest Ranch, from the translation of the Indian name for Waterpocket Fold. Now the ranch belongs to the park, but the former owners still live here. Pleasant Creek's perennial waters begin high on Boulder Mountain to the west and cut a scenic canyon completely through Capitol Reef. Hikers can head downstream through the three-mile-long canyon and then return the way they went in, or they can continue another three miles cross-country to Notom Road.

NORTH DISTRICT

Only the most adventurous travelers enter the remote canyons and desert country of the north. The few roads *cannot* be negotiated by four-wheel drive vehicles, let alone ordinary cars, in wet weather. In good weather, high-clearance vehicles (good clearance is more important than four-wheel drive) can enter the region from the east, north, and west. The roads lead through stately sandstone monoliths of Cathedral Valley, volcanic remnants, badlands country, many low mesas, and vast sand flats. Foot travel allows closer inspection of these features or lengthy excursions into the canyons of Polk, Deep, and Spring Creeks, which cut deeply into the flanks of Thousand Lake Mountain.

Mountain bikers enjoy these challenging roads as well, but they must stay on established roads. Much of the north district is good for horseback riding, too. **Cathedral Valley Campground's** five sites provide a place to stop for the night; rangers won't permit car camping elsewhere in the district. The campground is on the four-wheel drive Cathedral Valley loop road about 36 miles from the visitors center (from the park entrance, head 12 miles east on Hwy. 24, then turn north and ford the Fremont River and follow Hartnet Road about 24 miles to the campground); check on road conditions at the visitor center before heading out. The **Upper Cathedral Valley Trail,** located just below the campground, is an enjoyable one-mile walk offering excellent views of the Cathedrals. Hikers with a backcountry permit must camp at least half a mile from the nearest road. Guides to the area can be purchased at the visitors center.

SOUTH DISTRICT
Notom-Bullfrog Road

Capitol Reef is only a small part of the Waterpocket Fold. By taking the Notom-Bullfrog Road, you'll see nearly 80 miles of the fold's eastern side. This route crosses some of the younger geologic layers, such as those of the Morrison Formation that form colorful hills. In other places, eroded layers of the Waterpocket Fold jut up at 70-degree angles. The Henry Mountains to the east and the many canyons on both sides of the road add to the memorable panoramas. The road has been paved as far as Notom, and about 25 miles are paved on the southern end near Bullfrog. The rest of the road is dirt and gravel. Most cars should have no trouble negotiating this road in good weather. Keep an eye on the weather before setting out, though; the dirt-and-gravel surface is usually okay for cars when dry but can be dangerous for *any* vehicle when wet. Sandy spots and washouts may present a problem for low-clearance vehicles; contact the visitors center to check current conditions. Have a full gas

Waterpocket Fold is a vast rock wrinkle nearly 100 miles long.

THE ESCALANTE REGION

© W. C. MCRAE

tank and carry extra water and food because no services are available between Hwy. 24 and Bullfrog Marina. Purchase a small guide to this area at the visitors center. Features and mileage along the drive from north to south include the following:

- **Mile 0.0:** The turn-off from Hwy. 24 is 9.2 miles east of the visitors center and 30.2 miles west of Hanksville (another turn-off from Hwy. 24 is three miles east).

- **Mile 2.2:** Pleasant Creek; the mouth of the canyon is 5–6 miles upstream, although it's only about three miles away if you head cross-country from south of Notom. Hikers can follow the canyon three miles upstream through Capitol Reef to Pleasant Creek Road (off the Scenic Drive).

- **Mile 4.1:** Notom Ranch is to the west; once a small town, Notom is now a private ranch.

- **Mile 8.1:** Burrow Wash; hikers can explore the narrow canyon upstream.

- **Mile 9.3:** Cottonwood Wash; another canyon hike just upstream.

- **Mile 10.4:** Five Mile Wash; yet another canyon hike.

- **Mile 13.3:** Sheets Gulch; a scenic canyon lies upstream here, too.

- **Mile 14.1:** Sandy Ranch Junction; high-clearance vehicles can turn east 16 miles to the Henry Mountains.

- **Mile 14.2:** Oak Creek Access Road; the creek cuts a two-mile-long canyon through Capitol Reef and makes a good day hike. Backpackers sometimes start upstream at Lower Bowns Reservoir (off Hwy. 12) and hike the 15 miles to Oak Creek Access Road. The clear waters of Oak Creek flow year-round but are not potable.

- **Mile 14.4:** Oak Creek crossing.

- **Mile 20.0:** Entering Capitol Reef National Park; a small box has information sheets.

- **Mile 22.3:** Cedar Mesa Campground to

the west; the small five-site campground is surrounded by junipers and has fine views of Waterpocket Fold and the Henry Mountains. Free sites have tables and grills; there's an outhouse but no drinking water. Red Canyon Trail begins here, heads west into a huge box canyon in Waterpocket Fold, and is four miles round-trip.

- **Mile 26.0:** Bitter Creek Divide; streams to the north flow to the Fremont River; Halls Creek on the south side runs through Strike Valley to Lake Powell, 40 miles away.

- **Mile 34.1:** Burr Trail Road Junction; turn west up the steep switchbacks to ascend Waterpocket Fold and continue to Boulder and Hwy. 12 (36 miles). Burr Trail is the only road that actually crosses the top of the fold, and it's one of the most scenic in the park. Driving conditions are similar to the Notom-Bullfrog Road—okay for cars when dry. Pavement begins at the park boundary and continues to Boulder. Although paved, the Burr Trail still must be driven slowly because of its curves and potholes. The section of road through Long Canyon has especially pretty scenery.

- **Mile 36.0:** Surprise Canyon Trailhead; a hike into this narrow, usually shaded canyon takes 1–2 hours.

- **Mile 36.6:** The Post; a small trading post here once served sheepherders and some cattlemen, but today this spot is just a reference point. Park here to hike to Headquarters Canyon. A trailhead for Lower Muley Twist Canyon via Halls Creek lies at the end of a half-mile-long road to the south.

- **Mile 37.5:** Leaving Capitol Reef National Park; a small box has information sheets. Much of the road between here and Glen Canyon National Recreation Area has been paved.

- **Mile 45.5:** Road junction; turn right (south) to continue to Bullfrog Marina (25 miles) or go straight (east) for Starr Springs Campground (23 miles) in the Henry Mountains.

• **Mile 46.4:** The road to the right (west) goes to Halls Creek Overlook. This turn-off is poorly signed and easy to miss; look for it 0.9 mile south of the previous junction. Turn in and follow the road three miles, then turn right at a fork 0.4 mile to the viewpoint. The last 0.3 mile may be too rough for low-clearance cars. A picnic table is the only "facility" here. Far below in Grand Gulch, Halls Creek flows south to Lake Powell. Look across the valley for the double Brimhall Bridge in the red sandstone of Waterpocket Fold. A steep trail descends to Halls Creek (1.2 miles one-way), and it's possible to continue another 1.1 miles up Brimhall Canyon to the bridge. A register box at the overlook has information sheets on this route. Note, however, that the last part of the hike to the bridge requires difficult rock-scrambling and wading or swimming through pools. Hikers looking for another adventure might want to follow Halls Creek 10 miles downstream to the narrows. Here, convoluted walls as high as 700 feet narrow to little more than arm's length apart. This beautiful area of water-sculpted rock sometimes has deep pools that require swimming.

• **Mile 49.0:** Colorful clay hills of deep reds, creams, and grays rise beside the road. This clay turns to goo when wet, providing all the traction of axle grease.

• **Mile 54.0:** Beautiful panorama of countless mesas, mountains, and canyons. Lake Powell and Navajo Mountain can be seen to the south.

• **Mile 65.3:** Junction with paved Hwy. 276; turn left (north) for Hanksville (59 miles) or right (south) to Bullfrog Marina (5.2 miles).

• **Mile 70.5:** Bullfrog Marina (see *Glen Canyon National Recreation Area* in the *Canyonlands* chapter).

Lower Muley Twist Canyon

"So winding that it would twist a mule pulling a wagon," said an early visitor. This canyon has some of the best hiking in the southern district of the park. In the 1880s, Mormon pioneers used the canyon as part of a wagon route between Escalante and new settlements in southeastern Utah, replacing the even more difficult Hole-in-the-Rock route.

Unlike most canyons of the Waterpocket Fold, Muley Twist runs lengthwise along the crest for about 18 miles before finally turning east and leaving the fold. Hikers starting from Burr Trail Road can easily follow the twisting bends down to Halls Creek, 12 miles away. Two trailheads and the Halls Creek route allow a variety of trips.

You could start from Burr Trail Road near the top of the switchbacks (2.2 miles west of Notom-Bullfrog Road) and hike down the dry gravel streambed. After four miles, you have the options of returning the same way, taking the cutoff route east 2.5 miles to Post Trailhead (off Notom-Bullfrog Road), or continuing eight miles down Lower Muley Twist Canyon to its end at Halls Creek. Upon reaching Halls Creek, turn left (north) five miles up the creek bed or the old jeep road beside it to the Post. This section of creek lies in an open, dry valley. With a car shuttle, the Post would be the end of a good two-day, 17-mile hike, or you could loop back to Lower Muley Twist Canyon via the cutoff route and hike back to Burr Trail Road for a 23.5-mile trip. It's a good idea to check the weather beforehand and avoid the canyon if storms threaten.

Cream-colored sandstone cliffs lie atop the red Kayenta and Wingate formations. Impressively deep undercuts have been carved into the lower canyon. Spring and autumn offer the best conditions (summer temperatures can exceed 100°F). Elevations range from 5,640 feet at Burr Trail Road to 4,540 feet at the confluence with Halls Creek to 4,894 feet at the Post.

An information sheet available at the visitors center and trailheads has a small map and route details. Topographic maps of Wagon Box Mesa, Mount Pennell, and Hall Mesa, and the 1:100,000-scale Escalante and Hite Crossing maps are sold at the visitors center. You'll also find this hike described in David Day's *Utah's Favorite Hiking Trails*, or in the small, spiral-bound *Explore Capitol Reef's Trails*, by the Capitol Reef Natural History Association, available at the visitors center. Carry all water for the trip because natural sources are often dry or polluted.

Upper Muley Twist Canyon

This part of the canyon has plenty of scenery. Large and small natural arches along the way add to its beauty. Upper Muley Twist Road turns north off Burr Trail Road about one mile west from the top of a set of switchbacks. Cars can usually go in half a mile to a trailhead parking area; high-clearance four-wheel drive vehicles can head another 2.5 miles up a wash to the end of the primitive road. Look for natural arches on the left along this last section. **Strike Valley Overlook Trail** (0.75 mile round-trip) begins at the end of the road and leads to a magnificent panorama of Waterpocket Fold and beyond. Return to the canyon, where you can hike as far as 6.5 miles to the head of Upper Muley Twist Canyon.

Two large arches lie a short hike upstream; Saddle Arch, the second one on the left, is 1.75 miles away. The **Rim Route** begins across from Saddle Arch, climbs the canyon wall, follows the rim (good views of Strike Valley and the Henry Mountains), and descends back into the canyon at a point just above the narrows, 4.75 miles from the end of the road. (The Rim Route is most easily followed in this direction.) Proceed up-canyon to see several more arches. A narrow section of canyon beginning about four miles from the end of the road must be bypassed to continue; look for rock cairns showing the way around to the right. Continuing up the canyon past the Rim Route sign will take you to several small drainages marking the upper end of Muley Twist Canyon. Climb a high, tree-covered point on the west rim for great views; experienced hikers with a map can follow the rim back to Upper Muley Road (no trail or markers on this route). Bring all the water you'll need because there are no reliable sources in Upper Muley Twist Canyon.

HIKING

Fifteen day-hike trails begin within a short drive of the visitors center. Of these, only Grand Wash, Capitol Gorge, Sunset Point, and Goosenecks are easy. The others involve moderately strenuous climbs and travel over irregular slickrock. Signs and rock cairns mark the way, but it's all too easy to wander off if you don't pay attention to the route.

Although most hiking trails can easily be done in a day, backpackers and mountain hikers might want to try longer trips in Chimney Rock/Spring Canyons in the north or Muley Twist Canyon and Halls Creek in the south. Obtain the required backcountry permit (free) from a ranger and camp at least one-half mile from the nearest maintained road or trail. (Cairned routes like Chimney Rock Canyon, Muley Twist Canyon, and Halls Creek don't count as trails but are backcountry routes.) Bring a stove for cooking because backcountry users may not build fires. Avoid camping or parking in washes at any time—torrents of mud and boulders can carry away everything!

HIKES ALONG HIGHWAY 24

Stop by the visitors center to pick up a map showing hiking trails and trail descriptions. These trailheads are along the main highway through the park and along the Fremont River. Note that the Grand Wash Trail cuts west through the reef to the scenic drive.

Chimney Rock Trail

The trailhead is three miles west of the visitors center on the north side of the highway. Towering 660 feet above the highway, Chimney Rock is a fluted spire of dark red rock (Moenkopi Formation) capped by a block of hard sandstone (Shinarump Member of the Chinle Formation). A 3.5-mile loop trail ascends 540 feet from the parking lot (elev. 6,100 feet) to a ridge overlooking Chimney Rock; allow 2.5 hours. Panoramic views take in the face of Capitol Reef. Petrified wood along the trail has been eroded from the Chinle Formation (the same rock layer found in Petrified Forest National Park in Arizona). It is illegal to take any of the petrified wood.

it downstream. A sign marks Chimney Rock Canyon, which is 2.5 miles from the start. Turn right 6.5 miles (downstream) to reach the Fremont River. A section of narrows requires some rock-scrambling (bring a cord to lower backpacks), or the area can be bypassed on a narrow trail to the left above the narrows. Farther down, a natural arch high on the left marks the halfway point.

Upper Chimney Rock Canyon could be explored on an overnight trip. A spring (purify before drinking) is located in an alcove on the right side about one mile up Chimney Rock Canyon from the lead-in canyon. Wildlife use this water source, so camp at least one-quarter mile away. Chimney Rock Canyon, the longest in the park, begins high on the slopes of Thousand Lake Mountain and descends nearly 15 miles southeast to join the Fremont River.

© PAUL LEVY

The trail to Chimney Rock starts right on Highway 24.

Spring Canyon Route

This moderately difficult hike begins at the top of the Chimney Rock Trail. The wonderfully eroded forms of Navajo sandstone present a continually changing exhibition. The riverbed is normally dry; allow about six hours for the 10-mile (one-way) trip from the Chimney Rock parking area to the Fremont River and Hwy. 24. (Some maps show all or part of this as "Chimney Rock Canyon.") Check with rangers for the weather forecast before setting off because flash floods can be dangerous, and the Fremont River (which you must wade across) can rise quite high. Normally, the river runs less than knee-deep to Hwy. 24 (3.7 miles east of the visitors center). With luck you'll have a car waiting for you. Summer hikers can beat the heat with a crack-of-dawn departure. Carry water; this section of canyon lacks a reliable source.

From the Chimney Rock parking area, hike Chimney Rock Trail to the top of the ridge and follow the signs for Chimney Rock Canyon. Enter the unnamed lead-in canyon and follow

Sulphur Creek Route

This moderately difficult hike begins by following a wash across the highway from the Chimney Rock parking area, descending to Sulphur Creek, then heads down the narrow canyon to the visitors center. The trip is about five miles long (one-way) and takes 3–5 hours. Park rangers sometimes schedule guided hikes on this route. Warm weather is the best time because you'll be wading in the normally shallow creek. Three small waterfalls can be bypassed fairly easily; two falls are just below the goosenecks, and the third is about one-half mile before coming out at the visitors center. Carry water with you. The creek's name may be a mistake because there's no sulphur along it; perhaps outcrops of yellow limonite caused the confusion. You can make an all-day eight-mile hike in Sulphur Creek by starting where it crosses the highway between mileposts 72 and 73, five miles west of the visitors center.

Hickman Natural Bridge, Rim Overlook, and Navajo Knobs Trails

The trailhead is two miles east of the visitors center on the north side of the highway. The graceful Hickman Natural Bridge spans 133 feet across a small streambed. Numbered

THE ESCALANTE REGION

stops along the self-guided trail correspond to descriptions in a pamphlet available at the trailhead or visitors center. Starting from the parking area (elev. 5,320 feet), the trail follows the Fremont River's green banks a short distance before gaining 380 feet in the climb to the bridge. The last section of trail follows a dry wash shaded by cottonwood, juniper, and piñon pine trees. You'll pass under the bridge (eroded from the Kayenta Formation) at trail's end. Capitol Dome and other sculptured features of the Navajo sandstone surround the site. The two-mile round-trip hike takes about 90 minutes. Joseph Hickman served as principal of Wayne County High School and later in the state legislature during the 1920s; he and another local man, Ephraim Pectol, led efforts to promote Capitol Reef.

A splendid overlook 1,000 feet above Fruita beckons hikers up the **Rim Overlook Trail.** Take the Hickman Natural Bridge Trail one-quarter mile from the parking area, then turn right two miles at the signed fork. Allow 3.5 hours from the fork for this hike. Panoramic views take in the Fremont River valley below, the great cliffs of Capitol Reef above, the Henry Mountains to the southeast, and Boulder Mountain to the southwest.

Continue another 2.2 miles and more than 500 feet higher from the Rim Overlook to reach **Navajo Knobs.** Rock cairns lead the way over slickrock along the rim of Waterpocket Fold. A magnificent panorama at trail's end takes in much of southeastern Utah.

Cohab Canyon and Frying Pan Trails

Park at Hickman Natural Bridge Trailhead, then walk across the highway bridge. This trail climbs Capitol Reef for fine views in all directions and a close look at the swirling lines in the Navajo sandstone. After three-quarters of a mile and a 400-foot climb, you'll reach a trail fork: Keep right one mile to stay on Cohab Canyon Trail and descend to Fruita Campground or turn left onto Frying Pan Trail to Cassidy Arch (3.5 miles away) and Grand Wash (four miles away). The trail from Cassidy Arch

to Grand Wash is steep. All of these interconnecting trails offer many hiking possibilities, especially if you can arrange a car shuttle. For example, you could start up Cohab Canyon Trail from Hwy. 24, cross over the reef on Frying Pan Trail, make a side trip to Cassidy Arch, descend Cassidy Arch Trail to Grand Wash, walk down Grand Wash to Hwy. 24, then walk (or car shuttle) 2.7 miles along the highway back to the start (10.5 miles total).

Cohab is a pretty little canyon in the Wingate sandstone overlooking the campground. Mormon polygamists supposedly used the canyon to escape federal marshals during the 1880s. Hiking the Frying Pan Trail involves an additional 600 feet of climbing from either Cohab Canyon or Cassidy Arch trail. Once atop Capitol Reef, the trail follows the gently rolling slickrock terrain.

Grand Wash

The trailhead is 4.7 miles east of the visitors center on the south side of the highway. One of only five canyons cutting completely through the reef, Grand Wash offers easy hiking and great scenery. There's no trail—just follow the dry gravel riverbed. Flash floods can occur during storms. Canyon walls of Navajo sandstone rise 800 feet above the floor and close in to as little as 20 feet in width. Cassidy Arch Trailhead (see *Grand Wash Road* under *Hikes Along the Scenic Drive*) is two miles away, and parking for Grand Wash from the scenic drive is one-quarter mile farther.

HIKES ALONG THE SCENIC DRIVE

These hikes begin from trailheads along the scenic drive that turns south from the visitors center. There is a $5 entrance fee to travel the scenic drive.

Fremont Gorge Overlook Trail

From the start at the Fruita blacksmith shop, the trail crosses Johnson Mesa and climbs steeply to the overlook about 1,000 feet above the Fremont River; round-trip distance is 4.5 miles.

Cohab Canyon Trail

The trailhead is across the road from the Fruita Campground, 1.3 miles from the visitors center. The trail follows steep switchbacks during the first one-quarter mile, then more gentle grades to the top, 400 feet higher and one mile from the campground. You can take a short trail to viewpoints or continue three-quarters of a mile down the other side of the ridge to Hwy. 24. Another option is to turn right at the top on Frying Pan Trail to Cassidy Arch (3.5 miles one-way) and Grand Wash (four miles one-way).

Fremont River Trail

From the trailhead near the amphitheater at the Fruita Campground, 1.3 miles from the visitors center, the trail passes orchards along the Fremont River (elev. 5,350 feet), then begins the climb up sloping rock strata to a viewpoint on Miner's Mountain. Sweeping views take in Fruita, Boulder Mountain, and the reef. The round-trip distance of 2.5 miles takes about 90 minutes; the elevation gain is 770 feet.

Grand Wash Road

Turn left off the scenic drive 3.6 miles from the visitors center. This side trip follows the twisting Grand Wash for one mile. At road's end, you can continue on foot 2.25 miles (one-way) through the canyon to its end at the Fremont River.

Cassidy Arch Trail begins near the end of Grand Wash Road. Energetic hikers will enjoy good views of Grand Wash, the great domes of Navajo sandstone, and the arch itself. The 3.5-mile round-trip trail ascends the north wall of Grand Wash (Wingate and Kayenta Formations), then winds across slickrock of the Kayenta Formation to a vantage point close to the arch, also of Kayenta. Allow about three hours because the elevation gain is nearly 1,000 feet. The notorious outlaw Butch Cassidy may have traveled through Capitol Reef and seen this arch. Frying Pan Trail branches off Cassidy Arch Trail at the one-mile mark, then wends its way across three miles of slickrock to Cohab Canyon.

Old Wagon Trail

Wagon drivers once used this route as a shortcut between Grover and Capitol Gorge. Look for the trailhead 0.7 mile south of Slickrock Divide, between Grand Wash and Capitol Gorge. The old trail crosses a wash to the west, then ascends steadily through piñon and juniper woodland on Miners Mountain. After 1.5 miles, the trail leaves the wagon road and goes north one-half mile to a high knoll for the best views of the Capitol Reef area. The four-mile (round-trip) hike climbs 1,000 feet.

Capitol Gorge

Follow the well-maintained dirt road to the parking area in Capitol Gorge to begin these hikes. The first mile downstream is the most scenic: Fremont petroglyphs (in poor condition) appear on the left after 0.1 mile; narrows of Capitol Gorge close in at 0.3 mile; a "pioneer register" on the left at one-half mile consists of names and dates of early travelers and ranchers scratched in the canyon wall; and natural water tanks on the left at three-quarters of a mile are

© JUDY JEWELL

Just a short scramble above Capitol Gorge is a series of natural waterpockets.

THE ESCALANTE REGION

typical of those in Waterpocket Fold. Hikers can continue another three miles downstream to Notom Road.

The **Golden Throne Trail** also begins at the end of the scenic drive. Instead of heading down Capitol Gorge from the parking area, turn left up this trail for dramatic views of the reef and surrounding area. Golden Throne is a massive monolith of yellow-hued Navajo sandstone capped by a thin layer of red Carmel Formation. The four-mile round-trip trail climbs 1,100 feet in a steady grade to a viewpoint near the base of Golden Throne; allow four hours.

MOUNTAIN BIKING

Ditch the car and really get to know this country with a big loop tour. From Hwy. 24 near Capitol Reef, take the Notom-Bullfrog Road to Burr Trail Road, then Hwy. 12 over Boulder Mountain to Hwy. 24 and back to Capitol Reef. This is definitely the sort of trip that requires some touring experience and a decent level of training. (Boulder Mountain is quite a haul.) Expect the 125-mile loop to take several days.

In the remote northern section of the park, cyclists can ride the challenging Cathedral Canyon Loop. The complete loop is more than 60 miles long. Little water is available along the route, so it's best ridden in spring or fall, when temperatures are low. Contact the visitors center for more information on this and other routes.

ROCK CLIMBING

Rock climbing is allowed in the park. Climbers should check with rangers to learn about restricted areas, but registration is voluntary. Climbers must use "clean" techniques (no pitons or bolts) and keep at least 100 feet from rock-art panels and prehistoric structures. Because of the abundance of prehistoric rock art found there, the section of rock wall north of Hwy. 24 between the Fruita schoolhouse and the east end of Kreuger Orchard (Mile 81.4) is closed to climbing. Other areas closed to climbing are Hickman Natural Bridge and all other arches and bridges, Temple of the Moon, Temple of the Sun, and Chimney Rock.

The harder, fractured sandstone of the Wingate Formation is better suited to climbing than the more crumbly Entrada sandstone. However, the rock is given to flaking, so climbers should use caution. Be sure that chalk matches the color of the rock; white chalk is prohibited.

CAMPGROUNDS

Fruita Campground, located one mile south of the visitors center on the scenic drive, stays open all year and has drinking water but no showers or hookups ($10). November–April campers must get their water from the visitors center. The surrounding orchards and lush grass make this an attractive spot. Sites often fill by early afternoon in the busy May–October season. One group campground (by reservation only) and a picnic area are nearby. If you're just looking for a place to park for the night, check out the public land east of the park boundary off Hwy. 24. Areas on both sides of the highway (about nine miles east of the visitors center) may be used for free primitive camping.

The five-site **Cedar Mesa Campground** is in the park's southern district just off Notom-Bullfrog Road (dirt); campers here enjoy fine views of Waterpocket Fold and the Henry Mountains. Open all year; no water or fee. From the visitors center, go east 9.2 miles on Hwy. 24, then turn right 22 miles on Notom-Bullfrog Road (avoid this road if wet). **Cathedral Valley Campground** serves the park's northern district; it has five sites (no water or fee) near the Hartnet Junction, about 30 miles north of Hwy. 24. Take either Caineville Wash or Hartnet (has a river ford) Roads. Both roads are dirt and should be avoided when wet.

Torrey

Torrey (pop. 166) is an attractive little village with a real Western feel. Only 11 miles west of the Capitol Reef National Park visitors center, at the junction of Hwys. 12 and 24, it's a friendly and convenient place to stay, with several excellent lodgings and a good restaurant.

Other little towns lie along the Fremont River, which drains this steep-sided valley. Teasdale is a small community just four miles west, situated in a grove of piñon pines. Bicknell, a small farm and ranch town, is eight miles west of Torrey.

ACCOMMODATIONS
Under $50

There are a few small bunkhouse cabins at the center of town, at the **Torrey Trading Post** (75 W. Main St., 435/425-3716, www.torrey tradingpost.com, $28). They aren't loaded with frills—the toilets and showers are in men's and women's bathhouses—but the price is right and pets are permitted. The **Capitol Reef Inn and Cafe** (360 W. Main St., 435/425-3271, www .capitolreefinn.com, $48, closed in winter) has homey motel rooms and a good café serving breakfast, lunch, and dinner. In the front yard, the motel's owner and his brother have built a kiva resembling those used by Native Americans. It's obviously a labor of love, and a pretty cool place to explore.

In Bicknell, the **Aquarius Motel** (435/425-3835 or 800/833-5379, $47 and up) offers good-sized standard motel rooms, some with kitchens (you supply the kitchenware) and all with wireless Internet access. There's also a somewhat retro café open daily for breakfast, lunch, and dinner, and a glass-enclosed indoor pool.

$50-100

Immediately behind downtown Torrey's old trading post and country store in a grove of trees is **Austin's Chuck Wagon Lodge** (12 W. Main, 435/425-3335 or 800/863-3288,

© PAUL LEVY

Two local guys built this kiva in Torrey. It's in the front yard of the Capitol Reef Inn and Cafe.

THE ESCALANTE REGION

www.austinschuckwagonmotel.com, $69–135, closed Jan.–Feb.), with rooms in an older motel, a newer lodge-like building, or in two-bedroom cabins. There's also a pool and a hot tub.

In a pretty setting three miles south of town, **Cowboy Homestead Cabins** (Hwy. 12, 435/425-3414 or 888/854-5871, www.cowboy homesteadcabins.com, $69) has attractive, modern kitchenette cabins with outdoor gas barbeque grills.

The **Wonderland Inn** (junction of Hwys. 12 and 24, 435/425-3775 or 800/458-0216, www .capitolreefwonderland.com, $64 and up), just east of town near the turn-off for Boulder, is a larger motel with an indoor pool, a rather spacious greenhouse, and a restaurant serving breakfast, lunch, and dinner daily.

Farther east, the **Rim Rock Inn** (2523 E. Hwy. 24, 435/425-3388 or 888/447-4676, www.therimrock.net, $59 and up, closed Jan.–Feb.) does indeed perch on a rim of red rock. The motel and its two restaurants are part of a 120-acre ranch, so the views are expansive.

If you're looking for standard and comfortable motel rooms with perks like high-speed Internet access and an outdoor pool, a good choice is the **Best Western Capitol Reef Resort** (2600 E. Hwy. 24, 435/425-3761, www.bestwestern.com, $90 and up).

In Teasdale, four miles west of Torrey, **Pine Shadows** (125 S. 200 W., 435/425-3939 or 800/708-1223, www.pineshadowcabins.net, $69 and up) offers spacious, modern cabins equipped with bathrooms and kitchens in a piñon forest.

Over $100

The lovely **SkyRidge Inn Bed and Breakfast** (950 W. Hwy. 24, 435/425-3222 or 800/448-6990, www.skyridgeinn.com, $109–159) is located one mile east of downtown Torrey. The modern inn has been decorated with high-quality Southwestern art and artifacts; all six guest rooms have private baths. SkyRidge sits on a bluff amid 75 acres; guests are invited to explore the land on foot or bike.

The **C Lodge at Red River Ranch** (2900 W. Hwy 24, 435/425-3322 or 800/205-6343,

www.redriverranch.com, $140–225) is located between Bicknell and Torrey beneath towering cliffs of red sandstone on the banks of the Fremont River. This wonderful wood-beamed lodge sits on a working ranch, but there's nothing rustic or unsophisticated about the accommodations here. The three-story structure is newly built, although in the same grand architectural style of old-fashioned mountain lodges. The great room has a massive stone fireplace, cozy chairs and couches, and a splendid Old West atmosphere. There are 15 guest rooms, most decorated according to a theme, and all have private baths. Guests are welcome to wander ranch paths, fish for trout, or tinker in the gardens and orchards. Breakfast and dinner are served in the lodge restaurant, but are not included in the price of lodgings; box lunches can also be ordered.

Muley Twist Inn (294 West 125 St., Teasdale, 435/425-3640 or 800/530-1038, www.rof .net/yp/muley, $99–109), an elegantly decorated B&B, is on a 30-acre parcel with great views. It's another really wonderful place to come home to at the end of a day of driving or hiking.

Campgrounds

For campers, **Thousand Lakes RV Park** (435/425-3500, $15 tents, $21.50 RVs with full hookups), located one mile west of Torrey on Hwy. 24, has sites with showers, a laundry room, and a store, and is open late March–late October. Thousand Lakes also has cabins, ranging from Spartan ($31.50 without linens) to deluxe ($95, sleeps eight, linens provided) and Western-style cookouts on summer weeknights ($12.95–18.50). Right in town, the **Sand Creek RV Park** (540 W. Hwy. 24, 435/425-3577, $12 tents, $16–18 RVs with hookups, Apr.–mid-Oct.) has RV hookups and tent spaces in a pleasant grassy field.

The U.S. Forest Service's **Sunglow Campground** is just east of Bicknell at an elevation of 7,200 feet; sites are open with water mid-May–late October. The surrounding red cliffs really light up at sunset. Several other Forest Service campgrounds are on the slopes of Boulder Mountain along Hwy. 12 between Torrey and Boulder. These places are all above

8,600 feet, and usually don't open until late May or early June.

FOOD

Torrey's restaurant of note is **◖ Cafe Diablo** (599 W. Main, 435/425-3070, dinner nightly mid-Apr.–mid-Oct., $20–28). Their specialty is zesty Southwestern cuisine, with excellent dishes like fire-roasted pork tenderloin, eggplant-and-poblano-stuffed tamales, and pumpkin-seed trout. This is one of the few places you can order free-range rattlesnake meat, cooked into crabcake-like patties. Because there aren't many restaurants this good in rural Utah, this place is worth a detour.

Another pleasant surprise in this small town is the **Capitol Reef Inn and Cafe** (360 W. Main St., 435/425-3271, breakfast, lunch, and dinner daily, closed in winter, $10–15), where there's an emphasis on healthy and (when possible) locally grown food. It's easy to eat your veggies here—the ten-vegetable salad will make up for some of the less-nutritious meals you've had on the road.

West of Torrey, in Bicknell, **Alasdair's Stag and Heather Restaurant** (292 W. Main St., Bicknell, 435/425-2500, breakfast and dinner daily) had not yet opened when we were in the area, but it looked like it might be worth checking out. Chef Alasdair is Scottish, has cooked in upscale European restaurants, and managed a castle hotel in Scotland.

If you're heading east, between Capitol Reef and Hanksville is **Luna Mesa** (Hwy. 24, Caineville, 435/456-9122, breakfast, lunch, and dinner Mon.–Sat. May–Oct., $3–10), a welcome roadside spot for a burrito or a cold drink.

INFORMATION

The **Fremont River Ranger District** (138 South Main St., Loa, 435/836-2800, www .fs.fed.us/r4/fishlake, 8 A.M.–4:30 P.M. Mon.–Fri.) of the Fishlake National Forest has information about hiking, horseback riding, and road conditions in the northern and eastern parts of Boulder Mountain and the Aquarius Plateau.

East of Capitol Reef National Park

Hwy. 24 follows the Fremont River east from Capitol Reef National Park to a junction at Hanksville; from there you can head north toward I-70 (this is the best route to Moab) or south, skirting the eastern edge of the Henry Mountains to the upper reaches of Lake Powell. Hanksville is a good place to gas up if you're exploring the remote Henry Mountains or the southern San Rafael Swell. Goblin Valley State Park is worth a visit, and a good place to camp.

HANKSVILLE

Ebenezer Hanks and other Mormon settlers founded this out-of-the-way community in 1882 along the Fremont River, then known as the Dirty Devil River. The isolation attracted polygamists like Hanks and other fugitives from the law. Butch Cassidy and his gang found refuge in the rugged canyon country of "Robbers' Roost," east of town.

Even by Utah standards, Hanksville is pretty remote. The population is only about 360; most people work at ranching, farming (hay, corn feed, and watermelons), mining, or tourism. Several houses and the old stone church on Center, one block south of the highway, survive from the 19th century.

Travelers exploring this scenic region find Hanksville a handy if desultory stopover; Capitol Reef National Park lies to the west, Lake Powell and the Henry Mountains to the south, the remote Maze District of Canyonlands National Park to the east, and Goblin Valley State Park to the north.

Wolverton Mill

E. T. Wolverton built this ingenious mill

during the 1920s at his gold-mining claims in the Henry Mountains. A 20-foot waterwheel, still perfectly balanced, powered ore-crushing machinery and a sawmill. Owners of claims at the mill's original site didn't like a steady stream of tourists coming through to see the mill, so it was moved to the BLM office at Hanksville. Drive south a half mile on 100 West to see the mill and some of its original interior mechanism.

Accommodations
Whispering Sands Motel (68 East 100 North, 435/542-3238, $70) has spacious rooms with cable TV and phones.

In the center of town, **Red Rock Campground** (435/542-3235 or 800/894-3242, mid-Mar.–Oct., $12 tents, $18 RVs) has showers, laundry, and a restaurant.

Food
Hanksville's restaurants cluster at the south end of town; don't expect anything fancy. The **Red Rock** (26 E. 100 N., 435/542-3235, breakfast, lunch, and dinner daily Apr.–Oct., $8–22) is at the campground, with home cooking, beer, and wine. **Blondie's Eatery** (3 N. Hwy. 95, 435/542-3255, breakfast, lunch, and dinner daily, $5–13) is a casual sit-down place with chicken and burgers across from Whispering Sands motel. **Stan's Burger Shack** (140 S. Hwy. 95, 435/542-3441, breakfast, lunch, and dinner daily, $5–8), at the Chevron station, is more of a fast-food burger joint that's a step up from the chains.

Information and Services
The **Bureau of Land Management** (435/542-3461) has a field station a half mile south on 100 West from Hwy. 24, with information on road conditions, hiking, camping, and the buffalo herd in the Henry Mountains.

GOBLIN VALLEY STATE PARK
Thousands of spooky rock formations inhabit this valley (435/564-8110, 800/322-3770 or www.reserveamerica.com reservations, year-round, $6 day use, $15 camping). Little eye-like holes in the "goblins" make you wonder who's watching whom. All of the goblins have weathered out of the Entrada Formation, here a soft red sandstone and even softer siltstone. **Carmel Canyon Trail** (1.5-mile loop) begins at the northeast side of the parking lot at road's end, then leads into a strange landscape of goblins, spires, and balanced rocks. Just wander about at your whim; this is a great place for the imagination.

Curtis Bench Trail begins on the road between the parking lot and the campground and goes south to a viewpoint of the Henry Mountains; cairns mark the 1.5-mile (one-way) route.

The turnoff from Hwy. 24 is at milepost 137, 21 miles north of Hanksville and 24 miles south of I-70; follow signs west five miles on a paved road, then south seven miles on a gravel road.

Temple Mountain Bike Trail traverses old mining roads, ridges, and wash bottoms about 12 miles north of the state park. Popular hikes near the state park include the Little Wild Horse and Bell Canyons Loop, Chute and Crack Canyons Loop, and Wild Horse Canyon. The park is also a good base for exploring the **San Rafael Swell** area to the northwest.

SOUTHERN SAN RAFAEL SWELL
The massive fold and uplift of the earth's crust called the San Rafael Swell is crossed by I-70 about 19 miles west of Green River. The east face and "flat irons" of the Swell, known as the San Rafael Reef, rise dramatically 2,100 feet above the desert. Several view areas allow stopping for a look at the colorful rock layers. San Rafael Swell is 80 miles long (north to south) and 30 miles wide. (For a more complete discussion of the region's history and geology, see *The Castle Valley and North San Rafael Swell* section in the *Dinosaur Country* chapter.) For information, contact the BLM San Rafael Resource Area (125 South 600 West, Price, 435/636-3600, www.blm.gov/utah/price).

Black Dragon Canyon
Don't worry about the dragon; he doesn't bite.

This narrow canyon in the San Rafael Swell is just off I-70, 15 miles east of Green River. A quarter-mile walk up the streambed leads to a pair of pictograph panels of the dragon (he's actually red), human figures, a dog, and geometric designs. Continue farther up-canyon for more good scenery. To reach the trailhead, turn north on a dirt road from the I-70 westbound lane just past milepost 145; this isn't a regular exit and is not signed. If coming from the west, you'll have to turn around at the Hanksville Exit 147 and backtrack two miles. The dirt road crosses a wash (walk from here if it's filled with water), goes through a second gate, and crosses the streambed from Black Dragon Wash, 1.1 miles from I-70. Turn left 0.4 mile up the streambed (normally dry) to the canyon entrance. High-clearance vehicles can drive a short way up the canyon.

Hondoo Arch Loop

Dirt roads south of I-70 provide a scenic drive into some of the San Rafael's prettiest country. Either turn south and west 15 miles from I-70 Ranch Exit 129 or take the Goblin Valley State Park turnoff from Hwy. 24 and head west 20 miles to the beginning of the loop. The 29-mile loop drops into Reds Canyon with fine panoramas on the descent. Look for Hondoo Arch high in the cliffs across the Muddy River. Side roads off the loop go to Muddy River (beside Tomsich Butte), Hidden Splendor Mine, and other old mining areas. The Tomsich Butte area contains old cabins and uranium mines, which are dangerous to enter.

HENRY MOUNTAINS AND VICINITY

Great domes of intrusive igneous rock pushed into and deformed surrounding sedimentary layers about 70 million years ago. Erosion later uncovered the domes, revealing mountains towering 5,000 feet above the surrounding plateau. Mount Ellen's North Summit Ridge (elev. 11,522 feet) and Mount Pennell (elev. 11,320 feet) top the range. Scenic views and striking geologic features abound in and around the Henrys. Rock layers tilt dramatically in Water-pocket Fold to the west and in the Pink Cliffs on the south side of Mount Hillers. Sheer cliffs of the Horn, between Mount Ellen and Mount Pennell, attract rock climbers.

The arid land and rugged canyons surrounding the Henry Mountains so discouraged early explorers and potential settlers that the range wasn't even named or described until 1869, when members of the Powell River Expedition sighted it.

Buffalo, brought to the Henrys from Yellowstone National Park in 1941, form one of the few free-roaming herds in the United States. They winter in the southwestern part of the mountains, then move higher as the snow melts.

Exploring the Henry Mountains

Roads with panoramic views cross the range between the high peaks at Bull Creek, Pennellen, and Stanton Passes. Most driving routes are best suited for high-clearance vehicles. The road through Bull Creek Pass (elev. 10,485 feet) is snow-free only early July–late October. Rains, which peak in August, occasionally make travel difficult in late summer. Roads tend to be at their best after grading in autumn, just before the deer-hunting season. Travel at the lower elevations is possible all year, though spring and autumn have the most pleasant temperatures. Check in first with the BLM office in Hanksville before exploring the backcountry. Take precautions for desert travel, and have water, food, and extra clothing with you. The Henry Mountains remain a remote and little-traveled region.

Hiking

Countless mountain and canyon hiking possibilities exist in the range; most routes go cross-country or follow old mining roads. The **Mount Ellen Summit Route** is a good day hike and probably attracts the greatest number of hikers. The easiest way up is to follow the North Summit Ridge north from the road at Bull Creek Pass; there's an unsigned trail the first mile and on the final climb up Mount Ellen; elevation gain is 1,030 feet. Nearly all

THE ESCALANTE REGION

of this route lies above timberline with spectacular panoramas. Another popular approach begins from Dandelion Flat Picnic Area; a trail follows an old road that climbs the slopes part of the way, then it's cross-country; elevation gain is 3,400 feet. Either route is about four miles round-trip and takes half a day.

Little Egypt
Eerie rock formations similar to those in Goblin Valley, but covering a smaller area, lie east of the Henrys. Kids will enjoy exploring the area, and it's a fine place for a picnic. Turn southwest 1.5 miles from Hwy. 95 between mileposts 20 and 21; when dry, the gravel road is usually okay for cars. No facilities or even a sign mark the site, so note mileage from Hwy. 95.

Dirty Devil Canyon Overlook
The muddy waters of the Dirty Devil River have carved a deep canyon southeast of Hanksville. Views from the overlook at Burr Point take in some impressive scenery. Desperadoes around the turn of the century hid out in the rugged canyonlands of "Robbers' Roost" across the river. In 1869, when one of Powell's expedition members was asked if the waters had trout, he replied with disgust that the smelly and muddy river was "a dirty devil." An unpaved road winds east for 11 miles from Hwy. 95 (between mileposts 15 and 16). Cars with good clearance should be okay in dry weather. Park near where the road makes a sharp right just before the edge, or follow the road south for other views. Walking along the rim also affords different perspectives.

Campgrounds
The only easily accessible campsites in the Henry Mountains are at **Starr Springs Campground** (435/542-3461), off Hwy. 276 north of Ticaboo. The campground sits in an oak forest at the base of Mount Hillers. Sites (elev. 6,300 feet) stay open year-round and usually have water for an $8 fee early May–early October. **Panorama Knoll Trail** begins from the campground and makes a half-mile loop to an overlook. A good gravel road to Starr Springs Campground turns off Hwy. 276 near milepost 17 (23 miles north of Bullfrog and 43 miles south of Hanksville) and goes in four miles.

The handful of campgrounds along the Notom-Bullfrog Road route are described in *South District* in the *Capitol Reef National Park* section.

Glen Canyon National Recreation Area

This vast recreation area (520/608-6404, www.nps.gov/glca, $15 per vehicle or $7 per pedestrian or bicyclist for seven days, no charge for passing through Page on Hwy. 89) covers 1.25 million acres, most of which spreads northeast into Utah. Lake Powell stands as the centerpiece, surrounded by beautiful canyon country. Just a handful of roads approach the lake, so you'll need to do some boating or hiking to explore this unique land of water and rock. The recreation area also includes a beautiful remnant of Glen Canyon in a 15-mile section of the Colorado River from Glen Canyon Dam to Lees Ferry.

Note that *Arizona does not observe daylight savings time.* This means that mid-March–early November, the time in Page and surrounding areas will be an hour later than the time in Utah.

◖ LAKE POWELL
Conservationists deplored the loss of remote and beautiful Glen Canyon of the Colorado River beneath Lake Powell. Today, we have only words, pictures, and memories to remind us of its wonders. On the other hand, the 186-mile-long lake now provides easy access to an area most had not even known existed. Lake Powell is the second-largest human-made lake within the United States. Only Lake Mead, farther downstream, has a greater water-storage capacity. Lake Powell, however, has three times more shoreline—1,960 miles—and holds

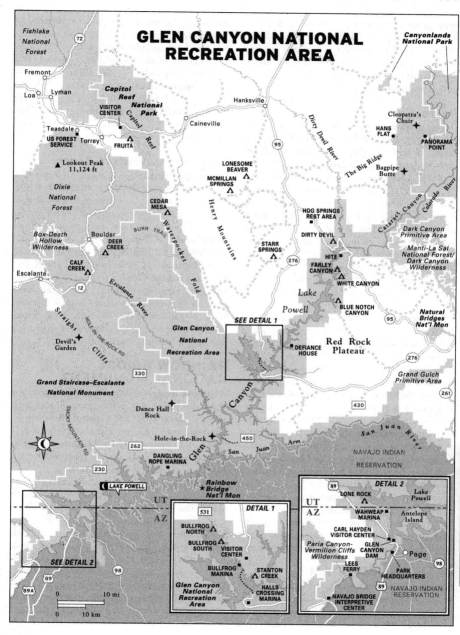

GLEN CANYON NATIONAL RECREATION AREA

Canyonlands National Park

© AVALON TRAVEL

THE ESCALANTE REGION

enough water to cover the state of Pennsylvania a foot deep. Just a handful of roads approach the lake, so access is basically limited to boats—bays and coves offer nearly limitless opportunities for exploration by boaters—or long-distance hiking trails.

Recreation

If you don't have your own craft, Wahweap and other marinas will rent a boat for fishing, skiing, or houseboating. Boat tours visit Rainbow Bridge (the world's largest natural bridge) and other destinations from Wahweap, Bullfrog, and Halls Crossing Marinas. Sailboats find the steadiest breezes in Wahweap, Padre, Halls, and Bullfrog Bays, where spring winds average 15–20 knots. Kayaks and canoes can be used in the more protected areas. All boaters need to be alert for approaching storms that can bring wind gusts up to 60 mph. Waves on open expanses of the lake are sometimes steeper than ocean waves and can exceed six feet from trough to crest.

Marinas and bookstores sell navigation maps of Lake Powell. You'll need an Arizona fishing license for the southern five miles of the lake and a Utah license for the rest of Lake Powell. Obtain licenses and information from marinas on the water or sporting goods stores in Page. Wahweap has a swimming beach (no lifeguards), and boaters can find their own remote spots. Scuba divers can swim underwater with the sizable bass. Hikers have a choice of easy day trips or long wilderness backpack treks, including trips up the canyons of the Escalante. Other good hiking spots within or adjacent to Glen Canyon NRA include Rainbow Bridge National Monument, Paria Canyon, Dark Canyon, and Grand Gulch. Most of the canyon country near Lake Powell remains wild and little explored—hiking possibilities are limitless. Be sure to carry plenty of water.

GLEN CANYON DAM

Construction workers labored 1956–1964 to build this giant concrete structure. It stands 710 feet high above bedrock, and its top measures 1,560 feet across. Thickness ranges from 300 feet at the base to just 25 feet at the top. As part of the Upper Colorado River Storage Project, the dam provides water storage (its main purpose), hydroelectricity, flood control, and recreation on Lake Powell. Eight giant turbine generators churn out a total of 1,150,000 kilowatts at 13,800 volts. Vertigo sufferers shouldn't look down when driving across Glen Canyon Bridge; cold, green waters of the Colorado River glide 700 feet below.

Carl Hayden Visitors Center

Photos, paintings, movies, and slide presentations in the visitors center (928/608-6404, 8 A.M.–6 P.M. daily in summer, 8 A.M.–4 P.M. daily in winter) show features of Glen Canyon National Recreation Area, including Lake Powell and construction of the dam. A giant relief map helps you visualize the rugged terrain surrounding the lake; look closely and you'll spot Rainbow Bridge. Guided tours inside the dam and generating room depart every half hour daily in summer. The Glen Canyon Natural History Association (928/645-3523) has books about the recreation area and its environs for sale next to the information desk.

RAINBOW BRIDGE NATIONAL MONUMENT

Rainbow Bridge (928/608-6200, www.nps .gov/rabr) forms a graceful span 290 feet high and 275 feet wide; the Capitol Building in Washington, D.C., would fit neatly underneath. The easiest way to Rainbow Bridge is by boat tour on Lake Powell from Wahweap, Bullfrog, or Halls Crossing Marina.

The more adventurous can hike to the bridge from the Cha Canyon Trailhead (just north across the Arizona–Utah border on the east side of Navajo Mountain) or from the Rainbow Lodge Ruins (just south of the Arizona–Utah border on the west side of Navajo Mountain). Rugged trails from each point wind through highly scenic canyons, meet in Bridge Canyon, then continue two miles to the bridge. The hike on either trail, or a loop with both (car shuttle needed), is 26–28 miles round-trip. Hikers must be experienced and self-sufficient; topo maps are available at the Carl Hayden Visitors Center and the National Park Service offers detailed directions and trail notes on their website.

No camping is allowed at Rainbow Bridge and no supplies are available. You may camp a half mile east of the bridge at Echo camp. The Dangling Rope Marina and National Park Service Ranger Station are 10 miles away, by water only. The best times to go are April–early June, September, and October. Winter cold and snow discourage visitors, and summer is hot and brings hazardous flash floods.

The National Park Service cannot issue hiking permits to Rainbow Bridge. Obtain the required tribal hiking permit ($5 per person per day) and camping permit (additional $5 per person per night) from the Cameron visitors center (not always open) or Navajo Parks Department (928/871-6451, www.navajonationparks.org).

Boat Tours to Rainbow Bridge

By far the most popular way to visit Rainbow Bridge is to sign on with a boat tour and take a half- or whole day trip to see the national monument. Most tours leave from Wahweap Marina (928/645-1070, www.lakepowell resorts.com, $124 adults, $84 children for full-day trip, reservations recommended), off U.S. 89. Tours run daily April–October, and on Saturdays during the off-season.

Once at Painted Arch, tour boats park at a floating dock, and you can walk to a viewing area beneath the arch, a distance of about a mile.

MARINAS

The **National Park Service** provides public boat ramps, campgrounds, and ranger offices at most of the marinas. Rangers know current boating and back-road conditions, primitive camping areas, and good places to explore. **Lake Powell Resorts and Marinas** (800/528-6154, www.lakepowell.com) operates marina services, boat rentals, boat tours, accommodations, RV parks, and restaurants; contact them for information and reservations (strongly recommended in summer). All the marinas stay open year-round; avoid crowds and peak prices

by coming in autumn, winter, or spring. Private or chartered aircraft can fly to Page Airport, San Juan County Airport near Bullfrog, or an airstrip near Halls Crossing.

Wahweap

The name means "bitter water" in the Ute language. Wahweap Lodge and Marina, Lake Powell's biggest, offers complete boaters' services and rentals, guided tours, deluxe accommodations, an RV park, and a restaurant. Wahweap is seven miles northwest of Page, five miles beyond the visitors center. **Lake Powell Resort** (800/528-6154, www.lakepowell.com, $128) is a very large complex of motel rooms, restaurants, and public areas run by the Aramark Corporation. There are different kinds of rooms, and they do a big business with bus tours. **Lake Powell Motel,** at Wahweap Junction (four miles northwest of Glen Canyon Dam on U.S. 89), has less-expensive rooms, starting at $94. Information and reservations are through Lake Powell Resorts and Marinas.

Wahweap Campground is operated on a first-come, first-served basis by Lake Powell Resorts and Marinas; tent sites have drinking water but no showers or hookups. Campers may use the pay showers and laundry facilities at the RV park. The RV park, campground, and a picnic area are between Wahweap Lodge and Stateline. Primitive camping (no water or fee) is available at **Lone Rock** in Utah, six miles northwest of Wahweap off U.S. 89; cars need to be very careful not to stray into loose sand areas. Boaters may also camp along the lakeshore, but not within one mile of developed areas. Public boat ramps are adjacent to the lodge and at Stateline, 1.3 miles northwest of the lodge and just into Utah. During summer (June–Sept.), you can also obtain recreation information from the **Wahweap Ranger Station** near the picnic area; at other times see the staff at Carl Hayden Visitors Center.

The marina offers **lake tours,** ranging from a short cruise around scenic Antelope Canyon ($31) to trips to Rainbow Bridge, 50 miles away ($119). The marina also offers a full range of watercraft rentals, including houseboats. For information on tours, call 928/645-1070.

Antelope Point Marina

Antelope Point Marina (800/255-5561, www .antelopepointlakepowell.com) is just north of Page and has complete boating facilities, including houseboat rentals, plus a swimming beach.

Dangling Rope Marina

This floating marina lies 42 miles uplake from Glen Canyon Dam. The only access is by boat. Services include a ranger station, store, minor boat repairs, gas dock, and sanitary pump-out station. A dangling rope left behind in a nearby canyon, perhaps by uranium prospectors, prompted the name. The dock for Rainbow Bridge is seven miles farther uplake in Bridge Canyon, a tributary of Forbidding Canyon.

San Juan

Boats can be hand-launched at **Clay Hills Crossing** at the upper end of the San Juan arm. An unpaved road branches 11 miles southwest from Hwy. 276 (road to Halls Crossing) to the lake; don't attempt the road after rains. River-runners on the San Juan often take out here; no facilities.

Halls Crossing

In 1880, Charles Hall built the ferry used by the Hole-in-the-Rock pioneers, who crossed the river to begin settlement in southeast Utah. The approach roads were so bad, however, that he moved the ferry 35 miles upstream to present-day Halls Crossing in the following year. Business continued to be slow, and Hall quit running the ferry in 1884.

Arriving at Halls Crossing by road, you'll first reach a small store offering three-bedroom units in trailer houses and an RV park. Continue for half a mile on the main road to the boat ramp and **Halls Crossing Marina** (435/684-2261). The marina has a larger store (groceries and fishing and boating supplies), tours to Rainbow Bridge, a boat-rental office (fishing, ski, and houseboat), a gas dock, slips, and storage. The

CROSSING LAKE POWELL BY FERRY

The Halls Crossing/Bullfrog Ferry Service, a car ferry that crosses Lake Powell between the two marinas, offers a good way to get out onto the lake and get a sense for the size and drama of the region. (Taking the ferry isn't required, as Highway 95 crosses the lake farther north, at Hite.) At the junction of Highway 276, a large sign lists the departure times for the ferry; note that these may be different than the times listed in the widely circulated flyer or on the website (www.nps.gov/glca/ferry). Confirm the departure times before making the 42-mile journey to Halls Crossing.

The crossing time from Halls Crossing to Bullfrog is 27 minutes (the crossing is only three miles, however). Fares for vehicles smaller than 19 feet 11 inches in length are $20, which includes the driver and all passengers. Bicycles are $5, and motorcycles are $10. Foot passengers are $5 per adult, but free for seniors over 65 and children under 5.

During the high summer season, May 15-

September 14, the ferries run on the hour daily beginning at 8 A.M. The final ferry from Halls Crossing departs at 6 P.M., and the final ferry from Bullfrog departs at 7 P.M. April 15-May 14 and September 15-October 31, the Halls Ferry begins operation at 8 A.M. and sails every two hours until 4 P.M. The Bullfrog ferry begins at 9 A.M. and sails every two hours until 5 P.M. The rest of the year, November 1-April 14, this same schedule continues, except the final trips of the day are at 2 P.M. and 3 P.M., respectively.

Note that if drought or downstream demand lowers the level of Lake Powell beyond a certain point, there may not be enough water for the ferry to operate. If this is the case, there will be notices about the ferry's status at just about every park visitors center in southern Utah.

For reservations and information regarding the ferries, lodging, tours, boating, and recreation at both Halls Crossing and Bullfrog Marina, contact **Lake Powell Resorts and Marinas** (800/528-6154, www.lakepowell.com).

ranger station is nearby, although rangers are usually out on patrol; look for their vehicle in the area if the office is closed.

Bullfrog Marina

On the western side of the lake, Bullfrog Marina (435/684-2233) is more like a small town, with a **visitors center** (435/684-2243), clinic, stores, service station, and a handsome hotel and restaurant. In addition to daily car ferries across to Halls Crossing, the marina offers tours to sights along Lake Powell, including **Rainbow Bridge,** April 15–October 31. It also offers boat rentals.

Defiance House Lodge (435/684-3000 or 800/528-6154, www.lakepowell.com) offers comfortable lake-view accommodations and the **Anasazi Restaurant** (breakfast, lunch, and dinner daily in summer). Rooms begin at $121 in summer (Apr. 1–Oct. 31) and $112 in winter. The front desk at the lodge also handles **housekeeping units** (trailers) and an **RV park.**

Showers, a laundry room, a convenience store, and a post office are at **Trailer Village.** Ask the visitors center staff or rangers for directions to primitive camping areas with vehicle access elsewhere along Bullfrog Bay.

Bullfrog Marina can be reached from the north via paved Hwy. 276. It's 40 miles between Bullfrog and the junction with Hwy. 95. At Ticaboo, 20 miles north of Bullfrog, is another good lodging option. The **Ticaboo Lodge** (435/788-2110 or 800/842-2267, $104) is a new hotel, restaurant, and service-station complex that pretty much constitutes all of Ticaboo.

For information on Bullfrog-Notom Road, see the *Capitol Reef Natinal Park* section.

Hite

Although a marina previously operated here, lake levels have dropped and services now are limited to a gas station and convenience store.

Page, Arizona

Wedged between the Arizona Strip to the west, Glen Canyon National Recreation Area to the north, and the Navajo Reservation to the east and south, Page is the largest community close to Lake Powell and offers travelers a variety of places to stay and eat. The town overlooks Lake Powell and Glen Canyon Dam; the large Wahweap Resort and Marina lies just six miles away.

In town, the **John Wesley Powell Memorial Museum** (corner of 6 N. Lake Powell Blvd. and N. Navajo Dr., 928/645-9496 or 888/597-6873, www.powellmuseum.org, 9 A.M.–5 P.M. Mon.–Fri., $5 adults, $3 seniors, $1 children 5–12) honors scientist and explorer John Wesley Powell. It's also a good place for local travel information.

ACCOMMODATIONS

Nearly all Page motels lie on or near Lake Powell Boulevard/Hwy. 89L, a 3.25-mile loop that branches off the main highway. Page is a busy place in summer, however, and a call ahead is a good idea if you don't want to chase around town looking for vacancies. Expect to pay top dollar for views of the lake. The summer rates listed here drop in winter (Nov.–Mar.). The 8th Avenue places lie in Page's historic district, a quiet residential area two blocks off Lake Powell Boulevard. These apartments date back to 1958–1959, when they housed supervisors and foremen for the dam; today some of the buildings have been fixed up as pensions and motels.

Under $50

C **Bashful Bob's Motel** (750 S. Navajo Dr., 928/645-3919, www.bashfulbobsmotel.com, $39) is a great little budget place with simple two-bedroom apartments, all with kitchenettes. **Debbie's Hide A Way** (117 8th Ave., 928/645-1224, www.debbieshideaway.com) is another place with a personal touch, with a quiet garden in back.

THE ESCALANTE REGION

Although most rooms are well over $50, you have a choice of rooms with shared bath and kitchen (from $39) or private suites (up to $159).

$50-100

Page Boy Motel (150 N. Lake Powell Blvd., 928/645-2416, $55) offers a swimming pool. **Empire Motel** (107 S. Lake Powell Blvd., 928/645-2406 or 800/551-9005, $60) is another good bet for a reasonably priced, though certainly not luxurious, motel with a pool.

Lake Powell Day's Inn and Suites (961 N. Hwy 89, 928/645-2800 or 877/525-3769, www.daysinn.net, $75) lies on the south edge of town beside U.S. 89, with an outdoor pool and spa.

Canyon Colors Bed and Breakfast (225 S. Navajo Dr., 928/645-5979 or 800/536-2530, www.canyon-country.com/colors, $95) has a pool, patio, and fireplaces.

Over $100

Holiday Inn Express (751 S. Navajo Dr., 928/645-9000 or 800/465-4329, www.lake powellhotels.com, $105) offers the comforts you'd expect in a good chain motel. **Courtyard by Marriott** (600 Clubhouse Dr., 928/645-5000 or 800/321-2211, $120) offers views, a restaurant, a pool, spa, exercise room, and adjacent 18-hole golf course.

FOOD AND ENTERTAINMENT

Dam Bar and Grill (644 N. Navajo Dr. 928/645-2161, dinner nightly, $8–25), in the Dam Plaza, serves up steak, barbecue, seafood, pasta, and sandwiches daily; it also has a sports bar. The adjacent **Gunsmoke Saloon** (928/645-2161, Tues.–Sat. 7 P.M.–2 A.M.) features country bands and other music.

Fiesta Mexicana (125 S. Lake Powell Blvd, 928/645-4082, $8–15) is a friendly little Mexican place (and here in Arizona, it's easy to get a margarita).

Bella Napoli Italia's Family Buffet (810 N. Navajo Dr., 928/645-2706, dinner nightly in summer, call for hours Oct.–Apr., $12–20) is a good spot for Italian cuisine.

CANYONLANDS

The Colorado River and its tributaries have carved extraordinary landscapes into the Colorado Plateau's vivid red and orange sandstone deposits that underlie southeastern Utah. Intricate mazes of canyons, delicate arches, and massive rock monoliths make this region seem primordial at times and lunar at others. It has a beauty and scenic drama that's unique, and first-time visitors often need a while to appreciate this strange land before they're won over by the infinite colors and variety of the sculptured rock. Two national parks—Arches and Canyonlands—preserve some of the most astounding of these landscapes, while numerous state parks, national monuments, and recreation areas protect other sights of great interest and beauty. At every turn, the landscape invites exploration, offering solitude, ruins of prehistoric villages, wildlife, and dramatic records of geologic history.

To best appreciate this landscape requires a brief refresher course in the unusual geology of the Colorado Plateau. About 300 million years ago, this land was at times a great Sahara-like desert and at others covered by water. Thick layers of sediment built up one on top of the other. During the last 50 million years, powerful forces within the earth slowly pushed the entire region a mile upward. The ancestral Colorado River and other streams appeared and began to carve the deep gorges seen today.

Ancient dunes, turned to stone, make up many of the sheer canyon cliffs, arches, and spires of the region. Delicate crossbedded lines of the former dunes add grace to these

© PAUL LEVY

HIGHLIGHTS

◖ Delicate Arch: Arches National Park is filled with astounding rock arches, but Delicate Arch, which rises directly from a slickrock bluff, is the most awe-inspiring. That it requires a bit of a hike to reach only makes the experience more rewarding (page 424).

◖ Mesa Arch Trail: It's a short, easy hike from Canyonlands park highway to the Island in the Sky cliffs, where a rock window opens up at the very edge of the precipice. It's a totally unlikely combination: a soaring arch over the void (page 432).

◖ Grand View Point: From this astounding spot, you'll see the trench-like canyon of the Colorado River from the top of thousand foot cliffs. Quite simply, this is the most dramatic vista in all of Utah – in fact, from here you'll feel that much of the state is spread out beneath your feet (page 433).

◖ Newspaper Rock Historical Monument: Perhaps this superlative example of ancient Native American rock art was like a newspaper to early residents of southern Utah. The meaning of the rock art has been lost (some images are more than 2,000 years old), but what remains here, at one of the best and most accessible rock art galleries, is beautiful, mysterious, and oddly meaningful (page 443).

◖ Hovenweep National Monument: The Anasazi masonry villages at Hovenweep were built around 900 years ago and formed the center of an extended agricultural community. The settlements were quickly abandoned, leaving behind these amazing ruins. Hovenweep is mostly unexcavated and largely unvisited, which means that you can explore the vast series of mysterious ruins on your own (page 448).

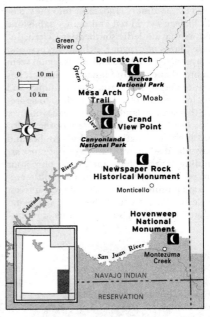

LOOK FOR ◖ TO FIND RECOMMENDED SIGHTS, ACTIVITIES, DINING, AND LODGING.

features. Volcanic pressures deep in the earth also shaped the land. Massive intrusions of magma bowed up overlying rock layers before cooling and solidifying. Erosion has since uncovered four of these dome-shaped ranges in southeastern Utah—the Henrys, the La Sals, the Abajos, and Navajo Mountain.

Despite its seemingly inhospitable terrain, this part of Utah has a long human history,

beginning about 5,000 years ago, when ancient hunter gatherers roamed this canyon country. Later, the Anasazi established many communities where they practiced farming and built stone dwellings along the cliffs; the extensive ruins at Hovenweep National Monument are especially well preserved. Then, about 800 years ago, the Anasazi abandoned their villages for unknown reasons, and except for roving

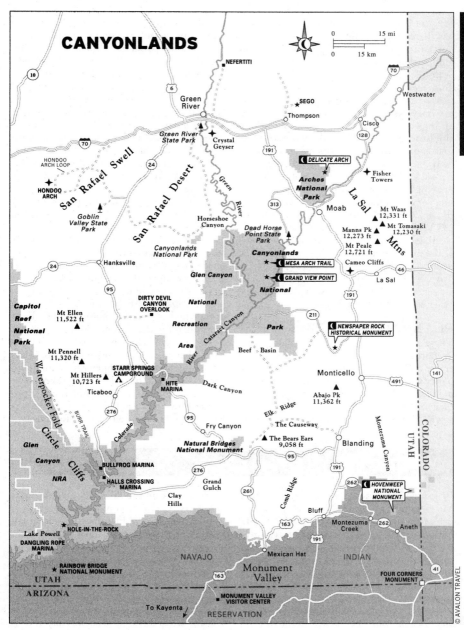

CANYONLANDS

CANYONLANDS

0   15 mi
0   15 km

NEFERTITI

Westwater

Green River

SEGO

Thompson

Cisco

Green River State Park

Crystal Geyser

DELICATE ARCH

Fisher Towers

HONDOO ARCH LOOP

San Rafael Swell

Arches National Park

La Sal

HONDOO ARCH

San Rafael Desert

Green River

Moab

Mt Waas 12,331 ft

Goblin Valley State Park

Horseshoe Canyon

Dead Horse Point State Park

Manns Pk 12,273 ft

Mt Tomasaki 12,230 ft

Canyonlands National Park

Canyonlands

Mt Peale 12,721 ft

Cameo Cliffs

Hanksville

Glen Canyon

MESA ARCH TRAIL

GRAND VIEW POINT

La Sal

National

DIRTY DEVIL CANYON OVERLOOK

National

Cataract Canyon

NEWSPAPER ROCK HISTORICAL MONUMENT

Capitol Reef National Park

Mt Ellen 11,522 ft

Recreation

Park

Area

Beef Basin

Mt Pennell 11,320 ft

River

Waterpocket Fold

Mt Hillers 10,723 ft

STARR SPRINGS CAMPGROUND

HITE MARINA

Dark Canyon

Monticello

Ticaboo

Abajo Pk 11,362 ft

Montezuma Canyon

COLORADO
UTAH

Glen

Canyon

Circle Cliffs

BURR TRAIL

Colorado

Fry Canyon

Elk Ridge

The Causeway

Blanding

Natural Bridges National Monument

The Bears Ears 9,058 ft

NRA

BULLFROG MARINA

HALLS CROSSING MARINA

Grand Gulch

Comb Ridge

HOVENWEEP NATIONAL MONUMENT

Clay Hills

Bluff

Lake Powell

HOLE-IN-THE-ROCK

Montezuma Creek

Aneth

DANGLING ROPE MARINA

NAVAJO

Mexican Hat

INDIAN

FOUR CORNERS MONUMENT

RAINBOW BRIDGE NATIONAL MONUMENT

UTAH
ARIZONA

Monument Valley

RESERVATION

To Kayenta

MONUMENT VALLEY VISITOR CENTER

bands of Utes and Fremont, this arid landscape has thereafter only intermittently supported human communities until the arrival of Mormon settlers in the 1850s and 1860s.

Besides the drama of the landscape, outdoor recreation is now what brings people to this corner of Utah: there are so many newly evolved outdoor sports and recreation options available here that plain old hiking almost seems passé. Moab is central for slickrock mountain biking, which brings people in from around the world to ride the area's red-rock cliffs and canyons. Another "sport" drawing legions of fans to the area is "off-roading," or exploration of the canyon backcountry on four-wheel drive and all-terrain vehicles (ATVs). The huge surge of popularity for off-roading has the BLM, which governs much of the non-park land in the area, considering restrictions on the number of people able to drive the backcountry, as the off-road vehicles are tearing up fragile ecosystems and causing other environmental damage.

PLANNING YOUR TIME

There are so many recreational opportunities in southeast Utah that many people spend an entire vacation in the area. With two national parks and myriad public lands, the hiker, mountain biker, or lover of the outdoors could easily fill a week with a diverse mix of recreation. Not everyone has that much time to spend, of course, but even more casual visitors should consider spending three days here. The national parks near Moab (Arches plus the Island in the Sky district of Canyonlands) will require a day to simply drive through, and the rest of Canyonlands and other national monuments in the extreme south (Hovenweep, Natural Bridges, Monument Valley) deserve at least a day. That leaves a single day to explore Moab itself, take a rafting trip down the Colorado River, or even go on a hike or mountain bike ride. Three days is a minimum unless you plan to drive straight through without stopping.

As for timing, the rugged character of the canyon country causes many local variations in climate, as do extremes in elevation between cliff rims and canyon bottoms. Fall and spring are the most popular times to visit, as daytime temperatures are moderate and outdoor recreation is comfortable. Real desert heat sets in late May or early June. Temperatures then soar into the 90s and 100s at midday, though the dry air makes the heat more bearable. Early morning is the choice time for summer travel. Autumn begins after the rains and lasts into November or even December; days are bright and sunny with ideal temperatures, but nights become cold. Winter lasts only about two months at the lower elevations. Light snows on the canyon walls add new beauty to the rock layers. Winter can be a fine time for travel.

Moab

By far the largest town in southeastern Utah, Moab (pop. 5,500) makes an excellent base for exploring Arches and Canyonland National Parks and the surrounding canyon country. Moab lies near the Colorado River in a green valley enclosed by high sandstone cliffs. The biblical Moab was a kingdom at the edge of Zion, and early Mormon settlers must have felt themselves at the edge of their world, too, being so isolated from Salt Lake City—the Mormon city of Zion. Moab's existence on the fringe of Mormon culture and the sizable gentile population gave the town a unique character.

In recent years, Moab has become nearly synonymous with mountain biking. The slickrock canyon country seems made for exploration by bike, and people come from all over the world to pedal the backcountry. River trips on the Colorado River are nearly as popular, and a host of other outdoor recreational diversions—from horseback riding to four-wheel jeep exploring to hot-air ballooning—

combine to make Moab one of the most popular destinations in Utah.

Moab is also one of the most youthful and vibrant communities in the state; thousands of young people travel to Moab for the recreation, while hundreds of others work here as guides and outfitters. Young, tanned, fit, and Lycra-clad bodies are the norm here, and the town's brewpubs, bike shops, and cafés do a booming trade.

As Moab's popularity has grown, so have concerns that the town and the surrounding countryside are simply getting loved to death. The landscape has always been a staple in car ads (remember those Chevy pickups balanced on a red-rock pinnacle?); now the landscape sells the "Just Do It" lifestyle for MTV, Nike, and other merchandisers of youth culture. On a busy day, hundreds of mountain bikers form queues to negotiate the trickier sections of the famed Slick Rock Trail, and more than 20,000 people crowd into town on busy weekends to bike, hike, float, and party. As noted in an article in *Details* magazine, "Moab is pretty much the Fort Lauderdale of the intermountain West." Whether this old Mormon town and the delicate desert environment can endure such an onslaught of popularity is a question of increasing concern.

Moab's recent history involves mineral extraction. Oil exploration in the 1920s caused some excitement, but nothing like that of the uranium boom that began in 1952. Moab's population tripled in just three years as eager prospectors swarmed into the canyons. One of these hopefuls, Charlie Steen, did hit it big. Experts had laughed at Charlie's efforts until he discovered the Mi Vida uranium bonanza about 30 miles south of town. An instant multimillionaire, he built a large mansion overlooking Moab and hosted lavish parties attended by Hollywood celebrities. Charlie Steen and most of the prospectors have moved on, but Moab has never been the same since.

SIGHTS

It's fair to say that Moab doesn't tempt travelers with a lot of traditional tourist establishments, but all you have to do is raise your eyes to the horizon. The locale is so striking that you'll want to get outdoors and explore, and the astonishing sights of Canyonlands and Arches National Parks are just minutes from town. But there's nothing wrong with just enjoying the enthusiastic vibe of the town.

Dan O'Laurie Museum

This regional museum (118 E. Center, 435/259-7985, www.grandcountyutah.net/museum .htm, 10 A.M.–6 P.M. Mon.–Fri., noon–6 P.M. Sat.–Sun. in summer, 10 A.M.–3 P.M. Mon.–Fri., noon–5 P.M. Sat.–Sun. in winter, ages 12 and older $3, families $7) tells the story of Moab's and Grand County's past, from prehistoric and Ute Indian artifacts to the explorations of Spanish missionaries. Photos and tools show pioneer Moab life, much of which centered on ranching or mining; here, too, you'll find displays of rocks and minerals, as well as bones of huge dinosaurs that once tracked across this land. A new resident is a replica of a 120-million-year-old *Gastonia burhei,* an 11-foot-long dinosaur that looks like a cross between a crocodile and a horned toad. Ask for a *Moab Area Historic Walking Tour* leaflet to learn about historic buildings in town.

Hole 'n the Rock

Albert Christensen worked 12 years to excavate his dream home (15 miles south of Moab on U.S. 191, 435/686-2250, www.theholein therock.com, 8 A.M.–dusk daily in summer, 9 A.M. daily in winter, adults $5, ages 5–10 $3.50) within a sandstone monolith south of town. When he died in 1957, his wife Gladys worked another eight years to complete the project. The interior has notable touches like a 65-foot chimney drilled through the rock ceiling, paintings, taxidermy exhibits, and a lapidary room. The 5,000-square-foot, 14-room home is open for tours daily, and has a gift shop, petting zoo, picnic area, and snack bar.

ENTERTAINMENT AND EVENTS
Nightlife

A lot of Moab's nightlife focuses on Moab's

CANYONLANDS

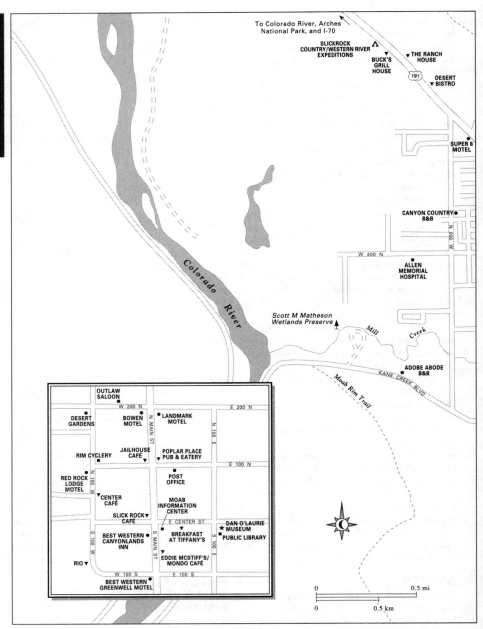

To Colorado River, Arches
National Park, and I-70

SLICKROCK
COUNTRY/WESTERN RIVER
EXPEDITIONS

BUCK'S
GRILL
HOUSE

THE RANCH
HOUSE

191

DESERT
BISTRO

SUPER 8
MOTEL

CANYON COUNTRY
B&B

N 500 W

W 400 N

ALLEN
MEMORIAL
HOSPITAL

Colorado River

Scott M Matheson
Wetlands Preserve

Mill   *Creek*

ADOBE ABODE
B&B

KANE CREEK BLVD

Moab Rim Trail

OUTLAW
SALOON

W 200 N

E 200 N

DESERT
GARDENS

BOWEN
MOTEL

N MAIN ST

LANDMARK
MOTEL

N 100 E

RIM CYCLERY

JAILHOUSE
CAFÉ

POPLAR PLACE
PUB & EATERY

E 100 N

RED ROCK
LODGE
MOTEL

N 100 W

POST
OFFICE

CENTER
CAFÉ

MOAB
INFORMATION
CENTER

SLICK ROCK
CAFÉ

E CENTER ST

DAN O'LAURIE
MUSEUM

S 100 E

S 100 W

BEST WESTERN
CANYONLANDS
INN

S MAIN ST

BREAKFAST
AT TIFFANY'S

PUBLIC LIBRARY

RIO

EDDIE MCSTIFF'S/
MONDO CAFÉ

W 100 S

E 100 S

BEST WESTERN
GREENWELL MOTEL

0   0.5 mi

0   0.5 km

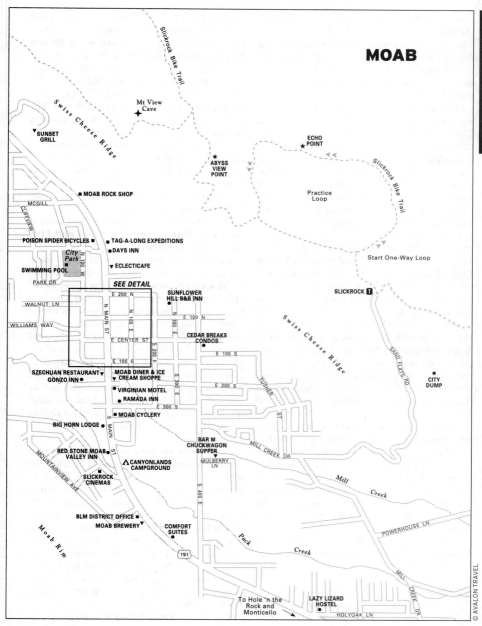

MOAB

Slickrock Bike Trail

Mt View Cave

Swiss Cheese Ridge

▼SUNSET GRILL

ECHO POINT

★ABYSS VIEW POINT

Slickrock Bike Trail

■ MOAB ROCK SHOP

Practice Loop

MCGILL

CLIFFVIEW

■ POISON SPIDER BICYCLES ■

City Park

■ TAG-A-LONG EXPEDITIONS

N 100 W

● DAYS INN

Start One-Way Loop

SWIMMING POOL

▼ ECLECTICAFE

PARK DR

SEE DETAIL

SLICKROCK 🆃

E 200 N

SUNFLOWER HILL B&B INN

WALNUT LN

N MAIN ST

N 100 E

N 300 E

E 100 N

WILLIAMS WAY

Swiss Cheese Ridge

SAND FLATS RD

E CENTER ST

CEDAR BREAKS CONDOS

S 200 E

E 100 S

■ CITY DUMP

SZECHUAN RESTAURANT▼

MOAB DINER & ICE

TUSHER ST

GONZO INN ●

▼ CREAM SHOPPE

S 300 E

E 200 S

● VIRGINIAN MOTEL

● RAMADA INN

E 300 S

■ MOAB CYCLERY

S MAIN ST

BIG HORN LODGE ●

BAR M CHUCKWAGON SUPPER

MILL CREEK DR

RED STONE MOAB●

VALLEY INN

S MAIN ST

MULBERRY LN

MOUNTAINVIEW AVE

▲CANYONLANDS CAMPGROUND

Mill Creek

■ SLICKROCK CINEMAS

S 400 E

■ BLM DISTRICT OFFICE ■

POWERHOUSE LN

Moab Rim

MOAB BREWERY▼

COMFORT SUITES

Pack Creek

MILL CREEK DR

191

LAZY LIZARD HOSTEL

To Hole 'n the Rock and Monticello

HOLYOAK LN

two brewpubs, the rowdy and well-loved **Eddie McStiff's** (57 S. Main in Western Plaza, 435/259-2337), and the posher **Moab Brewery** (686 S. Main St., 435/259-6333), more of a restaurant than a bar. But it's a pleasant place to sample good beer—you can also buy their microbrewed beer to go.

The following are private clubs, so you'll need to pay a minimal membership fee to get in. The **Outlaw Saloon** (44 W. 200 N., 435/259-2654) doesn't look like much from the outside (it's a Quonset hut) but the bar is spacious and DJs spin tunes on weekends. The Outlaw is also one of Moab's few places for late-night snacking—there's a "Midnight Menu" served until 12:30 A.M. **Rio Colorado** (2 South 100 W., 435/259-6666) has live music on weekends and a friendly and mellow hippie vibe during the week. The **Sportsman's Lounge** (1991 S. U.S. 191, 435/259-9972) and **Woody's Tavern** (221 S Main St., 435/259-9323) both have live bands on the weekends. Closing hours for bars and clubs in Moab change from night to night and season to season.

For a more family-friendly evening out, consider the **Bar-M Chuckwagon Live Western Show and Cowboy Supper,** a kind of Western-themed dinner theater that includes gunfights, live country music and other Old West entertainment in addition to a buffet chuck wagon dinner. For more information, see the *Casual Dining* section.

Another long-time tradition for evening entertainment is **Canyonlands by Night,** a cruise on the Colorado River that ends with a sound-and-light presentation along the sandstone cliffs. Dinner packages are available; children under 4 are not permitted per Coast Guard regulations. For more information, see *Motorboat Tours* in the *Moab Area Recreation* section.

For a selection of movies, head for **Slickrock Cinemas** (580 Kane Creek Blvd., 435/259-4441).

Events

To find out about local happenings and for details on events, contact the **Moab Information Center** (435/259-8825, www.discovermoab.com). Not surprisingly, Moab offers quite a few annual biking events. The **Moab Skinny Tire Festival** (435/259-2698, www.skinnytirefestival.com), held the first week of March, and the **Moab Century Tour,** held in early October, are both supported road bike events that benefit the Lance Armstrong Foundation. The mountain bike endurance race event **24 Hours of Moab** (www.grannygear.com/Races/Moab/index.shtml), held in mid-October, pits four-person relay teams against the rugged terrain of the Behind the Rocks area. This is one of North America's major events for mountain-bikers, bringing more than 500 teams and over 5000 spectators to Moab.

Other major annual athletic events include the **Canyonlands Half Marathon and Five Mile Run** in late March (third Sat.).

Moab's most popular annual event, more popular than anything celebrating two wheels, is the **Easter Jeep Safari** (www.rr4w.com/safari.html) which is the Sturgis or Daytona Beach of recreational off-roading. Upwards of 2000 four-wheel drive vehicles (it's not open just to Jeeps, though ATVs are not allowed) converge on Moab for a week's worth of organized back-country touring. "Big Saturday" (the day before Easter) is the climax of the event, when all participating vehicles parade through Moab. Reserve well ahead for lodging if you are planning to visit Moab during this event, as hotel rooms are often booked a year in advance.

June kicks up dust at the Spanish Trail Arena (just south of Moab at 3641 S. Hwy 191) with the professional **Canyonlands P.R.C.A. Rodeo** held the second weekend of the month, with rodeo, parade, dance, horse racing, and 4-H gymkhana. August means it's time for the **Grand County Fair,** with agricultural displays, crafts, and arts competitions. Most fair events are held at the Moab Arts and Recreation Center (111 E. 100 N., 435/259-6272) and include a pet parade, a "diaper derby" infant crawl contest, and a pie-eating competition, plus live music and entertainment.

The **Moab Music Festival** (435/259-7003,

www.moabmusicfest.org) got its start as a classical music festival but soon expanded to include other types of music, including jazz, bluegrass, and folk music. More than 30 artists are currently involved in the festival, which is held the first two weeks of September. Many of the concerts are held in dramatic outdoor settings. The **Moab Folk Festival** (www.moab folkfestival.com) is the town's other big annual musical event, attracting over a dozen nationally recognized performers to Moab the first weekend of November.

SHOPPING

Main Street, between 200 North and 200 South, has nearly a dozen galleries and gift shops with art and other gifts. **Hogan Trading Company** (100 S. Main, 435/259-8118, 10 A.M.–9 P.M. daily) has a great selection of Native American art; **Overlook Gallery** (83 E. Center, 435/259-3861, 10 A.M.–6 P.M. Mon.–Sat.) features local artists and photographers. **Back of Beyond Books** (83 N. Main,

435/259-5154) features an excellent selection of regional books and maps. A good selection of books and maps is also sold at **Times Independent Maps** (5 E. Center St., 435/259-7525, 9 A.M.–5 P.M. Mon.–Sat.).

RECREATION

The **city park** (181 West 400 North, 435/259-8226) has shaded picnic tables, a playground, and an outdoor swimming pool. **Lions Park** offers picnicking along the Colorado River two miles north of town. **Rotary Park,** on Mill Creek Drive, is family-oriented and has lots of activities for kids. **Moab Arts and Recreation** (111 East 100 North, 435/259-6272) sponsors year-round activities for kids; you don't need to be a resident to take part.

Moab Golf Club (2705 S. East Bench Rd., 435/259-6488) features an 18-hole course, a driving range, and a pro shop. Go south five miles on U.S. 191, turn left two miles on Spanish Trails Road, then right one-quarter mile on Murphy Lane.

© W. C. MCRAE

Moab's old downtown is filled with boutiques and gift shops.

ACCOMMODATIONS

Moab has been a tourist destination for generations and offers a wide variety of lodging choices, ranging from older motels to new upscale resorts. Luckily, lodgings are relatively inexpensive. The only time Moab isn't busy is in the dead of winter, November–February. At all other times, be sure to make reservations well in advance.

If you're having trouble finding a room, **Moab/Canyonlands Central Reservations** (435/259-5125, 800/748-4386, or 800/505-5343, www.moabutahlodging.com/reservations) can make bookings at 85 percent of Moab's accommodations, which include area bed-and-breakfasts, motels, condos, cabins, private houses, and luxury vacation homes. Another handy tool is www.moab-utah.com, which has a complete listing of lodging websites for the Moab area Summer rates are given; those in winter typically drop 40 percent.

Under $50

The **Lazy Lizard Hostel** (1213 S. U.S. 191, 435/259-6057, www.lazylizardhostel.com) costs just $9 per night for simple dorm-style accommodations. You won't need a hostel card, and all guests share access to a hot tub, kitchen, barbecue, coin-operated laundry, and common room with cable TV. Camping ($6 per person), showers for non-guests ($2), and private rooms ($26 double occupancy) are offered, too. New log cabins here can sleep two ($28) to four ($40) people. The Lazy Lizard sits one mile south of town, behind A-1 Storage; the turnoff is about 200 yards south of Moab Lanes.

$50-100

Each of the following offer basic but clean motel rooms at reasonable prices. The **Red Rock Lodge Motel** (51 N. 100 W., 435/259-5431 or 877/207-9708, $55 and up) has rooms with refrigerators and coffeemakers. It also includes a hot tub and a locked bicycle-storage facility. The **Red Stone Inn** (535 S. Main St., 435/259-3500 or 800/772-1972, $65 and up) is a newer, one-story motel; most rooms have efficiency kitchens. Other amenities include a

bicycle-maintenance area, covered patio with gas barbecue grill, hot tub, and guest laundry. Motel guests have free access to the hotel pool next door. Pets are permitted in smoking rooms only with a $5-per-night fee. The **Days Inn** (426 N. Main, 435/259-4468 or 800/329-7466, $68) has a pool and complimentary breakfast. For the same price, the **Big Horn Lodge** (550 S. Main, 435/259-6171 or 800/325-6171, $68) has a pool and restaurant. The **Bowen Motel** (169 N. Main, 435/259-7132 or 800/874-5439, $67 and up) is a pleasant, homey motel with an outdoor pool and free continental breakfast. The Bowen offers a variety of room types including three-bedroom family suites and an 1800-square-foot, three-bedroom home with full kitchen.

The **Landmark Motel** (168 N. Main, 435/259-6147 or 800/441-6147, www.landmarkinnmoab.com, $82 and up) is located right in the center of Moab and has a pool and a small waterslide, a hot tub, a guest laundry room, and three family units. At the **Virginian Motel** (70 E. 200 S., 435/259-5951 or 800/261-2063, $89), more than half the rooms have kitchenettes and pets are permitted. The local **Super 8 Motel** (889 N. Main, 435/259-8868 or 800/800-8000, $89) is north of downtown and has a pool, free high-speed Internet access, and complimentary breakfast, plus a hot tub.

The three two-bedroom cottages that compose **Desert Gardens** (123–127 W. 200 N., 435/259-5125 or 800/505-5343, $89 and up) each contain a full kitchen, bath, and living room. The cottages sit in a large shaded yard with access to a hot tub, barbecue, and nicely maintained gardens. A two-night-minimum stay is required.

Over $100

The **Ramada Inn** (182 S. Main, 888/989-1988 or 435/259-7141, $100) has nicely appointed rooms (some with balconies), a pool, spa, and facilities for small meetings.

South of downtown is the **Comfort Suites** (800 S. Main, 435/259-5252 or 800/228-5150, $100), an all-suites motel with large, nicely furnished rooms complete with microwaves and refrigerators. Facilities include an indoor pool, spa, exercise room, locked bike storage, and a guest laundry room.

Eight blocks from downtown, in a quiet property that backs up to Mill Creek and Nature Conservancy holdings, is **Adobe Adobe** (778 Kane Creek Blvd., 435/259-7716, www.adobeabodemoab.com, $129 and up), a newly constructed adobe inn with large guestrooms done up in handsome Southwest style. The inn also offers high-speed Internet access, a large and tasty breakfast, and a hot tub.

If you want seclusion in a wilderness setting, stay at the **Castle Valley Inn B&B** (located in Castle Valley, 18 miles east of Moab, 435/259-7830, www.castlevalleyinn.com, $100 and up). The inn adjoins a wildlife refuge in a stunning landscape of red-rock mesas and needle-pointed buttes. You can stay in one of the main house's five guest rooms or in one of the three bungalows with kitchens. For an additional fee and with advance notice, dinner is available for guests. Facilities include a hot tub. No children or pets are allowed, and a two-night stay is required on weekends. To reach Castle Valley Inn, follow Hwy. 128 east from Moab for 16 miles and turn south 2.3 miles toward Castle Valley.

The centrally located **Best Western Greenwell Motel** (105 S. Main, 435/259-6151 or 800/528-1234, $125 and up) has a pool, an on-premises restaurant, and some kitchenettes. The **Best Western Canyonlands Inn** (16 S. Main, 435/259-2300 or 800/528-1234, $125 and up) is also in the heart of Moab, with suites, a pool, fitness room and spa, restaurant, and bike-storage area.

One of the most interesting accommodations in Moab is the 【 **Gonzo Inn** (100 W. 200 S., 435/259-2515 or 800/791-4044, www.gonzoinn.com, $145 and up). With a look somewhere between an adobe inn and a postmodern warehouse, the Gonzo doesn't try to appear anything but young and hip. Expect large rooms with Day-Glo colors, a pool, and a friendly welcome.

Located in a lovely and quiet residential area, the 【 **Sunflower Hill Bed and Breakfast**

(185 N. 300 E., 435/259-2974 or 800/662-2786, www.sunflowerhill.com, $145–155 and up) offers high-quality accommodations in one of Moab's original farmhouses and in a newly built garden cottage with patios and balconies. All 12 rooms have private baths, air conditioning, and queen-size beds; there are also two suites. Guests share access to an outdoor hot tub, bike storage, patios, and large gardens. Children age eight and older are welcome, and it's open year-round.

Campgrounds

Spanish Trail RV Park (2980 S. U.S. 191, 435/259-2411 or 800/787-2751, $19 tents, $25 hookups, year-round) is about three miles south of Moab and has showers, laundry, and restrooms. More convenient to downtown is **Canyonlands Campground** (555 S. Main St., 435/259-6848 or 800/522-6848, $21–23 tents, $30–$32 Rvs, year-round); it has showers, a laundry room, store, and pool. Two-person air-conditioned cabins are also available for $42—bring your own bedding. **Slickrock Campground** (one mile north of Moab at 1301 1/2 N. U.S. 191, 435/259-7660 or 800/448-8873, $18 tents or RVs without hookups, $29 with hookups, $34 cabins with air-conditioning and heat, year-round) has showers, a store, an outdoor cafe, and a pool.

Moab Valley RV Resort (two miles north of Moab at 1773 N. U.S. 191 and Hwy. 128, 435/259-4469, tents $20, RVs $28 and up, year-round) has showers, a pool, a playground, and Wi-Fi access. There's also a selection of cabins ($39–$69) available, some simple sleeping rooms, others with bathrooms, refrigerators, and bedding. **Moab KOA** (four miles south of Moab at 3225 S. U.S. 191, 435/259-6682 or 800/562-0372, $20–$29 tents, RVs $26–$32, $42–$60 "kamping kabins," Mar.–Nov.) has showers, a laundry room, a store, mini-golf, and a pool.

The BLM requires that all camping along the Colorado River (accessible by road above and below Moab), Kane Creek, and near the Moab Slickrock Bike Trail *must* be in developed designated sites (with toilets) or undeveloped designated sites (no restrooms or fee). The following four camping areas are available along Hwy. 128 for a $10 fee. From the U.S. 191/ Hwy. 128 junction, you'll find **JayCee Park** at 4.2 miles, **Hal Canyon** at 6.6 miles, **Oak Grove** at 6.9 miles, and **Big Bend Recreation Site** at 7.4 miles. Contact the Moab Information Center for locations of additional campgrounds. You'll also find campgrounds farther out at Arches and Canyonlands National Parks, Dead Horse Point State Park, the La Sal Mountains, and Canyon Rims Recreation Area.

Guest Ranches

A short drive from Moab along the Colorado River's red-rock canyon is the region's premium luxury guest ranch, the **〖 Sorrel River Ranch** (17 miles northeast of Moab on Hwy. 128, 435/259-4642 or 877/359-2715, www.sorrelriver.com, $279 and up). The ranch sits on 240 acres in one of the most dramatic landscapes in the Moab area—located just across the river from Arches National Park and beneath the soaring mesas of Castle Valley.

Accommodations are in a series of beautifully furnished wooden lodges, all tastefully fitted with Old West–style furniture. All units have kitchenettes and a patio with porch swing or back deck overlooking the river (some rooms have both). Horseback rides are offered into the arroyos behind the ranch, and kayaks and bicycles can be rented. The ranch's restaurant, the River Grill, has some of the best views in Utah and an adventurous menu offering everything from steaks to grilled duck breast.

Sharing a similar view of the Colorado River and Castle Valley (though three miles closer to Moab) is **Red Cliffs Lodge** (Mile Post 14, Hwy 128, 435/259-2002 or 866/812-2002, www .redcliffslodge.com, $200 and up), a guest ranch and winery combo that offers "mini suites" in the main lodge building, plus a number of riverside cabins that can sleep up to six. The lodge offers a bar and restaurant, plus horseback rides and mountain bike rentals, and will arrange river raft trips. The lodge is also the headquarters for Castle Creek Winery; there's a tasting room in the lobby.

FOOD

Moab has the best restaurants in all of southern Utah; no matter what else the recreational craze has produced, it has certainly improved the food. Several Moab-area restaurants are closed for annual vacation in February.

Breakfast and Light Meals

Start the day at **Breakfast at Tiffany's** (90 E. Center, 435/259-2553, breakfast and lunch daily, $4–9), a happening coffee shop with fresh pastries and a deli. For a traditional breakfast, try the **Jailhouse Café** (101 N. Main St., 435/259-3900, breakfast and lunch daily, $5– 12). Another favorite is the **Mondo Café** (59 S. Main St., in McStiff's Plaza, 435/259-5551, breakfast and lunch daily, $3–7). They serve fresh baked goods, espresso drinks, and sandwiches for lunch. The **Moab Diner and Ice Cream Shoppe** (189 S. Main St., 435/259-4006, breakfast, lunch, and dinner daily, $6– 22) is a good place to know about—you'll find the breakfasts old-fashioned and abundant, a

© W. C. MCRAE

Saddle horses await their cowboys at Sorrel River Ranch.

Southwestern green-chili edge to the food, and the best ice cream in town. **EclectiCafe** (352 N. Main, 435/259-6896, breakfast and lunch daily, $5–9) has a good selection of organic and vegetarian dishes, mostly with ethnic roots.

Casual Dining

Unless otherwise noted, each of the following establishments has a full liquor license and entrees range $8–15.

For light meals and snacks, try the **Poplar Place Pub and Eatery** (Main and 100 N., 435/259-6018, lunch and dinner daily), which serves pizza, pasta, and deli sandwiches in a pub atmosphere. The **Slickrock Café** (5 N. Main, 435/259-8004, breakfast, lunch, and dinner daily) is another versatile restaurant. In a historic building downtown, the Slick Rock serves up-to-date food at reasonable prices, all with a spicy Southwestern or Caribbean kick.

The **Rio Colorado Restaurant** (2 S. 100 W., 435/259-6666, from 4–11 P.M. daily) can fill the bill for almost any appetite—sandwiches, Mexican food, steak, seafood, chicken, pasta, and salads. Only one restaurant in town serves Asian food: the **Szechuan Restaurant** (125 S. Main, 435/259-8984, breakfast, lunch, and dinner daily). Fortunately, the food is good, spicy, and inexpensive.

For a Western night out, consider **Bar-M Chuckwagon Live Western Show and Cowboy Supper** (541 South Mulberry Lane, 435/259-2276, http://barmchuckwagon.com, dinner Mon.–Sat. Apr.–Oct., $24 ages 11 and older, $12 children, beer only), located on the banks of Mill Creek just southeast of town. Tasty cowboy-style cooking is served up from chuck wagons, followed by a variety of live Western entertainment.

Brewpubs

After a hot day out on the trail, who can blame you for thinking about a cold brew and a good meal at a brewpub? Luckily, Moab has two excellent pubs to fill the bill. **Eddie McStiff's** (57 S. Main, 435/259-2337, lunch and dinner daily, $6–17) was the first brewpub in Moab and is an extremely popular place to sip a cool

one or eat a hearty meal of pasta, pizza, steaks, salads, chicken, and Mexican food. The pub is a convivial place to meet like-minded travelers; in good weather there's seating in a nice courtyard. You'd have to try hard not to have fun here.

There's more good beer and maybe better food at the **Moab Brewery** (686 S. Main St., 435/259-6333, lunch and dinner daily, $7–18), although this newer restaurant has yet to attract the kind of scene you'll find at Eddie McStiff's. The atmosphere is light and airy, and the food is good—steaks, sandwiches, burgers, and a wide selection of salads. There's deck seating when weather permits.

Fine Dining

The **Sunset Grill** (900 N. U.S. 191, 435/259-7146, dinner Mon.–Sat., $17–30) is located in uranium king Charlie Steen's mansion, situated high above Moab, with "million-dollar" sweeping views of the valley. Chefs offer steaks, fresh seafood, and a selection of modern pasta dishes.

Buck's Grill House (1393 N. U.S. 191, 435/259-5201, dinner nightly, $14–39) is a steakhouse with a difference. The restaurant features a pleasant Western atmosphere, and the food seems familiar enough—steaks, prime rib, roast chicken, seafood, grilled pork loin— but the quality of the preparation and the side dishes makes the difference. This is Western fine dining, with imaginative refinements on standard steakhouse fare. Dishes like pan-fried trout with apricot cilantro mayonnaise, duck tamales, and steaks with barbecue butter are excellent.

The **River Grill** (at Sorrel River Ranch, 17 miles northeast of Moab on Hwy. 128, 435/259-4642, three meals daily, dinner by reservation only, $18–32) has a lovely dining room that overlooks spires of red rock and the dramatic cliffs of the Colorado River. The scenery is hard to top, and the food is excellent, with a focus on prime beef and Continental specialties. Fresh fish and other seafood are flown in daily and form the basis for nightly specials.

Moab has two restaurants that feature

up-to-the-moment cuisine. The ◖ **Center Cafe** (60 N. 100 West, 435/259-4295, lunch Mon.–Fri, dinner nightly, $15–28) has been a long-time Moab favorite for its international menu and excellent service. The menu is eclectic, with a wide selection of pasta dishes (including several vegetarian choices) and other inventive fare that feature Continental influences and free-range and organic ingredients. There's also a market area for homemade breads, cheeses, and gourmet takeout.

The ◖ **Desert Bistro** (1266 N. U.S. 191, 435/259-0756, dinner nightly, $18–30.) has moved to the historic 1896 Ranch House at Moab Springs Ranch on the north end of Moab, where it continues to serve seasonal, sophisticated Southwest-meets-Continental cuisine featuring local meats and game, plus fresh fish and seafood. The patio dining here is the nicest in Moab.

INFORMATION

Moab is a small town, and people are generally friendly. Between the Moab Information Center and the county library—and the friendly advice of people in the street—you'll find it easy to assemble all the information you need to have a fine stay.

The **Moab Information Center** (Main and Center, 435/259-8825 or 800/635-6622, www.discovermoab.com, 8 A.M.–9 P.M. daily in summer, reduced hours the rest of the year) is the place to start for nearly all local and area information. The National Park Service, the BLM, the U.S. Forest Service, the Grand County Travel Council, and the Canyonlands Natural History Association are all represented here. Visitors needing help from any of these agencies should start at the information center rather than at the agency offices. Free literature is available, and a large selection of books and maps are sold. Especially useful is the free *Southeastern Utah Travel Guide*, which describes features of and opportunities for recreation in the Arches and Canyonlands National Parks. Included are comprehensive lists of tour operators, places to rent and purchase equipment, and campgrounds.

The **National Park Service office** (three miles south of downtown at 2282 Southwest Resource Blvd., Moab, UT 84532, 435/259-7164, 8 A.M.–4:30 P.M. Mon.–Fri.) is headquarters for Canyonlands and Arches National Parks and Natural Bridges National Monument. The **Manti-La Sal National Forest office** (435/259-7155, 8 A.M.–noon and 12:30–4:30 P.M. Mon.–Fri.) is at the same location. The **BLM District office** (82 E. Dogwood or P.O. Box 970, Moab, UT 84532, 435/259-8193, 7:45 A.M.–4:30 P.M. Mon.–Fri.) is on the south side of town behind Comfort Suites. Some land-use maps are sold here and this is the place to pick up river-running permits.

SERVICES

The **Grand County Public Library** (25 S. 100 E., 435/259-5421, 1–9 P.M. Mon.–Thurs., 1–5 P.M. Fri., 10 A.M.–2 P.M. Sat.) is a good place for local history and general reading. The library is for local residents, but others can use the services on a daily basis.

The **post office** is downtown (50 E. 100 N., 435/259-7427). **Allen Memorial Hospital** provides medical care (719 W. 400 N., 435/259-7191). For emergencies (ambulance, sheriff, police, or fire), dial 911.

TRANSPORTATION

US Airways Express (800/235-9292) provides daily scheduled air service between Canyonlands Field just north of Moab and Salt Lake International Airport, with one direct, round-trip flight Sunday–Thursday, and two on Fridays. The planes are Beech 1900D, a pressurized aircraft with a capacity of 19 passengers and 2 pilots. The Moab/Canyonlands Airfield is 16 miles north of Moab on U.S. 191.

The only other public transportation option to Moab is the ARK Shuttle run by Bighorn Express (888/655-7433, www.bighornexpress.com), which makes one minibus run daily between Moab and Salt Lake City. Advance reservations are required. One-way fare is $65.

For rental cars, contact **Certified Ford** (500 S. Main, 435/529-6107) or **Thrifty** (711 S. Main, 435/259-7317 or 800/847-4389), which has an office at the Moab airport. Shuttle services like **Roadrunner Shuttle** (435/259-9402, www.roadrunnershuttle.com) can also pick up and deliver passengers at the airport.

SCENIC DRIVES AND EXCURSIONS

Each of the following routes is at least partly accessible to standard low-clearance highway vehicles. If you have a four-wheel drive vehicle, you'll have the option of additional, off-road exploring.

Utah Scenic Byway 279

Hwy. 279 goes downstream through the Colorado River Canyon on the other side of the river from Moab. Pavement extends 16 miles past fine views, prehistoric rock art, arches, and hiking trails. A potash plant marks the end of the highway; a rough dirt road continues to Canyonlands National Park. From Moab, head north 3.5 miles on U.S. 191, then turn left on Hwy. 279. The highway enters the canyon at the Portal, 2.7 miles from the turnoff. Towering sandstone cliffs rise on the right, and the Colorado River drifts along just below on the left.

Stop at a signed pullout on the left 0.6 mile past the canyon entrance to see **Indian Ruins Viewpoint,** a small prehistoric Native American ruin tucked under a ledge across the river. The stone structure was probably used for food storage.

Groups of **petroglyphs** cover cliffs along the highway 5.2 miles from U.S. 191. These may not be signed; they are 0.7 mile beyond milepost 11. Look across the river to see The Fickle Finger of Fate among the sandstone fins of Behind the Rocks. A petroglyph of a bear is 0.2 mile farther down the highway. Archaeologists think that Fremont people and the later Utes did most of the artwork in this area.

A signed pullout on the right 6.2 miles from U.S. 191 points out **dinosaur tracks** and petroglyphs visible on rocks above. Sighting tubes help locate the features. It's possible to hike up the steep hillside for a closer look.

The aptly named **Jug Handle Arch,** with an opening 46 feet high and three feet wide, is

© W. C. MCRAE

Utah Scenic Byway 279

close to the road on the right, 13.6 miles from U.S. 191. The canyon opens up ahead.

At the **Moab Salt Plant,** mining operations inject water underground to dissolve the potash and other chemicals, then pump the solution to evaporation ponds. The ponds are dyed blue to hasten evaporation, which takes about a year. You can see these colorful solutions from Dead Horse Point and Anticline Overlook on the canyon rims.

High-clearance vehicles can continue on the unpaved road beyond the plant. The road passes through varied canyon country, with views overlooking the Colorado River. At a road junction in Canyonlands National Park (Island in the Sky District), you have a choice of turning left for the 100-mile White Rim Trail (four-wheel drive only past Musselman Arch), continuing up the steep switchbacks of the Shafer Trail Road (four-wheel drive recommended) to the paved park road, or returning the way you came.

Utah Scenic Byway 128

Hwy. 128 turns northeast from U.S. 191 just south of the Colorado River Bridge, two miles north of Moab. This exceptionally scenic canyon route follows the Colorado for 30 miles upstream before crossing at Dewey Bridge and turning north to I-70. The entire highway is paved. The Lions Park picnic area at the turnoff from U.S. 191 is a pleasant stopping place. Big Bend Recreation Site is another good spot 7.5 miles up Hwy. 128.

A network of highly scenic jeep roads branches off Castle Valley and Onion Creek Roads into side canyons and the **La Sal Mountains Loop Road.** This paved scenic road goes through Castle Valley, climbs high into the La Sals, then loops back to Moab. Allow at least three hours to drive the 62-mile loop. The turnoff from Hwy. 128 is 15.5 miles up from U.S. 191.

A graded county road, **Onion Creek Road,** turns southeast off the highway 20 miles from U.S. 191 and heads up Onion Creek, crossing it many times. *Avoid this route if storms threaten.* The unpleasant-smelling creek con-

tains poisonous arsenic and selenium. Colorful rock formations of dark red sandstone line the creek, and you'll cross an upthrusted block of crystalline gypsum. After about eight miles, the road climbs steeply out of Onion Creek to upper Fisher Valley and a junction with Kokopelli's Trail, which follows a jeep road over this part of its route.

The Gothic spires of **Fisher Towers** soar as high as 900 feet above Professor Valley. The BLM has a picnic area nearby and a hiking trail that skirts the base of the three main towers; Titan, the tallest, is the third one.

In 1962, three climbers from Colorado made the first ascent of Titan Tower. The almost-vertical rock faces, overhanging bulges, and sections of rotten rock made for an exhausting 3.5 days of climbing (the party descended to the base for two of the nights). Their final descent from the summit took only six hours. An unpaved road turns southeast off Hwy. 128 near milepost 21 (21 miles from U.S. 191) and continues two miles to the picnic area.

The modern two-lane concrete **Dewey Bridge** has replaced the picturesque wood-and-steel suspension bridge built in 1916. Here, the BLM has built the Dewey Bridge Recreation Site with a picnic area, trailhead, boat launch, and a small campground. Bicyclists and hikers can still use the old bridge; an interpretive sign explains its history. Drivers can continue on the highway to I-70 through rolling hills nearly devoid of vegetation.

Upstream from Dewey Bridge are the wild rapids of **Westwater Canyon.** The Colorado River cut this narrow gorge into dark metamorphic rock. You can raft or kayak down the river in one day or a more leisurely two days. Camping is limited to a single night. Unlike most desert rivers, this section of the Colorado also offers good river-running at low water levels in late summer and autumn. Westwater Canyon's inner gorge, where boaters face their greatest challenge, is only about 3.5 miles long; however, you can enjoy scenic sandstone canyons both upstream and downstream.

A bumpy four-wheel drive route, the **Top-of-the-World Road,** climbs to an overlook with outstanding views of Fisher Towers, Fisher Valley, Onion Creek, and beyond. Turn right (east) on Entrada Bluffs Road (just before crossing Dewey Bridge). After 5.5 miles, keep straight on a dirt road when the main road curves left, then immediately turn right (south) and go uphill 100 yards through a gate (gateposts are railroad ties) and continue about 4.5 miles on the Top-of-the-World Road to the rim. Elevation here is 6,800 feet, nearly 3,000 feet higher than the Colorado River.

Kane Creek Scenic Drive

This road heads downstream along the Colorado River on the same side as Moab. The four miles through the Colorado River Canyon are paved, followed by six miles of good dirt road through Kane Springs Canyon. This route also leads to several hiking trails (see the *Moab Area Recreation* section). People with high-clearance vehicles or mountain bikes can continue across a ford of Kane Springs Creek to Hurrah Pass and an extensive network of four-wheel drive trails.

LA SAL MOUNTAINS

The forests and lakes in Utah's second-highest mountain range provide a dramatic contrast to the barren slickrock and sands of the surrounding desert. Mount Peale (elev. 12,721 feet) crowns the range at a height nearly 9,000 feet above the Colorado River. Volcanic intrusions formed the La Sals about 30 million years ago, twisting and upturning surrounding rock layers at the same time. Streams and glaciers later carved knifelike ridges in the peaks and deep canyons in the foothills.

Wildlife you might see include black bear (one of the state's largest populations lives here), Rocky Mountain elk, mule deer, mountain lion, badger, ringtail cat, porcupine, pika, Merriam's turkey, and golden eagle. Native cutthroat and some brook and brown trout swim in streams at the middle to higher elevations. Reservoirs and Mill Creek contain rainbow trout. Early Spanish explorers, seeing the range when it was covered with snow, named it La Sal ("salt"). Other names include Salt Mountains and Elk Mountains. Gold fever peaked here at

the turn of the century with activity concentrated in Miners and Gold Basins. Old mines and ruins of former mining camps can still be found in these areas. Hiking trails cross the range from north to south and branch off to scenic lakes, basins, and canyons. Cross-country skiers often head to Miners Basin, Beaver Basin, Geyser Pass, Gold Basin, La Sal Pass, and Dark Canyon. Snowmobilers may also use the roads and trails in the mountains.

La Sal Mountains Loop Road

This paved road on the west side of the range provides a good introduction to the high country. Side roads and trails lead to lakes, alpine meadows, and old mining areas. Viewpoints overlook Castle Valley, Arches and Canyonlands National Parks, Moab Rim, and other scenic features. Vegetation along the drive runs the whole range from cottonwoods, sage, and

ISLANDS IN THE DESERT: ALPINE ECOSYSTEMS

Rising high above the desert are the La Sal, Henry, and Abajo Mountains. At elevations between 7,000 and 8,500 feet, the desert gives way to forests of aspen, Gambel oak, ponderosa pine, and mountain mahogany. Conifers dominate up to the tree line, at about 12,000 feet. Alpine flowering plants, grasses, sedges, and mosses cling to the windy summits of these mountains. Wildlife of the forests includes many of the desert dwellers, as well as elk, bear, mountain lion, marmot, and pika. A herd of bison roams freely in the Henry Mountains; the surrounding desert keeps them from going elsewhere. These high meadows, where temperatures rarely top 80°F, can be revivifying after broiling under the desert sun in the Colorado River canyon. Best of all, the high country of the La Sals and the Abajos are less than an hour's drive from Moab, Arches, or Canyonlands.

rabbitbrush of the desert to forests of aspen, fir, and spruce. The 62-mile loop road can easily take a full day with stops for scenic overlooks, a picnic, and a bit of hiking or fishing. Because of the high elevations, the loop's season usually lasts May–October. Stock up on supplies in Moab—you won't find any stores or gas stations after leaving town. Before venturing off the Loop Road, check current backroad conditions with the U.S. Forest Service office in Moab, and ask for a road log of sights and side roads.

DEAD HORSE POINT STATE PARK

The land drops away in sheer cliffs from this lofty perch west of Moab ($7 per vehicle day use). Nearly 5,000 square miles of rugged canyon country lie in the distance. Two thousand feet below, the Colorado River twists through a gooseneck on its long journey to the sea. The river and its tributaries have carved canyons that reveal a geologic layer cake of colorful rock formations. Even in a region of impressive views around nearly every corner, Dead

Horse Point stands out for its exceptionally breathtaking panorama.

A narrow neck of land only 30 yards wide connects the point with the rest of the plateau. Cowboys once herded wild horses onto the point, then placed a fence across the neck to make a 40-acre corral. They chose the desirable animals from the herd and let the rest go. According to one tale, a group of horses left behind after such a roundup became confused by the geography of the point. They couldn't find their way off and circled repeatedly until they died of thirst within sight of the river below. You may hear other stories of how the point got its name.

Besides the awe-inspiring views, the park also offers a visitors center (435/259-2614, 800/322-3770 reservations, 8 A.M.–6 P.M. daily May 16–September 15, 9 A.M.–5 P.M. the rest of the year), campground, picnic area, group area, nature trail, and hiking trails. The point has become popular with hang gliders. If you are lucky in timing your visit, you may see one or more crafts gliding back and forth above or below the viewpoint. Dead Horse Point is

© W. C. MCRAE

Dead Horse Point State Park rises above the Colorado River.

easily reached by paved road, either as a destination itself or as a side trip on the way to the Island in the Sky District of Canyonlands National Park. From Moab, head northwest 10 miles on U.S. 191, then turn left 22 miles on Hwy. 313.

Kayenta Campground (800/322-3770, www.reserveamerica.com, $15 camping fee,

$7 additional fee for reservations), just past the visitors center, offers sites with water and electric hookups but no showers. The campground nearly always fills up during the main season. Either make reservations ahead of time or try to arrive by early afternoon to ensure a space. Winter visitors may camp on the point; no hookups are available, but the restrooms have water.

Moab Area Recreation

Moab sits at the center of some of the most picturesque landscapes in North America. Even the most casual visitor will want to get outdoors and explore the river canyons, natural arches, and mesas. Mountain biking and river tours are the recreational activities that get the most attention in the Moab area, although hikers, climbers, and horseback riders will find plenty to do. If you're less physically adventurous, you can explore the landscape on scenic flights or on hot-air balloon trips, or follow old mining roads in four-wheel drive vehicles to remote backcountry destinations.

Contact the Moab Information Center (435/259-8825 or 800/635-6622) for full information about the area's recreational options; the center, at Main and Central in the center of town, has representatives from the National Park Service, the Bureau of Land Management (BLM), and the U.S. Forest Service on staff, and they can direct you to the adventure of your liking.

OUTFITTERS AND SPORTS AND EQUIPMENT RENTALS

It's easy to find outfitters and sports rental operations in Moab. It's the largest business segment in town. And there's a remarkable cohesion to the town's operations. It seems that everyone markets everybody else's excursions and services, so just ask the closest outfitter for whatever service you need, and chances are excellent you'll get hooked up with what you want.

Rim Cyclery (94 W. 100 North, 435/259-5333 or 888/304-8219, www.rimcyclery.com,

8 A.M.–8 P.M. daily) is Moab's oldest bike and outdoor gear store, offering mountain-bike sales, rentals, and service. Mountain-bike rentals and tours are also available at **Moab Cyclery** (391 S. Main, 435/259-7423 or 800/559-1978, www.moabcyclery.com, 8 A.M.–6 P.M. daily) and **Poison Spider Bicycles** (497 N. Main, 435/259-7882 or 800/635-1792, www.poisonspiderbicycles.com, 8 A.M.–6 P.M. daily). Expect to pay about $45 per day to rent a mountain bike and about $75–125 to join a group tour.

The place for rock climbing gear and information is **Pagan Mountaineering** (59 S Main St, 435/259-1117, www.paganmountaineering.com, 10 A.M.–8 P.M. daily). The friendly folks here also offer a climbing guide service to the local rock.

Canyon Voyages (211 N. Main St., 435/259-6007 or 800/733-6007, www.canyonvoyages.com, 8 A.M.–6 P.M.) and **Navtec Expeditions** (321 N. Main St., 435/259-7983 or 800/833-1278, www.navtec.com, 8 A.M.–6 P.M. daily) are two local rafting companies that rent rafts and kayaks for those who would rather organize their own river adventure. Canoe rental from **Red River Canoe Company** (497 N. Main St., 435/259-7722, www.redrivercanoe.com, 8 A.M.–6 P.M. daily) costs around $35 per day and includes necessary equipment.

You can rent jeeps and other four-wheel drive vehicles at a multitude of Moab outfits, including **Farabee Jeep Rentals** (1861 N. Hwy 191, 435/259-7734, www.moabjeeprentals.com, 8 A.M.–6 P.M. daily) or **Cliffhanger Jeep Rentals** (1551 North U.S. 191,

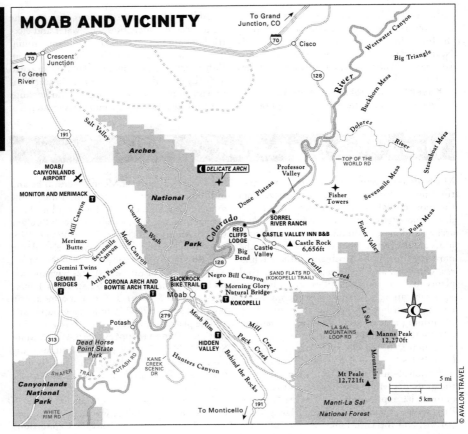

435/259-0889, www.cliffhangerjeeprental
.com, 8 A.M.–6 P.M. daily).

HIKING

To reach most of Moab's prime hiking trails
requires a short drive to trailheads; these routes
are all picturesque. For more options, pick up
the brochure *Moab Area Hiking Trails* at the
visitors center and turn to our sections on
Arches and Canyonlands National Parks.

Trails from Kane Creek
Scenic Drive and U.S. 191 South
The high cliffs just southwest of town provide

fine views of the Moab Valley, highlands of
Arches National Park, and La Sal Mountains.
The **Moab Rim Trail** turns off Kane Creek
Boulevard 1.5 miles downriver from Moab.
The total driving distance from the junction
of Main Street and Kane Creek Boulevard is
2.6 miles; look for the trailhead on the left 0.1
mile after a cattle guard.

You can see the sky through Little Arch
across the river from the trailhead. Four-wheel
drive vehicles can also ascend the Moab Rim
Trail, although the rough terrain is considered
difficult for them; the first 200 yards will give
drivers a feel for the difficulty. The trail climbs

northeast 1.5 miles along tilted rock strata of the Kayenta Formation to the top of the plateau. This hike is moderately difficult, with a gain of 940 feet and good views nearly all the way. Once on top, hikers can follow jeep roads southeast to Hidden Valley Trail and descend on a hiking trail to U.S. 191 south of Moab—a 5.5-mile trip one-way. Experienced hikers can also head south from the rim to **Behind the Rocks,** a fantastic maze of sandstone fins.

You'll see not only a "hidden valley" from the **Hidden Valley Trail** but also panoramas of the Moab area and Behind the Rocks. The moderately difficult trail ascends 500 feet in a series of switchbacks to a broad shelf below the Moab Rim, then follows the shelf (hidden valley) to the northwest. It then crosses a low pass and follows a second shelf in the same di-

rection. Near the end of the second shelf, the trail turns left to a divide, where you can see a portion of the remarkable fins of Behind the Rocks. This divide is one mile from the start and 680 feet higher in elevation. The trail continues one-third mile from the divide down to the end of the Moab Rim Trail, which is a jeep road and hiking trail. Instead of turning left to the divide, you can make a short side trip (no trail) to the right for views of Moab.

To reach the Hidden Valley Trailhead, drive south three miles on U.S. 191 from Moab, turn right 0.4 mile on Angel Rock Road to its end (the turnoff is just south of milepost 122), then right 0.3 mile on Rimrock Lane.

A look at the topographic map will show that something strange is going on at the area called **Behind the Rocks.** Massive fins of Navajo sandstone 100–500 feet high, 50–200 feet thick, and up to one-half-mile long cover a large area. Narrow vertical cracks, sometimes only a few feet wide, separate the fins. Archaeological sites and several arches are in the area. No maintained trails exist here, and some routes require technical climbing skills. The maze offers endless exploration routes. If you get lost (which is very easy to do), remember that the fins are oriented east–west; the rim of the Colorado River Canyon is reached by going west, and Spanish Valley is reached by going east. Bring plenty of water, a topographic map (Moab 7.5-minute), and a compass. Access routes are Moab Rim and Hidden Valley Trails (from the north and east) and Pritchett Canyon (from the west and south). Although it is only a couple of miles from Moab, Behind the Rocks seems a world away. The BLM is studying a possible wilderness designation to protect the solitude and character of this strange country.

Hikers along **Hunters Canyon** enjoy seeing a rock arch and other rock formations in the canyon walls and the lush vegetation along the creek. Off-road vehicles have made tracks a short way up; beyond that you'll be walking mostly along the creekbed. Short sections of trail lead around thickets of tamarisk and other water-loving plants. Look for Hunters Arch on the right about one-half mile up. Most

SEGO CANYON ROCK ART

If you approach Moab along I-70, consider a side trip to one of the premier rock-art galleries in Utah, just a short distance from the freeway junction with U.S. 191 to Moab. Sego Canyon is a showcase of prehistoric rock art – it preserves rock drawings and images that are thousands of years old. The Barrier Canyon Style drawings may be 8,000 years old; the more recent Fremont Style images were created in the last thousand years. Compared to these ancient pictures, the Ute etchings are relatively recent; experts speculate that they may have been drawn in the 1800s, when Ute villages still lined Sego Canyon. Interestingly, the newer petroglyphs and pictographs are more representational than the older ones. The ancient Barrier Canyon figures are typically horned ghostlike beings that look like aliens from early Hollywood sci-fi thrillers. The Fremont Style images depict stylized human figures made from geometric shapes; the crudest figures are the most recent. The Ute images are of buffaloes and hunters on horseback.

of the water in Hunters Canyon comes from a deep pool surrounded by hanging gardens of maidenhair fern. A dry fall and a small natural bridge lie above the pool. This pretty spot marks the hike's three-mile point and an elevation gain of 240 feet. At this point the hike becomes very brushy. To reach the trailhead from Moab, drive eight miles on Kane Creek Boulevard along the Colorado River and up Kane Creek Canyon. The road is asphalted where it fords Hunter Creek, but the asphalt is usually covered with dirt washed over it by the creek.

You can make a longer hike by going up Hunters Canyon and descending on Pritchett Canyon Road. The road crosses the normally dry creekbed just upstream from the deep pool. To bypass the dry fall above the pool, backtrack 300 feet down the canyon and rock-scramble up a short, steep slope—on your right heading upstream. At a junction just east of there, a jeep road along the north rim of Hunters Canyon meets Pritchett Canyon Road. Walk northeast one-half mile on Pritchett Canyon Road to a spur trail on the left leading to Pritchett Arch. Then continue 4.5 miles on Pritchett Canyon Road to Kane Creek Boulevard. This country is more open and desertlike than Hunters Canyon. A 3.2-mile car shuttle or hike is needed to return to Hunters Canyon Trailhead.

Trails from Highway 279

The **Portal Overlook Trail** switchbacks up a slope, then follows a sloping sandstone ledge of the Kayenta Formation to an overlook. A panorama takes in the Colorado River, Moab Valley, Arches National Park, and La Sal Mountains. The hike is 1.5 miles (one-way), with an elevation gain of 980 feet. This trail is a twin of the Moab Rim Trail across the river. Begin from Jaycee Park Campground on the right, 3.8 miles from the turnoff at U.S. 191; mulberry trees shade the attractive spot. Expect to share this trail with many mountain bikers.

The 1.5-mile (one-way) **Corona Arch and Bowtie Arch Trail** leads across slickrock country to these impressive arches. You can't see them from the road, although a third arch—Pinto—is visible. The signed trailhead is on the

right 10 miles from U.S. 191 (midway between mileposts 5 and 6); you'll see railroad tracks just beyond the trailhead. The trail climbs up from the parking area, crosses the tracks, and follows a bit of a jeep road and a small wash to an ancient gravel bar. Pinto (or Gold Bar) Arch stands to the left, although there's no trail to it. Follow cairns to Corona and Bowtie. Handrails and a ladder help in the few steep spots.

Despite being only a few hundred yards apart, each arch has a completely different character and history. Bowtie formed when a pothole in the cliffs above met a cave underneath. It used to be called Paul Bunyan's Potty before that name was appropriated for an arch in Canyonlands National Park. The hole is about 30 feet in diameter. Corona Arch, reminiscent of the larger Rainbow Bridge, eroded out of a sandstone fin. The graceful span is 140 feet long and 105 feet high. Both arches are composed of Navajo sandstone. If you have time for only one hike in the Moab area, this one is especially recommended.

Trails from Highway 128

Negro Bill Canyon is one of the most popular hiking destinations in the Moab Area. The route follows a lively stream pooled by beavers and surrounded by abundant greenery and sheer canyon cliffs. The high point of the hike is **Morning Glory Natural Bridge,** the sixth-longest natural rock span in the country at 243 feet. The trailhead is on the right just after crossing a concrete bridge three miles from U.S. 191. A trail leads upcanyon, along the creek in some places, high on the banks in others.

To see Morning Glory Natural Bridge, head two miles up the main canyon to the second side canyon on the right, then follow a good side trail one-half mile up to the long, slender bridge. The spring and small pool underneath keep the air cool even in summer; ferns, columbines, and poison ivy grow here. The elevation gain is 330 feet.

Experienced hikers can continue up the main canyon about eight miles and rock-scramble (no trail) up the right side, then drop into Rill Creek, which leads to the North Fork of Mill Creek and into Moab. The total distance is about 16 miles one-way; you'll have to find your own way between canyons. The upper Negro Bill and Rill Canyons can also be reached from Sand Flats Road. The Moab and Castle Valley 15-minute and Moab 1:100,000 topographic maps cover the route. This would be a good overnight trip, although fast hikers have done it in a day. Expect to do some wading and rock-scrambling. Water from the creeks and springs is available in both canyon systems, but be sure to purify it first.

A car shuttle is necessary between the Negro Bill and Mill Creek trailheads. You can reach Mill Creek from the end of Powerhouse Lane on the east edge of Moab, but *don't park here.* Vehicle break-ins are a serious problem. Either have someone meet or drop you off here or park closer to town near houses. A hike up the North Fork offers very pretty scenery. A deep pool and waterfall lie three-quarters of a mile upstream; follow Mill Creek upstream and take the left (north) fork. Negro Bill and Mill Creek Canyons are BLM wilderness study areas.

You can't miss the **Fisher Towers** as you

© W. C. MCRAE

The Fisher Towers are nearly 1,000 feet tall.

drive Hwy. 128. These spires of dark red sandstone rise 900 feet above Professor Valley. You can hike around the base of these needle rocks on a trail accessed from the BLM picnic area. Titan, the third and highest rock tower, stands one mile from the picnic area; a viewpoint overlooks Onion Creek 1.1 miles farther along. Carry water for this moderately difficult hike.

Trails North of Moab

The short **Mill Creek Dinosaur Trail,** with numbered stops, identifies the bones of dinosaurs who lived here 150 million years ago. You'll see fossilized wood, too. Pick up the brochure from the Moab Information Center or at the trailhead. From Moab, go 14 miles north on U.S. 191 (or four miles north of the Dead Horse Point turnoff), and turn left two miles on a dirt road, keeping right at a fork 1.1 miles in.

You'll find many other points of interest nearby. A copper mill and tailings dating from the late 1800s lie across the canyon. Halfway Stage Station ruins, where travelers once stopped on the Thompson–Moab run, are a short distance down the other road fork. Jeeps and mountain bikers can do a 13- to 14-mile loop to Monitor and Merimac Buttes (an information sign just in from U.S. 191 has a map and details).

BIKING

Moab is the West's most noted mountainbike destination. In addition to the famed and challenging slickrock trails (slickrock is the exposed sandstone that composes much of the land's surface here) that wind through astonishing desert landscapes, cyclists can pedal through alpine meadows in La Sal Mountains, while nearly abandoned four-wheel drive tracks open up the backcountry to the adventurous. Be aware that the most famous trails, like the Slickrock Bike Trail, are not for beginning mountain bikers. You'll need to be fit, as well as an expert in fat-tire technique to enjoy and, in some cases, make it all the way through these trails. Other trails are better matched to the skills of novices.

It's a good idea to read up on Moab-area trails before planning a trip here (heaps of books and pamphlets are available; see *Suggested Reading* in the *Resources* section). You can also hire an outfitter to teach you about the special skills needed to mountain bike in slickrock country, or join a guided tour. A good place to start is the Trails Illustrated *Bike Map #501* of the Moab area, which has mountain-bike routes color-coded according to difficulty. Or pick up a *Moab Area Mountain Bike Trails* map at the Moab Information Center.

Most people come to Moab to mountain bike mid-March–late May, and then again in fall, mid-September–October. Unless you are an early riser, summer is simply too hot for extended bike touring in these desert canyons. Be prepared for crowds, especially in mid-March, during spring break. In 1999, the Slickrock Trail alone attracted more than 150,000 riders.

If you've never biked on slickrock or in the desert, here are a few basic guidelines. Take care if venturing off a trail—it's a long way down some of the sheer cliff faces. A trail's steep slopes and sharp turns can be tricky, so a helmet is a must. Knee pads and riding gloves also protect from scrapes and bruises. Fat bald tires work best on the rock; partially deflated knobby tires do almost as well. Carry plenty of water—one gallon in summer, half a gallon in cooler months. Tiny plant associations, which live in fragile cryptobiotic soil, don't want you tearing through their homes; stay on the rock and avoid sand areas.

Dozens of trails thread the Moab area; some of the best and most noted are described here.

Slickrock Bike Trail

Undulating slickrock just east of Moab challenges even the best mountain bikers; this is not an area in which to learn mountain-bike skills. Originally, motorcyclists laid out this route, although now about 99 percent of riders rely on leg and lung power. The practice loop near the beginning allows first-time visitors a chance to get a feel for the slickrock. The "trail" consists only of painted white lines.

Riders following it have less chance of getting lost or finding themselves in hazardous areas. Plan on about five hours to do the 9.6-mile main loop, and expect to do some walking.

Side trails lead to viewpoints overlooking Moab, the Colorado River, and arms of Negro Bill Canyon. Panoramas of the surrounding canyon country and La Sal Mountains add to the pleasure of biking.

To reach the trailhead from Main Street in Moab, turn east 0.4 mile on 300 South, turn right 0.1 mile on 400 East, turn left (east) 0.5 mile on Mill Creek Drive, then left 2.5 miles on Sand Flats Road.

The practice loop also makes an enjoyable 2.5-mile hike. Steep drop-offs into the tributaries of Negro Bill Canyon offer breathtaking views. It's best to walk off to the side of the white lines marking the route. You'll reach the practice loop one-quarter mile from the trailhead.

Kokopelli's Trail

Mountain bikers have linked together a series of back roads through the magical canyons of eastern Utah and western Colorado. You can start on Sand Flats Road in Moab and ride east to Castle Valley (21.1 miles), Fisher Valley (44.9 miles), Dewey Bridge (62.9 miles), Cisco Boat Landing (83.5 miles), Rabbit Valley (108 miles), and Loma (140 miles). Lots of optional routes and access points allow for many possibilities. Campsites along the trail have tables, grills, and outhouses. See the small book *The Utah-Colorado Mountain Bike Trail System, Route 1—Moab to Loma,* by Peggy Utesch, for detailed descriptions. An excellent brochure, *Kokopelli's Trail Map,* is available free at the Moab Information Center.

Gimini Bridges (Bull Canyon) Trail

This 14-mile trail passes through tremendous natural rock arches and the slickrock fins of the Wingate Formation, making this one of the most scenic of Moab area trails; it's also one of the more moderate trails in terms of necessary skill and fitness. The trail begins 12.5 miles up Hwy. 313 (the access road to Dead Horse

A popular mountain bike trail leads to Monitor and Merimack mesas.

Point State Park), a total of 21 miles—all up-hill—from Moab, so a shuttle or drop-off is a good idea.

Monitor and Merimack Trail

A good introduction to the varied terrains in the Moab area, the 13.2-mile Monitor and Merimack Trail also includes a trip to a dinosaur fossil bed. The trail climbs through open desert and up Tusher Canyon, then explores red sandstone towers and buttes across slick-rock before dropping down Mill Canyon. At the base of the canyon, you can leave your bike and hike the Mill Canyon Dinosaur Trail before completing the loop to the parking area. Reach the trailhead by traveling 15 miles north of Moab on U.S. 191.

Guided Tours

Most of the bicycle rental shops in Moab offer daylong mountain bike excursions (see *Outfitters and Sports and Equipment Rentals* earlier in this section) while outfitters offer multi-day tours that vary in price depending

on the difficulty of the trail and the degree of comfort involved. The charge for these trips is usually $125–150 per day, including food and shuttles. Be sure to inquire whether rates include bike rental.

Dreamrides Mountainbike Tours (P.O. Box 1137, Moab, UT 84532, 435/259-6419, www .dreamride.com) focuses on leading small, customized group tours. Most packages are three- or five-day tours at roughly $150–200 per day, accommodations extra. **Rim Tours** (1233 S. U.S. 191, 435/259-5223 or 800/626-7335, www.rimtours.com) offers several half-day (around $85 with two or more cyclists), full-day (around $110 with two or more cyclists), and multi-day trips. **Escape Adventures** (operated out of Moab Cyclery, 391 S. Main, 435/259-7423 or 800/559-1978, www.escapeadventures .com) leads multi-day trips on mountain bikes; some of their tours combine cycling with rafting, climbing, and hiking.

Western Spirit Cycling (478 Mill Creek Dr., 435/259-8732 or 800/845-2453, www .westernspirit.com) offers 25 different bicycle

MOUNTAIN-BIKE ETIQUETTE

When mountain biking in the Moab area, don't expect an instant wilderness experience. Because of the popularity of the routes, the fragile desert environment is under quite a bit of stress; be considerate of the thousands of other people who share the trails. By keeping these rules in mind, you'll help keep Moab from being loved to death.

· **Ride only on open roads and trails.** Much of the desert consists of extremely fragile plant and animal ecosystems, and riding recklessly through cryptobiotic soils can destroy desert life and lead to erosion. If you pioneer a trail, chances are someone else will follow the tracks, leading to ever more destruction.

· **Protect and conserve scarce water sources.** Don't wash, swim, walk, or bike through potholes, and camp well away from isolated streams and water holes. The addition of your insect repellent, body oils, suntan lotion, or lubrication from your bike

can destroy the thronging life of a pothole. Camping right next to a remote stream can deprive shy desert wildlife of life-giving water access.

· **Leave all Native American sites and artifacts as you find them.** First, it's against the law to disturb antiquities; second, it's stupid. Enjoy looking at rock art, but don't touch the images – body oils hasten their deterioration. Don't even think about taking potsherds, arrowheads, or artifacts from where you find them. Leave them for others to enjoy or for archaeologists to decipher.

· **Dispose of human solid waste thoughtfully.** The desert can't easily absorb human fecal matter. Desert soils have few microorganisms to break down organic material, and, simply put, mummified turds can last for years. Be sure to bury human solid waste at least 6-12 inches deep in sand and at least 200 feet away from streams and water sources. Pack out toilet paper in resealable bags.

---

tours in the western United States, with about one-third in Utah. Moab area trips include the White Rim, the Maze, and the Kokopelli Trail.

Shuttle Services

Many mountain-bike trails are essentially one-way, and unless you want to cycle back the way you came, you'll need to arrange a shuttle service to pick you up and bring you back to Moab or your vehicle. Also, if you don't have a vehicle or a bike rack, you will need to use a shuttle service to get to more distant trailheads. **Roadrunner Shuttle** (435/259-9402, www.roadrunnershuttle.com) and **Acme Bike Shuttle** (435/260-2534) both operate shuttle services; depending on distance, the usual fare runs $15–25 per person. Both companies also shuttle hikers to trailheads or pick up rafters. Roadrunner also serves as a taxi service for groups.

ADVENTURE TOURS

Even a visitor with a tight schedule can get out and enjoy the canyon country on rafts and other watercraft. Outfitters offer both laid-back and exhilarating day trips, which usually require little advance planning. Longer, multiday trips include gentle canoe paddles along the placid Green River and thrilling expeditions down the Colorado River.

Reserve well in advance for most of the longer trips because the BLM and the National Park Service limit the number of trips through the backcountry, and space, especially in high season, is at a premium. Experienced rafters can also plan their own unguided trips, although you'll need a permit for all areas except for the daylong Fisher Towers float upstream from Moab.

The rafting season runs April–September, and jet-boat tours run February–November. Contact the Moab Information Center and the National

Park Service office for lists or brochures of tour operators; independent river-runners can also visit the center for Colorado River information, although you need to pick up permits from the BLM or National Parks offices. Most river-runners obtain their permits by applying in January and February for a March drawing; the Moab Information Center BLM Ranger can advise on this process and provide the latest information about available cancellations.

Moab Area Outfitters

Moab is full of river-trip companies, and most offer a variety of day and multi-day trips; in addition, many will combine raft trips with biking, horseback riding, hiking, or four-wheel drive excursions. Call for brochures or check out the many websites at www.discover moab.com/tour.htm. The list below includes major outfitters offering a variety of rafting options. Most of them lead trips to the major river destinations on the Colorado and Green Rivers as well as other rivers in Utah and the West. Inquire about special natural history or petroglyph tours.

- **Adrift Adventures:** 435/259-8594 or 800/874-4483, www.adrift.net

- **Canyon Voyages:** 435/259-6007 or 800/733-6007, www.canyonvoyages.com

- **Navtec Expeditions:** 435/259-7983 or 800/833-1278, www.navtec.com

- **Sheri Griffith Expeditions:** 503/259-8229 or 800/332-2439, www.griffithexp.com

- **Tag-A-Long Expeditions:** 435/259-8946 or 800/453-3292, www.tagalong.com

- **Western River Expeditions:** 435/259-7019 or 866/904-1163, www.westernriver.com

Moab Rafting and Kayaking Destinations

For most of the following, full-day rates include lunch and beverages, while part-day trips include just lemonade and soft drinks. On overnight trips you'll sleep in tents in backcountry campgrounds.

The **Colorado River** offers several exciting options. The most popular day run near Moab starts upstream near Fisher Towers and bounces through several moderate rapids on the way back to town. Full-day raft trips from Fisher Towers to near Moab generally cost $48–55 per person. Half-day trips run over much the same stretch of river (no lunch, though) and cost around $35–50 per adult.

For a more adventurous rafting trip, the Colorado's rugged **Westwater Canyon** offers lots of white water and several class III–IV rapids near the Utah–Colorado border. These long day trips are more expensive, typically $125–140 a day. The Westwater Canyon is also often offered as part of multi-day adventure packages. The **Dolores River** joins the Colorado about two miles upstream from Dewey Bridge, near the Colorado border. The Dolores River offers exciting white water in a narrow canyon during the spring runoff; the season is short, though, and the river is too low to run by mid-June. With plenty of class III and IV rapids, this trip usually takes 2–4 days and costs around $400–700 per person.

The **Cataract Canyon** section of the Colorado River, which begins south of the river's confluence with the Green River and extends to the backwater of Lake Powell, usually requires four days of rafting to complete. However, if you're in a hurry, some outfitters offer time-saving trips that motor (not float) through placid water and slow down only to shoot rapids, enabling these trips to conclude in as little as two days. This is the wildest white water in the Moab area, with big, boiling class III and IV rapids. Costs range $600–1000, depending on what kind of craft, the number of days, and whether you fly, hike, or drive out at the end of the trip.

The **Green River** also offers rafting opportunities, although they are milder than those on the Colorado. Trips on the Green make good family outings. Most trips require five days, leaving from the town of Green River and taking out at Mineral Bottom, just before Canyonlands National Park. Highlights of the Green River include Labyrinth Canyon and

Bowknot Bend. Costs range $600–850 for a five-day trip.

Rafting on Your Own

The Fisher Towers section of the Colorado is gentle enough for amateur rafters to negotiate on their own. Rent a raft or kayak from one of the rafting outfitters listed previously. A popular one-day raft trip with mild rapids begins from the Hittle Bottom Recreation Site, 23.5 miles up Hwy. 128 near Fisher Towers, and ends 14 river miles downstream at Take-Out Beach, 10.3 miles up Hwy. 128 from U.S. 191. You can rent rafts and the mandatory life jackets in Moab, and you won't need a permit on this section of river.

Experienced white-water rafters with permits can put in at the BLM's Westwater Ranger Station in Utah or at the Loma boat launch in Colorado. A start at Loma adds a day or two to the trip and the sights of Horsethief and Ruby Canyons. Normal take-out is at Cisco, although it's possible to continue 16 miles on slow-moving water through open country to Dewey Bridge.

Daily raft rentals begin at $85 or so; kayaks rent for $35.

Canoe Trips

Canoeists can also sample the calm waters of the Green River on multiday excursions with **Red River Canoe Company** (800/753-8216, www.redrivercanoe.com). It runs scheduled trips to four sections of the river. Red River Canoe also offers trips to calmer stretches of the Colorado and Dolores Rivers. The company also conducts white-water canoe workshops on the Colorado's Professor Valley and combination canoe and mountain-bike trips. Cost ranges $135–150 per person per day.

Jet Boat Tours

Guided jet-boat excursions through Canyonlands National Park start at around $70 for a half-day trip. **Tag-A-Long Expeditions** (435/259-8946 or 800/453-3292, www.tagalong.com) and **Adrift Adventures** (435/259-8594 or 800/874-4483, www.adrift.net) both offer half-day trips and full-day combination jet-boat/jeep excursions.

Motorboat Tours

Canyonlands by Night (435/259-5261, www.canyonlandsbynight.com, $49 adults, $39 ages 4–12, boats run Apr.–mid-Oct) tours leave at sunset in an open motorboat and go several miles upstream on the Colorado River; a guide points out canyon features. The sound and light show begins on the way back; music and historic narration accompany the play of lights on canyon walls. Package tours with chuck wagon dinners are available. Reservations are a good idea because the boat fills up fast. Trips depart from the Spanish mission–style office just north of Moab, across the Colorado River.

Four-Wheel Drive Touring

Road tours offer visitors a special opportunity to view unique canyonland arches and spires, indigenous rock art, and wildlife. An interpretive brochure at the Moab Information Center outlines the Moab Area Rock Art Auto Tour, which routes motorists to petroglyphs tucked away behind golf courses and ranches. You might also pick up a map of Moab area four-wheel drive trails: four rugged, 15- to 54-mile loop routes through the desert, which take 2.5–4 hours to drive. Those who left their trusty four-by-four and off-road-driving skills at home can take an off-road Jeep tour through a private operator. Most Moab outfitters offer Jeep tours, often in combination with rafting or hiking options. **Tag-A-Long Tours** (452 N. Main, 435/259-8946 or 800/453-3292, www.tagalong.com) and **Adrift Adventures** (378 N. Main, 435/259-8594 or 800/874-4483, www.adrift.net) have half-day (starting at $70) and full-day (starting at $110) Jeep tours with combination jet-boat or hiking options. Full-day tours include lunch.

You can also rent four-wheel drives from **Farabee 4X4 Adventures** (401 N. Main, 435/259-7494 or 800/806-5337) or **Slick Rock Jeep Rental** (284 N. Main, 435/259-5678).

ATV and Dirt Bike Touring

As an alternative to four-wheel drive touring in the backcountry, there's All Terrain Vehicle (ATV) and motorcycle "dirt biking," typically but not exclusively geared for the younger generation, or for families. Youths 8–15 years of age may operate an ATV provided they possess an Education Certificate issued by Utah State Parks and Recreation or an equivalent certificate from their home state. Much of the public land surrounding Moab is open to ATV exploration, with thousands of miles of unpaved roads and existing trails on which ATVs can travel. However, ATV and dirt bike riding is not allowed within either Arches or Canyonlands National Park.

One particularly popular area for ATVs is White Wash Sand Dunes, with many miles of dirt roads in a strikingly scenic location (48 miles northwest of Moab, reached by driving south 13 miles from Exit 175 on I-70, just east of Green River) The dunes are interspersed with large cottonwood trees and bordered by red sandstone cliffs. In addition to the dunes, White Wash is a popular route around three sides of the dunes.

ATVs and dirt bikes are available from a number of Moab area outfitters, including **High Point Hummer** (281 N. Main, 435/259-2972 or 877/486-6833, http://moab-utah.com/hummer) and **Moab Tour Company** (375 S Main, 435/259-4080, www.moabtourcompany.us). A half-day dirt bike or ATV rental starts around $110.

Air Tours

You'll have a bird's-eye view of southeastern Utah's incredible landscape from Moab's Canyonland Field with **Redtail Aviation** (P.O. Box 515, Moab, UT 84532, 435/259-7421 or 800/842-9251, www.moab-utah.com/redtail). Flights include Canyonlands National Park (Needles, Island in the Sky, and Maze Districts, $125). Longer tours are available, too. Rates are based on two or more persons. Flights operate all year. Also based at Canyonlands Field, **Slickrock Air Guides** (435/259-6216 or 866/259-1626, www.slickrockairguides.com) offers a one-hour tour over the Canyonlands area for $125 per person, and $350 for 3.5 hours over Canyonlands, Natural Bridges, Lake Powell, and the Capitol Reef area with a stop for lunch at the Marble Canyon Lodge (not included in rate).

Arches National Park

A concentration of arches of marvelous variety has formed within the maze of sandstone fins at this park, one of the most popular in the United States. Balanced rocks and tall spires add to the splendor. Paved roads and short hiking trails provide easy access to some of the more than 1,500 arches in the park. If you're short on time, a drive to the Windows Section (23.5 miles round-trip) allows a look at some of the largest and most spectacular arches. To visit all the stops and hike a few short trails would take all day. The entrance fee of $10 per vehicle ($5 bicyclists) is good for seven days at Arches only. The park brochure available at the entrance station and visitors center has a map of major scenic features, drives, trails, and back roads.

An unusual combination of geologic forces created the arches. About 300 million years ago, evaporation of inland seas left behind a salt layer more than 3,000 feet thick in the Paradox Basin of this region. Sediments, including those that later became the arches, covered the salt. Unequal pressures caused the salt to gradually flow upward in places, bending the overlying sediments as well. These upfolds, or anticlines, later collapsed when ground water dissolved the underlying salt. The faults and joints caused by the uplift and collapse opened the way for erosion to carve hundreds of freestanding fins. Alternate freezing and thawing action and exfoliation (flaking caused by expansion when water or frost penetrates the rock) continued to

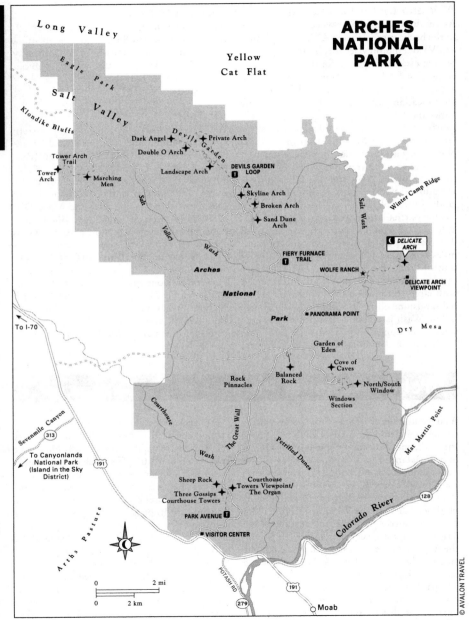

Long Valley

Eagle Park

Salt Valley

Klondike Bluffs

Yellow Cat Flat

ARCHES NATIONAL PARK

Devils Garden

Dark Angel • Private Arch •
Double O Arch •

Tower Arch Trail

Tower Arch •

• Marching Men

Landscape Arch •

DEVILS GARDEN LOOP

Salt

Valley

Wash

Skyline Arch •
• Broken Arch

• Sand Dune Arch

Winter Camp Ridge

Salt Wash

DELICATE ARCH

Arches

FIERY FURNACE TRAIL

WOLFE RANCH ★

DELICATE ARCH VIEWPOINT

National

Park

■ **PANORAMA POINT**

Dry Mesa

← To I-70

Garden of Eden

Cove of Caves •

Rock Pinnacles

• Balanced Rock

• North/South Window

Windows Section

Sevenmile Canyon

(313)

← To Canyonlands National Park (Island in the Sky District)

(191)

Courthouse

The Great Wall

Wash

Petrified Dunes

Mat Martin Point

(128)

Sheep Rock •

Three Gossips •
Courthouse Towers

Courthouse Towers Viewpoint/ The Organ

PARK AVENUE ❚

Arths Pasture

■ **VISITOR CENTER**

Colorado River

POTASH RD

(191)

(279)

0   2 mi

0   2 km

○ Moab

© AVALON TRAVEL

peel away more rock until holes formed in some of the fins. Rockfalls within the holes helped to enlarge the arches. Nearly all arches in the park eroded out of Entrada sandstone.

Eventually all the present arches will collapse, but we should have plenty of new ones by the time that happens. The fins' uniform strength and hard upper surfaces have proved ideal for arch formation. Not every hole in the rock is an arch. The opening must be at least three feet in one direction and light must be able to pass through. Although the term "windows" often refers to openings in large walls of rock, windows and arches are really the same. Water seeping through the sandstone from above has created a second type of arch—the pothole arch. You may also come across a few natural bridges cut from the rock by perennial water runoff.

Visitors Center

The entrance to Arches is five miles north of downtown Moab on U.S. 191. Located just past the entrance booth, the expansive new visitors center (435/719-2299, www.nps.gov/arch, 8 A.M.–4:30 P.M., extended hours spring–fall, $10 per vehicle, $5 bicyclists, motorcyclists, or pedestrians) provides a good introduction to what you can expect ahead. Exhibits identify the rock layers, describe the geologic and human history, and illustrate some of the wildlife and plants of the park. A large outdoor plaza is a good place to troll for information after hours. A short slide program runs regularly and staff members are available to answer your questions, issue backcountry permits, and sign people up for ranger-led tours in the Fiery Furnace area of the park. Look for the posted list of special activities; rangers host campfire programs and lead a wide variety of guided walks April–September. You'll also find checklists, pamphlets, books, maps, posters, postcards, and film here

---

EDWARD ABBEY: "RESIST MUCH, OBEY LITTLE"

Edward Abbey spent two summers in the late 1950s living in a trailer in Arches National Park. From this experience, he wrote *Desert Solitaire*, which, when it was published in 1968, introduced many readers to the beauties of Utah's slickrock country and the need to preserve it. In the introduction to this book, he gives a word of caution to slickrock pilgrims:

> Do not jump into your automobile next June and rush out to the Canyon country hoping to see some of that which I have attempted to evoke in these pages. In the first place you can't see *anything* from a car; you've got to get out of the goddamned contraption and walk, better yet crawl, on hands and knees, over the sandstone and through the...cactus. When traces of blood begin to mark your trail you'll see something, maybe.

This sense of letting the outdoors affect you – right down to the bone – pervades Abbey's writing. He advocated responding to assaults on the environment in an equally raw, gutsy way. Convinced that the only way to confront rampant development in the American West was by preserving its wilderness, he was a pioneer of radical environmentalism, a "desert anarchist." Long before Earth First!, Abbey's fictional characters blew up dams and created a holy environmentalist ruckus in *The Monkeywrench Gang*. Some of his ideas were radical, others reactionary, and he seemed deeply committed to raising a stir. Abbey's writing did a lot to change the way people think about the American West, its development, and staying true to values derived from the natural world.

Two fairly recent biographies, *Edward Abbey: A Life* (Tucson: University of Arizona Press, 2001), by James M. Cahalan, and the less academic *Adventures with Ed* (Albuquerque: University of New Mexico Press, 2002), by Abbey's good friend Jack Loeffler, help readers see the person behind the icon.

for purchase. See the ranger for advice and the free backcountry permit required for overnight trips. The easy 0.2-mile **Desert Nature Trail** begins near the visitors center and identifies some of the native plants. Picnic areas lie outside the visitors center and at Balanced Rock and Devils Garden.

A road guide to Arches National Park, available at the visitors center, has detailed descriptions that correspond to place names along the main road. Be sure to stop only in parking lots and designated pullouts. Watch out for others who are sightseeing in this popular park. With less than 30 miles of paved road in the park, the traffic density can be surprisingly high in the summer high season.

If your plans include visiting Canyonlands National Park plus Hovenweep and Natural Bridges National Monuments, consider the so-called Local Passport, which for $25 buys entry to each of these federal preserves. Purchase the pass at any of the park or national monument entrances.

Devils Garden Campground

The park's campground ($10, year-round, with water) is near the end of the 18-mile scenic drive, though in summer you must pre-register at the visitors center. Try to arrive early during the busy Easter–October season; only groups can reserve spaces. Elevation here is 5,355 feet. During summer evenings, rangers at the Campfire Circle tell about the park's geology, history, wildlife, flora, and environment.

Hiking, Biking, and Climbing

Established trails lead to many fine arches and overlooks that can't be seen from the road. You're free to wander cross-country, too, but please stay on rock or in washes to avoid damaging the fragile cryptobiotic soils. Wear good walking shoes with rubber soles for travel across slickrock. The summer sun can be especially harsh on the unprepared hiker—don't forget water, hat, and sunscreen. The desert rule is to carry at least one gallon of water per person for an all-day hike. Take a map and compass for off-trail hiking. Be cautious on the slickrock;

the soft sandstone can crumble easily. Also, remember that it's easier to go up a steep slickrock slope than to come back down.

You can reach almost any spot in the park on a day hike, though you'll also find some good overnight possibilities. Areas for longer trips include Courthouse Wash in the southern part of the park and Salt Wash in the eastern part. All backpacking is done off-trail. A backcountry permit must be obtained from a ranger before camping in the backcountry. Hiking regulations include no fires, no pets, camping out of sight of any road (at least one mile away) or trail (at least a half mile away) and at least 300 feet from a recognizable archaeological site or nonflowing water source.

Bicycles *must* stick to established roads in the park; cyclists have to contend with heavy traffic on the narrow paved roads and dusty, washboarded surfaces on the dirt roads. Beware of the deep sand on the four-wheel drive roads. Nearby, BLM and Canyonlands National Park areas offer much better mountain biking.

Rock climbers don't need a permit in Arches, although they should first discuss their plans with a ranger. Most features named on U.S. Geological Survey maps are *closed* to climbing. That means any of the arches and many of the most distinctive towers are off limits. There are still plenty of long-standing routes for advanced climbers to enjoy, although the rock in Arches is sandier and softer than other areas around Moab.

Several new climbing restrictions are in place, however. No new permanent climbing hardware may be installed in any fixed location. If an existing bolt or other hardware item is unsafe, it may be replaced. This effectively limits all technical climbing to existing routes or new routes not requiring placement of fixed anchors.

SIGHTS AND HIKES ALONG THE PARK ROAD

A road guide to Arches National Park, available at the visitors center, has detailed descriptions that correspond to place-names along the main road. Be sure to stop only in parking lots and designated pullouts. Watch out for others who are sightseeing in this popular park. The following are major points of interest.

Moab Fault

The park road begins a long but well-graded climb from the visitors center up the cliffs to the northeast. A pullout on the right after 1.1 miles gives a good view of Moab Canyon and its geology. The rock layers on this side of the canyon have slipped down more than 2,600 feet in relation to the other side. Movement took place about six million years ago along the Moab Fault, which follows the canyon floor. Rock layers at the top of the far cliffs are nearly the same age as those at the *bottom* on this side. If you could stack the rocks of this side on top of rocks on the other side, you'd have a complete stratigraphic column of the Moab area—more than 150 million years' worth.

Park Avenue

South Park Avenue Overlook and Trailhead are on the left 2.1 miles from the visitors center. Great sandstone slabs form a "skyline" on each side of this dry wash. A trail goes north one mile down the wash to North Park Avenue Trailhead (1.3 miles ahead by road). Arrange to be picked up there or backtrack to your starting point. The large rock monoliths of Courthouse Towers rise north of Park Avenue. Only a few small arches exist now, though major arches may have formed in the past.

Balanced Rock

This gravity-defying formation is on the right 8.5 miles from the visitors center. A boulder more than 55 feet high rests precariously atop a 73-foot pedestal. Chip Off the Old Block, a much smaller version of Balanced Rock, stood nearby until it collapsed in the winter of 1975–1976. For a closer look at Balanced Rock, take the 0.3-mile trail encircling it. There's a picnic area across the road. Author Edward Abbey lived in a trailer near Balanced Rock during a season as a park ranger in the 1950s; his journal became the basis for the classic *Desert Solitaire.*

© W. C. MCRAE

The aptly named Balanced Rock only looks precarious.

Windows Section

Turn right 2.5 miles on a paved road past Balanced Rock. Short trails (one-quarter to one mile long one-way) lead from the road's end to some massive arches. Windows Trailhead is the start for North Window (an opening 51 feet high and 93 feet wide), South Window (66 feet high and 105 feet wide), and Turret Arch (64 feet high and 39 feet wide). Double Arch, a short walk from a second trailhead, is an unusual pair of arches; the larger opening—105 feet high and 163 feet wide—is best appreciated by walking inside. The smaller opening is 61 feet high and 60 feet wide. Together, the two arches frame a large opening overhead, but this isn't considered a true arch.

Garden of Eden Viewpoint, on the way back to the main road, has a good panorama of Salt Valley to the north. Under the valley, the massive body of salt and gypsum that's responsible for the arches comes close to the surface. Tiny Delicate Arch can be seen across the valley on a sandstone ridge. Early visitors to the Garden of Eden saw rock formations

© W. C. MCRAE

Some of the park's largest arches are in the Windows section.

resembling Adam (with an apple) and Eve. Two other viewpoints of the Salt Valley area lie farther north on the main road.

◖ Delicate Arch

Drive north 2.5 miles on the main road from the Windows junction and turn right 1.8 miles to the Wolfe Ranch, where a bit of pioneer history survives. John Wesley Wolfe came to this spot in 1888, hoping the desert climate would provide relief for health problems related to a Civil War injury. He found a good spring high in the rocks, grass for cattle, and water in Salt Wash to irrigate a garden. The ranch that he built provided a home for him and some of his family for more than 20 years, and cattlemen later used it as a line ranch. Then sheepherders brought in their animals, which so overgrazed the range that the grass has yet to recover. A trail guide available at the entrance tells about the Wolfe family and features of their ranch. The weather-beaten cabin built in 1906 still survives. A short trail leads to petroglyphs above Wolfe Ranch; figures of horses indicate that

Utes did the artwork. Park staff can give directions to other rock-art sites; great care should be taken not to touch the fragile artwork.

Delicate Arch stands in a magnificent setting atop gracefully curving slickrock. Distant canyons and the La Sal Mountains lie beyond. The span is 45 feet high and 33 feet wide. A moderately strenuous hike to the arch begins at Wolfe Ranch and crosses the swinging bridge, climbs a slickrock slope, follows a gully, then contours across steep slickrock to the main overlook. Round-trip distance is three miles with an elevation gain of 500 feet; carry water. This is one of the most scenic hikes in the park. Just before the end of the trail, walk up to a small arch for a framed view of the final destination. The classic photo of Delicate Arch is taken late in the afternoon when the sandstone glows with golden hues.

Another perspective on Delicate Arch can be obtained by driving 1.2 miles beyond Wolfe Ranch. Look for the small arch high above. A steep trail (a half-mile round-trip) climbs a hill for the best panorama.

Fiery Furnace

Return to the main road and continue three miles to the Fiery Furnace Viewpoint and Trailhead on the right. Closely packed sandstone fins form a maze of deep slots, with many arches and at least one natural bridge inside. The Fiery Furnace can be fun to explore (with the required free permit, obtainable at the visitors center), though route finding is tricky. What look like obvious paths often lead to dead ends. Drop-offs and ridges make straight-line travel impossible. It's easy to get lost! Ranger-led hikes of about 90 minutes during the summer season provide the best way to see the wonders within. You'll need a reservation for this trip, obtainable in person only from the visitors center up to 48 hours in advance. The Fiery Furnace gets its name from sandstone fins that turn flaming red on occasions when thin cloud cover at the horizon reflects the warm light of sunrise or sunset. Actually, the shady recesses provide a cool respite from the hot summer sun.

To explore the Fiery Furnace you must join a ranger-led hike.

Broken Arches

The trailhead is on the right 2.4 miles past the Fiery Furnace turnoff. A short trail leads to small Sand Dune Arch (opening is eight feet high and 30 feet wide) tucked within fins. A longer trail (one mile round-trip) crosses a field to Broken Arch, which you can also see from the road. The opening is 43 feet high and 59 feet wide. Up close, you'll see that the arch isn't really broken. These arches can also be reached by trail from near comfort station 3 at Devils Garden Campground. Low-growing canyonlands biscuitroot, found only in areas of Entrada sandstone, colonizes sand dunes. Hikers can protect the habitat of the biscuitroot and other fragile plants by keeping to washes or rock surfaces.

Skyline Arch

Skyline Arch is on the right one mile past Sand Dune/Broken Arch Trailhead. In desert climates, erosion may proceed imperceptibly for centuries until a cataclysmic event happens. In 1940, a giant boulder fell from the opening of Skyline Arch, doubling the size of the arch in just seconds. The hole is now 45 feet high and 69 feet wide. A short trail leads to the base of the arch.

Devils Garden Trail

The trailhead, Devils Garden Picnic Area, and the campground all lie near the end of the main park road. Devils Garden offers fine scenery and more arches than any other section of the park. The trail leads past large sandstone fins to Landscape and six other named arches. Carry water if the weather is hot or if you might want to continue past the one-mile point at Landscape Arch. Adventurous hikers could spend days exploring the maze of canyons among the fins.

The first two arches lie off a short side trail to the right. Tunnel Arch has a relatively symmetrical opening 22 feet high and 27 feet wide. The nearby Pine Tree Arch is named for a piñon pine that once grew inside; the arch has an opening 48 feet high and 46 feet wide. Continue on the main trail to Landscape Arch, which has an incredible 306-foot span (six feet longer than a football field). This is one of the longest unsupported rock spans in the world. The thin arch (106 feet high) looks ready to collapse at any moment. A rockfall from the arch on September 1, 1991, worries some people who fear the end may be near. The distance from the trailhead is two miles round-trip, an easy one-hour walk.

The trail narrows past Landscape Arch and continues a quarter mile to Wall Arch, in a long wall-like fin. The opening is 41 feet high and 68 feet wide. A short side trail branches off to the left beyond Wall to Partition Arch (26 feet high and 28 feet wide) and Navajo Arch (13 feet high and 41 feet wide). Partition was so named because a piece of rock divides the main opening from a smaller hole eight feet high and 8.5 feet wide. Navajo Arch is a rock-shelter type; perhaps prehistoric peoples camped here. The main trail continues northwest and ends at Double O Arch (four miles round-trip from the trailhead). Double O has a large oval-shaped opening (45 feet high and 71 feet wide) and a smaller hole (21 feet high and 21 feet wide) underneath. Dark Angel is a distinctive rock pinnacle a quarter mile northwest; cairns mark the way. Another primitive trail loops back to Landscape Arch via Fin Canyon. This route goes through a different area of Devils Garden but adds about one mile to your trip (three miles back to the trailhead instead of two). Pay careful attention to the trail markers to keep on the correct route.

Klondike Bluffs and Tower Arch

Relatively few visitors come to the spires, high bluffs, and fine arch in this northwestern section of the park. A fair-weather dirt road turns off the main drive 1.3 miles before Devils Garden Trailhead, winds down into Salt Valley, and heads northwest. After 7.5 miles, turn left one mile on the road signed Klondike Bluffs to the Tower Arch Trailhead. These roads may be washboarded but are usually okay for cars in dry weather; don't drive on them if storms threaten. The trail to Tower Arch winds past the Marching Men and other rock formations; the distance is three miles round-trip. Alexander Ringhoffer, who discovered the arch in 1922, carved an inscription on the south column. The area can also be fun to explore off-trail (map and compass needed). Those with four-wheel drive vehicles can drive close to the arch on a separate jeep road. Tower Arch has an opening 34 feet high by 92 feet wide. A tall monolith nearby gave the arch its name.

Four-Wheel Drive Road

A rough road near Tower Arch in the Klondike Bluffs turns southeast past **Eye of the Whale Arch** in Herdina Park to Balanced Rock on the main park road, 10.8 miles away. The road isn't particularly difficult for four-wheel drive enthusiasts, though normal backcountry precautions should be taken. A steep sand hill north of Eye of the Whale Arch is very difficult to climb for vehicles coming from Balanced Rock; it's better to drive from the Tower Arch area instead.

Canyonlands National Park

The canyon country of southeastern Utah puts on its supreme performance in this vast park, which spreads across 527 square miles. The deeply entrenched Colorado and Green Rivers meet in its heart, then continue south as the mighty Colorado through tumultuous Cataract Canyon Rapids. These two rivers are administered as the park's River District. Addi-

tionally, they divide the main body of Canyonlands National Park into three other districts. Island in the Sky lies north between the rivers, the Maze is to the west, and Needles is to the east. In addition, a fifth district, the Horseshoe Canyon Unit with its trove of rock art, lies a dozen miles west of the park's main land block. Each district has its own distinct character. No bridges connect the three land districts in the main block, so most visitors have to leave the park to go from one region to another.

The huge park can be seen in many ways and on many levels. Paved roads reach a few areas, four-wheel drive roads go to more places, and hiking trails reach still more, yet much of the land shows no trace of human passage. To get the big picture, fly over this incredible complex of canyons (see *Air Tours* in the *Moab Area Recreation* section). However, only a river trip or a hike lets you experience the solitude and detail of the land. The park can be visited in any season of the year, with spring and autumn the best choices. Summer temperatures can get into the 100s; carrying (and drinking) water becomes critical then; carry at least one gallon per person per day. Arm yourself with insect repellent from late spring to midsummer. Winter days tend to be bright and sunny, though nighttime temperatures can dip into the teens or subzeros. Visitors coming in winter should inquire about travel conditions, as snow and ice occasionally close roads and trails at the higher elevations.

Visiting the Park

There are five districts of the park, each affording great views, spectacular geology, a chance to see wildlife, and endless opportunities to explore. You won't find crowds or elaborate park facilities—most of Canyonlands remains a primitive backcountry park.

Island in the Sky District has paved roads on its top to impressive overlooks and to Upheaval Dome, a strange geologic feature. If you're short on time or don't want to make a rigorous backcountry trip, this district is the best choice. The "Island," actually a large mesa, is much like Dead Horse Point on a giant scale; a narrow neck of land connects the north side with the "mainland." Hikers and those with suitable vehicles can drop off the Island in the Sky and descend about 1,300 feet to the White Rim 4WD Road, which follows cliffs of the White Rim around most of the island.

Few visitors make it over to the **Maze District,** some of the wildest country in the United States. Only the rivers and a handful of four-wheel drive roads and hiking trails provide access. Experienced hikers can explore the "maze" of canyons on unmarked routes. **Horseshoe Canyon Unit,** a detached section of Canyonlands National Park northwest of the Maze District, protects the Great Gallery, a group of pictographs left by a prehistoric culture.

Colorful rock spires prompted the name of the **Needles District.** Splendid canyons contain many arches, strange rock formations, and archaeological sites. Hikers enjoy day hikes and backpack treks on the network of trails and routes within the district. Drivers with four-wheel drive vehicles have their own challenging roads through canyons and other highly scenic areas. Overlooks and short nature trails can be enjoyed from the paved scenic drive in the park. South of Moab, Hwy. 211 branches off U.S. 191, providing easy access to the Needles District.

The **River District** includes long stretches of the Green and the Colorado. River-running provides one of the best ways to experience the inner depths of the park. Boaters can obtain helpful literature and advice from park rangers. Groups planning their own trip through Cataract Canyon need a river-running permit. Flat-water permits are also required, and there's a fee.

Admission to the park is $10 per vehicle, or $5 per bicyclist or pedestrian. In addition, fees are charged for backcountry camping, four-wheel drive exploration, and river-rafting. For information on the park, contact Canyonlands National Park (2282 S. West Resource Blvd., Moab, UT 84532, 435/719-2313, www.nps .gov/cany).

Visitors Centers and Information

Each of the land districts has a visitors center near the park entrance, but you may find it convenient to stop at the **Moab Information Center** (corner of Main and

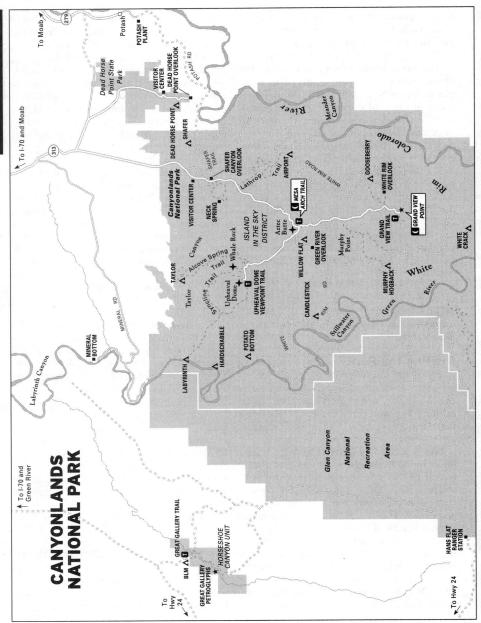

CANYONLANDS
NATIONAL PARK

CANYONLANDS

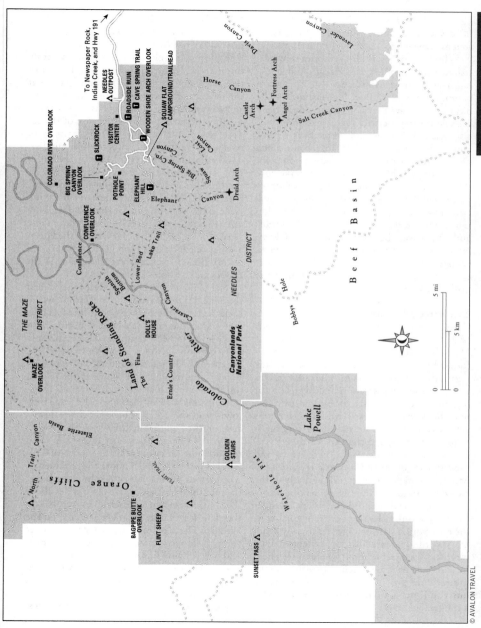

To Newspaper Rock,
Indian Creek, and Hwy 191

NEEDLES OUTPOST

ROADSIDE RUIN
CAVE SPRING TRAIL
WOODEN SHOE ARCH OVERLOOK
SQUAW FLAT CAMPGROUND/TRAILHEAD

VISITOR CENTER

SLICKROCK

COLORADO RIVER OVERLOOK

BIG SPRING CANYON OVERLOOK

POTHOLE POINT

ELEPHANT HILL

CONFLUENCE OVERLOOK

Confluence

THE MAZE DISTRICT

MAZE OVERLOOK

Land of Standing Rocks

The Fins

DOLL'S HOUSE

Ernie's Country

Spanish Bottom

Lower Red Lake Trail

Elephant Canyon

Druid Arch

Castle Arch
Angel Arch
Fortress Arch

Horse Canyon

Salt Creek Canyon

Lost Canyon

Squaw Canyon

Big Spring Cyn

Davis Canyon

Lavender Canyon

NEEDLES DISTRICT

Canyonlands National Park

Cataract Canyon

Colorado River

Beef Basin

Bobbys Hole

GOLDEN STAIRS

Lake Powell

Waterhole Flat

Elaterite Basin

North Trail Canyon

Orange Cliffs

BAGPIPE BUTTE OVERLOOK

FLINT SHEEP

FLINT TRAIL

SUNSET PASS

5 mi

5 km

0

0

© AVALON TRAVEL

Center, 435/259-8825 or 800/635-6622). The offices have brochures, maps, and books, as well as someone to answer your questions.

Vehicle camping is allowed only in established campgrounds and designated backcountry campsites. Except for the main campgrounds at Willow Flat (Island in the Sky) and Squaw Flat (Needles), you'll need a backcountry permit for overnight stays. There is a $15 fee for a backpacking permit and a $30 fee for a vehicle site permit. Each of the three districts has a different policy for backcountry vehicle camping, so make sure that you understand the details. Backcountry permits will also be needed for any technical climbing and trips with stock; check with a ranger for details. Pets aren't allowed on trails and must always be leashed. No firewood collecting is permitted in the park; backpackers need stoves for cooking. Vehicle and boat campers can bring in firewood but must use grills or fire pans.

Back-Road Travel

Canyonlands National Park offers hundreds of miles of exceptionally scenic jeep roads. Normally you must have a vehicle with both four-wheel drive and high clearance. Park regulations require all motorized vehicles to have proper registration and licensing for highway use (ATVs are prohibited); drivers must be licensed. It's essential for both motor vehicles and bicycles to stay on existing roads to prevent damage to the delicate desert vegetation. Carry tools, extra fuel, water, and food in case of breakdown in a remote area. Mountain bikers enjoy travel on many of the backcountry roads, too. Before making a trip, drivers and cyclists should talk with a ranger to register and to learn of current road conditions, which can change drastically from one day to the next. Also, the rangers will be more knowledgeable about where to seek help in case you become stuck. Primitive campgrounds are provided on most of the roads, but you'll need a backcountry permit from a ranger.

RIVER DISTRICT
River-Running Above the Confluence

The Green and Colorado Rivers flow smoothly through their canyons above the confluence of the two rivers. Almost any shallow-draft boat can navigate these waters: canoes, kayaks, rafts, and powerboats are commonly used. Any travel requires advance planning because of the remoteness of the canyons and the scarcity of river access points. No campgrounds, supplies, or other facilities exist past Moab on the Colorado River, or past the town of Green River on the Green. All river-runners must follow park regulations, which include the carrying of life jackets, use of a fire pan for fires, and packing out all garbage and solid human waste. The river flow on both the Colorado and the Green averages a gentle 2–4 mph (7–10 mph at high water). Boaters typically do 20 miles a day in canoes and 15 miles a day in rafts.

The Colorado has one modest rapid called the Slide, 1.5 miles above the confluence, where rocks constrict the river to one-third of its normal width; the rapid is roughest during high water levels in May and June. This is the only difficulty on the 64 river miles from Moab. Inexperienced canoeists and rafters may wish to portage around it. The most popular launch points on the Colorado are the Moab Dock (just upstream from the U.S. 191 bridge near town) and the Potash Dock (17 miles downriver on the Potash Road, Hwy. 279).

On the Green, boaters at low water need to watch for rocky areas at the mouth of Millard Canyon (33.5 miles above the confluence, where a rock bar extends across the river) and at the mouth of Horse Canyon (14.5 miles above the confluence, where a rock and gravel bar on the right leaves only a narrow channel on the left side). The trip from the town of Green River through Labyrinth and Stillwater Canyons is 120 miles. Launch places include Green River State Park (in Green River) and Mineral Canyon (52 miles above the confluence, reached on a fair-weather road from Hwy. 313).

No roads go to the confluence. The easiest

ENDANGERED FISH OF THE COLORADO RIVER BASIN

Colorado squawfish *(Ptychocheilus lucius):* Native only to the Colorado and its tributaries, this species is the largest minnow in North America. It has been reported as weighing up to 100 pounds and measuring six feet long. Loss of habitat caused by dam construction has greatly curtailed its size and range. Anglers often confuse the smaller, more common roundtail chub *(Gila robusta)* with the Colorado squawfish; the chub is distinguished by a smaller mouth extending back only to the front of the eye.

Humpback chub *(Gila cypha):* Scientists first described this fish in 1946 and know little about its life. This small fish usually weighs less than two pounds and measures less than 13 inches. Today the humpback chub hangs on the verge of extinction; it has retreated to a few small areas of the Colorado River, where the water still runs warm, muddy, and swift. The bonytail chub *(Gila robusta elegans)* has a similar size and shape, but without a hump; its numbers are also rapidly declining.

Humpback or razorback sucker *(Xyrauchen texanus):* This large sucker grows to weights of 10-16 pounds and lengths of about three feet. Its numbers have been slowly decreasing, especially above the Grand Canyon. They require warm, fast-flowing water to reproduce. Mating is a bizarre ritual in the spring: When the female has selected a suitable spawning site, two male fish press against the sides of her body. The female begins to shake her body until the eggs and spermatozoa are expelled simultaneously. One female can spawn three times, but she uses a different pair of males each time.

return to civilization for nonmotorized craft is a pick-up by jetboat from Moab by Tex's Riverways or Tag-A-Long Tours (see *Rafting and Boat Tours* in the *Moab Area Recreation* section). A far more difficult way out is hiking either of two trails just above the Cataract Canyon Rapids to four-wheel drive roads on the rim. Park rangers require that boaters above the confluence obtain a backcountry permit either in person from the Moab office or by mail (two weeks in advance). River notes on boating the Green and Colorado are available on request from the Moab office (435/259-3911).

River-Running Through Cataract Canyon

The Colorado River enters Cataract Canyon at the confluence and picks up speed. The rapids begin four miles downstream and extend for the next 14 miles to Lake Powell. Especially in spring, the 26 or more rapids give a wild ride equal to the best in the Grand Canyon. The current zips along (up to 16 mph) and forms waves more than seven feet high. When the excitement dies down, boaters have a 34-mile trip across Lake Powell to Hite Marina; most people either carry a motor or arrange for a powerboat to pick them up. Because of the real hazards of running the rapids, the National Park Service requires boaters to have proper equipment and a permit ($30). Many people go on a commercial trip in which everything has been taken care of (write the park for a list of boat companies). Private groups need to contact the Canyonlands River Unit (2282 W. Resource Blvd., Moab, UT 84532, 435/259-3911) far in advance for permit details.

ISLAND IN THE SKY DISTRICT

Panoramic views from the "Island" can be enjoyed from any point along the rim; you'll see much of the park and southeastern Utah. Short hiking trails lead to overlooks, Mesa Arch, Aztec Butte, Whale Rock, Upheaval Dome, and other features. Longer trails make steep, strenuous descents from the island to the White Rim 4WD Road below. Elevations on the island average about 6,000 feet. *Bring water for all hiking, camping, and travel on Island in the Sky.* No services are available, except at the visitors center in emergencies (bottled water is sold).

Visitors Center

Stop here (435/259-4351, 8 A.M.–4:30 P.M. daily, reservations made 12:30–4:30 P.M. Mon.–Sat., may close noon–1 P.M. in winter) for information about Island in the Sky and to see some exhibits; books and maps can be purchased. A $10 per-vehicle charge is made unless you have a receipt issued within the last seven days from the Needles District of Canyonlands. Obtain a backcountry permit ($15 for backpack camping, $30 for a vehicle campsite) if making an overnight hike or planning to stay at campgrounds along the White Rim 4WD Road (reservations by mail, phone, or in person are required for sites, $25 reservation fee). A bulletin board outside has park information. The visitors center is just before crossing "the neck" to Island in the Sky. From Moab, go northwest 10 miles on U.S. 191, turn left 15 miles on Hwy. 313 to the junction for Dead Horse Point State Park, then continue straight seven miles.

Shafer Canyon Overlook

Continue a half mile past the visitors center to this overlook on the left (just before crossing the neck). Shafer Trail Viewpoint, across the neck, provides another perspective a half mile farther. The neck is a narrow land bridge just wide enough for the road, and it's the only vehicle access to the 40-square-mile Island in the Sky. The overlooks have good views east down the canyon and the incredibly twisting **Shafer Trail Road.** Cattlemen Frank and John Schafer built the trail in the early 1900s to move stock to additional pastures (the "c" in their name was later dropped by mapmakers). Uranium prospectors upgraded the trail to a four-wheel drive road during the 1950s so that they could reach their claims at the base of the cliffs. Today the Shafer Trail Road connects the mesa top with White Rim 4WD Road and Potash Road 1,200 feet and four miles below. High-clearance vehicles should be used on Shafer,

preferably with four-wheel drive if you plan to climb up. Road conditions can vary considerably, so contact a ranger before starting.

Neck Spring Trail

The trail begins near the Shafer Canyon Overlook. A brochure should be available at the trailhead. This moderately difficult hike follows a five-mile loop down Taylor Canyon to Neck and Cabin Springs, formerly used by ranchers, then climbs back to Island in the Sky Road at a second trailhead a half mile south of the start. Elevation change is 300 feet. Water at the springs supports maidenhair fern and other water-loving plants. Also watch for birds and wildlife attracted to this spot. Bring water with you, as the springs aren't suitable for drinking.

Lathrop Trail

This is the only marked hiking route going all the way from Island in the Sky to the Colorado River. The trailhead is on the left 1.3 miles past the neck. The first 2.5 miles cross Gray's Pasture to the rim, then the trail descends steeply, dropping 1,600 feet over the next 2.5 miles to White Rim 4WD Road. Part of this section follows an old mining road past several abandoned mines, all relics of the uranium boom; don't enter the shafts, as they're in danger of collapse and may contain poisonous gases. From the mining area, the route descends through a wash to White Rim 4WD Road, follows the road a short distance south, then goes down Lathrop Canyon Road to the Colorado River, another four miles with a descent of 500 feet. Total distance for the strenuous hike is nine miles one-way, with an elevation change of 2,100 feet. The trail has little shade and can be very hot.

◖ Mesa Arch Trail

This easy trail leads to a dramatic arch that rises on the rim of a sheer 800-foot cliff. You'll marvel as to how this arch has survived at all in its precarious location (and gasp as adventurers climb the precipitous arch for photos). The

© W.C. MCRAE

An easy trail in Canyonlands' Island in the Sky District leads to Mesa Arch.

trailhead is on the left 5.5 miles from the neck. On the way, the road crosses the grasslands and scattered juniper trees of Gray's Pasture. A trail brochure, available at the start, describes the ecology of the mesa. Hiking distance is only a half-mile round-trip with an 80-foot elevation change. The arch, eroded from Navajo sandstone, frames views of rock formations below and the La Sal Mountains in the distance.

Murphy Point

Go straight at the road junction just past the Mesa Arch Trailhead for these and other spectacular viewpoints. After 2.5 miles, a rough dirt road turns right 1.7 miles to Murphy Point. Hikers can take **Murphy Trail,** which begins off the road to the point, to White Rim 4WD Road. This strenuous route forks partway down; one branch follows Murphy Hogback (a ridge) to Murphy Campground on the four-wheel drive road, and the other branch follows a wash to the road one mile south of the campground. A loop hike along both branches is nine miles round-trip with an elevation change of 1,100 feet.

◖ Grand View Point

Continue 2.5 miles on the main road past the Murphy Point turnoff to **Grand View Picnic Area,** a handy lunch stop. Two trails start here. **White Rim Overlook Trail** is an easy 1.5-mile hike (round-trip) east along a peninsula to an overlook of Monument Basin and beyond. **Gooseberry Trail** drops off the mesa and descends some extremely steep grades to the White Rim 4WD Road just north of Gooseberry Campground; the strenuous trip is 2.5 miles one-way with an elevation change of 1,400 feet.

Continue one mile on the main road past the picnic area to Grand View Point, perhaps the most spectacular panorama from Island in the Sky. Monument Basin lies directly below, and countless canyons, the Colorado River, the Needles, and mountain ranges are in the distance. **Grand View Trail** continues past the

© W. C. MCRAE

Grand View Point overlooks nearly all of the park.

end of the road for other vistas from the point, which is the southernmost tip of Island in the Sky. The easy hike is 1.5 miles round-trip.

Green River Overlook

Return to the road junction, turn west a quarter mile, then turn south 1.5 miles on an unpaved road to the overlook. Soda Springs Basin and a section of the Green River (deeply entrenched in Stillwater Canyon) can be seen below. Small **Willow Flat campground** is passed on the way to the overlook; it's open year-round (no water; $10 charge). Rangers present campfire programs here spring through autumn. Sites often fill except in winter; a sign near the visitors center indicates when they're full.

Aztec Butte Trail

The trailhead is on the right one mile northwest of the road junction. Aztec Butte is one of the few areas at Island in the Sky with Native American ruins; shortage of water prevented permanent settlement. An easy trail climbs 200

feet in half a mile to the top of the butte for a good panorama of the Island.

Whale Rock

The trailhead is on the right 4.4 miles northwest of the road junction. An easy trail climbs this sandstone hump near the outer rim of Upheaval Dome. Distance is a half mile round-trip with an ascent of 100 feet.

Upheaval Dome

Continue to the end of the road, 5.3 miles northwest of the road junction, for a look at this geological curiosity. There's also a small **picnic area** here. The easy **Crater View Trail** leads to overlooks on the rim of Upheaval Dome; the first viewpoint is a half mile round-trip, the second a one mile round-trip. A fantastically deformed pile of rock lies below within a crater about three miles across and 1,200 feet deep. For many years, Upheaval Dome has kept geologists busy trying to figure out its origin. They once assumed that salt of the Paradox Formation pushed the rock layers upward to form the dome. Now, however, there is strong evidence that a meteorite impact caused the structure. The surrounding ring depression (caused by collapse) and the convergence of rock layers upward toward the center correspond precisely to known impact structures. Shatter cones and microscopic analysis also indicate an impact origin. When the meteorite struck, sometime in the last 150 million years, it formed a crater up to five miles across. Erosion removed some of the overlying rock, perhaps as much as a vertical mile. The underlying salt may have played a role in uplifting the central section.

Energetic hikers can reach Upheaval Dome from the parking area at the overlook or from White Rim 4WD Road below. **Syncline Loop Trail** makes a strenuous eight-mile circuit completely around Upheaval Dome; elevation change is 1,200 feet. The trail crosses Upheaval Dome Canyon about halfway around from the overlook; walk east 1.5 miles up the canyon to enter the crater itself. This is the only nontechnical route into the center of the dome. A hike around Upheaval Dome with a side trip to the crater totals 11 miles; it's best done as an overnight trip. Carry plenty of water for the entire trip; this dry country can be very hot in summer. The Green River is the only reliable source of water. From near Upheaval Campsite on White Rim 4WD Road, you can hike four miles on **Upheaval Trail** through Upheaval Canyon to a junction with the Syncline Loop Trail, then another 1.5 miles into the crater; elevation gain is about 600 feet.

Alcove Spring Trail

Another hiking possibility in the area, the Alcove Spring Trail leaves the road 1.5 miles before the Upheaval Dome parking area and connects with White Rim 4WD Road in Taylor Canyon. Total distance is 10 miles one-way (five miles on the trail in Trail Canyon and five miles on a jeep road in Taylor Canyon); elevation change is about 1,500 feet. Carry plenty of water—the strenuous trail is hot and dry.

White Rim Four-Wheel Drive Road

This driving adventure follows the White Rim below the sheer cliffs of Island in the Sky. Travel along the winding road presents a constantly changing panorama of rock, canyons,

river, and sky. Keep an eye out for desert bighorn sheep. You'll see all three levels of Island in the Sky District, from the high plateaus to the White Rim to the rivers. Only four-wheel drive vehicles with high clearance can make the trip. With the proper vehicle, driving is mostly easy but slow and winding; a few steep or rough sections have to be negotiated. The 100-mile trip takes 2–3 days. Allow an extra day to travel all the road spurs. Mountain bikers find this a great trip, too; most cyclists arrange an accompanying vehicle to carry water and camping gear. Primitive campgrounds along the way provide convenient stopping places. Obtain reservations and a backcountry permit for the White Rim campsites from the Island in the Sky visitors center; this can be done in person, by mail from the park headquarters in Moab, or by phone (435/259-4351, Mon.–Sat. 12:30–4:30 P.M.). Demand exceeds supply during the popular spring and autumn seasons, when you should make reservations as far in advance as possible. A $25 fee per reservation applies for White Rim trips. No services or developed water sources exist anywhere on the drive, so be sure to have plenty of fuel and water with some to spare. Access points

© W. C. MCRAE

The White Rim Four-Wheel Drive Road snakes along the base of the Island in the Sky.

are Shafer Trail Road (from near Island in the Sky) and Potash Road (Hwy. 279 from Moab) on the east and Mineral Bottom Road on the west. White Rim sandstone forms the distinctive plateau crossed on the drive. A close look at the rock reveals ripple marks and crossbeds laid down near an ancient coastline. The plateau's east side is about 800 feet above the Colorado River. On the west side, the plateau meets the bank of the Green River.

MAZE DISTRICT

Only adventurous and experienced travelers will want to visit this rugged land west of the Green and Colorado Rivers. Vehicle access wasn't even possible until 1957, when mineral-exploration roads first entered what later became Canyonlands National Park. Today, you'll need a high-clearance four-wheel drive vehicle, a horse, or your own two feet to get around. The National Park Service plans to keep this district in its remote and primitive condition. An airplane flight, recommended if you can't come overland, provides the only easy way to see the scenic features here. However, the National Park Service is currently studying the future of such flights and they may be curtailed or discontinued. The names of erosional forms describe the landscape—Orange Cliffs, Golden Stairs, the Fins, Land of Standing Rocks, Lizard Rock, the Doll House, Chocolate Bars, the Maze, and Jasper Canyon. The many-fingered canyons of the Maze gave the district its name. Although not a true maze, these canyons give that impression.

Ranger Station and Information

Glen Canyon National Recreation Area borders the Maze District on the west with scenic canyons, cliffs, rock monuments, and overlooks of its own. The **Hans Flat Ranger Station** (435/259-2652, 8 A.M.–4:30 P.M. daily) for the Maze District lies inside Glen Canyon NRA. (In winter the station may close, but a ranger is usually available.) *There are no developed sources of water in the Maze District.* Hikers can obtain water from springs in some canyons (check with a ranger to find which are

flowing) or from the rivers; purify all water before drinking.

The Maze District has nine camping areas (two at Maze Overlook, seven at Land of Standing Rocks) with a 15-person, three-vehicle limit. A backcountry permit is needed for these or for backpacking. Note that a backcountry permit in this district is *not* a reservation—you may have to share a site with someone else, especially in the popular spring months. Also, as in the rest of the park, only designated sites can be used for vehicle camping. You don't need a permit to camp in the Glen Canyon NRA or on BLM land.

The Trails Illustrated topo map of the Maze District describes and shows the few roads and trails here; some routes and springs are marked on it, too. Agile hikers experienced in desert and canyon travel may want to take off on cross-country routes, which are either unmarked or lightly cairned. Extra care must be taken for preparation and travel in both Glen Canyon NRA and the Maze. Always talk with the rangers beforehand to find out current conditions. Be sure to leave an itinerary with someone reliable who can contact the rangers if you're overdue. Unless the rangers know where to look for you in case of breakdown or accident, a rescue could take weeks.

Dirt roads to the Hans Flat Ranger Station and Maze District branch off from Hwy. 24 (a half mile south of the Goblin Valley State Park turnoff) and Hwy. 95 (take Hite/Orange Cliffs Road between the Dirty Devil and Hite Bridges at Lake Powell). The easiest way in is the graded 46-mile road from Hwy. 24; it's fast, though sometimes badly corrugated. The Hite Road (also called Orange Cliffs Road) is longer, bumpier, and, for some drivers, tedious; it's 54 miles from the turnoff at Hwy. 95 to the Hans Flat Ranger Station via the Flint Trail. In winter or other times when the Flint Trail is closed, drivers must take Hite Road to reach the Maze Overlook, Land of Standing Rocks, and the Doll House areas. All roads to the Maze District cross Glen Canyon National Recreation Area. From Hwy. 24, two-wheel drive vehicles with good clearance can travel to Hans Flat Ranger Station and other areas near, but not actually in, the Maze District. (All the mileages given here come from the author's vehicle—they're not always the same as signs.)

North Point

Hans Flat Ranger Station, and this peninsula that reaches out to the east and north, lie at an elevation of about 6,400 feet. Panoramas from North Point take in the vastness of Canyonlands, including all three districts. From **Millard Canyon Overlook,** just 0.9 mile past the ranger station, you can see arches, Cleopatra's Chair, and features as distant as the La Sals and Book Cliffs. For the best views, drive out to Panorama Point, about 10.5 miles one-way from the ranger station. A spur road goes left two miles to Cleopatra's Chair, a massive sandstone monolith and area landmark. The trailhead for **North Trail Canyon** begins just down North Point Road (or 2.4 miles from the ranger station). Two-wheel drive vehicles can usually reach this spot, where hikers can follow the trail down seven miles (1,000-foot elevation change) through the Orange Cliffs, follow four-wheel drive roads six miles to the Maze Overlook Trail, then one more mile into a canyon of the Maze. Because North Point belongs to the Glen Canyon NRA, you can camp on it without a permit.

Flint Trail

This narrow, rough, four-wheel drive road connects the Hans Flat area with the Maze Overlook, Doll House, and other areas below. The road, driver, and vehicle should all be in good condition before driving it. Winter snow and mud close the road late December–March, as can rainstorms anytime. Check conditions first with a ranger. If you're starting from the top, stop at the signed overlook just before the descent to scout for vehicles headed up (the Flint Trail has very few places to pass). The top of the Flint Trail is 14 miles south of Hans Flat Ranger Station; at the bottom, 2.8 nervous miles later, you can turn left two miles to the Golden Stairs Trailhead or 12.7 miles to the

Maze Overlook; keep straight 28 miles to the Doll House or 39 miles to Hwy. 95.

The Golden Stairs

Hikers can descend this steep two-mile (one-way) foot trail to the Land of Standing Rocks Road in a fraction of the time it takes for drivers to follow roads. The trail offers good views of Ernies Country and the Fins but lacks shade or water. The upper trailhead is east two miles from the road junction at the bottom of the Flint Trail.

Maze Overlook

Now you're actually in Canyonlands National Park and at the edge of the sinuous canyons of the Maze. You can stay at primitive camping areas (backcountry permit needed) and enjoy the views. **Maze Overlook Trail** drops one mile into the South Fork of Horse Canyon; a rope helps to lower packs in a difficult section. Once in the canyon you can walk around to the Harvest Scene, a group of prehistoric pictographs, or do a variety of day hikes or backpacks. These canyons have water in some places; check with the ranger when getting your permits. At least four routes connect with the four-wheel drive road in Land of Standing Rocks (see the Trails Illustrated map). Hikers can also climb Petes Mesa from the canyons or head downstream to explore Horse Canyon (a dry fall blocks access to the Green River, however).

Land of Standing Rocks

Here, in the heart of the Maze District, strange-shaped rock spires stand guard over myriad canyons. Six camping areas offer scenic places to stay (permit needed). Hikers have a choice of many ridge and canyon routes from the four-wheel drive road, a trail to a confluence overlook, and a trail that descends to the Colorado River near Cataract Canyon. The well-named Chocolate Bars can be reached by a hiking route from the Wall near the beginning of the Land of Standing Rocks. A good day hike makes a loop from Chimney Rock to the Harvest Scene pictographs; take the ridge route (toward Petes Mesa) one direction and the canyon fork northwest of Chimney Rock the other. Follow your topo map through the canyons and the cairns between the canyons and ridge. Other routes from Chimney Rock lead to lower Jasper Canyon (no river access) or into Shot and Water Canyons and on to the Green River. Tall, rounded rock spires near the end of the road reminded early visitors of dolls, hence the name Doll House. The Doll House makes a delightful place to explore in itself, or you can head out on routes and trails. **Spanish Bottom Trail** begins here, then drops steeply to Spanish Bottom beside the Colorado River in 1.2 miles (one-way); a thin trail leads downstream into Cataract Canyon and the first of a long series of rapids. **Surprise Valley Overlook Trail** branches right off the Spanish Bottom Trail after about 300 feet and winds south past some dolls to a T junction (turn right for views of Surprise Valley, Cataract Canyon, and beyond); the trail ends at some well-preserved granaries; 1.5 miles one-way. The **Colorado/Green River Overlook Trail** heads north five miles (one-way) from the Doll House to a viewpoint of the confluence. See the area's Trails Illustrated map for routes, trails, and roads.

Getting to the Land of Standing Rocks takes some careful driving, especially on a three-mile stretch above Teapot Canyon. The many washes and small canyon crossings here make for slow going. Short-wheelbase vehicles have the easiest time, as usual. The turnoff for Land of Standing Rocks Road is 6.6 miles from the junction at the bottom of the Flint Trail via a wash shortcut (add about three miles if driving via the four-way intersection).

HORSESHOE CANYON UNIT

This canyon contains exceptional prehistoric rock art in a separate section of Canyonlands National Park. Ghostly life-size pictographs in the Great Gallery provide an intriguing look into the past. Archaeologists think that the images had religious importance, although the meaning of the figures remains unknown. The Barrier Canyon style of these drawings has been credited to an archaic Native American culture beginning at least 8,000 years ago

and lasting until about A.D. 450. Horseshoe Canyon also contains rock art left by the subsequent Fremont and Anasazi. The relation between the earlier and later prehistoric groups hasn't been determined.

Great Gallery

Horseshoe Canyon lies northwest of the Maze District. Two moderately difficult trails and a very rough jeep road lead down the canyon walls. In dry weather, cars with good clearance can be driven to a trailhead on the west rim. To reach this trailhead from Hwy. 24, drive to a junction a half mile south of Goblin Valley State Park turnoff, then turn east 30 miles on a dirt road (keep left at the Hans Flat Ranger Station/Horseshoe Canyon turnoff 25 miles in). From the rim, the trail descends 800 feet in one mile on an old jeep road, now closed to vehicles. At the canyon bottom, turn right two miles upstream to the Great Gallery. The sandy canyon floor is mostly level; trees provide shade in some areas.

A four-wheel drive road goes north 21 miles from Hans Flat Ranger Station and drops steeply into the canyon from the east side. The descent on this road is so rough that most people prefer to park on the rim and hike the last mile of road. A vehicle barricade prevents driving right up to the rock-art panel, but the 1.5-mile walk is easy. A branch off the jeep road goes to the start of **Deadman's Trail** (1.5 miles one-way), which is less used and more difficult.

Look for other rock art along the canyon walls on the way to the Great Gallery. Take care not to touch any of the drawings; they're very fragile as well as irreplaceable. (The oil from your hands will remove the paint.) Horseshoe Canyon also offers pleasant scenery and spring wildflowers. Carry plenty of water. Neither camping nor pets are allowed in the canyon, but you can stay on the rim. Contact the Hans Flat Ranger Station or the Moab office for road and trail conditions.

NEEDLES DISTRICT

The Needles District showcases some of the finest rock sculptures in Canyonlands National

Park. Spires, arches, or monoliths appear in almost any direction you look. Prehistoric ruins and rock art exist in greater variety and quantity than elsewhere in the park. Year-round springs and streams bring greenery to the desert. A paved road, several four-wheel drive roads, and many hiking trails offer a variety of ways to explore the Needles.

Needles Outpost

A general store just outside the park boundary offers a campground ($12 tent or RV without hookups), groceries, ice, gas, propane, snack bar, showers, jeep rentals and tours, and scenic flights. Call or write ahead, if possible, to arrange for jeep tours and scenic flights (P.O. Box 1107, Monticello, UT 84535, 435/979-4007). The season at Needles Outpost is mid-March–late October. Turnoff from Hwy. 211 is one mile before the Needles visitors center.

Visitors Center

Stop here (435/259-4711, 8 A.M.–5 P.M. daily) to find out about hiking, back roads, and other aspects of travel in the Needles. The staff has backcountry permits (required for all overnight stays in the backcountry), maps, brochures, and books. A $10 per vehicle charge is made unless you have a receipt issued within the last seven days from Island in the Sky of Canyonlands. Outside of office hours, get information at the bulletin board. To reach the Needles District, go 40 miles south from Moab (or 14 miles north of Monticello), turn west on Hwy. 211, and continue 38 miles.

Scenic Drive

The main road continues 6.5 miles past the visitors center to Big Spring Canyon Overlook. On the way, you can stop at several nature trails, turn off on four-wheel drive roads, or take short spur roads to trailheads and Squaw Flat Campground.

Roadside Ruin is on the left 0.4 mile past the visitors center. A one-third-mile loop trail goes near a well-preserved granary left by Anasazi. A trail guide available at the start tells about the Anasazi and the local plants.

POTHOLE ECOSYSTEMS

At Canyonlands it's easy to be in awe of the deep canyons and big desert rivers. But the little details of Canyonlands geology and ecology are pretty wonderful, too. Consider the potholes: shallow depressions dusted with wind-blown dirt. These holes, which range from less than an inch to several feet deep, fill after rainstorms and bring entire little ecosystems to life.

Pothole dwellers must be able to survive long periods of dryness, and then pack as much living as possible into the short wet periods. Some creatures, like the tadpole shrimp, live for only a couple of weeks. Others, like the spadefoot toad, hatch from drought-resistant eggs when water is present, quickly pass through the critical tadpole stage, then move onto dry land, returning to mate and lay eggs in potholes.

Though pothole dwellers are tough enough to survive in a dormant form during the long dry spells, most are very sensitive to sudden water chemistry changes, temperature changes, sediment input, being stepped on, and being splashed out onto dry land. Humans should never use pothole water for swimming, bathing, or drinking, as this can change the salinity or pH of a pool drastically. Organisms are unable to adapt to these human-generated changes, which occur suddenly, unlike slow, natural changes. While the desert pothole ecosystems may seem unimportant, they act as an indicator of the health of the larger ecosystems in which they occur.

Cave Spring Trail introduces the geology and ecology of the park and goes to an old cowboy line camp. Turn left 0.7 mile past the visitors center and follow signs about one mile to the trailhead. Pick up the brochure at the beginning. The 0.6-mile loop goes clockwise, crossing some slickrock; two ladders assist on the steep sections. Cowboys used the cave as a line camp from the late 1800s until establishment of the park in 1964; the line camp is just 50 yards in from the trailhead.

A road to **Squaw Flat Campground** and **Elephant Hill** turns left 2.7 miles past the ranger station. The campground, about a half mile in from the main road, has water and charges a $10 fee mid-March–September; it's open the rest of the year with no water or fee (water can be obtained year-round at the visitors center). Rangers present evening programs at the campfire circle on Loop A from spring through autumn. A **picnic area** is at the base of Elephant Hill, three miles past the campground turnoff and on the scenic drive. Hiking trails lead into wonderful rock forms and canyons from both the campground and picnic areas. Only experienced drivers in four-wheel drive vehicles should continue past the picnic area up Elephant Hill.

Pothole Point Nature Trail is on the left of the main road 5 miles past the visitors center. Highlights of this 0.6-mile loop hike are the many potholes dissolved in the Cedar Mesa sandstone. A brochure illustrates the fairy shrimp, tadpole shrimp, horsehair worm, snail, and other adaptable creatures that spring to life when rains fill the potholes. You'll also enjoy fine views of distant buttes from the trail.

Slickrock Trail begins on the right 6.2 miles past the visitors center. The trail makes a loop of 2.4 miles round-trip and takes you north to an overlook of the confluence of Big Spring and Little Spring Canyons. Hiking is easy and offers good panoramas.

Big Spring Canyon Overlook, 6.5 miles past the visitors center, marks the end of the scenic drive but not the scenery. The **Confluence Overlook Trail** begins here and winds west to an overlook of the Green and Colorado Rivers (see *Confluence Overlook Trail*).

Hiking

The Needles District has about 55 miles of backcountry trails. Many interconnect to provide all sorts of day and overnight trips. Cairns mark the trails; signs point the way at junctions. You can normally find water in upper Elephant Canyon and canyons to the east in

tromping through the desert in the Needles District

© PAUL LEVY

spring and early summer, though the remaining water often becomes stagnant by midsummer. Always ask the rangers about sources of water—don't depend on its availability. Treat water from all sources, including springs, before drinking. Chesler Park and other areas west of Elephant Canyon are very dry; bring all water. Mosquitoes, gnats, and deer flies can be very pesky from late spring to midsummer, especially in the wetter places—bring insect repellent. To plan your trip, obtain the small hiking map available from the visitors center, Trails Illustrated's Needles District map, or USGS topo maps.

Confluence Overlook Trail

This trail goes west 5.5 miles from Big Spring Canyon Overlook (at the end of the scenic drive) to a fine viewpoint overlooking the Green and Colorado Rivers 1,000 feet below. You might see rafts in the water or bighorn sheep on the cliffs. The trail crosses Big Spring and Elephant Canyons and follows a jeep road for a short distance. Higher points have good views of the Needles to the south. Except for a few short steep sections, this trail is level and fairly easy. A very early start is recommended in summer, as there's little shade. Carry water even if you don't plan to go all the way—this enchanting country has lured many a hiker beyond his or her original goal!

Hikes from Squaw Flat Trailhead

The main trailhead sits a short distance south of the campground and is reached by a separate signed road. You can also begin from a trailhead in the campground itself.

Peekaboo Trail winds southeast five miles (one-way) over rugged terrain, including some steep sections of slickrock (best avoided when wet, icy, or covered with snow). There's little shade; carry water. The trail follows Squaw Canyon, climbs over a pass to Lost Canyon, then crosses more slickrock before descending to Peekaboo Campground on Salt Creek 4WD Road. Look for Anasazi ruins on the way and rock art at the campground. A rockslide took out Peekaboo Spring, shown on some maps.

Options on this trail include a turnoff south through Squaw Canyon or Lost Canyon to make a loop of 8.75 miles or more.

Squaw Canyon Trail follows the canyon south for 3.75 miles one-way. Intermittent water can often be found until late spring. You can take a connecting trail (Peekaboo, Lost Canyon, and Big Spring Canyon) or cross a slickrock pass to Elephant Canyon.

Lost Canyon Trail, 3.25 miles one-way, is reached via Peekaboo or Squaw Canyon Trail and makes a loop with them. Water supports abundant vegetation; you may need to wade. Most of the way is in the wash bottom, except for a section of slickrock to Squaw Canyon.

Big Spring Canyon Trail crosses an outcrop of slickrock from the trailhead, then follows the canyon bottom to the head of the canyon, 3.75 miles one-way. You can usually find intermittent water along the way except in summer. At canyon's end, a climb up steep slickrock (hazardous if covered by snow or ice) takes you to Squaw Canyon Trail and back to the trailhead for a good 7.5-mile loop. Another possibility is to turn southwest to the head of Squaw Canyon, then hike over a slickrock saddle to Elephant Canyon for a 10.5-mile loop.

Hikes from Elephant Hill Trailhead

Drive west three miles past the campground turnoff to the picnic area and trailhead at the base of Elephant Hill. Sounds of racing engines and burning rubber can often be heard from above as vehicles attempt the difficult four-wheel drive road that begins just past the picnic area. All of the following destinations can also be reached by trails from the Squaw Flat Trailhead, though distances will be slightly greater.

Chesler Park is a favorite hiking destination. A lovely desert meadow contrasts with the red and white spires that gave the Needles District its name. An old cowboy line camp is on the west side of the rock island in the center of the park. Distance on **Chesler Park Trail** is about six miles round-trip. The trail winds through sand and slickrock before ascending a small pass through the Needles to

Chesler Park. Once inside, **Chesler Park Loop Trail** (five miles) circles completely around the park. The loop includes the unusual half-mile **Joint Trail,** which follows the bottom of a very narrow crack. Camping in Chesler Park is restricted to certain areas; check with a ranger.

Druid Arch reminds many people of the massive stone slabs at Stonehenge, popularly associated with the druids, in southern England. The arch is an 11-mile round-trip (15 miles if you start at Squaw Flat Trailhead). Follow the Chesler Park Trail two miles to Elephant Canyon, turn up the canyon 3.5 miles, then make a quarter-mile climb to the arch. Upper Elephant Canyon has seasonal water, but the narrow canyon is closed to camping.

Lower Red Lake Canyon Trail provides access to Cataract Canyon of the Colorado River. This is a long, strenuous trip best suited for experienced hikers and completed in two days. Distance from the Elephant Hill Trailhead is 19 miles round-trip; you'll be walking on four-wheel drive roads and trails. If you can drive Elephant Hill 4WD Road to the trail junction in Cyclone Canyon, the hike is only eight miles round-trip. The most difficult trail section is a steep talus slope that drops 700 feet in a half mile into the lower canyon. Total elevation change is 1,000 feet. The canyon has little shade and lacks any water source above the river. Summer heat can make the trip grueling; temperatures tend to be 5–10 degrees hotter than on other Needles trails. The river level drops between midsummer and autumn, allowing hikers to go along the shore both downstream to see the rapids and upstream to the confluence. Undertows and strong currents make the river dangerous to cross.

Upper Salt Creek Trail

Several impressive arches and many inviting side canyons attract adventurous hikers to the extreme southeast corner of the park. The trail begins at the end of the 13.5-mile four-wheel drive road up Salt Creek, then goes south 12 miles upcanyon to Cottonwood Canyon/Beef Basin Road near Cathedral Butte, just outside the park boundary. The trail is nearly level except for a steep climb at the end. Water can usually be found. Some wading and bushwhacking may be necessary. The famous "All American Man" pictograph, shown on some topo maps (or ask a ranger), is in a cave a short way off to the east at about the midpoint of the trail; follow your map and unsigned paths to the cave but don't climb in—it's dangerous to both you and the ruins and pictograph inside. Many more archaeological sites can be discovered near the trail; they're all fragile and need great care when visited.

Four-Wheel Drive Roads

A back-road tour allows you to see beautiful canyon scenery, arches, and Native American rock-art sites in the Needles District. Check with a ranger about special hazards before setting out. Also obtain a backcountry permit ($30 per vehicle) if you plan to use one of the campgrounds available along Salt Creek or in the area past Elephant Hill. Mountain bikers enjoy the challenge of going up Elephant Hill Road and the roads beyond. Colorado Overlook 4WD Road is good riding, too, but Salt Creek and the other eastern canyons have too much loose sand.

Salt Creek Canyon 4WD Road begins near Cave Spring Trail, crosses sage flats for the next 2.5 miles, then heads deep into this spectacular canyon. Round-trip distance, including a side trip to 150-foot-high Angel Arch, is 26 miles. Agile hikers can follow a steep slickrock route into the window of Angel Arch. You can also explore side canyons of Salt Creek or take the Upper Salt Creek Trail (the "All American Man" pictograph makes a good day-hike destination of 12 miles round-trip). **Horse Canyon 4WD Road** turns off to the left shortly before the mouth of Salt Canyon. Round-trip distance, including a side trip to Tower Ruin, is about 13 miles; other attractions include Paul Bunyan's Potty, Castle Arch, Fortress Arch, and side-canyon hiking. Salt and Horse Canyons can easily be driven in four-wheel drive vehicles. Usually Salt Canyon is closed due to quicksand after flash floods in summer and shelf ice in winter.

Four-wheel drive roads enter **Davis Canyon** and **Lavender Canyon** from Hwy. 211 east of the park boundary. Both canyons are accessed through Davis Canyon Road off Hwy. 211 and contain great scenery, arches, and Native American sites, and both are easily visited. Davis is about 20 miles round-trip and Lavender is about 26 miles round-trip. Try to allow plenty of time in either canyon, as there is much to see and many inviting side canyons to hike. You can camp on BLM land just outside the park boundaries—but not in the park itself.

Colorado Overlook 4WD Road begins beside the visitors center and follows Salt Creek to Lower Jump Overlook. Then it bounces across slickrock to a view of the Colorado River (upstream from the confluence). Driving is easy to moderate, though very rough the last 1.5 miles. Round-trip distance is 14 miles.

Elephant Hill 4WD Road begins three miles past the Squaw Flat Campground turnoff. Only experienced drivers with stout vehicles should attempt the extremely rough and steep climb up Elephant Hill (coming up the back side of El-

ephant Hill is even rougher). The loop is about 10 miles round-trip. Connecting roads go to the Confluence Overlook Trailhead (the viewpoint is one mile round-trip on foot), the Joint Trailhead (Chesler Park is two miles round-trip on foot), and several canyons. Some road sections on the loop are one-way. The parallel canyons in this area are grabens caused by faulting, where a layer of salt has shifted deep underground. In addition to Elephant Hill, a few other difficult spots must be negotiated. This area can also be reached by a long route south of the park using Cottonwood Canyon/Beef Basin Road from Hwy. 211, about 60 miles one-way. You'll enjoy spectacular vistas from the Abajo Highlands. Two *very* steep descents from Pappys Pasture into Bobbys Hole effectively make this section one-way; travel from Elephant Hill up Bobbys Hole is possible but much more difficult than going the other way and may require hours of road building. The Bobbys Hole route may be impassable at times—ask about conditions at the BLM office in Monticello or at the Needles visitors center.

Utah's Southeastern Corner

◖ NEWSPAPER ROCK HISTORICAL MONUMENT

At Newspaper Rock a profusion of petroglyphs depicts human figures, animals, birds, and abstract designs. These represent 2,000 years of human history during which archaic tribes and Anasazi, Fremont, Paiute, Navajo, and Anglo travelers have passed through Indian Creek Canyon. The patterns on the smooth sandstone rock face stand out clearly, thanks to a coating of dark desert varnish. Newspaper Rock lies just 150 feet off Hwy. 211 on the way to the Needles District of Canyonlands National Park. A quarter-mile nature trail introduces you to the area's desert and riparian vegetation. Picnic areas lie along Indian Creek across the highway. The park is relatively undeveloped; no drinking water or fee. From U.S. 191 between Moab and Monticello, turn west 10 miles on Hwy. 211.

Newspaper Rock preserves some of the richest and most fanciful prehistoric rock art in Utah.

© PAUL LEVY

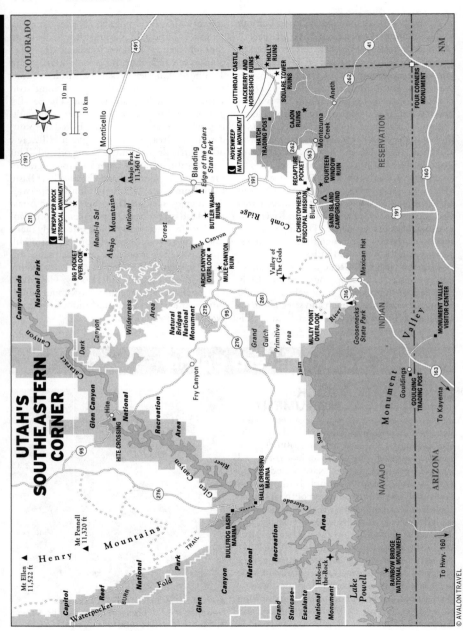

© AVALON TRAVEL

CANYON RIMS RECREATION AREA

Viewpoints atop the high mesa east of Canyonlands National Park offer magnificent panoramas of the surrounding area. The BLM has provided two fenced overlooks, two campgrounds, and good access roads. Other overlooks and scenic spots can be reached on jeep roads or by hiking. The 20-mile-long mesa, shown on maps as Hatch Point, features rock monoliths, canyons, slickrock, and rolling hills. You have a good chance of seeing the graceful antelope-like pronghorn that thrive in this high-desert country. The turnoff for Hatch Point of Canyon Rims is at milepost 93 on U.S. 191, 32 miles south of Moab and seven miles north of the Hwy. 211 junction for the Needles District. Canyon Rims Recreation Area has been greatly expanded recently to include surrounding BLM lands and the Beef Basin and Dark Canyon areas. Author and BLM volunteer Fran Barnes has written and published the large book *Canyon Country's Canyon Rims Recreation Area*, about exploring these areas. The book includes a 235-mile long "Canyon Rims Recreation Area Mountain Bike Challenge Route." For back-road travel in this area, you'll find Fran Barnes's book and separate map *Canyon Country Off-Road Vehicle Trails: Canyon Rims Recreation Area* very helpful. Cyclists will also find good info in Peggy and Bob Utesch's *Mountain Biking in Canyon Rims Recreation Area*. Also check out the website www.blm.gov/utah/moab/canyon_rims.html.

Needles Overlook

Follow the paved road 22 miles west to its end (turn left at the junction 15 miles in). The BLM has a picnic area and interpretive exhibits here. A fence protects visitors from the sheer cliffs that drop off more than 1,000 feet. You can see much of Canyonlands National Park and southeastern Utah. Look south for Six-Shooter Peaks and the high country of the Abajo Mountains; southwest for the Needles (thousands of spires reaching for the heavens); west for the confluence area of the Green and Colorado Rivers, the Maze District, the Orange Cliffs, and the Henry Mountains; northwest for the lazy bends of the Colorado River Canyon and the sheer-walled mesas of Island in the Sky and Dead Horse Point; north for the Book Cliffs; and northeast for the La Sal Mountains. The changing shadows and colors of the canyon country make for a continuous show throughout the day.

Anticline Overlook

Head west 15 miles on the paved road, then go straight (north) 17 miles on a good gravel road to the fenced overlook at road's end. Here you're standing 1,600 feet above the Colorado River. The sweeping panorama over the canyons, the river, and the twisted rocks of the Kane Creek Anticline is nearly as spectacular as that from Dead Horse Point, only 5.5 miles west as the crow flies. Salt and other minerals of the Paradox Formation pushed up overlying rocks into the dome visible below. Downcutting by the Colorado River has revealed the twisted rock layers. The Moab Salt Mine across the river to the north uses a solution technique to bring up potash from the Paradox Formation several thousand feet underground. Pumps then transfer the solution to the blue-tinted evaporation ponds. Look carefully on the northeast horizon to see an arch in the Windows Section of Arches National Park, 16 miles away.

You can reach **Pyramid Butte Overlook** by a gravel road that turns west off the main drive two miles before Anticline Overlook; the road goes around a rock monolith to viewpoints on the other side (1.3 miles round-trip). Vehicles with four-wheel drive can go west out to **Canyonlands Overlook** (17 miles round-trip) on rough unmarked roads. The turnoff, which may not be signed, is about 0.3 mile south of the Hatch Point Campground turnoff.

Campgrounds

Each camping area has water (mid-Apr.–mid-Oct.), tables, grills, and outhouses and charges a $10 fee. **Windwhistle Campground,** backed by cliffs to the south, has fine views to the north and a nature trail; follow the main road from U.S. 191 for six miles and turn left. At **Hatch Point Campground,** in a piñon-juniper woodland, you can enjoy views to the north. Go 24 miles in on the paved and gravel roads toward Anticline Overlook, then turn right one mile.

Trough Springs Trail

Hikers can follow this old livestock trail on the east side of Hatch Point. To reach the trailhead, turn east 0.6 mile on a dirt road five miles north of the Hatch Point Campground turnoff (or four miles south of Anticline Overlook). The trail begins from an abandoned well pad and follows the canyon to its mouth at Kane Creek Road. The first one-third mile follows a jeep road, then cairns mark the way. Carry water. The moderately difficult hike is five miles round-trip and has an elevation change of 1,200 feet.

Beef Basin

The rugged canyon country south of Canyonlands National Park's Needles District contains beautiful scenery, knock-out panoramas, and Anasazi pueblo ruins. You'll need a four-wheel drive, high-clearance vehicle, maps, camping gear, and emergency supplies to explore this remote region. Drive in from the east via County Road 104, or from the south over the Abajo Highlands of the Manti–La Sal National Forest. Although these approach roads are graded, high-clearance vehicles are still recommended. Snow and mud close the roads in winter and spring, especially from the Abajo Highlands. The Beef Basin Road drops from the forests into a series of grassy parks. Spur roads branch out to other canyons and parks and make a loop in Beef Basin.

Many Anasazi pueblos stand out in the open in Middle and Ruin Parks; others lie tucked into canyon alcoves. One road runs northwest past Ruin Park, makes two *very* steep and rough descents into Bobbys Hole, then continues to Elephant Hill in Canyonlands National Park. Only hard-core jeepers should consider this route into Canyonlands National Park. The road may be impassable in the reverse (uphill)

direction or totally impassable altogether; ask at the BLM office in Monticello or the Needles visitors center in the park.

Big Pocket Overlook

A rough jeep road branches north 2.5 miles from the Cottonwood Canyon/Beef Basin Road to spectacular panoramas of upper Salt and Lavender Canyons. Binoculars help to pick out natural arches and other details. The road, also good for hiking or mountain biking, makes a loop along the east side of this narrow peninsula. Although on BLM land, you'll be surrounded by some of the best views in the Needles District of Canyonlands National Park. A hiking trail into upper Salt Creek Canyon begins about one mile west of the Big Pocket Overlook turnoff.

MONTICELLO

This small Mormon town (pop. 1,900) is about 50 miles south of Moab and pretty much its polar opposite. Quiet and relatively non-touristy, it's the best place to stay if you're visiting the Needles District and don't want to camp. Monticello (pronounced mon-tuh-SELL-o) lies at an elevation of 7,050 feet just east of the Abajo Mountains. It's 46 miles east of the entrance to the Needles District of Canyonlands National Park.

Accommodations

Monticello has a number of comfortable and affordable motels. The **Best Western Wayside Inn** (197 E. Central St., 435/587-2261 or 800/633-9700, www.bestwestern.com, $73–80) is an easy place to land after a day of hiking, and it has a pool. The Monticello Inn (164 E. Central, 435/587-2274 or 800/657-6622, www.themonticelloinn.com, $55 and up) is a quiet and well-maintained older motel away from the main highway, with very clean rooms and a pleasant setting.

Food

Not only can you get a good cup of coffee and freshly made juice at **Peace Tree Juice Café** (516 N. Main, 435/587-5063, 9 A.M.–5 P.M.

daily, $4–9), but this is the only place this side of Moab that you're likely to get a vegetarian Thai wrap sandwich (and have it taste really good). You'll also find Internet access at this bright and cheery place.

More typical for the area, and a good bet for a big breakfast or dinner, is **MD Ranch Cookhouse** (380 S. Main, 435/587-3299, three meals daily, $6–22), where the Western atmosphere is a part of the appeal. The cowboy cooking is good, too, and includes steaks and buffalo.

Information and Services

The **San Juan County Multi-Agency Visitors Center** (117 S. Main, 435/587-3235 or 800/574-4386, www.southeastutah.com, 8 A.M.–5 P.M. Mon.–Fri. and 10 A.M.–5 P.M. Sat.–Sun. Apr.–Oct., 9 A.M.–5 P.M. Mon.–Fri. Nov.–Mar.) is on the side of the courthouse.

BLANDING

The largest town in San Juan County, Blanding (pop. 3,520) is also a handy travelers' stop. The state park on the northwest edge of town provides an excellent introduction to the Anasazi, who left behind many ruins in the Four Corners area. Mormon pioneers began work on an irrigation system in 1897 to bring water from the Abajo Mountains to the rich soil of White Mesa. The first families arrived at the town site, then known as Sidon, in 1905.

Edge of the Cedars State Park

Prehistoric Anasazi built at least six groups of pueblo structures between A.D. 700 and 1220 one mile north of present-day Blanding. The state park and museum (660 West 400 North, 435/678-2238, 9 A.M.–6 P.M. daily May 16–Sept. 15, 9 A.M.–5 P.M. daily the rest of the year, $3 per vehicle) features an excellent array of pottery, baskets, sandals, jewelry, and stone tools. The pottery collection on the second floor stands out for its rich variety of styles and decorative designs. The museum also has exhibits and artifacts of the people who followed the Anasazi—the Utes and Navajo and the early Anglo pioneers.

A short trail behind the museum leads past six clusters of ruins, each of which contains both rectangular rooms on the surface and circular depressions of underground kivas and pit houses. Only Complex 4 has been excavated and partly restored to give an idea of the village's appearance when the Anasazi lived here. You may enter the kiva by descending a ladder through the restored roof; the walls and interior features are original.

The Dinosaur Museum

This museum (754 South 200 West, 435/678-3454, 9 A.M.–5 P.M. Mon.–Sat. April 15–Oct. 15, $2 adults, $1 children and seniors) showcases the prehistoric plant and animal life of this corner of Utah. Exhibits include life-size models of dinosaurs as well as fossils and skeletons. Don't miss the History Hall of Hollywood Dinosaurs, which recounts the evolution of film's depictions of the thunder lizard.

Accommodations

The **Blanding Sunset Inn** (88 W. Center, 435/678-3323, $50 and up) is a good deal, with queen beds, cable TV, and a pool; pets allowed. The **Four Corners Inn** (131 E. Center, 435/678-3257 or 800/574-3150, $55 and up) has a restaurant, free continental breakfast, and children under 12 stay free. The **Comfort Inn** (711 S. U.S. 191, 435/678-3271 or 800/622-3250, $55 and up) has suites, guest laundry, indoor pool, hot tub, and exercise room. The area's newest lodging is the **Super 8** (755 S. Main, 435/678-3880 or 800/800-8000, $60 and up) has some family suites, some with three bedrooms. The **Gateway Inn** (88 E. Center, 435/678-2278 or 888/921-2279, $65 d) has an outdoor pool, complimentary breakfast, high speed Internet access and pets are welcome.

CAMPGROUNDS

At the south edge of town, **KamPark** (S. U.S. 191, 435/678-2770, $11 tent, $16 RV) has a store and showers; both tents and are RVs welcome. **Devil's Canyon Campground** ($11/night), elevation 7,100 feet, in the Manti–La Sal

National Forest has sites with water early May–late October (no water or fee off-season). A quarter-mile nature trail begins at the far end of the campground loop. Go north eight miles on U.S. 191, then west 1.3 miles on a paved road (turnoff is between mileposts 60 and 61).

Food

Yak's Center Street Café (140 N. U.S. 191, 435/678-2555, breakfast, lunch, and dinner Mon.–Sat., $5–17) is a long-time Blanding favorite (though in a new location) for good breakfasts and light meals. The best place for a full meal in an "Old West" setting is the **Old Tymer Restaurant** (733 S. Main, 435/678-2122, breakfast, lunch, and dinner, $10–18), with sandwiches, steak, prime rib, and chicken.

◙ HOVENWEEP NATIONAL MONUMENT

The Anasazi built many impressive masonry buildings during the early to mid-1200s, near the end of their 1,300-year stay in the area. A 25-year drought beginning in A.D. 1274 probably hastened their migration from this area. Several centuries of intensive farming, hunting, and woodcutting had already taken their toll on the land. Archaeologists believe the inhabitants retreated south in the late 1200s to sites in northwestern New Mexico and northeastern Arizona. The Ute word Hovenweep means "deserted valley," an appropriate name for the lonely high-desert country left behind. The Anasazi at Hovenweep had much in common with the Mesa Verde culture, though the Dakota sandstone here doesn't form large alcoves suitable for cliff-dweller villages. Ruins at Hovenweep remain essentially unexcavated, awaiting some future archaeologist's trowel.

The Anasazi farmers had a keen interest in the seasons because of their need to know the best time for planting crops. Astronomical stations (alignments of walls, doorways, and tiny openings) allowed the sun priests to determine the equinoxes and solstices with an accuracy of one or two days. This precision also may have been necessary for a complex ceremonial calendar. Astronomical stations at Hovenweep have been discovered at Hovenweep Castle and Unit-Type House of Square Tower Ruins and at Cajon Ruins.

Visitors Center

Hovenweep National Monument protects six groups of villages left behind by the Anasazi. The sites lie near the Colorado border southeast of Blanding. Square Tower Ruins Unit, where the visitors center is, has the greatest number of ruins and the most varied architecture. In fact, you can find all of the Hovenweep architectural styles here. The visitors center (970/749-0510, 8 A.M.–4:30 P.M. year-round, though the ruins are dawn–dusk year-round, $6 per vehicle or $3 per person) has a few exhibits on the Anasazi and photos of local wildlife. A ranger will answer your questions, provide brochures and handouts about various aspects of the monument, and give directions for visiting the other ruin groups. There's also a small campground at the monument ($10, no reservations).

One approach from U.S. 191 between Blanding and Bluff is to head east nine miles on Hwy. 262, continue straight six miles on a small paved road to Hatch Trading Post, then follow signs 16 miles. A good way in from Bluff is to go east 21 miles on the paved road to Montezuma Creek and Aneth, then follow signs north 20 miles. A scenic 58-mile route through Montezuma Canyon begins five miles south of Monticello and follows unpaved roads to Hatch and on to Hovenweep; you can stop at the BLM's Three Turkey Ruin on the way. From Colorado, take a partly paved road west and north 41 miles from U.S. 491 (the turnoff is four miles south of Cortez).

Square Tower Ruins

This extensive group of Anasazi towers and dwellings lines the rim and slopes of Little Ruin Canyon, a short walk from the visitors center. Obtain a trail guide booklet from the ranger station; the booklet's map shows the several loop trails and has good descriptions of Anasazi life and architecture and of the plants growing along the trail. You'll see towers

(D-shaped, square, oval, and round), cliff dwellings, surface dwellings, storehouses, kivas, and rock art. Take care not to disturb the fragile ruins. Keep an eye out for the prairie rattlesnake (a subspecies of the western rattlesnake), which is active at night in summer and during the day in spring and autumn. Please stay on the trail—don't climb ruin walls or walk on rubble mounds.

Other Ruins

You'll need a map and directions from a ranger to find the other Hovenweep ruins, as they aren't signed. One group, the Goodman Point, near Cortez, Colorado, has relatively little to see except unexcavated mounds.

Holly Ruins group is noted for its Great House, Holly Tower, and Tilted Tower. Most of Tilted Tower fell away after the boulder on which it sat shifted. Great piles of rubble mark the sites of structures built on loose ground. Look for remnants of farming terraces in the canyon below the Great House. A hiking trail connects the campground at Square Tower Ruins with Holly Ruins; the route follows canyon bottoms and is about eight miles round-trip. Hikers could also continue to Horseshoe Ruins (one mile farther) and Hackberry Ruins (one-third mile beyond Horseshoe). All of these lie just across the Colorado border and about six miles (one-way) by road from the visitors center.

Horseshoe Ruins and **Hackberry Ruins** are best reached by an easy trail (one mile round-trip) off the road to Holly Ruins. Horseshoe House, built in a horseshoe shape similar to Sun Temple at Mesa Verde, has exceptionally good masonry work. Archaeologists haven't determined the purpose of the structure. An alcove in the canyon below contains a spring and small shelter. A round tower nearby on the rim has a strategic view. Hackberry House has only one room still intact. Rubble piles and wall remnants abound in the area. The spring under an alcove here still has a good flow and supports lush growths of hackberry and cottonwood trees along with smaller plants.

Cutthroat Castle Ruins were remote even in Anasazi times. The ruins lie along an intermittent stream rather than at the head of a canyon like most other Hovenweep sites. Cutthroat Castle is a large multistory structure with both straight and curved walls. Three round towers stand nearby. Look for wall fragments and the circular depressions of kivas. High-clearance vehicles can go close to the ruins, about 11.5 miles (one-way) from the visitors center. Visitors with cars can drive to a trailhead and then walk to the ruins (1.5 miles round-trip on foot).

Cajon Ruins are at the head of a little canyon on Cajon Mesa in the Navajo Reservation in Utah, about nine miles southwest of the visitors center. The site has a commanding view across the San Juan Valley as far as Monument Valley. Buildings include a large multiroom structure, a round tower, and a tall square tower. An alcove just below has a spring and some rooms. Look for pictographs, petroglyphs, and grooves in rock (used for tool grinding). Farming terraces were located on the canyon's south side.

BLUFF

The 1880 Hole-in-the-Rock Expedition arrived here after an epic journey by wagon train from Escalante. Too tired to go any farther, they chose this section of the San Juan River Canyon in which to plant their fields and build new homes. They hoped that their presence here would secure the region for Mormon settlement and lead to conversion of the Native Americans. The settlers tried repeatedly to farm the fertile canyon soils, only to have the river wash their fields away. Most residents gave up and moved to more promising areas, but many of those who stayed prospered with large cattle herds.

Today Bluff is a sleepy community of about 300 inhabitants, nestled in a very striking physical location. Take the signed Bluff City Historic Loop to see pioneer houses along the back streets. Many visitors also drive to the cemetery atop a small hill to read inscriptions and enjoy views of the valley (turn in beside Turquoise RV Park, turn left just past the Decker Pioneer

House, and follow the paved road to the top). Native Americans from the Navajo Reservation across the river occasionally have dance performances, horse races, rodeos, and other get-togethers in Bluff.

In the past few years, Bluff has become a rather unlikely mecca for recreationists and escapees from urban congestion. The quality of lodging is better than almost any other town of this size in the state, and a growing number of outfitters make it easy to get out and enjoy the remarkable scenery hereabouts.

San Juan Footbridge and 14-Window Ruin

An easy walk of about two miles round-trip crosses a suspension bridge over the San Juan River and follows roads to this Anasazi cliff dwelling. From Bluff, drive east two miles on the paved road to St. Christopher's Episcopal Mission, continue straight 1.3 miles, and turn right a half mile on a dirt road (it may not be signed; keep right at a fork 0.1 mile in) to the footbridge. Walk across the bridge, follow dirt roads winding southeast about a half mile to a road running beneath the cliffs, turn right (west) a half mile, and look for the ruins in an alcove on the left. You can scramble up for a closer look, but don't enter the rooms—the ruins can easily be damaged. The walk passes farmlands on the Navajo Reservation; please resist the temptation to take shortcuts across the fields.

Floating the San Juan River

From the high San Juan Mountains in southern Colorado, this intriguing river winds its way into New Mexico, enters Utah near Four Corners, and twists through spectacular canyons before ending at Lake Powell. Sand waves spring up during flooding, usually in May and June. The waves can pop up out of flat water to heights of three feet and occasionally as much as seven or eight feet. Swift currents on the sandy bottom cause these harmless waves, which can migrate up or downstream before disappearing.

Below the town of Bluff, the muddy river picks up speed and dives deep within its canyon walls. Most boaters put in at Sand Island Campground near Bluff and take out at the town of Mexican Hat, 30 river miles downstream. This trip combines ancient Native American ruins, rock art, and a trip through Monument Upwarp and the Upper Canyon, with fast water for thrills (Class III rapids) and weirdly buckled geology to ponder. Longer trips continue on through the famous Goosenecks, the "entrenched meanders" carved thousands of feet below the desert surface, and through more Class III rapids on the way to Clay Hills Crossing or Paiute Farms (not always accessible) on Lake Powell. Allow at least four days for the full trip, though more time will allow exploration of side canyons and visits to Anasazi sites. Rafts, kayaks, and canoes can be used. The season now usually lasts year-round, because of Navajo Reservoir upstream.

Many commercial river-running companies offer San Juan trips. If you go on your own, you should have river-running experience or be with someone who does. Private groups need to obtain permits from the BLM San Juan Resource Area office (P.O. Box 7, Monticello, UT 84535, 435/587-2141) well in advance. The book *San Juan Canyons, A River Runner's Guide,* by Don Baars and Gene Stevenson, has a river log with detailed maps, practical advice, and background. Some people also like to run the river between Montezuma Creek and Sand Island, a leisurely trip of 20 river miles. The solitude often makes up for the lack of scenery. It's easy to get a river permit for this section because no use limits or fees apply.

If you're looking for a multiday trip on the San Juan, contact some of the larger Moab-based outfitters, who often offer a San Juan trip when interest allows. Or contact local **Wild Rivers Expeditions** (P.O. Box 118, Bluff, UT 84512, 435/672-2244 or 800/422-7654, www .riversandruins.com), which offers both day and multiday trips out of Bluff; trips run daily in summer and only a day's notice is usually needed to join a float. Eight-hour, 26-mile day excursions to Mexican Hat cost $150 adults,

$112 children 12 and under (motors may be used if water level is low). The office is on the main highway through town.

Accommodations

Attractive 【 **Desert Rose Inn** (701 W. Main St., 735/672-2303 or 888/475-7673, www .desertroseinn.com, $79 and up) is one of the nicest lodgings in all of southern Utah. The large, lodgelike log structure has two-story wraparound porches and rooms furnished with pine furniture, quilts, and Southwestern art. At the edge of the property are a number of handsome one-bedroom log cabins. Definitely a class act.

The other great place to stay is **Recapture Lodge** (220 E. Main St., P.O. Box 309, Bluff, UT 84512, 435/672-2281, $68 and up). For many years the heart and soul of Bluff, the lodge is operated by long-time outfitters and the lodge has an easy nonchalance that is immediately welcoming. Besides rooms and kitchenettes, Recapture Lodge has a swimming pool, hot tub, launderette, tours, and llama pack trips. You can also rent fully equipped homes in Bluff for families and groups.

The owners know of Native American ruins and scenic places in the backcountry. They offer free slide shows in the evenings during the season and can suggest places to go. Or you can take one of their organized full-day naturalist tours to Monument Valley, Comb Ridge, Recapture Pocket, and other locations. Guided camping trips can also be arranged in the canyon country of southeastern Utah. They also can provide a shuttle service for rafting trips.

Kokopelli Inn Motel (435/672-2322 or 800/541-8854, $55 and up), just next door, is a pleasant place to stay, though it pales in comparison to Bluff's unique lodges.

CAMPGROUNDS

Near the center of Bluff, **Cadillac Ranch R.V. Park** (U.S. 191, 435/672-2262 or 800/538-6195, $16) has RV hookups and tent sites. **Cottonwood R.V. Park** (U.S. 191, on the west end of Bluff, 435/672-2287, $11 tent, $16

RV) has both tent and RV sites. **Sand Island Recreation Area** is a primitive camping area along the San Juan River three miles south of town; large cottonwood trees shade this pretty spot. No drinking water or fee; tenters need to watch for thorns in the grass. River runners often put in at the campground. You can see a panel of pictographs along the cliff one-third mile downstream from the camping area along a gravel road.

Food

Cow Canyon Trading Post (435/672-2208, Thurs.–Mon. Apr.–Oct.) is a café that serves homemade dinners in an old trading post on the northeast edge of town. The trading post is open year-round with Native American crafts. **Twin Rocks Trading Post** (435/672-2341), just below the impossible-to-miss Twin Rocks, also has a cafe and a selection of high-quality Native American crafts, much of it produced locally by the Navajo.

WEST OF BLANDING

Hwy. 95 turns west from U.S. 191 four miles south of Blanding and crosses Comb Ridge, Cedar Mesa, and many canyons. Follow Hwy. 95 to Natural Bridges National Monument or continue on to Hite Marina, where a highway bridge crosses Lake Powell. Hwy. 261 turns south along Cedar Mesa before twisting down the hairpin curves of the Moki Dugway north of Mexican Hat (this section of the road is not paved).

Hwy. 276 turns off for Halls Crossing Marina and the car ferry across Lake Powell to Bullfrog Marina. At the junction of Hwys. 276 and 95, a large sign lists the departure times for the ferry service. Note that the times on the sign may be different than the times listed in the widely circulated flyer found in every tourist office. Confirm the departure times before making the 42-mile journey to Halls Crossing. For more information, see the sidebar *Crossing Lake Powell by Ferry* in the *The Escalante Region* chapter.

Fill up with gas before venturing out on Hwy. 95; you won't find any gas stations on the highway until Hanksville, which is 122 miles away. Hite and the other Lake Powell marinas do have gas and supplies, however.

Cedar Mesa and its canyons have an exceptionally large number of prehistoric Anasazi sites. Several groups of ruins lie just off the highway. Hikers will discover many more. If you would like to explore the Cedar Mesa area, drop in at the **Kane Gulch Ranger Station** (435/587-1532, 8 A.M.–noon daily, Mar.–mid.-Nov.) four miles south on Hwy. 261 from Hwy. 95. The BLM staff issues the permits required to explore the Cedar Mesa backcountry at $8 per person for overnight stays in Grand Gulch, Fish Creek Canyon, and Owl Creek Canyon. The number of people permitted to camp at a given time is limited, so call ahead. BLM people will also tell you about archaeological sites and their values, current hiking conditions, and locations of water. Day hikers will pay a $2 fee to hike certain sections of the monument. Check out www.blm.gov/utah/monticello for current information.

Butler Wash Ruins

Well-preserved pueblo ruins left by the Anasazi lie tucked under an overhang across the wash 11 miles west on Hwy. 95 (between mileposts 111 and 112) from U.S. 191. At the trailhead on the north side of the highway, follow cairns a half mile through juniper and piñon pine woodlands and across slickrock to the overlook.

Comb Ridge

Geologic forces have squeezed up the earth's crust in a long ridge running 80 miles south from the Abajo Peaks into Arizona. Sheer cliff faces plunge 800 feet into Comb Wash on the west side. Engineering the highway down these cliffs took considerable effort. A parking area near the top of the grade offers expansive panoramas across Comb Wash. The overlook is between mileposts 108 and 109, 2.5 miles west of Butler Wash Ruins. Scenic **jeep roads** between Hwy. 95 and U.S. 163 follow the west side of Comb Ridge through Comb Wash and the east side of Comb Ridge through Butler Wash. Another jeep road traces the route of the

1880 Mormon Hole-in-the-Rock Expedition between Hwy. 261 on Cedar Mesa and Comb Wash (a high-clearance vehicle is needed to go down, a four-wheel drive to go up).

Arch Canyon

This tributary canyon of Comb Wash has spectacular scenery and many Native American ruins. Much of the canyon can be seen on a day hike, but 2–3 days are needed to explore the upper reaches. The main streambeds usually have water (purify before drinking). To reach the trailhead, turn north 2.5 miles on a dirt road in Comb Wash (between mileposts 107 and 108 of Hwy. 95), go past a house and water tank, then park in a grove of cottonwood trees before a stream ford. This is also a good place to camp. The mouth of Arch Canyon lies just to the northwest (it's easy to miss!). Sign in at the register here. Look for a Native American ruin just up Arch Canyon on the right. More ruins lie tucked under alcoves farther upcanyon.

Arch Canyon Overlook

A road and short trail to the rim of Arch Canyon provide a beautiful view into the depths. Turn north four miles on Texas Flat Road (County 263) from Hwy. 95 between mileposts 102 and 103, park just before the road begins a steep climb, and walk east on an old jeep road about a quarter mile to the rim. This is a fine place for a picnic, although it has no facilities or guardrails. Texas Flat Road is dirt but okay when dry for cars with good clearance. Trucks can continue up the steep hill to other viewpoints of Arch and Texas Canyons.

Mule Canyon Ruin

Archaeologists have excavated and stabilized this Anasazi village on the gentle slope of Mule Canyon's South Fork. A stone kiva, circular tower, and 12-room structure can be seen, all originally connected by tunnels. Cave Towers, two miles to the southeast, would have been visible from the top of the tower here. Signs describe the ruin and periods of Anasazi development. Turn north 0.3 mile on a paved road from Hwy. 95 between mileposts 101 and 102. Hikers can explore other Native American ruins in North and South Forks of Mule Canyon; check with the Kane Gulch Ranger Station for advice and directions. You might see pieces of pottery and other artifacts in this area. Please leave *every* piece in place so that future visitors can enjoy the discovery, too. Federal laws also prohibit removal of artifacts.

NATURAL BRIDGES NATIONAL MONUMENT

Natural Bridges preserves some of the finest examples of natural stone architecture in the southwest. Streams in White Canyon and its tributaries cut deep canyons, then floodwaters sculpted the bridges by gouging tunnels between closely spaced loops in the meandering canyons. You can distinguish a natural bridge from an arch because the bridge spans a streambed and was initially carved out of the rock by flowing water. In the monument, these bridges illustrate three different stages of development, from the massive, newly formed Kachina Bridge to the middle-aged Sipapu Bridge to the delicate and fragile span of Owachomo. All three natural bridges will continue to widen and eventually collapse under their own weight. A nine-mile scenic drive has overlooks of the picturesque bridges, Anasazi ruins, and the twisting canyons. You can follow short trails down from the rim to the base of each bridge or hike through all three bridges on a nine-mile trail loop. The National Park Service offers a visitors center (435/692-1234, 8 A.M.–5 P.M. daily Mar.–Apr. and October, 8 A.M.–6 P.M. May–Sept., 9 A.M.–4:30 P.M. the rest of the year; closed holidays October–April, $6 per vehicle or $3 per person or bicyclist) and a small campground ($10).

Bridge View Drive

The nine-mile drive begins its one-way loop just past the campground. You can stop for

© PAUL LEVY

Owachomo Bridge is the most fragile and elegant of the monument's bridges.

lunch at a picnic area. Allow about 90 minutes for a quick trip around. To make all the stops and do a bit of leisurely hiking will take most of a day.

Sipapu Bridge viewpoint is two miles from the visitors center. The Hopi name refers to the gateway from which their ancestors entered this world from another world below. Sipapu Bridge has reached its mature or middle-aged stage of development. The bridge is the largest in the monument and has a span of 268 feet and a height of 220 feet. Many people think Sipapu the most magnificent of the bridges. Another view and a trail to the base of Sipapu are 0.8 mile farther. The viewpoint is about halfway down an easy trail; allow a half hour. A steeper and rougher trail branches off the viewpoint trail and winds down to the bottom of White Canyon, probably the best place to fully appreciate the bridge's size. Total round-trip distance is 1.2 miles with an elevation change of 600 feet.

Horse Collar Ruin, built by the Anasazi, looks as though it has been abandoned only a few decades, not 800 years. At 3.1 miles from the visitors center, a short trail leads to an overlook. The name comes from the shape of the doorway openings in two storage rooms. Hikers walking in the canyon between Sipapu and Kachina Bridges can scramble up a steep rock slope to the site. Like all ancient ruins, these are very fragile and must not be touched or entered. Only with such care will future generations of visitors be able to admire the well-preserved structures. Other groups of Anasazi dwellings can be seen in or near the monument too; ask a ranger for directions.

Kachina Bridge viewpoint and trailhead are 5.1 miles from the visitors center. The massive bridge has a span of 204 feet and a height of 210 feet. A trail, 1.5 miles round-trip, leads to the canyon bottom next to the bridge; elevation change is 650 feet. Look for pictographs near the base of the trail. Some of the figures resemble Hopi kachinas (spirits) and inspired the bridge's name. Armstrong Canyon joins White Canyon just downstream from the bridge; floods in each canyon abraded opposite sides of the rock fin that later became Kachina Bridge.

Owachomo Bridge viewpoint and trailhead are 7.1 miles from the visitors center. An easy walk leads to Owachomo's base—a half-mile round-trip with an elevation change of 180 feet. Graceful Owachomo spans 180 feet and is 106 feet high. Erosive forces have worn the venerable bridge to a thickness of only nine feet. Unlike the other two bridges, Owachomo spans a smaller tributary stream instead of a major canyon. Two streams played a role in the bridge's formation. Floods coming down the larger Armstrong Canyon surged against a sandstone fin on one side while floods in a small side canyon wore away the rock on the other side. Eventually a hole formed, and waters flowing down the side canyon took the shorter route through the bridge. The name Owachomo means "flat-rock mound" in the Hopi language; a large rock outcrop nearby inspired the name. Before construction of the present road, a trail winding down the opposite side of Armstrong Canyon provided the only access for monument visitors. The trail, little used now, connects with Hwy. 95.

Bridge View Drive is always open during daylight hours except after heavy snowstorms. A winter visit can be very enjoyable; ice or mud often closes the steep Sipapu and Kachina Trails, but the short trail to Owachomo Bridge usually stays open.

Photovoltaic Array

A large solar electric-power station sits across the road from the visitors center. This demonstration system, the largest in the world when constructed in 1980, has a quarter-million solar cells spread over nearly an acre and produces up to 100 kilowatts. Batteries, located elsewhere, store a two-day supply of power. The monument lies far from the nearest power lines, so the solar cells provide an alternative to continuous running of diesel-powered generators.

VICINITY OF NATURAL BRIDGES NATIONAL MONUMENT

Dark Canyon

This magnificent canyon system lies about 15 air miles north of Natural Bridges National Monument. Dark Canyon, with its many tributaries, begins in the high country of Elk Ridge and extends west to Lake Powell in lower Cataract Canyon. Steep cliffs and the isolated location have protected the relatively pristine environment. The upper canyons tend to be wide with open areas and groves of Douglas fir and ponderosa pine. Creeks dry up after spring snowmelt, leaving only widely scattered springs as water sources for most of the year. Farther downstream, the canyon walls close in and the desert trees of piñon pine, juniper, and cottonwood take over. At its lower end, Dark Canyon has a year-round stream and deep plunge pools; cliffs tower more than 1,400 feet above the canyon floor. Springs and running water attract wildlife, including bighorn sheep, black bear, deer, mountain lion, coyote, bobcat, ringtail cat, raccoon, fox, and spotted skunk.

Experienced hikers enjoy the solitude, wildlife, Anasazi ruins, and varied canyon scenery. Although it's possible to visit Dark Canyon on a day hike, it takes several days to get a feel for this area. To explore the entire canyon and its major tributaries would take weeks.

The upper half of the canyon system lies within Dark Canyon Wilderness, administered by the Manti–La Sal National Forest (P.O. Box 820, Monticello, UT 84535, 435/587-2041). The lower half of Dark Canyon, currently designated a primitive area, lies mostly within BLM land; the area is a candidate for wilderness status. Obtain a $2 day trip, $8 overnight permit from the BLM before visiting its lands.

The **Sundance Trail** is the most popular entry to lower Dark Canyon. The start of the trail can be reached on dirt roads that branch off Hwy. 95 southeast of the Hite Marina turnoff; this approach can be used year-round in dry weather. Cairns mark the trail, which drops 1,200 feet in less than one mile on a steep talus slope.

Grand Gulch Primitive Area

Within this twisting canyon system lies some of the most captivating scenery and largest concentrations of Anasazi ruins in all of southeastern Utah. The main canyon begins only about six miles southeast of Natural Bridges National Monument. From an elevation of 6,400 feet, Grand Gulch cuts deeply into Cedar Mesa on a tortuous path southwest to the San Juan River, dropping 2,700 feet in about 53 miles. Sheer cliffs, alcoves, pinnacles, Anasazi cliff dwellings, rock-art sites, arches, and a few natural bridges line Grand Gulch and its many tributaries.

Kane Gulch and Bullet Canyon provide access to the upper end of Grand Gulch from the east side. A popular loop hike using these canyons is 23 miles long (3–4 days); arrange a 7.5-mile car shuttle or hitch. Ask at the ranger station if a shuttle service is available. Collins Canyon, reached from Collins Spring Trailhead, leads into lower Grand Gulch from the west side. Hiking distance between Kane Gulch and Collins Spring Trailheads is 38 miles one-way (5–7 days). A car shuttle of about 29 miles (including eight miles of dirt road) is needed. Be sure to visit the BLM's Kane Gulch Ranger Station or Monticello office for a permit and information. You must have a day-use ($2) or overnight camping permit ($8) to enter the area.

Kane Gulch Ranger Station

The BLM provides permits, archaeological information, current hiking conditions, literature, and sales of maps and books at this bare-bones facility (8 A.M.–noon daily early Mar.–late Nov.). (Try to get maps in advance as rangers are sometimes out on patrol.) The station is at Kane Gulch Trailhead, four miles south on Hwy. 261 from Hwy. 95. No telephone, water, or trash collection is available. Normally this is the best place for firsthand information. You can also visit the BLM office

(435 N. Main, P.O. Box 7, Monticello, UT 84535, 435/587-1500, 7:45 A.M.–4:30 P.M. Mon.–Fri. year-round). Everyone visiting the Cedar Mesa backcountry should drop in for the required permit and to get the latest information. Permits run $5 per person for overnight camping and are limited to 12 persons. Note that groups of eight or more people with pack animals need to obtain permits at least three weeks beforehand from the ranger station or office. Help protect fragile desert soils by keeping all vehicles—including mountain bikes—on established roads. Campfires are not permitted in the canyons.

Fish Creek and Owl Creek Loop Hike

Varied canyon scenery, year-round pools, Anasazi ruins, and a magnificent natural arch make this an excellent hike. Fish Creek and its tributary Owl Creek lie east of Grand Gulch on the other side of Hwy. 261. A 1.5-mile trail atop Cedar Mesa connects upper arms of the two creeks to make a 15.5-mile loop. From the trailhead (elev. 6,160 feet), the path descends 1,400 feet to the junction of the two creeks. Opinions differ as to which direction to begin the loop, but either way is fine. Owl Creek might be the better choice for a day hike because it's closer to the trailhead and has the added attractions of easily accessible ruins just a half mile away and Nevill's Arch 3.5 miles farther (one-way). Contact the Kane Gulch or Monticello BLM offices for trail notes and current trail and water conditions. Permits cost $2 for day trips, $8 for overnight trips. Maps are essential for navigation, because it's easy to get off the route in some places.

The canyons have been carved in Cedar Mesa sandstone, which forms many overhangs where the Anasazi built cliff dwellings. Unfortunately, nearly all ruins sit high in the cliffs and can be hard to spot from the canyon bottoms (canyon depths average 500 feet). Binoculars come in handy for seeing the ruins, some of which are marked on the topo maps. Climbing equipment may not be used to reach the ruins.

The turnoff for the trailhead is between mileposts 27 and 28 of Hwy. 261, one mile south of Kane Gulch Ranger Station.

Slickhorn Canyon

Adventurous hikers enjoy the Native American ruins and impressive scenery in this rugged canyon south of Grand Gulch. Canyon depths along Slickhorn's 12-mile length range from about 300 feet in the northern reaches to 800 feet near the confluence with the San Juan River. Boulders, talus slopes, and pour-offs in the streambed hamper travel and discourage casual visitors. Allow about four days to explore Slickhorn Canyon and some of its tributaries. A more ambitious trip is to go down Slickhorn to the San Juan River, hike downstream along a high, narrow ledge to the mouth of Grand Gulch, then travel up to one of the Grand Gulch trailheads in a week or more of hiking. The BLM offices at Kane Gulch and Monticello have information sheets, trailhead information, and a map; overnight permits are $8.

John's Canyon

This varied canyon lies southeast of Grand Gulch and Slickhorn Canyons. A fingerlike network of deep narrow canyons in the upper drainages contrasts with a broad alluvial bottom downstream that's up to a mile wide. The main canyon is about 13 miles long and empties into the San Juan River. Canyon depths average about 1,000 feet. Experienced hikers will find the going relatively easy, as there are only a few boulder falls and small pour-offs in the upper canyons. High pour-offs in the lower canyon, however, effectively block access to the San Juan River. A map and information sheet available from the BLM offices have trailhead and spring information and a brief description of hiking in the canyon.

MEXICAN HAT

Spectacular geology surrounds this tiny community perched on the north bank of the San Juan River. Folded layers of red and gray rock stand out dramatically. Alhambra Rock, a jagged remnant of a volcano, marks the southern approach to Mexican Hat. Another rock, which looks just like an upside-down sombrero, gave Mexican Hat its name; you'll see this formation two miles north of town. The land has never proved good for much except its scenery; farmers and ranchers thought it next to worthless. Stories of gold in the San Juan River brought a frenzy of prospecting 1892–1893, but the mining proved mostly a bust. Oil, first struck by drillers in 1908, has brought mostly modest profits. The uranium mill across the river at Halchita gave a boost to the economy from 1956 until it closed in 1965. Mexican Hat now serves as a modest trade and tourism center. Monument Valley, Valley of the Gods Scenic Drive, Goosenecks State Park, and Grand Gulch Primitive Area lie only short drives away. The shore near town can be a busy place in summer as river runners on the San Juan put in, take out, or just stop for ice and beer.

Accommodations

The **San Juan Inn and Trading Post** (435/683-2220 or 800/447-2022, $80 and up), at a dramatic location above the river, just west of town, offers rooms, Native American trade goods, and a restaurant, the **Olde Bridge Bar and Grill** (435/683-2220, three meals daily, $9–15), serving American, Mexican, and Navajo food. **Canyonlands Motel** (435/683-2230, $55 and up) offers recently remodeled rooms; closed in winter. **Mexican Hat Lodge** (435/683-2222, $68 and up) offers rooms, a pool, and a restaurant with steaks and burgers daily for lunch and dinner.

CAMPGROUNDS

Valle's Trading Post and RV Park (435/683-2226, year-round, $12), has tent and RV sites with hookups. The trading post offers crafts, groceries, showers, vehicle storage, and car shuttles.

VICINITY OF MEXICAN HAT
Valley of the Gods

Great sandstone monoliths, delicate spires, and long rock fins rise from the broad val-

ley. This strange red-rock landscape resembles better-known Monument Valley but on a smaller scale. A 17-mile dirt road winds through the spectacular scenery. Cars can usually travel the road at low speeds if the weather is dry (washes are crossed). Allow 1–1.5 hours for the drive. The east end of the road connects with U.S. 163 at milepost 29 (7.5 miles northeast of Mexican Hat or 15 miles southwest of Bluff); the west end connects with Hwy. 261 just below the Moki Dugway switchbacks (four miles north of Mexican Hat on U.S. 163, then 6.6 miles northwest on Hwy. 261).

Goosenecks State Park

The San Juan River winds through a series of incredibly tight bends 1,000 feet below. So closely spaced are the bends that the river takes six miles to cover an air distance of only 1.5 miles. The bends and exposed rock layers form exquisitely graceful curves. Geologists know the site as a classic example of entrenched meanders, caused by gradual uplift of a formerly level plain. Signs at the overlook explain the geologic history and identify the rock formations. Goosenecks State Park is an undeveloped area with a few tables and vault toilets. Camping is available; no water or fee. From the junction of U.S. 163 and Hwy. 261, four miles north of Mexican Hat, go one mile northwest on Hwy. 261, then turn left three miles on Hwy. 316 to its end.

Muley Point Overlook

One of the great views in the Southwest lies just a short drive from Goosenecks State Park and more than 1,000 feet higher. Although the view of the Goosenecks below is less dramatic than at the state park, the 6,200-foot elevation provides a magnificent panorama across the Navajo Indian Reservation to Monument Valley and countless canyons and mountains. To get there, travel northwest nine miles on Hwy. 261 from the Goosenecks turnoff. At the top of the Moki Dugway switchbacks (an 1,100-foot climb on gravel roads with sharp curves and 5–10 percent grades), turn left (southwest) 5.3 miles on gravel County Road 241 (the turnoff may not be signed) and follow it toward the point. This road is not suitable for wet-weather travel.

MONUMENT VALLEY

Towering buttes, jagged pinnacles, and rippled sand dunes make this an otherworldly landscape. Changing colors and shifting shadows during the day add to the enchantment. Most of the natural monuments are remnants of sandstone eroded by wind and water. Agathla Peak and some lesser summits are roots of ancient volcanoes, whose dark rock contrasts with the pale yellow sandstone of the other formations. The valley lies at an elevation of 5,564 feet in the Upper Sonoran Life Zone; annual rainfall averages about 8.5 inches.

In 1863–1864, when Kit Carson was ravaging Canyon de Chelly in Arizona to round up the Navajo, Chief Hoskinini led his people to the safety and freedom of Monument Valley. Merrick Butte and Mitchell Mesa commemorate two miners who discovered rich silver deposits on their first trip to the valley in 1880. On their second trip both were killed, reportedly shot by Paiutes. Hollywood movies made the splendor of Monument Valley known to the outside world. *Stagecoach,* filmed here in 1938 and directed by John Ford, became the first in a series of Westerns that has continued to the present. John Wayne and many other movie greats rode across these sands.

The Navajo have preserved the valley as a tribal park with a scenic drive, visitors center, and campground. From Mexican Hat, drive 22 miles southwest on U.S. 163 and turn left 3.5 miles to the visitors center. From Kayenta, go 24 miles north on U.S. 163 and turn right 3.5 miles. At the junction of U.S. 163 is a village-worth of outdoor market stalls, where you can stop to buy Navajo art and crafts.

Visitors Center

An information desk (435/727-3287), exhibits, and a crafts shop are open 8 A.M.–7 P.M. daily May–September, then 8 A.M.–5 P.M. daily the rest of the year. Visitors pay a $5 fee per person

($2 ages 60 and over, free for children six and under), collected on the entrance road. Be prepared to run a gauntlet of Navajo entrepreneurs who will meet you at your car to offer you jeep or horseback tours of the monument for varying amounts of money.

Monument Valley Drive

A 17-mile, self-guided scenic drive (8 A.M.– 7 P.M. in summer, 8 A.M.–5 P.M. the rest of the year) begins at the visitors center and loops through the heart of the valley. Overlooks provide sweeping views from different vantage points. The dirt road is normally okay for cautiously driven cars. Avoid stopping and becoming stuck in the loose sand that sometimes blows across the road. Allow 90 minutes for the drive. No hiking or driving is allowed off the signed route. Water and restrooms are available only at the visitors center.

Valley Tours

Take one of several guided tours leaving daily year-round from the visitors center to visit sites such as a hogan, a cliff dwelling, and petroglyphs in areas beyond the self-guided drive. The trips last 2.5–3 hours and cost $20–32 per person. Guided horseback rides from near the visitors center cost around $20 for an hour; longer day and overnight trips can be arranged too. If you'd like to hike in Monument Valley, you must hire a guide; hiking tours of two hours to a day or more can be arranged at the visitors center.

Accommodations

Don't be surprised to find that lodgings at Monument Valley are expensive. The nearest mid-priced guest rooms are half an hour south in Kayenta, Arizona. **Best Western Wetherill Inn** (in the center of Kayenta on U.S. 163, 520/697-3231, $119 and up) has an indoor pool, complimentary breakfast and an on-site restaurant. The **Holiday Inn** (on U.S. 160 at the turnoff for Kayenta, 520/697-3221 or 800/465-4329, $119 and up) has expansive rooms, a restaurant, and pool. The adobe-style

Hampton Inn (on U.S. 160, 520/697-3170 or 800/426-7866, $127 and up) has a pool and very nicely furnished rooms.

Goulding's Lodge and Trading Post (435/727-3231 or 800/874-0902, www.gouldings.com, $175 and up) is by far the nicest place to stay in the Monument Valley area, though it's not cheap. Harry Goulding and his wife Mike opened this dramatically located trading post in 1924. It's tucked under the rimrocks two miles west of the U.S. 163 Monument Valley turnoff, just north of the Arizona–Utah border. Modern motel rooms offer incredible views of Monument Valley. Guests can use a small indoor pool; meals are available in the dining room. A gift shop sells souvenirs, books, and high-quality Native American crafts. The nearby store has groceries and gas pumps. Monument Valley tours operate year-round; $35 half day, $75 full day, with a six-person minimum (children under 12 half price). Horseback riding is also available. The lodge stays open year-round, though rates drop in winter and early spring. **Goulding's Museum,** in the old trading post building, displays prehistoric and modern artifacts, movie photos, and memorabilia of the Goulding family.

CAMPGROUNDS

Sites at **Mitten View Campground** (no phone) near the visitors center cost $14; coin-operated hot showers are available. The season is mid-March–mid-October. Tenters should be prepared for winds in this exposed location. **Monument Valley Campground** (435/727-3235, Apr.–Oct., $16 tents, $25 RVs with hookups) offers tent and RV sites a short drive west of the monument.

FOUR CORNERS MONUMENT

A concrete slab marks the point where Utah, Colorado, New Mexico, and Arizona meet. Five national parks and 18 national monuments are within a radius of 150 miles from this point and it's the only spot in the United States where you can put your finger on four states at once. More than 2,000 people a day are said to stop at the marker in the summer season. Average stay? 7–10 minutes. Native Americans, mostly Navajo with perhaps some Ute and Pueblo, set up dozens of crafts and refreshment booths in summer. Navajo Parks and Recreation collects a $2 per vehicle ($1 motorcycle) fee during the tourist season.

BACKGROUND

The Land

For many travelers, Utah's striking land forms and natural history provide the impetus for a visit to the state.

GEOGRAPHY

Utah's 84,990 square miles place it 11th in size among the 50 states. The varied landscape is divided into three major physiographic provinces: the **Basin and Range Province** to the west; the **Middle Rocky Mountains Province** of the soaring Uinta, Wasatch, and Bear River Ranges to the north and northeast; and the **Colorado Plateau Province** of canyons, mountains, and plateaus in the south.

Basin and Range Province

Rows of fault-block mountain ranges follow a north–south alignment in this province in the Great Basin west of the Wasatch Range and the High Plateaus. Most of the land lies at elevations between 4,000 and 5,000 feet. Peaks in the Stansbury and Deep Creek Mountains rise more than 11,000 feet above sea level, creating "biological islands" inhabited by cool-climate plants and animals.

Erosion has worn down many of the ranges, forming large alluvial fans in adjacent basins. Many of these broad valleys lack effective drainage, and none have outlets to the ocean. Terraces mark the hills along the shore of prehistoric Lake Bonneville, which once covered most of this province. Few perennial streams originate in these rocky mountains, but rivers from eastern ranges end their voyages in the Great Salt Lake, Sevier Lake, or barren silt-filled valleys.

© PAUL LEVY

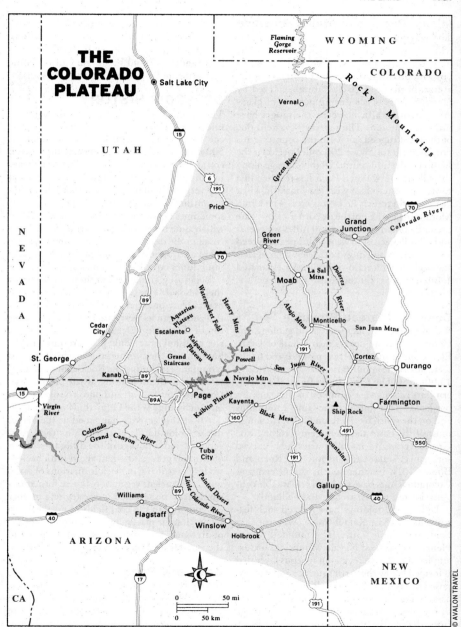

THE COLORADO PLATEAU

Salt Lake City

WYOMING

Flaming Gorge Reservoir

COLORADO

Rocky Mountains

UTAH

Vernal

NEVADA

Green River

Price

191

6

Grand Junction

70

Colorado River

Green River

70

15

Moab

La Sal Mtns

Dolores River

Aquarius Plateau

Waterpocket Fold

Henry Mtns

Abajo Mtns

Monticello

San Juan Mtns

89

Cedar City

Escalante

Kaiparowits Plateau

Lake Powell

San Juan River

Cortez

Durango

Grand Staircase

▲ Navajo Mtn

Kanab

89

St. George

15

89A

Page

Kaibito Plateau

Kayenta

Black Mesa

Chuska Mountains

▲ Ship Rock

Farmington

491

550

Virgin River

Colorado River

Grand Canyon

160

Tuba City

Painted Desert

Little Colorado River

191

Gallup

40

Williams

89

Flagstaff

Winslow

Holbrook

40

ARIZONA

17

NEW MEXICO

CA

0   50 mi

0   50 km

© AVALON TRAVEL

Middle Rocky Mountains Province

The Wasatch Range and the Uinta Mountains, which form this province, provide some of the most dramatic alpine scenery in the state. In both mountainous areas, you'll find cirques, arêtes, horns, and glacial troughs carved by massive rivers of ice during periods of glaciation. Structurally, however, the ranges have little in common. The narrow Wasatch, one of the most rugged ranges in the country, runs north–south for about 200 miles between the Idaho border and central Utah. Slippage along the still-active Wasatch Fault has resulted in a towering western face with few foothills. Most of Utah's ski resorts lie in this area. The Uinta Mountains in the northeast corner of the state present a broad rise about 150 miles west–east and 30 miles across. Twenty-four peaks exceed 13,000 feet, with Kings Peak (elev. 13,528 feet) the highest mountain in Utah. An estimated 1,400 tiny lakes dot the glacial moraines of the Uintas.

Colorado Plateau Province

World-famous for its scenery and geology, the Colorado Plateau covers nearly half of Utah. Elevations lie mostly between 3,000 and 6,000 feet, but some mountain peaks reach nearly 13,000 feet. The Uinta Basin forms the northern part of this vast complex of plateaus; it's bordered on the north by the Uinta Mountains and on the south by the Roan Cliffs. Although most of the basin terrain is gently rolling, the Green River and its tributaries have carved some spectacular canyons into the Roan and Book Cliffs. Farther south, the Green and Colorado Rivers have sculpted remarkable canyons, buttes, mesas, arches, and badlands.

Uplifts and foldings have formed such features as the San Rafael Swell, Waterpocket Fold, and Circle Cliffs. The rounded Abajo, Henry, La Sal, and Navajo Mountains are examples of intrusive rock—an igneous layer that is formed below the earth's surface and later exposed by erosion. The High Plateaus in the Escalante region drop in a series of steps known as the Grand Staircase. Exposed layers range from the relatively young rocks of the Black Cliffs (lava flows) in the north to the increasingly older Pink Cliffs (Wasatch Formation), Gray Cliffs (Mancos Shale), White Cliffs (Navajo Sandstone), and Vermilion Cliffs (Chinle and Wingate Formations) toward the south.

GEOLOGIC HISTORY

The land now contained in Utah began as undersea deposits when the North American continental plate sat near the equator, about 500 million years ago. The spectacular canyon country, now known as the Colorado Plateau, began as a basin of silt and sand deposits at the verge of a shallow sea. This basin sat on a continental plate that rose and fell; it was sometimes below the waters of ancient seas—at which time fossils of early marinelife were encased in the deposits—and sometimes, during more arid periods, above sea level, with vast sand dunes covering the landscape.

Beginning about 200 million years ago, in the Mesozoic era, the North American continental plate broke away from Europe and Africa and began its westward movement over the top of the Pacific Ocean seafloor. This massive collision of tectonic plates resulted in the buckling of rock formations—which formed mountains, including the Rockies and the Uintas—and in thrust faulting, where older formations were pushed up and onto younger rocks; one such range is the Oquirrh Mountains.

All of this activity happened at the verges of the Colorado Plateau, which by the Cretaceous period—the age of the dinosaurs, about 65 million years ago—had again sunk back to sea level, resulting in thick formations of sand, mud, and ancient vegetation. These formations would later be revealed in the region's mighty canyons and in the coal fields of northeastern Utah. In some places, fossilized mud footprints of dinosaurs provide unmistakable evidence of the era's far damper climate.

Basin and Range

In the Tertiary era, the new formations west of the old Colorado Plateau were shot through with volcanoes. Then, as the North American continental plate pivoted to the southwest,

© JUDY JEWELL

In the Eocene Gallery of the Utah Field House of Natural History State Park Museum, you'll see some lovely plant and fish fossils.

the earth's crust under this region—which would become the Basin and Range Province—stretched thinner and thinner. In fact, the Great Basin of Utah and Nevada is about twice as wide as it was about 18 million years ago. This stretching has resulted in a much thinner layer of underlying basement rock here than in other parts of the continent, and the entire area is riven by faults where parts of the crust have pulled apart. Given the differential forces at work in the earth's mantle, sometimes half of a fault would be pushed up to mountain heights while the other half would sink, causing a basin. The spectacular fault-block mountains of the Great Basin result from such parallel rising and falling along fault lines. The most famous instance of this type of formation is the rugged Wasatch Mountains, which rise directly above the basin of the Great Salt Lake.

To the east of this momentous fault-block mountain building, the old Colorado Plateau remained relatively undisturbed. However, within the last 10 million years the entire intermountain region bowed up in a broad arch,

elevating the old sandstones of the Colorado Plateau; this corner of Utah has risen 5,000 feet during this time. The rivers that once wound across the surface of eastern Utah were forced to cut ever deeper canyons as the formations rose. The erosive power of the Green, Colorado, San Juan, and other rivers and streams have cut down through hundreds of millions of years of rock.

Ice Age Utah

During the geologically recent Pleistocene era, ice-age mountain glaciers and climatic changes brought an abundance of moisture to Utah. The runoff and meltwater flooded the basins of fault-block mountain ranges, forming enormous lakes. The largest of these was Lake Bonneville, the name given to the ice-age predecessor of the Great Salt Lake. At its greatest extent, Lake Bonneville covered nearly all of northern and west-central Utah and was nearly 900 feet deeper than the current Great Salt Lake. Even at that depth, finding an outlet to the sea was not simple. It was only after the lake waters breached Red Rock Pass in Idaho that the lake found an outlet into the Snake and Columbia River systems, about 16,000 years ago.

After the ice ages ended, about 10,000 years ago, Lake Bonneville diminished in size and dropped below the level necessary to cut through Red Rock Pass, resulting in the saline Great Salt Lake. You can easily see the old lake shorelines along the Wasatch Front, and cities like Logan, Provo, and Salt Lake City sprawl along these stairstep-like ledges. Much of the old lake bottom west of Salt Lake City is salt desert and extremely flat. In the Bonneville Salt Flats, the valley is so flat and unbroken that the curvature of the earth can be seen.

CLIMATE

The hot summer sun awakens wildflowers in the mountains and turns desert areas brown. Autumn brings pleasant weather to all elevations until the snow line begins to creep down the mountain slopes. Winter snowfalls provide excellent skiing and add beauty to the landscape but cause many mountain roads to close. On those roads that don't close, you'll need chains or snow tires. Spring tends to be unpredictable—wet and windy one day, sunny and calm the next—but it's then you'll find the deserts at their greenest.

Utah's mid-continent location brings wide temperature variations between the seasons. Only a small part of the south experiences winter temperatures that average above freezing.

Precipitation

Most of Utah is dry, with an average precipitation of 13 inches. Precipitation varies greatly from place to place due to local topography and the irregularities of storm patterns. Deserts cover about 33 percent of the state; the driest areas are in the Great Basin, the Uinta Basin, and on the Colorado Plateau, where annual precipitation is around 5–10 inches. At the other extreme, the highest peaks of the Wasatch Range receive more than 50 inches of annual precipitation, most of it as snow.

Winter and Spring Weather Patterns

Periods of high-pressure systems broken by Pacific storm fronts shape most of Utah's winter weather. The high-pressure systems cause inversions when dense cold air flows down the snow-covered mountain slopes into the valleys, where it traps moisture and smoke. The blanket of fog or smog maintains even temperatures but is the bane of the Salt Lake City area. Skiers, however, enjoy bright, sunny days and cold nights in the clear air of the mountain peaks. The blankets of stagnant air in the valleys are cleaned out when cold fronts roll in from the Pacific. When skies clear, the daily temperature range is much greater until the inversion process sets in again.

Most winter precipitation arrives as snow, which all regions of the state expect. Fronts originating over the Gulf of Alaska typically arrive every 6–7 days and trigger most of Utah's snowfall.

Summer and Autumn Weather Patterns

During summer, the valleys still experience inversions of cold air on clear, dry nights, but with a much less pronounced effect than in winter. The canyon country in the south has higher daytime temperatures than do equivalent mountain elevations because there's no source of cold air in the canyons to replace the rising heated air. Also, canyon walls act as an oven, reflecting and trapping heat.

Thunderstorms are most common in summer, when moist warm air rises in billowing clouds. The storms, though they can produce heavy rains and hail, tend to be erratic and concentrated in small areas less than three miles across. Southeastern Utah sees the first thunderstorms of the season, often in mid-June; by mid-July, these storms have spread across the entire state. They lose energy as autumn approaches, and by October they're supplanted by low-pressure systems at high altitudes and Pacific storm fronts, which can cause long periods of heavy precipitation. Hikers need to be aware that the highest mountain peaks can receive snow even in midsummer.

Storm Hazards

Rainwater runs quickly off the rocky desert surfaces and into gullies and canyons. Flash floods can sweep away anything in their path, including boulders, cars, and campsites. Do not camp or park in potential flash-flood areas. If you come to a section of flooded roadway—a common occurrence on desert roads after storms—wait until the water goes down before crossing (it shouldn't take long). Summer lightning causes forest and brush fires, posing a danger to hikers foolish enough to climb mountains when storms threaten.

ENVIRONMENTAL ISSUES

Like many other western states, Utah is deeply conflicted about environmental issues. One of the most conservative states in the nation, Utah has always been very business oriented, especially toward the historic extractive industries such as mining, logging, and agriculture. Utah has also proved to be very friendly to the military; large portions of northeastern Utah are under Pentagon control as bases, weapons research areas, and munitions dumps.

On the other hand, tourism and high-tech industries are breathing life into Utah's economy. Tourism brings in 18 million visitors a year, making it the single largest employer in Utah. Wasatch Front cities are experiencing a phenomenal boom in population growth and new, low-environmental-impact industry. A large part of the reason for this modern migration is Utah's quality of life—pristine wilderness and world-class outdoor recreation are available right out the back door. The interests of the tourist industry and new residents are often at odds with the interests of the state's traditional power base. With supporters of resource extraction industries ensconced both in Washington and in Utah, the state finds itself in the crosshairs of the battle to save or level the West.

Water Use

The early Mormon pioneers came from well-watered New York and New England and the rich Midwestern prairies. When they arrived in Utah, they set about transforming the desert, following the scripture that says the desert will blossom as a rose. Brigham Young encouraged this endeavor, saying that God would change the climate, giving more water if the settlers worked to establish agriculture.

So the settlers planted fruit orchards, shade trees, and grass, turning the desert into an oasis. They built dams and created reservoirs. They dug canals, piping water from farther and farther away, turning the desert green.

Utah now has the second highest per-capita water use in the nation, despite having experienced many years of drought and being the second driest state in the United States.

Water conservationists maintain that Utah residents, including state officials in charge of water-use policy, have not let go of 19th-century ideals about water development and conservation. The state's current goal is to cut water use by 25 percent over the next 50 years, which environmentalists see as incredibly wishy-washy.

Meanwhile, many individuals view the drought as a wake-up call, and see water conservation and native-plant landscaping as the way of the new Utah pioneer.

ORV Overkill

Off-road vehicles, or ORVs (also known as ATVs—All Terrain Vehicles), have gone from being the hobby of a small group of off-road enthusiasts to being one of the fastest growing recreational markets in the country, and these dune-buggies-on-steroids are having a huge impact on public lands. The scope of the issue is easy to measure. In 1979, there were 9,000 ORVs registered in Utah. In 2005, there were 150,000. In addition, the power and dexterity of the machines has greatly increased. Now essentially military-style assault machines that can climb near-vertical cliffs and clamber on any kind of terrain, ORVs are the new "extreme sports" toys of choice, and towns like Moab are now seeing more visitors coming to tear up the back country on ORVs than to mountain bike. The problem is that the ORVs are extremely destructive to the delicate natural environment of deserts and canyonlands, and the more powerful, roaring, exhaust-belching machines put even the most remote and isolated areas within reach of large numbers of people.

Between the two camps—one which would preserve the public land and protect the ancient human artifacts found in remote canyons, the other which sees public land as a playground to be zipped over at high speed—is the BLM. The Moab BLM office has seemed to favor the ORV set, abdicating its role to protect the land and environment for all. Or so thought an alliance of eight environmental groups called the Southern Utah Wilderness Alliance (SUWA) who took the BLM to court to force it to comply with existing laws and create—and enforce—designated ORV trails in wilderness study areas. While lower courts found in favor of the environmental alliance, in 2004 the U.S. Supreme Court reversed the decision. Meanwhile, the Moab area, the San Rafael Swell near Hanksville, and the Vermillion Cliffs near Kanab are seeing unprecedented levels of ORV activity. Groups like the SUWA have regrouped and developed new strategies to force the BLM to comply with its own responsibility for environmental stewardship of public land. For more information see the SUWA website (www.suwa.org).

Flora and Fauna

A wide variety of plants and animals find homes within Utah's great range of elevations (more than 11,000 feet). Regardless of the precipitation, the environment is harsh, and most plants and animals have had to adapt to endure the challenging climate. To help simplify and understand the different environments, some scientists use the Merriam system of life zones, which offers a concise way to get an overview of Utah's vegetation and animal life. Because plants subsist on rainfall, which is determined largely by elevation, each life zone can be identified with an elevation range. These ranges are not exact, however, due to the different rainfall patterns and evaporation rates.

Utah's lowest elevations lie in the Lower Sonoran Life Zone (below 3,500 feet). This zone is found in the Mojave Desert, which extends into the southwest corner of the state. Most of Utah's northern deserts and canyonlands are considered part of the Upper Sonoran Life Zone (3,500–5,500 feet). As rainfall increases near mountain ranges, the Transition Life Zone (5,500–8,000 feet) begins. The Transition Zone is best developed on the High Plateaus and the Uinta Mountains and less so in the Great Basin and the Wasatch Range. At successively higher elevations are the Canadian Life Zone (8,000–10,000 feet), the Hudsonian Life Zone (10,000–11,000 feet), and the Alpine Tundra Life Zone (above 11,000 feet).

evening primrose, a common desert flower

© PAUL LEVY

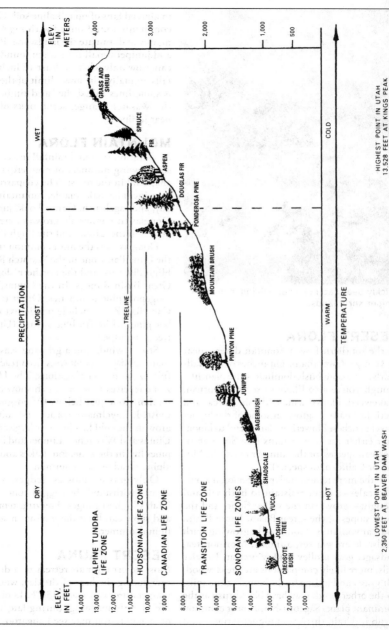

UTAH VEGETATION ZONES

PRECIPITATION

DRY   MOIST   WET

ELEV.
IN FEET

14,000
13,000
12,000
11,000
10,000
9,000
8,000
7,000
6,000
5,000
4,000
3,000
2,000
1,000

ELEV.
IN
METERS

4,000
3,000
2,000
1,000
500

ALPINE TUNDRA
LIFE ZONE

HUDSONIAN LIFE ZONE

CANADIAN LIFE ZONE

TRANSITION LIFE ZONE

SONORAN LIFE ZONES

TREELINE

GRASS AND SHRUB
SPRUCE
FIR
ASPEN
DOUGLAS FIR
PONDEROSA PINE
MOUNTAIN BRUSH
PINYON PINE
JUNIPER
SAGEBRUSH
SHADSCALE
YUCCA
JOSHUA TREE
CREOSOTE BUSH

TEMPERATURE

HOT   WARM   COLD

HIGHEST POINT IN UTAH
13,528 FEET AT KINGS PEAK

LOWEST POINT IN UTAH
2,350 FEET AT BEAVER DAM WASH

© AVALON TRAVEL

Prickly pear cacti eke out a living in arid juniper shrublands.

DESERT FLORA

In the southern Lower Sonoran deserts near St. George, fewer than eight inches of rain falls yearly. Creosote bush dominates the plantlife, though you're also likely to see rabbitbrush, snakeweed, blackbrush, saltbush, yucca, and cacti. Joshua trees grow on some of the higher gravel benches. Flowering plants tend to bloom after either the winter rains (the Sonoran or Mexican species) or the summer rains (the Mojave or Californian species).

In the more temperate Upper Sonoran Zone, shadscale—a plant resistant to both salt and drought—grows on the valley floors and the lower slopes of the Great Basin, Uinta Basin, and canyonlands. Commonly growing with shadscale are grasses, annuals, Mormon tea, budsage, gray molley, and winterfat. In salty soils, more likely companions are greasewood, salt grass, and iodine bush. Nonalkaline soils, on the other hand, may have blackbrush as the dominant plant. Sagebrush, the most common shrub in Utah, thrives on higher terraces and in alluvial fans of nonalkaline soil. Grasses are commonly found mixed with sagebrush and may even dominate the landscape. Piñon pine and juniper, small trees often found together, can grow only where at least 12 inches of rain falls annually; the lower limit of their growth is sometimes called the "arid timberline." In the Wasatch Range, scrub oaks often grow near junipers.

MOUNTAIN FLORA

As elevation rises and rainfall increases, you'll see growing numbers of ponderosa pine and chaparral in the forest. The chaparral association includes oak, maple, mountain mahogany, and sagebrush. Gambel oak, juniper, and Douglas fir commonly grow among the ponderosa in the Uintas and the High Plateaus.

Douglas fir is the most common tree within the Canadian Zone in the Wasatch Range, the High Plateaus, and the northern slopes of the Great Basin Ranges. In the Uintas, however, lodgepole pine dominates. Other trees of the Canadian Zone include ponderosa pine, limber pine, white fir, blue spruce (Utah's state tree), and aspen.

Strong winds and a growing season of less than 120 days prevent trees from reaching their full size at higher elevations. The Hudsonian Zone receives twice as much snow as the Canadian Zone just below. Often gnarled and twisted, Engelmann spruce and subalpine fir grow in the cold heights over large areas of the Uintas and Wasatches. Limber and bristlecone pines live in the zone, too. Lakes and lush subalpine meadows are common.

Only grasses, mosses, sedges, and annuals can withstand the rugged conditions atop Utah's highest ranges. Freezing temperatures and snow can blast the mountain slopes even in midsummer.

DESERT FAUNA

Most desert animals retreat to a den or burrow during the heat of the day, when ground temperatures can reach 130°F. Look for wildlife in early morning, during late afternoon, or at night. You may see kangaroo rat, desert cottontail, black-tailed jackrabbit, striped and spotted skunks, kit fox, ringtail cat, coyote, bobcat, mountain lion, and several species of squirrels and mice. Birds include the native Gambel's quail, roadrunner, red-tailed hawk, great horned owl, cactus wren, black-chinned and broad-tailed hummingbirds, and rufous-sided towhee. The endangered desert tortoise lives here, too, but faces extinction in a losing battle with livestock, which trample and graze on the tortoise's environment.

The rare Gila monster, identified by its beadlike skin with black and yellow patterns, is found in the state's southwest corner. Sidewinder, Great Basin, and other western rattlesnakes are occasionally seen. Also watch for other poisonous creatures; scorpions, spiders, and centipedes can inflict painful stings or bites. It's a good idea when camping to check for these unwanted guests in shoes and other items left outside. Be careful, too, not to reach under rocks or into places you can't see.

In the more temperate Upper Sonoran Zone, you'll see plenty of desert wildlife, though you might also see Utah prairie dog, beaver, muskrat, black bear, desert bighorn sheep, desert mule deer, and the antelope-like pronghorn. Marshes of the Great Basin have an abundance of food and cover that attract waterfowl; species include whistling swan, Great Basin Canada goose, lesser snow goose, great blue heron, seagull (Utah's state bird), common mallard, gadwall, and American common merganser. Chukar (from similar desert lands in Asia) and Hungarian partridge (from eastern Europe and western Asia) thrive under the cover of sagebrush in dry-farm areas. Sage and sharp-tailed grouse also prefer the open country. Rattlesnakes and other reptiles like the Upper Sonoran Zone best.

Not surprisingly, few fish live in the desert. The Great Salt Lake is too salty to support fish life; the only creatures that can live in its extremely saline water are bacteria, a few insect species, and brine shrimp, which are commercially harvested. The Colorado River, which cuts through southeastern Utah, supports a number of fish species, several of which are

rattlesnake warming against a rock

chukar at Kodachrome Basin State Park

endemic to the river and are now considered endangered.

MOUNTAIN FAUNA

In the thin forests of the Transition Zone, squirrels and chipmunks rely on pinecones for food; other animals living here include Nuttall's cottontail, black-tailed jackrabbit, spotted and striped skunks, red fox, coyote, mule deer, Rocky Mountain elk (Utah's state mammal), moose, black bear, and mountain lion. Moose did not arrive until the 1940s, when they crossed over from Wyoming; now they live in northern and central Utah. Merriam's wild turkey, originally from Colorado, is found in oak and ponderosa pine forests of central and southern Utah. Other birds of the Transition Zone include Steller's jay, blue and ruffed grouse, common poorwill, great horned owl, black-chinned and broad-tailed hummingbirds, gray-headed and Oregon juncos, white-throated swift, and the common raven. Most snakes, such as the gopher, hognose, and garter, are harmless, but you may also come across western rattlers.

Utah has more than 1,000 fishable lakes and numerous fishing streams. Species range from rainbow and cutthroat trout to large mackinaw and brown trout to striped bass, walleye, bluegill, and whitefish. Bear Lake in extreme northern Utah is home to the Bear Lake whitefish, Bonneville whitefish, Bonneville cisco, and Bear Lake sculpin—all are unique to Bear Lake and its tributaries. Because of their restricted range, they are vulnerable to extinction from habitat alteration due to water management of Bear Lake and its tributaries.

Deer and Rocky Mountain elk graze in the Canadian Zone but rarely higher. Smaller animals of the high mountains include northern flying squirrel, snowshoe rabbit, pocket gopher, yellow belly marmot, pika, chipmunk, and mice.

Even higher, in the Hudsonian Zone, on a bright summer day the trees, grasses, and tiny flowering alpine plants are abuzz with insects, rodents, and visiting birds. Come winter, though, most animals will have moved to lower, more protected areas. Few animals live in the true alpine regions. White-tailed ptarmigan, recently introduced to Utah, live in the tundra of the Uinta Mountains.

History

PRE-SETTLEMENT UTAH
Utah in Prehistory

Archaeologists have evidence that Paleo-Indians began to wander across the region that would become Utah about 15,000 years ago—hunting big game and gathering plant foods. The climate was probably cooler and wetter; food plants and game animals would have been more abundant than today. The early tribes continued their primitive hunting and gathering despite climate changes and the extinction of many big-game species about 10,000 years ago.

The first tentative attempts at agriculture were introduced from the south about 2,000 years ago and brought about a slow transition to a settled village life. The Fremont culture emerged in the northern part of the Colorado Plateau, the Anasazi in the southern part. Although both groups developed crafts such as basketry, pottery, and jewelry, only the Anasazi progressed to the construction of masonry buildings in their villages. Their corn, beans, and squash enabled them to be less reliant on migration and to construct year-round village sites. Thousands of stone dwellings, ceremonial kivas, and towers built by the Anasazi still stand. Both groups also left behind intriguing rock art, either pecked into the surfaces (petroglyphs) or painted on (pictographs). The Anasazi and the Fremont departed from this region about 800 years ago, perhaps because of drought, warfare, or disease. Some of the Anasazi moved south and joined the Pueblo tribes

ANASAZI OR ANCESTRAL PUEBLOAN?

As you travel through the Southwest, you may hear reference to the "ancestral Puebloans." In this book, we've chosen to use the more familiar name for these people – the Anasazi. The word *Anasazi* is actually a Navajo term that archaeologists chose, thinking it meant "old people." A more literal translation is "enemy ancestors." For this reason, some consider the name inaccurate. The terminology is in flux, and which name you hear depends on whom you're talking to or where you are. The National Park Service now uses the more descriptive term ancestral Puebloan. These prehistoric people who built masonry villages eventually moved south to Arizona and New Mexico, where their descendants, such as the Acoma, Cochiti, Santa Clara, Taos, and the Hopi Mesas, live in modern-day pueblos.

of present-day Arizona and New Mexico. The fate of the Fremont people remains a mystery.

About the same time, perhaps by coincidence, the nomadic Shoshoni in the north and the Utes and Paiutes in the south moved through Utah; none of these groups seemed to have knowledge of their sophisticated predecessors. Relatives of the Athapascans of western Canada, the seminomadic Navajo, wandered into New Mexico and Arizona between A.D. 1300 and 1500. This adaptable tribe learned agriculture, weaving, pottery, and other skills from their Pueblo neighbors and became expert horsepeople and sheepherders with livestock obtained from the Spanish.

The size of prehistoric populations has varied greatly in Utah. There were probably few inhabitants during the Archaic period (before A.D. 500), but many more during the time of the Anasazi and Fremont cultures (A.D. 500–1250), rising to a peak of perhaps 500,000. Except for the Athapascan-speaking Navajo,

all of Utah's historic tribes spoke Shoshonian languages and had similar cultures.

Explorers and Colonizers

In 1776, Spanish explorers of the Dominguez-Escalante Expedition were the first Europeans to visit and describe the region during their unsuccessful attempt to find a route west to California. Utes guided the Spanish expedition through the Uinta Basin.

Retreating to New Mexico, the explorers encountered great difficulties in the canyons of southern Utah before finding a safe ford across the Colorado River. This spot, known as the "Crossing of the Fathers," now lies under Lake Powell. Later explorers established the Old Spanish Trail through this area of Utah to connect New Mexico with California.

Adventurous mountain men seeking beaver pelts and other furs entered northern Utah in the mid-1820s. They explored the mountain ranges, the rivers, and the Great Salt Lake and blazed most of the trails later used by wagon trains, the Pony Express, telegraph lines, and the railroads. By 1830, most of the mountain men had moved on to better trapping areas and left the land to the Native Americans; some, however, returned to guide government explorers and groups of pioneer settlers.

Joseph Walker, who served under Captain Benjamin Bonneville, crossed the northwest corner of Utah in 1833 on a trip to California. He reported such difficult conditions that no one else attempted the route for the rest of the decade. California-bound wagon trains took heed and almost all followed a more northerly path through Idaho on the Oregon Trail.

In 1843, John C. Frémont led one of his several government-sponsored scientific expeditions into Utah. Frémont determined the salinity of the Great Salt Lake and laid to rest speculation that a river drained the lake into the Pacific Ocean. Two years later, he led a well-prepared group across the heart of the dreaded Great Salt Lake Desert despite warnings from the local Native Americans that no one had crossed it and survived. His accounts of the region described not only the salty lake and barren deserts but also the fertile valleys near the Wasatch Range. Mormon leaders planning a westward migration from Nauvoo, Illinois, carefully studied Frémont's reports.

Langsford Hastings, an ambitious politician, seized the opportunity to promote Frémont's desert route as a shortcut to California. Hastings had made the trip on horseback but failed to anticipate the problems of a wagon train. On this route in 1846, the Donner-Reed wagon train became so bogged down in the salt mud that many wagons were abandoned. Moreover, an 80-mile stretch between water holes proved too far for many of the oxen, which died from dehydration. Today, motorists can cruise in comfort along I-80 on a similar route between Salt Lake City and Wendover.

Native Americans vs. Settlers

The Paiutes and Utes befriended and guided the early explorers and settlers, but troubles soon began for these and other groups when they saw their lands taken over by farmers and ranchers. None of the tribes proved a match for the white population, which eventually drove the Native Americans from the most desirable lands and settled them on the state's five reservations.

The Navajo's habit of raiding neighboring tribes and white settlements brought about their downfall. In 1863–1864 the U.S. Army rounded up all the Navajo they could find and forced the survivors on "The Long Walk" from Fort Defiance in northeastern Arizona to a bleak camp in eastern New Mexico. This internment was a dismal failure, and the Navajo were released four years later.

In 1868, the federal government "awarded" to the Navajo land that has since grown to a giant reservation spreading from northeastern Arizona into adjacent Utah and New Mexico.

THE MORMON MIGRATION
The Early LDS Church

At the time of his revelations, the founder of the Church of Jesus Christ of Latter-day Saints, Joseph Smith, worked as a farmer in the state of New York. In 1830, he and his followers founded the new religion and published the first edition of the Book of Mormon. But Smith's revelations evoked fear and anger in many of his neighbors, and in 1831 he and his new church moved to Kirtland, Ohio. They set to work building a temple for sacred ordinances, developing a missionary program, and recruiting new followers. Mormons also settled farther west in Missouri, where they made plans for a temple and a community of Zion.

Persecution by non-Mormons continued to mount in both Ohio and Missouri, fueled largely by the church's polygamist practices, the prosperity of its members, and the Latter-day Saint claim that it was the "true" church. Missourians disliked the Mormons' anti-slavery views. Violence by gangs of armed men eventually forced church members to flee for their lives.

The winter of 1838–1839 found Joseph Smith in jail on treason charges and many church members without homes or legal protection. The Missouri Mormons made their way east to Illinois, not knowing where else to go. Brigham Young, a member of the Council of the Twelve Apostles, directed this exodus, foreshadowing the much longer migration he would lead eight years later.

Nauvoo the Beautiful

The Mormons purchased a large tract of swampy land along the Mississippi River in Illinois and set to work draining swamps and building a city. Joseph Smith, allowed to escape from the Missouri jail, named the Mormons' new home Nauvoo—a Hebrew word for "the beautiful location." Despite extreme poverty and the inability to secure reparations for the losses they had suffered in Missouri, the Mormons succeeded in building an attractive city. A magnificent temple, begun in 1841, rose above Nauvoo. Despite their success, the Mormons continued to face virulent opposition from those who objected to their religion.

Smith, who had withstood tarring and feathering, among other punishments, met his death in 1844 at Carthage, Illinois. He had voluntarily surrendered to authorities to stand trial for treason, but a mob stormed the jail and killed Smith and his brother Hyrum in a hail of bullets. Opponents thought that the Mormons would disband on the death of their leader. When they did not, their crops and houses were destroyed and their livestock was driven off. Brigham Young, who succeeded Smith, realized the Mormons would never find peace in Illinois. He and other leaders began looking toward the vastness of the West. They hoped the remote Rocky Mountains would provide a sanctuary from mobs and politicians. Plans for departure from Nauvoo began in the autumn of 1845.

The Exodus

Attacks against Nauvoo's citizens made life so difficult that they had to evacuate the following February despite severe winter weather. Homes, businesses, the temple, and most personal possessions were left behind as the Saints crossed the Mississippi into Iowa. (Mobs later took over the town and desecrated the temple; not a single stone of the structure is in its original position today.) The group slowly pushed westward through the snow and mud. Faith, a spirit of sharing, and competent leadership enabled them to survive.

Brigham Young thought it best not to press on all the way to the Rocky Mountains that first year, so the group spent a second winter on the plains. Dugouts and log cabins housed more than 3,500 people at Winter Quarters, near present-day Omaha. By the early spring of 1847, the leaders had worked out plans for the rest of the journey. The Salt Lake Valley, an uninhabited and isolated region, would be their goal. Mountain men encountered on the journey gave discouraging descriptions of this place as a site for a major settlement. Samuel Brannan, a Mormon who had settled on the West Coast, rode east to meet Brigham Young and present glowing reports of California. But Young wouldn't be swayed from his original goal. On July 24, 1847, Young arrived at the edge of the Salt Lake Valley and announced, "This is the right place."

The City of Zion

The pioneers immediately set to work digging irrigation canals, planting crops, constructing a small fort, and laying out a city. Nearly 2,000 more immigrants arrived that same summer of 1847.

These early citizens had to be self-sufficient; the nearest outposts of civilization lay 1,000 miles away. Through trial and error, farmers learned techniques of irrigating and farming the desert land. The city continued to grow—immigrants poured in; tanneries, flour mills, blacksmith shops, stores, and other enterprises developed under church direction; residential neighborhoods sprang up; and workers commenced raising the religious structures that still dominate the area around Temple Square.

The Colonization of Utah

Soon other areas in Utah were colonized: In 1849–1850, Mormon leaders in Salt Lake City took the first steps in exploring the rest of the state when they sent an advance party led by Parley P. Pratt to southern Utah. Encouraging reports of rich iron ore west of Cedar Valley and of fertile land along the Virgin River convinced the Mormons to expand southward.

Calls went out for members to establish missions and to mine the iron ore and supply iron products needed for the expanding Mormon empire. In 1855, a successful experiment in growing cotton along Santa Clara Creek, near present-day St. George, aroused considerable interest among the Mormons. New settlements soon arose in the Virgin River Valley. However, poor roads hindered development of the cotton and iron industries, which mostly ended when cheaper products began arriving on the transcontinental railroad.

In the 1870s and early 1880s, the LDS Church sent out calls for members to colonize lands east of the Wasatch Plateau. Though at first the land looked harsh and barren, crops and orchards eventually prospered with irrigation.

An Agrarian Paradise

By the end of the 19th century, the small agricultural settlements in Utah—mostly free of gentile influence—had by and large become the utopian religious communities envisioned by the religion's founders. Various tenets of the faith dictated nearly all aspects of life, from the width of the streets to social customs. Cultural homogeneity was greatly stressed; farmers and ranchers were discouraged from living on their land and encouraged instead to live in towns within range of the church. For a period, the church encouraged full-fledged communal and cooperative farm towns as the ideal social structure.

The Mormons were hardworking farmers and managed to convert an unyielding desert into a land of abundance. Streams were diverted into irrigation canals, and acres of orchards and fields blossomed. Little farm towns, all laid out with uniform street grids, were planted with trees and flowers; substantial homes of stone announced the prosperity of the LDS way of life.

The internal structure of the church—the ward (the parish) and stake (the diocese)—became the organizing principle of all religious and social life. Nearly all the social events of a small community were sponsored by the church. The overlap between church and civic authority was nearly complete.

The Road to Statehood

After many years of persecution, the early Latter-day Saints realized the importance of self-government. However, when the Mormon pioneers arrived in their new homeland of Zion, the land actually belonged to Mexico. However, after victory in the Mexican War in 1848, the United States took possession of a vast territory in the American West, including the land that would become Utah.

The LDS Church quickly assessed the positive benefits that statehood would bring the new territory, and in 1849 a convention was called "to consider the political needs of the community." The convention created the proposed state of Deseret, which encompassed a great swath of the West, including all or parts of the current states of Utah, Nevada, Arizona, Wyoming, Colorado, New Mexico, Oregon, Idaho, and parts of southern California. The convention

wrote a constitution, elected officials (Brigham Young was elected governor), and sent a delegate to the U.S. Congress. However, the House of Representatives declined to admit the delegate from Deseret, and the statehood was effectively quashed. In fact, LDS-dominated Utah would find it exceedingly difficult to attain statehood. Nearly 50 years would pass before Utah would finally become a state.

The federal Senate did pass legislation naming Utah as a territory in 1850; however, a number of factors—especially the thorny cultural and moral issues surrounding polygamy—worked to exacerbate tensions between the new territory and the federal government.

In 1857–1858, the U.S. government sent a 2,500-man army to occupy Salt Lake City and remove Brigham Young from the governorship (accompanying the army was Alfred Cummings, whom President Buchanan had selected as territorial governor). The army reached Salt Lake City to find it newly deserted, and Cummings assumed the governorship, ending at least in theory Utah's flirtation with theocracy. Cummings soon made peace with the Mormons, and residents returned to Salt Lake City.

Second and third attempts at statehood for Deseret were met with defeat in Washington and actually seemed to stir up anti-Mormon sentiment: Congress quickly passed legislation prohibiting polygamy in the territories. The same legislation also sought to unincorporate the LDS Church.

The building of the transcontinental railroad through Utah in the 1860s decreased Utah's isolation from the rest of the United States; however, greater contact with the outside world also meant increased Mormon-gentile hostility. In 1874, Congress passed a bill effectively disenfranchising LDS-controlled district courts. In 1879, the U.S. Supreme Court upheld legislation that made the practice of plural marriage a criminal offense. Subsequent federal legislation made it illegal for polygamists to vote, hold public office, or serve on juries. The result was persecution and pursuit of avowed polygamists, many of whom were forced into hiding or exile in Mexico. The federal government's anti-Mormon campaigns also had the effect of empowering the territory's non-Mormon minority far beyond its small power base.

In 1890, LDS president Wilford Woodruff issued the startling proclamation that henceforward he advised his brethren "to refrain from contracting any marriage forbidden by the law of the land." The new doctrine was published across the country, and while many doubted the proclamation's sincerity, it signaled a major shift in direction for the statehood movement. Finally, in 1894, Congress passed the Enabling Act, which set forth the steps Utah had to follow to achieve statehood (the act stipulated that the state constitution declare polygamy be banned forever). In 1896, President Cleveland proclaimed Utah the 45th state.

It's helpful to remember the long and rancorous disputes between Utah's LDS population and the federal government in the 19th century when trying to understand the state's fervid, ongoing anti-government tendencies. In some ways, the state's anger over the establishment of the Grand Staircase–Escalante National Monument is just an example of Utah's long memory of perceived past injustice.

MODERN TIMES

Utah's close-knit Mormon farm towns thrived from the late 19th century until the Depression years. The dust bowl years were particularly hard in Utah, as most farms were entirely dependent on irrigation and the decade-long drought greatly reduced the flow of already scarce water. Communities quickly rebounded during World War II, especially as federal money poured into military camps like Wendover Air Base in the deserts west of Salt Lake City.

The designation of five national parks (beginning with Zion in 1919), two huge national recreation areas, and the vast Grand Staircase–Escalante National Monument has brought an ever-increasing stream of tourists to the state. Today, tourism is the state's largest industry, dwarfing such stalwarts as mining and lumber. In 2002, the Winter Olympics were held in the Salt Lake City area, and the world spotlight shone on the state as never before.

People and Culture

One of the oddest statistics about Utah is that it's the most urban of America's western states. Eighty-five percent of the state's population of 2,316,000 citizens live in urban areas, and a full 80 percent reside in the Wasatch Front area.

A relatively young population, combined with the Mormons' emphasis on family life and clean living, has resulted in Utah's having one of the highest birth rates and lowest death rates in the country. Racially, the state largely reflects the northern European origins of Mormon pioneers; in 2000 the state was 89 percent white. The state's population includes Hispanics (9 percent), Native Americans (1.3 percent), Asians (1.7 percent), and African Americans (0.8 percent).

UTAH'S NATIVE AMERICANS
Shoshoni

Nomadic bands of Shoshoni occupied much of northern Utah, southern Idaho, and western Wyoming for thousands of years. Horses obtained from the Plains tribes—who had obtained them from the Spanish—allowed hunting parties to cover a large range. The great Chief Washakie led his people for 50 years and negotiated the tribe's treaties with the federal government. The Washakie Indian Reservation, near Plymouth in far northern Utah, belongs to the Northwestern band of Shoshoni, though few live there now. Tribal headquarters are in Rock Springs, Wyoming, south of the large Wind River Indian Reservation.

Goshute (or Gosiute)

This branch of the Western Shoshoni, more isolated than other Utah tribes, lived in the harsh Great Basin. They survived through intricate knowledge of the land and use of temporary shelters. These peaceful hunters and gatherers ate almost everything that they found—plants, birds, rodents, crickets, and other insects. Because the Goshute had to dig for much of their food, early explorers called the tribe Digger Indians. White men couldn't believe these people survived in such a barren land of alkaline flats and sagebrush. Also known as the Newe, the tribe now lives on the Skull Valley Indian Reservation in Tooele County and on the Goshute Indian Reservation along the Utah–Nevada border.

Ute

Several bands of Utes, or Núuci, ranged over large areas of central and eastern Utah and adjacent Colorado. Originally hunter-gatherers, they acquired horses in about 1800 and became skilled raiders. Customs adopted from Plains tribes included the use of rawhide, tepees, and the *travois* (a sled used to carry goods). The discovery of gold in southern Colorado and the pressures of farmers there and in Utah forced the Utes to move and renegotiate treaties many times. They now have the large Uintah and Ouray Indian Reservation in northeast Utah, the small White Mesa Indian Reservation in southeast Utah, and the Ute Mountain Indian Reservation in southwest Colorado and northwest New Mexico.

Southern Paiute

Six of the 19 major bands of the Southern Paiutes, or Nuwuvi, lived along the Santa Clara, Beaver, and Virgin Rivers and in other parts of southwest Utah. Extended families hunted and gathered food together. Fishing and the cultivation of corn, beans, squash, and sunflowers supplemented the diet of most of the bands. Today, Utah's Paiutes have a tribal headquarters in Cedar City and scattered small parcels of reservation land. Southern Paiutes also live in southern Nevada and northern Arizona.

Navajo

Calling themselves Diné, the Navajo moved into the San Juan River area about 1600. The tribe has proved exceptionally adaptable in learning new skills from other cultures: many Navajo crafts, clothing, and religious practices have come from Native American, Spanish, and Anglo neighbors. The Navajo tribe was the first in the area to move away from a hunting and gathering lifestyle, relying instead on the farming and shepherding techniques they had learned from the Spanish. The Navajo have become one of the largest Native American groups in the country, occupying 16 million acres of exceptionally scenic land in southeast Utah and adjacent Arizona and New Mexico. Tribal headquarters is at Window Rock in Arizona.

THE MORMONS

If you're new to the "Beehive State," you'll find plenty of opportunities to learn about Mormon history and religion. At least half of Utah's population actively participates in the Church of Jesus Christ of Latter-day Saints; three-quarters of the population were born into the faith. Temple Square in Salt Lake City offers excellent tours and exhibits about the church. You'll also find many other visitors centers and historic sites scattered around the state.

Members believe that God's prophets have restored teachings of the true Christian church to the world "in these latter days." They believe their church presidents, starting with Joseph Smith, to be prophets of God, and they hold both the Bible and the Book of Mormon as the sacred word of God. The latter, they believe, was revealed to Joseph Smith from 1823 to 1830. The text tells of three migrations from the Eastern Hemisphere to the New World and the history of the people who lived in the Americas from about 600 B.C. to about A.D. 400. The book contains 239 chapters, which include teachings Christ supposedly gave in the Americas, prophecy, doctrines, and epic tales of the rise and fall of nations. It's regarded by the church as a valuable addition to the Bible—but not a replacement.

Membership in the LDS Church requires faith, a willingness to serve, tithing, and obedience to church authorities. The church emphasizes healthful living, moral conduct, secure family relationships, and a thoughtful approach to social services.

RELIGION

The Church of Jesus Christ of Latter-day Saints is by far the dominant religion in Utah; about 65 percent of the population belongs to the church. Most major Christian denominations are represented in mid-sized towns, and in Salt Lake City there are small Jewish and Islamic congregations as well.

RELIGION IN UTAH

Quick, a little free-association test: When I say "Utah," what do you think? Most people, unsurprisingly, respond "Mormon." And Mormonism is inescapable for anyone traveling around Utah with eyes even half-open. Just as sensitive travelers would not denigrate Catholicism in Ireland or Buddhism in Thailand, travelers in Utah would do well to keep an open mind about Utah's predominant religion.

Remember that the church's proper title is the Church of Jesus Christ of Latter-day Saints, and that members prefer to be called "Latter-day Saints," "Saints" (usually this term is just used among church members), or "LDS." While calling someone a Mormon isn't *wrong*, it's not quite as respectful.

The religion is based in part on the Book of Mormon, the name given to a text derived from a set of "golden plates" found by Joseph Smith in 1827 in western New York. Smith claimed to have been led by an angel to the plates, which were covered with a text written in "reformed Egyptian." A farmer by upbringing, Smith translated the plates and published an English-language version of the Book of Mormon in 1830.

The Book of Mormon tells the story of the lost tribes of Israel, which, according to Mormon teachings, migrated to North America and became the ancestors of today's Native Americans. According to the Book of Mormon, Jesus also journeyed to North America, and the book includes teachings and prophecies that Christ supposedly gave to the ancient Native Americans.

Most people know that LDS members are clean-living, family people who eschew alcohol, tobacco, and stimulants, including caffeine. This can make it a little tough for visitors to feed their own vices (and indeed, it may make what formerly seemed like a benign habit feel a little more sinister). But Utah has loosened up a lot in the past few years, largely thanks to hosting the 2002 Winter Olympics, and it's really not too hard to find a place to have a beer with dinner, though you may have to make a special request. Towns near the national parks are particularly used to hosting non-Saints and attach virtually no stigma to waking up with a cup of coffee or settling down with a glass of wine.

Logan Tabernacle

Arts and Entertainment

MUSIC

Generally speaking, Salt Lake City is the center of the state's arts scene. The state's Mormon heritage is reflected in the city's love of and support for fine music. The glittering Abravanel Concert Hall is home to the noted Utah Symphony, and the tabernacle at Temple Square is often filled with concerts and recitals. The famed Mormon Tabernacle Choir performs here, as do various other church-related music groups. Best of all, all performances at Temple Square are free, making this a great opportunity for travelers to soak up culture at a good price.

Salt Lake City is also the state's major venue for rock and alternative music. A number of lively clubs host both local bands and traveling acts from both coasts. In most cases, music clubs are private clubs and you'll need to either buy a temporary membership or get sponsored by a member. Despite the rigmarole, the music's usually good and the crowds are interesting.

Come summer, there's fine music at more out-of-the-way places. Venues at Park City offer a full summer schedule ranging from rock concerts at The Canyons Ski Area to the Utah Symphony at classy Deer Valley Resort. In Logan's sparkling Capitol Theatre, the Utah Festival Opera puts on a summer season of grand opera.

THEATER AND DANCE

Again, Salt Lake City is the center of things theatrical in Utah. Several year-round theatrical troupes dish up everything from Broadway musicals to serious plays like Tony Kushner's *Angels in America*.

In the summer, Cedar City's Utah Shakespearean Festival (www.bard.org) offers eight different plays performed by a professional repertory company. Both Shakespearean and contemporary plays are featured; the Bard's works are presented under the stars in an outdoor theater.

Salt Lake City supports a number of dance troupes, all with excellent reputations. Ballet West performs a mix of classical and contemporary pieces, while the Ririe-Woodbury Dance Company has a more eclectic approach to dance.

CINEMA

While you'll be able to see most first-run films and some art-house fare in Salt Lake City and, to a lesser extent, in smaller cities in Utah, the real cinematic event in Utah is the Sundance Film Festival, held every January in Park City. Founded by actor Robert Redford as a forum for little-seen documentary and independent films, the festival has grown into a major showcase of new, high-quality cinema. Make lodging and ticket reservations well in advance if you want to attend. For more information and to get on the mailing list, call 801/328-FILM (801/328-3456).

MUSEUMS

Utah residents are very proud of their pioneer past, and nearly every community in the state has a Daughters of Utah Pioneers (DUP) museum, which recounts the story of local Mormon settlement. In fact, church history and state history are so closely interconnected that the primary state history museums are the various Temple Square institutions and the LDS-dominated Pioneer Memorial Museum. The museum at the Utah Historical Society isn't even in the same league.

Utah has a number of good museums dedicated to dinosaurs and other forms of ancient life. The area around Price and Vernal is rich in fossils, and both towns have good dinosaur museums; additionally, there are fossil digs with visitors centers at Dinosaur National Monument and at the Cleveland-Lloyd Dinosaur Quarry. The Museum of Ancient Life at Lehi has one of the largest collections of complete dinosaur skeletons in the country.

Ogden has converted its large and handsome

© JUDY JEWELL

The Utah Field House of Natural History State Park Museum is a must-see in Vernal.

railroad depot into a multi-museum complex with collections of minerals, fine art, firearms, and historic automobiles and train cars.

ART GALLERIES

Utah isn't exactly known for its fine-art collections, but the Salt Lake Art Center has a changing lineup of traveling shows that focus on regional artists. The universities in Salt Lake City, Provo, and Logan each have art galleries, and Ogden boasts the Myra Powell Art Gallery in the historic train depot. If you're looking for commercial art galleries, the state's richest pay dirt is in Park City. This small resort community has more fine art galleries than Salt Lake City.

EVENTS

Throughout Utah, the year's biggest event is **Pioneer Day** on July 24, with parades and fireworks in almost every Utah community. It commemorates the day in 1847 when Brigham Young said of the Salt Lake Valley "This is the place."

To most of the outside world, the biggest deal is January's **Sundance Film Festival,** in Park City, when you can see the best independent films shoulder to shoulder with the actors, directors, and press . . .tickets are hard to score, but it's possible. Likewise, be sure to book your room way in advance or be prepared for a long commute.

In June, the **Utah Shakespeare Festival** begins its summer-long run in Cedar City and, for a couple of weeks, little Manti becomes a hot spot with the performance of the **Mormon Miracle Pageant.**

July brings the **Utah Festival Opera** to Logan and, for six days in August, the Bonneville Salt Flats are the site of **Speed Week,** when vehicles ranging from motorcycles to diesel trucks "shoot the salt."

ESSENTIALS

Getting There and Around

Although Salt Lake City is well connected with the rest of the world and has a good public transportation system, to really explore the state, a car is the most realistic choice (though a case can be made for a bike and strong legs). However, if you're planning a winter trip with a focus on skiing the Wasatch ski areas, consider skipping the car rental and relying on shuttles or city buses.

GETTING THERE
By Air
More than a dozen major airlines serve Salt Lake City, which has the only major airport in the state. Salt Lake City is the western hub for Delta Air Lines, which provides the most international and regional links.

By Train
Amtrak runs one passenger train across Utah. The California Zephyr runs between Oakland and Chicago via Salt Lake City. For information and reservations, contact Amtrak (800/872-7245, www.amtrak.com).

By Bus
The **Greyhound** bus line offers interstate service to Utah on its routes along I-15, I-70, and I-80.

© SARAH BUTLER

By RV

Many foreign travelers enter Utah in RVs, which they rent to drive on a tour of the western national parks. It takes more planning to line up a rental RV than a car, but there are plenty of agencies in Los Angeles, Phoenix, Las Vegas, and Salt Lake City able to do the job. Most travel agents can help, or you can contact the local travel office in the city of your departure.

GETTING AROUND
By Air

Regional airlines connect Salt Lake City with other communities in the state. Regular scheduled flights link to Vernal, St. George, and Cedar City. The cost per mile of these short hops is high, but you'll often have excellent views.

By Train

Amtrak can get you to Price, Helper, Provo,

THE GREAT WESTERN TRAIL

As its name implies, the Great Western Trail, when completed, will traverse some of the West's most spectacular country. The Utah stretch, approximately 350 miles long, will link trails in Arizona and Idaho with others in New Mexico, Wyoming, and Montana (the Utah section is now over 90 percent complete). Planners envision a trail network stretching all the way from Mexico to Canada, providing travel possibilities for bicycles, horses, and motorized vehicles, as well as hikers. About 90 percent of the finished network will employ existing roads and trails.

The southernmost Utah section follows washes and canyons across land administered by the Bureau of Land Management; elevations drop as low as 4,800 feet. The Dixie National Forest section skirts the western edge of Bryce Canyon National Park and continues across high plateaus to Boulder Top, where it reaches elevations topping 11,000 feet. Fishlake National Forest has more fine alpine country and expansive views from Thousand Lake Mountain, Windstorm Peak, and the UM Plateau areas. In the Manti-La Sal National Forest, the trail ascends the lofty Wasatch Plateau and extends for 75 miles through rolling meadows and forest country. Uinta National Forest features lush forests beneath the jagged summits of the Wasatch Range's Mount Timpanogos and Lone Peak. The ups and downs of the Wasatch Range continue as the trail winds through the Wasatch-Cache National Forest high above Salt Lake City and the Great Salt Lake. The northernmost trail section in Utah climbs into the Bear River Range and meets the Idaho border near Beaver Mountain.

Note that some trail sections are open to off-road vehicles and pets and some aren't. You can obtain the latest trail information from www.gwt.org.

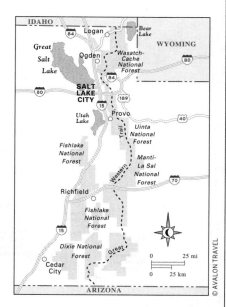

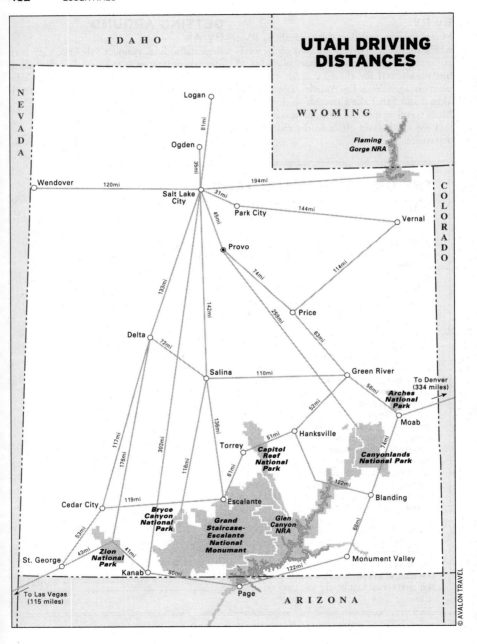

UTAH DRIVING DISTANCES

IDAHO

NEVADA

WYOMING

Flaming Gorge NRA

Logan

Ogden

81mi

35mi

Wendover — 120mi — 194mi

Salt Lake City

31mi — Park City — 144mi — Vernal

45mi

Provo

74mi

114mi

COLORADO

133mi

142mi

Price

259mi

63mi

Delta

72mi

Salina — 110mi — Green River

To Denver (334 miles)

58mi

Arches National Park

117mi

303mi

136mi

52mi

Moab

176mi

118mi

51mi — Hanksville

Torrey

Capitol Reef National Park

74mi

Canyonlands National Park

61mi

122mi

Cedar City — 119mi — Escalante

Blanding

Bryce Canyon National Park

53mi

Grand Staircase-Escalante National Monumant

Glen Canyon NRA

68mi

43mi

Zion National Park

41mi

St. George

Kanab — 80mi

Monument Valley

122mi

To Las Vegas (115 miles)

Page

ARIZONA

© AVALON TRAVEL

and Salt Lake City, but that's about all. Public transportation to other points of interest, such as the national parks, is notably absent.

By Bus

There's Greyhound bus service along Utah's interstate highways and U.S. 6 (between Green River and Provo), but these routes really don't get you close to the sorts of sights that most people come to Utah to see. The Wasatch Front area (from Provo to Ogden and from Salt Lake City out to Tooele) is served by Utah Transit Authority (UTA), a regional bus company with excellent service. Park City and other Salt Lake City ski areas are accessible via a number of ski-bus operations, some of which pick up at the airport.

By Car

Public transportation serves cities and some towns but very few of the scenic, historic, and recreational areas. Unless you're on a tour, you really need your own transportation. Cars are easily rented in any large town, though Salt Lake City offers by far the greatest selection. Four-wheel drive vehicles can be rented, too,

and will be very handy if you plan extensive travel on back roads.

Most tourist offices carry the Utah road map published by the Utah Department of Transportation; it's one of the best available and is free.

By Bicycle

Touring on a bicycle is to be fully alive to the land, skies, sounds, plants, and birds of Utah. The experience of gliding across the desert or topping out on a mountain pass goes beyond words. Some effort, a lightweight touring or mountain bike, touring gear, and awareness of what's going on around you are all that's needed. Start with short rides if you're new to bicycle touring, then work up to longer cross-country trips. By learning to maintain and repair your steed, you'll seldom have trouble on the road. An extra-low gear of 30 inches or less takes the strain out of long mountain grades. Utah has almost every kind of terrain and road condition imaginable; mountain bicyclists find the Moab area in the southeast especially challenging and scenic. Note that designated wilderness areas are closed to cycling.

Recreation

OUTDOOR ACTIVITIES

The best place to begin looking for information on recreational opportunities in Utah is the comprehensive www.utah.com website. The site contains information on most sports and activities and provides lots of links to yet more outfitters and sites.

Mountain Biking

Mountain biking has done much to put Utah on the recreation map. Trails in the slickrock canyon country near Moab attract more than 150,000 biking enthusiasts a year, and now nearly all corners of the state promote their old Forest Service or mining roads as a biking paradise. There's good info for planning bike trips at www.utah.com/bike, and excel-

lent biking guidebooks are available from bookstores.

In general, Utah summers are too hot for mountain biking. The peak season in Moab runs March–May and again September–November.

River-Running

Rafting or canoeing Utah's rivers is another favorite activity for tourists and adventurers. The most notable float trip is down the Colorado River between Moab and the backwaters of Lake Powell. This multiday trip passes through Cataract Canyon, and for spectacular adventure it's second only to trips through the Grand Canyon. The Green and San Juan Rivers are also popular. For these trips, plan well in

oarswoman and her crew on the Green River

slot canyon in Zion

advance, as spaces are limited and demand more than outstrips availability. In towns like Moab, Green River, Vernal, and Bluff, numerous outfitters provide exciting day trips that can usually take people with only a day's notice.

Hiking, Backpacking, and Camping

Utah offers lots of backcountry for those interested in exploring the scenery on foot. One increasingly popular activity is canyoneering—exploring mazelike slot canyons. Hundreds of feet deep but sometimes only wide enough for a hiker to squeeze through, these canyons are found in the southern part of the state, particularly near Escalante and in the Paria River area. You'll need to be fit to explore these regions—and watch the weather carefully for flash floods.

Hikers will find great trails in almost all parts of the state. The rugged Wasatch Range near Salt Lake City is a popular day-hike destination for urban residents of the Wasatch Front, while the lofty, lake-filled Uintas in northeastern Utah are perfect for long-distance trips. Much of the canyonlands of southern and southeastern Utah are accessible only by foot; visits to remote Anasazi ruins and petroglyphs reward the long-distance hiker.

Campers are in luck in Utah. The state has a highly developed network of campgrounds. During peak tourist season, make reservations or arrive at your destination early.

Skiing and Snowboarding

You may have noticed the legend on the license plates: "Ski Utah!" It is almost a command during the winter months. Skiing has always been excellent in the Wasatch Front ski areas near Salt Lake City and Park City, and since the 2002 Winter Olympics, the world knows about Utah's uncrowded slopes, which provide some of the best powder skiing in North America. If you've always wanted to ski or board Olympic-quality slopes, plan a trip to Utah: All the runs and facilities developed for the Olympics are still in place. For a good overview of Utah's ski areas and information on special package deals, check www.skiutah.com.

Fishing

The Wasatch and Uinta Ranges are dotted with lakes and drained by streams that are rich in rainbow and cutthroat trout. Fly-fishing is a major sport in many mountain communities, and most towns have at least one fly shop and an outfitter anxious to take you out to a stream. Favorite fishing spots include Bear Lake, with good fishing for lake and cutthroat trout; Flaming Gorge Reservoir on the Green River, offering good fishing for lake trout, smallmouth bass, and kokanee salmon; and Lake Powell, with good fishing for catfish, striper, and bass.

Horseback Riding

While guest ranches are the best places to experience a Western-style vacation on horseback, the ski areas at Park City also offer riding in summer. In winter, sleigh rides are featured.

Rockhounding

Utah is rich in curious stones, fossils, and gems. The lack of vegetation and the high level of erosion make rockhounding a relatively simple matter. One of the best places to plan a rock-hunting expedition is the Delta area, where you can explore for geodes, agates, garnets, and other treasures.

Golfing

There are dozens and dozens of golf courses across Utah. Notable courses dot the Salt Lake City area and also lie near Ogden, Logan, Provo, and Park City. The state's greatest concentration of courses, though, is in St. George, in the southern part of the state. Perhaps it's rhetorical to wonder which comes first, retirees or golf courses, but St. George's excellent courses amid magnificent red-rock formations certainly have contributed mightily to the town's reputation as a retirement haven.

NATIONAL PARKS AND MONUMENTS

Utah is home to five major national parks, seven national monuments, two national recreation areas, and one national historic site. Three of the crown jewels of the national park system—Zion, Arches, and Bryce Canyon—are here, as well as the less traveled Capitol Reef and Canyonlands parks. Just across the border in Nevada is Great Basin National Park, and just south in Arizona is the Grand Canyon. In 1996, Grand Staircase–Escalante National Monument added protection to 1.9 million acres of public land to Utah's inventory of scenic wild lands. These national park areas and national monuments are the state's largest tourist attractions.

The parks are all open year-round, though spring and fall are the best times to visit—you'll avoid the heat and crowds of high summer. The entry fee for the national parks has gone up greatly in the past few years; admission to Bryce Canyon is now $25 per vehicle. If you're planning on making the rounds of the Utah national parks, it's an excellent idea to purchase an America the Beautiful Pass ($80), which covers admission costs at national parks and other federal recreation sites.

STATE PARKS

Utah boasts 41 state parks, ranging from golf courses to fishing holes, from historic forts to Anasazi ruins. Entry fees to state parks vary, though in general there's a $5–7 per-vehicle day-use fee at the recreational parks. Many of these have campgrounds; you can make reservations at 800/322-3770 or www.reserve america.com. For general information on Utah's state parks, contact Utah State Parks (801/538-7220, http://stateparks.utah.gov).

WILDERNESS TRAVEL

As more people seek relief from the stress of urban life, wilderness areas are becoming increasingly popular. Fortunately, Utah has an abundance of this fragile and precious resource. The many designated wilderness areas have been closed to mechanized vehicles (including mountain bikes) to protect both the environment and the experience of solitude. Most designated areas lie within national forests or Bureau of Land Management lands, and many are free to visit without a permit; others require permits, and some have entrance fees. The national parks and monuments require backcountry permits for overnight stays.

Accommodations

Utah is a major tourist destination, and you can plan on finding high-quality, reasonably priced motels and hotels in most cities and towns. Reservations are a good idea in major centers like Salt Lake City, Park City, and Moab—especially on weekends. Along the national parks loop, off-season rooms are limited (some establishments are seasonal), so call ahead to make sure there's a room at the inn.

Hostels
Hostels are available only in Salt Lake City and Moab. They are open to travelers of all ages, and don't require membership cards. You may need to provide your own sleeping cloth.

Bed-and-Breakfasts
With its wealth of pioneer-era homes and mansions, Utah also offers travelers some comfortable bed-and-breakfast accommodations. If you're only familiar with British-style B&Bs, you'll discover that in American B&Bs are more like small, well-appointed inns—usually in historically or architecturally significant homes. Smoking and pets are restricted, some inns have rules against young children, and others are reserved for couples only. Most require advance booking.

In Utah's B&Bs you'll find a friendly welcome, personalized advice on sites and recreation, a chance to meet fellow travelers, and, of course, a fine breakfast.

For more information on bed-and-breakfasts, contact the visitors centers in the regions you plan to visit; contact B&B Inns of Utah Incorporated (www.bbiu.org), a membership organization representing bed-and-breakfasts across the state; or contact the Utah Travel Council (800/200-1160, www.utah.com) for a more general list.

Guest Ranches
Utah has fewer guest ranches than other Western states, but some have sprung up here and there. Most are family ranches that take in guests during the summer. These tend to be authentic, horse-powered operations where you'll work alongside the family and stay in no-frills cabins or bunkhouses. Others are more upscale and offer a dude-ranch atmosphere with a number of recreational options.

Most guest ranches ask for minimum stays, and prices include all meals and lodging. Advance reservations are usually required. If you're contemplating staying at a guest ranch, be sure to ask specific questions about lodgings and work requirements. Expectations of the guest and host can vary widely. The Utah Travel Council can provide a full listing of Utah guest ranches; it's also available from www.utah.com.

Food and Drink

Utah is not one of the culinary capitals of the world. Outside of Salt Lake City, Park City, and Moab, restaurants in Utah generally serve standard American fare, with family restaurants and grills setting the standards even in midsize towns. Even the steak house, omnipresent elsewhere in the West, is curiously absent here. Most towns have a vintage American-Chinese restaurant, which is usually the best bet for a vegetarian. After a couple of days on the road, you may be glad to note that Pizza Hut usually offers a salad bar and that you can get a fresh salad at McDonalds.

The good news is that in the three towns noted above, you can eat quite well. Park City has some excellent high-end restaurants. Moab offers a varied selection of restaurants, including two excellent brewpubs with complete dining facilities. Salt Lake City has restaurants to satisfy most every taste, including some excellent ethnic options.

Having a drink with your meal is easier in the above three cities than elsewhere in the state. Access to alcohol in restaurants varies quite a bit from community to community, and some towns are practically "dry"—alcohol-free.

Drinking Laws

The state's liquor laws are rather confusing and peculiar. Several different kinds of establishments are licensed to sell alcoholic beverages.

Taverns, which include brewpubs, can sell only 3.2 percent beer (not wine, which is classed as hard liquor in Utah). You don't need to purchase food or be a member of a private club to have a beer in a tavern. With the exception of brewpubs, taverns are usually fairly derelict and not especially cheery places to hang out.

Licensed restaurants sell beer, wine, and hard liquor but only with food orders. However, it's not always easy to tell if drinks are served, because a long-time—but now defunct—law forbade servers from asking customers if they cared for a drink. In many parts of the state, you still need to specifically ask for a drink or the drink menu to begin the process. In Salt Lake City, Moab, and Park City, most restaurants have liquor licenses. In other cities and towns, very few eating establishments offer alcohol.

Private clubs are essentially the same as bars in other parts of the United States. You can have drinks with or without food during opening hours. However, you must be a member to eat or drink in a private club. For the traveler, this doesn't present an insurmountable hurdle, as you can buy temporary memberships (a two-week membership usually costs around $5). If you're fond of a drink and nightlife, it might well be worth it. Most live music clubs are private clubs, for instance. Also, members of a club are able to sign in up to five friends on a nightly basis. You can ask a friendly-looking stranger to sign you in, or, if you're part of a group, one of you can become a member and sign the others in.

Nearly all towns have a state-owned liquor store, and 3.2 percent beer is available in most grocery stores. Carrying a bottle of your favorite beverage to your room may be the easiest way to enjoy an evening drink.

The state drinking age is 21.

Conduct and Customs

If you've never traveled in Utah before, you may find that Utah residents don't initially seem as welcoming and outgoing as people in other Western states. In many smaller towns, visitors from outside the community are a relatively new phenomenon, and not everyone in the state is anxious to have their towns turned into tourist or recreational meccas. The Mormons are very family- and community-oriented, and if certain individuals initially seem insular and uninterested in travelers, don't take it as unfriendliness.

Mormons are also very orderly and socially conservative people. Brash displays of rudeness or use of foul language in public will not make you popular.

Alcohol and Nightlife

Observant Mormons don't drink alcoholic beverages, and state laws have been drafted to make purchasing alcohol relatively awkward. If going out for drinks and nightclubbing is part of your idea of entertainment, you'll find that only Salt Lake City, Park City, and Moab offer much in the way of clubs and nightspots. Most towns have a liquor store; outside of the Wasatch Front and Moab, don't expect restaurants to have liquor licenses.

SAY IT RIGHT!

The following place-names are easy to mispronounce. Say it like a local!

Duchesne	du-SHANE
Ephraim	E-from
Escalante	es-kuh-LAN-tay
Hurricane	HUR-uh-kun
Kanab	kuh-NAB
Lehi	LEE-high
Manti	MAN-tie
Monticello	mon-tuh-SELL-o
Nephi	NEE-fi
Panguitch	PAN-gwich
Salina	suh-LINE-uh
Tooele	too-WILL-uh
Uinta	yoo-IN-tuh
Weber	WEE-ber

Private Clubs

Most drinking establishments—and certainly the ones that will seem most normal to outsiders—are private clubs. Clubs that serve hard liquor without food and feature live music or other entertainment are almost all private clubs, which means you need to be a member to get in. Thankfully, it's not an overwhelming obstacle. You can buy a two-week membership, usually for $5.

Smoking

Smoking is taboo for observant Mormons, and, as in many states, an Indoor Clean Air Act prohibits smoking in all public places (excluding taverns and private clubs). You're also not allowed to smoke on church grounds.

Tips for Travelers

FOREIGN VISITORS
Entering the United States

Citizens of Canada must now provide a passport to enter the United States. However, a visa is not required for Canadian citizens.

Citizens of 28 other countries can enter under a reciprocal visa waiver program. These citizens can enter the United States for up to 90 days for tourism or business with a valid passport; however, no visa is required. These countries include most of Western Europe, plus Japan, Australia, New Zealand, and Singapore. For a full list of reciprocal visa countries (and other late-breaking new for travelers to the United States), check out www.travel.state.gov. Visitors on this program who arrive by sea or air must show round-trip tickets back out of the United States within 90 days, and must be able to present proof of financial solvency (credit cards are usually sufficient). If citizens of these countries are staying longer than 90 days, they must apply for and present a visa.

Citizens of countries not covered by the reciprocal visa program are required to present both a valid passport and a visa to enter the United States. These are obtained from U.S. embassies and consulates. These travelers are also required to offer proof of financial solvency and provide a round-trip ticket out of the United States within the timeline of the visa.

Customs

U.S. Customs allows each person over the age of 21 to bring in one liter of liquor and 200 cigarettes duty free into the country. Non-U.S. citizens can bring in $100 worth of gifts without paying duty. If you are carrying more than $10,000 in cash or travelers checks, you are required to declare it.

Traveling in the United States

Once in the United States, foreign visitors can travel freely among states without restrictions. A few states maintain agricultural checkpoints at state borders to prevent transport of fruit or plants, but Utah is not one of these states.

GAY AND LESBIAN TRAVELERS

Gay travelers will find Utah even less welcoming to openly gay people than many of the surrounding Western states. There's a gay scene of sorts in Salt Lake City, but very little sign of support elsewhere in the state. In 1996, a bookstore owned by two gay men was burned in southern Utah and the owners were forced to leave town. Not surprisingly, Utah gays and lesbians tend to be extremely discreet.

Unfortunately, there aren't a lot of community resources for gay and lesbian travelers. Salt Lake City's two gay newspapers, *Q* and *Pillar,* are a good places to get a flavor for the Utah gay scene. Many of the support groups that do exist in the state are concerned with supporting gay and lesbian Mormons.

TRAVELERS WITH DISABILITIES

Travelers with disabilities will find Utah quite progressive when it comes to accessibility issues, especially in Salt Lake City and the heavily traveled national parks in southern Utah. Most parks offer all-abilities trails, and many hotels advertise their fully accessible facilities. The National Ability Center (435/649-3991, www.discoverNAC.org), based in Park City, provides recreational opportunities for people of all ages and abilities, including a skiing program at nearby Park City Mountain Resort.

Health and Safety

Utah has one of the lowest crime rates in the United States. Although parts of Salt Lake City look pretty scruffy, there's little reason to fear random violence unless you put yourself in unwise situations.

In emergencies, you can dial 911 in most communities in Utah; otherwise, use the emergency number listed on most telephones or dial a zero for an operator. Hospital emergency rooms offer the quickest help but cost more than a visit to a doctor's office or clinic. Hospital care is very expensive—medical insurance is recommended.

ANIMAL THREATS

Probably a greater threat to health are poisonous rattlesnakes and scorpions. When hiking or climbing in desert areas, never put your hand onto a ledge or into a hole that you can't see. Both are perfect lairs for snakes and scorpions. While snakebites are rarely fatal anymore, they're no fun, either. If you are bitten, immobilize the affected area and seek immediate medical attention.

If you do much hiking and biking in the spring, there's a good chance you'll encounter ticks. While ticks in this part of the United States don't usually carry Lyme disease, there is a remote threat of Rocky Mountain spotted fever, spread by the wood tick. If a tick has bitten you, pull it off immediately. Grasp the tick's head parts (as close to your skin as possible) with tweezers and pull slowly and steadily. Do not attempt to remove ticks by burning them or coating them with anything. Removing a tick as quickly as possible greatly reduces your chance of infection.

Utah is home to black bears, which aren't as menacing as their cousins the grizzly bear. However, black bears weigh more than most humans and have far sharper claws and teeth. An encounter with a black bear is rarely fatal, but it's something to be avoided.

If you encounter a bear, give it plenty of room and try not to surprise it. Wearing a fragrance while in bear country isn't a good idea because it attracts bears, as do strong-smelling foods. *Always store food items outside the tent,* and if you're in bear territory, sleep well away from the cooking area. Waking up with a bear clawing at your tent is to be avoided. Hanging food in a bag from a tree is a long-standing and wise precaution. If a bear becomes aggressive, try to drop something that will divert its attention while you flee. If that isn't possible, the next best bet is to curl up into a ball, clasp your hands behind your neck, and play dead, even if the bear begins to bat you around. Taking precautions and having respect for bears will ensure not only your continued existence, but theirs as well.

In recent years, as humans have increasingly moved into mountain lions' habitat (and as their numbers have increased), they have become a threat to humans, especially small children. Never leave children unattended in forests and never allow them to lag far behind on a family hike. Nearly every summer newspapers in the Western states carry tragic stories of children stalked and killed by mountain lions. Safety is in numbers.

HYPOTHERMIA

The greatest danger outdoors is one that can sneak up and kill with very little warning. Hypothermia—a lowering of the body's temperature below 95°F—causes disorientation, uncontrollable shivering, slurred speech, and drowsiness. The victim may not even realize what's wrong. Unless corrective action is taken immediately, hypothermia can lead to death. This is why hikers should travel with companions and always carry wind and rain protection. Space blankets are lightweight and cheap and offer protection against the cold in emergencies. Remember that temperatures can plummet rapidly in Utah's dry climate—a drop of 40°F between day and night is common. Be especially careful at high elevations, where summer sunshine can quickly change into freezing rain or a blizzard. Simply falling into a mountain stream while fishing can also lead to hypothermia and death unless proper action is taken. If you're cold and tired, don't waste time! Seek shelter and build a fire, change into dry clothes, and drink warm liquids. If a victim isn't fully conscious, warm him or her by skin-to-skin contact in a sleeping bag. Try to keep the victim awake and offer plenty of warm liquids.

HANTAVIRUS

Hantavirus is an airborne infectious disease agent transmitted from rodents to humans when rodents shed hantavirus particles in their saliva, urine, and droppings and humans inhale infected particles. It is easiest for a human to contract hantavirus in a contained environment, such as a cabin infested with mouse droppings, where the virus-infected particles are not thoroughly dispersed.

Simply traveling to a place where the hantavirus is known to occur is not considered a risk factor. Camping, hiking, and other outdoor activities also pose low risks, especially if steps are taken to reduce rodent contact.

The very first symptoms can occur anywhere between five days and three weeks after infection. They almost always include fever, fatigue, and aching muscles (usually in the back, shoulders, and/or thighs) and other flu-like conditions. Other early symptoms may include headaches, dizziness, chills, and abdominal discomfort (such as vomiting, nausea, and/or diarrhea). These are shortly followed by intense coughing and shortness of breath. If you have these symptoms, seek medical help immediately. Untreated infections of hantavirus are almost always fatal.

GIARDIA

Giardia, a protozoan that has become common in even the remotest mountain streams, is carried in animal or human waste that is deposited or washed into natural waters. When ingested, it begins reproducing, causing an intestinal sickness in the host that can become very serious and may not be cured without medical attention.

You can take precautions against giardia with a variety of chemicals and filtering methods or by boiling water before drinking it. The various chemical solutions on the market work in some applications, but because they need to be safe for human consumption they are weak and ineffective against the protozoan in its cyst stage of life (when it encases itself in a hard shell). Filtering may eliminate giardia, but there are other water pests too small to be caught by most filters. The most effective way to eliminate such threats is to boil all suspect water. A few minutes at a rolling boil will kill giardia even in the cyst stage.

THE SUN AND HEAT

Utah in summer is a very hot place. Be sure to use sunscreen, or else you risk having a very uncomfortable vacation. Heat exhaustion can also be a problem if you're hiking in the hot sun. Drink plenty of water; in midsummer, try to get an early start if you're hiking in full sun.

GETTING LOST

Part of the attraction of Utah's vast wilderness backcountry is its remoteness. And if you're hiking in the canyon country in the southern part of the state, you'll spend most of your time hiking at the bottom of narrow and twisting canyons. It's easy to get lost, or at least disoriented. Always carry adequate and up-to-date maps and a compass—and you need know how to use them if you're heading off into the backcountry. Always plan a route. Planning usually saves time and effort. Tell someone (like a family member or a ranger) where you are going and when you'll be back, so they know where and when to start looking for you in case you get into trouble. Always take at least one other person with you: *Do not* venture into the desert alone. Parties of four people (or two vehicles) are ideal, because one person can stay with the person in trouble, while the other two escort each other to get help. It's a good idea to carry your cell phone in case you need to make an emergency call or send an email.

FLASH FLOODS

Thunderstorms can wash hikers away and bury them in the canyons and washes of the Southwest. Flash floods can happen almost any time of year but are most prevalent in the summer months. Before entering slot canyon areas like Paria or the Escalante Canyons, check with rangers or local authorities for weather reports. And while you're hiking, read and heed the clouds. Many washes and canyons drain large areas, with their headwaters many miles away. The dangerous part is that sometimes you just can't tell what's coming down the wash or canyon because of the vast number of acres that these canyons drain, and because the cliff walls are too high to see out to any storms that may be creating flood potential upstream. At any sign of a threat, get out of the canyon bottom—at least 60 vertical feet up—to avoid water and debris. Since many of these canyons are narrow, there are places where it's not possible to get out of the canyon on short notice. Never drive a vehicle into a flooded wash. Stop and wait for the water to recede, as it usually will within an hour.

DRIVING HAZARDS

Summer heat in the desert puts an extra strain on both cars and drivers. It's worth double-checking your vehicle's cooling system, engine oil, transmission fluid, fan belts, and tires to make sure they are in top condition. Carry several gallons of water in case of a breakdown or radiator trouble. Never leave children or pets in a parked car during warm weather—temperatures inside can cause fatal heatstroke in minutes.

At times the desert has *too much* water, when late-summer storms frequently flood low spots in the road. Wait for the water level to subside before crossing.

Dust storms can completely block visibility but tend to be short-lived. During such storms, pull completely off the road, stop, and turn off your lights so as not to confuse other drivers.

If stranded, either on the desert or in the mountains, stay with your vehicle unless you're *positive* of where to go for help, then leave a note explaining your route and departure time. Airplanes can easily spot a stranded car (tie a piece of cloth to your antenna), but a person walking is more difficult to see. It's best to carry emergency supplies: blankets or sleeping bags, first-aid kit, tools, jumper cables, shovel, traction mats or chains, flashlight, rain gear, water, food, and a can opener.

Information and Services

MONEY

Prices of all services mentioned in this book were current at press time. You're sure to find seasonal and long-term price changes, so *please,* don't use what's listed here to argue with the staff at a motel, campground, museum, airline, or other office.

Banking

Cash machines or ATMs are available throughout Utah, even in the smallest towns. It's hard to exchange foreign currency or travelers checks outside of central Salt Lake City, so foreign travelers should exchange all they'll need before setting out for rural parts of the state. Credit cards are generally accepted at most businesses.

Taxes

A 6.25 percent sales tax is added to most transactions on goods, food, and services. Additional room taxes are added; these vary by community and can be quite steep.

Tipping

It's customary to tip 15–20 percent to food and drink servers; tips are almost never automatically added to the bill. Taxi drivers receive a 10–15 percent gratuity; bellhops get at least $1 a bag.

MAPS AND TOURIST INFORMATION

General tourist literature and maps are available from the **Utah Travel Council** (800/200-1160, www.utah.com). Utah's many chambers of commerce also have free material and are happy to help with travel suggestions in their areas. See the *Information* sections throughout this book for contact information. Also listed are national forest offices and other government agencies that have information on outdoor recreation in their areas.

The Utah Department of Transportation prints and distributes a free, regularly updated map of Utah. Ask for it when you call for information or when you stop at a visitors information office. If you're planning on extensive backcountry exploration, be sure to ask locally about conditions. Backcountry enthusiasts or back-road explorers should also pick up Benchmark Maps' *Utah Road and Recreation Atlas.*

Utah State Parks and Recreation

Obtain literature and the latest information on all of Utah's state parks from the Utah State Parks and Recreation office (801/538-7220, 877/887-2757, http://stateparks.utah.gov). If you're planning a lot of state park visits, ask about the $70 annual state park pass. Reservations for campgrounds and some other services can be made by at 800/322-3770 or www.reserveamerica.com; a reservation fee of $7 applies.

COMMUNICATIONS

Normal post office hours are 8:30 A.M.–5 P.M. Monday–Friday and sometimes 8:30 A.M.–noon Saturday. U.S. post offices sell stamps and postal money orders. Overnight express service is also available.

Utah has two area codes: 801 is the code for the greater Salt Lake City area, which includes suburbs as far south as Provo and as far north as Ogden. The rest of the state has the area code 435.

Toll-free numbers in the United States have an 800, 888, 877, or 866 area code. To obtain directory assistance, dial 411. In rural areas, you may need to dial the state area code, then 555-1212. Many airlines and motel chains have toll-free numbers; dial 800/555-1212 for toll-free information.

The cost of a call from a pay phone is usually $0.50. Phones that accept prepaid phone cards are only dependably available in the Salt Lake City and Park City areas.

Even in small towns, most hotels (and even many budget motels) offer wireless Internet access.

BUSINESS HOURS

In Utah, most commercial businesses are open 9 A.M.–6 P.M. Monday–Saturday. The biggest surprise to many travelers will be that nearly all businesses—and almost certainly those away from Salt Lake City, big recreational hubs, and the national parks—close on Sunday in Utah. *Again, almost all businesses in Utah, including restaurants, are closed on Sunday.* This includes local public transportation. Even in Salt Lake City it can be difficult to find a place to eat on Sunday; even fast-food restaurants are closed. Imagine how difficult it might be to find a bite to eat in— say—Monticello. If you're traveling outside the Wasatch Front on Sunday, ask your motel clerk if you'll be able to find a meal at your intended destination. Usually some gas stations along the interstates are open on Sunday, but in out-of-the-way places it's not guaranteed, so be sure to fill up on Saturday. Plan well ahead; it's easy to get stranded, hungry, and disappointed.

Note that many museums, recreation areas, and other tourist attractions close on Thanksgiving, Christmas, New Year's Day, and other holidays. These closings are not always mentioned in the text, so call ahead to check.

WEIGHTS AND MEASURES
Time Zones

The state is in the mountain time zone and goes on daylight saving time (advanced one hour) May–October. Nevada is in the Pacific time zone (one hour earlier); all other bordering states are in the mountain time zone. An odd exception is Arizona, which stays on mountain standard time all year (except for the Navajo Reservation, which goes on daylight saving time to keep up with its Utah and New Mexico sections).

Electricity

As in all of the United States, electricity is 110 volts. Plugs have either two flat or two-flat-plus-one-round prongs. Older homes and hotels may have outlets that only have two-prong outlets, and you may well be traveling with computers or appliances that have three-prong plugs. Ask your hotel or motel manager for an adapter; if necessary, you may need to buy a three-prong adapter, but the cost is small.

RESOURCES

Suggested Reading

DESCRIPTION AND TRAVEL

Benchmark Maps. *Utah Road and Recreation Atlas.* Medford, OR: Benchmark Maps, 2002. Shaded relief maps emphasize landforms, and recreational information is abundant. Use it to locate campgrounds, back roads, and major trailheads, though there's not enough detail to rely on it for hiking.

Huegel, Tony. *Utah Byways: 65 Backcountry Drives for the Whole Family, including Moab, Canyonlands, Arches, Capitol Reef, San Rafael Swell, and Glen Canyon.* Berkeley, CA: Wilderness Press, 2000. If you're looking for off-highway adventure, then this is your guide. The book includes detailed directions, human and natural history, outstanding photography, full-page maps for each of the 65 routes, and an extensive how-to chapter for beginners.

Porter, Eliot. *The Place No One Knew: Glen Canyon on the Colorado.* San Francisco: Sierra Club Books, 2000. Beautiful color photos show a world now lost to the waters of Lake Powell. Thoughtful quotations from many individuals accompany the illustrations.

Roylance, Ward J. *Utah: A Guide to the State.* Layton, UT: Gibbs Smith Publishers, 1998. An updated version of the book published by the W.P.A. Writers Program in 1941. Much of the original material and format has been preserved. The comprehensive introduction to Utah's people and history is followed by 11 tours of the state.

Rutter, Michael J. *Fun with the Family in Utah: Hundreds of Ideas for Day Trips with the Kids.* Old Saybrook, CT: Globe Pequot Press, 2004. Comprehensive guide to events, recreation, history, and activities with the family in mind.

Stegner, Wallace, ed. *This Is Dinosaur: Echo Park Country and Its Magic Rivers.* Niwot, CO: Roberts Rinehart, Inc., 1985. Essays on this rugged land—its geology, dinosaurs, wildlife, Native Americans, explorers, river-running, and visiting Dinosaur National Monument.

Zwinger, Ann. *Wind in the Rock: The Canyonlands of Southeastern Utah.* Tucson: University of Arizona Press, 1986. Well-written accounts of hiking in the Grand Gulch and nearby canyons. The author tells of the area's history, archaeology, wildlife, and plants.

RECREATION

Adkison, Ron. *Hiking Grand Staircase–Escalante and the Glen Canyon Region.* Helena, MT: Falcon Publishing Company, 1998. The vast Escalante/Glen Canyon area of southern Utah is nearly roadless, and hiking is about the only way you'll have a chance to visit these beautiful and austere canyons. This guide includes detailed information on 59 hikes, including Paria Canyon and Grand Gulch, in addition to the Grand Staircase–Escalante National Monument.

Allen, Steve. *Canyoneering the San Rafael Swell.* Salt Lake City: University of Utah Press, 1992. Eight chapters each cover a different area of this exceptional, though little-known, canyon country. Trail and route descriptions cover adventures from easy rambles to challenging hikes. The author provides some climbing notes, too. Detailed road logs help you get there, whether by mountain bike, car, or truck.

Belknap, Buzz and Laura Evans Belknap. *Belknap's Waterproof Dinosaur River Guide.* Evergreen, CO: Westwater Books, 2007. Topo maps show the canyons and points of interest along the Green and Yampa Rivers in Dinosaur National Monument of north-eastern Utah and adjacent Colorado. Includes Lodore, Whirlpool, and Split Mountain Canyons of the Green River. The Belknaps' other river guides are also go-to guides.

Bjørnstad, Eric. *Desert Rock I: Rock Climbs in National Parks.* Helena, MT: Falcon Publishing, 1996. One of several excellent climbing guides by one of Utah's most respected climbers.

Bomka, Gregg. *Mountain Biking Utah.* Helena, MT: Falcon Publishing Company, 1999. Detailed route descriptions of more than 100 rides, from the Salt Lake City area through Moab and Brian Head. Easy-to-use maps and elevation profiles included.

Brinkerhoff, Brian. *Best Easy Day Hikes Salt Lake City.* Helena, MT: Falcon Publishing Company, 1999. More than 20 short hikes in the Wasatch Front canyons near Salt Lake City.

Campbell, Todd. *Above and Beyond Slickrock.* Salt Lake City: Wasatch Publishers Inc., 1999. Exploring the slickrock country of southeastern Utah.

Crowell, David. *Mountain Biking Moab.* Helena, MT: Falcon Publishing Company, 2003. A handy guide to the many trails around Moab, from the most popular to the little explored, in a handy size: small enough to take on the bike with you.

Day, J. David and David Day. *Utah's Favorite Hiking Trails.* Provo, UT: Rincon Publishing, 2002. Good selection of trips within Utah, with simple but very clear maps.

Green, Stewart M. *Rock Climbing Utah.* Helena, MT: Falcon Publishing Company, 1998. Comprehensive guide to climbing routes throughout the state. Route maps are superimposed over photographs to make sure climbers find the right route.

Kelsey, Michael R. *Canyon Hiking Guide to the Colorado Plateau.* Provo: Kelsey Publishing, 1999. Classic guide to hiking in southeastern Utah's canyon country. The author persists in using only the metric system, and the layout is a bit dense, but it's certainly comprehensive. Kelsey is also incredibly prolific—he has written many guides to the southwest, and if you like this one, you should search for his others.

Lambrechtse, Rudi. *Hiking the Escalante.* Salt Lake City: Wasatch Publishers Inc., 1999. Introduction to history, geology, and natural history of the Escalante region in southern Utah, with descriptions of 42 hikes.

Probst, Jeffrey and Brad Probst. *High Uintas Backcountry.* Outland Publishing, 1999. Nearly 100 hiking trails from easy to long-distance, and information on the area's 600 lakes.

Wharton, Gayen and Tom Wharton. *Foghorn Outdoors Utah Camping.* Emeryville, CA: Avalon Travel Publishing, 2001. The best guide to public and private campgrounds across the state. A great resource if you're planning on doing any backcountry exploration.

MEMOIRS

Abbey, Edward. *Desert Solitaire.* Ballantine Books, 1991. A meditation on the Red Rock Canyon Country of Utah. Abbey brings his fiery prose to the service of the American outback, while excoriating the commercialization of the West.

Childs, Craig. *The Secret Knowledge of Water.* Boston: Back Bay Books, 2000. Childs looks for water in the desert, and finds plenty of it.

Meloy, Ellen. *Raven's Exile.* New York: Henry Holt and Company, 1994. Throughout a summer of Green River raft trips, Meloy reflects on natural and human history of the area.

Williams, Terry Tempest. *Refuge: An Unnatural History of Family and Place.* New York: Vintage Books, 1992. A memoir of a family devastated by cancer (caused by federal government atomic testing), overlain with a natural history of birdlife along the Great Salt Lake. Haunting, deeply spiritual, and beautifully written.

HISTORY AND CURRENT EVENTS

Bennet, Cynthia Larsen. *Roadside History of Utah.* Missoula, MT: Mountain Press Publishing Co., 1999. A very readable account of the state's history organized by driving tours. Full of great stories, yarns, and amazing human stories.

Krakauer, Jon. *Under the Banner of Heaven: A Story of Violent Faith.* New York: Doubleday Books, 2003. The story of two fundamentalist, polygamous brothers who killed their sister-in-law and nephew upon receiving what they considered to be a message from God.

Stegner, Wallace. *Beyond the Hundredth Meridian: John Wesley Powell and the Second Opening of the West.* New York: Penguin Books, 1992 (first published in 1954). Stegner tells the story of Powell's wild rides down the Colorado River, then goes on from there to point out why the United States should have listened to what Powell had to say about the American Southwest.

ARCHAEOLOGY

Lister, Robert, and Florence Lister. *Those Who Came Before.* Tucson: Southwest Parks and Monuments, 1993. A well-illustrated guide to the history, artifacts, and ruins of prehistoric Southwest Native Americans. The author also describes parks and monuments containing archaeological sites.

Slifer, Dennis. *Guide to Rock Art of the Utah Region: Sites with Public Access.* Albuquerque: University of New Mexico Press, 2000. The most complete guide to rock-art sites, with descriptions of more than 50 sites in the Four Corners region. Complete with maps and directions, and with an overview of rock-art styles and traditions.

NATURAL SCIENCES

Chronic, Halka. *Roadside Geology of Utah.* Missoula, MT: Mountain Press Publishing Co., 1990. Utah's geology as seen by following major roadways.

Fagan, Damian. *Canyon Country Wildflowers.* Helena, MT: Falcon Publishing Company, 1998. A comprehensive field guide to the diverse flora of the Four Corners area.

Williams, David. *A Naturalist's Guide to Canyon Country.* Helena, MT: Falcon Publishing, 2000. If you want to buy just one field guide, this is the one to get. It's well written, beautifully illustrated, and a delight to use.

Internet Resources

Although a virtual visit to Utah cannot replace the real thing, you'll find an enormous amount of helpful information on the World Wide Web. Thousands of websites interlink to cover everything from ghost towns to the latest community news.

TRAVEL

Utah Travel Council
www.utah.com

The Utah Travel Council is a one-stop shop for all sorts of information on Utah. It takes you around the state to sights, activities, events, maps, and offers links to local tourist offices. The accommodations listings are the most up-to-date source for current prices and options.

Visit Salt Lake City
www.visitsaltlake.com

Find the scoop on all aspects of visiting Salt Lake City, including accommodations (sometimes with special deals), events, and activities ranging from genealogical research to bird-watching. It's also a good place to find special deals on ski passes.

Ski Utah
www.skiutah.com

If you're thinking snow, glide over to Ski Utah, where you'll also find summer activities at the ski resorts.

Ghost Towns
www.ghosttowns.com/states/ut/ut.html

Histories and photos of Utah's loneliest towns.

THE GREAT OUTDOORS

The National Park Service
www.nps.gov

The National Park Service offers pages for all their areas at this site, where a click-on map will take you to Utah's parks. You can also enter this address followed by a slash and the first two letters of the first two words of the place (first four letters if there's just a one-word name); for example, www.nps.gov/brca takes you to Bryce Canyon National Park and www.nps.gov/zion leads to Zion National Park.

Utah State Parks
http://stateparks.utah.gov

The Utah State Parks site offers details on the large park system.

Desert USA
www.desertusa.com

Desert USA's Utah section discusses places to visit and what plants and animals you might meet there. Find out what's in bloom at www.desertusa.com/wildflo/wildupdates.

U.S. Forest Service
www.fs.fed.us/r4

Utah falls within U.S. Forest Service Region 4. From this site you can navigate to a particular national forest.

Reserve America
www.reserveamerica.com

Use this website to reserve campsites in state campgrounds. It costs a few extra bucks to reserve a campsite, but compare that with the cost of being skunked out of a site and having to resort to a motel room.

Federal Recreation Reservations
www.recreation.gov

If a campground is operated by the federal government, this is the place to make a reservation. Again, you can expect to pay a few dollars for this convenience.

NEWS AND SPORTS

Salt Lake Tribune
www.sltrib.com

The *Salt Lake Tribune* is the state's newspaper of record.

Deseret Morning News
www.desnews.com

Salt Lake's other major newspaper, the *Deseret Morning News,* has good regional and LDS coverage.

SL Weekly
www.slweekly.com

Salt Lake City's alternative weekly newspaper has online event listings and in-depth articles on city issues.

Index

A

Abbey, Edward: 421
Abbey of Our Lady of the Holy Trinity: 139
Abravanel Concert Hall: 43, 51
accommodations: 486; see also specific place
aerial tours: 419
Agua Canyon: 269
air travel: 480, 481
alcohol: 487
Alcove Spring Trail: 435
Alpine Scenic Loop: 18, 193
Alpine Slide: 101
Alta Ski Area: 16, 93-96
altitude sickness: 89
American West Heritage Center: 147
Anasazi people: 471
Anasazi State Park: 27, 347
Ancestral Puebloans: 471
animals: 468-470
animal threats: 489-490
Antelope Island: 22, 126
Antelope Island State Park: 126
Antelope Point Marina: 388
Anticline Overlook: 445
archaeological sites: Anasazi State Park 347;
    Antelope Island State Park 126; Beef Basin
    446; Boulder 364; Cedar Mesa 452; Dark
    Canyon 455; Edge of the Cedars State
    Park 447; Grand Gulch Primitive Area 455;
    Horse Collar Ruin 454; Hovenweep National
    Monument 448-449; Mule Canyon Ruin 452;
    Owl Creek Loop Hike 456
Arch Canyon: 452
Arches National Park: 23, 26, 419-426
architecture, Salt Lake City: 46
art galleries: 479
Ashley National Forest: 226, 241
Aspen Mirror Lake: 329
Assembly Hall: 38
ATV trails: 174, 206, 255, 275-276, 359, 419
ATV use, devastation from: 465
Aviary, Tracy: 50
Aztec Butte Trail: 434

B

backpacking: general discussion 484; Bryce
    Canyon National Park 271; Canaan Mountain
    307; Deep Creek Range 171; Devil's Kitchen
    Geologic Area 197; Diamond Mountain 225;
    Escalante River 352-355; House Range
    177-178; Islands in the Sky District 432;
    Kane Gulch Ranger Station 455; Lone Peak

Wilderness 194; Moab 413; Paria Canyon 350,
    357; precautions 491; Rainbow Bridge National
    Monument 386; ski touring 203; Snow Canyon
    State Park 315; Stansbury Mountains 163-164;
    Uinta Mountains 216; Upper Paria River
    Canyon 352; Wah Wah Mountains 182
Baker Dam Recreation Site: 317
Balanced Rock: 423
Basin and Range Province: 460, 462-463
Bass, Dick: 88
Bear Lake: 17, 154-156
Bear Lake Monster: 156
Bear Lake National Wildlife Refuge: 155
Bear Lake State Park: 155
Bear River Migratory Bird Refuge: 143
Beaver: 201-202
Beaver Mountain Ski Area: 153-154
bed-and-breakfasts: 486; see also specific place
Beef Basin: 446
Beehive House: 43
Behunin Cabin: 368
Belmont Springs: 143
Benson Grist Mill: 165
Best Friends Animal Sanctuary: 282
Big Bend: 293
Big Cottonwood Canyon: 82-88
Big Fill Walk: 145
Big Pocket Overlook: 446
Big Rock Candy Mountain: 208
Big Water: 349
biking: 483; see also specific place; mountain
    biking
bird-watching: Antelope Island State Park 127;
    Bear Lake National Wildlife Refuge 155; Bear
    River Migratory Bird Refuge 143; Browns
    Park National Wildlife Refuge 226; Clear
    Lake State Waterfowl Management Area 179;
    Fish Springs National Wildlife Refuge 168;
    Otter Creek State Park 209; Ouray National
    Wildlife Refuge 238; Pelican Lake 239;
    Sheeprock Mountains 174; Willard Bay State
    Park 142; Willow Park and Zoo 147
bison: 126
Black Dragon Canyon: 382
Blacksmith Fork Canyon: 153
Blanding: 447-448
Bluff: 23, 449-451
Bluffs, The: 137
boating: 109, 137; see also specific place
Bonneville Race Track: 61
Bonneville Salt Flats International Speedway:
    17, 162

Bonneville Seabase: 163
Boulder: 347, 364-366
Boulder Creek: 354
Boulder Mountain Scenic Drive: 365
Bowington (Boynton) Arch: 354
Box Elder Tabernacle: 143
Boyd Pony Express Station: 169
Boynton Overlook: 29, 346
Braithwaite Fine Arts Gallery: 323
Brian Head: 330, 331
Brian Head-Panguitch Lake Scenic Byway 143: 330-332
Brian Head Peak: 330
Brian Head Resort: 330
Bridge View Drive: 453-454
Brigham City: 143
Brigham City Museum-Gallery: 143
Brigham Young Cemetery: 43
Brigham Young Monument: 41
Brigham Young University: 18, 186
Brigham Young winter home: 311
Brighton Lakes Trail: 87
Brighton Ski Resort: 86-87
Bristlecone Loop Trail: 271
Bristlecone Pine Trail: 328
Broken Arches: 425
Browning Firearms Museum: 130
Browning-Kimball Car Museum: 129
Bryce, Ebenezer: 276
Bryce Canyon National Park: 18, 23, 27, 265-275; accommodations 272-274; food 274; highlights 262; hiking 269-272; maps 263, 266; scenic drives 267; winter visits 269
Bryce Point: 268
Buckskin Gulch: 358
Bullfrog Marina: 389
Bullion-Beck Mine: 173
Bull Valley Gorge: 350
Burr Trail Road: 348
business hours: 493
bus travel: 480, 482; *see also specific place*
Butch Cassidy Festival: 201
Butler Wash Ruins: 452

C
Cache Valley Historical Museum: 147
Cajon Ruins: 449
Calf Creek Falls Trail: 24, 27, 356
Calf Creek Recreation Area: 346, 356
Callao: 169
Camp Floyd: 167
Camp Floyd Stagecoach Inn State Park: 192
camping: general discussion 484; Alpine Scenic Loop 193; Antelope Island State Park 126; Bear Lake 156; Beaver 201; Big Cottonwood Canyon

88; Blacksmith Fork Canyon 153; Canyon Mountains 176; Deer Creek State Park 118; Delta 176; East Canyon State Park 116; Echo Reservoir 116; Fillmore 199; Hobble Creek-Diamond Fork Loop 196; itinerary 24-25; Jordanelle State Park 118; Little Cottonwood Canyon 97; Little Sahara Recreation Area 174; Logan 151; Logan Canyon 154; Minersville Reservoir Park 180; Ogden 140; Pahvant Range 200; Park City 114; Provo 190; Raft River Mountains 145-146; Rockport State Park 116; Salt Lake City 67-68; San Pitch Mountains 204; Sheeprock Mountains 174; Squaw Peak Road 196; Stansbury Mountains 163-164; Strawberry Reservoir 119; Tushar Mountains 202; Wasatch Mountain State Park 118; Willard Bay State Park 142; Yuba State Park 198
Canaan Mountain: 307
canoeing: 60, 239
Canyonlands National Park: 19, 23, 26, 426-443; Horseshoe Canyon Unit 438; Islands in the Sky District 431-436; maps 393, 428-429; Maze District 436-438; Needles District 438-443; trip planning 394; visitors center 426
Canyon Mountains: 176
Canyon Overlook Trail: 300
Canyon Rims Recreation Area: 445
Canyon Road: 256
Canyons Resort, The: 104-105
Canyon Station: 169
Capitol Gorge: 370, 377
Capitol Reef National Park: 19, 24, 27, 29, 366-378
Capitol Theatre: 51
Carl Hayden Visitors Center: 386
Car Museum, Browning-Kimball: 129
car travel: 482
Cascade Falls National Recreation Trail: 328
Cascade Springs: 195
Cassidy, Butch: 208
Cassidy Arch Trail: 377
Castle Dale: 253-254
Castle Rock Campground: 208
Castle Valley: 250-256
Cataract Canyon: 431
caves: 193, 283
Cecret Lake Trail: 97
Cedar Breaks National Monument: 18, 332
Cedar City: 321-326
Cedar City Cowboy Gathering: 323
Cedar Mesa: 452
Cedar Mountain Driving Tour: 253
Chase Home Museum of Utah Folk Art: 51
Chase Mill, The: 50
children's activities: Children's Garden 50; Clark Planetarium 44; Hogle Zoo 50;

Lagoon Amusement Park 39; Salt Lake City 39; Seven Peaks Resort Water Park 190; Thanksgiving Point 191; Willow Park and Zoo 147; Wolf Mountain Family Ski Area 142
Chimney Rock Trail: 374
cinema: 478; see also specific place; Sundance Film Festival
City Creek Canyon: 59
City Creek Center: 40
Clark Planetarium: 44
Clear Lake State Waterfowl Management Area: 179
Cleveland-Lloyd Dinosaur Quarry: 18, 25, 252-253
Clifton: 170
climate: 464
Coalville: 116
Cohab Canyon: 376
Cohab Canyon Trail: 377
College of Eastern Utah Prehistoric Museum: 243-244
colonization: 471-472
Colorado Plateau: 461, 462
Colorado River: 23, 430
Comb Ridge: 452
communications: 492
conduct, social: 487
Conference Center: 41
Confluence Overlook Trail: 441
Confusion Range: 178
Coral Pink Sand Dunes State Park: 285
Cottonwood Canyon Road: 349, 351
Cottonwood Canyon Scenic Back Road: 343
Council Hall: 45
Court of the Patriarchs Viewpoint: 291, 296
Cove Fort: 200
Coyote Buttes: 358
Coyote Gulch: 24, 356
cross-country skiing: Alta Ski Area 94; Ashley National Forest 226; Bryce Canyon National Park 269; Duck Creek Village 329; Flaming Gorge National Recreation Area 228; Historic Union Pacific Rail Trail State Park 107; Logan 150; Mirror Lake Highway 217; Nebo Scenic Loop 197; Ogden 134; Salt Lake City 57; Scofield State Park 248; Skyline Drive 203-204; Snowbasin Ski Area 141; Soldier Hollow 117; Solitude Mountain Resort 84; Strawberry Reservoir 119; Tushar Mountains 203; Wasatch Mountain State Park 118; White Pine Touring 107
Crystal Geyser: 259
Currant Creek Reservoir: 119
customs, immigration and: 488
customs, social: 487
Cutthroat Castle Ruins: 449

D

dance: 478
Dance Hall Rock: 346
Dangling Rope Marina: 388
Dan O'Laurie Museum: 395
Dark Canyon: 455
Daughters of Utah Pioneers Museum (Panguitch): 278
Daughters of Utah Pioneers Museum (St. George): 311
Daughters of Utah Pioneers Museum (Tooele): 165
Daughters of Utah Pioneers Museum (Vernal): 222
David Eccles Conference Center: 131
Days of '47 Celebration: 54
Dead Horse Point State Park: 408
Death Hollow: 353, 355
Deep Creek Range: 170
Deer Creek State Park: 118
Deer Valley Resort: 16, 101-104
Delicate Arch: 23, 30, 424
Delta: 175-176
Desert Peak Wilderness Area: 164
Desolation Canyon: 249-250, 257
Devils Garden (Arches National Park): 23, 425; campground 422
Devil's Garden (Grand Staircase-Escalante National Monument): 27, 345
Devil's Kitchen Geologic Area: 197
Dewey Bridge: 406
Diamond Mountain: 225
dinosaur country: 18, 211-260; Castle Valley and North San Rafael Swell 250-256; Dinosaur National Monument: 233-238; Flaming Gorge National Recreation Area 227-233; itinerary for visiting 25-26; maps 213; Price 243-246; trip planning 211-212; Uinta Mountains 214-219; Vernal 220-224
Dinosaur Museum, The: 447
Dinosaur National Monument: 18, 233-238
Dinosaur Quarry: 233
dinosaur sites: Big Water 349; Cleveland-Lloyd Dinosaur Quarry 252-253; College of Eastern Utah Prehistoric Museum 243-244; Dinosaur Museum, The 447; Dinosaur National Monument 233-238; Dinosaur Trackway 225; Eccles Dinosaur Park and Museum 132; Fort Pearce Dinosaur Tracks 309; Mill Creek Dinosaur Trail 413; Museum of Ancient Life 192; St. George Dinosaur Discovery Site 308; Utah Scenic Byway (Hwy. 279) 405
Dirty Devil Canyon Overlook: 384
disabilities, travelers with: 489
Discover Gateway: 39
Dividend: 173

Donner-Reed Pioneer Museum: 162-163
drinks: 486
driving hazards: 491
Dry Fork of Coyote Gulch: 27, 355
Dry Fork Petroglyphs: 30, 222
Duchesne: 241
Duck Creek Campground: 328
Duck Creek Village: 329
Dugway Proving Ground: 161
dune buggying: 174
Dutch John: 231, 232

E

Eagle Gate: 43
Earth Science Museum: 188
East Canyon State Park: 116
Eccles Community Art Center: 132
Eccles Dinosaur Park and Museum: 132
Eccles Railroad Center: 130
Echo Canyon Trail: 298
Echo Park: 236
Echo Reservoir: 116
ecosystems: alpine 407; pothole 439
Edge of the Cedars State Park: 447
electricity: 493
Electric Lake: 251-252
Elephant Trail: 441
Elkhorn Campground: 210
Emerald Pools Trail: 27, 297
Emery County Pioneer Museum: 253
Enterprise Reservoirs: 318
entertainment: 478-479
environmental issues: general discussion 465-466; endangered fish 431; Leave No Trace hiking 349; mountain bike etiquette 416
Ephraim: 204
Escalante Canyons: 338
Escalante Canyon Trailheads: 353
Escalante Petrified Forest State Park: 24, 344
Escalante region: 19, 23, 24, 334-390; Capitol Reef National Park 366-378; Escalante (town) 344-345, 360-364; maps 336-337; trip planning 334
Escalante River: 352
Escalante River Canyon: 349
Escalante (town): 344-345, 360-364
essential oils: 197
Eureka: 172

F

Fairview: 204
Fairview Museum of History and Art: 204
Fairyland Loop Trail: 270
Fairyland Point: 268
Falcon's Ledge: 241
Family History Library: 40

FamilySearch Center: 41
farmers markets: 131, 142
Farview Point: 268
fauna: 291, 468-470
ferries, Lake Powell: 388
Ferron: 256
festivals: 28-29, 53, 54, 109, 479; see also specific place
Fiery Furnace: 425
Fillmore: 198-199
fish: 431
Fish Creek: 248, 456
Fisher Towers: 406
fishing: general discussion 485; Alpine Scenic Loop 193; Ashley National Forest 226; Baker Dam Recreation Site 317; Bear Lake State Park 155; Blacksmith Fork Canyon 153; Browne Lake 233; Canyon Mountains 176; Deer Creek State Park 118; East Canyon State Park 116; Escalante Petrified Forest State Park 344; Ferron 256; Grantsville Reservoir 164; Green River 231; Gunlock Lake State Park 317; Hobble Creek-Diamond Fork Loop 196; Huntington Canyon 251-252; Huntington State Park 251; Jordanelle State Park 118; Kolob Reservoir 295; Lake Powell 386; Minersville Reservoir Park 180; Navajo Lake 328; Otter Creek State Park 209; Palisade State Park 205; Panguitch Lake 330; Park City area 109; Pine Valley Recreation Area 318; Pineview Reservoir 137; Quail Creek State Park 320; Red Fleet State Park 225; Roosevelt area guest ranches 241; Scofield State Park 248; Sheeprock Mountains 174; Spirit Lake 232; Starvation State Park 242; Steinaker State Park 225; Strawberry Reservoir 119; Uinta Mountains 214; Utah Lake State Park 188; Yuba State Park 198
Fish Lake: 209-210
Fish Springs National Wildlife Refuge: 168
Flaming Gorge Dam: 229
Flaming Gorge National Recreation Area: 18, 227-233
flash floods: 491
Flight of the Canyons Gondola: 105
Flink Trail: 437
floods, flash: 491
flora: 291, 466-468
fly-fishing: see fishing
food: 486
Fort Buenaventura State Park: 132
Fort Deseret: 179
Fort Douglas Military Museum: 49
Fort Pearce Dinosaur Tracks: 309
Fossil Mountain: 179
fossils, digging for: 175, 177

Four Corners Monument: 459
14-Window Ruin: 450
four-wheel drive exploration: 359, 418, 426, 430, 435, 442
Frémont, John C.: 168
Fremont Gorge Overlook Trail: 376
Fremont Indian State Park: 207
Fremont Petroglyphs: 368
Fremont River Trail: 377
Fremont River Waterfall: 368
Frisco: 180
Frontier Movie Town: 283
Fruita: 27, 369
Fruita Campground: 24, 378
Fruita Schoolhouse: 368
Frying Pan Trails: 376

G

Gallivan Center: 28, 54
Garden City: 154
Garden of Eden Viewpoint: 423
gardens: International Peace Gardens 51; Nephi Rose Garden 197; Red Butte Garden and Arboretum 49; Thanksgiving Point 192
Gardner Village: 56
Gates of Lodore: 237
Gateway, The: 55
gay and lesbian travelers: 489
gear: 21, 56, 61
gems, digging for: 175
geography: 93, 460-462
geology: 224, 288, 292, 342, 462-464
ghost towns: general discussion 17, 247; Clifton 170; Eureka area 173; Frisco 180; Gold Hill 170; Grafton 307; Iosepa 163; Jacob City 165; Kimberly 208; Mercur Gold Mine 166; Newhouse 181; Ophir 166; Pariah Townsite Road 348; Sego Canyon 260; Silver Reef 320; south of Vernal 238; Topaz Camp 176
giardia: 490
Gilgal Gardens: 46
Gimini Bridge (Bull Canyon) Trail: 414
Glen Canyon Dam: 23, 386
Glen Canyon National Recreation Area: 384-389
Glendale: 280-281
Goblin Valley State Park: 25, 382
Golden Spike National Historic Site: 22, 144-146
Golden Stairs: 437
Golden Throne Trail: 378
Gold Hill: 170
golf: general discussion 485; Beaver 201; disc golf 84; Ferron 256; Hurricane 308; Logan 150; Moab 399; Nephi 197; Ogden 134; Palisade State Park 206; Park City 107; Price 245; Provo 190; Salt Lake City 60; St. George 312; Tooele 165; Vernal 223

Gooseberry Reservoir Canyon: 252
Goosenecks: 368
Goosenecks State Park: 457
Goshute Indian Reservation: 169, 476
Grafton: 307
Grand Gulch Primitive Area: 455
Grand Staircase-Escalante National Monument: 19, 27, 338-360; geology 342; hiking 349-358; history 338-340; maps 340-341; visitors center 340
Grand View Point: 433
Grand Wash: 369, 376
Grand Wash Road: 377
Granite Creek: 170-171
Grantsville: 162-163
Gray Canyon: 249-250, 257
Great Basin Desert: 17, 157-182
Great Basin Museum: 175
Great Gallery: 30, 438
Great Salt Lake: 22, 125-127
Great Salt Lake Desert: 160-164
Great Salt Lake State Park: 125-126
Great Stone Face: 179
Great Western Trail: 481
Great White Throne: 293
Greek Festival: 55
Green River: 18, 222, 227, 237, 249-250, 430
Green River Overlook: 434
Green River Scenic Drive: 259
Green River (town): 25, 256
Greyhound Gathering: 283
Grosvenor Arch: 338, 344
Grotto, The: 292
guest ranches: 241, 242, 402, 486
Gulch, The: 354
Gunlock Lake State Park: 317
Gunnison: 206
gyms (Salt Lake City): 60

H

Hackberry Ruins: 449
Halls Crossing: 388
hang gliding: 408
Hanksville: 381-382
Hans Flat Ranger Station: 436-437
hantavirus: 490
Hardware Ranch: 153
Harpers Corner Road: 236
Harris Fine Arts Center: 186
Harris Wash: 355
Hatch: 280
hazards: 489-491
health: 89, 489-491
Heber City: 117-120
Heber Valley Historic Railroad: 117
Hell's Backbone: 363

Helper: 246
Helper Arts Festival: 246
Henry Mountains: 383-384
Hickman Natural Bridge: 375
Hidden Canyon: 298
Highway 18: 317
Highway 148 Junction: 328
Highway 128: 412
Highway 24: 368-369
Highway 279: 412
hiking: *see specific place*
Hill Aerospace Museum: 132
Historic Gifford Homestead: 369
Historic Union Pacific Rail Trail State Park: 107
history: 35, 470-475
Hite: 389
Hobble Creek-Diamond Fork Loop: 196
Hogle Zoo: 50
Hog's Back: 347
Hole-in-the-Rock Road: 345
Hole n' the Rock: 395
Holly Ruins: 30, 449
Homestead Crater: 117
Hondo Arch Loop: 383
hoodoos: 253, 266, 293
horseback riding: general discussion 485;
    Antelope Island State Park 126; Bryce Canyon
    National Park 272; Canyons Resort 105;
    Historic Union Pacific Rail Trail State Park 107;
    Kodachrome Basin State Park 343; Park City
    108; Park City Mountain Resort 101; Roosevelt
    area guest ranches 241; Snowbird Ski and
    Summer Resort 90; Zion National Park 303
Horse Collar Ruin: 454
horse races: 201
Horseshoe Canyon Unit: 30, 427, 438
Horseshoe Ruins: 449
hostels: 486
hot air ballooning: 105, 109
Hotel Utah: 41
hot springs: 117, 143
House Range: 176
Hovenweep National Monument: 23, 29, 448-449
Huber Wash: 300
Humbug Overlook Driving Tour: 253
Hundred Hands Pictograph: 346
Huntington: 251
Huntington Canyon: 251-252
Huntington State Park: 251
Hurricane: 308
hypothermia: 490
Hyrum State Park: 151-152

I

Ibapah: 169
Ice Age geology: 463

Ice Cave: 329
ice fishing: Millsite State Park 256; Strawberry
    Reservoir 119
ice-skating: 60, 133, 150, 189, 209
Indian Farm Canyon: 171
Inspiration Point: 268
International Peace Gardens: 51
international travelers: 488
Iosepa: 163
Iron Mission State Park Museum: 321
Irontown: 320
Islands in the Sky District: 26, 427, 431-436

J

Jacob Hamblin Home: 311
Joes Valley Reservoir: 255
John Hutchings Museum of Natural History: 191
John Jarvie Ranch: 225-226
John's Canyon: 456
Johnson Canyon: 342, 350-351
Johnson Canyon Road: 348
John Wesley Powell River History Museum:
    257, 389
Jones Hole National Fish Hatchery: 225
Jordanelle State Park: 25, 118
Jordan River State Park: 60
Joseph Smith Memorial Building: 41
Josie Morris Cabin: 235
Jug Handle Arch: 405
Junction: 208-209

K

Kachina Bridge: 454
Kamas: 216
Kanab: 282-285
Kanab Heritage House: 283
Kane Creek Scenic Drive: 407, 410
Kane Gulch Ranger Station: 455
kayaking: 417
Kimball Art Center: 99
Kimberly Scenic Drive: 208
Klondike Bluffs: 426
Kodachrome Basin State Park: 24, 343
Kokopelli's Trail: 414
Kolob Arch: 300
Kolob Canyons: 294
Kolob Canyons Road: 294
Kolob Canyons Visitors Center: 287, 294
Kolob Reservoir: 295
Kolob Terrace: 294

L

Labyrinth Canyon: 257
Ladies of the White House Doll Collection: 222
Lagoon Amusement Park: 39
Lahrop Trail: 432

Lake Bonneville: 160
Lake Powell: 19, 27, 384, 388
land, the: 460-464
Land of Standing Rocks: 437
La Sal Mountains: 407
La Sal Mountains Loop Road: 406
Latter-Day Saints: 477; Brigham Young
    University 186; Salt Lake City 36-43;
    see also specific place
Latter-Day Saints Office Building: 43
Lava Point: 294, 301
laws, drinking: 487
LC Ranch: 241
lesbian and gay travelers: 489
Liberty Park: 50, 59
Lick Wash: 351
Little Cottonwood Canyon: 88-97
Little Egypt: 384
Little Grand Canyon: 255
Little Sahara Recreation Area: 174
Logan: 17, 22, 28, 146-151
Logan Canyon: 153-154
Logan Tabernacle: 28, 146
Lone Peak Wilderness: 194
Lone Rock: 387
Long Valley: 280
Lower Calf Creek Falls: 346
Lower Muley Twist Canyon: 373-374

M
Madeleine Arts and Humanities Program: 28, 53
Mammoth: 173
Mammoth Cave: 331
Mammoth Springs: 331
Manila: 232
Manti: 205
Manti Temple: 205
map resources: 492
Markagunt Plateau: 326-333
Markagunt Scenic Byway: 327
Maze District: 427, 436-438
Maze Overlook: 437
melons: 256
Mercur Gold Mine: 166
Merimack Trail: 415
Mesa Arch Trail: 432
Mexican Hat: 456-457
Middle Rocky Mountains province: 462
Miles Goodyear Cabin: 131
Milford: 179-180
Mill Creek Canyon: 58
Million-Dollar Road: 347
Millsite State Park: 256
Mineral Fork Trail: 87
minerals, digging for: 175
Minersville Reservoir Park: 180

Mining Museum, Tintic: 172
Mirror Lake Highway: 216-219
Moab: 19, 23, 394-409; accommodations
    400-402; entertainment 395-399; food
    402-404; maps 396-397; recreation 399,
    409-419; sights 395; summer music festivals
    28; transportation 404
Moab Fault: 423
Moab Folk Festival: 29, 399
Moab Music Festival: 28, 398
Moab Salt Plant: 406
money: 492
Monitor Trail: 415
Monrovian Park: 207
monster, Bear Lake: 156
Monte L. Bean Life Science Museum: 188
Monticello: 446-447
Monument Valley: 19, 23, 458
Moon Lake Resort: 241
Moqui Cave: 283
Mormon Miracle Pageant: 205
Mormons: 476
Mormon settlers: 35, 472
Mormon Tabernacle (Salt Lake City): 16, 38
Mormon Tabernacle Choir: 38, 53
Morning Glory National Bridge: 412
Mossy Cave Trail: 271
motorboat tours: 418
mountain biking: general discussion 483;
    Antelope Island State Park 126; Arches
    National Park 422; Brian Head 330; Bryce
    Canyon National Park 272; Canyons Resort
    105; Capitol Reef National Park 371, 378;
    Deer Valley Resort 102; etiquette 415;
    Flaming Gorge National Recreation Area
    231; Goblin Valley State Park 382; Grand
    Staircase-Escalante National Monument
    359; Historic Union Pacific Rail Trail State
    Park 107; Mill Creek Canyon 58; Moab
    413-416; Park City 101, 107; Powell Point 276;
    Red Canyon 275; Snowbasin Ski Area 141;
    Snowbird Ski and Summer Resort 90; Soldier
    Canyon 165; Solitude Mountain Resort 84;
    Vernal 223; Zion National Park area 302
mountaineering expeditions: 91
Mountain Man Rendezvous: 155
Mountain Meadows Massacre Historic Site: 317
Mount Carmel Junction: 281
Mount Nebo Wilderness: 197
Mount Timpanogos Wilderness: 195
Mule Canyon Ruin: 452
Muley Point Overlook: 457
Murphy Point: 433
Museum of Ancient Life: 26, 192
Museum of Art: 186
Museum of Church History and Art: 40

Museum of Human History: 290
Museum of Peoples and Cultures: 188
Museum of the San Rafael: 254
museums: 478; *see also specific museum; specific place*
music concerts: 36, 478
music festivals: 28-29

N

Narrows, The: 299
national parks: 26-27, 485; *see also specific park*
native peoples: 475-476
Natural Bridge (Bryce): 269
Natural Bridges National Monument: 27, 453-454
Natural History Museum: 130
Nauvoo: 472
Navajo Knobs Trails: 375
Navajo Lake: 328
Navajo Loop Trail: 270
Navajo people: 476
Navajo Reservation: 23, 449
Navajo Sandstone: 292
Nebo Scenic Loop: 197
Neck Spring Trail: 432
Needles District: 26, 427, 438-443
Needles Outpost: 439
Needles Overlook: 445
Nephi: 197
Newhouse: 181
Newspaper Rock Historical Monument: 23, 26, 30, 443
nightlife: 487; *see also specific place*
Nine Mile Canyon: 30, 248
Nine Mile Canyon Backcountry Byway: 248-249
No Mans Mesa: 351
Nora Eccles Harrison Museum of Art: 148
North Dragon Road: 255
North Point: 437
North San Rafael Swell: 250-256
North Visitor Center: 38
Notch Peak: 178
Notom-Bullfrog Road: 371-373

O

Oak Grove Campground: 321
Observation Point Trail: 297
O.C. Tanner Amphitheater: 304
off-road vehicles: see ATV trails
Ogden: 17, 22, 127-137; accommodations 134-135; entertainment 133; food 135-136; history 127; maps 128, 138; recreation 134; sights 129-133
Ogden Amphitheater: 131
Ogden Canyon: 137
Ogden Nature Center: 132
Ogden Temple and Tabernacle: 131-132

Old Deseret: 50
Old Lyric Repertory Theatre: 28, 149
Old Wagon Trail: 377
Olympic Park, Utah: 106
Onion Creek Road: 406
Ophir: 166
Oquirrh Mountains ghost towns: 166
Orangeville: 253
orchards: 369
Otter Creek State Park: 209
Ouray Indian Reservation: 239
Ouray National Wildlife Refuge: 238
outdoor activities: 483-485; *see also specific activity; specific place*
Owachomo Bridge: 454
Owl Creek Loop Hike: 456

P

packing: 21
Page (Arizona): 389-390
Pahvant Butte: 179
Pahvant Range: 200
Pahvant Valley: 175
Paiute All-Terrain Vehicle Trail: 207
Paiute Restoration Gathering: 323
Paiute people: 476
Palisade State Park: 205
Panguitch: 278-280
Panguitch Lake: 330, 331
Panguitch Lake Scenic Byway 143: 330-332
Panorama Point: 368
Paria Canyon: 348, 350, 356
Pariah Townsite Road: 348
Paria River Canyon: 338
Paria View: 268
Park Avenue: 423
Park City: 16, 22, 97-116; accommodations 111-114; Canyons Resort 104-105; Deer Valley Resort 101-104; entertainment 109-111; food 114-115; maps 81, 98; Park City Mountain Resort 99-101; recreation 106-109; sights 99; summer music festivals 28; transportation 115-116
Park City Film Series: 110
Park City International Music Festival: 28, 110
Park City Mountain Resort: 16, 99-101
Park City Museum: 99
Parowan: 326
Parowan Gap: 29, 326
Pa'rus Trail: 296
Paunsagaunt Wildlife Museum: 276
Peekaboo Loop Trail: 270
Peery's Egyptian Theater: 131
Pelican Lake: 239
performing arts: 52
Peruvian Gulch-Hidden Peak Trail: 97

petrified wood: 300, 344
petroglyphs: 27; Capitol Gorge 370; Dry Fork Petroglyphs 222; Fremont Petroglyphs 368; itinerary for visiting 29-30; Moab area 405; Newspaper Rock Historical Monument 443; Parowan Gap 326; Quarry to Josie Morris Cabin Drive 235; "Swelter Shelter" 233
Phipps Wash: 354
Photovoltaic Array: 454
pictographs: Diamond Mountain 225; Great Gallery 438; Horseshoe Canyon Unit 438; Hundred Hands Pictograph 346; itinerary for visiting 29-30; Land of Standing Rocks 437; Maze Overlook 437; San Rafael Campground 255
Pine Valley Mountains: 318-321
Pine Valley Recreation Area: 318
Pine Valley Wilderness: 318
Pineview Reservoir: 137
pioneer log cabin: 175
Pioneer Memorial Museum: 16, 45
Pioneer Village: 39
Piute State Park: 209
plant life: 466-468
Pleasant Creek Road: 370
Ponderosa Canyon: 269
Pony Express: 17, 167
pothole ecosystems: 439
Powder Mountain Winter Resort: 142
Powell Point: 276
powwows: 117, 240
precipitation: 464
prehistory: 470-471
Price: 243-246
Price Canyon Recreation Area: 247
Price mural: 244
Promontory Point: 145
Provo: 18, 186-192
Provo River: 109
Provo Tabernacle: 188
Provo Temple: 188

QR

Quail Creek State Park: 320
Quarry to Josie Morris Cabin Drive: 233
Queen's Garden Trail: 270
Quilt Walk: 278
rafting: general discussion 483; Grand-Staircase Escalante National Monument 359; Gray Canyon 257; Green River 222, 230, 237; Moab 417-418; Provo River 109; River District 430; San Juan River 450; San Rafael Swell 255; White River 239
Raft River Mountains: 145-146
rain: 464

Rainbow Bridge National Monument: 386
Rainbow Point: 269
ranches: see guest ranches
Raspberry Days Festival: 155
recreation: 483-485; see also specific place
Recreational Equipment Inc. (REI): 56
Red Butte Garden and Arboretum: 49, 58
Red Canyon: 275-276
Red Canyon Visitors Center: 229
Red Cedar Creek: 171
Red Cliffs Recreation Site: 320
Red Cloud Loop Scenic Drive: 226
Red Fleet State Park: 225
Red Mountain: 171
religion: 477
Richfield: 206
Riggs Spring Loop: 271
Rim Overlook: 375
Rim Route: 374
Rim Trail: 270
River District: 427
river hiking: 299
Riverside Walk: 27, 298
rock art: Dry Fork 222; Fremont Indian State Park 207; Green River canyons 249-250; itinerary for visiting 18, 29-30; Nine Mile Canyon Backcountry Byway 248-249; Sego Canyon 260, 411; see also petroglyphs; pictographs
Rock Church: 321
Rock Cliff Reservoir: 25, 118
rock climbing: Arches National Park 422; Capitol Reef National Park 378; Rockreation 61; Zion National Park 295, 302-303
rockhounding: 17, 175, 485
Rockport State Park: 116
rodeos: Days of '47 Celebration 54; Heber City 117; Logan 149; Nephi 197; Northern Ute Indian Pow Wow and Rodeo 240; Park City 111; Price 245; St. George 311; Vernal 222
Ronald V. Jensen Living Historical Farm: 147
Roosevelt: 240
Rose Wagner Performing Arts Center: 51
Rush Lake: 165
RVs: 481

S

sailboarding: 109, 165, 205
sailing: 116
Salina: 206
Saltair Resort: 126
Salt Island Adventures: 126
Salt Lake Art Center: 43
Salt Lake Bees: 61
Salt Lake City: 16, 22, 24, 31-78; accommodations 61-68; architecture 46;

entertainment 51-55; food 68-74; highlights 32; history 35-36; maps 33, 34, 42, 48, 62, 69; recreation 56-61; services 75-77; shopping 55-56; sights 36-51; summer music festival 28, 54; tourist information 75; transportation 77-78; trip planning 33-34
Salt Lake Temple: 37
Salt Palace Convention Center: 44
Sand Bench Trail: 296
Sand Creek: 353
sandstone, Navajo: 292
San Francisco Mountains: 180
San Juan: 388
San Juan Footbridge: 450
San Juan River: 450
San Pitch Mountains: 204
San Rafael Campground: 255
San Rafael Swell: 255, 382
Sawtooth National Forest: 145-146
Scandinavian Festival: 204
scenic drives: Alpine Scenic Loop 193; Ashley National Forest 226; Boulder Mountain Scenic Drive 365; Bryce Canyon National Park 267; Canaan Mountain 307; Capitol Reef National Park 369; Cedar Breaks National Monument 332; Cleveland-Lloyd Dinosaur Quarry 253; Cottonwood Canyon Road 349; Cottonwood Canyon Scenic Back Road 343; Crouse Canyon 226; Echo Park 236; Green River Scenic Drive 259; Harpers Corner Road 236; Hell's Backbone 363; Hobble Creek-Diamond Fork Loop 196; Hole-in-the-Rock Road 345; Hondo Arch Loop 383; House Range 177; Kimberly Scenic Drive 208; Kolob Canyons Road 294; Logan Canyon 153-154; Markagunt Scenic Byway 327; Million-Dollar Road 347; Mirror Lake Highway 216-219; Moab 405-407; Monument Valley Drive 458; Nebo Scenic Loop 197; Needles District 439; Nine Mile Canyon Backcountry Byway 248-249; Notom-Bullfrog Road 371-373; Pole Creek (Elkhorn) Scenic Loop 241; Promontory Trail Auto Tour 144-145; Quarry to Josie Morris Cabin Drive 233; Red Cloud Loop Scenic Drive 226; San Rafael Swell 255; Sheep Creek Canyon Geological Area 229; Skyline Drive 203-204; Squaw Peak Road 196; St. George 315; Tushar Mountains 202; Uinta Mountains 214; Wasatch Mountain State Park 118; West Tavaputs Plateau 242; Wildlife Through the Ages Scenic Byway 224; Zion National Park 287
Scofield: 248
Scofield State Park: 248
scuba diving: 117, 163, 225, 228
sculpture gardens: 46
seasonal weather: 464
seasons: 20-21
Seely, Mrs. Orange: 214
Sego Canyon: 30, 260
Shafer Canyon Overlook: 432
Shakespearean Festival, Utah: 323
Sheep Creek Canyon Geological Area: 229
Sheepdog Championship, International: 117
Sheeprock Mountains: 174
Shoshoni people: 475
Silver City: 173
Silver Falls Creek: 355
Silver Island Mountains: 162
Silver Reef: 320
Simpson Springs: 168
Sipapu Bridge: 454
skiing: Beaver Mountain Ski Area 153-154; Brighton Ski Resort 86-87; Ogden 134; Powder Mountain Winter Resort 142; Salt Lake City 57; Ski Utah Interconnect 57, 107; Snowbasin Ski Area 141; Snowbird Ski and Summer Resort 88-93; Solitude Mountain Resort 83-86; Sundance Resort 196; transportation between resorts 86; Wolf Mountain Family Ski Area 142; see also cross-country skiing
Ski Utah Interconnect: 57, 107
Skutumpah Road: 342, 350-351
Skyline Arch: 425
Skyline Drive: 203-204, 252, 256
sleigh rides: 107, 153
Slickhorn Canyon: 456
Slickrock Bike Trail: 414
Smith, Jedediah: 168
Smokey Mountain Road: 345, 349
smoking: 488
snorkeling: 117
snow: 93, 464
Snowbasin Ski Area: 141
Snowbird Ski and Summer Resort: 16, 88-93
snowboarding: see skiing
Snow Canyon State Park: 24, 315-317
snowmobiling: Cedar Breaks National Monument 332; Duck Creek Village 329; Flaming Gorge National Recreation Area 228; Logan 150; Mirror Lake Highway 217; Nebo Scenic Loop 197; Skyline Drive 203-204; Snowbasin Ski Area 141; Strawberry Reservoir 119; Wasatch Mountain State Park 118
snowshoeing: 107, 269, 332
Soldier Hollow: 117
Solitude Mountain Resort: 83-86
Sorrel River Ranch: 23, 402
Southern Utah University: 323

South Visitor Center: 38
spas: 312
Speed Week: 162, 479
Spirit Lake: 232
Spring Canyon Route: 375
Springdale: 28, 304-307
springs: Big Rock Candy Mountain 208; Crystal Geyser 259; hot 117, 143; Kolob Arch 301; Mammoth Springs 331
Springville Museum of Art: 189
Square Tower Ruins: 448-449
Squaw Flat: 441
Squaw Peak Road: 196
Squaw Trail: 282
Stagecoach Inn State Park: 167
Stansbury Mountains: 163-164
Starvation State Park: 242
State Capitol: 44-45
state parks: 485
Steinaker State Park: 225
Stewart Lake State Waterfowl Management Area: 238
St. George: 28, 309-315
St. George Art Museum: 311
St. George Dinosaur Discovery Site: 26, 308
St. George Tabernacle: 311
St. George Temple: 310
Stillwater Canyon: 257
storm hazards: 465
Strawberry Point: 329
Strawberry Reservoir: 119
Strike Valley Overlook Trail: 374
Sugarhouse Park: 60
Sulphur Creek Route: 375
Sundance Film Festival: 16, 110, 111, 479
Sundance Institute: 196
Sundance Resort: 18, 195
Sundance Trail: 455
Sunrise Point: 268
Sunset Point: 268
sunstroke: 491
Swasey Peak: 178
Swett Ranch: 230
swimming: 125-126

T
Tabernacle Hill: 199
Tanner Amphitheater: 28, 304
taxidermy: 276
Taylor Creek Trail: 300
temperatures: 464
Temple of Sinawava: 293
Temple Square: 16, 22, 28, 36-43, 51
tennis: 60, 312, 324
Territorial Statehouse State Park: 198-199

Thanksgiving Point: 191
theater: 52, 110, 478
Thiokol: 145
"This is the Place" State Park: 49
Thousand Lake Mountain: 210
time zones: 493
Timpanogos Cave National Monument: 18, 193
Tintic Mining Museum: 172
toboggan tracks: 101
Toms Creek: 171
Tooele: 164-166
Tooele Army Depot: 161, 164
Tooele Railroad Museum: 164-166
Topaz Camp: 176
Torrey: 27, 379-381
tourist information: 492
tours: adventure 416-419; backcountry ski 57; Bryce Canyon National Park 272; Grand Staircase-Escalante National Monument 360; guided river trips 237, 257; jet-boat 418; Lake Powell 387; Moab bike 415; Monument Valley 458; Temple Square 37; Zion National Park 290; see also specific place
Tower Arch: 426
TP Gallery: 56
Tracy Aviary: 50
train travel: 480, 481
tram rides: 90
transportation: 480-483; see also specific place
Trappist Monks: 139
travel, wilderness: 485
travel tips: 488
trip planning: 20-21
Trolley Square: 55
Tropic: 276
Trough Springs Trail: 446
Trout Creek: 171
Tuacahn Amphitheater: 28, 317
Tushar Mountains: 202-203
25th St. (Ogden): 130

U
U-Bar Wilderness Ranch: 241
Uintah Indian Reservation: 239
Uinta Mountains: 18, 214-219, 242
Under-the-Rim Trail: 271
Union Station Museums: 129
United Order of Enoch: 280-281
University of Utah: 47, 61
Upheaval Dome: 434
Upper Cathedral Valley Trail: 371
Upper Muley Twist Canyon: 374
Upper Salt Creek Trail: 442
U.S. 191: 410, 413

U.S. 89 (Grand Staircase-Escalante National Monument): 348-350
U.S. 89 (Panguitch to Kanab): 278-281
Utah Festival Opera: 28, 149, 479
Utah Field House: 25, 220-222
Utah Jazz: 61
Utah Lake State Park: 188
Utah Museum of Fine Arts: 48
Utah Museum of Natural History: 48
Utah Olympic Park: 106
Utah Opera Company: 53
Utah Scenic Byway 128: 406
Utah Scenic Byway 279: 405
Utah Shakespearean Festival: 323, 479
Utah State Capitol: 16, 44-45
Utah State Fair: 55
Utah State University: 148
Utah Symphony: 28, 53, 109
Utah Training and Test Range: 161
Ute Mountain Fire Lookout Tower: 233
Utes: 476

VW

Valley of the Gods: 457
vegetation: 466-468
Vermillion Cliffs National Monument: 348, 356
Vernal: 18, 220-224
Veyo Resort: 317
Virgin River Rim Trailhead: 328
Wah Wah Mountains: 181-182
Wahweap: 387
Wasatch-Cache National Forest: 75
Wasatch Mountain State Park: 25, 117-118
Wasatch Range: 16, 79-120; Big Cottonwood Canyon 82-88; Heber City 117-120; highlights 80; maps 81; Park City 97-116; skiing 79; trip planning 80
Watchman Trail: 24, 296
Waterpocket Fold: 19, 371
water-skiing: Bear Lake State Park 155; Echo Reservoir 116; Flaming Gorge National Recreation Area 227; Huntington State Park 251; Lake Powell 386; Minersville Reservoir Park 180; Pineview Reservoir 137; Provo River 109; Scofield State Park 248; Steinaker State Park 225; Yuba State Park 198
water use: 465
Watson, George: 93
weather: 464
Weber County Daughters of Utah Pioneer Museum: 131
Weber State University: 133
Wedge Overlook: 255

Weeping Rock: 293
Weeping Rock Trail: 297
Wendover: 160
Western Heritage Museum: 222
Western Mining and Railroad Museum: 246
West Rim Trail: 297
Westwater Canyon: 406
Whale Rock: 434
Wheeler Historic Farm: 39
Whiskey Springs Picnic Area: 119
White Pine Touring: 107
White Rim 4WD Road: 435
White River: 239
white-water rafting: see rafting
wilderness travel: 485
wildlife: 468-470
Wildlife Through the Ages Scenic Byway: 224
Willard Bay State Park: 142
Willis Creek Narrows: 350
Willow Flat Campground: 434
Willow Park and Zoo: 147
Windows Section: 423
Wire Pass: 358
Wolf Mountain Family Ski Area: 142
Wolverine Creek: 355
Wolverton Mill: 381-382
Wrather Canyon Arch: 358

XYZ

Yampa River: 237
yoga: 109, 308
Young, Brigham: 41, 43, 280, 311
Young Living Family Farm: 197
Yovimpa Point: 269
Yuba State Park: 198
Zion Canyon: 290-293
Zion Canyon Field Institute: 296
Zion Canyon Giant Screen Theatre: 304
Zion Canyon Visitors Center: 290
Zion Lodge: 292, 303
Zion Mountain Resort: 281
Zion-Mt. Carmel Highway: 27, 293
Zion-Mt. Carmel Tunnel: 293
Zion National Park: 18, 23, 24, 27, 285-304; camping 303; hiking 295-302; history 289; maps 263, 286; shuttle bus 289; Zion Canyon 290-293
Zion Nature Center: 290
Zion Overlook: 328
Zip Rider: 101
zoos: Hogle Zoo 50; petting zoos 191; Willow Park and Zoo 147

www.moon.com

For helpful advice on planning a trip, visit www.moon.com for the **TRAVEL PLANNER** and get access to useful travel strategies and valuable information about great places to visit. When you travel with Moon, expect an experience that is uncommon and truly unique.

MAP SYMBOLS

▦▦▦ Expressway	◖ Highlight	✗ Airfield	⚲ Golf Course
▦▦▦ Primary Road	○ City/Town	✈ Airport	▣ Parking Area
▦▦▦ Secondary Road	◉ State Capital	▲ Mountain	⬟ Archaeological Site
▪ ▪ ▪ Unpaved Road	⊛ National Capital	✦ Unique Natural Feature	▮ Church
- - - - - Trail	★ Point of Interest		▯ Gas Station
············ Ferry	• Accommodation	⬞ Waterfall	◌ Glacier
⊢⊢⊢ Railroad	▼ Restaurant/Bar	▲ Park	Mangrove
▨▨▨ Pedestrian Walkway	■ Other Location	⬔ Trailhead	Reef
▥▥▥ Stairs	⋀ Campground	⛷ Skiing Area	Swamp

CONVERSION TABLES

$^{\circ}C = (^{\circ}F - 32) / 1.8$
$^{\circ}F = (^{\circ}C \times 1.8) + 32$
1 inch = 2.54 centimeters (cm)
1 foot = 0.304 meters (m)
1 yard = 0.914 meters
1 mile = 1.6093 kilometers (km)
1 km = 0.6214 miles
1 fathom = 1.8288 m
1 chain = 20.1168 m
1 furlong = 201.168 m
1 acre = 0.4047 hectares
1 sq km = 100 hectares
1 sq mile = 2.59 square km
1 ounce = 28.35 grams
1 pound = 0.4536 kilograms
1 short ton = 0.90718 metric ton
1 short ton = 2,000 pounds
1 long ton = 1.016 metric tons
1 long ton = 2,240 pounds
1 metric ton = 1,000 kilograms
1 quart = 0.94635 liters
1 US gallon = 3.7854 liters
1 Imperial gallon = 4.5459 liters
1 nautical mile = 1.852 km

MOON UTAH

Avalon Travel
a member of the Perseus Books Group
1700 Fourth Street
Berkeley, CA 94710, USA
www.moon.com

Editor: Naomi Adler Dancis
Series Manager: Kathryn Ettinger
Copy Editor: Kay Elliott
Graphics Coordinator: Elizabeth Jang
Production Coordinator: Elizabeth Jang
Cover Designer: Elizabeth Jang
Map Editor: Albert Angulo
Cartographers: Kat Bennett, Mike Morgenfeld,
    Suzanne Service, Tim Lohnes
Proofreaders: Jamie Andrade, Tiffany Watson
Indexer: Rachel Kuhn

ISBN-10: 1-56691-838-3
ISBN-13: 978-1-56691-838-1
ISSN: 1078-5280

Printing History
1st Edition – 1988
8th Edition – May 2008
5 4 3 2 1

KEEPING CURRENT

If you have a favorite gem you'd like to see included in the next edition, or see anything
that needs updating, clarification, or correction, please drop us a line. Send your
comments via email to feedback@moon.com, or use the address above.